The Inauguration of Organized Political Warfare

Cold War Organizations

sponsored by the
National Committee
for a Free Europe /
Free Europe Committee

Introductory Chapter read by A. Ross Johnson

An imprint of
Helena History Press, LLC
PO Box 838
Saint Helena, CA
USA 94574
Email: editor@helenahistorypress.com
Website: www.helenahistorypress.com

Order From
Central European University Press
11 Nador utca
Budapest, Hungary H-1051
Email:ceupress@ceu.hu
Website: www.ceupress.com

ISBN: 978-0-9859433-0-1
Production Manager: Peter Strausz
Copy Editor: Jill Hannum
Graphic Designer: Book Jacket & Text: Sebastian Stachowski
Graphic Designer: Photo Gallery: Zsolt Gembela
Printed in Hungary by Prime Rate Kft, Budapest

The Inauguration of Organized Political Warfare

Cold War Organizations

sponsored by the National Committee for a Free Europe / Free Europe Committee

Edited by Katalin Kádár Lynn

HHP

Contents

Each of the essays in this volume focuses on an organization or activity that was funded through the National Committee for a Free Europe, Inc. (NCFE) during the war of ideas and ideals between the United States and the Soviet Union that came to be known as the Cold War. This US government-sponsored organization existed between 1949 and 1971 and was known as the Free Europe Committee, Inc. (FEC) after 5 March 1954. It represented but one aspect of America's policy regarding Soviet expansionism – a policy that encompassed both containment and an aggressive stance. Archival records on the NCFE offer a rich source of information that has not yet been thoroughly mined by scholars. In May 1948 US statesman and Cold War strategist George Kennan outlined the NCFE's original charge to the National Security Council in a policy paper titled "The Inauguration of Organized Political Warfare". The NCFE was to be the principal tool in waging the "organized political warfare" that became the ideological basis of US policy during the Cold War. In large part, this effort involved the US-based exiles from the nations of Central and East Europe that had become Soviet satellites after World War II. The plan to organize the NCFE originated in the Central Intelligence Agency's Office of Policy Coordination in 1948, and it was formally incorporated on 17 May 1949. Throughout its twenty-two year existence it was operated and funded covertly through American intelligence channels as an ostensibly private, not for profit entity funded by donations from the American public.

The archival records of Radio Free Europe (RFE) and Radio Liberty, always the highest profile of the NCFE divisions, were acquired by the Hoover Institution Archives at Stanford University in 2000 and have since been the focus of most NCFE-related scholarship. There is additional archival material that documents the much wider range of Cold War activities that the NCFE established, sponsored and funded, but until now, these non-radio activities have received little attention. This is due in part to the fact that, as of this writing, a portion of the primary archival material relating to the parent organization remains classified. Despite this challenge, each of this book's contributors has successfully researched an activity or organization sponsored by the NCFE, Inc or its later incarnation, the FEC, Inc.

Of primary interest to scholars will be the histories of the national councils/committees that represented the US-based exile leadership from Hungary, Czechoslovakia, Romania, Bulgaria, Poland and the Baltic States. The NCFE's founders intended for these nationalities' groups and their leaders to lead the propaganda battle against the growth of worldwide communism. In outlining the NCFE's mission Kennan wrote that it should "encourage the formation of a public American organization which will sponsor selected refugee committees so that they may act as the focus of national hope and revive a sense of purpose among political refugees from the Soviet World; provide an inspiration for continuing popular resistance within the countries of the Soviet World; and serve as a potential nucleus for allout liberation movements in the event of war." The many nationalities' committees were provided with operating funds for their domestic and international offices, publications and activities as well as for salaries for their leadership.

However, NCFE sponsorship was not limited to these committees; its organizations numbered well over one hundred, circled the globe and were represented not just in the United States but in Europe, Latin America and Asia as well. The major sponsored organizations ranged from the Assembly of Captive European Nations, Free European University in Exile, Crusade for Freedom and International Peasant Union to various propaganda programs, including those that sponsored cultural and sports activities and organizations. The history of the Assembly of Captive European Nations and that of the Free Europe University in Exile, Inc. are also addressed in this volume.

The introductory chapter gives an overview of the genesis of the US program that inaugurated "organized political warfare". It also attempts to show the extent of the range of activities and organizations sponsored through funds disbursed by the NCFE/FEC, although the larger history of these programs remains to be written. The chapter's aim is not only to illustrate the number of lives that were touched for the better part of two decades by these organizations and programs but also to ponder the lasting legacy of this US investment in organized political warfare.

The NCFE and its Cold War activities remain one of the last aspects of US Cold War policy that has not been thoroughly researched, and Cold War scholarship will not be complete until the remaining material is declassified. This volume takes a first step in that direction, but there is still much more material to be uncovered.

This work has been many years in the making. Not for lack of scholarly interest but because the archival resources have been fragmentary or missing. As the Cold War recedes into the past, archival material has become increasingly available – still in fragmentary form but now in enough depth to allow research on these topics. In addition to the Corporate Records of RFE, the Hoover Institution also houses considerable material related to the Romanian, Czechoslovak, Polish, Bulgarian and Hungarian national councils and the political leadership that was involved in those émigré groups. Without the valuable resources of the Hoover Institution Archives, this book could not have been written.

I first happened upon the NCFE while researching my doctoral dissertation more than a decade ago and have continued to pursue it at the urging of Dr Stephen Fischer-Galati, Distinguished Professor Emeritus of History at the University of Colorado. I thank him for his suggestion that this volume compile works by emerging and established scholars who focus on Cold War history. This volume is dedicated to him and honors his more than sixty-year contribution to the field of Central and East European history through the publications he founded and edited, *East European Monographs* and *East European Quarterly*.

All of the authors also owe a great debt of gratitude to Carol Leadenham, Anatol Shmelev and the entire team at the Hoover Institution Archives, all of whom have assisted our diverse research for many years. Many of the contributors to this volume have also benefitted from the generous assistance provided by A. Ross Johnson, distinguished historian, Research Fellow at the Hoover Institution and Senior Scholar at the Woodrow Wilson Institute Center. He has been a pioneer in this field and our work is all the richer for the interest he has taken in it.

In addition to the Hoover Institution, the contributors have received support and cooperation from a range of other archives and private collections and from the generous individuals listed below:

Francis Raska, author of the chapter on the Council of Free Czechoslovakia, wishes to acknowledge the cooperation of the late Mojmir Povolný, the last president of the Council of Free Czechoslovakia.

Archival research for the chapters written by Anna Mazurkiewicz was made possible by the Kosciuszko Foundation and the Foundation for Polish Science as well as by the generous hospitality of the Immigration History Research Center at the University of Minnesota, Minneapolis.

Marius I. Petraru, author of the history of the Romanian National Council, extends his thanks to Irena Czernichowska of the Hoover Institution Archives and Justin Liuba, former director of Radio Free Europe and founder and president of the Iuliu Maniu Foundation.

The author of the history of the Free European University in Exile, Veronika Durin-Hornyik, wishes to thank Wojciech Sikora, director of the Institut Litteraire Kultura, and his colleague Leszek Czarnecki for their help and friendly spirit, and to thank as well a former FEUE fellow who provided invaluable help but wishes to remain anonymous.

Jonathan L'Hommedieu, author of the history of the Baltic Freedom Committees, would like to acknowledge the assistance of Daniel Necas of the Immigration History Research Center and Kimmo Rentola and Marko Lehti of the University of Turku, Finland.

Maria Kokoncheva, who wrote the chapter on Georgi Dimitrov, extends her thanks to Dimitrov's daughter, Mrs. Anastasia Moser, for the archival material and the personal insights she so generously provided.

The history of the Hungarian National Sports Federation was written by Toby Charles Rider, who extends his thanks to Gladys and Paul Szapary for access to their personal archives. Jim Leyerzapf, Chalsea Millner, Catherine Cain and Valoise Armstrong at the Eisenhower Library. Bob Barnes and the staff at the International Olympic Committee Archives and the International Centre for Olympic Studies at the University of Western Ontario for their support.

In addition to the archivists at the Hoover Institution whose assistance was invaluable to me and to my fellow researchers, I would like to personally thank Ferenc Földesi, the director of the archives at the National Széchényi Library (Országos Széchényi Könyvtár, OSZK) in Budapest for allowing me to use the Hungarian National Council archival material which has not yet been catalogued. I am grateful for the gracious assistance the entire staff provided me during the three years that I worked with the HNC material.

Ultimately the form that any anthology such as this takes depends not just on the voice of the researchers but on that of the editors as well. We all would like to thank Jill Hannum, our skilled and erudite copy editor who helped shape this volume, and Peter Strausz, our production manager in Budapest, who brought the book to print. Our distribution partner, Central European University Press, ably led by its director, Krisztina Kós, is also to be thanked for generously providing advice and resources to all involved with our fledging imprint. We are grateful for all of the assistance provided by them and for their enthusiasm for our mission.

Katalin Kádár Lynn
Editor

I

At War While at Peace: United States Cold War Policy and the National Committee for a Free Europe, Inc.

Katalin Kádár Lynn

"The National Committee for a Free Europe is engaged in active ideological warfare against communism and soviet totalitarianism."
NCFE, Inc. Secretary Frederic Dolbeare, May 15, 1952

At War While at Peace

Sixty-eight years after the end of World War II, it seems fitting to begin to examine more thoroughly the other, more unconventional war, the psychological war for "men's minds" that shortly was to follow the armistice. Termed the "Cold War", it was fought with great intensity by all sides while the world was at "peace". It pitted the Soviet Union and the world wide Communist movement against the forces of democracy led by the United States in a propaganda war that lasted the better part of four decades. This Cold War between the two world superpowers was at the peak of its intensity during the first decade after its inception, having been fueled by the realization by the United States that one conflict had, to a degree, been replaced by another and by the ideological fervor of the anti-communist movement in the United States.

The Cold War sprang from the realization by the West that the political vacuum created by the Axis defeat was quickly being filled by the Soviet Union and the world wide Communist movement, and that this represented a very real threat to the survival of democracies, particularly in politically fragile areas of the Far East, the Indian sub-continent,

Latin America and even in Europe, where the communist movement emerged with great strength from the ashes of WWII.

This essay will discuss the events that led to the onset of the Cold War and how United States policy makers chose to develop a plan of "organized political warfare"[1] to counteract Soviet influence in Europe. It will describe in general the tactics utilizing psychological warfare that were chosen and the programs put in place as part of this strategy. It will also describe the various institutions created to fight this battle as it related to the nations that by 1947–1948 had become Soviet satellites in Central and East Europe.

To this day, there are still programs and organizations put in place as a result of the Truman Doctrine that have not been fully researched. These programs were the outgrowth of policies arising from the policy of containment and an aggressive stance against Soviet expansionism that the Truman Doctrine espoused. This essay will introduce how refugees fleeing from the Soviet takeover of their nations constituted a tool for the United States to wage psychological warfare via the National Councils, Radio Free Europe, Radio Liberty and the organizations termed "the internationals". It will also illustrate the wide range of US-sponsored activities related to all of these organizations, both in the United States and abroad. While the history of "the radios" has been extensively researched and written about, that of the other sponsored entities has not, leaving a void in the history of the Cold War.

The Run-Up to War's End

Several years before the end of the war, Washington policy makers were already secretly discussing post war relations with the Soviet Union, and by 1943 their conversations included the structure of the postwar world and relations among its leading powers. Warnings of Soviet ambitions for world domination were voiced by experienced Soviet hands such as William Bullitt, the first US Ambassador to the Soviet Union, and Charles E. Bohlen, who served with Bullitt in Moscow and as US President Franklin Delano Roosevelt's interpreter at the Teheran Conference and at Yalta.[2] Their warnings were swept aside.

During the conduct of the war, the relationship between the three Great Powers was never quite one of trust and comfort. Early on in their relationship, Roosevelt thought he could bring his considerable charm to bear on Soviet Premier Joseph Stalin and said to Bullitt, "I have just a hunch that Stalin doesn't want anything but security for his country, and I think that if I give him everything I possibly can and ask nothing in return, noblesse oblige he won't try to annex anything and will work for a world of democracy and peace."[3] Despite Roosevelt's misplaced confidence in his ability to sway Stalin not to "try to annex anything and … work for a world of democracy and peace", and although Stalin was called "Uncle Joe" in the US press, not many would have made the case for his being a proponent of democracy. This, despite the fact that wide-ranging Soviet propaganda efforts during the war had ensured that the US public at large was reminded daily of the sacrifices being made by the Soviet Union.

The Western Allies' "marriage" with the USSR during the war had been one of convenience in which both partners jockeyed for dominance in the alliance. By the end of the war, Great Britain found itself a poor third in the uneasy alliance, having to focus its priorities on reconstructing its economy and society and leaving the two remaining Great Powers to face each other in the Cold War power struggle, which was to last for the next four decades.

Stalin's Eastern European Ambitions

From the onset of the USSR's entry into the Allied partnership, Stalin demanded that the Soviet Union be given a sphere of influence in continental Europe, the parameters of which were initially discussed at the 1943 Teheran Conference when the Big Three, Stalin, British Prime Minister Winston Churchill and Roosevelt, first met to discuss the war in Europe.[4] Churchill's subsequent meeting with Stalin in Moscow in October 1944 produced a one-page, hand written agreement on East and West percentage shares in Eastern Europe. The Yalta Conference held February 4–11, 1945, resulted in an attempt by the US State Department to resolve the fate of Eastern Europe in which Roosevelt submitted to Churchill and Stalin a document relating to the region titled "Declaration on Liberated Europe", which all three powers signed. Charles Bohlen's memoirs detail the subsequent fate of the declaration.

> The declaration was adopted. Had it been implemented by the Soviet Union, it would have radically changed the face of Eastern Europe. Almost all of the protests over Soviet policies in Eastern Europe contained a reference to the declaration. But all Soviet actions, from Vishinsky's forcing of a communist-dominated government on Rumania [sic] within a week after the close of the Yalta Conference to moves in Poland, Bulgaria, Hungary, and Czechoslovakia, were made without even a semblance of consultation with Britain or the United States. [5]

Archival materials and personal memoirs uncovered since the end of WWII have revealed that Stalin had intended from the outset to dominate as much of continental Europe as possible as a result of Soviet participation in the Allied effort. Robert C. Tucker, Stalin's biographer, writes of Stalin's intentions as reflected in his political report given at the 18th Party Congress on March 10, 1939. In the report

> … he was projecting … a scenario that had lain in his own mind since at least 1925 and animated his diplomacy subsequently. It envisaged a war between two European coalitions with the USSR remaining neutral until an advantageous moment and then intervening to advance the Communist cause. The task of diplomacy was to help this division of Europe to come about … .[6]

"This, Stalin could calculate, would enable Hitler to unleash aggression and him, [Stalin] while remaining neutral, to take over territories in Eastern Europe on an agreed- upon basis."[7] While Eastern Europe was in its sights, the Baltic Nations were as well, as the letters of Georgi Dimitrov, the long term head of the Comintern and one of Stalin's closest associates, attest: "on 25 December 1939 Stalin remarked to Dimitrov that 'we think that in the mutual assistance pacts (with Estonia, Latvia, Lithuania) we have found the form that will allow us to bring a number of countries into the sphere of influence of the Soviet Union'."[8] In speaking of the Soviets' plans at war's end, Allen Dulles, the first civilian director of the US Central Intelligence Agency (1953–61), candidly stated "... it is wise to remember that the Communist program was well under way by the time of our peace talks with them at Yalta and Potsdam. Then they were thinking not of peace but of how they could use the common victory, and their zones of military occupation, for further Communist conquest."[9]

While Russia hands in the State Department might have suspected Stalin's plans for a sphere of influence in Europe, those plans were definitely a major cause for concern for the countries of Central and Eastern Europe and the Baltics, which had dealt with the colossus to their east in a variety of ways prior to the onset of WWII and during the war. The Czechoslovaks, under former Prime Minister Eduard Beneš's leadership, tried to make an ally of the USSR and thought they had succeeded.[10] The Hungarians on the other hand, having had a taste of communist government during the six-month Béla Kun regime in 1919, were desperate to form alliances with any of the major powers other than the Soviets. The Poles knew that the victorious Soviets were going to gain a major portion of their territories and were simply attempting to minimize Soviet control of Poland. However, Bohlen tells us that Stalin managed to resist the attempts by Churchill and the US "to modify his grasp on Poland, thus ensuring his domination of Eastern Europe ... ."[11]

When Hitler's launched his surprise Operation Barbarossa campaign against the Soviet Union in June 1941, it broke the Soviet–German Alliance[12] that Stalin had signed in August 1939 with the express plan of utilizing the alliance to parcel out Eastern Europe. Stalin then allied with the West to accomplish what he could not achieve in league with Hitler.[13] And in the main he was wildly successful. He was able to execute his plan with little or no interference from the United States and Great Britain, whose pragmatic practice during WWII was to acquiesce to Soviet demands.[14] And indeed, the sacrifice made by the USSR was a powerful argument for appeasement. There is no question, however, that the West's reluctance to challenge Stalin granted him many strategic and diplomatic victories and advantages. He was often able to prevail with Roosevelt, as, for example, in two issues agreed upon at the Teheran Conference —the redrawing of the Polish borders to give the Soviet Union a third of eastern Poland and the Soviet takeover of the Baltic States.[15] Also agreed upon, according to Charles Bohlen's recounting of Stalin's plan for a post-war Europe in his memoirs, was that

> Germany was to be broken up and kept broken up. The states of eastern, southeastern and central Europe will not be permitted to group themselves into any federations or association. France is to be stripped of her colonies and strategic bases beyond her borders and will not be permitted to maintain any appreciable military establishment....the result would be that the Soviet Union would be the only important military and political force on the continent of Europe. The rest of Europe would be reduced to military and political impotence.[16]

The War's End

In 1945 Washington policymakers formulated a three-point plan: 1. to support the United Nations and make its agencies operational; 2. to work out methods of collaboration with Stalin and his associates, considered essential to making the UN a reality; 3. to rely on the British to deal with the wide array of political problems arising from the chaos of two wars just twenty years apart. "Only a minority at this point (mostly anti-communist European émigrés) thought that the principal problems of the postwar period would be caused by the Soviet Union, which had borne a major share of the burden of defeating Hitler" and had lost 20 million people during the war.[17]

Only a year later, however, US President Harry S. Truman received what came to be known as "the Long Telegram" from George F. Kennan, a long-time State Department expert on the USSR who had been posted in Moscow after the war. Kennan's February 22, 1946, message warned the Truman administration about Soviet expansionist policies and urged the US to develop a policy of "containment". Shortly after Kennan's telegram, Churchill also warned of Soviet expansion and colonialism in his Iron Curtain speech at Westminster College in Fulton, Missouri. The speech was delivered on March 5, 1946, the year the curtain began to descend on the countries of Central and Eastern Europe. However, on August 21, 1944, long before the war ended, Churchill's private physician, Lord Moran, had already noted in his diary: "Winston never talks about Hitler these days; he is always harping on the dangers of Communism. He dreams of the Red Army spreading like a cancer from one country to another. It has become an obsession – he seems to think of little else."[18]

In September 1946, Truman's aide, Clark M. Clifford, presented the president with an important state paper on the issue of US relations with the Soviet Union. It outlined every detail of the wartime relationship with the Soviet Union and accurately predicted the postwar relationship between the nations. Clifford's comments also outlined the postwar prospects for US foreign relations and the "shape and thrust of Truman's subsequent programs, the Greek–Turkish aid legislation or Truman Doctrine, the Marshall Plan, and the North Atlantic Alliance [NATO]." Clifford framed the situation as follows:

> The gravest problem facing the United States today is that of American relations with the Soviet Union. The solution of that problem may determine whether or not there will be a third World War. Soviet leaders appear to be conducting their nation on a course of aggrandizement designed to lead to eventual world domination by the USSR. Their goal, and their policies designed to reach it, are in direct conflict with American ideals, and the United States has not yet been able to persuade Stalin and his associates that world peace and prosperity lie not in the direction in which the Soviet union is moving but in the opposite direction of international cooperation and friendship.[19]

After his return to the US, Kennan expanded on the same theme in an article published under the pseudonym "X" in the July 1947 issue of

Foreign Affairs.[20] Kennan's expertise and the growing recognition of the Soviet threat meant that his perspective was taken very seriously by the US administration. The case made to Truman by his advisors and the professional "Russia hands" in the State Department, coupled with the uncomfortable partnership among the allies throughout the war, added impetus to the president's decision to implement what became known as the Truman Doctrine. What added further impetus was that the nations of Central and East Europe were being Sovietized at an alarming rate, and national leaders whose lives were in mortal danger were fleeing to the West. Nikola Petkov, an anti-communist parliamentary leader in Bulgaria was arrested on June 6, 1947, and after a show trial was hanged on September 23 of that year. The exodus of freely elected political leaders included Stanislaw Mikolajczyk, deputy prime minister of Poland, Ferenc Nagy, prime minister of Hungary, and Msgr. Béla Varga, speaker of the Hungarian parliament – all of whom had fled to the West by June 1947.

Post World War II US Foreign Policy

The Onset of the Cold War and the Truman Doctrine

The policy the Truman administration put in place was later defined as follows by Paul Nitze, who followed George Kennan as head of the State Department's Policy Planning Staff:

> For over forty years the foreign and defense policies of the United States were guided by a central theme, a well-defined basic policy objective. That goal, throughout the Cold War, was for the United States to take the lead in building an international world order based on liberal economic and political institutions, and to defend that world against communist attack.[21]

While this was the official policy of the United States, successive post war administrations interpreted it differently, and its implementation varied considerably.[22]

What did Truman face as the euphoria of victory diminished and post war reality sank in? The Soviets were disinclined to repay even a portion of the Lend-Lease funds the USSR owed to the United States, or of the funds expended for Red Cross and US–Russian war relief efforts. The Soviet Union also pressured all of its European satellites to reject the Marshall Plan that the US was rolling out to help the war torn nations of Europe effect their recovery. The Soviet Army now occupied much of Europe and wasn't going to go home; Communist agitators were disrupting governments and free elections in most European countries; Greece and Turkey were in danger of toppling into the Communist camp; and France and Italy already had powerful Communist parties. This latter was no surprise. As Roosevelt had told Archduke Otto Habsburg in August 1944 at the Second Anglo-American Quebec Conference, during the war the Soviets had negotiated an agreement that any Allied decision to provide support for WWII underground movements had to be unanimous. Thus, the Allies had funded principally the communist and leftist underground, and requests for aid to centrist and rightist partisan groups were regularly refused because of Soviet objections.[23]

Realizing that he needed to deal with the crisis of Soviet aggression, on March 12, 1947, Truman spoke before a joint session of Congress outlining what became known as the Truman Doctrine. His purpose was to ask Congress for funds to counterattack against Communist infiltration of European countries, specifically Turkey and Greece, where communist guerrillas were operating and an imminent overthrow of civil society was feared. "Totalitarian regimes imposed on free peoples by direct or indirect aggression, undermine the foundations of international peace and hence the security of the United States," Truman said. "I believe it must be the policy of the United States to support free peoples who are resisting attempted subjugation by armed minorities or by outside pressures … . I believe that we must assist free peoples to work out their own destinies in their own way."[24]

Truman's speech reinforced policy expressed years earlier by Churchill and Roosevelt at the August 14, 1941, joint issuing of the Atlantic Charter. The charter made two important statements that continued to give hope to the beleaguered nations of Europe throughout the war. It stated in Point 2 that the signatories "desire to see no territorial changes that are not in accord with the freely expressed wishes of the peoples concerned"; and Point 3 advocated that the signatories "respect the right of all peoples to choose the form of government under which they will live; and they wish to see sovereign rights and self government restored to those who have been forcibly deprived of them."[25] Perhaps more important to his constituency, Truman's speech also addressed the increased concern among the American public "that we, as signatories of the Yalta Agreements owed a debt to these people [Central & East Europeans] for having let them down by failing to force the Soviet Union to live up to its promise of free elections in the countries they had liberated or conquered."[26]

Acknowledging the threat and the need to support the president, Congress provided Truman with the funds he requested to support the reconstruction of Europe and fund the Marshall Plan, as well as to deploy large numbers of US troops to military bases throughout Europe and to establish the North Atlantic Treaty Organization (NATO), founded in April 1949. In 1950, 32 percent of the total number of US troops was deployed in foreign countries, with 52 percent of those troops deployed in Europe. From the early 1950s until early 1990, West Germany hosted a quarter of a million US military personnel. Smaller numbers of US troops were posted in the rest of Europe, with the greatest number in France (70,000) in the 1950s.[27] These numbers illustrate the strong US presence on the continent from 1950 onward, and they highlight the fact that military response on the continent was in fact available to support any democratic uprising.

As the US ramped up its presence on the world stage and the Cold War became a reality, US foreign policy officials went into high gear to do everything and anything, publicly and covertly, to support the nation's policy of "containment" of the Soviet Union.

Implementation of the Truman Doctrine: Planning organized political warfare

The official US policy statement creating this program was as much a statement for "liberation" as for "containment". In 1947 Soviet expert George Kennan was appointed the first director of the State Department's Policy Planning Staff. Together with Dulles, William "Wild Bill" Donovan and Charles "Chip" Bohlen, as well as Clark Clifford of Truman's staff,[28] Kennan led the move to convince the administration to establish an agency to undertake "covert psychological operations to counteract Soviet and Soviet inspired activities which constitute a threat to world peace and security, or are designed to discredit and defeat the United States in its endeavors to promote a world peace and security."[29]

In a Top Secret memorandum dated April 30, 1948, Kennan presented to the National Security Council (NSC) a State Department position paper titled "The Inauguration of Organized Political Warfare", which became the ideological basis for this policy. In his report, Kennan speaks of the historical precedent for political warfare as practiced by the Soviet Union and by the British. About the latter he writes:

> ... the creation, success, and survival of the British Empire has been due in part to the British understanding and application of the principles of political warfare.... We have been handicapped however by a popular attachment to the concept of a basic difference between peace and war, by a tendency to view war as a sort of sporting contest outside of all political context, by a national tendency to seek for a political cure-all, and by a reluctance to recognize the realities of international relations – the perpetual rhythm of [sentence incomplete].This government has of course, in part consciously and part unconsciously, been conducting political warfare. Aggressive Soviet political warfare has driven us overtly prior to the Truman Document to ERP then to sponsorship of Western Union. [Two lines redacted here.] This was all political warfare and should be recognized as such ... Having assumed greater international responsibili-

> ties than ever before in our history and having been engaged by the full might of the Kremlin's political warfare, we cannot afford to leave unmobilized [sic] our resources for covert political warfare.[30]

Kennan then goes on to propose a three-point program of support for "liberation committees, underground activities behind the Iron Curtain and support of indigenous anti-Communist elements in threatened countries of the Free World". The liberation committees' purpose would be: "To form centers of national hope and revive a sense of purpose among political refugees from the Soviet World; to provide an inspiration for continuing popular resistance within the countries of the Soviet World; and to provide a potential nucleus for all-out liberation movements in the event of war."[31]

In describing how the committees would be formed and supported, Kennan further elaborates the operation he proposes:

> This is primarily an overt operation which, however, should receive covert guidance and possibly assistance from the Government. It is proposed that trusted private American citizens be encouraged to establish a public committee which would give support and guidance in US interests to national freedom movements publicly led by outstanding political refugees from the Soviet World, such as Mikolajczyk and Nagy.[32] The American Committee should be so selected and organized as to cooperate closely with this Government. The functions of the American Committee should be limited to enabling selected refugee leaders to keep alive as public figures with access to printing presses and microphones. It should not engage in underground [sic][33]
>
> What is proposed here is an operation in the traditional American form: organized public support of resistance to tyranny in foreign countries. Throughout our history, private American citizens have banded together to champion the cause of freedom for people suffering under oppression. (The Communists and Zionist have exploited this tradition to the extreme, to their own ends to our national det-

> riment, as witness the Abraham Lincoln brigade during the Spanish Civil War and the current illegal Zionist activities.) Our proposal is that this tradition be revived specifically to further American national interests in the present crisis.[34]

Kennan then outlines the second of the three proposals, "Underground Activities behind the Iron Curtain", the purpose of which would be to "maintain contact with, sustain, and influence underground movements in the Soviet World resisting Kremlin domination."[35] Here Kennan envisions that, in contrast to CIA operations, which involved the American government directly with clandestine activities, the project would follow the example set by the Soviets and British in political warfare; to wit, "remote and deeply concealed official control of clandestine operations so that governmental responsibility cannot be shown."[36] While the government would provide direction and funding, a private American organization or organizations led by someone such as Allen Dulles would execute the plans. The organizations, having set up offices in Europe and Asia would establish contact with clandestine services in those countries and use them to "pass on assistance and guidance to the resistance movements behind the Iron Curtain".[37]

The third of these proposed areas of action was "Support of Indigenous Anti-Communist Elements in Threatened Countries of the Free World". The purpose in this case was to "strengthen indigenous forces combatting communism in countries where Soviet political warfare is threat to our national security." Again, this was to be "a covert operation utilizing private intermediaries. To insure cover, the private American organizations conducting the operation should be separate from the organizations mentioned in previous projects."[38]

Further on in his report Kennan recommends that while "covert political warfare" must be controlled by the State Department, the direction should not be physically located therein. In part because the funds needed for an operation such as the one proposed could not be hidden in the department's budget. "Therefore, this operation must find cover elsewhere."[39]

Concluding his report, Kennan points out that the time had arrived "for the creation of a covert political warfare operations directorate within the Government". He recommends that if the department were to be established, it should be under unified direction with one person as "boss". He recommends immediate establishment of a directorate of political warfare operations under the cover of the National Council Secretariat.

Acting on Kennan's recommendations, on June 18, 1948, President Truman's National Security Council passed NSC 10/2 creating within the CIA an Office of Special Projects, later called the Office of Policy Coordination (OPC).[40] The passage of the NSC directive gave the new division the ability to undertake a full range of covert activities "incident to the conduct of secret political, psychological and economic warfare together with preventive direction action (paramilitary activities) – all within the policy direction of the Departments of State and Defense."[41]

Organized Political Warfare

Formally established on September 1, 1948, the directive creating the Office of Special Projects took note of the "vicious covert activities of the USSR" and gave the new division "a loose charter to undertake the full range of covert activities incident to the conduct of secret political, psychological and economic warfare together with preventive direction action (paramilitary activities) all within the policy direction of the Departments of Sate and Defense."[42]

As Gerald Miller described in his report on the first four years of Office of Special Projects/OPC activities,

> … to the United States and to OPC the conduct of political and psychological warfare in peacetime was a new art. Some of the techniques were known but doctrine and experience were lacking. OPC was to learn by doing. By 1952 OPC had built an organization capable of executing covert action on a worldwide scale … . The secret

> war provided an immediate area of confrontation and, as a consequence, there was much governmental pressure to "get on with it".[43]

The word soon got out to intelligence services, groups and individuals that there was "a force abroad in the world around which they could rally and gain support in their own opposition to Communism."[44] This was a new type of warfare, involving "commitment without capability", which relied on technology and psychological techniques.[45]

Miller continued in his report:

> The first priority of the State Department was the need to deal with the political leadership of the many thousands of refugees and émigrés who had fled to the West from the satellite nations and Russia. The most immediate problem was how to deal with them outside of the Iron Curtain. They could not be endorsed to head governments in exile as pragmatically the US needed to recognize the Communist regimes that had assumed power; but these political figures could be utilized in campaigns of psychological and political warfare behind the Iron Curtain.[46]

Malcolm Proudfoot's seminal work on the post WWII refugee problem gives us some idea of the scope of that problem. He reports that the Preparatory Commission of the International Refugee Organization (1947–1951) and the International Refugee Organization (IRO) that succeeded it were responsible for resettling 1,039,601 displaced persons and refugees from the Iron Curtain countries, including the Baltic States and the USSR, from 1947–1951. Of this number, 329,301 were resettled in the United States and Australia; Canada and Israel each accepted over one hundred thousand refugees. Coupled with the émigrés from these nations who were already in the United States, it was estimated that persons in this category composed 11 percent of America's population – a force to be reckoned with at the ballot box and in formulating future foreign policy.[47]

Establishment of the Committee for Free Europe, Inc.

In Notes from a Memorandum of Conversation dated August 26, 1948, "CIA, State Department, Defense Department, and OPC officials discuss establishing a philanthropic organization to sponsor radio broadcasts and other activities of East European émigrés."[48] Those notes show that Rear Admiral Roscoe H. Hillenkoetter (Director of Intelligence), George Kennan, Charles W. Thayer, Col. Ivan Yeaton, Frank Wisner, Maynard Barnes and _____ Ruddock (name redacted) met to a) "consider the establishment of a democratic, philanthropic organization in New York under some such name as the American Committee for Free Europe which in turn would b) organize a committee of responsible foreign language groups now in the western Zones of Germany and provide them with facilities for communication with their homelands."[49] The memorandum further detailed what the Office of Special Projects would provide in addition to covering financial and material support (details on the form of controls to be used are redacted from the file copy): "the New York Committee would provide direction to the refugee committee in Germany, making arrangements for émigré leaders now in Western Europe and the US to participate in the informational activities of the refugee organization. The refugee committee would operate the radio and printing facilities, providing all necessary technical personnel."[50] The closing paragraph states the principal problems in connection with implementation of the program: "a) Soviet reaction b) US response to Soviet reaction, c) the allocation of wave-bands to the refugee committees, and the d) countermeasures to be taken to minimize the effects of Soviet jamming; and e) precautions to protect OSP and the US Government from any attributable connection with the New York or Germany organizations."[51] It is clear then from this organizing document that the intention on the part of US intelligence leaders from the start was to use the newly established corporation to mount, as the primary mission of the organization, a clandestine radio campaign beamed to the Soviet Satellites.

Peter Grose tells us in his biography of Dulles that at the same time the intelligence leaders were meeting

> ... bored in his law practice...[Dulles]was already embarked as a private citizen on a mission of his own in a domain that the public mind could not yet recognize. He quietly conceived the idea of a network of 'fronts' for the coming battle against communism, the national interest as Allen perceived it. With the zeal that came to mark the Cold War generation, he led a like-minded group of public citizens in creating the means for psychological warfare and subversion. Nothing useful could be expected from the sluggish CIA and its lackluster holdovers from abandoned careers. What was needed, instead, was a structure of public organizations that could carry to the world the virtues of democracy without the baggage of bureaucracy. With fanfare he [Allen Dulles] presided for the formation of such innocuous-sounding groups such as the Free Europe Committee ... .[52]

While Grose's depiction of the formation of the Free Europe Committee may appear to contradict the organizational goals and plans outlined above in the August 26, 1948 Memorandum of Conversation, it should instead be taken as an indication that Dulles may have been the catalyst for the formation of the FEC. Not only was he involved from its inception (he was named president of the FEC, Inc. when it was formed and chair of the NCFE, Inc executive committee when it was renamed a few days later) but some key individuals who joined the organization at its inception were also his choices – among them Frederic Dolbeare, Royall Tyler, Jay Lovestone and Carmel Offie. This indicates his depth of interest and his influence in the new organization.[53]

The Committee for Free Europe, Inc. was incorporated in the state of New York on May 11, 1949, as a not for profit corporation. "Shortly thereafter the incorporators decided the name 'National Committee for Free Europe, Inc.' would be preferable and an application was made to the Secretary of State of New York in this sense, and the Certificate of Change of Name was filed with the Secretary of State on May 19,

1949."[54] Allen Dulles was elected as its president at its first board meeting on May 17, 1949. [55] In New York on June 1, 1949, Joseph C. Grew announced to the press that the NCFE had been established as a private organization of "freedom loving Americans" as part of the US initiative to counter the threat of the spread of Communism worldwide.[56] In 1954 NCFE, Inc. was renamed the Free Europe Committee, Inc. (FEC) [reverting to the name of the original incorporating organization]. NCFE, Inc. operated under the stewardship of the State Department and the Department of Defense and was covertly funded through the Central Intelligence Agency (CIA) for the life of the organization, from 1949–1971.[57]

A *New York Times* headline of June 2, 1949, trumpeted the NCFE's formation: "New Group Formed to Assist Refugees; Unit led by Grew; Plan to Help Prepare Leaders for Time When Iron Curtain Lifts; Public Fund Drive is Set; Committee Will Be Independent of the Government but Will Supplement Its Work".[58]

Many exile groups from Central and Eastern European nations were formed during and immediately after the war, both in the US and abroad. During the war, the Polish and Czechoslovakian governments in exile, headquartered in London, were recognized by the Allied powers; the exiled leaders from nations fighting on the Axis side never achieved the same recognition. However, after Yalta and Potsdam, on July 6, 1945, even the Polish government in exile in London, which had provided over two hundred thousand troops to fight under British command on the Allied side during the war, had its recognition withdrawn by Great Britain and the United States. The onset of the Cold War reversed this hands-off policy radically, and most of the recently formed, post war national council programs were then folded into the sphere of NCFE, Inc. The first individual to serve as NCFE, Inc.'s president, DeWitt C. Poole, acknowledged this in a September 28, 1950, letter to Allen Dulles, chair of the executive committee, referring to "the concept of national councils we inherited".[59]

The first meeting of the incorporators and subscribers of the newly formed organization was held on May 17, 1949, after which a statement was issued to the public in which the founders announced that they "join in announcing the National Committee for Free Europe, Inc." and proclaimed:

- We will seek to further the cause of freedom everywhere –
- By supporting those democratic leaders who have escaped to the United States from Communist oppression in Eastern Europe…
- We will assist those leaders:
- To maintain themselves in useful occupations during their enforced stay in the United States;
- To come to know the people of the United States and to understand their spirit and aims;
- To engage in efforts by radio, press and other means to keep alive in their fellow citizens in Europe the ideals of individual and national freedom;
- To establish effective means of cooperation with like-minded European leaders in the United States, and to coordinate their plans with those of similar leaders abroad.
- We will encourage these leaders to maintain in this country National Committees which will stand as symbols of democratic hope to their peoples – the peoples of Bulgaria, Czechoslovakia, Hungary, Poland, Rumania and Yugoslavia to whom at Yalta in 1945 we promised *free elections and the fundamental freedoms.*
- Arms and economic aid are indispensable but by themselves are not enough. Only in the field of ideas and spiritual values can victory be lasting.

A new operation begins in the American defense and counter-attack against the Communist assault. Money is needed to finance the fight.

We call on all Americans to join us by sending an urgently needed contribution. As the Communists like to remind us: "*It is later than you think.*"[60]

As of June 20, 1949, the NCFE officers were: Joseph C. Grew, board chairman; DeWitt C. Poole, president; Frank Altschul, treasurer; Frederic R. Dolbeare, secretary; and Allen W. Dulles, chairman of the executive committee. The committee members included: A. A. Berle Jr., Francis Biddle, Robert Wood Bliss, James B. Carey, William L. Clayton, Hugh A. Drum, Dwight D. Eisenhower, Mark F. Ethridge, James A. Farley, William Green, Charles R. Hook, Arthur Bliss Lane, Henry R. Luce, Joseph V. McKee, Arthur W. Page, Spyros Skouras, Charles M. Spofford, Charles P. Taft, DeWitt Wallace, W.W. Waymack, Matthew Woll, Darryl Zanuck and Virginia Gildersleeve.[61]

The chairman, Grew, was a professional diplomat and had served as US ambassador to Japan during the 1930s and held that post when war broke out between the US and Japan. Post-war he was one of the first diplomats to speak out regarding the danger that the USSR posed to American security interests, and he is quoted as saying that "Moscow 'will constitute in future as great a danger to us as did the Axis'."[62] Poole was a former diplomat, a Russia hand who had served as US chargé d' affaires in Moscow and Archangel during the first years of the Bolshevik Revolution. He had the earliest contact with the Bolsheviks and a first hand view of how they seized power in Russia. "Thirty years later, Poole still identified Bolshevism as a deadly threat to civilization, a new form of barbarism that pursued its interests unrestrained by moral or ethical standards."[63]

As can be seen from the names listed, the committee members reflected not just the world of diplomacy but leaders from the military and the worlds of commerce and entertainment as well. The committee leadership reflected a range of political ideologies – A. A. Berle was a New Dealer, while Ambassador Grew and General Dwight D. Eisenhower, soon to be elected president of the United States, were conservatives. What they all had in common was their belief that the world wide communist movement was a threat to the United States and that its progress could only be halted with an aggressive program that included psychological warfare.

Sources of Funding

Covertly funded through the CIA and supported in its efforts by the NSC and the Department of Defense, NCFE, Inc. established a base in

New York City and very quickly became a global operation with thousands of employees and offices in Paris, London, Vienna and Frankfurt. It bears repeating that referencing the name of the committee has always been problematic for scholars, as the incorporation was originally filed as Committee for Free Europe Inc, then almost immediately renamed National Committee for Free Europe. The organization name remained National Committee for Free Europe, Inc. until it was changed slightly on April 11, 1950, to the National Committee for a Free Europe, Inc., and then on March 5, 1954, to the Free Europe Committee, Inc.[64] In 1949, its first year of operation, NCFE received $69,000 in funding from the US government; the sum jumped to over $3 million in 1950, and by 1971 the government's annual contribution was slightly under $20 million. When coupled with a small percentage of additional funds from public and corporate contributions, that year's budget totaled just over $20 million.[65] Over the life of the organization, 70 percent of the funds were for the operation and maintenance of Radio Free Europe.[66]

After the government source of funding of the Free Europe organization became a matter of public knowledge and discussion ensued in Congress on continuing funding and on what basis, [67] a Government Accounting Office (GAO) record of the revenues provided to fund the organization was summarized in a report dated May 25, 1972, for the Committee on Foreign Relations of the United States Senate. From its inception in May 1949 through June 30, 1971, it received a total of $356.9 million. The major source of income was the US government, from which Free Europe received $306.8 million, 86 percent of its income. Its next major source of income was public contributions, which totaled about $46 million through public fundraising campaigns such as the Crusade for Freedom. The remaining revenues, about $4.2 million, were received from the sale of fixed assets, interest income and miscellaneous income. In addition to the grants it provided to Free Europe, the US government provided the Radio Europe Fund a total of $16.5 million in operating expenses; a practice it halted after June 30, 1968.[68]

The costs for what was termed Non Radio Activities totaled about $76.1 million. These funds supported exile relations, publications and the re-deployment of Eastern Europeans. Of the $76.1 million, $29.2 million included payment of stipends to exiles and support to organizations formed by the exiles. The GAO's breakdown for these funds was as follows:

Committee for National Councils: $2,665,000
Exile Relations Program: (later exile political organization division) $19,438,000
Citizen Services: $1,466,000
Free Europe Organizations and Publications: $3,090,000
West European Operations Division: $2,508,000
Total: $29,167,000[69]

The Publication Division included printed materials, a monthly magazine, *East Europe*, and various other publications on Western affairs and the Western way of life, and distribution of these materials to the countries of East Europe and to Eastern Europeans in the West. Funds for the Publication Division also covered the cost of the controversial balloon program, which dropped millions of printed propaganda leaflets and materials behind the Iron Curtain. The total expenditure for publications was $26.6 million and included:

Publications Program (later publications and special projects): $12,252,000
Free Europe Press: $11,769,000
Free Europe Organizations and Publications: $1,765,000
Communist bloc operations: $786,000[70]

Under the heading of Redeployment of Eastern Europeans was a range of activities organized in the 1950s and 1960s that were essentially intended to help "exiles maintain themselves in suitable occupations". The largest investment in this division was for the organization and funding of the Free Europe University in Exile, which shared a teaching facility with the University of Strasbourg. The FEUE provided refugees of college age with an opportunity to continue their education in the West and in no small part was also intended to indoctrinate the students with "Western" values and to encourage them to look toward a future return to their homelands to establish democratic governments and institutions.[71]

Additional funds included under the "redeployment" heading were: scholarships to young exiles; the Mid-European Studies Center, which was staffed by exiles engaged in scholarly research on East European economic, social, historical and legal topics; and development projects, chiefly in underdeveloped nations. Expenses under this category totaled $16.1 million and broke out as follows:

Committee for Intellectual Cooperation: $5,853,000
Committee for American Contact: $204,000
Support of Free Europe University in Exile: $4,874,000
Free Europe Organizations and Publications: $2,501,000[72]
West European Operations Division: $627,000
Free-world Operations Division: $996,000
Phase out of Program: $1,028,000 (funding a successor organization to FEC, Inc., the International Development Foundation.)[73]

Under the heading Other Expenses Incurred, the GAO reported that FEC, Inc. spent about $2.1 million on Designated Projects funded by contributors who specified a designated purpose. FEC, Inc. also spent $2.2 million additional funds on "small projects that related to projects listed above".[74]

Organizational Structure of NCFE, Inc.

NCFE, Inc.'s original organizational structure in 1949 included three divisions:[75]

1) the Committee on Intellectual Cooperation, chaired by A. A. Berle, Jr, a Harvard-educated corporate lawyer and law professor, member of Franklin Delano Roosevelt's original "Brain Trust" and former assis-

tant secretary of state for Latin American affairs; 2) the Committee on Radio and the Press, chaired by Frank Altschul, III, a powerful New York investment banker; 3) the Committee on American Contacts, chaired by staff member Charles M. Spofford. At the time of its founding, Division 3 included the working groups of exiled leaders that would be the "special concern" of Allen Dulles, and the Crusade for Freedom, which was the special concern of Arthur W. Page.[76]

The Committee on Intellectual Cooperation's original efforts in 1949 included establishing a Division of Jurists and Miscellaneous Research at the Library of Congress, which was staffed by qualified exiles. The division provided interim jobs for exiled scholars until they were able to secure positions in Western research centers or universities. Exile scholars were also made available to the New York Public Library and the Library of Congress to assist in cataloging their collections on Eastern Europe. The second project of the Committee on Intellectual Cooperation was the Danubian Inquiry Project, funded by a generous grant from the Carnegie Endowment for International Peace and later through cooperation with New York University (NYU) faculty, who became joint sponsors of the project at a research center founded at Washington Square. In 1950 these two groups were merged into the Mid-European Studies Center, and as a result of financial support from NYU were able to lease a headquarters at 154 East 62nd Street in Manhattan. The Committee on Intellectual Cooperation was also responsible for "miscellaneous and individual projects", which included commissioning books and research by East European scholars as well as securing funding for placement of faculty at Harvard University and the University of Virginia.[77]

The Committee for Radio and the Press had as its assignment developing a propaganda network through public media. It became the sponsoring arm of Radio Free Europe, which by "1950 went on the air with a mobile 7.5 kilowatt shortwave transmitter located in Germany and a total programming schedule of ten hours a week. By the end of 1950, RFE was broadcasting to the people of Rumania[sic], Poland, Czechoslovakia, Bulgaria and Hungary."[78]

As the radio broadcasts developed their audiences, it was realized that broader coverage was needed, and in 1951 RFE negotiated with the government of Portugal for permission to organize the Sociedade Anonima de Raio-Retranmissao, SARL (RARET), to establish and operate facilities to relay RFE programs. By July 1951, RFE began transmitting from Portugal. They also had two transmitters at sites in Germany, and RFE's main news and broadcasting facilities were located in Munich, in the American Zone of West Germany. At the peak of its operating capability while under the sponsorship of US intelligence, RFE's network consisted of 32 transmitters having an aggregate power of over 2.2 million watts. Programming was broadcast 20 hours a day to Czechoslovakia, 19 hours to Poland and Hungary, 12 hours to Romania and 8 hours to Bulgaria. Additionally, RFE broadcast music programs on Saturdays and Sundays. By 1971 RFE estimated its listening audience in Central and East Europe to be 31 million out of an adult population of some 60 million.[79]

The Committee on American Contacts originally had two divisions, the American Contacts Division, overseen by Spofford, and the National Councils Division, overseen by Dulles. The former served the Polish, Czechoslovak, Hungarian, Romanian and Bulgarian communities of exiles, while the latter included all of the American Contacts Division countries plus Albania. The American Contacts Division introduced exile leadership to American audiences in a process intended to familiarize the émigrés with American culture but also to help promote public support for US Cold War propaganda objectives. The National Councils Division coordinated the national councils' efforts abroad and in their native lands.

The organizational structure of the divisions changed over the years the NCFE, Inc./ FEC, Inc. existed, reflecting the changes in the political landscape. The onset of attempts at "peaceful co-existence" or détente between the two Great Powers, the stalemate in the nuclear arms race, the uprisings in East Germany in 1953, Hungary in 1956 and Czechoslovakia in 1968 all impacted how the organizations' resources were deployed during their existence. Some of the key divisions, such as the Mid-European Studies Center and its publishing arm, the Free Europe

Press, evolved and increased in importance as the NCFE, Inc./FEC found its niche. The Congress for Cultural Freedom, while an organization peripheral to that of most of the exiles, served among the intelligentsia world wide as a propaganda tool against the communist threat. Its "mission was to nudge the intelligentsia of Western Europe away from its lingering fascination with Marxism and Communism towards a view more accommodating of 'the American way'."[80] The Free Europe University in Exile emerged from ideas that resulted from problem solving amongst the board regarding the issue of young refugees and their education, coupled with a desire on the part of the NCFE leadership to devise a program that would promote a pro-Western outlook amongst future young leaders who had emigrated from the satellite nations. Still other divisions, such as the Assembly of Captive European Nations (ACEN), arose from the problematic relations existing within émigré communities and the lack of cohesion amongst and within the national councils. Suffice it to say that regardless of the shifts in public policy, the primary mission of the organization remained the same throughout its life.

The Non-Radio Divisions: The National Councils

By far, the National Councils were the divisions of the NCFE/FEC organizational structure that most touched the lives of the greatest number of refugees from behind the Iron Curtain. While millions of their compatriots in their homelands were listening to RFE, it was the various organizations and economic, cultural and political groups that the national councils sponsored – directly or indirectly – with the funds provided to them that offered an immense variety of services to Eastern European refugees, and did so for the better part of two decades – even longer in some cases. In addition to being an informational touchstone and lobbying organization for the best interests of their compatriots, in many instances the national councils supplemented the work of the international NGOs that assisted refugees making the transition from their homelands to new lives in the West, helping many hundreds of thousands of individuals in the process.

Post WWII, the status of the political refugees from Eastern Europe was known to be grave, as most did not have the financial resources to maintain themselves in the West. Hundreds of thousands of Displaced Persons were already in Europe's refugee camps when the Iron Curtain began to fall, and many thousands of newly arrived refugees soon swelled their ranks. Among them were hundreds of political leaders from the satellite nations. The nationality groups began to organize themselves while still in Europe, some along military lines, some along political lines, but it was not until after their leadership arrived in the United States and US Cold War policy was newly minted that these émigré groups became influential factors in their respective communities in the US and abroad.

In 1947 the State Department had informally reversed its position discouraging the formation of émigré groups. While they did not publicly provide official support to them they had been encouraged to organize "With the knowledge and acquiescence of the Department of the Department of State, before NCFE came into being four national Councils of Committees had been formed and were in active existence." [81] Hungarian émigré leaders had been among the first to organize announced the formation of their group on November 18, 1947. The Bulgarian National Committee, the Council of Free Czechoslovakia and the Rumanian [sic] National Committee were also formed prior to the NCFE becoming operational.[82] All had been provided with funding to enable their establishment by the Department of State as the Cold War became reality. "As soon as the NCFE received its charter and commenced operations it was requested to take over the foregoing Committees as far as payments concerned and to work closely with the Committees in order to develop their activities along useful lines."[83]

However, by 1949, as Gerald Miller recounts,

> Highest on the State Department's priorities was the need to deal with the political leadership of the countless thousands of refugees and émigrés who had fled to the West from Russia and the satellite countries. The immediate problem was to deal with them outside of the Iron Curtain. These leaders could not be endorsed to head

> governments- in-exile for the realities of the situation ultimately demanded recognition of the Communist regimes that had assumed power; but they could be employed in the conduct of PP operations behond[sic] the Curtain.[84]

NCFE's chairman, Joseph Grew, put American's reasoning in supporting the political exiles on a much more elevated plane in an introductory statement to the press issued on June 2, 1949:

> In an immediate sense, our enterprise derives from Yalta. There in 1945 you will recall, the United States joined with the United Kingdom and the USSR in promising to the peoples liberated from the Nazi tyranny free elections and the fundamental freedoms. The peoples in question are those of Poland, Czechoslovakia, Hungary Rumania, Yugoslavia and Bulgaria. That promise has not been kept. On the contrary, a new oppression has arisen; and from that oppression the democratic leaders of the six nations mentioned have escaped abroad, so far as they could. A good number have arrived in the United States and are among us as exiles and refugees; more may come.
> Our program begins with the tangible fact of the presence here of these exiles and refugees. There is an American tradition of hospitality to political refugees. The promise which we gave at Yalta remains unredeemed. More than that we have a definite self-interest in helping to keep alive, and in full vigor, political leaders who share our view of life – leaders who have refused to knuckle under, men who have not hesitated to risk their lives for their democratic faith. [85]

Whether the reasons for the US policy were pragmatic or idealistic, it was a boon to the newly formed national councils With the newly formed NCFE the leadership of the émigré groups was provided with bountiful funding, office space, salaries and support systems for their organizations.

The NCFE, Inc. leadership considered the Hungarian group to be the most successful of the national councils, and that group can serve as an example to track the development of the exile committees.[86] After it's founding, the Hungarian National Council (HNC) announced its mission and the establishment of a national council composed of Hungarian citizens.[87] The executive committee chairman was Msgr. Béla Varga, a Roman Catholic priest and the last freely elected speaker of the Hungarian Parliament (until May 31, 1947) who had not resigned his post when he fled to the West. The executive committee also included the prime minister of Hungary, Ferenc Nagy, who had recently been forced into exile, and other major political leaders.[88] By 1954 the HNC had 76 members, including all of the exiled former leaders from Hungary, among them two former prime ministers, several ministers and the former leaders of all the political parties purged between 1947 and 1949. The former Royal Hungarian Legations in Portugal and in Spain operated as the council's representatives as a result of those nations not having recognized the communist led Hungarian government and continued to so operate and issue passports into the 1960s. And while denials abounded on the part of NCFE, Inc. that these were not undeclared governments in exile, in many ways the Hungarian executive committee functioned as such, as did the national councils of Poland, Bulgaria, Romania and Czechoslovakia.[89] Because rivalry among opposition groups carried over from their home countries into emigration, the committees were rife with competition and infighting, and some nationalities' representation in émigré life included rival groups. But only the Polish émigrés carried their rivalry to the point that they were represented by two groups in some of the major bodies sponsored by NCFE, Inc.[90]

To illustrate the extent of NCFE's sponsorship for just one small nation under its umbrella, consider that at the peak of its activities the Hungarian National Council had offices in Washington, D.C. and New York City and satellite groups and offices in eighteen countries. Their entire budget, like that of most of other national councils and émigré groups, was funded through the NCFE. That the revenues originated from the Office of Policy Coordination at the CIA remained secret. John Foster Leich, who served as the assistant director of the National Councils Division for over a decade, writes that "the exiles without exception assumed that government funds were involved, and were glad of this evidence of United States interest in their cause."[91] However he does not say that the exiles were aware that their funding came from US intelligence. In his article on the national councils he makes clear that although he was an experienced foreign service officer when he came to the NCFE, he personally was only made aware "after an appropriate probationary period – that government funds were involved, but that this was officially to be denied. The precise origin, means of transmission, or obligations which this funding imposed upon the Committee were never discussed with any staff member who did not have a direct 'need to know' and had not been 'cleared' for that purpose."[92] That this was a topic that was not broached even within the committee itself is made clear by Leich and by this author's review of the archival material related to the NCFE and FEC, including the minutes of the Executive Committee meetings.[93]

The national councils had various organizational structures, but with few exceptions most of their leadership was composed of pre-communist era former political leaders or diplomats. Each of the committees had a staff in New York or Washington DC (for a brief period some had offices and staff in both) that included an office manager and someone to handle bookkeeping (usually English speaking to be able to converse with the NCFE staff and auditors). The committees typically published a bulletin or newsletter – in the national language (and/or in English) – which was distributed within the US and abroad. The committees were conduits of information regarding their respective nations, and questions in that regard were referred to them. There were specific job descriptions assigned to members that included lobbying, liaison with their nationality groups, assistance with visas and job or legal problems arising within the émigré community.[94] Were any involved with intelligence behind the Iron Curtain? Leich, who had firsthand experience, tells us that some exiles "were specifically entrusted with keeping contact with the homeland, a process with which the NCFE was not directly concerned and into which we did not pry. It was my impression that such intelligence services as the committee undertook were delivered directly to interested American governmental agencies."[95]

In addition to the national councils and their infrastructures, the NCFE from its inception provided financial support for "meritorious exiles" from the satellites. The list reads like a Who's Who of Central and Eastern Europe's diplomatic and political elite. These individuals were not necessarily expected to perform any tasks (although many worked extensively on behalf of the NCFE) but received stipends as a result of their position in the émigré hierarchy. They received regular compensation from NCFE, Inc./FEC, Inc. until that support was terminated on November 30, 1957.[96] We do not know how many other exiles where supported or subsidized by the organization in some manner that is not transparent and of which there are no records available.

Although the composition of NCFE, Inc.'s leadership was public information, it was not well known that many of its members had prior intelligence service affiliations or were directly or indirectly involved with the intelligence community or the military. De Witt Poole and Whitney H. Shepardson served in the OSS, as did C.D. Jackson of the Luce publishing empire. John Chambers Hughes also served in the OSS during WWII and was later chief of mission to NATO and European Regional Organizations in Paris during the Eisenhower Administration. General Dwight D. Eisenhower and Rear Admiral Harold Blaine Miller were, of course, military leaders. Significant in the organization's makeup was that the chairmanship of the executive committee was held by Allen W. Dulles, also formerly of the OSS, as were the two individuals who were to serve as heads of the National Councils Division: Frederic Dolbeare (1949–1957) and Bernard Yarrow (1957–1973). Minutes of the meetings show that representatives of both the CIA and the Department of Defense were present at some of the NCFE board meetings.[97]

In its primary role as a propaganda organization, NCFE, Inc. used its leadership's prestige and media contacts from the onset to announce its formation, its purpose and its planned activities.[98] The board included prominent members of the media who helped publicize the work of NCFE, Inc., such as DeWitt Wallace, founder and chairman of *Readers Digest* and Mark F. Ethridge, editor and publisher of the *Louisville Courier Journal and Times*, chairman of the US Advisory Commission on Information from 1948–1950 and former president of the National Association of Broadcasters.[99]

The Public Activities

In its first organizational structure, NCFE, Inc. provided sponsorship for the institutions and organizations already mentioned. As organizational plans were laid, it also began to explore ways in which the propaganda or psychological warfare campaign against Communism could be exported to the American public, which, although having been exposed to media coverage recounting the dangers of communism, was not really familiar with what it meant to be under communist control. But by 1950, after the outbreak of civil war heralded the strong possibility of a communist takeover on the Korean peninsula – a prospect the US had deployed troops to prevent – the American public was more fully aware of the dangers of communism. The public knew that the governments of Central and East Europe were controlled by Soviet puppets and in many cases were occupied by hundreds of thousands of Soviet troops; and by then many Americans had perhaps encountered some of the three hundred thousand or more Displaced Persons who had left their homelands for the US, not for economic but for political reasons. However, there was no denying that two oceans separated the American public from nations that had fallen to communism, so the question of how to engage them and encourage their support was a challenge NCFE, Inc.'s organizers took on. The challenge was addressed by the formation of the Crusade for Freedom, which became the public face of the campaign to support the work of NCFE, Inc. and RFE.

The Crusade for Freedom

In addition to the various national councils incorporated into NCFE, Inc., that organization's leadership began plans in 1949 to take on another huge financial commitment, the establishment of two new broadcast entities Radio Free Europe and Radio Liberty. In April 1950 the Crusade for Freedom, which took the Liberty Bell as its symbol, was established as a not for profit organization whose mission was to raise funds from the general public for the NCFE, but primarily for Radio Free Europe.[100] Its secondary but perhaps more important function was to influence American public opinion in support of the anti-communist crusade. A press release issued by Poole on April 26, 1950, announced that General Lucius D. Clay had agreed to chair the new organization. "The Crusade, in which every American citizen will be invited to participate, will carry our message of freedom and friendship to the oppressed and threatened people overseas and give the lie to Kremlin propaganda that our goal is world domination and war."[101]

President Truman's May 1, 1950, letter of congratulation to General Grew on the Crusade's launch reads:

> Dear Joe, your telegram of April twenty-eight, advising me that the National Committee for a Free Europe is launching a nationwide crusade for freedom, meets with my heartiest approval. I hope that all Americans will join with you in dedicating themselves to this critical struggle for men's minds. I am deeply gratified by your prompt response to my appeal of April twentieth, in which I emphasized the important role of private groups and organizations in the great endeavor.[102]

The roster of the Crusade's regional chairmen included a Who's Who of American business and finance – A.P. Giannini, founder and president of the Bank of America, Palmer Hoyt, publisher of the *Denver Post*, Harry A. Bullis, board chairman of General Mills, Frank R. Denton, vice-chairman of Mellon National Bank and Trust, Walter H. Wheeler Jr., president of Pitney Bowes, Inc. – and the Crusade's influence in communities throughout America cannot be underestimated.[103] While there were Crusade fundraisers at, for example, the Metropolitan Opera in New York, its primary fundraising efforts targeted the general American public. In 1950 $1,288,000 was raised, the bulk of it in contributions "of under one dollar".[104] Supplementing the activities of the professional fundraising staff was a large number of grass roots supporters – "there is a group of approximately 1000 business leaders headed by the national chairman and by 59 State chairmen or cochairmen."[105] It was said that "the Crusade's real strength rested in the thousands of volunteers around the country."[106]

Although it never raised more than a small part of the NCFE's budget, the Crusade's publications, advertising, parades, public forums and annual fundraising slogans (such as, "Fight the Big Lie with the Big Truth" and "Help Truth Fight Communism") helped to mobilize American support for the Cold War. The Crusade's campaign symbol, the ten-ton Freedom Bell (designed to replicate the Liberty Bell), was emblazoned with a laurel wreath symbolizing peace and a frieze of five figures representing the five races of humankind passing the torch of freedom. Its inscription quoted Abraham Lincoln: "That this world under God shall have a new birth of freedom." The bell arrived from its British foundry to a ticker tape parade in New York City and then toured 21 US cities, where over one and half million Americans signed a Freedom Scroll to be delivered and presented along with the bell at its final destination in West Berlin.[107] In West Berlin, the bell was installed in City Hall on October 24, 1950, in a ceremony with over 400,000 Berliners present, including West German Chancellor Konrad Adenauer, the mayor of West Berlin, Dr. Ernst Reuter, and General Maxwell D. Taylor, commander of US military forces in Germany. It was fitting that General Clay, a hero of the 1948 Berlin airlift as well as chairman of the Crusade, started the bell ringing. It is said that it could be heard ten miles away, throughout East Berlin and into East Germany as well.[108]

The Crusade received strong support from the general public in the early 1950s, but after several years it began to downplay its grass roots campaign in order to concentrate on corporate donors, which had become increasingly important as the organization matured. As an example, the Crusade fundraising committee in 1953 was chaired by Henry Ford II, chairman of the Ford Motor Company, simultaneously with his service as chairman of the board of trustees of the American Heritage Foundation. Ford incorporated the Crusade fundraising drive into the Heritage

Foundation's program with a goal of raising $4 million in the 1952/53 campaign.[109] By 1956 when the radios received public criticism for their performance during the Hungarian Revolution, the public campaign was discontinued while the corporate fundraising effort to support the radios continued unabated: the 1957 campaign sought to raise $10 million; and in 1958 a group of 56 US community leaders went on tour to Europe. Their itinerary including the RFE facilities in Germany and Portugal, the Czechoslovak border, where they saw "the barbed wire fringe of the Iron Curtain", and a reception in Paris at the Allied Powers' Supreme Headquarters. "After returning to the United States, they were expected to give more than 1000 speeches on radio and television describing what they saw."[110] Later, as the Cold War waned and the Eisenhower administration began to reject harsh anti-communist rhetoric, the direction of the FEC changed, and the Crusade for Freedom was renamed the Free Europe Fund.

The Radios

The NCFE Committee began planning Radio Free Europe and Radio Liberty in 1949. These new US propaganda vehicles were modeled on the successful RIAS-Radio in the American Sector of Berlin, which went on the air in 1946 and was of major importance not just during the 1948 Berlin Blockade but also in broadcasting news commentary and cultural programs that were unavailable through the German Democratic Republic's censored outlets.[111] NCFE Inc. provided large amounts of funding to establish the two radios, first in New York and then at a new headquarters in Munich, West Germany. It was thought initially that RFE would be an extension of the exile national councils, but that proved problematic operationally, and after its first year, RFE was operated as a separate division. "[NCFE] attaches a considerably LESS role to the political exiles than NCFE did in 1949: RFE was then basically the mouthpiece and instrument of the national councils."[112]

RFE's first broadcast was on July 4, 1950, a half hour program beamed to Czechoslovakia. RFE/Radio Liberty broadcast directly to each of the satellite countries, mostly employing native former journalists who had emigrated to the West. By 1952 RFE operated twenty transmitters broadcasting in seven languages to six satellite countries for more than 1500 hours per week.[113] The broadcast content focused on information that was withheld from citizens of satellite countries, where the press was totally controlled by communist governments. The broadcasts' effectiveness could be judged in part by a statement in a May 3, 1957, memorandum on the Council of Europe Special Committee on Radio Free Europe investigation: "There is sufficient evidence to prove the effectiveness of Radio Free Europe. We think of the statements given by the continuous stream of refugees, of the letters smuggled through the Iron Curtain and of Communist attacks on Radio Free Europe which indicate the reds are seriously troubled by its influence."[114]

In addition to the radio broadcasts, it was decided to put balloons to use to distribute propaganda behind the Iron Curtain. In 1948 the CIA Special Procedures Group (SPG), using the code name Project ULTIMATE, had acquired a printing press and a stockpile of meteorological balloons, with the intent of delivering propaganda leaflets inside Eastern European countries in the event of war. From October 1951 to November 1956, the skies of Central Europe carried more than 350,000 balloons sent from West Germany to carry over 300 million "friendship" leaflets, posters, books and other printed matter to Poland, Czechoslovakia and Hungary.[115] The balloons also contained aluminum medals; one recipient reported finding one that pictured the Liberty Bell and had the legend "Hungarians for Freedom – all the Free World for Hungarians".[116] The effectiveness of such efforts can be measured, to a degree, by a report stating that "according to the 1957 RFE survey of Hungarian defectors, fifteen percent of the population relied on leaflets for their news."[117]

Communist authorities denounced the balloon leaflet program, and on one occasion Red Army units in Austria opened fire on the airborne propaganda with anti-aircraft guns. On May 24, 1954, the Czech government delivered an official protest against the balloon leafleting program to the US embassy in Prague; and in 1956 it attributed the crash of a Czech airliner and the death of 22 passengers to a propaganda balloon.[118]

The balloon program and the broadcasts crossed what might be considered a provocative line – on the one hand, they provided information to news-starved millions; on the other, they indirectly gave the impression that if citizens behind the Iron Curtain rose against their communist oppressors, the West would support them.

After the general strikes in June 1956 in Poznan, Poland, and the emergence of the Gomulka government's reform leadership, recently appointed RFE Director W.J. Convery Egan received a warning from Bill Griffith, his chief policy advisor in Munich, that émigré broadcasters should be directed to mute the organization's support for reform leaders in communist countries lest the RFE provide fuel for armed insurrections. From his desk in New York, Egan instead demanded an all out propaganda offensive.[119]

Richard Helms, the longest-serving director of the CIA (1966–73), recalls in his memoirs that "one of the least remembered RFE [intelligence] achievements came in late summer 1956 when William Griffith, the Munich-based policy advisor, and his deputy, Paul Henze, spotted a changing mood in Eastern Europe, and gave warning of a likely confrontation between the indigenous populations and the Soviet Forces in East Germany, Poland and Hungary." CIA Director Dulles was briefed on this speculation by Cord Meyer of the OPC, who attempted to get this impression across to the analysts at State and the CIA. "Neither Dulles nor the reigning specialists were convinced by the RFE analysis. When the outbreak of violence in Poland and open revolt in Hungary proved the RFE analysts were correct, Allen Dulles rebuked Cord for not having pressed the RFE position hard enough."[120]

The Hungarian Revolution of 1956 began on October 23 at a peaceful march organized by students of the Budapest Technical University in support of the reform government of Poland. The march grew spontaneously into a crowd of 100,000, violence erupted when the Hungarian secret police fired into the crowd, killing a number of people and wounding others.[121] The revolution ultimately resulted in some 2500 Hungarian deaths, the capture and execution of an additional 350 people and the flight of close to 250,000 refugees to neighboring neutral

Austria, many with just the clothes on their backs. The reprisals for those remaining in Hungary assumed a massive scale.[122]

In some of the worldwide press of the day, RFE's Hungarian broadcasting was said to have been responsible for encouraging Hungarian resistance, and the media attention resulted in investigations launched by the United Nations, the West German government, a United States congressional subcommittee and the Council of Europe. Ultimately, RFE was cleared of the charge of fomenting the uprising, although it was criticized for giving the impression that Western aid would be forthcoming.[123] What has not been discussed and needs to be evaluated is whether the Hungarian National Council and its extensive network of activities worldwide on behalf of Hungarian freedom was also a factor in instigating the revolt. While it appears that the council could not do a great deal to influence events in Hungary once the revolution broke out, did it play a role preceding the revolution in fomenting or sowing the seeds of dissatisfaction that sparked the revolution? A comprehensive study of the intelligence activities of the HNC prior to the revolution has yet to be done to adequately answer that question.[124]

What is clear is that until October 1956 the liberation of Captive Nations through the combined efforts of all of the above organizations was a consistent component of all high level US political pronouncements, which were subsequently transmitted to Eastern Europe by the various propaganda organizations, particularly RFE. The accusation that the RFE broadcasting staff was itself principally responsible for producing the rhetoric and inciting the Hungarian and other satellite revolts is not accurate, given that the organizational structure of the radios clearly had the Free Europe Committee overseeing the ideological basis of program content, which has been described as "a muscular brand of political warfare".[125] As can be seen from various NCFE documents relating to national liberation and the role of the national councils in US liberation policy, during its early years of operation and up until the Hungarian Revolution, a clear and aggressive propaganda program aimed at the Soviet Satellites was the *basis* of NCFE/FEC policy. Its goal was to transmit the message of liberation to the satellites. The parent organization's program was implemented by the national councils, endorsed and funded by the US government. As a division of the NCFE/FEC, RFE was the mouthpiece for that policy.

A study prepared for US Army Intelligence in January 1956, "Hungary: Resistance Activities and Potentials", examines Hungary "as a potential theater for Special Forces operations". The study illustrates that the US military was actively looking for ways to exploit the shortcomings of the regimes in Eastern Europe.[126] Coupled with the strong US military presence on the continent, the Crusade for Freedom had made fighting communism a major priority for the American public. And US support of émigré organizations – whether political, educational or cultural, in Europe or the US – also served to create the impression, not only in Eastern Europe and the US but throughout the world, that the United States had a new focus. Despite having shown very little interest in the region historically, it now appeared that the US was focusing on the liberation of East European nations as a key feature of its foreign policy and of East–West relations in general.

Public impressions aside, however, and this point needs to be stressed in evaluating the legacy of the NCFE/FEC, United States foreign policy of this era was based on a pragmatic perspective that recognized the post-WWII European status quo and accepted the prevailing balance of power with the Soviet Union. Regardless of the anti-Communist rhetoric of the NCFE/FEC, US foreign policy was based on "avoidance at all cost of superpower conflict",[127] particularly after the US learned that the Soviet Union had developed intercontinental ballistic missiles that could reach the United States.[128] It is notable that while the US began to make a substantial financial investment in the area of organized political warfare as early as 1947, there was a distinct imbalance to the US's reach. Its commitment to the aggressive anti-communist campaign led by the NCFE/FEC was counterbalanced by its lack of willingness to take military action to support any of the uprisings within the Soviet Satellites. As a case in point in terms of investment, historian Charles Gati writes that while thousands were employed at the US-funded RFE headquarters in Munich, there was only one bona fide CIA officer on the ground in Hungary when the Hungarian Revolution broke out.[129]

What then were the citizens of the Captive or Iron Curtain countries expected to think when they heard the US-originated messages being broadcast to their countries promoting the idea of national self-determination and liberty? The United States funded and maintained their exile leaders and exile organizations; it provided funds to enable support of émigré media; news and propaganda daily reinforced the message that those behind the Iron Curtain had not been forgotten by the West. The United States spent hundreds of millions of dollars to promote the "Western viewpoint" but in the end proved totally unwilling to take action when confronted with the fruits of its successful propaganda, that is, whenever protests broke out in the satellite nations.

Few will dispute that until the Hungarian revolution failed for lack of Western support, and a good percentage of the satellites' citizens truly believed such support would have been forthcoming. In 1957 Elmo Wilson of International Research Associates, Inc. conducted a study of the uprising among 1000 Hungarian refugees. It showed that "96 percent of the respondents expected Western aid in general and 77 percent of these also expected military aid."[130] Examination of the archival material regarding the extensive, expensive and long-term US-funded programs – including those that supported the national councils and the various other "liberation" organizations and activities – leaves no doubt that responsibility for encouraging Hungary's revolution lies in no small part with the methods US intelligence used to fight the Cold War and to implement the US foreign policy of the period.

Irrespective of the true nature of RFE's role in fomenting uprisings in Hungary and Poland and the criticisms leveled at it in the press and at the UN, upon investigation RFE was absolved of any blame in instigating the uprising, and its US government funding and support continued, although RFE was "placed under an unprecedented degree of government oversight".[131]

Activities sponsored through the National Councils

While focusing on the radio broadcasts, which were the primary proponents of US Cold War policy, scholarship has all but ignored the perhaps equally influential activities that the NCFE sponsored through the National Councils and for which RFE served – not always, but in great part – as a mouthpiece. The influence of the exile political group network was extensive, and its activities had enormous propaganda clout within the exile communities. Some of the hundreds of organizations around which daily émigré life revolved included the national councils, the Mid-European Study Center, headquartered in Manhattan, the Assembly of Captive European Nations and the Free Europe University in Exile as well as the International Peasant Union and the Christian Democratic Union of Central and Eastern Europe.[132]

From early in their development the national councils had regular ongoing contact with each other, whether informally, as many members had served as diplomats and political figures and thus were acquainted with one another, or formally through the Central and Eastern European Conference in which they participated. Starting in the late 1940s Gregoire Gafencu, the former foreign minister of Romania, had organized the exile leaders, who met informally on the first Tuesday of every month in New York. This group became known as the Tuesday Panel and it was at their initiative that a demonstration of exile solidarity was planned in Philadelphia in 1951. By then exile leadership realized that they would have a great deal more political clout if they collaborated on reaching their common goals. Under the sponsorship of the NCFE the Central and East European Conference held its first gathering on February 11, 1951 at Independence Hall. Participating were 195 Central and East European exile leaders as well as Alexander Kerensky, head of the Russian Provisional Government of July–November 1919.[133] It resulted in the following "Declaration of the Aims and Principles of the Liberation of the Central and Eastern European Peoples" and was signed by the participants on February 11:

> The peoples of Central and Eastern Europe are eager to take their natural place in the great movement of free peoples towards better relationship and closer union. They are desirous of establishing among themselves strong ties of a federal character and of joining in the formation of a United Europe. Such a fraternal federation must prize and respect the distinctive values of each nation, for the common good of our European civilization and for the cultural heritage of mankind throughout the world.[134]

In 1952 the Conference set about organizing a meeting in the House of Burgesses Chamber in Williamsburg, Virginia, timed to coincide with the anniversary of the signing of the Virginia Bill of Rights on June 12, 1776.[135] The meeting was attended by "the leaders in exile from the countries now under communist dictatorship and held in Soviet bondage behind the Iron Curtain". The keynote speaker was A. A. Berle of the NCFE, who noted, "The Free peoples will establish between themselves strong regional ties and by this join in the formation of a United States of Europe." Berle declared that "unity for these peoples is no longer a vague desire of theorists" but noted that there was pressing need "that a commonwealth of free nations must now become fact, if any of these nations or any individual within them shall survive. Without unity freedom of any small nation may well be only the freedom of a castaway ship on a strong sea."[136]

The meeting produced what became known as the Williamsburg Declaration of 1952. Its signatories included former leaders from Albania, Bulgaria, Czechoslovakia, Estonia, Hungary, Latvia, Lithuania, Poland, Romania and Yugoslavia. It endorsed the principles set forth in the Virginia Bill of Rights and demanded that those rights be restored to the citizens of the captive nations upon their liberation.

While there was general agreement that the Williamsburg meeting and the Declaration were a success, noted educator Levering Tyson, the president of the Free Europe University in Exile, suggested in a follow up letter to NCFE President Miller that it had occurred to him at the signing ceremony that "these men, practically all of ancient vintage, could not hope themselves [Tyson's emphasis] ever to carry out the terms of the

Declaration. Obviously what they were doing was symbolic and powerfully so." Tyson went on to suggest that exile youths at FEUE in Strasbourg should supplement the Declaration with their own document. "I believe we could use advantageously some ceremony at Strasbourg, or here jointly, at which exile youth could make a ringing declaration, but it will all have to be considered carefully."[137]

After the successes of the Philadelphia and Williamsburg conferences, the exile groups' next attempt at self-organization would be more permanent and would work on their behalf on an ongoing basis. The Assembly of Captive European Nations (ACEN) was established in 1954 with the intent of incorporating all the "Captive Nations". From the start, it was bureaucratic (on the UN model), and its leadership generally mirrored that of the respective national councils; however, it was the most successful of the umbrella organizations sponsored by the NCFE. When it was founded the ACEN was composed of representatives of Albania, the Baltic States, Bulgaria, Czechoslovakia, Hungary, Poland and Romania as well as non-voting representatives from the Christian Democratic Union of Central and Eastern Europe and the International Peasant Union. It met in General Assembly sessions at the same time as the United Nations. It should be noted that to avoid a confrontation with the Soviet Union and in order not to encourage separatist groups within it, the US State Department and policy makers insisted that delegations from Russia, Belorussia and the Ukraine be excluded from participation, Also excluded were the Yugoslav émigrés who applied for membership but were "never invited to join" due to US policymakers fears of alienating Marshall Tito.[138] What ACEN accomplished was to provide a forum in which the Captive Nation leaders could have ongoing dialogue with each other and cooperate as a block to counter actions in the UN by the Soviets and their satellites.[139] This was remarkable in and of itself, as the nationalities that comprised the ACEN had not just historical animosities between their nations to overcome but also conflicts of the recent past, including Hungary's seizure of a third of Romania, Poland re-taking of a portion of the Teschen area of Czechoslovakia and the Bulgarians participation in the dismemberment of Yugoslavia.[140]

The ACEN and NCFE leaders made full use of their power within the immigrant communities and as propaganda vehicles to promote anti-communism at home and abroad. For a time, there were visual expressions of their aggressive anti-Communist stance in the form of banners hung adjacent to the ACEN headquarters, which was located directly across the street from the UN. These caused the USSR and its UN diplomats much embarrassment and negative press. One such banner, read "United Nations: We demand the withdrawal of all Soviet Forces and Free Elections – Help Us!"[141] As long as its activism coincided with US policy, the ACEN had considerable political clout, although its members were not US citizens and the organization had to remain at arms length from partisan politics. However, after the Hungarian Revolution and the Eisenhower administration's foreign policy shift toward increasingly peaceful co-existence, US foreign policy and the ACEN's goals went increasingly divergent ways. Regardless of their internal squabbles and problems within the delegations, the ACEN mission always remained liberation of their nations, and the organization worked in collaboration with its members' national councils and even extensively with some of the nationalities not represented in its membership.

The Legacy of the NCFE/FEC

When speaking specifically of NCFE/FEC and the Eastern European satellites, the question arising from the perspective of history is this: If not liberation, then what *was* the US political agenda or reasoning in sponsoring national councils of émigré leadership from the Iron Curtain countries for twenty-two years and spending millions of dollars annually on Radio Free Europe and Radio Liberty? At the onset of its efforts, it was "liberation" that the NCFE had as its goal. Indeed, in a letter written on December 1, 1952, to A. A. Berle, Robert L. Lang, the director of RFE, referred to the exile leaders as "Cold storage reservoirs for the day of liberation". [142] Among the NCFE leadership's propaganda goals was that the organizations and individuals under its sponsorship would influence public opinion in their homelands and would form the basis of civil democratic societies when those homelands were liberated.

To answer the question of when the NCFE policies began to shift, we need to consider the foreign policy changes that occurred during the first years of its operation. By 1954 US policy objectives changed from seeking "liberation" of the Soviet satellites to the pragmatic realization that freeing any of the satellites could result in warfare with the Soviet Union. Between the time of the NCFE's 1949 launch as a vehicle of organized political warfare and 1954 the world dynamic had changed and the growth of communism and communist influence on the world stage had become undeniable. While the Central and Eastern European nations were being absorbed as Soviet satellites, the communist Chinese army finally defeated the Kuomintang in 1949 and took control of the world's most populous country. The Korean War, fought essentially as a proxy war in which both North and South were sponsored by external powers, ended in 1953 with an unsatisfactory armistice that left North Korea as a Communist nation. The Indochina War ended in1954, after which the French were expelled from Vietnam and that country was partitioned into North and South, with the North coming under communist control. The change in US policy was a result of a realization of the limitations of US power coupled with the heightened arms race between the two super powers and fear of nuclear war. Thus, the Free Europe Committee, Inc. – as renamed in 1954 – took as its primary focus a broad program of psychological warfare and the further development of the radios and their propaganda program, as these were thought to be of paramount importance in implementing US policy goals.

While the foreign policy objectives of the US were shifting, the national councils and the émigré populations remained hard liners, not just against the communist threat but also against any steps toward rapprochement with the Soviet Union short of liberation of their homelands. Thus the ideological split between the nationality groups and their sponsor began to manifest itself – at first slowly but later more dramatically.[143]

The role of the FEC, Inc. was defined in a policy memo of December 1954: "The primary interest of FEC being the attainment of its political warfare objectives behind the Iron Curtain, and RFE and FEP[Free Europe Press] being its instruments for the definition and attainment of those objectives … ."[144] After the FEC goals were rewritten, the leadership still encouraged development of non-radio activities, for example, the establishment of the ACEN. Perhaps it was because some Cold War hard liners in positions of importance in the departments of State and Defense and in US intelligence simply continued on the previous trajectory, regardless of the fact that US foreign policy and US actions abroad were entering a period of détente. Or perhaps it was simply an effort on the part of the FEC to take the generally unwieldy and rather difficult groups of individuals and committees with which it had to deal and try to incorporate them into a single working organization that would be easier to direct and monitor.

The results of the broad range of efforts expended by NCFE/FEC's directly- and indirectly-sponsored organizations are not easily quantifiable or measureable by means as traditional as, for example, RFE listener analysis. As its most basic function and in accord with the primary original intent of its founders, the NCFE/FEC-sponsored organizations provided employment for émigré leaders sympathetic to US policy and kept those leaders' activities under the watchful eye and control of the US for more than two decades.

And while to those outside the émigré groups it might have appeared that NCFE/FEC just provided "make work" jobs for refugee political figures, there was nonetheless a definite reaction and response to the efforts of those "employees". As Dr. Béla Fabian, a member of the Hungarian National Council's executive committee, wrote in the *Washington Post* on March 18, 1951, the national councils' activities did have influence behind the Iron Curtain:

> … resistance keeps flaring up sporadically. The governments of the Iron Curtain countries are sensing connections between the patriots and the National Councils in exile…The vehement agitation deployed by the various governments of the Soviet-satellite states against the National Councils in the United States and their mem-

> bers, clearly shows what nuisance they are to them. The National Councils are the hope of the subjugated peoples behind the Iron Curtain. ...The underground movements of the Iron Curtain countries have in them a fixed point whereon to focus their aims; the peoples themselves concentrate their longing in their direction.[145]

As to the awareness behind the Iron Curtain of the aid extended to their nationals by the councils, one only has to read a letter to Paul Auer, head of the Paris office of the HNC, from the widow of Endre Bajcsy Zsilinszky, who was martyred by the Nazis. Dated September 13, 1956, the letter asks Auer to please send "aid packages" to her in Budapest.[146] A list of some of the many refugee organizations supported by the FEC in just two European nations follows, but it must be remembered it wasn't just émigrés in the West who counted on help from these exile committees; those behind the Iron Curtain also received hundreds of thousands of care packages sent by their countrymen in exile abroad. [147]

Even as US foreign policy changed direction, the organizations spawned as a result of US Cold War policy continued on their original mission. Despite the U.S's failure to live up to its own propaganda in East Germany, Poland, Hungary and Czechoslovakia, the anti-communist propaganda machine did not lose its impetus. In 1957 many of the national committees found their support increased when the FEC, Inc. budget went up by $2.2 million over the prior year, while the radios budget remained static.

A brief recounting of the range of assistance provided to Central and East European refugees on the continent alone offers an idea of the enormous scope of the help made available. Refugee centers established under the auspices of NCFE/FEC-sponsored national councils operated in Vienna, Salzburg, Munich, Rome and Paris and even in Washington, New York and various cities of Latin America and Australia. They disbursed financial aid and helped hundreds of thousands of émigrés negotiate the bureaucracy of the countries they found themselves in. They acted as employment bureaus, helped provide translators for paperwork and locate relatives and friends lost in the maze of exile. They promoted cultural and social activities within the émigré communities, supported schools and religious institutions, and established sporting clubs and sporting facilities for the immigrants.

In addition to funding each of its in-country offices, as of June 1959 the FEC also provided monthly financial support to organizations in France, Belgium, Italy, Holland, Sweden, Norway, Denmark, England, West Germany and Austria.[148]

As an example, in West Germany alone these organizations included: for Czechoslovaks, the Czechoslovak Refugee Service, the Committee of Czechoslovak Students in Exile, *Sklizen* (a publication); for Estonians, the Estonian Central Committee, EESTI RADA (a publication); for Hungarians, the Hungarian Cultural Association, Hungarian Refugee Service (Munich), Hungarian Students Federation; for Latvians, the Latvian Central Committee, LATVIJA (a publication); for Lithuanians, the Lithuanian Central Committee, EUROPOS LIETUVIS (a publication); for Poles, the Union of Polish Refugees in Germany; for Romanians, the Union of Rumanians in Germany, Union of Rumanians in Southern Germany. In addition, the FEC sponsored the Baltic Students Union in West Germany.

In Austria the FEC supported a list of aid agencies that the RFE corporate files indicate included Caritas, Catholic Bahnhofsmission, Österreichiescher Bundesjugendring, Arbeitsgemeinschaft "Junges Leben", Österreichische Hochschlerschaft, Pfadfinder Österreichs, as well as one college and research institute, Österreichisches College and Osteuropa Institut.[149]

There was also support for the nationality groups in Austria. Polish organizations included ZPA Union of Poles in Austria, Polish Supplementary Schools in Vienna, Graz, Ebensee, Salzburg, Enns, Villach, Pairc, Vienna III, Polish Students Vienna. Support for Hungarians included the World Federation of Hungarian Refugee Sportsmen (including funds for the water polo team), the Malteser Library, the Philharmonia Hungarica, the Hungarian Puppet Players, the Hungarian Theater. Funding was also provided to the Hungarian Refugee Farmers, *Bécsi Magyar Hirado* (a Vienna weekly newspaper in Hungarian), *Nemzetör* (an organ of Hungarian student writers), the Hungarian Verein Vienna, Hungarian Catholic Priests, Hungarian Scouts, and most importantly, the UFHD/HRS Hungarian Refugee Service, with offices in Vienna, Graz, Innsbruck and Voralberg.[150]

Bulgarians in Austria had support for the Bulgarian Verein Vienna and one-time support for the Bulgarian Christian Community. Additionally in Austria, five Czechoslovak and three Romanian organizations received financial support. Some organizations were funded on three continents (in Europe, Asia, Latin America and the US). These included the International Institute of Youth Affairs, the International Federation of Free Journalists, PEN in Exile and the International Features Service (for the press).[151]

Schools were established at all levels for children and youth who arrived in the West speaking only their native language. In Europe, the Free Europe University in Exile was established in Strasbourg, France – through a sizeable grant from the Ford Foundation. Over 5500 university-age refugees from the satellite nations were given the opportunity to begin or continue their studies there from 1951 to 1958, when it was decided to disband the program as it was felt that the funds could be applied toward RFE for a better return.[152]

While this volume focuses on illustrating the wide range of support provided to refugees from Communist tyranny and details the history of some of those organizations, the NCFE/FEC sponsored other sizeable international organizations that deserve a research paper of their own – for example, the International Peasant Union. Originally founded in 1922 in Paris by peasant parties of Central and Eastern Europe, it was re-established post WWII first by Georgi Dimitrov of Bulgaria, who was joined by Ferenc Nagy of Hungary upon his arrival in the US and by other exiled peasant or agrarian party leaders. It then began its activism on behalf of the peasant populations that were being forced into collectives by the communist governments. With the arrival in the US of Stanislaw Mikolajczyk, the leader of the Polish Peasant Party, the organization was re-organized with a new set of by-laws in 1948. Prior to the establishment of many of the national councils, it served as an international organization that represented the interests of agrarian and peasant citizens behind the Iron Curtain. From its re-activation until 1950 the organization was funded by its leadership, and budgetary constraints thus limited its activities. In 1950, however, the NCFE decided to bring the International Peasant Union into the fold and began to support it in a generous manner. It was one of the three "internationals" supported by the NCFE, another of which was the International Center of Free Trade Unionist in Exile, which was founded in 1947 in Paris and represented exiled pre-war trade unionists of Poland, Hungary, Rumania, Yugoslavia, Bulgaria, Lithuania, Latvia, Estonia and Ukraine. It was first funded by the Free Trade Union of the American Federation of Labor (AFL) and from 1951 on by the NCFE.[153] The third of the "internationals" the NCFE supported from its founding in 1950 onward was the Christian Democratic Union of Central Europe, which came into being as the exiled representatives of the Christian Democratic Parties started their work in the West. "They worked first within the framework of the Nouvelles Equipes Internationales, founded in 1947 as a Christian democratic and conservative bourgeois organization for European integration. Swiss, French and Belgian parties were included in the NEI's formation but exile groups from Bulgaria, Romania, Lithuania, Hungary, Poland, Czechoslovakia and Yugoslavia also took part. Later when they found themselves in the United States, they organized the Christian Democratic Union of Central Europe, officially set up on July 26, 1950."[154] All three of these international organizations collaborated with the national councils, and when the ACEN was formed they worked in concert with them as well.

As the partial list of sponsored organizations attests, a decade after NCFE, Inc. was founded there existed a great number of organizations funded in part in or in full by the FEC that were aiding refugees and enhancing the life of émigrés. Unfortunately for the cause of the exiles, by 1961 the communist delegations from all the Soviet satellites had been recognized and seated at the UN. The United States worked very hard to keep the "issue of Hungary" alive in the United Nations through its collaboration with Sir Leslie Munro, the representative from New

Zealand and a former president of the UN General Assembly who had been charged in December 1956 with the task of enforcing UN resolutions on Hungary, but ultimately the US was unsuccessful in making any progress toward that goal. Munro's dedication to keeping the issue of Hungary alive in the UN was key to causing discomfort to the Soviet Union and the puppet Kádár government.[155] It needs to be noted that during this period the leadership of all of the national councils offered extensive support and lobbying on the Hungarian Issue, an example of successful collaboration and support for each other's issues amongst the exile groups that a few years previously would have been considered impossible.

The Deactivation of the FEC, Inc.

The issue of the origins of NCFE/FEC, Inc.'s financial support was raised any number of times in the American press and even by the Soviet Union during its lifetime. During the height of the Cold War, it was the far-right that questioned whether the organization was soft on communism and was being run to support a group of leftish émigrés. Fulton Lewis, an arch-conservative syndicated columnist, wrote over one hundred newspaper columns in the 1950s asking such questions and stating outright that the CIA was funding the NCFE/FEC. However, in those times his assertions did not cause the alarm that they would a decade later. In the 1950s America's Cold War policy objectives of waging organized political warfare were still secure. However,

> ... by the late 1960s, the anti-communist consensus that had enabled the United States and Europe to maintain a more or less unified policy of containment had clearly broken down. A shift toward a vague kind neutralism was particularly noticeable among the parties of the liberal Left. In varying degrees, the Democrats in America, the British Labor Party, and the social democratic parties of the Nordic countries were beginning to distance themselves from a foreign policy ideology grounded in anti-communism.[156]

In the United States, *Ramparts* magazine, a "freewheeling forum of New Left journalism",[157] published an article in February 1967 that questioned the CIA's role as the funding agency for non-governmental political organizations. The article's focus was on the National Students Association, which had been receiving CIA funding for a number of years. The *Ramparts* article prompted questioning of the CIA's other domestic projects, and further dialogue ensued in the press. Questions about the source of federal funds covertly bankrolling Radio Free Europe and the Free Europe Committee were not far behind. As the story emerged, the real scandal, in most Americans' minds, was that the Free Europe Fund and the Crusade for Freedom before it had shamelessly exploited the American public in their efforts to raise donations for an organization that was covertly funded by US intelligence. However, as Richard Helms recounts in his autobiography, one of the ironies of the situation was that even as Mike Wallace of CBS News protested the subterfuge used by the Free Europe Committee, the corporate president of CBS, his employer, was chairman of the executive committee of the Free Europe Fund.[158] The issue clearly had a polarizing effect within American society.

A strong case was made for totally disbanding the radios, with Senator J. William Fulbright leading the charge in the Senate. Of course, if the radios were to be disbanded, the ancillary organizations sponsored through the FEC would have to be disbanded as well. President Lyndon Johnson, wanting to rid himself of another foreign policy thorn in his side, appointed Undersecretary of State Nicholas Katzenbach to form a committee that included Richard Helms of the CIA and Secretary of Health, Education and Welfare John Gardner. Johnson asked them to make recommendations as to the disposition of the CIA assets. Helms recounts that while the president was well versed in all the ongoing agency operations in Eastern Europe and Russia, "his enthusiasm was never more than tepid."[159] Indeed the recommendation of the committee was that "no federal agency shall provide any covert financial assistance or support, direct or indirect, to any of the nation's educational or private voluntary organizations."[160] The committee did note that covert assistance to private American groups was necessary in order to counteract the work of the communist front organizations, but that was a point ignored in the press coverage. Unfortunately, the pressure of the press and in the editorial pages made it necessary to terminate all such secret grants, which meant that support would have to be terminated not just for Radio Free Europe and Radio Liberty but for all the exile groups that were still receiving funding for activities within their communities.

The recommendation of the Katzenbach Committee was accepted by the president in March 1967. However, the threat of communism was still all too real for many, as the 1968 Soviet invasion of Czechoslovakia and the US involvement in the ongoing war in Vietnam were to attest, and the issue was not fully resolved until 1971, when funding was finally terminated. The radios were ultimately saved by a mandate to establish a public/private mechanism to provide public funds openly for organizations deemed deserving of public support, and the Board for International Broadcasting was established in 1973 (transition funds had been authorized to keep the radios operating for the three year interim period). The real casualties were the émigré groups whose social, educational and cultural services all fell victim to the policy change.

Most of the national committees were not fully disbanded until June 30, 1971, when FEC, Inc. was defunded; but even after its funding was terminated, any number of organizations continued to operate with public and corporate support, some of them until the fall of the communist regimes throughout Central and East Europe in 1989. By the end of its sponsorship of NCFE/ FEC Inc., the United States had spent $306,849,269 on the record and countless millions more untraceable funds to support Free Europe, Inc.[161]

It needs to be noted that it was only when the origin of the supporting funds became public that the FEC was finally shut down. Had its source of funding not come to light and created public outrage, it is not hard to imagine that, like some of its sponsored organizations, the FEC could have continued until 1989 and the liberation of the Soviet satellites.

What then can be said to be the legacy of America's policy of "organized political warfare"? Did the National Committee for a Free Europe/

Free Europe Committee make a real contribution or difference on either side of the "curtain"?

Surprisingly, and despite its other failures, the answer is a resounding yes because from a human point of view, beyond the ideology, propaganda and East–West Cold War competition, the NCFE/FEC provided for each of the national councils a foundation on which to provide assistance to the refugees from their homelands. For this, if for no other reason, the committees should be lauded. Additionally, their activities and propaganda reminded the Western public on a daily basis of the nations and people trapped behind the Iron Curtain, people who had not chosen to live under communism or under communist puppet governments propped up by Soviet occupying forces.

It also must be noted that any number of organizations that the NCFE/FEC sponsored or for which they provided underwriting continued their efforts after the FEC's demise in 1971. Amongst them were the national councils of Poland, Czechoslovakia and Romania, the Assembly of Captive European Nations and any number of cultural and civic institutions operating in émigré communities in the United States and abroad.

Thus, its foreign policy "mission" to wage a propaganda war against Communist expansion aside, the enduring positive legacy of the NCFE/FEC is in fact centered in the day in, day out assistance it provided to refugees from the satellite nations from 1949 onward. By its very existence, the NCFE/FEC played a large part in keeping intact the exiles' national spirit, their cultures and languages. It might even be argued that these exiles and their children, who stayed in touch with friends and family in their homelands, kept the hope of democratic change alive in hearts behind the Iron Curtain. One could posit that this helped hasten the final disintegration of the Soviet occupation of Central and East Europe. Perhaps this was the true legacy of the funds expended by the United States in support of the Captive Nations of Europe.

Epigraph: RFE Corporate Files, Hoover Institution Archives. Stanford, CA. Box 188, folder 1: Mr. Dolbeare's suggestions for additions to Mr. Phenix' letter. Draft May 15, 1952.

Endnotes

1 Cold War International History Project: Digital Archive Collection; Radio Free Europe/ Radio Liberty e-Dossier No. 32. Document: Organizing Political Warfare: www.wilsoncenter.org/digital-archives. Accessed 21 November 2012.

2 Bohlen also served as President Truman's interpreter at the Potsdam Conference.

3 William C. Bullitt, "How We Won the War and Lost the Peace," *Life*, 30 August 1948, 94.

4 Teheran, Iran, November 28–December 1, 1943.

5 Charles E. Bohlen, *Witness to History 1929–1969* (New York: W.W. Norton Co, Inc., 1973) 193.

6 Robert C. Tucker. *Stalin in Power: The Revolution from Above, 1928–1941*(London, New York: W.W. Norton, 1990) 592.

7 Ibid.

8 Alexander Dallin and F.I. Firsov, eds., *Dimitrov & Stalin 1934–1943: Letters from the Soviet Archives* (New Haven & London: Yale University Press, 2000) 166.

9 Allen W. Dulles. *The Craft of Intelligence* (Guilford, CN: The Lyons Press, 1964) 221.

10 Beneš's relationship with the Soviet Union was complex, and an explanation of it requires more space than this chapter allows. However, Beneš's secret pact of friendship and postwar cooperation with the Soviet Union made on his trip to Moscow in December of 1943 was a culmination of the Czech's throwing in their lot with the USSR. See Stephen Borsody, *The Tragedy of Central Europe, Nazi and Soviet Conquest and Aftermath* (New Haven: Yale Concilium on International and Area Studies, 1980) 187.

11 Bohlen, *Witness to History*, 200.

12 Treaty of Non-Aggression between Germany and the Soviet Union, also known as the Molotov–Ribbentrop Pact, was signed in Moscow on 23 August 1939.

13 Planning for Operation Barbarossa began in December 1940, just three months after the signing of the non-aggression pact. The actual campaign began on 22 June 1941.

14 Bohlen speaks quite candidly about the fact that "the first sharp words uttered during the war by an American President to a high Soviet official" were those of Harry Truman to Molotov in April 1945, *Witness to History*, 213.

15 "Roosevelt never explained his attitude in my presence, but his apparent belief that ganging up on the Russians was to be avoided at all cost was, in my mind a basic error." Ibid, 146.

16 Ibid, 153.

17 Paul Nitze, "America: An Honest Broker," *Foreign Affairs*, 69, no. 4 (Fall 1990) 1–14.

18 Lord Moran, *Churchill: Taken from the Diaries of Lord Moran. The Struggle for Survival 1940–1965* (Boston: Houghton Mifflin Company; Cambridge: The Riverside Press, 1966) 185.

19 Gerald Miller. Office of Policy Co-ordination 1948–1952. CIA Historical Study, 2. www.foia.cia.gov. Accessed 1 October 2008. In September 1947 the USSR launched the Communist Information Bureau (Cominform) which "marked a resumption of the process of international revolution which purportedly had been discarded by the dissolution of the Communist International (Comintern) in 1943. This subversive formation was viewed by the American people as a portent of aggressive Russian intentions." Miller, Office of Policy Coordination, 3.

20 "The Sources of Soviet Conduct, by X", *Foreign Affairs*, July 1947. Reprinted in *Foreign Affairs* 65, no. 4 (Spring 1987) 854–868.

21 Paul Nitze, "America: An Honest Broker", *Foreign Affairs* 69, no. 4 (Fall 1990) 1–14.

22 US Department of State: Office of the Historian. www.history.state.gov/milestones/ 1969–1976/Detente. Accessed 28 December 2012. The hard line policies of the Truman Doc-

trine gave way to a policy of détente, which resulted in a limited Test Ban Treaty by 1963 and a Nuclear Non Proliferation Treaty by 1968.

23 Dr. Otto von Habsburg, interview by the author at Pöcking, Germany, 23 October 2003, in Katalin Kádár Lynn, *Tibor Eckhardt. His American Years* (Boulder, CO: East European Monographs, 2007)108.

24 Truman Presidential Museum and Library. Truman Doctrine Documents. Address of the President of the Congress: Recommendation for Assistance to Greece and Turkey, 12 March 1947. www.trumanlibrary.org Accessed 1 January 2008.

25 The National Archives of the United States. Records of the office of government reports. Record Group 44. Arc. 513885. http://www.archives.gov/education/lessons/fdr-churchill/images/atlantic-charter.gif. Accessed 1 December 2012.

26 John Foster Leich, "Great Expectations: The National Councils In Exile: 1950–1960", *The Polish Review* 35, nos. 3/4 (1990) 183–196 , 184.

27 Tim Kane, Global US Troop Deployment, 1950–2003. Center for Data Analysis Report #04-11. The Heritage Foundation 2004. www.heritage.org/research/nationalsecurity Accessed 21 November 2012.

28 Miller, Office of Policy Co-ordination 1948–1952, 1.

29 Hugh Wilford, *The CIA, the British Left and the Cold War: Calling the Tune?* (London: Frank Cass Publishers, 2003) 84.

30 Cold War International History Project Digital Archive: Collection: Radio Free Europe/Radio Liberty: e-Dossier No. 32 Document 1: Organizing Political Warfare www.wilsoncenter.org/digital-archive. Accessed 21 November 2012.

31 Cold War International History Project: Digital Archive: Collection Radio Free Europe/Radio Liberty: e-Dossier No. 32 Document 1: Organizing Political Warfare: www.wilsoncenter.org/digital-archive Accessed 21 November 2012.

32 Stanislaw Mikolajczyk, Deputy Prime Minister of Poland and former Prime Minister of the WWII London Polish Government, and Ferenc Nagy, Prime Minister of Hungary, both went into exile in 1947 as the Soviet Union closed the vise on their countries.

33 The sentence ends with "underground"; there is no further text nor punctuation that follows. It is clear from reading the document that the last line of text on pages 1, 3, 4, 5 is missing from the scan of the original document.

34 Cold War International History Project: e-Dossier No. 32 Document 1.

35 Ibid.

36 Ibid.

37 Ibid.

38 Ibid.

39 Ibid.

40 The OPC, then called the Office of Special Projects, was formally established on 1 September 1948 and continued operating until its 1 August 1952 merger with the CIA's Office of Special Operations (OSO) into a combined directorate that became the CIA Clandestine Service. Miller, "Office of Policy Coordination, 1948–1952", 7. www.foia.cia.gov/docs. Accessed 21 December 2012.

41 Ibid.

42 Ibid.

43 Ibid., 10–11.

44 Ibid., 12.

45 Larry Dwayne Collins, "The Free Europe Committee, An American Weapon of the Cold War". Unpublished dissertation, Carleton University, November 1973, 1.

46 Miller, Office of Policy Co-ordination 1948–1952, 12–13.

47 Malcolm J. Proudfoot, *European Refugees: 1939–1952* (Evanston, IL: Northwestern University Press, 1956) 427. Bohlen also mentions in *Witness to History* (188–190) that it would irritate Stalin when Roosevelt would discuss the fact that the fate of Poland was important to the US because of the sheer numbers of Polish émigrés and their power at the ballot box.

48 Cold War International History Project. Digital Archive. Collection Radio Free Europe/ Radio Liberty e-Dossier No.32 Document 2: USG Officials Discuss Émigré Broadcasts to Eastern Europe.

49 Ibid.

50 Ibid.

51 Ibid.

52 Peter Grose, *Gentleman Spy: The Life of Allen Dulles* (Boston, New York: Houghton Mifflin Company, 1994) 299–300.

53 Ibid.

54 RFE Corporate Files: Box 1536 (temporary numbering) Minutes of a Special Meeting of the Board of Directors of National Committee for Free Europe, Inc. 2 June 1949. Hoover Institution Archives. Stanford University. Stanford, CA (hereafter HIA).

55 RFE Corporate Files. Box 1536 (temporary numbering). FEC Corporate Minutes. HIA At the first meeting of the Committee for a Free Europe, Inc. corporation on May 17, 1949. Allen W. Dulles was elected President of the corporation, DeWitt C. Poole, Vice-President, Frank Altschul, Treasurer, Frederic R. Dolbeare, Secretary, and Robert E. Tarhaar was elected Assistant Treasurer.

56 Grose, *Gentleman Spy*, 299–300.

57 Hugh Wilford. *The CIA, the British Left and the Cold War: Calling the tune?* (London: Frank Cass Publishers, 2003) 85–87.

58 "New Group Formed to Assist Refugees", *New York Times*, 2 June 1949.

59 Letter to Allen W. Dulles from DeWitt C. Poole re: The NCFE Position to be Re-examined 28 September 1950. Freedom of Information Act Releases. www.foia.cia.gov. Accessed 22 November 2012. De Witt C. Poole was then the president of the National Committee for Free Europe, Inc. Dulles was practicing law in the New York firm of Sullivan & Cromwell and was chairman of the executive committee of NCFE.

60 RFE Corporate Files. Box 188, Folder 1: Free Europe Committee General Files 1949–1957. HIA.

61 Radio Free Europe Corporation Papers: Box 188, Folder 1 FEC General 1949–1957. HIA.

62 Arch Puddington, *Broadcasting Freedom: The Cold War Triumph of Radio Free Europe and Radio Liberty* (Lexington, KY: The University Press of Kentucky, 2000) 12.

63 Puddington, *Broadcasting Freedom*, 9.

64 Radio Free Europe Corporate Files, Box 188: Folder1: Free Europe Committee-General 1949–1957. HIA. Memorandum to the staff, Whitney H. Shepardson, dated March 9, 1954. "Please take note that effective March 5, 1954 the name of National Committee for a Free Europe, Inc has been legally changed to Free Europe Committee, Inc." Box 1536 (temporary) Minutes of a Special Meeting of the Board of Directors National Committee for Free Europe, Inc., June 2, 1949. "The chairman stated that the original incorporation was applied for under the name "Committee for Free Europe, Inc." Shortly thereafter, the incorporators came to the opinion that the name "National Committee for Free Europe, Inc." would be preferable. A resolution was passed "that the action of the members in causing the name of the Corporation to be changed to National Committee for Free Europe, Inc. is in all respects hereby ratified, confirmed and approved."

65 Comptroller General of the United States: US Government Monies provided to Radio Free Europe and Radio Liberty: NARA RG 263- CIA Archives. 01 25 May 1972. 102–104. (Hereafter, "US Government Monies".) In this report the statistics on the budgets are shown as bar charts and as such are not specific on increments between the levels, which are shown in two million dollar increments. A very small portion of the 1971 funding is shown as "private and other" sources of funds. Twenty million in 2012 dollars adjusted for inflation is in excess of $114 million.

66 Ibid., 14–18.

67 Benjamin Welles, "Ban Sought on CIA Aid for Radio Free Europe", *New York Times*, 24 January 1971.

68 "US Government Monies", 14–18.

69 Ibid.

70 Ibid.

71 See Chapter 10 in this volume for a well-researched and comprehensive history of the Free Europe University in Exile, authored by Veronika Durin-Hornyik.

72 Refers to publications produced by the Mid-European Studies Center related to Free Europe organizations. Several divisions had their own publishing arms, each having something to do with the various sponsored organizations.

73 "US Government Monies", 14–18.

74 Ibid. The above report also provides (19–37) a break down of details of the expenditures of the FEC, Inc. for fiscal year 1971, including wages, pensions, insurance, termination programs and labor contracts, providing an interesting insight into how the funds were actually allocated in any given year. As the report on US Monies for the life of the NCFE/FEC operations was produced in 1972, one must accept these findings prepared for the Senate Foreign Relations Committee by the Government Accounting Office. However, it needs to be pointed out that these budgets were not necessarily completely transparent. As an example, the Free Europe, Inc. budget for the year ending 30 June 1952, shows a Special Fund of $300,000 without any further indication of its purpose. RFE Corporate Files: Box 189, Folder 5: FEC Budget 1949–1968.

75 RFE Corporate Files: Box 188, Folder 1: Free Europe Committee General 1949–1957 NCFE, Inc. Memorandum on Organization and Operations 25 July 1949. Further details of the National Councils Division and the sub-committee were agreed upon at the Special meeting of the Board of Directors 4 August 1949. A. A. Berle Papers. FDR Presidential Library. Box 222 Folder: Executive Committee 1949–1953.

76 As of the annual report of NCFE for 1952, the divisions of NCFE had been further divided into the following: Division of Exile Relations (or National Councils Division), Radio Free Europe, Division of Intellectual Cooperation, Research and Publications Service, Crusade for Freedom (a separate corporation), General Administration. NCFE President's Report 1952. www.foia.cia.gov Accessed 22 December 2012.

77 Papers of A. A. Berle Jr. Franklin Delano Roosevelt Presidential Library. Box 222. Folder: Executive Committee 1949–1953 President's Report for the Year 1950, 6–7.

78 "US Government Monies", 7.

79 Ibid.

80 Frances Stoner Saunders, *The Cultural Cold War: The CIA and the World of Arts and Letters.* (New York: The New Press, 1999) 1.

81 RFE Corporate Files: Box 2319 (temporary).Binder Number 3: 17 March 1952–10 September 1952. Minutes of the Executive Committee of the Board of Directors of the NCFE, Inc. 17 July 1952.

82 A. A. Berle, Jr. Papers. Franklin Delano Roosevelt Presidential Library, Hyde Park, NY. Box 222 President's Report for the Year 1950: National Committee for a Free Europe, Inc., 11.

83 RFE Corporate Files: Box 2319 (temporary) Binder Number 3. Minutes of the Executive Committee of the Board of Directors of the NCFE, Inc. 17 July 1952.

84 Miller, Office of Policy Coordination 1948–52, 12.

85 Országos Széchényi Könyvtár. OSZK. Hungarian National Library Archives. Budapest. Fond 488: Box 39: Portion of Introductory Statement to the Press by Joseph C. Grew, 1 June 1949. National Committee for Free Europe, Inc.

86 Dewitt C. Poole to Allen W. Dulles 28 September 1950. "…only the Hungarian [council] is anywhere near satisfactory." www.foia.cia.gov. Accessed 22 November 2012.
"We always cited the Hungarian National Council … as the model of an efficient and cohesive national exile organization." Leitch, "Great Expectations" 186.

87 Kádár Lynn, *Tibor Eckhardt. His American Years*, 218–219. The original proclamation is reproduced in Hungarian and English: The announcement of the formation of the Hungarian National Council, November 18, 1947. "Proclamation to the Hungarian People" (Kiáltvany a Magyar Néphez).

88 The founding members of the Hungarian National Council were: Msgr. Béla Varga, Ferenc Nagy, Tibor Eckhardt, Dezső Sulyok and Zoltán Pfeiffer.

89 In 1950 the president's Report shows that the NCFE was still operating on the notion that the exiles would soon be returning home: "In the interim pending liberation such a working committee can stand before the world, under the name of National Council, as a symbol its country in the democratic aspect." President's Report for the Year 1950 National Committee for a Free Europe, Inc., 5 January 1951, 10. A. A. Berle Papers, FDR Presidential Library, Box 222. Folder NCFE President's Report 1950.

90 A well researched and illuminating essay on this topic by Polish historian Anna Mazurkiewicz follows in a succeeding chapter; as do chapters on the Romanian National Council, authored by Marius Petraru, the Council for Free Czechoslovakia by Francis Raška, the Bulgarian National Council by Maria Kokoncheva and the Baltic Freedom Committees by Jonathan L'Hommedieu.

91 Leich, "Great Expectations", 185.

92 Ibid.

93 The issue of the exile leaders' knowledge of the sources of NCFE funding seems to have been distorted since the revelations of the origins of its funding by the CIA. Some historians have taken the position that everyone knew that the funding for NCFE /FEC came through US intelligence, yet there is no evidence to prove that – other than a few émigré leaders who had ongoing contacts with US intelligence – this was the case. Leich's article tells us it was an open secret that the US government was providing the funding, not that it was US intelligence.

94 Leich, "Great Expectations", 186.

95 Ibid.

96 Papers of Ferenc Marosy. HIA. Radio Free Europe Corporate Files, Box 235, Folder 12. Letter dated 6 October1958 from General Crittenberger (President of FEC) to Bernard Yarrow, Vice President of the FEC.

97 Memorandum for: Deputy Director of Central Intelligence 22 November 1950. Subject. Radio Free Europe. "At the meeting of the directors of the National Committee for a Free Europe in New York on Thursday evening, November 2nd, attended by the Deputy Director of Central Intelligence and the Assistant Director for Policy Coordination…" www.foia.cia.gov CO1123655. Accessed 27 November 2012.

98 "'Free Europe' Unit Formed", *Washington Post*, June 2, 1949; "New Group Formed to Assist Refugees", *New York Times*, June 2, 1949.

99 A. A. Berle Papers, Box 222, Folder Executive Committee: 1949–1953. Members of the NCFE, Inc. Board.

100 Later known as the Radio Free Europe Fund. A second radio organization in addition to RFE, Radio Liberty, originally named Radio Liberation, was inaugurated on 1 March 1 1953 with programming directed to the Soviet Union. Radio Liberty was "conceived as a weapon of psychological warfare during the darkest days of the anti-Stalin struggle." Puddington, *Broadcasting Freedom*, 153.

101 A. A. Berle Papers. Box 222 Folder: Crusade for Freedom 1950, 1951, 1952.

102 RFE Corporation Papers, Box 166, Folder: 13: Crusade for Freedom General: January–June 1950. HIA.

103 Ibid. Crusade for Freedom Campaign Letter #1 from Lucius D. Clay to committee members Frank Altschul, Allen W. Dulles, Arthur W. Page, DeWitt C. Poole, Major General C. L. Adcock (Vice chairman).

104 Papers of A. A. Berle. Franklin D. Roosevelt Presidential Library. Hyde Park, NY. Box 222. Folder: Crusade for Freedom 1950, 1951, 1952. Letter from General Lucius D. Clay to A. A. Berle, 20 December 1950.

105 "Government Monies", 11.

106 Puddington, *Broadcasting Freedom*, 23.

107 Lucius D. Clay to DeWitt C. Poole December 20, 1950. "The number of signatures of Americans on the Freedom Scroll has passed the fifteen million mark: 15,507,877." RFE Corporate Files, Box 166. Folder 14: "Crusade for Freedom." HIA. It should be noted that in 1950 the population of the United States was 152 million – which means that fully 10 percent of the entire population participated in the Crusade for Freedom Campaign.

108 Puddington, *Broadcasting Freedom*, 20–22.

109 "Ford Named Head of Freedom Drive: Heritage Foundation, Which is Taking Over Crusade, Wins Eisenhower's Praise", *New York Times*, May 15, 1953. The 1950/51 campaign resulted in $3.5 million dollars in revenues.

110 "US Group in Lisbon", *New York Times*, October 26, 1958.

111 Puddington, *Broadcasting Freedom*, 13.

112 Papers of Adolf A. Berle. Franklin D. Roosevelt Presidential Library. Box 222. Folder: NCFE Executive Committee – 1949–1953. Letter from Robert L. Land, Director of RFE to A. A. Berle re: Exile Politics, 1 December 1951.

113 Whitney H. Shepardson (President NCFE) to Allen W. Dulles re: The President's Report for the NCFE 1952. 10.4.1953 Report reproduced in full. www.foia.cia.gov Accessed 29 November 2012.

114 Memorandum for the Honorable Robert G. Murphy, Deputy Under-Secretary of State, Dept of State, May 2, 1957. Subject: Radio Free Europe, 4. www.foia.cia.gov. Accessed 10 February 2013.

115 Richard H. Cummings, "Balloons over East Europe. The Cold War Leaflet Campaign of Radio Free Europe". Extract from "Attacks from the East Against Radio Free Europe/Radio Liberty." Paper presented at the 5th Annual Meeting of the International Intelligence History Study Group, 18–20 June 1999, Tunzing, Germany. In *Falling Leaf Journal of the Psywar Society*. www.psywarsoc.org. Accessed 22 November 2012.

116 James A. Michener, *The Bridge at Andau* (New York: Random House, 1957) 251.

117 László Borhi, *Hungary in the Cold War Between the United States and the Soviet Union: 1945–1956* (Budapest: CEU Press, 2004) 284.

[118] Walter L. Hixson, *Parting the Curtain: Propaganda, Culture and the Cold War 1945–1961* (New York, St. Martin's Griffin, 1997) 66.

[119] Cissie Dore Hill, "Voices of Hope: The Story of Radio Free Europe and Radio Liberty." *Hoover Digest* 4 (October 30, 2001). www.hoover.org/publications/hoover-digest/article/6270. Accessed 29 November 2012.

[120] Richard Helms and William Hood, *A Look over My Shoulder: A Life in the Central Intelligence Agency* (New York: Random House, 2003) 363.

[121] United Nations General Assembly, *Special Committee on the Problem of Hungary* (1957). Chapter II, 20, paragraph 56.

[122] György Litván, ed. *The Hungarian Revolution of 1956: Reform, Revolt and Repression: 1953–1963* (London: Longman, 1996) 145.

[123] Arthur J. Olsen, "Free Radio Denies Inciting Hungary", *New York Times*, 9 December 1956, 3. See also: Internal Memorandum 5 December 1956 by RFE Political Advisor William Griffith. Policy Review for Voice for Free Hungary Programming, October 23–November 23, 1956.. The George Washington University National Security Archive.

[124] CIA, The Clandestine Service Historical Series. Hungary, volume II: External Operations 1946–1965. May 1972. www. foia.cia.gov. Accessed 7 January 2013.

[125] Puddington, *Broadcasting Freedom*, 14.

[126] US Army Military Institute. Carlisle Barracks, PA. Georgetown University, Washington DC research project, under contract to G2 Department of the Army. "Hungary, Resistance Activities and Potentials" Project No. 9570. 5 January 1956. www.gwu.edu/~nsarchiv/NSAEBB/NSAEBB76/doc.pdf. Accessed 26 November 2012.

[127] Litván, *The Hungarian Revolution of 1956*, 46.

[128] Cissie Dore Hill, "Voices of Hope". Accessed 29 November 2012.

[129] Charles Gati, *Failed Illusions: Moscow, Washington, Budapest and the failed 1956 Hungarian Revolt.* (Washington, DC: Woodrow Wilson Center Press: Stanford University Press, Stanford, CA, 2006) 93.
Although there may have been vestiges of the Grombach-Pond Network which operated in Central and East Europe from 1942–1954, still in contact with the West. Until its deactivation, the Grombach Network had a wide-ranging radio communication network and hundreds of operatives working behind the Iron Curtain. Katalin Kádár Lynn, "Tibor Eckhardt and the Grombach Organization: Hungarian Émigré Politics and United States Intelligence 1941–1955 "in Anna Mazurkiewicz, ed., *East Central Europe in Exile: Patterns of Transatlantic Migration* (London: Cambridge Scholars Publishing, 2013 [forthcoming]).

[130] RFE Corporate Files: Box 211. Folder 4: Hungary 1949–1957. To: Thomas H. Brown from Henry O. Hart, July 8, 1959. Quoting the findings in a report titled "Hungary and the 1956 Uprising," published by International Research Associates, Inc in 1957. "This study carried out by Elmo C Wilson of the above institution has the advantage of being an independent investigation based on a relatively large sample (1000 respondents), which was representative of the parent population at least along three lines, namely, sex, age and religion."

[131] Puddington, *Broadcasting Freedom,* 116.

[132] In addition to the history of the Czechoslovak, Hungarian, Polish, Bulgarian, Romanian and Bulgarian national councils in this work, the history of several of the key organizations sponsored by the NCFE/FEC, Assembly of Captive European Nations (ACEN), the Free Europe University in Exile as well as NCFE support for exile cultural and sport organizations are recounted in this volume, providing the reader with a comprehensive range of NCFE/FEC sponsored activities. .

[133] Leich, "Great Expectations", 194.

[134] A. A. Berle Papers. FDR Presidential Library. Box 224: Folder NCFE: Williamsburg Declaration.

[135] Regular meetings were held by the exile groups in preparation for the Williamsburg Conference, as minutes from meetings from May 22 and May 27 of the General Committee of the Central and Eastern Conference attest. Papers of the Hungarian National Council (Magyar Nemzeti Bizottmany), Hungarian National Library (OSZK) Archives. Fond 488, Box 44. Folder: Williamsburg Conference.

[136] A. A. Berle Papers. FDR Presidential Library. Box 224: Folder NCFE. A. A. Berle, Jr. speech June 12, 1952, 2–3.

[137] A. A. Berle Papers, FDR Presidential Library. Box 224, Folder: Williamsburg Declartion. Levering Tyson to Admiral Miller with copies to Mr. Wright and Dr. Berle on June 16, 1952.

[138] Anna Mazurkiewicz, "The Voice of the Silenced Peoples", in Ieva Zake, ed., *Anti-Communist Minorities in the US: Activism of Ethnic Refugees* (New York: Palgrave McMillan, 2000).
By the time of the Second Session of the 94th Congress and the annual observance of "Captive Nations Week" in the US Congress, instituted in 1959 by public law 86–90, the list of nations considered "captive" had been expanded to 30 and included Asian and Southeast Asian countries. *The Bicentennial Salute to the Captive Nations, 1976* (Washington, DC: US Government Printing Office, 1977) 7.

[139] Assembly of Captive European Nations Papers 1953–1972. Immigration History Research Center. University of Minnesota, Historical Sketch, 1. "The Assembly of Captive European Nations was a coalition of representatives from nine nations under Soviet domination after WWII. Membership in the organization consisted of government and cultural leaders from Albania, Bulgaria, Czechoslovakia, Estonia, Hungary, Latvia, Lithuania, Poland and Romania." Founded on 20 September 1954, the ACEN was established to "symbolize in one name both the plight and the aims of the Central and East European Nations" which were either unrepresented or misrepresented in the United Nations". See Anna Mazurkiewicz's chapter on the ACEN in this volume and her essay on the ACEN in *Anti-Communist Minorities*, cited above.

[140] Leich, *"Great Expectations"*, 194.

[141] Mazurkiewicz, "The Voice of the Silenced Peoples", 174.

[142] A. A. Berle Jr. Papers, Box 224, File: Mid-European Studies Center 1952–1955, Franklin D. Roosevelt Presidential Library. Hyde Park, NY.

[143] Anna Mazurkiewicz's essay in Chapter 9 of this volume on the campaign against Khruschev's visit to the United States in 1959 describes this schism in detail.

[144] RFE Corporate Files. Box 188. Folder 6: Free Europe Committee Administration 1949–1954. HIA. Memorandum of Agreement on Exile Activities in the United States Sponsored or Stimulated by FEC. 20 December 1954.

[145] Béla Fábián, "Embers Behind the Curtain", *Washington Post*, 18 March 1951, B4.

[146] Hungarian National Council Papers. Box 22, Folder: Paul Auer. Széchényi National Library Archives. Budapest.

[147] However, whatever aid was allowed had to be purchased through organizations controlled by the communist governments, which not only used these agencies' sales to acquire hard currency but also shamelessly marked up the cost of the packages' contents.

[148] RFE Corporate Files. Box 185. File 6: Exile Organizations. HIA. Memorandums dated June 30, 1959 and July 8, 1950, Exile Organizations supported or assisted by FEC in Europe.

[149] Ibid.

[150] Ibid.

[151] Ibid.

[152] Hixson, 66. For a well researched and comprehensive history of the Free Europe University in Exile, see Veronika Durin-Hornyik's essay, Chapter 10 in this volume.

[153] A. A. Berle Papers, Box 222, Folder NCFE Executive Committee 1949–1953. Letter dated 16 July 1951 from Leon Dennen to CD Jackson, then president of NCFE.

[154] Papers of Stanislaw Mikolajczyk. HIA. Box 133. International Peasant Union. Folder 15: Cooperating Organizations: Christian Democratic Union. Report of the Secretary General of the Christian Democratic Union of Central Europe presented by Konrad Seiniewicz at the First International Congress of the Christian Democratic Union of Central Europe. New York, March 13, 1953, 4.

[155] "4 Years Failure on Hungary Cited: Munro, in UN Report says Soviet Occupations shows Peril to Small Nations", *New York Times*, December 3, 1960. www.nytimes.com. Accessed 12 April 2012.

[156] Puddington, *Broadcasting Freedom*, 175.

[157] Ibid., 188.

[158] Helms, *A Look over My Shoulder*, 368.

[159] Ibid.

[160] Ibid., 369.

[161] Comptroller General of the United States, Report to the Committee on Foreign Relations United States Senate: US Government Monies Provided to Radio Free Europe and Radio Liberty. NARA. Record Group 263-10. FOIA Records of the CIA, May 25, 1972.

Select Bibliography

Archives:

Radio Free Europe Corporate Files, Hoover Institution Archives, Stanford, CA

A great body of archival materials related to Romanian, Polish, Bulgarian Hungarian and Czech émigré organizations and leaders during the Cold War are located in the HIA.

Papers of A. A. Berle Jr. Franklin Delano Roosevelt Presidential Library, Hyde Park, NY

ACEN Archives: Immigration History Research Center. University of Minneapolis, Minneapolis, MN.

Cold War International History Project, Digital Archive Collection. www.wilsoncenter.org/digital-archives

Articles:

John Foster Leich: "Great Expectations: The National Councils In Exile: 1950–1960". The Polish Review 35 nos. 3/4 (1990) 183–196

George Kennan. "The Sources of Soviet Conduct" by X, Foreign Affairs, July 1947 Reprinted in Foreign Affairs, 65, no. 4 (Spring 1987) 854–868

Anna Mazurkiewicz. "The Voice of the Silenced Peoples", in Ieva Zake ed., *Anti-Communist Minorities in the US: Activism of Ethnic Refugees* (New York. Palgrave McMillan, 2000)

Paul Nitze. "America, An Honest Broker", Foreign Affairs, 69 no.4 (Fall 1990) 1–14

Unpublished Manuscripts:

Larry Dwayne Collins, "The Free Europe Committee, An American Weapon of the Cold War". Unpublished dissertation. Carleton University. 1973.

Books:

Charles E. Bohlen. *Witness to History, 1929–1969* (New York, WW Norton, Co. Inc. 1973)
Walter Hixson. *Parting the Curtain: Propaganda, Culture and the Cold War, 1945–1961* (New York, St. Martin's Griffin, 1997)
Arch Puddington. *Broadcasting Freedom: The Cold War Triumph of Radio Free Europe and Radio Liberty* (Lexington, KY, The University Press of Kentucky, 2000)
Hugh Wilford. *The CIA, the British Left and the Cold War: Calling the Tune?* (London, Frank Cass Publishers, 2003)

11

History of the Council of Free Czechoslovakia

Francis D. Raška

Introduction-formation of the Council of Free Czechoslovakia

After the Communist takeover of the Czechoslovak government in February 1948, a large group of non-Communist Czechoslovak politicians sought exile in the West. A large proportion of them left their homeland out of a justified fear of Communist persecution. In fact, some of the non-Communist politicians in Czechoslovakia had already been arrested in February 1948 but were released following the personal intervention of President Edvard Beneš. Most of those who escaped initially found refuge in the western zones of Germany, and others in Austria. As time progressed, significant groups of exiles formed in Britain, France and the United States. Smaller groups formed in Belgium, Italy and other countries as well. At first, most of the refugees were interned in various refugee camps, where living conditions were very poor. Their situation improved somewhat in the summer months of 1948 when the refugee camps were placed under the jurisdiction of the International Refugee Organization.[1]

Prominent individuals such as former government members or parliamentary deputies were housed at the so-called Alaska House in Frankfurt. Among the early residents were National Socialists Ota Hora, Alois Čížek, Jaroslav Stránský and Vladimír Krajina; People's Party deputy Ivo Ducháček; Judge Jaroslav Drábek and editor, Ivan Herben. Their first significant activity was initiating a meeting of the representatives of four parties (National Socialist, Social Democratic, Slovak Democratic and People's) in Paris, followed by another meeting on 10 April in London. The main purpose was an agreement to form a central Czechoslovak organ in exile, which would also help provide for a growing number of Czechoslovak refugees.[2]

Three National Socialist deputies, accompanied by the Minister of Defense in the wartime Czechoslovak Exile Government, Sergej Ingr, visited Winston Churchill, who tried to arrange a presentation by them in the House of Commons.[3] But, the meeting at the House of Commons never took place. At that time, a Social Democrat, Blažej Vilím, used his access to the Labour government and tried to organize a meeting of thirty escaped Czechoslovak parliamentary deputies prior to the Czechoslovak elections scheduled for 30 May. It should be mentioned that Vilím had to assure the British authorities that there was "no intention to set up any committees, least of all a government-in-exile."[4] A Foreign Office official, C.P. Mayhew, added this: "My own view is that this is the 'thin end of the wedge' and that if we do not intend to use Czech refugees for propaganda and intelligence purposes, we would not be wise to open our doors to these Czech MPs." C.F.A. Warner, Mayhew's colleague, indicated his agreement: "I think most of these MPs will drift on to America before they become out of date (and therefore valueless) and have become much of a nuisance here."[5] R.M.A. Hankey at the Foreign Office recommended that the Czechoslovak MPs should be given the visas.[6]

The meeting was finally scheduled for 28 May 1948 at Caxton Hall in London. Prior to the meeting, the Czech delegation failed to obtain a reception with the Speaker of the British Parliament. The meeting adopted a two-page resolution deploring the Communist takeover of 25 February and declared that, regardless of party, they would strive "with all our efforts in brotherly unity for the return of freedom and democracy to our country in the spirit of the humanitarian, democratic and socialist principles of our president-liberator, T.G. Masaryk."[7]

The role of these Czechoslovak politicians was difficult indeed because nobody seemed to care much about their predicament. A confidential appraisal of the meeting for the Foreign Office stated:

> ...having depended so long upon their leader, Dr. Beneš, and been deserted by him at the crucial moment, these Czechoslovak exile politicians are almost at a total loss as to where to go from here. There is no leader of inspiration among them, at least for the moment.[8]

In the United States, early attempts to organize an exile movement were undertaken by diplomats rather than politicians because most politicians had not yet made it to the United States. The first meeting, which took place on 14 June 1948 in New York, consisted of eight people, seven of whom were Slovaks.[9] They issued a public declaration and informed the American authorities of their intention to organize a central organ of Czechoslovak resistance, namely the Council of Free Czechoslovakia.[10] A press conference ensued on 29 June 1948, during which a memorandum was presented by Dr. Štefan Osuský, a major rival of Beneš's during the Second World War. The most important meeting took place on 17–18 July in New York. The British Foreign Office, which was closely monitoring the situation, concluded that the Preparatory Committee of the Council of Free Czechoslovakia was composed of fairly harmless individuals, except for Dr. Osuský.[11]

Yet another center of Czechoslovak exile activity was established in Paris. This consisted mainly of Agrarians, National Democrats and Smallholders (the three parties not reinstated in Czechoslovakia after the 1945 liberation). The People's Party had its representatives there as well, and the National Socialist leader, Hubert Ripka, also joined the group.

Both the summer and autumn months of 1948 witnessed frantic activities in both London and Paris. The representatives of individual parties tried to form various coalitions with other parties while, at the same time, excluding others.[12]

On 17 September 1948, the British authorities concluded that an agreement had been reached among all political parties to form the Council of Free Czechoslovakia, which would include representatives of all parties of the "National Front" as well as the Republicans, as the Agrarians now referred to themselves.

The British could not have been more mistaken. The negotiations would last for a long time yet. The working charter document stated that all the future members would be government ministers and parliamentary deputies, representing all Czechoslovak political parties recognized since 1 January 1935. The British desk officer at the Foreign Office considered this unfortunate. "For the Communists will make much good propaganda if the old reactionary parties are deliberately revived by the émigrés."[13]

A regional meeting took place in Paris in early January with little unity among the parties.[14] Rudolf Kopecký, a National Democrat who worked at the BBC in London, summarized his unhappiness as follows:

> I think that our entire group still lives in domestic conditions and that they are awarding ministerial posts instead of admitting that now it is necessary to work together to ensure the possibility of awarding such posts in the future...This reminds me of another mistake on the part of the Czechoslovak exiles. I will use the metaphor of sports terminology. The majority of our politicians think it is a sprint, whereas I declare that it is a marathon. If I am wrong, then I will arrive at the finish line late. But, if our politicians are wrong, and perhaps they see that they are, they will never reach the finish line. To speculate that war is imminent and that we will return home leads us to erroneous conclusions, which are the reasons for our failure to unite... The task of the politician is to assure for his nation peace, tranquility, a satisfying way of life, and prosperity. We know that, to give this to our people, we have to liberate our country. Therefore, no matter what pacifists we are, we are not afraid of war. Put yourself in the position of a British or American minister. Does he need to assure this for his nation? You may call me a pessimist, but I am not. Life has taught me. I liken everything that took place in Paris to playing with toy soldiers.[15]

The final meeting of the Preparatory Committee was called for 11 February 1949. It took place at All Souls Unitarian Church in Washington, D.C., and resulted in an agreement ten days later to form the Council of Free Czechoslovakia. The formation was announced on 25 February 1949 in a declaration sent to thirty-nine governments. Twenty-one of them, including the United States, United Kingdom and France, acknowledged the notification in writing.[16]

The declaration is an impressive document written by prominent Czech journalist and writer, Ferdinand Peroutka. Its conclusion states:

> Even if the Communist regime rages with madness, please preserve spotless the character of the nation. Do not allow yourselves to be deceived so as not to be able to recognize what is freedom and what is tyranny, what is right and what is wrong. In your thinking, be free men. Educate your children to be honest citizens. Teach them, and you yourselves never forget, to distinguish between good and evil. If the character of the nation is preserved, everything else will be restored.[17]

Petr Zenkl was elected chairman of the Council of Free Czechoslovakia. Jozef Lettrich (Slovak) and Václav Majer were elected vice-chairmen. The presidium consisted of twelve members, and the executive committee had thirty. In addition, there was to be a consultative body consisting of about 100 members.[18] Among exiles, reactions to the Council's establishment were mixed. The *New York Times* published a terse announcement on 26 February 1949: "Yesterday, on the one-year anniversary of the Communist takeover in Prague, the newly formed Council of Free Czechoslovakia announced its determination to liberate its country from the yoke of Communist tyranny."[19]

The formation of a central organ of Czechoslovak exile resistance was an important event. The road to the establishment of such an organization, however, was complicated by controversy, striking disagreements between Czech and Slovak representatives respectively, and friction among the political parties. The domination of the Council by the parties of the post-1945 National Front did not go unrecognized by other parties in exile. Future developments showed that these conflicts would be ignored only temporarily. Indeed, personal rivalries within the Council would have a negative impact on the organization's effectiveness and even its cohesion.

Early Years

By the end of 1950, the presidium of the Council had met thirty-seven times in either New York or Washington. These meetings resulted in the adoption of a number of formal declarations on conditions in Czechoslovakia. Communist terror was deplored, especially the executions of General Heliodor Píka and Dr. Milada Horáková. The Council also protested Communist aggression in Korea.

From the outset, the Preparatory Committee had difficulties financing its activities. In March 1949, the situation improved when funds began arriving from "anonymous" donors, surrounded in secrecy. Some members of the Council were uncomfortable with the funding situation and began to question the source of the funds.[20]

During the late 1960s evidence began to emerge regarding the funding of exile groups by U.S. intelligence organizations, and it became clear that the funds the exiles questioned had actually come from the United States Central Intelligence Agency. They were later funneled through the "non-profit" organization known as the National Committee for a Free Europe (NCFE). It remains unclear exactly who at this time knew where the funds were originated. Some members were at this time receiving personal support ranging from two hundred to four hundred dollars (at first called "stipends" and later "compensation"). In the summer of 1950, the NCFE asked the Council to present a budget proposal. Discussions concerning this took place at a meeting of the presidium on 16 July 1949.[21] Although the proposed budget was $29,200 per month, the NCFE initially agreed to provide $8,900 per month.

A Council report on its activities of November 1950 summarized the state of the Council as exceptionally satisfactory: "The Council finds understanding and sympathies everywhere...The relationship to the American representatives is based on close cooperation with the

NCFE. This collaboration is driven by the unity of goals of both organizations…"[22] The report also stated the following about Radio Free Europe (RFE): "Even before the broadcasts of RFE began in July 1950, the Council expressed its interest in establishing close collaboration with RFE…"[23] Indeed, participation in Radio Free Europe's activities probably represented the most effective aspect of the Council's anti-Communist activities.

Regional Committees of the Council were established in London and in Paris. Unlike in the United States, where the Council enjoyed NCFE support, the Regional Committees received no such support from the British and French Governments and the effectiveness of these bodies was hampered accordingly. Their membership was declining because many members were in the process of moving to North America. In London, vice-chairman of the Council, Václav Majer, sent a list of the London Committee's membership to the Foreign Office on 1 April 1949, and the Foreign Office duly noted that of the fourteen members, three had already moved to Canada or the United States.[24] Requests for financial support from the British were denied.

In Paris, the chairman of the local board, Dr. Hubert Ripka, was voted out on 23 January 1950. The Washington-based presidium of the Council refused to acknowledge this result.[25] The split in the Paris Regional Committee should have been recognized as a harbinger of things to come in Washington.

In October 1950, a rift developed between the Council's chairman, Petr Zenkl, and his first deputy, Dr. Jozef Lettrich. A meeting of the Executive Committee was called for 6 January 1951.[26] On 5 January 1951, the Council received an ultimatum from the chairman of the NCFE, C.D. Jackson.[27] It concluded: "It is honest to announce to you, your colleagues, and legally empowered functionaries, that the NCFE will fundamentally reexamine its relationship with the Council of Free Czechoslovakia in light of the results accomplished at this meeting."[28]

The meeting of the Council was affected by Jackson's ultimatum. Lasting two weeks, the meeting presented a picture of disunity and personal invectives. The ultimate catastrophe was brought about by a discussion of the terms of office, a proposal that was rejected by the National Socialists, who abruptly left the meeting. The Executive Committee split into two groups. The opinion of the majority was presented by Ferdinand Peroutka, who killed any chances of Zenkl's reelection as chairman. A minority group of thirteen dissenting members declared that the Council was dissolved and left the meeting. The majority group, however, continued the Council's activitiesCouncil. The dissenters subsequently announced the formation of a new organization, the National Committee of Free Czechoslovakia, with Petr Zenkl as its chairman.[29] The majority (seventeen members) of the original Executive Committee empowered Peroutka to negotiate a meeting with Frederick Dolbeare and C.D. Jackson of the NCFE in order to set up a meeting with a duly elected delegation led by Václav Majer. NCFE support for the Council continued, despite the obvious disagreements within the organization.

The breakup of the Council received sharp criticism from other members of the Czechoslovak exile community. Pressure slowly mounted for the two groups to reconcile their differences and unite, but this did not happen in 1951. On the occasion of the opening of the Munich station of Radio Free Europe, the Council of Free Czechoslovakia together with several members of the National Committee of Free Czechoslovakia, including its chairman, Petr Zenkl, made a joint statement on 30 April 1951.[30]

An attempt to bring the two organizations together in May 1951 failed, and their respective representatives continued their mutual accusations of pettiness and position-seeking. On 26–27 January 1952, the two organizations formed a twenty-four member committee on the basis of an agreement that had been reached on 15 January 1952.[31]

The Council adopted statutes which based its organization along party lines and also allowed for a body of personalities unaffiliated with any political party. After difficult and stormy meetings, the Council was reunited. The chairman of the Executive Committee was Petr Zenkl, whereas the Chairman of Deputies was Štefan Osuský. The remaining fifteen years of the Council's existence were marked by a continuing crisis and attempts to find solutions. Yet, in spite of party rivalries and personal conflicts, the Council would play an important role in the fight against communism.

The most effective tactic in the fight against Communism was the participation of Council members in Radio Free Europe. Ferdinand Peroutka became the head of the Czechoslovak Section. Between 1 May 1951 and 25 December 1976, Peroutka wrote more than one thousand commentaries for listeners in Czechoslovakia. Most of these commentaries can be found in the archives of the Hoover Institution at Stanford. Except for during the first year, the majority of these commentaries focused on international events and presented and defended the interests and policies of the United States. The Communist government in Czechoslovakia paid close attention to Peroutka's activities and spent considerable resources on a program of systematic jamming of RFE broadcasts. Peroutka's position at Radio Free Europe gave him extraordinary powers on the Council. It was he who decided who would speak on the program to Czechoslovakia, which was not only important for exile politicians, but also provided honoraria. As program director, Peroutka especially valued a young and very talented journalist and People's Party member, Pavel Tigrid. Tigrid was brilliant but abrasive and soon developed conflicts with some older socialist politicians. Peroutka thus fired Tigrid and replaced him with National Socialist, Julius Firt. After overcoming some hardships, Tigrid began to publish the periodical *Svědectví (Testimony)* in Europe. *Svědectví* gained a wide circulation and succeeded in its goal to undermine systematically Communist policies.

The Americans appreciated Peroutka's talents and did not hesitate to use him in order to pressure the Council. Peroutka soon found out that it was the Americans, not he, who controlled the Czechoslovak program of RFE. The best example was the fate of his own piece of work on former president, Edvard Beneš.[32] The most striking was his change of tune with respect to the issue of the Sudeten Germans. The NCFE was very sensitive to this political group (Sudeten Germans), which was becoming politically influential in West Germany and very closely followed the RFE program. The Council's political program of 1952 stated: "We consider the transfer of Germans from Czechoslovakia to be definitive. It was implemented on the basis of agreements among the American, British and French governments and in accordance with the declarations of the Potsdam conference…"[33]

The NCFE leadership was concerned about this statement and about the statement regarding the renewal of Czechoslovakia within its pre-Munich frontiers.[34] The Council's position on transfer gradually softened due to pressure exerted by the NCFE, in spite of the fact that some Council leaders had been the moving force behind the Czechoslovak Exile Government's transfer plans during the war. Along these lines, it is imperative to note that, at variance with the wishy-washy position of the NCFE in the 1950s, the United States Government's position on the issue of transfer was unequivocal, and the transfer was defended as "…an historical fact based on the Potsdam conference and the United States is confident that no country wishes to call it into question."[35]

On 20 April 1953, Peroutka met with a representative of Dr. Rudolf Lodgman von Auen (leader of the revisionist Sudetendeutsche Landsmannschaft based in Munich) and during the meeting stated: "I cannot imagine a permanent solution of matters without the return of the Germans."[36] Peroutka's dialogue with representatives of Sudeten German organizations continued. In an interview with a German newspaper, in New York, Staatszeitung und Herold, Peroutka stated, "My personal view is that the almost complete expulsion of the Sudeten Germans was a mistake. Moreover, what happened during the implementation of it is a shame."[37]

This statement provoked a storm of protests, but Peroutka refused to stop.

Also a major source of conflict among members of the Council was the relationship between the two predominant nationalities, namely the Czechs and Slovaks. This issue was never resolved satisfactorily, and the post-Communist history of Czechoslovakia, which survived a mere three years after the return of democracy, demonstrates the depth of the problem, which ended in the division of Czechoslovakia into two countries on 1 January 1993. It should be noted that sub-Carpathian Ruthenia, which had been ceded by Czechoslovakia to the Soviet Union in 1945, was discussed briefly in Council deliberations, as was the ethnic Hungarian minority in Slovakia, but a general consensus emerged (with a handful of dissenters) that these issues did not represent a Council priority.

Another major activity of the Council was participation in various international bodies. The European Movement is worthy of mention, but the most important organization the Council took part in was the Assembly of Captive European Nations (ACEN). ACEN was founded in the summer months of 1954 as a representative body of Central and East European countries under Communist and Soviet domination. These included Albania, the Baltic States, Bulgaria, Czechoslovakia, Hungary, Poland and Romania. Czechoslovak participation started with a bang. Dr. Štefan Osuský (the head of the first delegation) chaired the meeting of 22 October 1954. The program focused upon Soviet aggression toward and oppression of the "captive nations", violations of peace treaties by Hungary, Romania and Bulgaria, and the forced militarization of captive nations. In addition, religious persecution in captive nations and forced labor behind the Iron Curtain were discussed.[38] Czechoslovak participation received much publicity in the Czech and Slovak press in the West.[39] Representatives from the Council presented a number of fundamental contributions to the deliberations of ACEN. Unfortunately, as was the case with almost all other Council activities, its participation in ACEN soon deteriorated due to factionalism and personal rivalries.

Already in 1956, problems arose with respect to the Czechoslovak delegation.[40]

As already mentioned, the Council ultimately split, and Czechoslovak representation in ACEN was awarded to a new body called the Committee of Free Czechoslovakia. This organization adhered to the statutes of ACEN, which prohibited representatives from accepting the citizenship of other countries. Arguments between competing factions of Czechoslovak exiles may seem ridiculous today, but they exerted a negative influence on the effectiveness and international standing of their cause.

The archives are filled with documents attesting to an almost uninterrupted crisis in the Council of Free Czechoslovakia. It should be stressed that a number of members proposed remedial actions but to no avail.

Among them, we should mention Miloslav Rechcígl, a pre-war parliamentary deputy of the Agrarian Party, and Václav Hlavatý, a famous mathematician. Above all, however, a great effort to resolve quarrels among Council members was made by representatives of the young generation of Czechoslovak exiles, who wrote in a declaration: "The basis of real leadership in exile has to be a program and not personal sympathies or antipathies. We wish that work was the only requirement for membership in the leadership."[41]

On 29 March 1955, Peroutka informed Bernard Yarrow of the NCFE about the sorry shape of the Council and proposed corrective measures.[42] Julius Firt's response to Peroutka in a letter of 22 September 1956 is revealing.

> I understand your disgust, but I think you cannot pull back and leave everything to these gangs. I think we would have to bite into the unpleasant, but important problem. The Council needs to be placed on an entirely new foundation and the old one needs to be put on some sort of reservation where the old stags are not hunted, but also cannot be allowed to cross the fence.[43]

The NCFE's support for the Council came to an end in 1957. It had finally lost patience and concluded that the Council's internal differences were irreconcilable. Once NCFE funding was terminated, the Council had to rely on member contributions as its main source of income. However, NCFE funding for the Czechoslovak delegation to ACEN continued. Quarrels emerged, which ultimately resulted in another split of the Council that occurred between 1959 and 1961, and it was a serious one. In 1959, a Political Committee directed by Dr. Jozef Lettrich and Arnošt Heidrich was established within the Council. This body soon came into conflict with the Executive Committee led by Petr Zenkl. The dispute concerned the composition of the Czechoslovak delegation to ACEN. The Political Committee wrote a protest letter to the president of ACEN complaining that the Executive Committee could not represent the Council because it did not contain any Slovaks and that some members had already acquired a new citizenship and thus could not represent exiles. Zenkl's reply clearly challenged the letter, and the dispute between the two committees became public. Then in September 1961 the Political Committee proclaimed itself as a new organization, the Committee of Free Czechoslovakia, and adopted its own statutes.[44] The Committee then succeeded in replacing the Council of Free Czechoslovakia as the official Czechoslovak member of ACEN. This new organization had sixteen members: Vilém Bernard, Dr. Vladislav Brdlík, Dr. Josef Černý, Vasily L. Fedinec, Arnošt Heidrich, Fedor M. Hodža, Václav Holub, Dr. Martin Kvetko, Dr. Jozef Lettrich, Theodor Lipčík, Václav Majer, Jozef Mrázek, Dr. Štefan Osuský, Dr Adolf Procházka, Leopold Slíva and Marie Tumlířová.[45]

The Road to Reunification

After the split, the remaining Council members concentrated around Petr Zenkl. At this time, some of the elderly original members were already deceased and others took retirement from political life. Petr Zenkl himself was already approaching his eighties. Several members of the "younger" generation remained active (Jiří Horák, Radomír Luža, Emil Ransdorf, Čeněk Torn and Mojmír Povolný). The activities of the Council, however, were slowly declining to a point that dissolving the organization was actually under consideration. The reasons for considering dissolution were complex and reflected the situation at home as well as in the West. At home, the Communist regime in the 1960s was falling into political and economic crisis. Under Nikita Khrushchev's rule (1953–1964), the Soviet regime underwent some degree of liberalization. In Czechoslovakia, the dissociation from Stalinism took the form of searching for a new face of socialism. The reform movement, led from the top of the Communist Party establishment, was split into two factions within the Party. The "conservatives" wished to improve the old system, whereas "progressives" sought to create a new socialist model. The Council sympathized with the reform movement and supported it on the international scene. However, the exiles did not believe in reforming the Communist regime. They still held out some hope for the development of a civic movement in Czechoslovakia, which would result in the overthrow of the Communist regime altogether.[46] This hope, however, was crushed by the Soviet invasion of Czechoslovakia in August 1968, which guaranteed the defeat of attempts at reform. On 20 September 1968, the Council issued a proclamation in Washington, D.C., in which appeals were made to all governments faithful to humanitarian ideals, to the intelligentsia throughout the world, to workers, to the youth of the world, and to the conscience of every man and woman, to show to the Soviet Union their solidarity with the Czechoslovak people, already suffering for one month under Soviet occupation.[47]

The West's passive acceptance of the new reality was a painful disappointment to Council members. In the ensuing months, the Council faced the critical decision of whether to terminate its activities and existence altogether. The "Normalization" process at home (as the post-1968 clampdown initiated in 1969 was referred to) without a doubt contributed to the deep sense of despair. It was again Petr Zenkl, now over eighty years old, who in 1971 provided the impulse to resurrect the Council and continue its original mission.

In November 1971, Zenkl sent a letter to members of the the Council assembly informing them of his intention to call a meeting of the Executive Committee and asking them for comments and proposals concerning the Council's future. In the letter, Zenkl explained the reasons for what many members perceived as stagnation and lack of activity on the part of the Council. He described the splitting of the organization, the passing away of many previously active members, and the need to involve the democratically-minded members of the post-1968 emigration in Council activities. To this end, Zenkl therefore suggested that a meeting of the Assembly be convened in order to elect a new Executive Committee and admit new members to the organization. It is obvious that Zenkl understood that adherence to principles based on political parties within the Council was outdated, as younger or new members lacked experience and were not familiar with the workings of a multiparty system. Instead, he stressed the importance of recruiting young people, students and workers, with an emphasis on their character and on democratic inclinations.[48]

Nearly a year passed before the meeting of the Assembly of the Council was held in Washington, D.C. beginning on 10 November 1972. In order to maximize attendance, this date was selected to coincide with the annual congress of the Czechoslovak Society of Arts and Sciences. A meeting of the Executive Committee, chaired by Petr Zenkl, preceded the meeting of the Assembly called by vice-chairman, Čeněk Torn. The previous night Adolf Klimek had already called for a "confidential" planning meeting of several members (Radomír Luža, Mojmír Povolný, Jiří Horák, Ransdorf, Ján Papánek). How important this meeting was for the remaining members is obvious from a letter from Čeněk Torn to Mojmír Povolný dated 3 November 1972. Torn wrote:

> Years ago, the younger ones left. Many of our contemporaries have died and the gap between us is ever growing. I come to you, dear Mojmír, with a request that only a friend can make: return to us. In about a week, a meeting will take place, called by Dr. Zenkl, at which we want to resurrect the activity of the Council in spite of stubbornly adverse circumstances and to transfer the Council alive into better times.[49]

According to the minutes of the meeting, recorded by Adolf Klimek, all ten participants (Zenkl, Hora, Horák, Luža, Klimek, Papánek, Povolný, Ryšavý, Torn, Ransdorf) agreed on the following:

- to maintain the continuity of the Council of Free Czechoslovakia;
- to establish a Working Committee with a mandate to create a new statutory and personal structure of the Council;
- to fulfill all the political tasks of the Council;
- to establish contacts with other Czechoslovak exile organizations in other parts of the world and to try to coordinate activities with them;
- to prepare a position paper defining the Council's opinion on questions to be addressed by the European Conference on Security.[50]

This Working Committee consisted of Papánek, Horák, Luža, Povolný, Ransdorf, Hora and Klimek. Dr. Zenkl would remain the chairman of the Council. Dr. Ryšavý would take care of financial matters, and Dr. Klimek would assist Dr. Zenkl.[51]

This new beginning was not without problems. By December 1972, Ota Hora, in his letter to the Working Committee, was already criticizing the Working Committee for being too slow and ineffective, namely in producing a position paper for the Conference on European Security. Hora pointed to the fact that the ethnic organization, the Czechoslovak National Council of America as well as the Czechoslovak Advisory Council in Western Europe had already produced their position papers. He also reminded the Working Committee of the necessity to analyze the Council's financial situation and try to find new sources of support.[52] By this time, all that the Council could rely on were membership dues and donations from a dwindling number of supporters. It became obvious that the Council's lack of a functional central office with a permanent employee represented a substantial obstacle in keeping administrative operations effective and interpersonal communications prompt and reliable. Yet another problem that was perceived by several members of the Working Committee was the absence of leadership by the now-ailing Dr. Zenkl. In one of his letters to Mojmír Povolný, Adolf Klimek described how much Zenkl had done in the past for the Council organizationally and politically—indeed, Klimek called Zenkl the backbone of the organization— and how much these qualities were lacking at the moment. Klimek tried to convince Zenkl to prepare the organization for his successor, but Zenkl insisted that "until his last breath, until the end of his life, he will consciously and fully perform all duties for which he went into exile and which were entrusted in him by the chairmanship of the Council of Free Czechoslovakia."[53]

In 1973, however, Petr Zenkl gradually stepped aside for health reasons. Between 1972 and 1974, the activities of the Council were affected by a lack of both leadership and financial support. In spite of these circumstances, the members of the Working Committee pursued a number of goals.

In late 1971, Dr. Papánek prepared a memorandum to be sent on behalf of the Council to President Richard Nixon before his upcoming May 1972 summit with Soviet leaders in Moscow. The memo outlines the importance of three principles essential for peace and stability in Europe: sovereign equality of all European states, including non-intervention in the internal affairs of any state; independence and the right of self-determination of any state; renunciation of the use of force against any state. It also recalls the occupation of Czechoslovakia in 1968 and the violation of the Czechoslovak-Soviet Treaty of 1943 by the Soviet Union.[54]

It became obvious that the Council would have to establish a better connection with European-based Czechoslovak exile organizations formed by the "newer exiles" who arrived in the West after 1968, as well as to maintain contact with European exile organizations fighting for freedom in their respective countries. Especially instrumental in this context were Radomír Luža, Adolf Klimek and Mojmír Povolný. Upon his return to the United States from Europe in 1972, Luža wrote to Povolný how successful Jiří Pelikán's action (*Listy* Group) had been in attracting attention to Czechoslovakia in connection with the so-called "normalization trials".[55] Mojmír Povolný understood well the increasing importance and influence of European exile groups, and during his one-year stay in Europe (1973–1974), he invested considerable effort in the coordination of some exile activities.[56] The ultimate hope, that all organizations would come under the umbrella of the Council of Free Czechoslovakia, however, did not materialize.

Not all members of the Working Committee were prepared to welcome the "new" exile generation. As is apparent from the meeting of the Committee on 17–18 March 1973, two members of the Committee (Ryšavý and Hora) were categorically opposed to any collaboration with the post-1968 generation of exiles. This was due to deep distrust of the post-1968 generation, many of whom had been Communist functionaries. The final agreement reached by meeting participants was to maintain contact with the new exiles, but to postpone any co-opting of other groups for the future. At the same meeting, unhappiness was expressed about the existence of the Czechoslovak Advisory Committee in Western Europe, directed by Council of Free Czechoslovakia member, Edmund Řehák. It was felt that this exile organization should be under the Council's umbrella and thus present as a unified body.[57]

In March 1974, a draft of new bylaws was accepted and a meeting of the Assembly to elect new Council organs was called for September 1974. The new Council bylaws accepted the principle of the federal arrangement of Czechoslovakia since 1968 and called for parity in chairmanships of all Council organs. The September elections indeed resulted in a new leadership. Mojmír Povolný (Czech) became the chairman of the Executive Committee and Martin Kvetko (Slovak) became vice chairman. Jiří Horák (Czech) was elected the general secretary. Rudolf Fraštacký (Slovak) became chairman of the Council Assembly and Čeněk Torn its vice chairman. In his memoirs, *Ma cesta dvacátým stoletím (My Journey through the Twentieth Century)*, Professor Povolný cites the names of all members of the Executive Committee, the majority of whom remained in the Council until the fall of totalitarianism in Czechoslovakia in 1989.[58] The membership of the Executive Committee included: Mojmír Povolný (chairman), Martin Kvetko (vice chairman), Jiří Horák (general secretary), as well as members Ján Behárka, Pavol Blaho, Libuše Drobílková, Vlastislav Chalupa, Ján Horváth, Alois Čížek, Anna Faltusová, Mikuláš Ferjenčík, Ota Hora, Karel Hrubý, Čestmír Ješina, Josef Jonáš, N. Jíša, Karel Jeřábek, Adolf Klimek, Ľudovít Linczényi, Radomír Luža, Ján Mrázek, Michal Múdrý-Šebík, Štefan Pagáč, Josef Pejskar, Ota Rambousek, Edmund Řehák, Alois Rozehnal, Vavro Ryřavý, Michal Srnec, František Schwarzenberg, František Slíva, Jiří Škvor, Eduard Táborský and Felix Uhl. Erazim Kohák declined to become a member. Later, the following individuals became influential Executive Committee members: Vilém Brzorád, Bohumír Bunža, Milan Fabry, Vladimír Kabeš, Miloš Knorr, Milan Ondruš, Jiří Nápravník, Vlado Šimko and Ivan Viest.[59]

Activities of the reunited council

Immediately after the election, a new chapter in the life of the organization began. Povolný prepared a speech for Radio Free Europe and began to organize broadcasting on a regular schedule. He also started working on a new periodical called *Za svobodu,* which would be edited and published by Jiří Škvor (chief editor) in Montreal. Unfortunately, Škvor was at that time employed by the Canadian Broadcasting Corporation (CBC) and, as a state employee, he had great difficulties functioning as an editor of a political exile publication. He did an excellent job as editor of and as a contributor to the first issue of *Za svobodu*, which was published in January 1975; after that, he was compelled to give up his association with the periodical.[60] *Za svobodu* was replaced in 1976 by *Czechoslovak Newsletter*, which was published in New York on a quarterly basis.

As mentioned earlier, Povolný was well aware of the need to collaborate with other exile organizations, including the Czechoslovak Society of Arts and Sciences, and also with ethnic Czechoslovak organizations. After being elected chairman of the Executive Committee, Povolný contacted a number of organizations and informed them of the new direction the Council intended to take. Especially important for the exile cause was the Czechoslovak Advisory Committee in Western Europe, headed by Edmund Řehák. In his letter, Povolný explained the profound changes underway in the Council and signaled his intention to seek new methods of work and collaboration.[61] In March 1975, a representative of the Council, Martin Kvetko, met in Munich with representatives of the Czechoslovak Advisory Committee in Western Europe in order to establish rules for collaboration. In reaction to Povolný's efforts, Řehák issued a statement to all members of his organization about collaboration with the Council of Free Czechoslovakia. In the years that followed, Řehák became one of the important sources of information for fellow exiles about the situation in Europe. From Povolný's correspondence, it is apparent that he attempted to strengthen ties with the Council's European members and to reestablish the European base. He envisaged

Dr. Karel Hrubý (Switzerland) functioning as the European secretary of the Council in close collaboration with Felix Uhl (Switzerland).[62]

The financial state of the Council was dismal. Vavro Ryšavý was put in charge of the finances and was also expected to improve the Council's fundraising. As previously mentioned, United States funding via the National Committee for a Free Europe (NCFE) had ended in 1957. The only resources were contributions from Council members and the Canadian-based Baťa company.

Povolný also asked Papánek, who chaired the American Fund for Czechoslovak Refugees and, as a former ambassador to the United Nations, was well connected, for help in establishing personal contact with officials in the State Department responsible for Czechoslovak affairs.[63]

Some members of the Council were not happy about the changes in its bylaws and overall course. In a letter to a member of the Executive Committee, Libuše Drobílková, Povolný explained why the composition of the Council, initially created on the basis of political parties, no longer worked. Povolný saw the importance of political parties as mediators between the state and the people, necessary for the democratic manner of governance. He pointed out the reality that the exile members came from different political parties and did not represent a state and did not govern any people. Instead, the main goal of the exile was to speak for the people at home who were not in a position to speak freely.[64] Obviously, forfeiting the party adherence principle was difficult, especially for older members of the Council.

The renewed Council would undergo yet another profound change. In previous years, the major focus had been on gaining the support of Western democracies for the restoration of democratic Czechoslovakia and ending the Soviet occupation of the country. From the early 1970s onward, the issue of human rights became a major topic between the East and West blocs, especially after the signing of the Helsinki Final Act on 1 August 1975 and subsequent international meetings of the Conference on Security and Cooperation in Europe (CSCE). The ratification of the Helsinki Final Act on 1 August 1975 provided an international framework for future Czechoslovak exile activities. It deserves to be noted, however, that respect for human rights was a Council priority long before Helsinki. The new leadership of the Council immediately initiated debate on the strategy they should adopt in light of the Helsinki process. In a memorandum dated 20 February 1975, the Council leaders pointed out violations by the Czechoslovak government of the spirit of the proposals presented at the Geneva Conference on European Security and Cooperation, calling for "a guarantee of basic human rights and freedoms".[65]

In a memorandum sent to American President Gerald Ford shortly before his departure to sign the Helsinki Declaration, the Council's leaders urged:

> As the lights on human rights and freedoms go off in one country after another throughout the world, we implore you, Mr. President, as the representative of the greatest Western democracy and of our entire civilization,
> (1) to proclaim publicly and solemnly in Helsinki that the cause of human rights and freedoms in Central and Eastern Europe is, as it was thirty years ago, of paramount interest to the United States because it is inseparable from a genuine international détente and cooperation;
> (2) to establish a system for the monitoring of the implementation of the provisions of the Geneva declaration;
> (3) to set in motion preparations for a new conference of all the countries which participated in the Conference on European Security and Cooperation that would be concerned exclusively with the issue of specific human rights and freedoms...[66]

At that time, they also requested help from Senator Henry Jackson.[67] A new strategy was proposed by a European member of the Council, Frank Uhlíř, from Munich:

> I would say that Helsinki offers a new opportunity. I am sure that you have weighed the options. What if in addition to or instead of our traditional position, we did the opposite? What if we were to

> jump onto the détente bandwagon, which is slowing down anyhow? The situation offers several positive openings, which could be of use to us. We could prepare a position paper for the signing of the Helsinki declaration or after it. We ought to point out, without engaging in polemics with the facts, that a new situation is emerging. We should state that while countries and governments must stick with the idea of peaceful coexistence in their relations, in the clash of ideas and cultural interpretations, however, a new competition has begun. The West refers to it as "openings to the East, whereas East European signatories speak of "the continuation of the irreconcilable ideological struggle up until the complete and final victory of socialism." In this case, I feel that the Council, as one of the small players in the West, can offer Western signatories its energy, knowledge, and experiences in the formulation of the West's response to the irreconcilable struggle of the Communists.[68]

Uhlíř urged Povolný that the so-called „third basket" of the Helsinki Protocol (which deals with human rights) should be elevated to as high as "the Jewish emigration from the USSR is today".[69] Povolný summarized the position of the Council in a letter to Čeněk Torn:

> We must use the Helsinki Declaration to our advantage. As we agreed in Toronto, we will monitor its implementation in cooperation with Amnesty International. We will do our utmost to convince the Senate to adopt a position on the issue. We will write a fundamental statement on the entire text of the Declaration and make it available to all participating governments. The main thing is to take the offensive on this issue now because during the entire proceedings in Geneva, the West was defensive and our offensive position was not taken into consideration.[70]

The official position of the Czechoslovak Government on the Helsinki Accords, however, was best summarized by the deputy chairman of the National Front (the Communist-dominated coalition that ruled

Czechoslovakia since the 1948 coup), Tomáš Trávníček: "The interpretation of Helsinki principles is the sovereign right of any state and any society. Our interpretation proceeds consistently from class positions."[71]

After the codification of the Helsinki Final Act by all signatories (including the Czechoslovak and Soviet governments) into law, dissidents in Czechoslovakia saw an opportunity to challenge the Communist authorities on the grounds that the Czechoslovak government was violating its own laws. In September 1976, the Czechoslovak authorities arrested the members of the music band Plastic People of the Universe and charged them with forming an illegal organization. Dissidents Václav Havel (whose politically-inspired plays would receive much attention in the West) and Catholic theologian Jiří Němec publicized the band's trial and this was followed by the publication of an open letter from a number of dissident lawyers stating that the authorities were in direct violation of the Helsinki Accords.[72] Western leaders became aware of the matter and began to voice their concerns. Clearly sensitive to Western criticism, the Czechoslovak authorities released a number of political prisoners. This motivated dissidents to organize, and on 1 January 1977, Charter 77 was founded by 242 signatories who produced a document citing human rights violations and calling for dialogue with the Communist regime regarding how human rights could be safeguarded.[73] Among the original signatories were former foreign minister Jiří Hájek, the renowned philosopher, Professor Jan Patočka (who would soon die as a consequence of harsh police interrogations), and Václav Havel. Charter 77 was unique in that it claimed to be neither a formal organization nor an opposition party and its signatories came from all walks of life and harbored a variety of political opinions. In its "Founding Declaration", Charter 77 publicly announced its inception as "a free, informal, and open community of people of different convictions, different faiths and different professions united by the will to strive, individually and collectively, for the respect of civil and human rights in our own country and throughout the world." Despite a harsh crackdown on Charter 77 members by the Czechoslovak authorities, the founding of Charter 77 was immediately publicized in the West. Charter 77 members established contacts with political representatives and human rights activists in the West and went on to publish numerous documents that appeared in Western newspapers up until the collapse of the totalitarian regime in 1989.

The Council of Free Czechoslovakia was quick to respond to Charter 77's appearance and closely identified itself with the ideals expressed in the "Founding Charter Document" and with the plight of its signatories. For Professor Povolný and other Council members, Charter 77 was seen as a crucial partner inside Czechoslovakia that greatly aided Council efforts to expose human rights violations in the country. The Council thus devised a public relations strategy based upon Principle VII of the Third Basket of the Helsinki Final Act, and this became the cornerstone of Council activities during the remaining years of Communist rule in Czechoslovakia.

The first main Council activity after the genesis of Charter 77 was to disseminate the "Founding Document" to major North American newspapers.[74] The *Toronto Globe and Mail* published its full text and credited the chairman of the Council assembly, Rudolf Fraštacký, with providing it. Likewise, the *Free Trade Union News*, the journal of the American Federation of Labor and the Congress of Industrial Organizations (AFL-CIO) in Washington, D.C., published the Charter's "Founding Document", with an introduction written by the Council's general secretary, Jiří Horák.[75]

The Council then issued an international appeal concerning the violation of human rights and basic civil liberties in Czechoslovakia, which stated that "the family of civilized nations cannot close its eyes in the wake of this new wave of repression without threatening the basis of the international order it strives for, namely a system of peace, security, freedom, and justice." This appeal was sent to numerous North American politicians and leaders of international organizations, many of whom reacted forcefully.[76] The Conference on Security and Cooperation in Europe (CSCE), for example, requested testimony from Council representatives on the violations of the Helsinki Accords.[77] The success of the appeal emboldened the Council of Free Czechoslovakia to work harder in support of Charter 77. Other Czechoslovak exile groups and ethnic organizations also joined the effort.[78] The Czechoslovak National Council of America, a Czechoslovak ethnic organization based in Chicago (particularly its Washington representative, Anna Faltus), translated Charter 77 documents into English and passed them on to the State Department and the U.S. Congress. In Western Europe, the Listy Group (led by former 1968 reformer and later European Parliament Socialist MP, Jiří Pelikán) disseminated first-hand information from Czechoslovakia provided by Western European statesmen, diplomats and other officials who had recently visited the country.[79] Paris-based Council of Free Czechoslovakia member Edmund Řehák facilitated contact between the Assembly of Captive European Nations and the Council of Europe concerning Czechoslovak matters. Exiled Charter 77 signatory Ivan Medek (based in Vienna) kept the Council of Free Czechoslovakia as well as European institutions up to date on the latest activities of Charter 77. Ordinary Czechoslovak exiles were informed of events in Czechoslovakia by the journal *Svědectví* (*Testament*), whose chief editor, Pavel Tigrid, was in a position to obtain reliable current information from Czechoslovakia. Fundraising activities for Charter 77 in the West were undertaken by exiled nuclear physicist František Janouch, who founded the Charter 77 Foundation in Stockholm.[80]

The first CSCE meetings and negotiations following the signing of the Helsinki Final Act took place in Belgrade between October 4, 1977 and March 8, 1978. In preparation for the Belgrade gathering, the Council assembly assigned Canada-based Czechoslovak exile Viktor Miroslav Fic the task of preparing the lengthy document "Violations of Civil and Political Rights in Czechoslovakia and the HelsinkiAccord".[81] Fic's work in composing the document was assisted by fellow 1948-era exiles Rudolf Fraštacký, Jiří Horák, Vladimír Krajina, Martin Kvetko, Josef Pejskar, Mojmír Povolný, Jaroslav Rouček and the 1968-era exile writer and publisher Josef Škvorecký. The Council of Free Czechoslovakia was in constant contact with the Czechoslovak Desk at the U.S. State Department[82] and the U.S. Congressional Committee for Security and Cooperation in Europe.[83] In addition, human rights violations were reported to both Canadian prime minister Pierre Elliott Trudeau and the Canadian parliament by pro-Charter 77 activists in Canada.[84]

In order to place matters in historical context, it is necessary to note that U.S. President Jimmy Carter's administration did not at this time advocate confrontation with the Soviet Union or its European satellite states over human rights violations, and the attitude of other Western governments was similar. Luckily, the U.S. Congress applied pressure on the White House and, thanks to prominent Democratic politician and former Supreme Court justice Arthur Goldberg, the issue of human rights and basic liberties in the Soviet bloc was presented in Belgrade, despite reservations by Secretary of State Cyrus Vance and U.S. allies in Western Europe.[85] However, as a result of power politics and a lack of support from Tito's Yugoslavia, there was no mention of human rights in the final protocol of the Belgrade conference (the text of which required consensus among all signatories, from East and West alike).[86] The Council of Free Czechoslovakia and other Czechoslovak exile organizations were disappointed with the outcome of the Belgrade meeting, but the American delegation did not view the results of Belgrade so pessimistically. Matthew Nimetz at the State Department summarized the results of the Belgrade meeting in a long letter to Jiří Horák:

> That the Final Act, particularly its human rights and human contacts provisions, was discussed in such detail was an historic breakthrough. Building on the accomplishments of the June preparatory meeting, a precedent has been set and procedures established which should encourage future efforts to implement the Final Act more concretely and more fully. As Ambassador Goldberg said in his enclosed concluding speech, "Belgrade has tested the validity and flexibility of the CSCE process. It has not been an easy passage, but we have delineated the scope of that process and added to its depth. Most important of all, we have given our commitment to preserving the process and to making its growth our common enterprise."
>
> The CSCE process will not be an easy or quick one. It is unrealistic to expect that systems of controls developed over decades and

> reflecting Communist theories of the role of party, state and industry will be relaxed in a couple of years. The Final Act and the Belgrade meeting have demonstrated, however, that it is legitimate to discuss human rights and they have put the Soviet Union and other Eastern states on notice that we will not shy away from such frank discussion. Indeed, we view it as our responsibility under the terms of the Final Act.[87]

His letter continued:

> A word is in order about the negotiations which led to the final document at Belgrade. While harboring some reservations about specific provisions of a rather detailed text put forward by neutral and nonaligned participants, we and the Allies supported fully their efforts to negotiate a substantive final document that would have taken note of the review that had taken place, of the successes and failures in implementation, and mentioned the work still to be done in human rights, military, economic and other areas. The Soviets and some of their allies made it quite clear, however, that they would not accept any document that referred to failures of implementation or human rights. We made clear that without such language a detailed document would be incomplete, unbalanced and misleading.

The Council thanked Nimetz and promised to keep the CSCE commission informed of all violations of the Helsinki Final Act in preparation for the next CSCE meeting in Madrid.[88] This signified a continuation of the Helsinki Process, and it was assumed that the free atmosphere in post-Franco Spain would not permit the issue of human rights to be ignored, as had largely been the case in Belgrade. Escalating Cold War tensions, particularly Western dismay at the Soviet invasion of Afghanistan, meant that the West was more likely to fight harder over the issue of human rights. The White House issued a statement on the disappointing results of Belgrade, which concluded: "…We intend to continue pressure on the Soviet Union to fulfill its obligations concerning human rights..." In a letter to President Carter, the Council expressed the view that this statement "is a guarantee of focused attention on the issue of human rights".[89]

The beginning of 1978 saw an initiative on the part of thousands of democratic Czechoslovak exiles who prepared a petition to be presented to the Human Rights Committee of the United Nations on 21 August 1978 and sent to 35 signatory states of the Helsinki Accords.[90] The text of "Petition '78" reads as follows:

> The year of 1978 has a historical significance for the nation of Czechoslovakia because it marks three important mile stones in their existence.
> 60 years ago, in 1918, Czechoslovakia became an independent state which was based upon the democratic and humanistic ideas of T.G. Masaryk.
> 30 years ago, in 1948, the democratic parliamentary order in the country was destroyed; this interrupted its peaceful and democratic evolution and led to the entrenchment of Stalinism which sapped the national will, spirit and resources for many years.
> 10 years ago, in 1968, the armed forces of the Soviet bloc invaded the country in order to arrest the process of regeneration of national culture and humanization and democratization of its public life; and this resulted in a massive violation of fundamental civil and political rights.
> REMEMBERING THESE THREE ANNIVERSARIES THE PETITIONERS
> (1) DEMAND the withdrawal of Soviet troops from Czechoslovakia and restoration of independence, sovereignty and of the right of the people to self-determination according to Articles I, II, III, IV and VII of the Helsinki Accord of 1975.
> (2) SUPPORT Charter 77 in demanding from the Government of Czechoslovakia to implement the civil and political rights as defined in the Helsinki Accord as well as in Law 120/75 adopted by the Federal Parliament on November 11, 1975.

(3) CALL upon the Government of Czechoslovakia to desist from persecuting the Chartists and other citizens who merely demand that the government observes the Czechoslovak laws and international conventions on civil and political rights which it has signed.
(4) CALL upon the Government of Czechoslovakia to remove or reform all laws which either violate or limit the enjoyment of civil and political rights as defined in the Helsinki Accord.
(5) CALL upon the Human Rights Committee of the United Nations to hold the Government of Czechoslovakia accountable for periodical reports on the measure undertaken to implement the International convention on Civil and Political Rights in the country.
(6) CALL upon all signatory states of the Helsinki Accord to hold the Government of Czechoslovakia accountable for the full implementation of the Accord and of all international agreements which the Accord invokes.
New York, January 1, 1978

Jiří Horák urged the Council of Free Czechoslovakia to endorse "Petition '78" and proposed its further distribution.[91]

The Czechoslovak exiles' fight for human rights was helped by the increasing sympathy expressed by the U.S. Congress (in particular Erika Schlager) as well as the support of U.S. Helsinki Watch Committee activist Jeri Laber, and writer Arthur Miller, who had taken up the cause of exiled Czechoslovak writer Pavel Kohout. The restive labor movement in Poland (which ultimately led to the foundation of Solidarity), the election of the Polish Pope, John Paul II, and the increased persecution of dissidents in the Soviet Union also aided the struggle for human rights in Communist Europe, including Czechoslovakia.[92] The founding in Czechoslovakia of the Committee for the Defense of the Unjustly Prosecuted (VONS) after the Belgrade conference ended in 1978 signified that the fight for human rights in Czechoslovakia continued.

On 6 November 1978, Charter 77 together with VONS sent an open letter to United Nations Secretary General Kurt Waldheim and to heads of state of signatories of the Helsinki Final Act.[93] The Council of Free

Czechoslovakia endorsed this letter and wrote to President Carter and multiple other heads of state asking that "Czechoslovakia should fulfill its international and constitutional obligations in the area of human rights and basic freedoms of its citizens…"[94]

In Europe, the cause of Charter 77 and VONS was taken up by the periodical *Listy*, published in Rome by former Communist Party functionary and director of Czechoslovak state television, Jiří Pelikán, who also founded the exile organization, Listy Group. The Charter declaration was published in its entirety in the first 1977 issue of *Listy*. Thereafter, *Listy* published practically all Charter 77 and VONS documents, usually in their complete form.[95] Upon closer analysis, Charter 77 activities mirrored the ideas of the 1968 Prague Spring. Pelikán believed that Charter 77 represented the most significant change in Czechoslovakia since the beginning of "normalization" (and thus permitted *Listy* to be used as a forum to disseminate Chartist documents to Czechoslovak émigrés in the West.[96]

It should be mentioned that on the thirtieth anniversary of the founding of the Council of Free Czechoslovakia in 1979, the Council unequivocally expressed its support for the activities of Charter 77 and VONS.[97] On 18 April 1979, the Council was invited to an informal meeting concerning the future of U.S. relations with Czechoslovakia by State Department official Robert L. Barry. Human rights were discussed at this and similar meetings and it became obvious that the violation of human rights in the Soviet bloc would be on the agenda in Madrid.[98] Charter 77 was supported at a seminar organized by the group Opus bonum in Franken, Germany. This seminar was attended by about a hundred representatives of various factions of the Czechoslovak exile community, including many exiled signatories of Charter 77.[99]

In Czechoslovakia, ten representatives of Charter 77 were arrested in June 1979 and accused of anti-state activities.[100] On 23 October, six members of Charter 77 and VONS were convicted on charges of "subversion of the Republic" and sentenced to prison terms.[101] A protest demonstration was held in New York on 24 October, sponsored by the international human rights organization Helsinki Watch and the PEN-

American Center. The Council of Free Czechoslovakia also issued a protest declaration.[102]

In 1979, Jiří Pelikán was elected to the European Parliament. The leadership of the Council of Free Czechoslovakia sent a congratulatory letter to all elected European deputies, including Pelikán, along with a request that they monitor human rights in Czechoslovakia and form a committee to monitor compliance with the Helsinki Accords.[103] Pelikán thanked Povolný, Zich, and Horák of the Council for their congratulations and assured them of his interest in productive collaboration with the Council.[104] Ten days later, Pelikán explained in a letter to Povolný that his proposal to form a committee to monitor Helsinki compliance had failed to gain the European Parliament's support, but he pointed to the resolution it adopted condemning the prosecution of Charter 77 members.[105] While some Council members saw the need to work in harmony with Pelikán on the grounds that "he can advance our agenda in the European Parliament",[106] others vehemently protested the idea. The strongest opposition came from Felix Uhl, who reminded his Council colleagues of Pelikán's checkered past[107] and even drafted a protest letter from the Council to European Parliament president Simone Veil.[108] This draft was rejected by the Council and never sent. On the fourth anniversary of the signing of the Helsinki Final Act, President Carter specifically mentioned the violation of human rights and persecution of Charter 77 members in Czechoslovakia. A number of congressmembers did the same. In addition, the Council issued an appeal from Toronto in September 1979 to world leaders and international organizations protesting the persecution of Czechoslovak dissidents.[109]

The CSCE conference in Madrid lasted from 11 November 1980 until 9 September 1983. Czechoslovak exile organizations started preparing materials for the conference as early as 1979. On 24 October 1979, representatives of "East European ethnic groups in the USA" met with Matthew Nimetz, an advisor to the Secretary of State, to discuss preparations for Madrid. Czechoslovaks were represented by the Czechoslovak National Council of America in the person of Anna Faltusová.

The Council of Free Czechoslovakia, however, was not invited.[110] This fact prompted Council member Jaroslav Zich to analyze the situation and to point out a number of tactical errors the Council had made. He summarized these in a letter to fellow Council members Povolný, Kvetko and Horák. Zich wrote: "I believe it is imperative to start preparations for Madrid somewhat more specifically. So far, at our meetings we have had only general discussions. Over the year, we have formed a special committee, but, overall, we have accomplished nothing…" [111]

In a New Year's message to Czechoslovakia, the Council reiterated its intention to prepare for the Madrid meeting "to determine whether international law can assure human dignity and respect for human rights even when laws and regulations of a specific country are in conflict with this international agreement".[112]

In January 1980, the Czechoslovak National Council of America issued a "Situation Report on the Compliance in Czechoslovakia with the Helsinki Accords".[113] This document systematically identified violations of individual principles of the agreement, most notably of Principle 7: Respect for Human Rights and Fundamental Freedoms. The "Report" focused on the recent trial of six Charter 77 signatories and members of VONS as well as on breaches of Czechoslovak "justice" abroad in the form of stripping human rights activists of their Czechoslovak citizenship. The Council published an even stronger document, "Czechoslovakia since Belgrade", in April 1980.[114]

The exile group Czechoslovak Advisory Committee in Western Europe, represented by Dr. Rudolf Václavík, also sent a memorandum to the signatories of the Helsinki Final Act.[115] This document contained two parts: 1) Persecution of Chartists 77 and their Sympathizers; and 2) Withdrawal (sic.) Czechoslovak citizenship. Appended to this document were multiple verdicts or refusals by Czechoslovak courts and officials.

The Council of Free Czechoslovakia appealed on 29 September to all democratic Czechoslovak exile organizations around the world to prepare a joint appeal to the Madrid Conference that would be made public at the conference of the Czechoslovak Society of Arts and Sciences in

Washington on 17 October 1980. The proposed appeal was prepared by Mojmír Povolný and it concluded:

> We bring this appeal as representatives of the Czechoslovak democratic tradition. We are aware that we speak for all our brothers and sisters in Czechoslovakia, that fulfillment of the obligations and promises of the Final Act by all signatories is of vital significance for the well-being of every citizen, that the question of human rights and liberties is an international question and that the fate of Europe and our civilization rests on compliance with it and its defense.[116]

Twenty-one Czechoslovak exile organizations in North America, Western Europe, Australia and New Zealand signed the appeal.

On 9 October 1980, the Council addressed all countries participating in the Conference on Security and Cooperation in Europe[117] by letter and appended a 21-page document compiled by Charter 77 titled "Violations of the Helsinki Accords in Czechoslovakia".[118] Particular attention was also devoted to a letter from Charter 77 to Czechoslovak President Gustáv Husák in which Marie Hromádková and Miloš Rejchrt asked that "the state of which we are citizens contribute in a positive way to negotiations concerning the problems of human rights and fundamental freedoms and of the so-called Basket Three in general..."[119]

The Czechoslovak exile representation at the Madrid Conference included Mrs. Betka Papánek (a member of the Czechoslovak National Council of America), who was an official member of the American delegation. Mrs. Papánek was accompanied by her husband, the former Czechoslovak ambassador to the United Nations, Ján Papánek. The selection process for the other Czechoslovak members of the United States delegation was, however, unacceptable to the Council. Special Assistant to the President [Carter] for Ethnic Affairs Stephen R. Aiello arranged for the inclusion into the delegation of Mrs. Cecilia Sarocky of the Ladies Pennsylvania Slovak Catholic Union upon the recommendation of Michael Krajsa. Not only was this selection made at the very late stage of the selection process, while candidates submitted by the

Council some six months earlier were refused for being submitted too late, but Krajsa was known to advocate in the Slovak community in America for the dismemberment of the Czechoslovak Republic. Povolný expressed the views of the Council in his letter to Mr. Aiello, writing:

> In the first place, we all question the wisdom of placing a person representing the tradition advocated by Mr. Krajsa on a delegation that will be primarily concerned with the issue of human, civil, and political rights. It is not important what views Mrs. Sarocky holds personally; what is important is the perception of her association with the cause for which Mr. Krajsa's organizations and newspapers stand. Secondly, you have handed the Czechoslovak Communist delegation to Madrid an easy and effective weapon against the United States because the Czechoslovak delegation will be able to accuse the United States of undermining the integrity of the Czechoslovak state by sending to Madrid an opponent of the union of Czechs and Slovaks.
>
> Thirdly, the Czechoslovak National Council of America has, since the days of the First World War, represented the ideals, views, and interests of Americans of Czech and Slovak origin most faithfully, and it was simply overlooked in your "political" calculation. It was denied the place and the recognition that it deserves in American politics more than any other ethnic organization.
>
> Finally, you must have forgotten how much support American Czechs and Slovaks of Czechoslovak persuasion have historically given to the Democratic Party. Let us remind you only of Chicago and New York. Your overcalculated step has shaken their confidence not only in the way in which you administer ethnic affairs for the President, but in the President's administration itself...
>
> I am sending a copy of this letter to President Carter, Mr. White, and Mr. Valuchek of the Democratic National Committee, Mrs. Ridgway and Mr. Johnson of the Department of State and I shall share it with my friends in the Czechoslovak community in the United States...[120]

As is apparent from this document, the Council was deeply committed to the preservation of the Czechoslovak state. The reaction to Povolný's letter from Rosanne Ridgway at the State Department was very positive: "The United States has no desire to see Czechoslovakia divided..."[121]

Mojmír Povolný was granted observer status at the conference and he reported to the Council on his experience in Madrid.[122] In the report, he emphasized the contributions of Pavel Tigrid, the Czechoslovak National Council of America and the Czechoslovak National Association of Canada.

Future events in Madrid would be influenced by the fact that President Carter lost his bid for reelection in November 1980, and his successor, Ronald Reagan, was determined to pursue a tougher line against the Soviet Union and its satellite states. Thanks in part to an appeal by the Council of Free Czechoslovakia, the final protocol of the Madrid Conference did mention human rights violations, and it called for a special conference of CSCE human rights experts to be held in 1985 in Ottawa. United States Secretary of State George Shultz's speech at the closing of the Madrid Conference praised as heroes the Polish workers, Czech intellectuals, East German clergy members and Soviet dissidents from all walks of life who risked their lives and livelihoods for freedom. It can be said that Madrid represented clear progress in the West's willingness to fight for human rights, and Czechoslovak dissidents as well as Czechoslovak exiles in the West were encouraged by the results.[123]

The Council of Free Czechoslovakia soon began its preparations for the next CSCE meeting in Vienna. On the occasion of the Ottawa CSCE meeting of human rights experts in 1985, the Council supported the intervention of the Czechoslovak National Association of Canada, which once again documented human rights violations in Czechoslovakia. On the tenth anniversary of the signing of the Helsinki Accords, the Council issued an appeal to the CSCE that it insist on the upholding of human rights in Czechoslovakia.[124] On 10 September 1985, the Council sent a memorandum to President Reagan prior to his meeting with Mikhail Gorbachev, which stated:

> The Communist authorities in Czechoslovakia harshly repress the Czechoslovak people's civil and political rights, persecute members of Charter 77 and of the Committee for the Defense of the Unjustly Prosecuted and, in general, maintain a repressive internal system seriously violating every citizen's freedom of conscience, religion, expression, and association.[125]

The letter urged Reagan to demand that Gorbachev begin to work with the United States in order to achieve an end to these violations.

The Council was not alone in advancing the issue of human rights. The first 1985 issue of the periodical *Listy* contained sixteen pages of Charter 77 documents entitled "Eight Years of Charter 77".[126] In the United Kingdom, the issue of Czechoslovak human rights violations was addressed by at least two émigré organizations. The first was Palach Press, founded in 1974 by Jan Kavan to provide "prompt and accurate information on developments in Czechoslovakia", especially information obtained from a variety of Czechoslovak non-governmental sources, to Western journalists, human rights organizations, etc.[127] From January 1978 on Palach Press published a pamphlet "Information on Charter 77". It disseminated the full texts of all Charter 77 documents and of VONS statements. An official background note to the British Prime Minister's office regarding Palach Press stated:

> Among its directors are Mr. Jiří Pelikán, a former Director-General of Czechoslovak Television and a leading émigré living in Rome, and Mr. Jan Kavan, a leader of the Czech student movements in 1966. The latter is apparently the real driving force behind this organization.[128]

Another organization that brought attention to human rights violations was the Free Central European News Agency headed by Josef Josten. It was Josten who brought the VONS issue to the attention of the British Minister of State at the Foreign and Commonwealth Office.[129] In an official background note from the British Information Research Department, Josten was characterized as "a Czech Jewish refugee and an able organizer and businessman". The note concluded, however: "Although his heart is unquestionably in the right place, we keep him at arm's length because his emotionalism tends to be counter-productive here and he does not always check his material with sufficient care and discrimination."[130]

Another significant act undertaken by the Council was the initiation of negotiations with the London-based Polish Exile Government, which resulted in a joint memorandum of 19January 1986 pledging that both organizations would work together to fight Communism. Both the Council and the Polish Exile Government also held a press conference on 3 November 1986 inVienna reiterating their determination to collaborate with one another.

The CSCE meeting in Vienna took place between 4 November 1986 and 19 January 1989. Czechoslovak exile organizations made careful preparations for the Vienna conference. On 21 May 1986, the designated leader of the U.S. delegation invited Mojmír Povolný to a CSCE forum on 5 June 1986, organized jointly by the State Department and the Appeal of Conscience Foundation at St. James Church in New York.[131] The Czechoslovak National Council of America prepared a memorandum for the Vienna meeting dated 10 June 1986.[132] That same month, another document appeared titled "Situation in Czechoslovakia since the Madrid Review Meeting concerning Compliance with the Helsinki Final Act and the Madrid Concluding Document", which was prepared by the Committee for the Support of Human Rights in Czechoslovakia.[133] Human rights were also addressed in several articles in the *New York Times*. An opinion article by Warren Zimmerman, head of the U.S. delegation to the Vienna conference, titled "Making Moscow pay the Price for Human Rights Abuses", was the most decisive, but it contained no specific information on Czechoslovakia.[134]

The Czechoslovak National Council of America suggested that the Council of Free Czechoslovakia organize a public demonstration in Vienna on the occasion of the opening of the CSCE meeting on 4 November. Mojmír Povolný appealed to dozens of democratic exile organizations around the world to participate.[135] The gathering took place on the evening of 3 November and was broadcast by Austrian television. The Council of Free Czechoslovakia also organized a press conference at Vienna's Presseclub Concordia on 3 November. In addition to the Council of Free Czechoslovakia, the Polish Government-in-Exile, the Ukrainian Government-in-Exile, and Free Romanians were represented. There were Hungarian and Byelorussian representatives as well.[136] The conference was disrupted, however, by Slovak separatists and Sudeten German representatives.

The Council of Free Czechoslovakia presented the Conference with a "Joint Memorandum of the Council of Free Czechoslovakia and the Polish Government-in-Exile",[137] which urged the participants to consider eight points designed to guarantee Czechoslovak and Polish citizens their human rights and civic freedoms. It also asked for the establishment "within the framework of the CSCE of an institution to which dissident groups could address their grievances and through which they could seek redress."

In addition, the Czechoslovak National Council of America presented a conference within the Sakharov Institute titled "An Invisible Oppression: Methods of Social Control in a Mature Totalitarian System". The speakers included Francis Schwarzenberg, Vlastislav Chalupa, Ivan Gaďourek, Mojmír Povolný, Jiří Němec and Dagmar Vaněček.[138]

The Council, together with the Czechoslovak National Council of America and sixteen other exile organizations, presented the CSCE meeting with a joint petition calling for the withdrawal of the Soviet army from Czechoslovakia and the recognition of Charter 77 as a non-governmental monitoring organization overseeing the fulfillment of the responsibilities of the Helsinki Final Act.[139]

The Executive Committee of the Council of Free Czechoslovakia met in December 1986 to evaluate the results of the Vienna conference and issued a memorandum demanding that all democratic signatories of the Helsinki Final Act ensure that commitments regarding human rights and basic liberties be adhered to in Czechoslovakia.[140]

On 7 January 1987, the Council, together with the Czechoslovak National Council of America, sent a special memorandum to U.S. ambassador Warren Zimmerman. The memorandum addressed specific violations of the Helsinki Final Act in Czechoslovakia, but also pointed out:

> We have also observed that on the part of the West European, American, and Canadian delegations to the Vienna follow-up meeting there has been a tendency to focus their eyes on Soviet violations, while its violations and disregard by the Central and East European Communist states fail to receive the same attention...[141]

In January 1987, the U.S. Commission on CSCE nominated Charter 77 for the Nobel Peace Prize. The nomination letter was signed by Steny Hoyer (chairman) and the fourteen members of Congress who were members of the Commission.[142]

In March 1987, the Council protested against the persecution of Jan Dus, Petr Pospíchal and the Jazz Section of the musicians' union by the Czechoslovak justice system.[143] Also in 1987, the Council of Free Czechoslovakia sent several letters to President Reagan ahead of Reagan's upcoming meeting with Soviet leader, Mikhail Gorbachev.[144] The last letter, sent after the summit meeting, expressed the Council*'s* disappointment with the meeting:

> ...We are, however, especially disappointed that on no occasion in your meetings with General Secretary Gorbachev the question of Soviet domination of Central and Eastern Europe was raised. This is even more disappointing since the centerpiece of this summit meeting was the removal of intermediate and short-range missiles from Europe, that is, in political terms, the question of Europe, European security, and European order...

In addition, the Czechoslovak National Council of America sponsored a "Joint Statement of Czechoslovak Organizations in the Free World":

> It is in the West's power to support the democratization efforts of the disenfranchised population of the communist states through infor-

> mation, culture exchange, and diplomatic action; withhold economic help and technical assistance to such an extent as would pressure communist governments to expand their citizens' rights and fundamental freedoms; pursue vigorously the development of a strong defense capability, especially the S.D.I. [Strategic Defense Initiative], effectively assist democratic liberation movements to block the Soviet Union from consolidating its conquests in the contested areas." The statement offers specific recommendations "based on past, recent, and present experiences of our members with the communist regime in Czechoslovakia...[145]

The statement was signed by the following organizations: the Alliance of Czechoslovak Democratic Associations in Australia and New Zealand; the American Fund for Czechoslovak Refugees; the Association of Czechoslovak Legionnaires; the Council of Free Czechoslovakia; the Czechoslovak Association of Canada; the Czechoslovak National Council of America; the K-231 Club of Former Czechoslovak Political Prisoners; the National Alliance of Czech Catholics U.S.A.; the National Council of Women of Free Czechoslovakia; the Naarden Movement, United Kingdom; and the Permanent Conference of Slovak Democratic Exiles.

In March 1988, the Council of Free Czechoslovakia pointed out the renewed severity and brutality of the measures with which the Communist authorities in Czechoslovakia responded to Czechoslovak citizens' calls for greater religious freedom.[146]

On the twentieth anniversary of the Soviet invasion of Czechoslovakia (21 August 1988), President Reagan issued a statement that read, in part:

> Brave men and women within the country, such as the signatories of Charter 77, continue to struggle for freedom and long-overdue reforms which remain the fervent hopes of Czechs and Slovaks. We take the occasion of this anniversary to salute those people and to express firm agreement with their conviction that, in the end, truth will prevail...[147]

The Czechoslovak government proposed that the economic follow-up meeting of CSCE take place in Czechoslovakia. The head of the U.S. delegation, Warren Zimmerman, rejected this proposal because of the Czechoslovak authorities' suppression of the Prague symposium "Czechoslovakia 88".[148] The Council of Free Czechoslovakia also endorsed the U.S. conditions for a possible CSCE meeting in Moscow in 1991.[149] In Vienna, the attitude of the U.S. delegation was even more sympathetic than had been the case in Madrid.

On the twentieth anniversary of the Soviet invasion of Czechoslovakia, the Council of Free Czechoslovakia published a proclamation demanding the removal of Soviet armed forces from Czechoslovakia and an end to all discrimination against dissidents. At the end of 1988, the Council issued a proclamation to Czechoslovak citizens urging them to demand the renewal of democracy in Czechoslovakia.[150] The Vienna conference ended on 19 January 1989. Three days prior to that date, the *New York Times* wrote: "35 Nations Issue East-West Pact to Protect Broad Human Rights".[151]

The situation in Czechoslovakia, however, despite some advances of perestroika in the Soviet Union, was not encouraging. The Council of Free Czechoslovakia sent a letter to president-elect George H.W. Bush asking for assistance with fourteen points "which, we are convinced, are in harmony with the interests of the United States."[152]

For human rights activists in Czechoslovakia, the year 1989 did not begin well. In January, a demonstration in commemoration of the twentieth anniversary of Jan Palach's self-immolation was brutally suppressed by the police. On 21 February, Václav Havel was sentenced to nine months in prison for "antistate activities". A day later, seven human rights activists were also convicted of participating in the January ceremony in remembrance of Palach.[153] In the meantime, the United States Helsinki Commission nominated Václav Havel for the 1989 Nobel Peace Prize.[154]

In early April 1989, Radio Free Europe aired a declaration by the Council of Free Czechoslovakia on recent developments in Czechoslovakia. The declaration condemned the attitude of the Czechoslovak Communist Party towards calls to investigate police brutality connected with the civic demonstrations commemorating the anniversary of Jan Palach's death and asked for the release of all those imprisoned after that event.[155]

Eastern Europe was rapidly changing in 1989. The decision by the Hungarian Communist authorities to allow East Germans to escape to West Germany through the newly opened border between Hungary and Austria represented a major turning point. The critical step took place in Prague when East German and Czechoslovak officials decided to permit East German refugees who had taken refuge in the West German Embassy in Prague to leave for West Germany. On 9 November, the Berlin Wall came down. The conservative Czechoslovak Communist government, however, held its ground. On 17 November, the police attacked a government-sanctioned demonstration by university students commemorating the fiftieth anniversary of the murder of medical student Jan Opletal by the Nazis. This resulted in mass demonstrations calling for the resignation of the Communist authorities. The Council of Free Czechoslovakia held a meeting in New York on 17 November and a cable was sent to Prime Minister Ladislav Adamec that read in part:

> The Council of Free Czechoslovakia protests against the brutal attempt to suppress the manifestation for freedom and democracy in Prague on 17 November... We demand that those responsible for this act be immediately suspended and members of the security forces who committed brutal acts be punished.[156]

The Communist regime in Czechoslovakia collapsed on 24 November when the general secretary of the Czechoslovak Communist Party, Milouš Jakeš, resigned during a live television address to the nation.

On 28 November, the Council of Free Czechoslovakia sent a letter to the leader of Civic Forum, Václav Havel, which concluded:

> We are happy that our position, in principle, agrees with your demands and thus brings evidence of unity of our thoughts... Your

> success has to be a great encouragement and source of strength for future activities...You can count on our full support and willingness to help wherever we can...[157]

The Council continued to follow the unfolding events in Prague and on 3 December deplored the composition of the "new government".[158] Later, it endorsed the caretaker government led by Marian Čalfa and congratulated Václav Havel on his election to the presidency on 29 December.[159] Four decades of Communist totalitarian rule had come to an end, and the dream of the Czechoslovak exile for a free country had materialized.

Conclusion

A scathing criticism of the Council's early activities was presented in the final issue of volume V of the exile periodical *Skutečnost (Reality)*. Its editor, Jan Hanuš Hájek, wrote:

> Among organizations striving to acquire the character of an exile government, the first place belongs to the Council of Free Czechoslovakia; it is composed on one hand of independent intellectuals belonging to the older generation and, on the other hand,-and this is regrettably the majority-of escaped "people's democratic" politicians who have always been incompetent in the field they selected as their career...The program of the Council of Free Czechoslovakia is, of course, the liberation of Czechoslovakia from Communism, etc. An objective observation of the Council's activities indicates that there is little more than empty phrases...[160]

Later, the Council was also criticized by other exile organizations, in particular those in favor of Slovak separatism.

To be critical of the Council of Free Czechoslovakia today, however, would be very simplistic and most unfair. It is true that the accomplishments of the Cold War-era Czechoslovak exiles do not compare well with those of the two previous Czechoslovak exiles, both of which formed during a major world war. The situations of the earlier Czechoslovak exiles, however, were completely different. They occurred during hostilities of world wars with defined lines of conflict and were relatively brief. Even so, the plans of the first two Czechoslovak exiles changed in accordance with the evolving plans of the major powers.

In contrast, the Czechoslovak exiles of 1948 and 1968 entered the Cold War struggle in which the democratic powers felt compelled to observe the democratic niceties and were aware that the Soviet yoke over Central Europe basically had been agreed to at the Teheran and Yalta conferences. Professional diplomats showed little sympathy for Czechoslovak exiles and no real support, except for propaganda purposes. The often cited personal rivalries among exile politicians had deep historical roots. Despite their democratic declarations, politicians of the post-war National Front in Czechoslovakia had not permitted the reestablishment of pre-war civic parties in 1945 and remained silent when the leaders of civic parties were persecuted in various ways. Some National Front politicians had been hostile to wartime Slovak opponents of President Beneš. In addition, there was mutual mistrust between the 1948 and 1968 generations of exiles.

The personal conflicts were also a reflection of the exiles' frustration with their new existences and the hopelessness of their cause, which was overshadowed by the interests of the major powers. They were patriots who were powerless in their role in what, for them, represented a never-ending struggle. Initial hopes for an early return to Czechoslovakia behind U.S. tanks did not materialize. The outcome of the Hungarian revolt of 1956 taught the Czechoslovak exiles that the interests of the major powers supersede those of small nations. The post-1948 exiles would witness the Soviet occupation of Czechoslovakia in 1968, which would trigger a new wave of refugees who had actually lived under Communism, and, as already mentioned, both the composition and the political outlook of the two exile generations were completely different. Those exiles who survived had to wait until 1989 for Communism to collapse, an event to which they contributed relatively little, despite their noble efforts. However, it must be reiterated that the Council did its utmost to bring to the West's attention to the persecution of dissidents by the Czechoslovak Communist authorities, and it demanded that Communist Czechoslovakia honor the terms of the Helsinki Accords.

Although the personalities of individual Czechoslovak exiles are often the subject of criticism by journalists in today's Czech Republic, Professor Igor Lukeš of Boston University concludes his essay on the first years of the Czechoslovak political exile as follows:

> Let us assume that the Czechoslovak exile group would have a Czech Roosevelt, Churchill, and DeGaulle and the rest would be composed of Masaryks. All of them would have been thrown into the reality of the divided world faced by the real leaders of the Council of Free Czechoslovakia. Would they have succeeded in overthrowing the totalitarian regime in Prague and restored democracy? I think not.[161]

This author agrees with Professor Lukeš's conclusions, which can be applied to both generations of Cold War-era Czechoslovak exiles. Despite their obvious shortcomings, the exiles who formed the Council of Free Czechoslovakia could not have done much better, and their memory deserves to be honored.

Endnotes

1. Zdeněk Jirásek and Miloš Trapl, *Exilová politika v letech 1948–1956* (Olomouc: Centrum pro československá exilová studia; Moneta-FM, 1996) 16–17.
2. Bořivoj Čelovský, *Politici bez moci* (Tilia: Šenov u Ostravy, 2000) 17.
3. National Archives (London), PRO, FO371/71331, Churchill to Ernest Bevin, 25 April 1948.
4. Mayhew to CFA Warner, 28 April 1948, Ibid.
5. Warner to Northern Department, 29 April 1948, Ibid.
6. Hankey to Warner, 6 May 1948, Ibid.
7. Resolution made by Free Members of the Czechoslovak National Constitutional Assembly, London, 28 May 1948, Ibid.
8. Shaw to Hankey, 31 May 1948, Ibid.

9 Čelovský, *Politici*, 21.
10 Hoover Institution (HI) (Stanford), Osuský Collection, Box 79, File 79/12, 16 June 1948.
11 PRO, FO371/71331, Elliott's minute, 26 August 1948.
12 Immigration History Research Center (IHRC) (Minneapolis), Rechcígl Collection, Box 7, Rechcígl to Kopecký, 27 January 1949.
13 Elliott's minute, 21 October 1948, Ibid.
14 IHRC, Rechcígl Collection, Box 7, Rechcígl to Kopecký, 27 January 1949.
15 Kopecký to Rechcígl, 31 January 1949, Ibid.
16 Rada svobodného Československa-stručná zpráva o činnosti, Washington, D.C., November 1950, Ibid.
17 PRO, FO371/77251, Declaration of the Council of Free Czechoslovakia, 12 March 1949.
18 Jan Stránský to Hankey, 7 March 1949, Ibid.
19 *New York Times*, 26 February 1949.
20 Čelovský, *Politici*, 48–49.
21 Ibid., 52–53.
22 IHRC, Rechcígl Collection, Rada svobodného Československa-stručná zpráva o činnosti, 4.
23 Ibid.
24 PRO, FO371/77251, Wilkinson's minute, 7 April 1949.
25 IHRC, Rechcígl Collection, Box 9, Zpráva o činnosti oblastního sboru v Paříži, 1950.
26 PRO, FO371/86228, Majer to Foreign Office, 14 December 1950.
27 IHRC, Rechcígl Collection, Box 9, NCFE to the Council of Free Czechoslovakia, Czech translation, January 1951.
28 Ibid.
29 Stránský's declaration, 25 January 1951, Ibid.
30 HI, Osuský Collection, Box 78, File 78.5, Statement on the Opening of Radio Free Europe Broadcasts.
31 IHRC, Rechcígl Collection, Box 9, Communique, Washington, 28 January 1952.
32 Pavel Kosatík, *Ferdinand Peroutka, pozdější život* (Prague: Paseka, 2000) 172.
33 IHRC, Rechcígl Collection, Box 9, Council of Free Czechoslovakia Program, 1952.
34 Čelovský, *Politici*, 114–115.
35 Matějka, Dobroslav (ed.), *Právní aspekty odsunu sudetských Němců* (Prague: Ústav mezinárodních vztahů,1996) 103.
36 HI, Peroutka Collection, Box 2, Peroutka's Note on Meeting with Simon, 20 April 1953.
37 Hermann W Gaertner, "Zum tschechisch-sudetendeutschen Verhältnis", in: *Staatszeitung und Herold*, New York, 11 March 1956. (As cited in Čelovský, *Politici*, 114–115.)
38 IHRC, ACEN Collection, Box 36, *Exulantské Spojené národy*, in: *Nový svět*, Cleveland, 11 November 1954.
39 Council of Free Czechoslovakia, Šturm to Coste, 3 March 1955, Ibid.
40 Ibid., Box 35, Multiple memoranda, 29 March–28 September 1956.
41 HI, Peroutka Collection, Box 1, Declaration of the Representatives of the Young Generation of Czechoslovak Exiles, October 1954.
42 Peroutka to Yarrow, "Present Situation of the Council of Free Czechoslovakia and Possible Ways of Rectification", 29 March 1955, Ibid.
43 Firt to Peroutka, 22 September 1956, Ibid.
44 IHRC, ACEN Collection, Box 35, Heidrich and Lettrich to Sidzikauskas, 14 September 1961.
45 IHRC, ACEN Collection, Box 36, Ján Papánek, Committee for Free Czechoslovakia-Statutes.

46 Mojmír Povolný, *Zápas o lidská práva: Rada svobodného Československaa helsinský proces* (Brno: Stylus Press, 2007).
47 Ibid., 90–91.
48 Centrum pro československá exilová studia (CČSES), Univerzita Palackého, Olomouc, Fond Rady svobodného Československa, November 1971.
49 Torn to Povolný, 3 November 1972 , Ibid.
50 Adolf Klimek, Minutes, 10 November 1972, Ibid.
51 Adolf Klimek, Minutes, 10 November 1972, Ibid.
52 Hora to Horák et al, 24 December 1972, Ibid.
53 Klimek to Povolný, 28 July 1973, Ibid.
54 Draft memorandum to President Nixon, late 1971 (undated), Ibid.
55 Luža to Povolný, 26 September 1972, Ibid.
56 Torn to Povolný, 31 May 1974, Ibid.
57 Minutes of the meeting, 17–18 March 1973, Ibid.
58 Mojmír Povolný, *Má cesta dvacátým stoletím* (Brno: Nakladatelství Šimon Ryšavý, 2001) 56.
59 Ibid., 56.
60 Škvor to Povolný, 15 January 1975, CČSES, Povolný Collection.
61 Povolný to Řehák, 25 February 1975, Ibid.
62 CČSES, Rada svobodného Československa Collection, Povolný to Uhl, 31 December 1975.
63 Povolný to Papánek, 9 October 1974, Ibid.
64 Povolný to Drobílková, 20 January 1975, Ibid.
65 Declaration by the Council of Free Czechoslovakia, 20 February 1975, Ibid.
66 M. Povolný and R. Fraštacký to President G. Ford, 22 July 1975, Ibid.
67 M. Povolný to Senator H.M. Jackson, 26 July 1975, Ibid.
68 F. Uhlíř to M. Povolný, 17 July 1975, Ibid.
69 F. Uhlíř to M. Povolný, 19 July 1975, Ibid.
70 M. Povolný to Č. Torn, 31 July 1975, Ibid.
71 Czechoslovak Newsletter #2, April 1976, Ibid.
72 Barbara J Falk, *The Dilemmas of Dissidence in East-Central Europe* (Budapest: CEU Press, 2003) 84–87.
73 H. Gordon Skilling, *Charter 77 and Human Rights in Czechoslovakia* (London: George Allen & Unwin, 1981).
74 CČSES, Rada svobodného Československa Collection, The Charter 77 Declaration (English translation).
75 Czechoslovak Newsletter, III/1, 20 January 1977; III/2, 31 January 1977, Ibid.
76 A Memorandum on the Non-Compliance by the Government of Czechoslovakia with the Provisions of the Final Act of Helsinki, 14 May 1977, Ibid.
77 D.B. Farrell of the CSCE and Congress of the United States to V. Ryšavý, 29 April 1977, Ibid.
78 Zprávy československého svazu křesťanských pracujících Švýcarsko, January/February 1977, Ibid.
79 Francesco Caccamo, *Jiří Pelikán a jeho cesta socialismem 20. století* (Brno: Doplněk, 2008) 52–65.
80 *Václav Havel-František Janouch Korespondence 1978–2001*, ed. Jirí Suk (Prague: Akropolis, 2007) 12–15.
81 CČSES, Rada svobodného Československa Collection, Violations of Civil and Political Rights in Czechoslovakia and the Helsinki Accord, Report presented to the 2nd session of the CSCE, Belgrade, Yugoslavia, June 1977.
82 M. Povolný to M. Nimetz, 1 September 1977, Ibid.
83 C. Cosman to J. Horák, 10 November 1977, Ibid.

84 C.L. Cacca to L. Urban and J.G. Corn, 19 December 1977; L Urban and J.G. Corn to P.E. Trudeau, 17 March 1977, Ibid.
85 M. Nimetz to J. Horák, 8 November 1977, Ibid.
86 Povolný, *Zápas*, 167.
87 CČSES, Rada svobodného Československa Collection, M. Nimetz to J. Horák, 3 April 1978.
88 J. Horák and M. Povolný to M. Nimetz, 5 May 1978, Ibid.
89 Letter from the Council of Free Czechoslovakia to President Carter, 8 March 1978, Ibid.
90 Petition '78, 1 January 1978, Ibid.
91 J. Horák to the leadership of the Council of Free Czechoslovakia, 30 January 1978, Ibid.
92 Povolný, *Zápas*, 168–173.
93 CČSES, Rada svobodného Československa Collection, Open letter from Charter 77 and VONS to Kurt Waldheim and the heads of state who signed the Helsinki Declaration, 6 November 1978.
94 Solidarita s Chartou 77, Council of Free Czechoslovakia Press Release IV/24, 4 December 1978, Ibid.
95 Dušan Havlíček, *Listy v exilu* (Olomouc: Burian a tichák, 2008) 41.
96 Caccamo, *Jiří*, 56.
97 CČSES, Rada svobodného Československa Collection, *Projev předsedy výkonného výboru RSČ na schůzi zastupitelstva v New Yorku*, 24 February 1979; *Prohlášení zastupitelstva RSČ*, 25 February 1979.
98 Povolný, *Zápas*, 176–186.
99 CČSES, Rada svobodného Československa Collection, Seminář o Chartě 77 ve Frankenu 29.3–1.4.1979; Council of Free Czechoslovakia Press release V/12, 6 June 1979.
100 Nová persekuce v Československu, 6 June 1979, Ibid.
101 Czechoslovak Newsletter, IV, No. 9–10, 8, Ibid.
102 Declaration by the Council of Free Czechoslovakia, 24 October 1979, Ibid.
103 Council of Free Czechoslovakia Press Release, V/15, Dopis poslancům evropského parlamentu, 17 July 1979, Ibid.
104 J. Pelikán to M. Povolný, J. Zich, and J. Horák, 7 July 1979, Ibid.
105 J. Pelikán to M. Povolný, 17 July 1979, Ibid.
106 E. Řehák to M. Povolný, 11 September 1979, Ibid.,
107 F. Uhl to M. Povolný a R. Fraštacký, 5 September 1979, Ibid.
108 Draft of an unsent letter from the Council of Free Czechoslovakia to Simone Veil, 30 September 1979, Ibid.
109 Povolný, *Zápas*, 190–192.
110 CČSES, Rada svobodného Československa Collection, Minutes of the meeting of the Czechoslovak National Council of America, 6 November 1979.
111 J. Zich to M. Povolný, M. Kvetko, and J. Horák, 15 December 1979, Ibid.
112 Council of Free Czechoslovakia press release V/24, Novoroční pozdrav domovu, 11 December 1979, Ibid.
113 Situation Report on the Compliance in Czechoslovakia with the Helsinki Accords, Czechoslovak National Council of America, January 1980, Ibid.
114 Czechoslovakia since Belgrade, Czechoslovak National Council of America, 2 April 1980, Ibid.
115 Memorandum of the Czechoslovak Advisory Committee in Western Europe, 21 March 1980, Ibid.
116 Letter from the Council of Free Czechoslovakia to 20 democratic Czechoslovak exile organizations throughout the world, 29 September 1980, Ibid.

117 Memorandum of the Council of Free Czechoslovakia, 9 October 1980, Ibid.

118 Violations of the Helsinki Accords in Czechoslovakia, Charter 77 document, Ibid.

119 Letter from Charter 77 to President G. Husák, 17 September 1980, Ibid.

120 Povolný to Aiello, 28 October 1980, Ibid.

121 Horak, Jiří, Report on the Activities of the Council of Free Czechoslovakia, January 1981, Ibid.

122 Zpráva předsedy výkonného výboru Mojmíra Povolného o účasti na konferenci o bezpečnosti a spolupráci v Evropě v Madridu, 23 March 1981, Ibid.

123 Povolný, *Zápas*, 221–222.

124 225–229, Ibid.

125 CČSES, Rada svobodného Československa Collection, Letter from the Council of Free Czechoslovakia to President R. Reagan, 10 September 1985.

126 *Listy*, Volume 15, Attachment to Issue 1, 1985, Ibid.

127 London School of Economics (LSE) Archives and Rare Books, European Nuclear Disarmament (END) Collection, Palach Press Infoch Summary and Subscription Order Form.

128 National Archives (London), Public Record Office (PRO), File FCO28/3298, Background note to letter from Tom McNally (political advisor to the Prime Minister) to Karen Ingall of Palach Press, 8 August 1978.

129 J. Josten to P. Blaker, 1 November 1979, FCO28/3717, Ibid.

130 Confidential report on Mr. Josef Josten prepared by Merwyn Jones, IRD, 4 March 1975, Ibid.

131 CČSES, Rada svobodného Československa Collection, Invitation to M. Povolný from W. Zimmerman, 21 May 1986.

132 Memorandum on the Vienna meeting of the CSCE by the Czechoslovak National Council of America, 10 June 1986, Ibid.

133 Committee for the Support of Human Rights in Czechoslovakia, Situation inCzechoslovakia since the Madrid Review Meeting concerning Compliance with the Helsinki Final Act and the Madrid Concluding Document, 30 June 1986, Ibid.

134 W. Zimmerman, Making Moscow Pay the Price for Human Rights Abuses, *New York Times*, 1 August 1986, Ibid.

135 Letter and questionnaire to Czechoslovak exile organizations, 10 September 1986, Ibid.

136 Invitation to the international press conference at the Presseklub Concordia, 3 November 1986, Ibid.

137 Joint Memorandum of the Council of Free Czechoslovakia and the Polish Government-in-Exile for the Review Meeting of the CSCE, Vienna, 3 November 1986, Ibid.

138 Invitation to the scientific symposium Invisible Oppression, Methods of Social Control in a Mature Totalitarian System, 6 November 1986; Memorandum prepared by Czechoslovak National Council of America on Invisible Oppression in Czechoslovakia, 6 October 1986, Ibid.

139 Povolný, *Zápas*, 258

140 Ibid., 265–269.

141 CČSES, Rada svobodného Československa Collection, A Memorandum on the Early Phase of the Vienna Follow-Up Conference of CSCE, 27 December 1986.

142 CSCE News Release: Helsinki Commission nominates Charter 77 for Nobel Peace Prize, 30 January 1987, Ibid.

143 The Real Violations of Human Rights in Czechoslovakia: The Jazz Section, the Reverend Jan Dus, and Petr Pospíchal, 15 March 1987, Ibid.

144 M. Povolný and R. Fraštacký to President R. Reagan, 1 September 1987, 11 November 1987, and 14 December 1987, Ibid.

[145] Czechoslovak Newsletter, No. XII (134), November 1987, Ibid.
[146] Letter from Council of Free Czechoslovakia to President R. Reagan, 20 March 1988, Ibid.
[147] The White House, Statement by the President, 20 August 1988, Ibid.
[148] M. Povolný to R.H. Frowick, 28 December 1988. Ibid.
[149] M. Povolný to W. Zimmerman, 1 December 1988, Ibid.
[150] Povolný, *Zápas*, 275–283.
[151] 35 Nations issue East–West Pact to protect Broad Human Rights, *New York Times*, 16 January 1989.
[152] CČSES, Czechoslovak Newsletter, XIV, No. 1 (148), Letter to President-elect George Bush, 4 January 1989.
[153] Czechoslovak Newsletter, XIV, No. 2/3 (149/150), February/March 1989, Ibid.
[154] Congressional Record, Vol. 135, No. 12, Helsinki Commission Chairman nominates Czechoslovak Human Rights Activist for Nobel Peace Prize, 7 February 1989.
[155] Povolný, *Zápas*, 287–289.
[156] Ibid., 294–295.
[157] CČSES, Rada svobodného Československa Collection, Council of Free Czechoslovakia to Václav Havel, 28 November 1989.
[158] Povolný, *Zápas*, 296.
[159] Ibid., 296–298.
[160] Zdeněk Pousta (ed.), *Rozchod 1948. Rozhovory s českými poúnorovými exulanty* (Prague: Karolinum, 2006) 17.
[161] Igor Lukeš, Československý politický exil za studené války: první roky, *Střední Evropa* 119 (February 2004) 12. Available at www.sweb.cz/stredni.evropa/editor/clanek119.pdf . Accesed: 8 July 2012.

Select bibliography

Čelovský, Bořivoj. *Politici bez moci*. Tilia: Šenov u Ostravy, 2000.

Povolný, Mojmír. *Má cesta dvacatým stoletím*. Brno: Šimon Ryšavý, 2001.

Povolný, Mojmír. *Zápas o lidská práva. Rada svobodného Československa a helsinský proces*. Brno: Stylus Press, 2007.

Raška, Francis D. *Fighting Communism from Afar: The Council of Free Czechoslovakia*. Boulder: East European Monographs, 2008.

Raška, Francis D. *The Long Road to Victory: A History of Czechoslovak Exile Organizations*. Boulder: East European Monographs, 2012.

The History of the Romanian National Committee: 1947–1975

Marius Petraru

After the fall of the Iron Curtain and of the Communist regime in Romania, most historians focused their attention on the history of Communism and on the Ceaușescu regime, but Romanian historiography has never addressed the subject of the Romanian government in exile after 1947. This issue continues to be taboo not only in Romanian modern historiography but abroad as well. In the United States there have been only a few articles about this subject in journals published by the American Romanian Academy of Arts and Sciences, where many of the members or contributors were direct witnesses to some of the events in Romania before and during the institution of the Communist regime in 1947.

This article intends to analyze and identify the most important moments at the time of the foundation of the Romanian National Committee (RNC), its purpose, by-laws and activity, as well as its relations with National Committee for a Free Europe (NCFE). The RNC's activities were made possible mostly by funding provided by the US State Department and from private funds and those of the Romanian legations in Lisbon and Madrid. The financial support allowed it to develop its activity not only in the United States but through its representatives in the most important Western European countries and Latin America as well. The funding also enabled its extensive cultural and political activities in the capitals of the Western European countries, especially in Paris through the re-establishment of the Carol I University Foundation. This article also analyses the circumstances that lead to the division and reorganization of the National Committee, as well as its relations with the other national committees. For the communist authorities in Romania, the RNC represented a constant and uncomfortable opposition that was the very expression of the interests of the Romanian nation in relation to the great Western democracies and of the supreme desire for freedom from the Soviet communist regime.

Romania's Calvary: From Antonescu's Regime to Popular Democracy (1944–1948)

The coup d'état that took place on August 23, 1944, overthrew the pro-Nazi dictatorship of Marshal Ion Antonescu and brought Romania into the antifascist coalition. With the political support of the National Peasant Party (NPP), National Liberal Party, the Social-Democrat Party (SDP) and the Romanian Communist Party (RCP), King Michael commissioned General Constantin Sănătescu to form a new government on August 23, 1944, taking Romania from the side of the Axis to that of the Allied Powers.[1] By then, Soviet troops were at the eastern Romanian borders and were going to reach Bucharest in a few days. Due to the Soviet presence, the Communist party – made legal again after the coup and with fewer than 1,000 members – was able to obtain political superiority within the government coalition, which they would have been unable to achieve through their own electoral forces. Communist leaders were soon installed in important ministerial positions: Lucrețiu Pătrășcanu was named justice minister and Gheorghe Gheorghiu-Dej transportation minister.[2] The presence of Soviet troops on Romanian territory played a crucial role in the transformation of the communist minority into a dynamic pressure group. During 1944–1945 the general strategy of the Eastern European communist parties, as well as many of their concrete actions, were coordinated or ordered by the Kremlin.[3]

During this time, a few major changes occurred that would decisively influence Romania's future for the next decades. The first was the unrelenting economic pressure exerted by Soviet civilian and military officials, which lead to the erosion of the economy, already weakened by three years of war. This situation caused Mircea Ionnițiu, King Michael's personal secretary, to declare: "I saw how the Soviet Union caused, by its demands, a complete economic chaos, that lead to severe food shortage and social disturbances."[4]

The second factor was the duality shown by the Communist party, which, while an element in the cabinet, was, with the help of its political allies, conducting a campaign to subvert the social and political structure of the country.

The third factor was what some in the Romanian leadership called the American "policy of no policy".[5] They felt that the United States, which refused to make any deals while the war was going on, was indifferent to Eastern Europe or did not want to get involved. Given that the State Department remained aloof to making plans in the region, US military leaders were opposed to making any commitment. This reinforced Stalin's assertion that "whoever occupies a territory also imposes his own social system".[6]

The Communist Party's objective was to gain control over the key ministries and impose Communists leaders on the departments important to the war effort and the administrative and economic control of the country. The threatening and demonization of adversaries and the wooing of industrial workers were a few of the means the Communists used to achieve their goals. An important role in this process was played by the USSR's deputy minister for external affairs, Andrei Ianuarievici Vishinsky, the man named by Stalin to deal with Romanian affairs.[7]

After Vishinsky's visit to Bucharest in October 1944, the Communist Party engaged in an active campaign to disrupt economic and industrial life, and create social strife. Prime Minister Sănătescu's attempts to restrain the disturbances caused the fall of the government, due to complaints from the Allied Control Commission. A second Sănătescu-coalition government was then formed, but, unlike the first, it contained a full range of politicians: 4 National Peasants, 4 Liberals, 3 Socialists, and 1 Communist. As before, the party leaders were ministers without portfolio. However, the second Sănătescu government lasted only a month.[8] Communist agitators, spurred on by the Soviets, staged demonstrations throughout the country, directing their criticism especially at Interior Minister Nicolae Penescu, a National Peasant Party leader. All police authority was vested in that ministry, making that post a prime Communist target throughout Eastern Europe. A crisis developed at the end of November, when Penescu used troops to insure peace and order. The Communists vociferously attacked Penescu as a protector of Fascists. In the face of mounting pressure, Sănătescu was forced to resign.[9]

A new government under General Nicolae Rădescu (December 6, 1944–February 28, 1945) enjoyed a brief spell of calm before the Communist party resumed its campaign. An elderly officer known for his anti-German views during the war, Rădescu had the approval of Soviet authorities. Upon his appointment, Rădescu, acting under Soviet pressure, made what was termed "an important concession to the Communists" by rejecting an interior minister from the National Peasant, Liberal or Socialist parties and appointing himself to the post. Moreover, Rădescu appointed Teohari Georgescu, a member of the Communist Party's Central Committee, as undersecretary in the Interior Ministry. According to Ghiță Ionescu, the Communists used this post to introduce into the police and security forces "as many as possible of the agents trained in the patriotic guards in the last three months by Emil Bodnăraș and the Soviet NKVD supervisors."[10] In commenting on this government, Prof. Stephen Fischer-Galați, wrote: "The composition of this government showed an increase in the number of Communist and pro-Communist members. Under instructions from Moscow, the Communist members of the Rădescu cabinet sabotaged its operations by promoting anti-government demonstration."[11]

The violence throughout the country created an intolerable situation, and the king, after consulting with the leaders of the political parties, believed that replacing general Rădescu could defuse the tension. At the same time, Andrei Vishinsky arrived in Bucharest and met with the king on February 27 to obtain his approval to dismiss Rădescu. The king stated that he was bound to follow constitutional procedures and the principles agreed upon at Yalta. Vishinsky bluntly responded: "The Yalta declaration does not mention the Rădescu government."[12] The next day, speaking of the Rădescu government, Vishinsky shouted to King Michael in the royal palace: "I state officially that we cannot tolerate such a government. You do not appreciate the gravity of the situation… .The government must be replaced immediately. … Today, by six o'clock, the resignation of the cabinet must be announced and immediately after, somebody should be charged to form a new government."[13]

The Petru Groza "government" was imposed by the Soviet Union on March 6, 1945, through the might of its occupation forces, contrary to the obligations it assumed at Yalta, and in gross violation of every principle of international law. Once installed, the Groza government of the so-called Romanian People's Republic proceeded to suppress all liberties, dissolve and destroy all political parties, arrest all who at any time had been prominent in public life, and carry out so-called elections. The elections were subsequently described officially by the governments of the United States and Great Britain as "the most fraudulent elections known to history".[14]

In the collective memory of Romanians, it was Vishinsky who transformed their country into a potential Soviet colony. In 1946–1947, Romanian Communists benefited from the false pluralism of the Groza regime. As a result of Western pressure, historical parties were represented in his government, but for a short period of time and at a minor level.[15]

Important steps towards the total destruction of the official opposition began to be taken, starting with the falsification of the parliamentary elections of November 19, 1946. The Communists obtained low results in the elections, despite the involvement of prefects that were complicit with of Teohari Georgescu (the Communist minister of internal affairs) and despite the "revolutionary" gangs that terrorized the electors. The real winner in that election was the NPP, which the Communists correctly perceived to be the nucleus of the resistance to the sovietization of the country.[16]

Over time, the opposition was effectively destroyed by the measures described above. On December 30, 1947, King Michael was forced to abdicate and leave the country. The next day a "People's Republic" was proclaimed. According to Romanian Communist historians and political theorists, the advent of the Groza Government on March 6, 1945, signified the installation of the "popular democratic" regime in Romania, to be followed by the second phase of conquest, the dictatorship of the proletariat, starting on December 31, 1947.[17]

Summarizing Romania's seven months of coalition governments in which Communists participated, Ionescu declared: "From the day on which King Michael dismissed Antonescu to that on which Soviet Russia imposed the Groza government on him, there were three Rumanian governments. All tried to solve the problem of genuine collaboration between an independent Rumania and Soviet Russia. The first two were under the presidency of General Sănătescu; the third under that of General Rădescu. All three failed because of the direct and indirect refusals of Soviet Russia to deal with any but a communist-controlled government."[18]

World War II had already driven many people into exile. Later, according to Astrid Suhrke, "the singular effect of the Cold War was not to politicize the refugee phenomenon, but to globalize this process and connect it to the dominant rivalry between the superpowers. Refugees became instruments of and parties of the Cold War, representing increments of power that were counted in the balance between East and West. In an age of mass politics and under the terms of ideological rivalry during the Cold War, refugees who crossed over to the West represented a political asset..."[19] Therefore, one cannot speak about exile and its strategies without considering the specifics of the ideological warfare between East and West and the crucial importance of cultural aspects, which were perceived as an effective weapon to be utilized by both sides through propaganda.

There is no doubt that the Romanian political emigration played an important role during World War I. After Romania was defeated and forced to sign the peace treaty, the National Committee of Romanian Unity was formed in Paris at the initiative of Take Ionescu. The Committee was immediately recognized by England, France and Italy, creating a favorable situation at the Paris peace conference and keeping the Allies' sympathy for Romania alive.[20]

The installation in fall 1940 of the Antonescu regime and a new government dominated by the Iron Guard, as well as Romania's involvement on the Axis side in World War II, led to a new wave of Romanian political emigration. In September 1940, after the abdication of King Carol II, the Free Rumanian Democratic Committee/Romanian National Committee started taking shape in London. Its aim was to coordinate all Romanian international activities, initially for the liberation of the country from the control of Nazi Germany, later from that of Soviet Russia. A secret report from Witold Mieczysławski, Poland's foreign affairs minister before World War II, to Professor Stanisław Kot (vice president in Sikorski's government) informed Kot that the sender had met with Viorel Tilea on November 8, 1940. During this meeting, Tilea, a former Romanian ambassador to the United Kingdom, informed Mieczysławski of his intentions to form the Romanian Front and the Romanian Free Movement (the Free Demmocratic Committee), to be composed of people from among the fairly large numbers of Romanian émigrés in Canada and the United States.[21] It is clear from the same report that Tilea had close relations with the former military attaché of the Republic of Poland in Bucharest, Jan Kowałewski, who, starting in 1940, was the head of the center of Polish intelligence in Lisbon.[22]Through his mediation, Tilea had close relations with the Polish minister in Istanbul, Tomasz Arcziszewski, who was constantly in touch with some of the Romanian political leaders. In order to implement his plans, Tilea managed to obtain the support of Jean Pangal, the former Romanian ambassador in Lisbon,[23] and Grigore Gafencu, Romania's plenipotentiary minister in Moscow at that time. He also gained the support of a great number of Romanian politicians who were already in exile, such as plenipotentiary Minister Dimitri D. Dimăncescu,[24] former foreign affairs counselor Alexandru Gurănescu, former plenipotentiary minister to Yugoslavia and Austria Richard Franasovici, who was established in Bern, and the plenipotentiary minister to the Vatican (and former ambassador to Warsaw and Paris and then plenipotentiary minister in Bern), Nicolae Petrescu Comnen.[25]

Mieczsyławski also specified in his report that the committee, once formed, would represent the interests of all Romanians, and that its aim was to fight for the restoration of Romanian territories occupied by force in the summer of 1940, for the liberation of King Michael I from the hostile situation in which he found himself and for restoring his rights as the monarch. The committee also predicted that in the future, only the creation of a confederation of Eastern and South-Eastern European countries having the same interests toward Germany and the Soviet Russia could result in peaceful coexistence.[26]

Tilea admitted that, taking into account the internal political and military situation, it was imperative that cooperation with the democratic forces be accomplished only with the help of Iuliu Maniu, the former prime minister of Romania and the leader of the National Peasants' Party, who represented "the only moral and political authority in Romania" at that time. In order to inform Maniu of the committee's intentions without arousing suspicion, Tilea proposed that Constantin Angelescu, executive president of Urbana Bank of Bucharest, be the only contact person between Maniu and the committee.[27] This group of Romanian political emigrants would constitute the first nucleus of the future RNC.

The RNC's Predecessors

The predecessor to the RNC was formed at Bern in 1946, and its goals and conditions led to the later group's formation in the United States. In a June 16, 1942, letter to the Polish Minister of Foreign Affairs in London, Polish Colonel H. Gano noted that other groups of political emigrants from the Southern Eastern European countries were located in the United States and Canada and had started to develop plans to support the liberation of Europe from German occupation, but in general they had received no attention from the Department of State. However, among these groups the Department of State's attention was drawn to the organization called the "Free Romanians", which was divided into two fractions that had no common ideology and were in permanent conflict.[28]

The first and oldest faction, the "Free Roumanian Committee", was created by the Romanian clergy in the United States and Canada and led by two priests, Glicherie Moraru and Alexandru Opreanu. They chose as president of the Committee King Carol II, then in exile in Mexico, and intending to form a "government in exile".[29] Although US Undersecretary of State Sumner Wells refused to grant the former king a visa to enter the United States, the Committee was quite active, issuing, among other things, three publications: *Glasul Românesc* (The Romanian Voice), *Solia* (The Messenger, by the Romanian-American Orthodox Diocese), and a monthly publication in English, *The Free Roumanian*, which appeared only for three issues.[30] *The Free Roumanian* was also supported by a small fraction of the Romanian-American Jewish community, represented by the former vice-president of United Romanian Jews of America, Leon Fischer. Although Fischer tried in a few articles to convince American Romanians of the former sovereign's good democratic intentions, his readers could not forget Carol II's relations with the Iron Guard regarding the naming of the fascist Goga-Cuza government, nor the relations the Free Roumanian Committee had with Viorel Tilea and about his close relations with Carol II.

The second faction, the "Independent Romanians" movement, was led by Carol Cilla Davila and was also known as the "Alliance of Romanian Americans for Democracy" (of which the United Romanian Jews was also a part). Davila, a well-known politician, was close to Iuliu Maniu, who had sent him to Washington in 1928 to fill the position of plenipotentiary minister. This group edited a newspaper in Romanian entitled *America*, which was known for its anti-Nazi and pro-democratic views. Having the support of the greater part of the Romanian-American Jewish community, and known for its democratic views, which were supported by the majority of American Romanians, Washington regarded this group with great sympathy and trust.[31]

In 1947 the Romanian political exile leadership in the United States formed a coalition, but this did not mean that its rifts were healed. In 1947, Grigore Gafencu arrived in the United States. The Romanian secret police, the "Securitate", considered him "the main representative of the Romanian reactionary movement abroad".[32] Together with other political leaders, he attempted to organize a Romanian government in exile, which created difficulties for the US authorities.[33]

After Communist regimes were installed in Eastern Europe, the US government realized the emigrants' value as a force against those regimes and began to recruit from among the writers, politicians, economists, and intelligentsia, hoping to pave the way for reinstalling democratic governments in Eastern Europe. Because the Western powers quickly recognized most of the postwar political regimes in Central and Eastern Europe, there was no possibility of acknowledging official governments in exile. However, the West did assist and subsidize unofficial national committees, through the National Committee for a Free Europe, Inc. (NCFE, which became the Free Europe Committee, Inc., FEC, in 1954). This organization was incorporated to provide support for émigré leaders from Eastern Europe to form organizations to fight a propaganda battle against communist rule of their homelands.

The Romanian National Committee was founded in 1949. King Michael remembered, after almost half a century, the positive and negative aspects of the RNC and his relations with the head of its governing committee, General Nicolae Rădescu, underlining the fact that, "This Committee was, from the beginning to the end, in crisis, because it itself was the expression of a crisis."[34] Crisis characterized the activities of the other national committees as well, primarily resulting from the differences in political ideology of the groups they represented. The situation was further complicated by the challenge of organizing new political groups outside the home country, which required new strategies and new human and financial resources.

The first generation of Romanians in exile after WWII had a heterogeneous political composition and was made up of several important politicians, covering the whole political spectrum. According to a Radio Free Europe report, there were four main political groups of Romanians abroad during the first decade of the Cold War. The first group was comprised of the supporters of the Romanian National Peasant's Party, the second of National Liberals, the third of socialists, and the fourth of Iron Guard members and sympathizers.[35] Between them, they mirrored the divisions at home and generated competing political organizations, such as the Romanian National Committee and the League of

Free Romanians in London. None of these political figures in exile succeeded in bringing the exiles together.

It should also be noted that the greatest part of the Romanian political class in exile was concentrated in the United States, while the majority of the intellectual and artistic exiles remained in Europe, largely in Paris. After fleeing the country in the first years after 1945, some Romanians chose to go to France and the French occupation zone in Germany because most of the first generation felt a kinship of language and educational background. Spain was another preferred destination, in particular for former extreme right-wing activists.[36]

The Organization and Legitimacy of the Romanian National Committee

For most Romanian political leaders who played an important role in the democratic politics of interwar/pre-WWII Romania, the events of 1947 were the cruel beginning of exile. Those who left did not, however, abandon the hope of returning someday to a free and democratic Romania.

The Romanian National Committee was formed in the United States on May 10, 1949. The matter of forming a Romanian political organization in exile had been discussed since 1947 and was put into motion after the act of force committed by the Groza government against King Michael.

From the discussions that took place at the US Department of State between the political exiles from various countries behind the Iron Curtain, it was clear as early as the summer of 1948 that even though the US was willing to maintain diplomatic relations with the so-called "satellite" countries, and so was unable to accept "exile governments" on its territory, it still regarded with favor the formation of National Committees made up of people representing those countries.

An agreement to form the Romanian Democrat Parties Council was made on January 31, 1948, between General Rădescu and representatives of the National Peasant Party, Social-Democrat Independent Party and

National Liberty Party. King Michael was aware of the agreement by that February. The declaration, signed by Rădescu, Grigore Niculescu-Buzeşti and Mihail Fărcăşanu, states the council's purpose:

> Recent international circumstances indicate the need of intensifying and organizing Romanian political actions abroad, and since the Geneva group could not be automatically transformed into a national political and representative committee, we agreed to initiate a proposal to His Majesty the King to constitute such a committee. Regarding the Geneva group, it will end its function upon the formation of this committee and will be considered dissolved thereafter.[37]

Based on this agreement, on August 5, 1948, the king made some recommendations regarding the formation of a "Romanian Coordination Committee". After several meetings, and following King Michael's recommendations, on April 6, 1949, a new agreement was signed that supported the January 31, 1948, agreement to form the national committee.[38] This decision was finally sanctioned by the king on April 23, 1949, and on May 5 of that year General Rădescu officially informed US Secretary of State Dean Acheson of that event.[39]

The national committee was based on a formula proposed by King Michael, namely: a body of 10 persons, formed of 5 representatives of the democrat political parties (National Peasant, Liberty and Social-Democrat Independent) named by the Romanian Democrat Parties Council in exile (a body formed in Paris on March 31, 1948) and 5 persons who did not belong to political parties.[40] Besides General Rădescu, who was elected president, the other members elected to form the Committee were Grigore Niculescu Buzeşti (former foreign minister), Augustin Popa (former member of the Romanian parliament), Cornel Bianu (former member of the Romanian parliament) as representatives of the National Peasant Party, Mihail Fărcăşanu (president of the Romanian Liberal Youth Organization) representing the National Liberty Party, and Iancu Zissu representing the Social-Democrat Independent Party. To these were added: Niculae Caranfil (former minister of aviation),

Alexandru Cretzianu (former Romanian minister in Ankara), Grigore Gafencu (former foreign minister) and Constantin Vişoianu (former foreign minister).[41]

On the occasion of its formation, the RNC issued a proclamation on May 10, 1949, outlining its objectives and the role it would play in the international political arena, especially with regard to setting Romania free from Soviet influence:

> The Committee undertakes to fight for the independence of Romania and to restore the human rights and fundamental freedoms destroyed by the Bucharest puppet government at the dictation of Moscow; to keep alive the hope of salvation in the enslaved Romanian people unable through terror to voice their distress; to inform Western public opinion about the ways and methods by which Communist Russia is pursuing its policy of ever expanding domination.
> The Committee also appeals to Western European countries working for a United Europe to bear in mind that Romania by her history, culture and economics is an integral part of Europe.
> It further expresses its desire to collaborate closely with free representatives of all nations under Moscow's domination in order to lay the basis of new patterns of democratic life. It accepts, for this purpose, new forms of regional organizations which may lead to the unification of Europe.[42]

The same day, King Michael addressed the country in a message that was broadcast by Voice of America. At the end of his speech, the king added: "I have the pleasure to give my approval today for the formation of the Romanian National Committee, which will dedicate all its power to the fight for the liberation of our country."[43]

The RNC's formation received extensive coverage in the Romanian-American newspaper *America*, which gave the historic act special attention. The event was also announced in the American publication the *Evening Star* on May 10, 1949. The *Evening Star* was to cooperate with the committee and would cover the most important of the RNC's activities. Agence France Presse also announced the Committee's formation, emphasizing the role of the king and of the Romanian martyrs in communist prisons who supported the political act of Romanian emigration: "A Romanian national committee has been formed in the United States with the support of King Michael. ... Convinced that real peace will not be ensured with a regime of terror existing in a part of Europe", the Committee intends to "cooperate closely with the free representatives of the countries behind the Iron Curtain to the service of their common ideal of independence." The Committee specified that "its action will be inspired by the martyrdom of great Romanian democrats, such as Iuliu Maniu, Mihai and Titel Petrescu, who lie in prisons."[44]

The RNC's formation was also very well received by the Turkish political class, which had had relations with Romania during the negotiation of the armistice and knew the role Alexandru Cretzianu played in the secret discussions with the Allies. Thus, in a May 11, 1949, article in *Tasvir-I Efkar* by Selim Sabit titled "The True Representatives of the Romanian Nation", one could read a detailed description of the members of the Committee and the role played by King Michael.[45]

The problem of national representation in exile unleashed vehement controversies in all the emigrations. Representing all factions of the emigration, the RNC formed "National Nuclei" composed of legitimate elements found in exile. The alliance pronounced that it had "the right of representation of a national conscience". Benefiting from freedom of speech, the RNC felt itself to be the spokesman for those who living under the Soviet controlled regime in Romania. Their presentation of the Romanian nation abroad was to be composed of "legitimate factors" in exile, such as King Michael, representatives of the last legal government (dismissed by Vishinsky on March 6, 1945) and Romanian refugees.[46]

For Romanians, the monarchy represented permanence and continuity; the sovereign, as head of state, represented a necessary element constituting national representation. According to the 1923 Romanian constitution, the king held hereditary power and "reigns and does not govern", which is why he was joined by the representatives of the last legal government, who continued to exercise "executive power" in the name of the sovereign. After the events of March 6, 1945, the entire Romanian political class questioned the Groza government's legitimacy – given its having been imposed under the pressure of the presence of Russian troops at a time when Romania was deprived of the free exercise of its constitutional functions. King Michael's refusal to recognize the Groza government provided the RNC's mandate in exile. The committee itself fulfilled some of the provisions of the Romanian Constitution of 1923 and received the right to apply them. In article 87 it stated: "no act of the king can have force unless undersigned by a Minister, who in this way becomes responsible for that act." Article 91 stated: "the king has no other rights than those given to him by the constitution." Thus, the representatives of the last legal government were those who, in exile, formed the legitimate entity that would fulfill the sovereign's responsibility according to the requirements of the constitution.

On his return to Romania in April 1992, King Michael spoke with writer Mircea Ciobanu about the RNC's legitimacy and the role this played in the fight for Romania's liberation from Soviet influence:

For us, the National Committee represented the Romanian government in exile. The Committee was conceived as a government in exile; the Americans would not have accepted having such a political formulation on their territory. And yet Romanians were accepted at Washington with this Committee, the Department of State knew the role it played and the role we had given it. They understood exactly what we were doing. Nicolae Rădescu was the first president of the government; General Rădescu had been the last prime minister in the country, named by us in freedom. That is exactly why we named him. We wanted it to be known that there is continuity in the way we see things. Representatives of all the parties that had entered the last democratic government from Bucharest took part in constituting the Committee. We acted this way so that the Romanians and the authorities in Washington would have no doubt about our orientation, which had to remain a democratic one.[47]

There is no doubt that during times of extreme stress, as during World War II, circumstances unexpectedly bring together different personalities, some driven by noble and unselfish sentiments and others just by the primal urge to survive. The RNC was composed of persons of importance from interwar Romanian politics who had had ministerial functions or served in parliament before 1947. Their concern for the future of the country drew them into a government that fought for Romania's sovereignty, and when it was lost, they went into exile.

A few studies have been published about the first RNC president, General Nicolae Rădescu, but not about the other RNC members.[48] One individual who played an important role in the August 23, 1944, drama was Grigore Niculescu-Buzești. Those who today still lament Romania's dramatic departure from the Axis camp in 1944 regard Buzești as a sinister character. They accuse him of having undermined the bulwark that kept the Red Army out of Europe, ignoring the fact the German war machine was already on its way to destruction in August 1944. But for the majority of people, who supported King Michael's actions, understood the historical realities and were neither vocal nor bigoted, Niculescu-Buzești was an "extremely interesting figure, a militant for democracy and freedom. He tried, with the support of a group of his colleagues in the Foreign Office and the support of the leaders of the political parties, to ensure the continuity of the foreign policy initiated by Nicolae Titulescu prior to World War II."[49]

After having been admitted to the prestigious Mănăstirea Dealul military school from Târgoviște, Buzești would (because of a chronic disease of which he would later die) continue his career at the School of Law in Bucharest, where he graduated in 1927. At the same time, he managed to pass all the exams for a position in the Foreign Ministry. In 1933, when Nicolae Titulescu was elected president of the League of Nations, Buzești was transferred to Geneva to support the diplomatic mission. His work was greatly appreciated, but when Titulescu was removed from power by King Carol II in order to signal a shift to the right in Romania's foreign policy, Buzești was recalled and sent to diplomatic posts in the Scandinavian countries. When Romania was drawn into the war, he was recalled to Bucharest by Alexandru Cretzianu, the secretary general of the Foreign Office. He was appointed director of codes and ciphers, a position he held until King Michael named him foreign minister on August 23, 1944.[50]

Buzești was part of a small group of patriots who advised the king during the critical hours of the war, and he showed the same resolution in his later relations with the Soviets. In November 1946, when Iuliu Maniu asked him to run on the National Peasant slate in the national elections, he accepted without hesitation, fully aware of the dangers that awaited an opposition candidate in a Communist-run election. The constant threats hurled at him by the Communist groups forced Buzești to seek refuge abroad. When, in spite of his wife's serious illness, the government refused to issue him a passport so he could visit her in Switzerland, Buzești left the country illegally. Catherine, his wife, died shortly after his arrival, and, grieving deeply, he moved to New York, where he carried out with fervor his assignment to speak for freedom in the name of Romania's political parties. In New York, he participated in the RNC's organization.[51] During that time, a letter smuggled out of Romania confirmed that Iuliu Maniu had decided to entrust Buzești with the leadership of the National Peasant Party, in case he himself was unable to lead it.[52] But on October 4, 1949, the leukemia Buzești had fought for so many years got the upper hand and he passed away in a New York hospital. The obstacles encountered while fighting for the independence of Romania, the tragic loss of his wife, and the difficulties in organizing the activities of free Romanians had exhausted his reserves. His position in the RNC leadership was filled by Anton Crihan,[53] born in Bessarabia, a member of the National Peasant Party and a former undersecretary of state who had left Romania illegally in 1949.[54]

The most active and prolific of all the RNC leaders was Constantin Vișoianu, who succeeded General Rădescu as president on November 4, 1950.[55] Vișoianu began his career as a secretary of the mixed arbitration courts created by the peace treaties after World War I. While in that position he came to the attention of Niculae Titulescu, who secured his appointment as a member of the League of Nations General Secretariat in Geneva. He was then named minister to the Hague and later to Warsaw. After Titulescu was deposed in August 1936, Vișoianu left the

Romanian diplomatic service and became the foreign policy counselor to Iuliu Maniu and Ion Mihalache, the leaders of the National Peasant Party. In 1944 Maniu sent Vişoianu and Barbu Ştirbey to Cairo to take part in the secret armistice negotiations with the Allies. After the coup of August 23, 1944, Vişoianu entered the second Sănătescu government and then the Rădescu government that followed, occupying the position of minister of foreign affairs. He left that post on February 27, 1945, when the Groza government was installed. At the end of 1946, Vişoianu managed to leave Romania illegally for the United States.[56]

Cornel Bianu was another member of the RNC and of the National Peasant Party. He was born in Transylvania, was close to Iuliu Maniu, and served as a member in the Romanian parliament. In 1941 he went to London, where he spent the entire war as a special delegate of Maniu. After its formation, Bianu was active in the RNC until spring 1965.[57]

Another good friend of Maniu, Augustin Popa, was one of the most active and long-serving RNC members, contributing both to its foundation and its functioning. Born in Transylvania and a supporter of the peasant doctrine, in 1929 Popa was a deputy of the National Peasant Party in Blaj and held the position of general secretary of the General Association of the Greek-Uniate Church, which was founded in Blaj on November 23–24.[58] After the August 1944 coup, Popa edited the National Peasant newspaper, *The Courier*, until 1946, when the Soviet authorities ordered the publication closed and the arrest of its manager. Popa left the country illegally and emigrated to the United States, where he continued his efforts on behalf of Romanian independence. He died in New York on November 1, 1974.[59]

The National Peasant Party formed a majority among the refugee politicians in the West. The National Liberty Party had few members in exile and consequently was represented on the committee by just one person, Mihail Fărcăşanu, who held a PhD in political science from the University of Berlin. He had been very active in organizing the Liberty Youth in Romania, where he had been regarded as the great hope for his party's future. When the RNC was formed, he was recruited by the other members, and among his other assignments he was in charge of providing program materials to the radio stations that broadcast programs in Romanian in the United States, England, France, Italy, Greece, Turkey and Spain as well as overseeing the relationships between the RNC and the NCFE.[60]Because of a dispute within the RNC during the summer of 1950, Fărcăşanu presented his resignation[61] and his position went to Gheorghe Assan, a member of the National Liberty party and a former undersecretary of state and minister in Copenhagen.[62]

Few representatives of the Social Democrat Independent Party took part in the discussions leading to the RNC's formation. Most of that party's leaders who were in the West, such as Eftimie Gherman and Sacha Volman, refused to have any relations with the other parties. Still, a few Social Democrats took part in the negotiations, including Iancu Zissu, a lawyer from Galati who was representing Constantin Titel Petrescu.[63]

Among the participants who were not politicians, Niculae Caranfil deserves mention. He was a corresponding member of the Romanian Academy with vast knowledge in the fields of economics and ethnology and also had extraordinary organizational skills. Caranfil had been a representative of the Romanian Society of the Free Red Cross, a non-profit organization that represented the interests of the Romanian Red Cross abroad, which had been dissolved and replaced with a new organization approved by the new regime in Bucharest. Through the summer of 1950, in addition to his other obligations, Caranfil was part of the RNC financial commission until he was replaced by Cornel Bianu.[64]

Another figure who left his mark on the RNC's decisions and activities was Sabin Manuilă (1894–1964), director of the first Central Institute of Statistics of Romania (1934–1947) and a member of the Romanian Academy. He was also a member of the International Institute of Statistics and vice-president of the Royal Society of Heredity. A former Rockefeller Foundation fellow, he received financial support from that foundation to organize the first demographic census of Romania in 1930. Manuilă took up residence in New York in 1948 and was recruited into the RNC a year later. He was also active on the Commission for Refugees' Help.[65] In 1950 he became a charter member of the

Iuliu Maniu American Romanian Relief Foundation.[66] In the summer of 1954, he and his wife, Veturia, began their participation in the Assembly of Captive European Nations (ACEN) as part of its Social Commission.[67] Manuilă made an important contribution toward solving some of the serious social problems being studied by ACEN – problems related to population structure, public and social health, social security, and youth as well issues related to refugees. He maintained a very close relationship with Romanian colleagues and friends, and with the support of the former president of the Federation of Jewish Communities of Romania, he wrote the first scholarly work enumerating the population patterns of Jews in Romania between 1930 and 1956. Manuilă's study was presented at Stockholm on the occasion of the thirtieth session of the International Institute of Statistics, of which he was a member.[68]

Alexandru Cretzianu (1895–1979) was one of the architects of Romanian foreign policy between the two world wars and after World War II. Romanian historiography mentions almost nothing about his diplomatic activity. There is no bibliography dedicated to this great Romanian diplomat. After successful postings at the Romanian legation in London, Rome and Berne, Cretzianu continued his work under Nicolae Titulescu at the League of Nations between 1929 and 1932. In 1933 he began serving as chief of the political division of the Foreign Ministry, a post he held until 1938 and was then its secretary general until 1941. Called back to his post in September 1943, he was sent as minister to Ankara, where he initiated the armistice negotiations and dealt with transmitting messages regarding the armistice – messages between King Michael and Iuliu Maniu, on the one hand, and between the delegates from Cairo on the other.[69] Cretzianu was greatly appreciated in both the Romanian and the international diplomatic worlds and was considered by some analysts "the grey eminence of Romanian foreign policy".[70] Despite his success in international diplomacy, a few Romanian historians and writers consider Cretzianu to have been largely responsible, together with Vișoianu, for the "evaporation" of a huge amount of money Antonescu had deposited in a special fund in Switzerland. Known as the "Mihai Antonescu Fund" or the "Switzerland Fund", according to the same sources it was what caused the discord that led to the split in the RNC in the summer of 1950.[71]

In order to provide the RNC with greater legitimacy, most of those participating in its formation felt that King Michael, as the ultimate decision maker, should approve its members. Throughout the RNC's existence most decisions were made by the members after asking the sovereign for counsel. Not having his own cabinet, the king relied upon his personal secretary, General C. Petre-Lazăr, who signed all the king's correspondence with politicians, making it difficult to determine how much of a letter's content was the king's exact opinion and how much was the general's opinion and interpretations. Although he was criticized by his contemporaries for his rigid way of communicating and his negative influence on the king's political life, King Michael described his relationship with Petre-Lazăr in the following way:

> He was close to us; he worked for our family his entire life. He was extremely loyal to me. Those who did not know General C. Petre-Lazăr speak ill of him. The others cherished him a lot. ... It is true, he could be quite severe, but not with everybody. ...We received all kind of documents, many from the CNR – letters, people asking for an audience, some in good faith, others with all sorts of schemes. Petre Lazăr responded harshly to some. ... He was not an obstacle to any Romanian who wanted to see me or to work with us. ... Some friction could not be avoided. ... General Lazăr did not like mixed, ambiguous relations. That is for sure. He had conflicts with Vişoianu too...."[72]

After being formally established, the RNC passed operating by-laws, which set the guidelines for formation of the general secretariat, as well as for the allocation of responsibilities among the departments. Fărcăşanu and Cretzianu were the main authors of the first draft of the by-laws, which were distributed to all the members on May 19, 1949,[73] and went through several revisions during 1949 and the beginning of 1950. After consulting King Michael, Petre-Lazăr suggested in a letter dated October 30, 1949, in Washington, that the by-laws be organized to address the issues presented in preceding drafts.[74] Fărcăşanu and Cretzianu wrote the final draft of the by-laws, which was approved at the meeting on November 29, 1949.[75] In a letter written on December 16, 1949, Petre-Lazăr informed the Committee that the by-laws had been reviewed and approved by the sovereign, with the specification that: "His Majesty believes that according to the regulations, the National Committee will only be able to function legitimately with the participation of at least two thirds of its members, namely 7 members..." In a letter addressed to all the members, General Rădescu informed them about the modifications resulting from King Michael's input as well as about "the procedure for the Committee to follow to change its operating structure". He also expressed his regret that he could not take part in the extraordinary meeting on December 27, as they had requested.[76] Table 1 at the conclusion of this text, By-laws of the Romanian National Committee, presents a detailed analysis of the RNC's operating regulations and can be consulted in order to understand the decisions and measures taken by the members that will be referred to in this study.

In the meeting of January 26, 1950, Gafencu proposed an amendment to article 12, namely that the RNC general secretary be named by a two-thirds majority. Vişioanu, Fărcăşanu and Cretzianu opposed this, finding no need for a two-thirds majority and stating that asimple majority was enough. The meeting also decided to form a secretariat in New York[77] and another in Washington, D.C. Each was to be responsible for operations in its area. It was also specified that all original correspondence be presented to the RNC president in New York and then returned to the secretariat in Washington.[78]

At the February 25, 1950, meeting, the RNC decided to reorganize its activities by limiting its members' spheres of activity. From the tasks and activity areas outlined, one can see that the focus was to be on diplomatic and foreign policy and on propaganda. These priorities were the result of external realities and US foreign policy towards Soviet Russia. The Department of State supported the national councils functioning in the United States and used their propaganda activity to support US political and military agendas against the Soviet Union. Vişoianu and Gafencu chaired the committee on foreign policy from its inception. Vişoianu was in charge of relations with the Department of State, with the ambassadors and ministers of fellow governments recognized by Washington, with the other national committees headquartered in Washington, and with the political exiles who settled in Washington. Gafencu coordinated relations with the United Nations and the European Federal Movement, as well as with all the other political exiles in New York.[79]

Popa chaired the committee on foreign media and propaganda, supervised the publication of the RNC's books and brochures as well as relations with the international media, and also supervised the organization and management of the RNC media office. Fărcăşanu was responsible for cooperation with all the radio stations that broadcast in Romanian and with the National Committee for Free Europe. He was also in charge of the problems related to the organization and activities of the Romanian Orthodox Church in exile and the Romanian cultural foundations and institutions abroad.[80]

Cretzianu's responsibilities included gathering information from Romania and about Romania and producing a bi-monthly bulletin that would keep King Michael informed. He was also to coordinate the activities of the RNC representatives abroad. Material and legal assistance provided to the Romanian refugees was overseen by Nicolae Caranfil.[81]

At the meeting of February 25, a commission was formed to be led by Cornel Bianu and composed of Caranfil, Fărcăşanu, Gafencu, Vişoianu and Zissu. Its objective was to form a plan regarding the first measures to be adopted the moment Romania was liberated. Another important decision made at that meeting was to name Emil Ghilezan[82] as general secretary to replace Cretzianu, who had temporarily occupied the position since May 1949.

The Division and Reorganization of the Romanian National Committee

Differences in ideology and political views were among the most significant reasons for dissension within the RNC. Characterizing his collaboration with Rădescu, King Michael noted that at some points he had difficulty getting along with the old general:

> Throughout our collaboration, he could not by any means come to terms with the fact that the people he worked with– Vișoianu, Caranfil, Gafencu, Cretzianu, Niculescu Buzești, Zissu, Fărcășanu, Ghilezan and others –represented parties or, even if they were independent, that they sympathized with one party or another. The General worked with the members of the Committee in a tense atmosphere. One year after the Committee was constituted, General Rădescu complained to me in a letter about all the difficulties that had arisen as a result of his agreement to work with the representatives of the parties rather than with the independents, as he would have wished.[83]

In the summer of 1949, immediately after the RNC was established, Rădescu began informing the king of internal Committee disagreements and animosities as well as about the difficulties he encountered in dialogue with other members. At the September 9, 1949, meeting, he expressed his regret for having written a letter he had sent to the king to inform him about problems within the Committee:"I regret that a personal letter such as mine, which was not directed to the Committee, could be interpreted to indicate that I considered the Committee unable to do its work."[84]

The deterioration of relations among the RNC members began soon after the committee was established. On September 13, 1949, Cretzianu and Vișoianu sent a letter to Rădescu complaining that all the minutes of the meetings taken to that date contained many errors and had been incorrectly and incompletely edited.[85] RNC meeting protocol took its permanent form starting in October 1949, following those complaints. Another main cause of dissent among the RNC members, which has often been overlooked, was Rădescu's relationship with the prominent Romanian industrialist Nicolae Malaxa and his having been called to testify on Malax's behalf in the "Coplon trial". On March 6, 1949, FBI agents in Manhattan arrested Judith Coplon, a clerk at the US Department of Justice. In her bag, agents found 34 top secret documents, which she intended to turn over to

Gubişev Valentin, a Soviet NKVD agent working undercover in New York as an official in the UN Secretariat. Among the documents was a memorandum by the FBI addressed to the CIA on May 11, 1948, regarding Nicholas Malaxa, who emigrated to the US after 1947. It stated that Malaxa was the subject of extensive investigation by the FBI and CIA and was suspected of operating as a security agent in Bucharest. At Coplon's trial, at the request of the judge, the FBI was forced to bring the documents found in her bag to court, which resulted in extensive media coverage of Coplon's spying and cast doubt on Malaxa's character.[86]

Taking note of statements and accusations made by Bianu, Buzeşti, Cretzianu, Popa, Vişoianu and Zissu, in the September 9, 1949, meeting, Rădescu denied any political ties to Malaxa but admitted that before the RNC was constituted he had received funds from Malaxa, which he had made available for refugees and Romanian students. Rădescu refused to acknowledge that his relationship with Malaxa might have jeopardized RNC activitites, given that all the members were already aware of it. Caranfil, Fărcăşanu and Gafencu supported the general's statement, noting:

> The confessions in the Coplon trial regarding our Committee referred to facts that had already been known by the American authorities. The members of the Committee also knew these facts, even before the Committee was constituted. Consequently, the so-called confessions could not influence or alter in any way the rapport between the American authorities and the [RNC] President or the Romanian Committee, or the rapport among the members of the Committee. Actually relations between the American Free Europe Committee and the President, namely our Committee, have strengthened of late.[87]

A few days after that meeting, Cretzianu asked Caranfil to transmit a brief to Rădescu responding to declarations the general had made at that meeting. They asked that it be attached to the minutes being sent to the king. In one of the points made in the brief, Cretzianu contradicts Rădescu regarding the Coplon trial and his relations with Malaxa:

> The statement that the members of the Committee knew the facts that were disclosed during the Coplon trial is not correct. The members of the Committee did not know –there was no way they could have known – that on May 5, 1948, General Rădescu declared to the American authorities (the Federal Bureau of Investigation) that he made the decision for the astronomical amount of compensation, in dollars, that the Romanian State had given to Mr. Malaxa, of which none of the victims in Romania received a cent. During the September 9 meeting of the Committee, I read the text of Mr. Rădescu"s declaration: "Rădescu pointed out that although the decree which returned Malaxa to control of his factories and reimbursed him for their use by the Rumanian Government, and although the seizure of the tube mill by the Russians was signed after he was deposed as Prime Minister, he was responsible for its passage. He also pointed out that although the pro-Communist Government of Peter Groza was in power at that time, they did not have complete control, and there was still a semblance of democratic procedure. He was unable to explain why this decree called for Malaxa to be reimbursed in foreign currency.
> In a previous meeting of the Committee, I showed that the secret Central Intelligence Agency Memorandum of May 11, 1948, revealed at the Coplon trial, literally states: "Rădescu had proposed that this organization transmit certain funds, amounting to only a few thousand dollars, to certain of his adherents abroad. In view of Rădescu's association with Malaxa, his proposal was rejected."[88]

In the same letter, Cretzianu recounts the aversion Malaxa had towards the RNC and his request that the money sent to Rădescu not finance RNC activities:

> I had another discussion with Mr. Rădescu regarding his statement that Mr. Malaxa remitted those sums to him with no conditions. I showed him that his own testimony, made to the National Committee on June 24, 1949, states that Mr. Malaxa set the condition that the funds remitted by no means be entrusted to the National Commit-

> tee. I also need to add, regarding some offers which would have been made by Mr. Rădescu after the September 9 meeting, that this matter should not have appeared in the minutes of that meeting.[89]

The basic reasons for the schism within the committee appear in a letter entitled "The End" signed on September 14, 1950, by Rădescu, Caranfil, Fărcăşanu and Gafencu. It was sent to the other members of the Committee on October 4, 1950. After first briefly reviewing the important steps that led to establishing the RNC's operating agreements, the writers state their decision to resign from the Committee based on a letter sent to General Petre-Lazăr on September 4, 1950. Contrary to the RNC's operational by-laws, the provisions in the letter had gone against the members' decisions and had led to a revision of the by-laws and the breaking of relations among the members. Following this internal RNC crisis, the letter's signers cite the reasons for their decision to resign, mentioning a series of issues and disputes:

> … in the desire to ensure fruitful and harmonious cooperation in the Committee, we requested that the person of the President be respected, who, as His Majesty the King himself indicated, enjoys great popularity in the country by virtue of his age and his past history; and as the last Romanian Prime Minister he has the respect of the Romanian public and government. The undersigned also requested, in the desire to give the National Committee a representative and national character, that it be completed and invigorated by adding new and valuable elements. Thus, we proposed expanding the Committee in order to ensure fair and real representation of all the democratic parties, and which would encompass politicians who have recently left the country as well as others who, through their merits, have proved to be particularly useful to our national cause.[90]

The idea of expanding the Committee by incorporating a larger political and national representation is elaborated on by Aurel S. Marinescu in the first volume of *A Contribution to the History of the Roma-*

nian Exile. According to Marinescu, among those who were dissatisfied that they had not been recruited to be part of the RNC was Emil Ghilezan, for whom a new position of general secretary of the Committee was specially created in February 1950.[91] At the same time, the position of military counselor was created for Major Bazil Rațiu, who was later replaced by General Puiu Petrescu. Willy Filderman, the former president of the Jewish Community of Romania, was also dissatisfied with not being recruited by the Committee, as was Carol Citta Davilla, a former member of the Romanian Legation in Washington. Davilla was not admitted on the pretext that he was involved in financial fraud and sympathized with the Soviets. Viorel V. Tilea, a former member of the Romanian legation in London, was also not on the list of Committee members. Tilea was suspected of sympathizing with King Carol II and was a declared enemy of Iuliu Maniu.[92] There is no documentation to support Marinescu's statements about this list. But there were definitely discussions among the Committee members regarding naming Vintilă Brătianu to the position vacated by the death of Niculescu-Buzești, who had been appointed as a representative of the National Peasant's Party together with Bianu and Popa. But as Brătianu was a member of the Liberty Party, the other two Peasant members initially delayed acting on this proposal and then rejected it, arguing that the by-laws had to be modified in order to accept it. For his part, Fărcășanu, the only representative of the Liberty Party on the Committee, joined other members in supported the naming of Brătianu, arguing that: "The National Liberty Party is insufficiently represented numerically on the Committee, and this situation is to the disadvantage of cooperation both among the representatives of the political parties and between the members of the Committee."[93]

The writers of the September 14 letter also asked "that all available financial means be gathered under the control of the Committee and be made available to it. We requested that all available amounts that originated in public funds and were currently in the possession of some members of the Committee [referring to the fund retained by Cretzianu] or of some former public clerks, be brought to the Committee to be used exclusively for the purposes shown in the by-laws and according to the decisions of the Committee."[94]

The letter ends on a pessimistic note that would put an end to the Committee after just one year and four months of operation: "After all that has been demonstrated, the undersigned take note that the National Committee, formed based on the act of April 6, 1949, has ceased to exist. There is no other political foundation and no statuary right that would allow a group of members to hold discussions and make decisions in the name of the National Committee."[95]

Another factor that perpetrated the split took place the month before the "The End" letter, when President Rădescu repeatedly refused to convoke a meeting of the Committee. Willing to reach a solution and with the support of the royal house, Cretzianu, Popa and Vișoianu addressed a letter to Rădescu on August 26, formally asking him to convoke the Committee. He replied on August 29 through general secretary Ghilezan, that he could not honor their request. On August 31, Cretzianu renewed the request, informing him that in case of another refusal, according to the operating by-laws, the Committee meeting would have to be convoked within 10 days of the date of the request.[96] That same day, the request was transmitted verbatim to the other members, Gafencu, Caranfil, Fărcășanu, Zissu and Bianu. Gafencu, Fărcășanu and Caranfil supported Rădescu's refusal to agree to convoke a meeting on September 9.

The report written by General Secretary Ghilezan after the September 9 RNC meeting, which was eventually forced to convene, reveals more behind the scene details about the division. In a letter to Vișoianu on October 2, 1950, Ghilezan expressed his indignation that the minutes that had initially been written based on notes taken during the meeting had been altered.[97]Ghilezan wrote that his minutes showed that:"during the following days Mr. A. Popa and C. Visoianu would follow the reconciliation proceedings decided upon in the morning meeting, towards Mr. N. Caranfil and M. Fărcășanu." He writes that he noted that, following a meeting of Popa and Vișoianu with Rădescu, Rădescu declared that he was ready to discuss ways to apply Lazăr's letters of August 10 and September 4, on condition that expanding the number of RNC members and making the funds in individual members' possession available to the Committee also be discussed.[98]

The altered version of the minutes specified:"Mr. Popa and Vișoianu inform the Committee about the negative result of these meetings [theirs with Rădescu and Vișoianu's with Gafencu]. Mr. General Rădescu and Gr. Gafencu maintained their refusal to participate in the Committee operations within the provisions of the royal letters.[99]

The second part of the September 9 meeting discussed naming Crihan to fill Buzești's position and Ghilezan's decision to resign as general secretary was also noted. The altered minutes do not specify the real reasons for Ghilezan's resignation or the point of view of the Political Parties Council regarding naming Crihan and increasing the number of Committee members:

> The Committee takes note of this [Popa's] communication [naming Crihan to succeed Buzești] and decides, unanimously, to forward it to His Majesty the King for approval.
> ... Mr. Em. Ghilezan presents his resignation from the position of General Secretary, declaring that his resignation is motivated by internal Peasant's Party matters, of which he is a member. He requests the naming of a successor.[100]

Ghilezan's letter to Vișoianu clearly shows the reasons for his resignation, as well as who authorized the alterations of the minutes, which were sent to the king, who would make the final decision on the reorganization. Ghilezan writes that after Popa's proposal of Crihan as Buzești's successor was accepted, he presented his resignation as secretary general:

> My resignation was and is motivated by the fact that the proposition to recruit Mr. A. Crihan is not in conformity with the decision of the National Peasant's Party, which conditioned it on the simultaneous recruitment of other leaders of Romanian democratic political parties.

> My resignation was also motivated by the fact that the proposition is not in agreement with the decision of the Political Parties Council, which I am part of, since the Council, in its turn, subscribed completely to the National Peasant's Party's decision. I considered and still consider that disregarding the decisions of these organizations not only abuses the terms of the by-laws but could also cause severe prejudice to the political organizations that constitute the Political Parties Council and inestimable trouble within them.
>
> When I received, in New York, the minutes containing the alterations I describe above, I called Mr. Naum Ionescu on the phone to ask for explanations. He put me through to Mr. Al. Cretzianu, who, at my question regarding the last alteration, communicated that: "You do not have a deliberative vote in the Committee… according to the procedures, the minutes should record what we want it to… if you wish you can address a letter to the National Committee, but you cannot alter the minutes."[101]

On October 9, 11 and 13, 1950, a now-smaller number of members participated in a post-split RNC meeting. After noting the "resignation out of their own free will" of Rădescu, Caranfil, Fărcăşanu and Gafencu, the Committee unanimously proposed to King Michael that he name Vişoianu as RNC president to replace Rădescu.[102] On the Peasant Party's advice, the king did so, after which they filled the other vacancies. Crihan took Buzeşti's place as a "representative of Bessarabia", and Gh. Aassan was recruited to fill Fărcăşanu's place. At the first meeting after the naming of the new president, at Vişoianu's suggestion, the Committee decided to ask King Michael to approve the continued use of the name "Romanian National Committee".[103]

After a period of inactivity after leaving the RNC, on November 27, 1950, Rădescu founded a new Romanian organization in exile called the "Association of Free Romanians in the United States of America", headquartered in New York. Rădescu's purpose was to draw other elements from the exile groups to this organization in order to isolate and weaken the RNC. Rădescu was president of the new organization, and four counselors, a secretary and a treasurer were elected from among the 19 members.[104] Although there were some disagreements between the two organizations, they began to collaborate successfully starting in the summer of 1954, when the Assembly of Captive European Nations was first constituted. Due to the good offices of Raoul Bossy, former Romanian ambassador to Rome and Berlin, and also to the spirit of cooperation and understanding fostered by Vişoianu, the leaders of the two Romanian exile groups presented a united delegation to ACEN that proved to be a most valuable ACEN asset.[105]

Aware that the RNC's prestige had declined among Romanian exiles as a result of the September 1950 schism, Vişoianu attempted to develop the Committee's relations with the other Romanian associations and organizations in order to bring in new elements to strengthen the RNC's position with the Free Europe Committee. At its January 18, 1951, meeting, the RNC discussed Vişoianu's idea of strengthening ties with Romanian-American organizations and Vişoianu took on the task of contacting people who might constitute a council of action for the liberation of Romania. This council would be formed of representatives of the Romanian-American National Committee, the Union and League of the Societies of Romanian-Americans, the Orthodox-, Greek-Catholic and Baptist churches, United Roumanian-Jews and the organization of Romanian-American women, in addition to RNC representatives.[106] The new council's purpose was to support the liberation of Romania by appearing at American forums and influencing public opinion in the US.

The year 1955 brought new changes in the RNC's composition, with the inclusion of new members. In addition to Crihan, who had been proposed by the old committee, George Assan, Alexandru Bunescu, Dimitrie N. Ciotori, Sabin Manuilă and Mihai Răutu were brought in. After taking the oath to the king,[107] the new committee informed the Free Europe Committee representative, Cloyce K. Huston, about the responsibilities of each new member and about the Committee's activities with Radio Free Europe.[108]

The composition of the Committee changed again in 1959, when Ionescu resigned as general secretary and was replaced by Ion Vardala, who served in that capacity until spring 1975. The reduction in the number of Committee members reduced the group's activities as well, which is reflected in the reports and minutes issued after 1970. In 1973 Ion Stere joined the Committee as secretary and Miron Butariu as treasurer, joining Vișoainu, Popa, Bunescu and Vardala. Because of financial difficulties resulting from the 1971 disbanding of the Free Europe Committee and the loss of their principal funding, the Committee moved its headquarters, and after March 1973 continued its operations in an apartment made available by Ion Stere, where its archive was located.[109] In April 1974 Vișoianu traveled to Geneva, where he met King Michael to discuss, among other things, the problem of expanding the Committee through naming new members. Even after their meeting, Vișoianu continued to send requests to the king on that topic.[110]

King Michael's interview with Mircea Ciobanu also addresses that issue:

> Vișoianu was asking us to reinvigorate the National Committee; people were growing old, they were losing their strength for action. In 1972, Vișoianu presented the Committee's crisis to me, the difficult conditions they had to work in, the cessation of support from the Free Europe Committee, the need to recruit new members. The criteria [for membership] were very much to their disadvantage: 1. Only people who had not obtained foreign citizenship were able to be active – a great number of capable Romanians had received foreign citizenship and were eliminated from being considered; 2. [members needed] To have a job … since the Committee could not provide compensation; 3. The moral criteria.[111]

Vișoianu made a desperate attempt to save the Committee by asking Professor Brutus Coste to take the initiative in forming an exiles' action committee.[112] But with Popa's death on November 1, 1974, Vișoianu was forced to consider ending the Committee's activities, a decision he would implement a few months later.[113]

The Romanian National Committee's Activities

In addition to naming its representatives, one of the main points on the RNC agenda for October 26 and 27, 1949, was the organization of Committee activity outside the United States. It was decided that this would be done through representatives, delegates and correspondents. In countries that would recognize the RNC delegates' official status as representatives of Romania, they would bear the title of chargé d'affaires. Representatives were named for England, France, Greece and Turkey. Delegates were named for Argentina, Belgium, Brazil, Canada, Chile, Cuba, Switzerland, Israel, Holland, Peru, Portugal, Spain, Venezuela and other countries. Delegates and correspondents were named only for Austria, Germany and Italy.[114]

An official document outlining their responsibilities was sent to all RNC representatives abroad.[115] Among their obligations and tasks were:

> 1. In the political arena, the person appointed would be the Committee's representative for that country's government and local authorities, as well as for the Romanians in that country who did not acknowledge the Communist Government in Bucharest;
> 2. In the area of foreign propaganda, the mission was to organize and lead actions to inform public opinion in that country on all Romanian matters. For this purpose, the objective was to establish good contacts with journalists, press agencies and radio stations;
> 3. Regarding the area of propaganda in Romania, it was decided that in countries with radio stations broadcasting programs in Romanian (London, Paris, Rome, Istanbul, Athens, Madrid, etc.), the representative would stay in constant touch with the Romanian department of those stations in order to formulate suggestions and critiques as well as to gather materials to be presented for Romania's listeners. In addition, the representatives would use any means possible to smuggle RNC publications into Romania.
> 4. In the field of public information, the representative had the duty of informing the Committee in detail about the political and eco-

nomic situation of the country he was in. He would also organize the gathering and classifying of all information about Romania from the available newspapers and magazines published in Romania and the official bulletin of the RNC, as well as bulletins of the press agencies and radio stations and declarations from persons who had recently come from Romania. The representative would also gather from refugees recently arrived from Romania information regarding ways to escape, the method they had used, details regarding border security and control, what sort of units and formations ensured border security and what means they used to do so. Starting on March 15, 1950, the Committee used such information to publish a bi-monthly *Information Bulletin.*[116] Initially published in Romanian, at Cretzianu's suggestion this appeared in English starting with issue No. 14 in October 1950 and was distributed to various publications and members of the US Congress.[117] These bulletins represented the real situation in Romania through the complex and detailed information gathered by the representatives, and created a list of credible information provided a foundation for the Romanian exiles' continued activities.

5. Together with the areas listed above, refugees' protection and assistance was a major objective of the representatives, who were responsible for the census of all the Romanian refugees in their region. Individual files were created that were required to include the refugee's military experience and skills. These were sent to the Committee to be used later in the fight for Romania's liberation. Cretzianu suggested that the RNC consider providing each representative with assistance from a Consultative Council formed of Romanian exiles in a given country, who would bring forward their problems and needs.[118]In addition, the representative would work with local social assistance organizations and the administration in order to help the Romanian refugees. There was a particular focus on Romanian students, for whom the RNC would try to obtain scholarships and financial aid from the local government, universities and/or organizations.[119]

Nomination of the RNC representatives to serve outside the United States was based on professional criteria and not political ones. Most of those named had been businessmen or diplomats in the Romanian Foreign Ministry before 1947. The first nominations were presented to King Michael for approval on December 1, 1950: in Belgium – Alexandru Stănescu, former consul in Brussels; in Brazil – Comandor Ion Economu, former naval attaché in Turkey, having Ed Ressel and Mircea Bunescu as his assistants; in Chile – Henry Helefant, who had been commercial counselor in Madrid; in Peru – Grigore Cugler, former legation secretary in Sweden; in Portugal – Alexandru Totescu, former chargé d'affaires in Lisbon; and in Turkey – Aurel Decei, former cultural attaché in Istanbul.[120]

The nominations continued in 1951. In a letter to King Michael on February 2, 1951, Vişoianu and Cretzianu asked him to approve these new nominations: in England – Cornel Bianu, RNC member and deputy representative, assisted by Grigore Constantinescu, former minister in Teheran and first counselor of the Romanian legation in the United Kingdom; in Canada – Niculae Timiraş, former chargé d'affaires in the Vatican; and in Venezuela – Petre Maxim, legation secretary.[121] After the February 26 and 27 meetings and after seeing the reports from the representatives who had been named the previous year, the Committee proposed additional nominations to King Michael. Thus, Nicolae Petrescu-Comnen, former foreign affairs minister and Romanian minister was proposed as representative to the Vatican, and Miron Giuroiu, former legation secretary in Sweden, for Stockholm. Professor Virgil Veniamin was named for Paris. Together with other Romanian professors, Veniamin would be responsible for the reopening of Carol I University. In Germany, the Committee proposed Raoul Bossy, who had been legation chief in Berlin from 1941–1943; and in Buenos Aires, Argentina C. Vălimarescu.[122] Vălimarescu's nomination was reviewed at the April 18, 1951, meeting, as was G. Anastasiu's nomination in Switzerland, and Traian Gallin's in Bonn. Gallin was former general consul in Lwow, Hamburg and Bern. To further consolidate relations with the state of Israel, and taking into account that many Romanian Jews had left Romania after World War II, Vişoianu consulted Wilhelm Fildermann, the former president of the Jewish Community of Romania, to find the right candidate for the RNC position in Israel.[123]

Additional representatives were nominated in the second half of 1951, especially in order to develop relations with the Mediterranean countries, which had absorbed a considerable number of Romanian exiles and had a special connection with the Roman and Greek Catholics from Romania. According to statistics and information received from Romania, Catholics were subject to unprecedented persecution by the Communist authorities in Bucharest. The RNC asked King Michael to consider the nomination of Radu Scarlat Arion, former chargé d'affaires in Athens, as a representative in Greece; and Vladimir Ionescu, former general consul in Florence, and Canonic Tăut as deputy members in Italy, namely the Vatican. In Rome Ionescu was going to cooperate with Lazăr Schineanu, who was in charge of the Romanian programs of Radio Rome.[124] In West Germany, the Committee decided to name one more representative in addition to Gallin, Minister Constantin Hiott. The decision to have two representatives resulted from the foundation and operation there of multiple associations established by Romanian exiles and a great wave of Saxon and Székely repatriates from Transylvania, who considered themselves Romanians.[125] The situation in Spain proved a bit delicate because after the Committee had originally proposed Constantin Antoniade as representative, the Spanish government acknowledged de facto Niculae Dimitrescu, former minister of Romania in Madrid, as the most qualified person for this position. The Committee eventually agreed on this nomination, after receiving a message from the Spanish ambassador in London that his government was ready to receive a representative of King Michael in Madrid.[126] Beginning in fall 1952, the Committee started to cooperate with the United Nations as well, appointing Sabin Manuilă as its representative.[127]

Very few details are known about the RNC representatives' activities abroad. From its inception, the RNC monthly and annual budgets had included finances for their work abroad. In the finance committee's budget projections for October 1949, $3,100 was allocated for expenses outside the US.[128] The Committee also financed the Information Bulletins, which contained information the representatives gleaned about the internal situation in Romania. In 1952 the RNC specified in its annual activity report:

> The activity of the National Committee in Washington was doubled by its representatives in the European and South-American capitals. They did their best to maintain contact with the local governments, with the media groups, and also dealt with the administrative assistance of Romanian refugees. Several representatives, especially those in France, Turkey and Greece, sent precious information to the National Committee about the evolution of the political and economic situation in Romania. The information was gathered from persons who have recently left Romania.[129]

In 1957 when the Free Europe Committee's funding for the RNC was reduced, the representatives started to face financial and logistic problems,[130] but in spite of the difficulties, they continued to fulfill their mandate. Thus, Veniamin, the representative in Paris, arranged in November 1958 for two T-Deums to be held on the king's name day, one at the Orthodox Church and the other one at the Uniate Church in Paris. On the anniversary of Maniu's condemnation, Veniamin gave two talks, one broadcast on Radio Free Europe and the other on Radio Paris. He also attended the ACEN meetings and those at the Franco-Austrian Cultural Center, where he spoke about the problem of refugees in neutral countries. He also had various contacts with the representative of the High Commissioner for Refugees, Henry Tremaud, and with the French authorities. He discussed with them the situation of the elderly refugees who would be admitted to a newly-created old age home in the south of France.[131]

Ed Ressel, the RNC representative in Brazil, organized a protest against the acceptance at the United Nations of the Hungarian Communist delegation's credentials. He secured an audience with the Brazilian foreign minister, to whom he submitted a memorandum on this question. In Greece, representative Arion saw many public figures and numerous Greek refugees who had been expelled from Romania in the fall of 1958 and were able to give him interesting news and reliable information concerning that country. He assisted many of them in their appeals to the Greek Red Cross and the American authorities. He also attended meetings at the Ministry of Health and Welfare with respect to aid and food parcels to be sent to Romania.[132]

Despite the ongoing financial difficulties, in late 1958 the representatives abroad continued to carry out their usual duties, including providing information for the newspaper *Romania*. In Buenos Aires, Radu Cutzarida, together with former Romanian ambassador Vălimarescu and former Romanian consul Titu Mihăilescu, had an audience on December 3 with the under secretary of state of Argentina's Foreign Office and with the director for political affairs. The purpose of the meeting was to discuss blocking the acceptance of the Hungarian Communist delegation at the United Nations. Their intervention was successful, and Argentina's UN delegate was instructed to support any motion to refuse the Hungarians' credentials and in general to vote for any motion blocking Communist actions. Also during December, Cutzarida attended various meetings of the Romanian colony in Argentina, distributed gifts for needy Romanian children at a Christmas celebration at the Romanian Church and secured an entrance visa to Argentina for a Romanian Orthodox priest who would officiate at the Greek Orthodox Church built in Buenos Aires by a wealthy member of the Romanian colony.[133]

In Rio de Janeiro, Ressel was decorated by the Brazilian Red Cross for his activity as president of the Association of Refugees in Brazil. Together with the Brazilian Red Cross, from 1945 on this association provided assistance to more than one million refugees from behind the Iron Curtain.[134] On March 15, 1959, Cutzarida participated at the laying in Buenos Aires of the corner stone of South America's first Greek-Orthodox Church.[135] Together with Mihăilescu, Cutzarida, a former press counselor in Argentine, initiated a campaign denouncing the RPR delegation in Buenos Aires for espionage. In consequence, the Romanian cultural attaché and the Soviet first counselor were declared persona non grata by the Argentine government and had to leave the country.[136]

The representatives' gathering and sharing of propaganda materials from the Bucharest government was facilitated through the relations and trust they were accorded by the associations of Romanian exiles and the local authorities. In his May 1959 report to the Committee, Radu Arion provided information about the propaganda initiated by the Romanian Communist government through its legation in Athens:

> Persons now living in Greece who once served the Romanian State and therefore have a right to an old age pension have to go in person to the Legation with the requisite papers to prove their rights; delegates from claimants living in distant localities are also admitted. Through this stratagem, the RPR Legation seeks to know the whereabouts and activity of the many Romanians living now in Greece and to bribe them with the above mentioned pension. This propaganda action is very ingenious."[137]

During all of 1959 and the beginning of the next year, the Committee received reports about its representatives' activities in the important European and South American capitals, most notably those of the representation in Paris.

A focal point of Romanian exile and RNC activity in France was the development of a cultural nucleus in the capital that would be dedicated to the preservation and continuation of the Romanian spirit, unspoiled by communist propaganda and ideology. Beginning in 1950, all Parisian-Romanian cultural life was concentrated around the Carol I University Foundation. It had been created in March 1895[138]at the initiative of King Carol I but was closed by the Communist regime through Decree 136 of 1948. For the Royal House and the young King Michael the Carol I Foundation was a symbol of the perpetuation of the monarchy and its identification with all that was holier and nobler, the Romanian people. Much affected by the Communists' measures to close the foundation, King Michael asked the RNC to analyze the possibility of forming a similar institution in Paris.[139]

For the second time in its history, the French capital was to host a "forty-eighters generation" of Romanian intellectuals who considered

Paris their second spiritual home.[140] With the support of the entire Romanian elite, Veniamin and Professor Petre Sergescu planned torevive the Carol I University Foundation[141] with the aim of helping Romanian students who were studying in the French capital, and in 1959 they would organize the first congress of Romanian intellectuals.[142]

At its December 21, 1949, meeting, the RNC approved re-establishing the Foundation and allocated 7 million French Francs from the Alexandru Totescu Fund, also known as the Lisbon Fund (detailed below under Financial Resources of the RNC). The funds were managed by Totescu according to payment orders issued by the Committee. The majority was to be used to establish the Carol I University Foundation in Paris, but also the funds were partly to cover grants to Romanian students in Paris[143] for the university year January 1, 1951, to January 1, 1952.

A commission made up of Fărcăşanu, Popa and the general secretary was charged with presenting plans for the Foundation's organization and realization, in cooperation with the Paris Association of Professors, of which Petre Sergescu was president.[144]At the September 9, 1950, meeting, the new National Committee submitted a few propositions to King Michael for approval, among them the naming of a commission composed of Professors Constantin Marinescu, Sergescu and Veniamin that would prepare the Foundation's by-laws and operating procedures.[145] In a letter of November 16, 1950, Veniamin announced Sergescu, Basil Munteanu and Marinescu as the members of the Foundation's executive committee and proposed G. Ciorănescu as secretary.[146] Noting Veniamin's announcement, at the November 22 meeting the Committee submitted for the king's approval his list and the tasks for which the proposed executive committee was responsible.[147]

After the final details regarding the opening of the Foundation were settled, the University Foundation Committee analyzed, two months later, the matter of the Romanian Studies Institute at the Sorbonne University, which had been functioning for more than 10 years and until 1943 had been called the Romanian Philology Institute. When the funding provided to it by Romania ceased, the RNC, through Rădescu, provided funds for its operation for a period of two years. In a letter from Sergescu to Vişoianu dated February 16, 1951, the president of the Committee was asked to allocate 200,000 French Francs to support the institute.[148] The Committee approved the request at the February 27 meeting, stipulating that the amount be taken from the budget of the Carol I Foundation.[149]

With the agreement of the financial commission, the RNC, and President Vişoianu, in January–February 1951 Totescu would transfer FF 2,650,000 to the University Foundation account that had been opened at the Société Général bank. On March 6, 1951, Totescu transferred an additional FF 1,600,000[150] and on June 2, FF 1,250,000.[151] These funds would ensure the Foundation's budget until 1955. The first signs that the Lisbon Fund was diminishing appeared in 1953, when Totescu had about $30,000 left under his management. During the November 11, 1953, Committee meeting, Vişoianu notified King Michael of the Foundation's critical financial situation and of the procedures to be followed in order to clear the amount remainingin the fund managed by Totescu.[152] Towards the end of 1955, the Lisbon Fund was depleted and no funds remained to cover the budget of the Carol I University Foundation in Paris[153]or to support financially other projects started by the Committee. From then on, although theoretically it was directed by the National Committee, the Carol I University Foundation functioned independently until January 1974, when it ceased all activity due to lack of funds.

Another highlight of Veniamin's tenure was that due to his efforts, along with Gheorghe Răut, president of the Cultural Association of the Romanian Church in Paris, the Romanian Orthodox Church reopened in Paris in 1951.[154]

After prestigious activity during almost two decades in the service of Romanian exiles in Paris, in January 1974 Veniamin resigned from his position as president of Carol I Foundation and implicitly, his position as RNC representative. His resignation was accepted after French counterintelligence services discovered that he was working as an agent for the RPR embassy, to which he had given information about exiles for six years.[155] After his resignation, the activities of the RNC representative in France were continued by Constantin Amăriuţei, together with the Korne-Filitti group of friends, who, among other things, would continue publication of the Committee newspaper, *La Nation Roumaine*.[156]

Romanian Refugee Assistance, and Cooperation with other National Committees in the United States

In addition to its regular meetings, the Committee's activities in the US consisted of conferences, occasional programs on radio stations, declarations, memorandums to the United Nations, cooperation with other national committees from the US and Western Europe and with ACEN, and gathering and editing materials about the communist governments in the RPR and USSR. From its inception, the Committee concentrated on diplomacy and propaganda, initiating a few types of actions, such as assistance for refugees from Romania, writing reports that would present the real situation in Romania, and cooperating with the committees that represented other countries under the influence of the Soviet Union.

The refugees and deportees from Romania immediately after 1947 were one of the Committee's main preoccupations beginning in 1949, when the desperate situation of Romanian refugees in Paris, Rome and Geneva prompted some Committee members to suggest providing immediate assistance through the Totescu Fund. During the September 26–27, 1949, meeting, Rădescu brought forward an August 31 appeal from the Committee of Assistance to Romanians in Paris requesting $2,500 for urgent needs. Also brought forward at this meeting was a September 8 letter from N. Caranfil asking the Committee to consider providing food and clothing to the families of the fighters who were imprisoned or had disappeared. The finance sub-committee was authorized to take up to $1,500 from the Lisbon fund and arrange for it to be distributed through several specialized agencies, maintaining the greatest secrecy about the sender and recipients.[157]

Thus, on October 28 the Committee applied to the State Department to intervene on behalf of the Romanians refugees in Yugoslavia. A sort of agreement had been reached between the International Red Cross and the authorities in Belgrade, according to which hospitalized Romanians who possessed visas for Western countries had the authorization to leave Yugoslavia, and those without visas would have a blind eyed turned when they passed the frontier clandestinely. Nonetheless, the RNC had information that it was still the case that people considered "fascist" or "in the service of imperialist capitalism" were sent back to Romania. The Committee applied to the US government to intervene with Yugoslavia to end such procedures.[158]

Another delicate matter the RNC brought to the attention of the State Department was the situation of refugees who could not be registered on the lists of the International Refugees' Organization (IRO), which was going to be liquidated on June 1, 1950. According to its provisions, refugees who applied after October 15, 1949, could not be registered. This would impact Romanian refugees who had left Romania from July through October 1948 and had been detained by the Yugoslavian authorities. Those who reached Trieste, the free zone, after October 15 would not being accepted by the IRO authorities in Italy. The Committee proposed two solutions to the US government. One was that the IRO in Italy be authorized to handle these cases directly, and another was to make an agreement with the International Red Cross to take these refugees under its protection.[159]

In addition to assisting refugees in the United States, the RNC also had relations with the Romanian refugee organizations in Western Europe. When he visited Italy in 1956, Popa wrote in his report presented to the National Committee at the November 14 meeting, he met with representatives of the Romanian refugees in Rome. Monsegnieur C. Capros, the head of the Vatican department that dealt with assistance for Romanians, told him that 312 refugees located in 8 cities were listed in his registers. In addition, in Italy there were about 22,000 "Italians" repatriated from Romania, most of whom were Romanized and were Romanian citizens who had organized into the "Association of Italian Refugees from Romania", whose president was Antonio Dozzi. Popa also learned that over 300 copies of the Committee's newspaper, *Romania*, were distributed among the members of that association.[160]

Popa arrived in Germany on October 9, 1956, where he had contacts with the leaders of the Free Europe Committee and the Romanian department of Radio Free Europe and later with German authorities and the leaders of the organizations of German refugees from Romania, as well as with the leaders of the Romanian organizations in Germany. Among the German public figures Popa met in Munich were a Dr. Wagner, a member of the Bavarian parliament (born in Bucovina), Prof. Hans Koch, principal of the East-European Institute, Hans Hartl, a famous journalist (born in Transylvania), and the leaders of the organizations of Germans born in Romania, namely Blass and Hans Prelitsch, brothers from the Landsmannschaft der Bukovinaer Deutschen, and a Mr. Plesch, the spokesperson of the Saxons from Transylvania.[161]

In Bonn, Popa met with Minister Teodor Oberlaender of the Ministry of Refugees, with whom he discussed the problems facing Romanian refugees in Germany. He also had meetings with the leaders of different organizations of Romanian refugees from Germany, among them George Racoveanu, the president of the Free Romanians Association from Germany, founded in 1955comprised of more than 2,500 Romanian refugees, and Colonel Alexandrescu, Virgil Popa, and Aureliu Lepadatu.[162]

One of the RNC's most daring projects was to found a military organization, a Romanian army in exile. The idea was that of General Dumitru Petrescu, who had consulted with Rădescu when he visited Europe in September 1949. In a memorandum written on November 14, 1949, in Paris, Petrescu refers to the number of Romanian refugees with professional military experience, a few hundred persons, and also mentions that "the president of the Romanian National Committee ordered the establishment of a 'Military Headquarters' in Paris, with the mission of studying and proposing the organization of the Romanian military element, as far as the situation and the current financial means allow."[163] This military organization would function according to the laws and regulations of the Romanian Army established on March 6, 1945, and would be under King Michael as supreme commander. The proposed monthly budget of this organization appeared at the end of the memorandum: FF 117,000 a month for regular expenses, as well as a permanent fund of FF 90,000 for temporary financial assistance for those serving in the military.[164]

Rădescu brought the memorandum to the attention of the RNC members at the November 28–29 meeting. They eventually agreed to analyze its content in a subsequent meeting.[165] Because of the crises within the Committee, the discussion was not resumed until November 13–14, 1950, when the members also asked the king's opinion on appointing Petrescu to head the military organization.[166] After the king's positive response, the Committee also considered the possibility that there would be local difficulties with the title "military organization" and agreed it would be more appropriate to call it a "Military Science Society".[167] There is little information about military actions taken after this decision, and the forming of military units in exile never materialized.

For many East European exiles, New York was the Mecca of their hopes for liberating European countries from Soviet domination, and the place where the candle of freedom burned in the hearts of those who still hoped to go back to their home countries. The dreams of the great Eastern European democratic politicians started to be realized in New York through alliances and agreements that had the coordinated mission of bringing down the Iron Curtain. That common mission is why, since the first months of its operation, the Committee developed very close relations with the other National Committees and international organizations.

The onset of the Cold War created a vacuum of information about Eastern Europe and dealing with the tragedies and rigors of life under the Soviet system. That is why the first measure taken by the NCFE was to organize, coordinate and distribute news and articles about the countries behind the Iron Curtain to the US media. The RNC appointed Cretzianu and Teodor Trancu as its representatives for relations with the NCFE and the other National Committees and to the meetings that began in September 1949. At these meetings, the NCFE noted that information about Romania, Bulgaria and Poland was almost nonexistent in the US media and proposed that those countries' committees delegate press representatives to establish relationships with the US mass media in order to provide information about their countries of origin.[168]

On September 17, 1949, Vişoianu represented the RNC at a reception organized by Peter Zenkl, president of the Czechoslovak National Committee, in honor of the members of the Albanian National Committee, which had recently been formed under the presidency of Midhat Frasheri. Representatives of the Free Czechoslovakia Committee (Zenkl and vice-president Lieutenant Lettrich) and the Hungary National Council's delegation (President Bela Varga and members Ferenc Nagy, Tibor Eckhardt and Baron Bakach Bessenyey) joined with the RNC representatives on the tenth anniversary of the beginning of World War II to express their solidarity with the efforts of the US administration to fight for Eastern Europe's liberation. RNC representatives Cretzianu and Fărcăşanu also participated in September 1949 at the Arlington National Cemetery's annual ceremony, together with Bulgarian National Committee representative General Marin Pundev, its secretary, Constantin Fotitch, former ambassador of Yugoslavia in Washington, Michael Kwapiczewski, representing Jan Ciechanowski, former ambassador of Poland in the United States, Vladko Machek, head of the Croatian Peasant's Party, representing the Agricultural International Union, and Mr. Adamczyk, representing the workers from Eastern Europe.[169]

Beginning in the fall of 1949, the NCFE organized a series of anticommunist conferences in New York aimed at the American public and sustained by the leaders of the National Committees active in the US. On November 8, 1949, the NCFE presented a series of anti-communist speeches in New York's Town Hall at which Grigore Gafencu, former foreign minister of Romania, spoke on the topic "Communism versus Man". Other speakers were Stanisław Mikolajczik, former prime minister of Poland, Stefan Osusky, former minister of Czechoslovakia in Paris, G. N. Dimitroff, president of the Bulgarian National Committee, Bela Fabian, member of the Hungarian National Council, Arthur Bliss Lane, former ambassador of the United States in Poland, and Professor George Counts from Columbia University.[170]

On the occasion of starting its work in October 1951, the Conference of National Committees and Councils of Central and Eastern European Countries and Diplomatic Representatives of the Baltic States and their National Committees reiterated its special collaboration with the NCFE, underlining that:

> We are fully convinced, moreover, that such a collaboration would also be of the greatest advantage to the NCFE in its own endeavors. The NCFE can at all times find in the Conference the source of the best available knowledge and understanding of the state of our countries' spirit, of susceptibilities and trends as they develop among our several peoples. The powerful means available to the NCFE, backed with this knowledge and understanding, may be relied upon to result in the most appropriate and efficacious action at all times.[171]

One of Vişoianu's main preoccupations was to form a group that would represent all the countries under Soviet control. In order to strengthen the solidarity among political exiles from East-Central Europe, on February 11, 1951, 168 exile leaders gathered at Independence Hall in Philadelphia, Pennsylvania, where they signed a Declaration of the Aims and Principles of Liberation of the Central and Eastern European Peoples affirming the right of the subjugated peoples to freedom and democracy.

After long preliminary negotiations, the Assembly of Captive European Nations (ACEN) came into existence in the summer of 1954 when, under the guidance of the Exiles Relation Department of the Free Europe Committee (the FEC, i.e., the recently renamed NCFE), the political exiles from East-Central Europe reached an agreement. ACEN's formation can be considered a success because 160 exiles, divided by all kinds of personal antagonisms and political opinions, formed an organization to represent the desire of a hundred million people to be free and to expose the Kremlin's ruthlessness to world opinion. To the public at large and the news media, ACEN was nonetheless a "True Voice of the Enslaved People", or the "Little United Nations". One of ACEN's aims was "to work for the liberation from the Communist dictatorship and Soviet domination of the nine captive nations...to affirm the right of the CN [captive nations] to be represented in the U.N. and to strive, to preserve and foster democratic ideals in the hearts and minds of the enslaved peoples."[172]

Starting in 1954, the RNC's activity was mainly conducted in agreement with the other committees and various RNC representatives active in ACEN, among them Brutus Coste, general secretary of ACEN (1955–1965)[173] and Miron Butariu, treasurer and accountant (1954–1972).[174]

On September 26, 1949, British Foreign Minister Ernest Bevin gave a speech in the UN General Assembly that caused confusion and tension for the RNC and other National Committees. He repeated his view that he would be ready to buy the security of Western Europe by sacrificing the East to Russia. Detailing the acts of aggression committed by the Soviet Union in the satellite countries, he admitted at the end of his talk, "if all these represent the price of peace, we have to admit it is a very high price."[175] In a letter to Minister Bevin dated October 8, 1949, the RNC reminded him of the permanent rights and interests of the Romanian nation and asked Great Britain once again for its support for the liberation of Romania.

Also in October 1949, the RNC aired its opinion regarding the discussion of human rights violations in Romania with the UN General Assembly in a report titled "Suppression of Human Rights in Rumania". Several copies were sent to each delegation on the occasion of hearings held throughout October by the Ad-Hoc Political Commission and the United Nations General Assembly on a resolution presented by the US, Canada and Bolivia regarding the violation of human rights and liberties in Romania, Bulgaria and Hungary.[176] The RNC report was very well received and commended as "extremely well organized and valuable and quite handsomely produced."[177] The Romanian delegation's report had a huge impact in the US media, including an article by Anne O'Hare McCormick in the October 17 issue of the *New York Times*. At the request of Representative John Lodge, on October 18, 1949, that article was inserted into the Congressional Record, the official bulletin of the US Congress.[178]

In 1950, the RNC sent four reports to the UN General Assembly. One of these, written by Vișoianu and dated October 1, exposing the

USSR's violations of international rights and treaties. The others, put together by Cretzianu, Popa and Zissu, addressed the prisoners of war detained in the USSR and the request for establishment of international legal revue for political refugees. The following year, the RNC again sent similar reports to the General Assembly. On October 19, 1951, the Central and Eastern European Conference, the collaborative organ of the National Committees and Councils, presented a memorandum to the United Nations and its member nations concerning the inhumane deportations carried out by the governments imposed on those countries by the Soviet Union.[179]

The RNC continued to send reports and make formal protests throughout 1952 as well, following the deterioration of conditions for prisoners of war and political prisoners detained in Romania's forced labor camps. On January 7, 1952, the RNC sent all the non-communist countries represented in the UN a letter exposing the reasons the so-called Romanian Popular Republic should not be admitted to the United Nations. A few days later, the RNC sent a memorandum to the president of the UN Commission for War Prisoners, Jose Gustavo Guerrero, regarding the Romanian war prisoners remaining in the Soviet Union. This memorandum was actually a follow-up to an RNC protest made on October 1, 1950.[180]

Not having succeeded in annihilating the elements it considered "hostile" to the communist regime, on February 28, 1950, the Communist party in Romania had decided to establish forced labor units to "reeducate elements that are enemies of the RPR and to prepare them to integrate into social life under the conditions of popular democracy and for the construction of socialism."[181] In reaction, on March 30, 1952, the RNC sent a report on forced labor in Romania to the UN Special Committee on Forced Labor, and on June 23 that committee received Cretzianu and Zissu and took their reports detailing the institution of forced labor in Romania under the communist regime and the situation for all Romanian workers.[182]

The Financial Resources of the RNC

Problems related to funding the RNC's work were raised when it was first organized. First, it was necessary to provide compensation for the Committee members, since none of them had a source of income or the means to support the Committee's activity financially. In addition to the headquarters in Washington, the founders had to consider opening a secretariat in New York and then expanding to Paris, London and Lisbon. Actions the Committee planned to initiate also required financial support, and the most important actions had to be selected. All this led to heated debate.

The members organized a financial sub-committee to coordinate the existing resources and those yet to be identified and establish the related regulations. This sub-committee would have four members chosen from among the RNC members for a three year term with the right to be reelected. The sub-committee would manage the RNC's resources and be in charge of proposing the budget for the following year at least one month before the end of the fiscal year. It was also in charge of gathering funds and controlling expenditures by the members. When the sub-committee was formed, the RNC also ordered the naming of a treasurer, who would work with the General Secretariat and be in charge of managing the funds. They also established an account with Union Trust Bank.[183]Formed on August 18, 1949, the first sub-committee included Cretzianu, Popa, Caranfil and Fărcășanu. Naum Ionescu was treasurer.[184]

The Alexandru Totescu Fund, also known as the Lisbon Fund, was a source of emergency finances available to the Committee. Since the US State Department had not yet prepared the budget to be dedicated to RNC activities, and since the situation of the refugees and of the Romanian students in Germany and Paris was considered critical, the Committee asked Alexandru Totescu, chargé d'affaires of the Romanian legation in Lisbon, to make available the fund that was under his administration. Its value of about CHF 400,000 was later supplemented by CHF 700,000 from the Romanian legation in Madrid, which was transferred to Lisbon by Scarlat Grigoriu, first secretary of the legation. (Both legations had at their disposal funds that pre-dated the communist regime in Romania.) In light of the international post-war economic situation and the depreciation of various currencies, the financial sub-committee took measures to safeguard the fund's value. These included transferring one third of the Lisbon fund to the US and exchanging it for US dollars in the Union Trust account. The other two thirds would remain in Lisbon. The committee advised Totescu to exchange half of this amount for gold coins and asked him to take measures so that the funds could not be blocked in case death or accident made him unable to act.[185]

The case of the Romanian National Fund or the Mihai Antonescu Fund – known later as the Al. Cretzianu Fund– was one of the most controversial issues in Romanian exile history and especially in the history of the RNC, which had de facto remained the only official Romanian democratic organ in exile. Although it occasioned a great deal of controversy in Romanian historiography after 1989, the odyssey of the Cretzianu Fund remains an enigma for most historians, and there are, to this date, many unanswered questions about it.

This fund was created in the tumult of the 1944 events, when Romania was in conflict with Soviet troops and the political class realized that occupation was imminent. The experience of 1917, when the Romanian treasury was removed to Moscow and, after the Bolshevik Revolution, the Soviets "forgot" to return it to Romania, was also taken into account. But the most eloquent example was that of the Polish political and military migration after September 1939, when Poland was occupied first by German troops and then the Soviets. Due to unilateral peace and cooperation treaties, the Poles received permission to pass the Polish treasury through Romania with the assistance of the government and civilian and military refugees. With the intention of saving and funding that part of the Romanian political and intellectual elite that was going to leave the country, at the initiative of the vice-president of the ministerial council, Mihai Antonescu, a special law was passed in the spring of 1944 regarding Funds for Special State Interests. It was decided that a special fund in the amount of twenty million Swiss francs be deposited at the Romanian legation in Bern. The funds were administered by the Foreign Affairs Ministry and its disposition was in the hands of the foreign affairs minister, in person.

Right after Antonescu's arrest in August 1944, the foreign affairs minister was Grigore Niculescu Buzești, who ordered the Swiss account to be cleared, and almost half the funds were sent back to Romania. On January 12, 1945, Vișoianu, who had only just replaced Buzești as foreign affairs minister, wrote to the fund custodian, Romanian chargé d'affaires in Bern George Anastasiu, to transfer CHF 6 million of the remaining funds to the personal account of Alexandru Cretzianu, Romanian minister in Ankara.[186]

In a memorandum to King Michael dated December 9, 1970, Visoianu briefly retells what happened after Cretzianu was entrusted with the money:

> The amount of 6 million Swiss francs was made available for Mr. Cretzianu who, afterwards, cashed 3 million Swiss francs, which he deposited in a secret fund in a bank in Switzerland. With the other half, namely 3 million Swiss francs, Mr. Cretzianu supported the activity of a group of Romanians who, together with him, went to Paris during the time of the Peace Conference in order to inform the American and English delegates about the situation in Romania and about our country's rights, which had been violated by the Soviet Russia. Then, for some time, he helped the Romanian National Committee, which had been formed in the United States, and which, at that time, received no help from the Free Europe Committee. I never knew how much of the 3 million Swiss francs he spent.[187]

Vișoianu goes on to accuse Cretzianu of giving no accounting of the money after receiving it. So, according to Vișoianu, Cretzianu took possession of the 6 million Swiss francs, to which we also have to add the funds from the Ankara legation. Regarding just the initial 3 million, which Vișoianu says were used to finance the group that acted at the Peace Conference, that sum can be considered to have been embezzled, since it was not made available for exile institutions and, especially, given that the expenses were not accounted for, not even to Vişoianu.

Regarding the remaining 3 million Swiss francs, Vişoianu writes:

> I have to inform Your Majesty that, during the trial,[188] Mr. Cretzianu maintained that the amount was not his personal property, that he didn't have to give any account to the Foreign Affairs Minister at that time, Mr. Gh. Tătărăscu, and that he had no obligation except towards Mr. Vişoianu, even if he was no longer Foreign Affairs Minister. Before withdrawing the funds Mr. Cretzianu informed me that he was going to create a trust composed of three or four persons who would manage the national funds. After withdrawing the funds, he no longer wanted to form the trust and continued to manage the amount according to his own criteria, without giving me any accounting of it. I have to confess to Your Majesty the mistake I might have made in not asking Mr. Cretzianu to constitute the trust on a firmer basis or at least to give me a regular accounting of that money's management. I made this mistake because, together with all my colleagues, I trusted Mr. Cretzianu's honesty. I am not going to list all the difficulties and refusals I encountered whenever I asked him to direct some of the funds to the purpose for which they had been designated.[189]

In this letter Vişoianu does admit that Cretzianu supported him whenever he had to travel to Europe or Brazil and also supported the publication of a few of the books produced by the Committee or the Carol I Foundation in Paris: "He would give me a monthly amount that covered the expenses of travel from Washington to New York, or helped me travel abroad in order to fulfill my mission as President of the Romanian National Committee."[190]

Vişoianu's letter to the king ends with a firm conclusion about what Cretzianu had done: "Sire, I am writing this report to Your Majesty with a grieving heart and am still full of amazement that a Romanian, a former minister with the reputation for honesty that he had, committed such a severe crime against our country's interests."[191]

The denunciation of Cretzianu in December 1970 was closely tied to the dramatic financial problems the RNC was experiencing under Vişoianu's leadership. The former foreign affairs minister recalled the reason he had transferred the country's money into the account of an individual and accused Cretzianu of not making the money available to the RNC. But the history of the RNC's rise and fall shows that Cretzianu had been asked since 1949 to make the money available to the Committee.[192] But in every case, he was defended by Vişoianu. Even though the Committee was in full financial crisis and did not receive material support from the Free Europe Committee, the Carol I University Foundation in Paris continued to function, in large part due to modest funds provided by King Michael and funds allocated by Cretzianu from the money taken from the National Fund. After Veniamin, the president of the Foundation, resigned in the spring of 1974, Cretzianu informed Vişoianu that starting that summer he would no longer contribute monthly amounts from the National Fund.[193] At that time, Cretzianu was also using money from this fund to support celebrations of the Romanian national holidays (January 24, May 10, and December 1) in the amount of about $700 for each holiday. He also supported the newspaper *La Nation Roumanie* and, for some time, the newspaper *Romania*.[194]

Of all the funds that were available to the Committee from its inception to the end of its activity in spring 1975, it was the Totescu Fund and the Cretzianu Fund that allowed its formation and its refugee assistance activities, and the re-establishment of the Carol I Foundation in Paris as well. The RNC did not depend entirely on funding from the Free Europe Committee, as is evidenced by its members' activities, the big projects accomplished by its representatives and, especially, the coordination of the cultural activity of the Romanian exiles in Paris. The other National Committees did not have such a large amount of private material support available to them, but the vulnerability of these private funds in the wrong hands affected and limited the Committee's intentions and activity, especially after 1971.

The NCFE transferred its initial funding of $1,500 to the RNC in summer 1949, which Rădescu received a few months before the budget that would be sent to NCFE was drafted. Cretzianu sent Rădescu a letter on December 19, 1949, as a member of the financial sub-committee, asking the general to account for the amounts he had received from the NCFE during July, August and September, amounts which, according to the RNC's account registers, were supposed to cover office expenses and the president's travel expenses.[195]

In October 1949 NCFE New York provided funds totaling $4,800 and asked the RNC to present during that month a budget proposal for monthly funding starting November 1. The first preliminary budget the financial sub-committee prepared stipulated $15,750 for monthly expenses; $6,850 for expenses within the United States, $3,100 for the representatives and agencies of the Committee abroad, $1,800 for the Committee newspaper in Romanian, and $4,000 for refugee assistance.[196] All monies were transferred to the RNC account at Union Trust Bank in Washington, and checks for payments from this account were signed by the Committee treasurer, Naum Ionescu, and co-signed by Cretzianu and Fărcăşanu.[197] Also in fall 1949, NCFE representative Frederic Dolbeare expressed his intention to intervene with the US authorities to free part of the Romanian assets confiscated by the United States during World War II.[198]

In exchange for NCFE's financial assistance, the RNC financial sub-committee, represented by Cretzianu, committed to make available all the data regarding the status and use of those funds. According to the legal regulations of operation and cooperation with the NCFE, Cretzianu was to inform President Rădescu of the criteria set by the NCFE and about his attendant obligations as the RNC's representative to the American organization. Thus, in a letter dated January 24, 1950, Cretzianu wrote:

> In the January 9, 1950, letter from the National Committee for Free Europe, referring, among other things, to the funds which I manage and which were remitted to me … it is stated that: "In order to evaluate the amounts which would be necessary for effective operations, it would be useful for the National Committee for Free Europe to know, at regular intervals, the situation of those funds and their destination."

> In the interest of close cooperation between the National Committee for Free Europe and the Romanian National Committee, of which I am a member, I declare once again that I agree to provide information at regular intervals to the National Committee for Free Europe about the status and destination of those funds. Since those are "secret funds", I will provide the information through the Financial Sub-Committee of the Romanian National Committee, and that Sub-Committee, will, at the same time, provide that information to the National Committee, taking all measures to honor the confidential nature of this information.[199]

Based on this commitment, Cretzianu informed RNC Secretary Ghilezan about the amounts and destinations of the funds he was entrusted with in January 1950 by the NCFE. In his letter to Ghilezan, Cretzianu specified:

> Taking note of the FEC letter of June 29, 1950, I have the honor to ask you to take notice of the following directions which I consider should be included in a possible reply by the National Committee to that letter:
> 1. The Department of Information from Romania of the National Committee has published, starting on March 15 of this year, a bi-monthly confidential Bulletin of Information, which is also sent to the Research and Information Center of NCFE. The cost and mailing of this bulletin so far has been $105.77 and was paid from the funding provided by the NCFE for the office expenses of the National Committee Secretariat.
> 2. Last fall [1949] the Romanian National Committee published two brochures: "Suppression of Human Rights in Rumania" and "Persecution of Religion in Rumania". ... The printing of these two brochures cost $4,230.45 and was paid from the Romanian funds that were entrusted to me personally in January 1950 ... .Their mailing cost $440.33 and was paid from the funding given by the NCFE for office expenses.[200]

The relations between the RNC and NCFE/FEC continued in the following years, and the Committee continued to receive funding from the State Department, despite the division of the Committee and the crises created by the resignation of some key members of the leadership. Referring to the RNC, on December 1, 1950, the "Information Bulletin of Exiled Romanians", which appeared bi-monthly in Paris, wrote: "Free Europe is the body that supports financially and morally the resistance against Communists."[201] The RNC continued to be recognized both by the NCFE/FEC and by the State Department as "the only representative forum of the Romanians in exile". In 1951, the Committee sent only two memoranda to the head of the NCFE presenting in detail the activities, budgets and organizational plans for the new projects for 1952. In the memorandum covering April–June 1951, Popa and Bianu reiterated the requests for financial support from NCFE.[202]

The US economic situation during 1953–1955 lead to a decrease in NCFE funds and initiated a review of its expense policies and its strategy of providing assistance to the National Committees. In a letter dated August 15, 1955, Vișoianu informed George Assan –one of the three RNC representatives in Paris –about the difficulty of negotiating with the NCFE to obtain the amounts necessary to continue the RNC representatives' activity in Paris and the members' activity in New York. He also outlined the new requirements for cooperation imposed by the NCFE:

> With this letter you will also receive a check representing the monthly assistance Free Europe gives to the members of the Committee. This check is in the amount of $700 and represents the funding for July and August. I had great difficulty in obtaining this support for you from NCFE. Consequently, please take all measures to come as soon as possible because I can give you no guarantee that Free Europe will continue to pay for your expenses abroad.
>
> On the other hand, NCFE requests that each member of the Committee continue to show positive results.They did not want to provide funding before receiving from me a list of all the tasks each member

of the Committee has, as well as my guarantee that these tasks will be fulfilled. …[203]

Please believe me that I encountered great difficulty and it took a lot of work to reach an agreement with Free Europe, and it is not yet over. The result is that our Committee will be closely supervised by FEC regarding its internal solidarity and its activity.[204]

A few months later, in November 1955, Committee President Vişoianu wrote to King Michael in very optimistic terms about the existing relations between the two organizations:

The relations of the Romanian National Committee with the Free Europe Committee have developed in a satisfactory atmosphere and are on the way to achieve more and more useful results regarding the support of the Romanian National Committee's regular activity. Your Majesty knows that the Romanian National Committee unfortunately has to seek not only the moral and political support of the Free Europe Committee but also its material support. Because of this, we are constantly in discussion with the Free Europe Committee in order to obtain greater material support, which would allow the National Committee to undertake a large number of activities it considers necessary. For now, based on the Free Europe Committee's material support, the National Committee has a headquarters in New York, where – in response to the Free Europe Committee's firm and persistent request– it has established its main administrative office. I have to admit that these offices in New York are greatly useful, since they allow us, on the one hand, to ensure faster cooperation with the Free Europe Committee, the Captive Nations Assembly [ACEN], and the other National Committees that have, almost all of them, their headquarters in New York. The official headquarters of the Romanian National Committee remains in Washington, where we no longer have office support available. I divide my activity between New York and Washington, spending three days of the week in New York and three in Washington.[205]

The meetings and discussions between the representatives of the two organizations eventually led to finding the financial means to support the RNC for the year 1956. In discussions in November and December 1955, FEC representatives Cloyce Huston and Bernard Yarrow assured Vişoianu regarding the financial assistance and finding the funds necessary to purchase a larger headquarters in Paris for the newspaper *La Nation Roumaine*, the RNC representatives and the Carol I Foundation.[206]

On December 14, 1955, on the occasion of the opening of the New York headquarters,[207] the RNC held a reception, with the support of the FEC, at the Carnegie Endowment Building. Several hundred people took part, including William Crawford, the State Department's official representative, FEC President Whitney Shepardson, FEC executives Yarrow and Huston, and members of the Romanian colony, the Committees and the groups of East-European exiles in the United States. Princess Helen of Romania was also present. In his opening speech Vişoianu expressed the Committee's gratitude to the FEC for the understanding it had shown regarding the organization's needs. In his turn, FEC President Shepardson reiterated the RNC's role and ended, "Let's be sure that nothing we do or we don't do will diminish the trust the captive nations have in us. This is the meaning of our meeting today and in this spirit, Mr. Vişoianu, we will continue to help the enhancement and strengthening of the efforts of the Romanian National Committee."[208]

In his January 18, 1956, letter to King Michael, Vişoianu wrote:

> The Free Europe Committee communicated to us that starting January 1, they gave approval to other requests we had, such as:
> a) Supplying a monthly amount of $500 for the "King Carol I" University Foundation
> b) Supplying a monthly amount of $900 for the publication of a newspaper in Romanian
> c) Supplying funding to rent a small apartment, reimburse a secretary, and purchase a typewriter for the RNC Representation in Paris
> d) Supplying a monthly amount for the reimbursement of a secretary.

> I am glad that this way we can increase the activity of the Romanian National Committee and that part of our requests have been satisfied by the Free Europe Committee.
> On the other hand, the same committee communicated to us that they are considering the acquisition or rental of a house in Paris, where the Royal Foundation, the Committee Representation, the *La Nation Roumaine* newspaper and other Committee activities would be installed. Also, the Free Europe Committee let us know that they hope to obtain soon, from their headquarters, approval of funding for the assistance of our representatives in various countries.[209]

The great changes in the international political arena following the new orientation of Soviet policy towards the United States, as well as the dramatic changes inside the Polish Communist Party and the revolution in Hungary in 1956 all had a decisive influence on the tactics the US adopted in its relations with the Soviet Union. Policy changes at the State Department and the FEC affected their relations with the National Committees and their financial support. The RNC was among the first victims of the FEC's new orientation, causing Vişoianu to addressing a desperate letter to George Assan in Paris presenting him with the catastrophic budget the FEC had given to the Committee in the summer of 1957:

> I am very upset that the Fee Europe Committee not only did not give us the financial means they had promised but that they also cut some of the current budget. They are at a stage of big cuts and we are some of the victims. … Free Europe tells me these cuts are temporary and they hope to review them in a few months. I doubt it. The Free Europe Committee informed me again that this is the last pay check you will receive abroad.[210]

In another letter, sent one month later to Niculae D. Ciotori in Paris, Vişoianu was more blunt in exposing the real motives of the new FEC policy towards all the National Committees, the Voice of America and Radio Free Europe:

> I agree with you regarding your thoughts on the American policy. It is indeed a new American policy, which stems from the President's [Eisenhower] sick fear of warand from his illusions that one can reach an agreement with Soviet Russia. This new policy is manifested in all forms. Even the National Committees fell victim. Our budgets have been cut significantly. The Voice of America as well as Radio Free Europe have been transformed into neutered stations. None of them is allowed to attack the Communist regimes in our countries anymore or to upset Khrushchev in any way.[211]

The consequences of this policy are also reflected in the desperate situation in which the Committee found itself a few years later, when, in 1962, the RNC presented a memorandum to the FEC listing its requests and needs in order to continue its activity:

> I) Newspaper *Romania* from New York: We now receive $625.00 per month, for 6 issues per year. We need $1,000.00 per month (i.e. a $4,500.00 per year increase), for 12 issues per year, over 7,300 copies.
> II) Newspaper *La Nation Roumaine* from Paris: We now receive $775.00 per month, which covers only 6 issues yearly. We need $1,000.00 per month (i.e. an increase of $2,700.00 per year), for 12 issues, over 6,000 copies.
> III) "Special Meetings": We now receive $10.00 monthly (we received $35.00 until December 31, 1961). We need an increase for attending special meetings of Rumanian American groups and organizations and for maintaining permanent contacts with these groups and outstanding political figures in America and Europe.
> IV) "Books, Publications, Clippings": We now received $50.00 monthly. We need more.
> V) Emergency Assistance: We need some money for such eventualities, which are frequent.
> VI) Representatives of the Committee Abroad: Now they pay from their own pocket expenses incurred as Representatives. We should like to be able to reimburse them for such expenses.

VII) A Handbook about Rumania (geography, history, economy, culture, etc.) is often requested by students at American High Schools and Colleges.
VIII) Commemoration of important historical events, especially in New York and Paris.
IX) Printing of the Memorandum addressed to the United Nations ($400.00)
X) Remuneration of the Committee's members.[212]

Between 1962 and 1971, the Committee's activities were hampered, on the one hand by the indifference of the younger generations of East European refugees to the fate of their parents' homeland, and on the other hand by US foreign policy, which had turned its attention mostly to Vietnam. Members of the Senate, among them J. W. Fulbright, the chairman of the Foreign Affairs Committee, were very vocal in asking President Nixon to discontinue CIA funding for Radio Free Europe and Radio Liberty. Therefore, a high level government decision was reached by President Nixon and Secretary of State Henry Kissinger to cut allocations to the National Committees and the ACEN, and Congress was asked to fund Radio Free Europe and Radio Liberty.

On November 1, 1971, Nixon issued Presidential Determination Letter Nr. 72-6, under which he authorized the secretary of state to transfer and make available $1,850,000 for use pursuant to section 2 (c) of the Migration and Refugee Assistance Act of 1962. The Free Europe Committee bought 62 insurance policies from the Pennsylvania Mutual Life Insurance Company valued at a total of $1,850,000. Each of 62 individuals named as beneficiaries in the policies received an annuity of $350.00 a month. From the Romanian group, only six people were eligible to receive the annuity, which required that the recipient be over 56 years of age and be a member of the Committee or of the ACEN.[213]

The cut in Free Europe Committee funds was the prelude to the cessation of RNC activity. From 1972 on, it continued its activities anemically through self-funding and sporadic donations it received for the continued publication of *The Romanian*.

The Agony of the Romanian National Committee

At the beginning of the 1960s the Committee's various activities diminished and the members showed less and less interest. Because of their age, many of them retired. The minutes of each meeting show no more than five participating members until the early 1970s, when their number was reduced to four. This situation can be explained first by the political position of the United States, the new stance of peaceful coexistence, the lessening of the international tensions that might have led to a conflict with global consequences. The reestablishment of the West's relations with the USSR and the opening of Romanian Popular Republic embassies in the United States, France and Germany made the Committee's relations with Western democraciesvery difficult.

Second, as a consequence of the State Department's new policy orientation, the funds distributed to the RNC through the FEC were substantially reduced starting in 1957. Since the US objective was for these Cold War organizations to cease their activity, which had started to conflict with US foreign policy, the American authorities significantly reduced the Committees' budgets until December 1971, when they were cut for good. On December 30, 1971, Vişoianu wrote to G. Constantinescu, the Committee representative in London, telling him about the RNC's unpleasant financial situation:

> The funding allocated to the national Committees and to the Assembly of Captive European Nations is so little for the American budget that nobody can believe that it was cut due to economic needs. Surely ... this measure is of a political nature and was taken because of the American President's visit to Moscow, to please Brezhnev and Kosygin.[214]

As a consequence of this measure, starting in 1972 the new RNC headquarters were in the basement of Ion Stere's house, where they occupied a room and a lobby, and where Vişoianu, Popa, Bunescu and Vardala would meet every two or three months.[215]Without the FEC funding and in an effort to resolve the RNC's terrible financial situation, Vişoianu registered the Rumanian National Committee, Inc. at Albany, New York, in April 1973. He would name Ion Stere as secretary and Miron Butariu as treasurer for both the RNC and the Rumanian National Committee, Inc.[216] Through this action, Vişoianu was hoping to obtain new funds from the American authorities and from private organizations, especially for the financial support of *Romania*. At the same time he was trying to recruit new members to the Committee and to regain the trust of the Romanian exiles.

Vişoianu's trip to Europe in April 1974 and his meetings with King Michael regarding reviving the Committee's activity and naming new members had no positive results. The report sent to the king on July 15, together with a letter of September 18, 1974, did not succeed in reviving the Committee.[217] After Popa's death on November 1, the number of Committee members was reduced to three –Vişoianu and Bunescu in the United States and Veniamin in Paris. This caused Vişoianu to submit the Committee's resignation to His Majesty King Michael at the meeting of December 18, 1974.[218] At the beginning of May 1975, General Petre Lazăr wrote to Vişoianu informing him that the king approved the RNC's resignation and asking him to send suggestions for new members who would be part of a new Committee to be constituted later. Taking note of the sovereign's decision, Vişoianu proposed to the king that during the period of reorganization, the RNC's activities should be led by a temporary Committee for a period of at least three months.[219] Since more than seven months had passed since the May 8 meeting, and since they had received no answer from the king, the Committee had a last meeting on December 8, when it was decided to end their activity completely.[220]

The validity of the approval of the resignation of the National Committee's president is controversial. As already mentioned, General Lazar informed Vişoianu that the king gave his consent for the resignation of the Committee, but in two interviews with His Majesty conducted after 1989, the king denied having approved the decision to depose Vişoianu and the Committee. In the weekly *Free World*, which appeared in New

York for a short period of time, Liviu Valenaş interviewed the king in April 1998. When asked about the activity and the abolition of the Committee after 1965, the king stated, "This national committee has never been abolished, but it practically ceased to exist since 1970."[221] In another interview, this time with Mircea Ciobanu in 1995, the king maintained, "If you consider things well, RNC has never been abolished; Vişoianu's resignation was not approved. There is no document about its dissolution."[222]

In conclusion, the RNC was a democratic political organization, established in reaction to the repressive communist regime installed by the Soviet Union and maintained by its occupation troops. Recognized and supported by the large Western democracies and denigrated by the Communist government in Bucharest, the RNC was the voice of the Romanian exile, a legitimate organization authorized by the feeble opposition within Romania, as well as by the leaders of the Romanian exile community, who had always looked for an authority that would represent their rights and hopes about the liberation of Romania. Above all, the RNC was the Romanian government in exile, which accomplished its duties as much as it was allowed, perfectly integrated into the US and West European strategies and actions of annihilating and stopping Communism.[223]

Table. The Romanian National Committee By-laws

Subject	Regulations	Contents
Constitution	Art. 1.	The National Committee was constituted through the April 6, 1949 minutes, based on the criteria in the King's communication on August 5, 1948, and confirmed by the sanction of the King of April 23, 1949.
Objective	Art. 2.	The objective of the Romanian National Committee is to: • Represent the Romanian nation and protect its interests until the moment of national liberation; • Lead by all means actions for the liberation of Romania and re-establishment of a democratic system of government; • Coordinate and support the assistance of Romanian refugees; • Guide the cooperation of Romanian diasporas for the achievement of these objectives.
Vacancies	Art. 3.	Regarding the filling of vacancies in the National Committee, the Committee will propose to the Sovereign the nominations made according to the criteria that are at the foundation of the constitution and existence of the Committee itself.
Structural Modifications	Art. 4.	The Committee will be able to propose to the Sovereign any suggestion or proposition referring to the structure of the National Committee.
By-Laws Modifications	Art. 5.	The current by-laws can be modified through the decision of the Committee, taken by a majority of 2/3, and with the approval of the Sovereign.
Vote	Art. 6.	With the exception of the art. 5 provisions, the decisions of the Committee will be taken with an absolute majority of its members votes.
Absent Members	Art. 7.	Since the vote is personal and direct, it cannot be delegated. An absent member can still vote directly and personally, in writing, if he has knowledge about the matter that is discussed.
Members	Art. 8.	The members of the Committee work with equal power and responsibilities. They have the obligation to keep secret the subject of the debates, and of the decisions taken, when the Committee decides so. Each member had the right to be informed about the continuous proceeding of the action of the Committee.
President	Art. 9.	The president of the Committee: • Presides over the National Committee; • Signs the important correspondence of the Committee; • Represents the Committee on official occasions. In case he is unable to perform his duties, he will ask the Committee to name a substitute.

Departments. Consultative bodies.	Art. 10.	The Committee will be able to organize its activity by departments, trusting those departments to one or more of its members. The Committee will also be able, for any of these departments of activity, to appoint consultative and executive bodies that can be also be led by persons who are not part of the Committee. The delegates will present a monthly report of their activity.
Headquarters	Art. 11.	The headquarters of the Committee is in Washington. The president will be able to call meetings in other locations too.
General Secretariat	Art. 12.	The Committee will be able to appoint a General Secretary who will be responsible for the administrative work of the Committee. The General Secretariat staff will be approved by the Committee. The General Secretariat is permanently at the disposal of the president and of the members of the Committee, in fulfilling their tasks.
Minutes	Art. 13.	Minutes will be read at the beginning of the meeting and subject to the approval of the present members.
Calling Meetings	Art. 14.	The president calls the meetings of the Committee. In case the president receives a request to call a meeting signed by 1/3 of the members of the Committee, he will call a meeting within 10 days from the date of the request. Regular meetings will be held once a month, namely on the first Tuesday of every month, and as often as necessary.
Agenda	Art. 15.	The text of the calling to a meeting will contain the agenda. Any member of the Committee has the right to propose for the agenda any matters he considers necessary.

Endnotes

1 Nicolette Franck, "Defeat in Victory: How the Kingdom of Romania Became a Popular Republic (1944–1947)", *Journal of the American Romanian Academy of Arts and Sciences,* nr. 6–7 (1985): 232–247; John Keegan, *The Second World War* (New York: Penguin Books, 1990) 504.

2 Henry Kissinger, *Diplomacy* (New York: Simon & Schuster, 1994) 437–439.

3 See Leonid Gibianski, "URSS Şi câteva aspecte ale formării blocului sovietic în Europa Orientală", in *6 martie 1945. Începuturile comunizării României* (Bucureşti, Enciclopedică, 1995) 254–256; Norman Naimark and Leonid Gibianski, *The Establishment of Communist Regimes in Eastern Europe, 1944–1949* (Boulder: Westview Press, 1997).

4 Mircea Ionnitiu, "The Takeover of Romania, 6 March 1945", *Journal of the American Romanian Academy of Arts and Sciences,* nr. 8–9 (1986) 80.

5 Ibid.

6 Ibid.

7 Radu Ciuceanu, Ioan Chiper, Florin Constantiniu, *Misiunile lui A.L. Vîşinski în România. Din istoria relaţiilor româno-sovietice, 1944–1946. Documente secrete* (Bucureşti, Institutul Naţional pentru Studiul Totalitarismului, 1997).

8 Ionescu Ghiţă, *Communism in Rumania, 1944–1962*, (Oxford: Oxford University Press, 1964) 99.

9 Ionescu, *Communism in Rumania*, 103; Ionniţiu, "The Takeover", 83.

10 Ionescu, *Communism in Rumania*, 103.

11 Stephan A. Fischer-Galaţi, ed. *Romania* (New York: Frederick A. Praeger, 1957) 65.

12 Constantin Vişoianu, "Rumania's Tragedy", *Evening Star*, 16 February 1965, sec 1, p. 8; Ionniţiu, "Communism in Rumania", 83; Roy Melbourne, "Witness to the Start of the Cold War: The view from Romania", in Paul D. Quinlan (ed.), *The United States and Romania. American-Romanian Relations during the Twentieth Century* (Woodland Hills, CA: American Romanian Academy of Arts and Sciences, 1988) 97–104.

13 Ionniţiu, *Communism in Rumania*, 83–84.

14 On November 16, at the meeting of the Political Committee of the General Assembly of the United Nations, the Soviet Foreign Affairs Minister emphasized the statement made by Warren Austin, the United States' representative, before the Committee, regarding the ultimatum presented by Vishinsky to King Michael on February 28, 1945. Using extremely aggressive words, Vishinsky had given a firm disclaimer to Austin, agreeing to bring before the Assembly a witness who would confirm his declarations. Taking note of these declarations, General Nicolae Rădescu, the president of the Romanian National Committee at the time, in a letter addressed to Carlos Romulo, the president of the General Assembly of the United Nations at the time, specified that he was ready to appear as witness to Vishinsky's act of force in Rumania on February 28, 1945. Moreover, he called a press conference on November 25, in which he gave detailed explanations regarding the circumstances in which Vishinsky's ultimatum was produced. In his declarations, general Rădescu was supported by the telegram and the letter addressed to Austin by Vişoianu about the methods used by Vishinski in his audience with King Michael on February 28, 1945. See Constantin Vişoianu's declaration to the United Nations Organization on January 7, 1952, Comitetul National Roman (Romanian National Committee, hereafter CNR), box 1, folder 1, Hoover Institution Archive (hereafter HIA); also see Darea de seamă asupra activităţii Comitetului Naţional Român din 16 Noiembrie 1949, CNR, box 1, folder 1, HIA; Paul D. Quinlan, *Clash Over Romania. British and American Policies Towards Romania: 1938–1947* (Los Angeles: American Romanian Academy of Arts and Sciences, 1977) 105–131.

15 Ionescu, *Communism in Rumania*, 105. Regarding the events that took place in 1945, the "king's strike" of King Michael and the Anglo-American and Soviet reactions that led to Groza's "false pluralism", see the introductory study in Dinu C. Giurescu (coord.), *Imposibila încercare. Greva regală, 1945* (Bucureşti: Enciclopedică, 1999) 7–91.

16 Quinlan, *Clash Over Romania*, 153–155; Keith Hitchins, *Rumania, 1866–1947* (Oxford: Clarendon Press, 1944) 530–534. Regarding the events of 1946 also see Romulus Rusan (ed.), *Anul 1946- Începutul sfârşitului* (Bucureşti: Fundaţia Academia Civică, 1996); Constatntin Sănătescu, *Jurnal* (Bucureşti: Humanitas, 1993) 238–240.

17 Ionescu, *Communism in Rumania*, 107.

18 Ibid., 94.

19 Astrid Suhrke, "Uncertain Globalization: Refugee Movement in the Second half of the Twentieth Century," in Wang Gungwu, *Global History and Migrations* (Boulder: Westview Press, 1997) 217–239.

20 Take Ionescu, CNR, box 1, folder 1, HIA.

21 Notatka opracowana dla Prof. Kota na podstawie telegramów MSZ., informacjj ppłk. Kowałewskiego z Lizbony oraz moich rozmów z p. Tilea, Register of the Poland Ministerstwo Spraw Zagranicznych Records, 1919–1947, series 3, box 2, folder 11, HIA. (hereafter, RPMSZR).

[22] Jan Kowałewski was of invaluable service to the former Romanian King Carol II, enabling him to escape from Romania and leave Spain for Lisbon, See: Mjr Zdzisław Żórawski, *Dziennik obrońcy Warszawy wrzesień 1939 r.,* Tomasz Szarota, ed. (Warszawa: Rytm, 2011) 22–29.

[23] Jean Pangal was a Romanian centrist politician and former Romanian envoy to Lisbon. Pangal was dismissed at the end of 1941 by Romanian leader Ion Antonescu because of his pro-Allied stance. Pangal remained in Lisbon and became a collaborator with Polish intelligence in Allied attempts to win over the Third Reich's allies – Hungary, Romania, Finland and Italy.

[24] While serving as a diplomat in London, he chose in 1941 to resign from the service when the Antonescu dictatorship was established in collaboration with the Nazi government. He soon co-founded the Romanian Free Movement led by Ambassador Tilea. At the same time, he was invited by Prime Minister Winston Churchill to serve in political intelligence against the Germans in Romania. At war's end he re-entered diplomatic service during the period of post-war treaty negotiations at the Paris and New York conferences. In 1947 he went into exile after the communist coup and lived in Marrakech, Morocco, for eight years before emigrating with his family to the United States in 1956.

[25] Notatka opracowana dla Prof. Kota na podstawie telegramów MSZ., informacjj ppłk. Kowałewskiego z Lizbony oraz moich rozmów z p. Tilea, RPMSZR, series 3, box 2, folder 11, HIA.

[26] Ibid.

[27] Ibid.

[28] "Wolni Rumuni" na terenie U.S.A. I Kanady, RPMSZR, series 3, box 12, folder 12, HIA.

[29] Ibid.; Carol in pilgrim's guise visit to U.S.A.?, RPMSZR, series 3, box 12, folder 12, HIA; Robert Lewis Taylor, "Carol and Lupescu Down Mexico Way", *Saturday Evening Post,* July 25, 1942, 11,97.

[30] Ibid.

[31] Ibid.; Who are the "Free Romanian"?, RPMSZR, series 3, box 12, folder 12, HIA; Democratic Romania Looks Ahead, RPMSZR, series 3, box 12, folder 12, HIA.

[32] Lavinia S. Stan, "The Cultural and Political Strategies of Exile: Romanians in the Cold War," in Ausna Cindina and Jonathan Osmond, *Power and Culture. Hegemony, Interaction and Dissent* (Pisa: Edizioni Plus, 2006) 150.

[33] Ibid.

[34] Aurel Sergiu Marinescu, *O Contribuție la Istoria Exilului Românesc*, vol. 1 (București: Vremea, 1999) 377.

[35] Stan, "The Cultural and Political Strategies", 149.

[36] Ibid., 150.

[37] Comitetul Național Român, CNR, box 1, folder 6, HIA.

[38] Procesul-Verbal din 6 aprilie, 1949, CNR, box 1, folder 3, HIA. Some circumstances also in the background of the formation of the National Committee were the Romanian political events of 1947, as well as the fact that several political figures left the country. The dissolution of the Romanian consultative group from Geneva on April 30, 1949 added to this background.

[39] Comitetul Național Român, CNR, box 3, folder 2, HIA. In the letter written to General Rădescu on April 23, 1949, transmitted from Lausanne by General C. Petre-Lazăr (personal secretary to King Michael), King Michael was giving his consent for the formation of the National Committee. See: Comitetul Național Român, CNR, box 1, folder 6, HIA.

[40] Comitetul Național Român, CNR, box 1, folder 6, HIA.

[41] Ibid.; Aurel Sergiu Marinescu, *O Contribuție,* 341–342.

[42] Summary of the Proclamation of the Rumanian National Committee, CNR, box 1, folder 6, HIA; Rumanians Form Free exile Group: Creation of a Committee for Country's "Independence" is disclosed by Ex-Premier, *New York Times*, May 10, 1949, 18.

[43] Ibid.; Marinescu, *O Contribuție*, 349.

[44] Constitution D'un Comité National Roumain, *Agence France-Presse*, Paris, May, 10 1949.

[45] See: Adevărații reprezentanți ai națiunii române, CNR, box 1, folder 6, HIA.

[46] Dreptul de reprezentare în exil, CNR, box 4, folder 1, HIA.

[47] Mircea Ciobanu, *Noi convorbiri cu Regele Mihai I al României* (București: Humanitas, 1992) 35–92.

[48] See: Dinu C. Giurescu, *Guvernarea Nicolae Rădescu* (București: All, 1996); Mircea Ionnițiu, "Two Brave Forgotten Men: General Nicolae Rădescu and Grigore Niculescu-Buzești", *Journal of the American Romanian Academy of Arts and Sciences*, nr. 13–14 (1990) 214–218.

[49] Ionnițiu, "Two Brave Forgotten Men", 218.

[50] Ibid.

[51] "Nicolescu-Buzești, Rumanian Exile, 41. Former Foreign Minister and Peasant Party Leader Dies Here-Foe of Communists", *New York Times*, October 5, 1949.

[52] Ionnițiu, "Two Brave Forgotten Men", 218.

[53] Proces-Verbal al Ședințelor Comitetului Național Român din 9, 11 și 13 Octombrie 1950, CNR, box 3, folder 2, HIA.

[54] Comitetul Național Român, CNR, box 1, folder 6, HIA.

[55] Proces-Verbal al Ședințelor Comitetului Național Român din 13 și 14 Noiembrie 1950, CNR, box 3, folder 2, HIA.

[56] Comitetul Național Român, CNR, box 1, folder 6, HIA.

[57] Ibid.

[58] A.G.R.U.-Congresul General de Constituire din Blaj, *Curierul Creștin*, Gherla, 15 Noiembrie 1929, nr. 22, 184–186.

[59] Comitetul Național Român, CNR, box 1, folder 6; Proces-Verbal al Ședinței Comitetului Național Român din 18 Decembrie 1974, CNR, box 4, folder 4, HIA.

[60] Darea de seamă asupra activității Comitetului Național în cursul lunilor Decembrie 1949, Ianuarie și Februarie 1950, CNR, box 1, folder 6, HIA.

[61] Proces-Verbal al Ședintelor Comitetului Național Român din 9, 11 și 13 Octombrie 1950, CNR, box 3, folder 2, HIA.

[62] Proces-Verbal al Ședințelor din 4 și 5 Decembrie 1950, CNR, box 3, folder 2, HIA.

[63] Comitetul Național Român, CNR, box 1, folder 6, HIA.

[64] Proces-Verbal al Ședințelor Comitetului Național Român din 9, 11 și 13 Octombrie 1950, CNR, box 3, folder 2, HIA.

[65] Darea de seamă asupra activității Comitetului Național în cursul lunei Septembrie 1949, CNR, box 1, folder 1, HIA.

[66] Rozeta Metes, *The Iuliu Maniu American-Romanian Relief Foundation. A Quarter Century of Activity. 1951–1976* (Cleveland, Ohio: America Newspaper/America Calendars, 1977) 6.

[67] Miron Butariu, "Assembly of Captive European Nations. The Little United Nations – The Voice of the People", *Journal of theAmerican Romanian Academy of Arts and Sciences,* nr.10 (1987) 131.

[68] Sabin Manuilă, Regional Development of the Jewish population in Romania, CNR, box 2, folder 10, HIA.

[69] Comitetul Național Român, CNR, box 1, folder 6, HIA.

[70] Marinescu, *O Contribuție*, 352.

71 Ibid., 281–322; See: S Marinescu, *O contribuție la Istoria Exilului Românesc,* vol. 2 (București: Vremea, 2002) 603–686.

72 Mircea Ciobanu, *În fața neamului meu-Convorbiri cu MS Regele Mihai* (Iași: Princeps, 1995) 177–185.

73 Statutul Comitetului Național Român din 19 .V. 1949, CNR, box 1, folder 6, HIA.

74 Statutul Comitetului Național Român din 3 .VI.1949, CNR, box 1, folder 6, HIA; Scrisoarea adresată generalului N. Rădescu în data de 30.X. 1949, CNR, box 1, folder 6, HIA.

75 Statutul Comitetului Național Român din 29.XI. 1949, CNR, box 1, folder 6, HIA; Ordinea de zi a ședinței din 25 Noiembrie 1949, CNR, box 3, folder 2, HIA; Proces-Verbal Nr. 22. Sesiunea din 28 și 29 Noiembrie 1949, CNR, box 3, folder 4, HIA.

76 Proces-Verbal Nr. 24.Sesiunile din 21, 22, 23, 27 și 28 Decembrie 1949, CNR, box 3, folder 2, HIA.

77 Proces-Verbal al Ședințelor Comitetului Național Român din 12 și 13 Octombrie 1949, CNR, box 3, folder 2, HIA.

78 Textul Statutului Comitetului Național Român stabilit în principiu cu prilejul consfătuirii din 26 Ianuarie 1950, CNR, box 1, folder 6, HIA; Regulament interior pentru funcționarea organelor Secretariatului general al Comitetului Național Român, CNR, box 1, folder 6, HIA.

79 Dare de seamă asupra activității Comitetului Național în Cursul Lunilor Decembrie 1949, Ianuarie și Februarie 1950, CNR, box 1, folder 6, HIA.

80 Ibid.

81 Ibid.

82 Ibid; Proces-Verbal Nr. 23. Ședința din 15 Decembrie 1949, CNR, box 3, folder 4, HIA.

83 Marinescu, *O Contribuție*, vol.1, 377.

84 Proces-Verbal Nr. 17 din 9 Septembrie 1949, CNR, box 3, folder 4, HIA.

85 Proces-Verbal Nr. 18. Ședințele din 26 și 27 Septembrie 1949, CNR, box 3, folder 2, HIA.

86 "Spy Aid Hinted", *Spokane Daily Chronicle,* 10 June 1949, Empire Edition, nr. 225, p.2.

87 Proces-Verbal Nr. 17 din 9 Septembrie 1949, CNR, box 3, folder 4, HIA.

88 Scrisoarea lui Al. Cretzianu din 19 Septembrie către N. Caranfil, CNR, box 3, folder 4, HIA.

89 Ibid.

90 Încheiere, CNR, box 3, folder 2, HIA.

91 Dare de seamă asupra activității Comitetului Național în cursul lunilor Decembrie 1949, Ianuarie și Februarie 1950, CNR, box 1, folder 1, HIA

92 Marinescu, *O Contribuție*, vol.1, 350.

93 Proces-Verbal Nr. 23. Ședința din 15 Decembrie 1949, CNR, box 3, folder 4, HIA.

94 Încheiere, CNR, box 3, folder 2, HIA.

95 Ibid.

96 Scrisoarea lui Al. Cretzianu către Generalul N. Rădescu din 31 August 1950, CNR, box 3, folder 2, HIA.

97 See, Scrisoarea lui Emil Ghilezan către Constantin Vișoianu din 2 Octombrie 1950, CNR, box 3, folder 2, HIA.

98 Ibid.

99 Proces-Verbal al Ședinței Comitetului Național Român din ziua de 9 Septembrie 1950, CNR, box 3, folder 3, HIA.

100 Ibid.

101 Scrisoarea lui Emil Ghilezan către Constantin Vișoianu din 2 Octombrie 1950, CNR, box 3, folder 2, HIA; Scrisoarea lui Emil Ghilezan către Naum Ionescu din 22 Septembrie 1950, CNR, box 3, folder 2, HIA.

[102] Proces-Verbal al Ședințelor Comitetului Național Român din 9, 11 și 13 Octombrie 1950, CNR, box 3, folder 3, HIA; Scrisoarea către Regele Mihai din 14 Octombrie 1950, CNR, box 3, folder 2, HIA.

[103] Proces-Verbal al Ședințelor Comitetului Național Român din 13 și 14 Noiembrie 1950, CNR, box 3, folder 2, HIA; Proces-Verbal al Consiliului Partidelor Politice Democratice Române. Secțiunea din Statele Unite din Ședințele din 4 și Decembrie 1950, CNR, box 3, folder 2, HIA; Deciziune din 10 Decembrie a Comitetului Național Român, CNR, box 3, folder 2, HIA.

[104] Întrunirea de la New York din 27 Noiembrie 1950, CNR, box 3, folder 2, HIA; Proiect de Statute ale "Asociațiunii Românilor Liberi Din Statele Unite ale Americii", CNR, box 3, folder 2, HIA.

[105] Butariu, "Assembly of Captive European Nations", 129.

[106] Proces-Verbal al Ședinței Comitetului Național Român din ziua de 18 Ianuarie 1951, CNR, box 3, folder 3, HIA.

[107] Proces-Verbal al Ședinței Comitetului Național Român din 23 Iulie 1955, CNR, box 3, folder 5, HIA.

[108] Dare de seamă asupra activității Comitetului Național Român în cursul lunilor Iulie-Noiembrie 1955, CNR, box 3, folder 5, HIA; Scrisoarea către Cloyce K. Huston din 30 Iulie 1955, CNR, box 3, folder 5, HIA.

[109] Proces-Verbal al Ședinței Comitetului Național Român din 29 Martie 1974, CNR, box 4, folder 2, HIA.

[110] Proces-Verbal al Ședinței Comitetului Național Român din 1 Iunie 1974, CNR, box 4, folder 2, HIA.

[111] Marinescu, *O contribuție*, vol. 1, 379.

[112] Proces-Verbal al Ședinței Comitetului Național Român din 18 Septembrie 1974, CNR, box 4, folder 2, HIA.

[113] Proces-Verbal al Ședinței Comitetului Național Român din 18 Decembrie 1974, CNR, box 4, folder 2, HIA.

[114] Proces-Verbal Nr. 20. Sesiunea din 26 și 27 Octombrie 1949, CNR, box 3, folder 4, HIA.

[115] Atribuțiile Reprezentanților Comitetului Național Român, CNR, box 1, folder 6, HIA.

[116] Buletin Informativ Nr 1, Washington, 15 Martie 1950, CNR, box 1, folder 4–5, HIA.

[117] Proces-Verbal al Ședinței Comitetului Național Român din ziua de 9 Septembrie 1950, CNR, box 3, folder 2, HIA.

[118] Proces-Verbal al Ședinței Comitetului Național Român din ziua de 15 Iunie 1951, CNR, box 3, folder 4, HIA.

[119] Atribuțiile Reprezentanților Comitetului Național Român, CNR, box 1, folder 6, HIA.

[120] Proces-Verbal al Ședinței Comitetului Național Român din 1 Decembrie 1950, CNR, box 3, folder 2, HIA.

[121] Scrisoarea către Majestatea Sa Regele Mihai de la 2 Februarie 1951, CNR, box 3, folder 4, HIA.

[122] Proces-Verbal al Ședințelor Comitetului Național Român din zilele de 26 și 27 Februarie 1951, CNR, box 3, folder 4, HIA. Constantin Vălimarescu fulfilled this function until April 1952 when he resigned because he had become a citizen of Argentina. The vacancy was filled by Radu Cutzarida. See: Proces-Verbal al Ședinței Comitetului Național Român din ziua de 1 Aprilie 1952, CNR, box 3, folder 4, HIA.

[123] Proces-Verbal al Ședinței Comitetului Național Român din ziua de 18 Aprilie 1951, CNR, box 3, folder 4, HIA.

[124] Proces-Verbal al Ședinței Comitetului Național Român din ziua de 16 Iulie 1951, CNR, box 3, folder 4, HIA.

[125] Proces-Verbal al Ședinței Comitetului Național din ziua de 17 Decembrie 1951, CNR, box 3, folder 4, HIA.

[126] Proces-Verbal al Ședinței Comitetului Național Român din ziua de 1 Aprilie 1952, CNR, box 3, folder 4, HIA. Also see: Proces-Verbal al Ședintei Comitetului Național Român din ziua de 9 Septembrie 1952, CNR, box 3, folder 4, HIA.

[127] Proces-Verbal al Ședinței Comitetului Național Român din ziua de 9 Septembrie 1952, CNR, box 3, folder 4, HIA.

[128] Dare de seamă asupra activității Comitetului Național în cursul lunii Octombrie 1949, CNR, box 1, folder 1, HIA.

[129] Activitatea Comitetului Național Român în Anul 1952, CNR, box 1, folder 1, HIA.

[130] Proces-Verbal al Ședinței Comitetului Național Român din ziua de 6 Noiembrie 1957, CNR, box 4, folder 1, HIA.

[131] Activity Report for the month of November. 1958, CNR, box 4, folder 5, HIA.

[132] Ibid.

[133] Activity Report for the month of December, 1958, CNR, box 4, folder 5, HIA.

[134] Ibid.

[135] Activity Report for the month of March, 1959, CNR, box 4, folder 5, HIA.

[136] Activity Report for the Month of April, 1959, CNR, box 4, folder 5, HIA.

[137] Activity Report for the Month of May, 1959, CNR, box 4, folder 5, HIA.

[138] Paul Lindenberg, *Regele Carol I al României* (București: Humanitas, 2006) 281.

[139] Proces-Verbal Nr. 22. Sesiunea din 28 și 29 Noiembrie 1949, CNR, box 3, folder 4, HIA.

[140] Matei Călinescu, "The 1927 Generation in Romania: Friendships and Ideological Choices (Mihail Sebastian, Mircea Eliade, Nae Ionescu, Eugene Ionesco, E.M. Cioran)", *East European Politics and Socities* 15, nr 3, 649–677.

[141] Chestiunea Fundațiunii Universitare Carol I, CNR, box 11, folder 20, HIA.

[142] The Congress of Rumanian Intellectuals. January 24–26, 1959. Paris-France, CNR, box 11, folder 4, HIA.

[143] Proces-Verbal Nr. 24. Sesiunile din 21, 22, 23, 27 și 28 Decembrie 1949, CNR, box 3, folder 2, HIA.

[144] Ibid.

[145] Proces-Verbal al Ședinței Comitetului Național Român din ziua de 9 Septembrie 1950, CNR, box 3, folder 2, HIA; Raport asupra reînființări la Paris a Fundațiunii Culturale Regele Carol I, CNR, box 11, folder 20, HIA.

[146] Chestiunea Fundațiunii Universitare Carol I, CNR, box 11, folder 20, HIA.

[147] Adaos la Procesul-Verbal al Ședințelor Comitetului Național Român din 13 și 14 Noiembrie 1950, CNR, box 3, folder 2, HIA.

[148] Scrisoarea lui P Sergescu către C. Vișoianu din 16 Februarie, 1951, CNR, box 11, folder 20, HIA.

[149] Proces-Verbal al Ședințelor Comitetului Național Român din zilele de 26 și 27 Februarie 1951, box 3, folder 4, HIA.

[150] Primul Raport Financiar al Fundației Universitare Carol I, 1 Decembrie 1950–1 Martie 1951, CNR, box 11, folder 20.

[151] Referat asupra sumelor trimise de A. Totescu Fundației Universitare Carol I, CNR, box 11, folder 21; Proces-Verbal al Ședinței Comitetului Național Român din ziua de 18 Ianuarie 1951, CNR, box 3, folder 3, HIA.

[152] Proces-Verbal al Ședinței Comitetului Național Român din ziua de 11 Noiembrie 1953, CNR, box 3, folder 4, HIA.

[153] Proces-Verbal al Ședinței Comitetului Național Român din ziua de 8 Noiembrie 1955, CNR, box 3, folder 5, HIA.

[154] Proces-Verbal al Ședințelor Comitetului Național Român din 13 și 14 Noiembrie 1950, CNR, box 3, folder 2, HIA.
[155] Aurel Sergiu Marinescu, *O Contribuție,* vol.2, 573.
[156] Proces-Verbal al Ședinței Comitetului Național Român din 14 Ianuarie, CNR, box 4, folder 4, HIA.
[157] Proces-Verbal al Ședintelor din 26 și 27 Septembrie 1949, CNR, box 3, folder 2, HIA; Proces-Verbal Nr. 24. Sesiunile din 21, 22, 23, 27 și 28 Decembrie 1949, CNR, box 3, folder 4, HIA; Proces-Verbal Nr. 21. Ședința din 9 Noiembrie 1949, orele 16, CNR, box 3, folder 4, HIA.
[158] Dare de seamă asupra activității Comitetului Național în cursul lunei Octombrie 1949, CNR, box 1, folder 1, HIA.
[159] Ibid; Proces-Verbal al Ședințelor Comitetului Național Român din 12 și 13 Octombrie 1949, CNR, box 3, folder 2, HIA.
[160] Proces-Verbal al Ședinței Comitetului Național Român din ziua de 14 Noiembrie 1956, CNR, box 3, folder 6, HIA.
[161] Ibid.
[162] Ibid; Rumanian Exile Association in West Germany, CNR, box 13, folder 11, HIA.
[163] Memoriu privind organizarea unei Direcțiuni Militare a Refugiaților Români, CNR, box 2, folder 1, HIA.
[164] Ibid.
[165] Proces-Verbal Nr 22. Sesiunea din 28 și 29 Noiembrie 1949, CNR, box 3, folder 4, HIA.
[166] Proces-Verbal al Ședințelor Comitetului Național Român din 13 și 14 Noiembrie 1950, CNR, box 3, folder 2, HIA.
[167] Proces-Verbal al Ședinței Comitetului Național Român din 1 Decembrie 1950, CNR, box 3, folder 2, HIA.
[168] Dare de seamă asupra activității Comitetului Național în cursul lunei Septembrie 1949, CNR, box 1, folder 1, HIA.
[169] Ibid.
[170] Dare de seamă asupra activității Comitetului Național în cursul lunei Noiembrie 1949, box 1, folder 1, HIA.
[171] Ibid.
[172] Butariu, "Assembly of Captive European Nations", 128–129.
[173] Ibid; Stefan Issărescu, "A Life Dedicated To Romania: Brutus Coste", *Journal of the American Romanian Academy of Arts and Sciences,* nr. 8–9 (1986) 75–78.
[174] Ibid.
[175] Ibid.
[176] Dare de seamă asupra activității Comitetului Național în cursul lunei Octombrie 1949, CNR, box 1, folder 1, HIA.
[177] Ibid.
[178] Ibid.
[179] Memorandum on Deportations in Rumania, CNR, box 1, folder 1, HIA; Pamphlet of the "Central and Eastern European Conference" Washington D.C. 1951, CNR, box 2, folder 15, HIA.
[180] Activitatea Comitetului Național Român în anul 1952, CNR, box 1, folder 1, HIA.
[181] Comisia Prezidențială Pentru Analiza Dictaturii Comuniste Din România. Raport Final (București: Humanitas 2007) 276–279.
[182] Activitatea Comitetului Național Român în anul 1952, CNR, box 1, folder 1, HIA.
[183] Regulamentul financiar al Comitetului Național, CNR, box 1, folder 6, HIA; Regulament Interior Pentru Funcționarea Organelor Secretariatului General Al Comitetului Național Român, CNR, box 1, folder 6, HIA.

184 Dare de seamă asurpa activității Comitetului Național în Cursul Lunei Septembrie 1949, CNR, box 1, folder 1, HIA; Dare de seamă asupra activității Comitetului Național în Cursul Lunilor Decembrie 1949, Ianuarie și Februarie 1950, CNR, box 1, folder 6, HIA.

185 Proces-Verbal. Ședințele din 26 și 27 Septembrie 1949, CNR, box 3, folder 2, HIA.

186 Marinescu, *O Contribuție*, vol. 1, 352.

187 Scrisoarea lui C. Vișoianu domniei sale Domnului General C. Petre Lazăr din Casa Majestății Sale Regelui Mihai I, CNR, box 13, folder 6, HIA; Marinescu, *O Contribuție*, vol. 1, 408–412.

188 Ibid. Gheorghe Tătărăscu, appointed foreign minister in the Petru Groza government, immediately tried to recover the Romanian National Fund, addressing a complaint against Cretzianu in a Swiss court on November 17, 1945. See, Marinescu, *O Contributie*, vol. 1, 390.

189 Ibid.

190 Ibid.

191 Ibid.

192 Proces-Verbal Nr. 17 din 9 Septembrie 1949, CNR, box 3, folder 4, HIA.

193 Proces-Verbal al Ședinței Comitetului Național Român din 29 Martie 1974, CNR, box 4, folder 2, HIA.

194 Marinescu, *O Contribuție*, vol. 1, 387.

195 Scrisoarea către General N. Rădescu din 19 Decembrie 1949, CNR, box 3, folder 2, HIA.

196 Dare de seamă asupra activității Comitetului Național în Cursul Lunei Octombrie 1949, CNR, box 1, folder 1, HIA.

197 Dare de seamă asupra activității Comitetului Național în Cursul Lunei Septembrie 1949, CNR, box 3, folder 2, HIA.

198 Scrisoarea lui Al. Cretzianu către Barbu Niculescu din 14 Noiembrie 1949, CNR, box 2, folder 2, HIA.

199 Declarațiune făcută de Dl. Al. Cretzianu în cursul ședinței din 9 Octombrie 1950 a Comitetului Național, CNR, box 2, folder 5, HIA.

200 Scrisoarea lui Al. Cretzianu către Emil Ghilezan din 10 Iulie 1950, CNR, box 2, folder 2, HIA.

201 Marinescu, *O Contribuție*, vol. 1, 387.

202 Proces-Verbal al Ședinței Comitetului Național Român din ziua de 15 Iunie 1951, CNR, box 3, folder 4, HIA.

203 See: Letter from Vișoianu to Cloyce K. Huston of July 30, 1955 on the personal work of each member of the Romanian National Committee, CNR, box 3, folder 5, HIA.

204 Scrisoarea lui C. Vișoianu către George Assan din 15 August 1955, CNR, box 2, folder 1, HIA.

205 Scrisoarea președintelui C. Vișoianu către Regele Mihai din 15 Noiembrie 1955, CNR, box 3, folder 5, HIA.

206 Proces-Verbal al Ședinței Comitetului Național Român din ziua de 13 Decembrie 1955, CNR, box 3, folder 5, HIA; Proces-Verbal al Ședinței Comitetului Național Român din ziua de 18 Octombrie 1955, CNR, box 3, folder 5, HIA.

207 From the beginning of October 1955, the Romanian National Committee also had an official headquarters in New York City situated at 157 West 57th Street. See: Dare de seamă asupra activității Comitetului Național Român în cursul lunilor Iulie-Noiembrie 1955, CNR, box 3, folder 5, HIA.

208 Dare de seamă asupra activității Comitetului Național Român. Decembrie 1955, CNR, box 3, folder 5, HIA; Recepția din 14 Decembrie de la New York a Comitetului Național, CNR, box 3, folder 5, HIA.

209 Marinescu, *O contribuție*, vol. 1, 406–407.
210 Scrisoarea lui C. Vișoianu către George Assan din 26 Iulie 1957, CNR, box 2, folder 1, HIA.
211 Scrisoarea lui C. Vișoianu către Niculae D. Ciotori din 8 August 1957, CNR, box 2, folder 1, HIA.
212 Memorandum concerning the present needs of the Rumanian National Committee, CNR, box 2, folder 11, HIA.
213 Butariu, "Assembly of Captive European Nations", 147.
214 Marinescu, *O Contribuție*, vol. 2, 581.
215 Proces-Verbal al Ședinței Comitetului Național Român din 12 Aprilie 1973, CNR, box 4, folder 4, HIA.
216 Ibid; Criza Comitetului Național Român.Declarațiile Domnului George Serdici, Georges de Serdici, box 9, folder 32, HIA.
217 Proces-Verbal al Ședinței Comitetului Național Român din 18 Septembrie 1974, CNR, box 4, folder 4, HIA.
218 Ibid.
219 Proces-Verbal al Ședinței Comitetului Național Român din 8 Mai 1975, CNR, box 4, folder 4, HIA.
220 Proces-Verbal al Ședinței Comitetului Național Român din 8 Decembrie 1975, CNR, box 4, folder 4, HIA.
221 Marinescu, *O Contribuție*, vol. 1, 376.
222 Ibid., 383.
223 Some avenues of inquiry regarding the RNC have not been taken in this paper and will be the subjects of future analysis. These include, the Committee's relations with Romanian-American organizations; its memorandums and reports to the United Nations regarding religious prosecution in Romania and the problem of war deportees and prisoners; the social assistance of refugees and exiles in Europe and the US; an analysis of communist propaganda in the Romanian Orthodox church in the United States and France and inside the Romanian cultural associations and organizations in exile; details of the RNC's cooperation with the other National Committees; and the exodus of the German and Jewish population from Romania.

Select bibliography

Archive resources

Hoover Institution Archives, Stanford University, Stanford, California

Register of the Comitetul Național Român Records, 1945–1975.
Register of the Poland Ministerstwo Spraw Zagranicznych Records, 1919–1947, series 3.
Register of the Georges de Serdici, baron, papers, 1947–1990.

Articles:

Miron Butariu, "Assembly of Captive European Nations. The Little United Nations-The Voice of the People", *Journal of the American Romanian Academy of Arts and Sciences,* nr. 10, (Davis, California, 1987)

Matei Călinescu, "The 1927 Generation in Romania: Friendships and Ideological Choices (Mihail Sebastian, Mircea Eliade, Nae Ionescu, Eugene Ionesco, E.M. Cioran", *East European Politics and Socities* 15, nr 3,

Nicolette Franck, *Defeat in Victory: How the Kingdom of Romania Became a Popular Republic (1944–1947)*, in *"Journal of the American Romanian Academy of Arts and Sciences"*, nr. 6–7 (Davis-California, 1985)
Mircea Ionnitiu, "The Takeover Of Romania 6 March 1945", Journal of the *American Romanian Academy of Arts and Sciences*, nr. 8–9 (Davis- California, 1986)
Mircea Ionnitiu, "Two Brave Forgotten Men: Generalul Nicolae Rădescu and Grigore Niculescu-Buzești", *Journal of the American Romanian Academy of Arts and Sciences*, nr. 13–14 (Davis, California, 1990)
Stefan Issărescu, "A Life Dedicated To Romania: Brutus Coste", *Journal of the American Romanian Aacademy of Arts and Sciences*, nr. 8–9 (Davis, California, 1986)

Newspapers:
Curierul Creștin, Gherla, 15 Noiembrie 1929, nr. 22
Evening Star, 16 February, 1965
New York Times, 10 May 1949, October 5, 1949
Saturday Evening Post, 25 July 1942, vol. 215, Issue 4
Spokane Daily Chronicle (Spokane), 10 June, 1949, Empire Edition, nr. 225

Books:
Mircea Ciobanu, În *fața neamului meu-Convorbiri cu MS Regele Mihai* (Iași:Princeps, 1995)
Mircea Ciobanu, *Noi convorbiri cu Regele Mihai I al României* (București: Humanitas, 1992)
Stephan A. Fischer-Galați, ed. *Romania* (New York: Frederick A. Praeger, 1957)
Ionescu Ghiță, *Communism in Rumania, 1944–1962*, (Oxford: University Press, 1964)
Keith Hitchins, *Rumania, 1866–1947*, (Oxford, Clarendon Press, 1944)
Paul Lindenberg, *Regele Carol I al României* (București: Humanitas, 2006)
Aurel Sergiu Marinescu, *O Contribuție la Istoria Exilului Românesc*, (București, Vremea, 1999), vol. 1
Aurel Sergiu Marinescu, *O Contribuție la Istoria Exilului Românesc* (București, Vremea, 2002), vol. 2
Roy Melbourne, "Witness to the Start of the Cold War: The view from Romania", in Paul D. Quinlan (ed.), *The United States and Romania. American-Romanian Relations During the Twentieth Century*, (Woodland Hills, California, 1988)
Rozeta Metes, *The Iuliu Maniu American-Romanian Relief Foundation* (Cleveland, Ohio, 1977)
Paul D. Quinlan, *Clash Over Romania. British and American Policies Towards Romania: 1938–1947*, (Los Angeles 1977)
Lavinia S.Stan, "The Cultural and Political Strategies of Exile: Romanians in the Cold War," in Ausna Cindina, Jonathan Osmond, Power and Culture. Hegemony, Interaction and Dissent (Pisa:Edizioni Plus, 2006)
Astrid Suhrke, "Uncertain Globalization: Refugee Movement in the Second half of the Twentieth Century," in Wang Gungwu, *Global History and Migrations* (Boulder, 1997)

IV

The Baltic Freedom Committees: Politics and Policies of an Exile Community

Jonathan H. L'Hommedieu

Introduction

When describing one of the methods of engaging in psychological warfare against the Soviet Union in 1948, the director of the State Department's Policy Planning Staff, George F. Kennan, proposed that the United States should support the establishment of "liberation committees" that would serve as "foci of national hope" for political refugees, "provide inspiration" for popular resistance within the Soviet Union, and "serve as a potential nucleus for all-out liberation movements in the event of war."[1] Within the context of National Security Council directive 10/2, these proposed liberation committees were to be overt operations guided by trusted American citizens and receive covert guidance and possible financial assistance from the United States government.[2] By 1949 policymakers engaged in serious debate about whether such liberation committees should be established and how they should function, it was decided that the United States would establish an organization that would organize émigrés into liberation committees, would receive "confidential or unvouchered [sic] fund" from the CIA, and receive policy guidance from the State Department.[3]

Joseph C. Grew, former American ambassador to Japan, held a press conference in New York City on 1 June 1949 announcing that the National Committee for Free Europe, Inc. had been created with the assistance of a number of noteworthy private American citizens on its board, including Dwight D. Eisenhower, DeWitt Wallace, publisher of Reader's Digest, and Henry Luce, publisher of Time, Fortune, and Life magazines. The ostensibly private organization was created by "freedom loving Americans" as part of an effort to counter the threat of communism.[4]

Initially, the National Committee for Free Europe, Inc. (NCFE) divided its activities into three discrete units: 1) Committee on Intellectual Activity [its name belies its function, as its purpose was to "find suitable employment for escaped political and intellectual leaders"]… 2) Committee on Radio and the Press; 3) Committee on American Contacts and the National Councils as a section separate of the other 3 committees. "They actively assist the NCFE to accomplish the purposes already outlined for committees 1, 2 and 3."[5] Within a few years after the establishment of Radio Free Europe, the emphasis of the organization shifted and Radio broadcasting became the most important NCFE activity. However, the organization also sponsored a plethora of other exile activities that ranged from the establishment of a Free Europe University in Strasbourg France to the Free Europe Press that published the prominent exile literature and scholarship.[6] Perhaps one of the most important short-term projects that the NCFE started was the Mid-European Studies Center (MESC) in New York City. The MESC's goal was to assist exiled academics' transition into academic positions at American institutions of higher education.[7] In return, the NCFE hoped that its activities would foster a sense of political solidarity among Eastern European exiles that could be eventually tapped as a useful resource to combat the Soviet Union.

The Soviet Union's annexation of the Baltic States of Estonia, Latvia, and Lithuania in the summer of 1940 represented one the earliest examples of Soviet territorial aggrandizement and aggression in Eastern Europe. One of the greatest legacies of World War II for these three small states was the demographic tragedy associated with German and Soviet deportations, the Holocaust, wartime fatalities, and the flight of thousands of Estonians, Latvians, and Lithuanians to the West. From 1942 to 1945, roughly 60,000 Estonians, 100,000 Latvians, and 50,000 Lithuanians fled.[8] Baltic Displaced Persons refused to repatriate to the Soviet Union from the American and British zones of occupation in Germany during the postwar period. This not only resulted in the establishment of vibrant exile communities in the United States, Australia, and Western Europe due to migration but also served as a potential pool of recruits for American officials who sought to use political exiles from Eastern Europe as weapons against the Soviet Union in the early Cold War.

In many respects, the Estonian, Latvian, and Lithuanian exiles residing in United States and Western Europe shared many of the same goals as other Eastern European exiles during the late 1940s. There was a rejection of the Soviet influence over their homelands as well as a belief that the United States would become a strong ally in their attempts to undermine Soviet hegemony. The diplomatic status of the Baltic States from the perspective of the United States, however, was markedly different from that of the satellite nations of the Soviet bloc. While the United States maintained diplomatic relations with nations such as Poland, it continued a policy of non-recognition towards the Baltic States, which dated back to the initial Soviet annexation in 1940.[9] Nevertheless, the preconditions were present for the Free Europe Committee to work alongside Baltic exiles in their campaign against the Soviet Union.

Despite this seeming convergence of interests between Baltic exiles and the Free Europe Committee, the initial attitude of NCFE officials towards the Baltic States was ambiguous at best. This ambiguous relationship, in addition to the fact that Baltic exiles were the only nationality groups whose homelands were constituent republics of the Soviet Union, made the Baltic Freedom Committees, which were eventually established, unique among the national freedom committees sponsored by the NCFE. This ambiguity can best be understood through the context of the diplomatic status of the Baltic republics, the small size of the Baltic republics relative to other states, and the financial costs of starting Baltic committees relative to their small size. This chapter will broadly explore political developments within and surrounding the Committees for a Free Estonia, Free Latvia, and Free Lithuania. More specific questions that will be addressed include: How did contacts between Baltic exiles and the National Committee for a Free Europe begin and develop over time? What were the reactions within the broader Baltic exile communities towards the Baltic Freedom Committees and how they did they affect unity within the communities? How did the debate over NCFE-sponsored radio broadcasts impact the Baltic Freedom Committees? Who were the audiences to which the committees directed their activities, particularly within the United States? How did international events undermine the rationale for continued sponsorship of the Baltic Freedom Committees?

Initiation of Contacts & Establishment of Panels

Considering that the NCFE was viewed from the outside as an organization that private American citizens created to give voice to Eastern European exiles and that the organization provided material assistance to prominent exiles through employment and transition assistance, it was inevitable that exile communities that were not initially brought under the NCFE umbrella would rapidly begin lobbying all facets of American society for inclusion. By the spring of 1950, Estonians, Latvians, and Lithuanians began pursuing such contacts. Although myriad Baltic organizations in the United States attempted to influence the NCFE to open lines of communication with the Estonian, Latvian, and Lithuanian exiles, it was the Baltic diplomats accredited to the United States and the American Lithuanian Council (ALT) that were the most influential in this endeavor. The first contacts between the Baltic diplomatic missions and the NCFE occurred during the late spring and summer of 1950.[10] The main argument that the diplomats used with their interlocutors was that Baltic panels associated with the NCFE would help unify the diasporas whose constituents perceived themselves as temporary refugees in the United States and hoped to return to their homelands as soon as possible to reassert "democratic standards."[11]

On 17 March 1950, the Lithuanian American Information Center (LAIC) submitted their first formal protest against the omission of the Baltic States from NCFE activities.[12] On 24 September 1950, the ALT's Congress passed a resolution stating: "Whereas, Lithuania, Latvia, and Estonia, are in urgent need of support of the cause of liberation... [Therefore,] be it resolved that the Lithuanian Organizations of Chicago appeal and request the NCFE to include Lithuania, and the other two Baltic States, in the Committee's plans and National Program for the liberation of Soviet-enslaved and dominated Europe."[13]

Unknown to Baltic activists, the NCFE had begun making plans in order to collaborate with Baltic exile groups. PROJECT 1-1951 was created on 15 March 1950 with the intention of coordinating "Baltic States' Activities within the NCFE."[14] The initial proposal called for the creation of consultative panels and groups of individuals that would work with the Mid-European Studies Center, American Contacts Division, and Radio Free Europe. The plan proposed that after the successful creation of panels, by 31 March 1950 Baltic scholars would be employed by the Mid-European Studies Center, the American Contacts Division would hire Baltic lecturers Baltic lecturers, and Radio desks would be established.[15]

Officials acknowledged to the Baltic diplomats their reasons behind initial reticence towards initiating such projects. First, FEC officials viewed the non-recognition policy of the Soviet annexation of Estonia, Latvia, and Lithuania as being a net positive for the emigrations, since they continued to have diplomatic representation of the "democratic side" as opposed to the "totalitarian side" as in the cases of Poland and Hungary.[16] On 25 May 1950, a NCFE official asked Latvian Chargé d'Affaires Jules Feldmans if it was in his interest to support a Latvian panel, as it might prove to be inimical to his own diplomatic position in Washington.[17] Second, NCFE officials acknowledged that they had limited resources and had decided to give larger countries that lacked any sort of democratic diplomatic representation in the West the organization's top priorities.[18] Ultimately, in August 1950, the NCFE contacted the State Department's policy planning staff to give further guidance on the issue, as their first impression was to "doubt the advisability of forming national councils along the lines of those in the satellite countries in view of the existence of diplomatic representation acceptable to us."[19]

Despite the initial setback, Feldmans continued to make preparations to begin cooperative efforts with the FEC. On 25 July, the NCFE received a letter from Feldmans with a list of potential Latvian exiles who could form an NCFE committee.[20] Although the list of names largely represented officials of the former authoritarian government, and not the pre-1934 democratic elements, on 5 October a meeting between the two factions of Latvian diplomats took place in London, where it appeared as though there would be some reconciliation.[21] Meanwhile, the NCFE gave instructions to its staff to go ahead with preparations for the creation of Baltic panels.

On 2 October 1950, the NCFE asked the State Department if it would be appropriate to informally approach Feldmans about creating an advisory body to utilize Baltic refugees more effectively. The FEC argued that such a solution would combine the legal continuity of the exiled diplomats with the broad-based representative nature of a national council.[22] Conditions were placed on how such an advisory body should be created if it were to receive NCFE funding. As a way of promoting unity among the competing political factions in the emigration, financial assistance would only be granted to a "genuinely representative" group that represented both the official elements of the Latvian government and the pre-1934 democratic elements.[23] The three consultative panels, as envisaged by the NCFE, would consist of seven members and have similar functions as the national councils that already represented countries such as Hungary. All panel members necessarily had to be exiles, but members of the Baltic diplomatic corps would be excluded. Further, it would not duplicate the activities of the Baltic diplomatic missions in the United States. The panels would receive a budget of roughly $60,000 annually.[24]

NCFE officials met with Feldmans on 28 December to propose the idea of creating a Latvian Consultative Panel. Feldmans considered it to be an excellent solution to the problem of fostering a closer relationship between the Latvian emigration and the FEC and agreed that no members of the Latvian diplomatic corps should be members. The question of broad representation among the various political factions in the Latvian Diaspora proved to be contentious. Feldmans held the opinion that exiled political parties had absolutely no relevance in either the situation existing in territorial Latvia or the political situation that would exist in a future independent Latvia, implying that exiled political parties had no role in any cooperation with NCFE.[25] The NCFE official stressed that if any political faction felt under-represented, the resulting open hostility to the Latvian panel would undermine its effectiveness.[26] Feldmans conceded the point but stressed that political orientation should only play a minor part in creating the panel.

After receiving a positive answer from the Latvian diplomat, NCFE officials subsequently contacted the Estonian Consul General in New York, Johannes Kaiv, on 12 January and the Lithuanian minister in Washington, Povilas Žadeikis, on 25 January to discuss the creation of Estonian and Lithuanian consultative panels.[27] Both Kaiv and Žadeikis confirmed their willingness to work towards the creation of their respective panels and were presented with suggestions relevant to their diasporas' political situation. Kaiv argued that a consultative panel was a better idea than a national council, due to the complicated political situation of the Baltic States, and the FEC official suggested that one or two members of the panel should be drawn from members of the Estonian emigration residing in Sweden, since the largest group of Estonian exiles resided there.[28] During the meeting with Žadeikis, the Lithuanian diplomat submitted a list of eighteen names that he thought should be considered as members of the Lithuanian consultative panel, which was eventually reduced to seven members.[29]

Meanwhile, Kaiv and Feldmans submitted lists of their own candidates that should participate in the first iteration of the Estonian and Latvian panels. On 19 January, Kaiv and Kaarel Pusta submitted the names of Ernst Ein, Leonhard Vahter, Adolf Perandi, Ilma Raamot, and Aksel Mei to the NCFE for consideration as members of the Estonian Panel.[30] The Estonians considered it wise to begin with five names and increase it to seven at a later date, depending on whether or not to include exiles residing outside the United States. Feldmans submitted eight names to the NCFE on 22 January and reaffirmed his opinion that consultative panels were more appropriate compared to national committees. He was under a great deal of pressure from a plethora of Latvian nationals who viewed the creation of a national committee as an excellent way to promote a government-in-exile, but this was a concept that Feldmans disapproved of "as it represented nothing."[31]

In January 1951, the NCFE gave both written and verbal approval that the Baltic States should be included within the scope of the organization's activities.[32] After the NCFE and leading Baltic exiles completed the assembly of the consultative panels, the NCFE promised to move forward with creating radio desks to broadcast to each Baltic nation and to include Baltic exiles in the full portfolio of activities that the organization had created. Although the NCFE had created its own independent list while deliberating internally over whether or not to reach out to the Baltic diasporas, the Estonian, Latvian, and Lithuanian diplomats had a significant role in deciding who would ultimately sit on the consultative panels. For instance, the eight members of the Lithuanian panel, led by Vaclovas Sidzikauskas, were all of the same generation – born in the late nineteenth or early twentieth centuries; were all former members of government or inter-war Lithuania's academia; each represented a political party that existed in Lithuania prior to 1926; and all had resided in the United States for fewer than three years.[33]

On 24 May, 1951 permission was granted for the formal creation of Estonian, Latvian, and Lithuanian consultative panels, despite not yet having a solution to the radio funding issue. The primary goal of the Baltic consultative panels was to work "under the auspices of the NCFE, to work hard for the emancipation of the Lithuanian people from aggressive Soviet imperialism and for the restoration of human rights in our country."[34] Although the long-term objective of the consultative panels was to prepare for the eventual liberation and re-democratization of Estonia, Latvia, and Lithuania, there were three main activities of consequence that the panels participated in over the short-term. First, the Americans hoped that the Baltic consultative panels would serve as a unifying factor among the Estonian, Latvian, and Lithuanian emigrations, which was seen as an important precondition to the liberation of East and Central Europe. Second, the panels were to cooperate with other organs of the NCFE, specifically RFE broadcasts. Third, the panels took it upon themselves to provide accurate information about the political, economic, and social conditions in the Soviet republics.

From Panels to Committees: Attempts to Unify the Emigrations

The primary rationale for the establishing of national committees by the NCFE, and of consultative panels (in the case of the Baltic republics) was to foster rapprochement among various political factions within each nationality, in the hope of promoting a unified opposition front of exiles against communism. Although the Baltic diplomats, leading exiles, FEC officials, and the State Department attempted to mollify political factionalism through providing politically balanced charter panels, the initial attempts at fostering cooperation by means of each diaspora was decidedly mixed.

In response to the composition of the Estonian Panel, the World Federation of Free Estonians (VEKO), based in Stockholm, issued a strong protest. VEKO argued that not one of its members had been included on the panel while two members of the competing organization in Stockholm, the Estonian National Committee (ERN) had been included. They continued by stating that VEKO has a larger membership than the ERN and that they were suffering from unfair discrimination. FEC officials responded to VEKO's chairman that members of the Estonian Consultative Panel did not serve as representatives of any party or organization. Discussions between Kaiv, the FEC, and the Estonian Consultative Panel in August 1951 resulted in an agreement that the Consultative Panel would directly negotiate with VEKO to insure that there would be a settlement that was satisfactory to all concerned.[35]

The Latvian exile community was equally displeased with the initial composition of the Latvian Consultative Panel. The most significant concern that Latvians had was that the panel had too many members and was composed of right-wing Latvians at the expense of the left-wing and the Social Democrats. Additional concern came from religiously devout Latvians. Lutherans were upset that the Lutheran Church, as an institution, was not represented on the panel, and exiles from Latgale were concerned that Catholics were not represented. Finally, a small organization, the Latvian Liberal Union in Sweden, was upset that no member from their organization was represented. The NCFE response to all of these concerns was that the political criticism was unfounded since the panel was composed of liberals, the Peasant Party, and those not affiliated with a particular party, but held liberal or socialistic views. The Lutherans were told that all of the members of the panel were Lutherans. The Catholics were told that there were plans to have Bishop Rancans from Latgale sit on the panel, but he had not been able to accept as he had not yet received permission from Church hierarchy. Finally, the Latvian Liberal Union was told that that panel did not represent any particular organization.[36] On the other hand, the Lithuanian immigration was generally pleased with the composition of its Consulative Panel. NCFE officials argued that this was the case because the panel consisted of eight members (as opposed to the five Estonians and seven Latvians) who represented each of Lithuania's political parties, plus one individual from Memelland.[37]

Despite the inherent problems that the Baltic panels had in fostering a high-level of cooperation among the disparate groups in the Baltic exile community, on 27 February, 1952, the NCFE decided that the panels had succeeded in their initial portfolio of activities. The NCFE argued that the panels had achieved a position of importance in the Baltic exile communities and established a good working relationship with the diplomatic representatives in the United States. It was stated that "they have now achieved a position where it would be possible to no longer designate them simply as Consultative Panels to the Fund, but as National Committees for a Free Estonia, Latvia, and Lithuania.[38]

The Radio Free Europe and Voice of America Debate

Throughout 1950 and 1951, State Department officials and leading Baltic exiles were engaged in vigorous discussion about the proper broadcasting avenue to reach the relatively few speakers of the Baltic languages. At the highest level, there was general agreement between the Americans and their Baltic counterparts that Estonian, Latvian, and Lithuanian-language broadcasts were an important component to further American policy towards the Baltic republics but there were three main issues that proved contentious. First, official American policy towards the Baltic republics, which held that that the non-recognition policy placed Baltic radio broadcasts in a separate category from other parts of the Soviet bloc. Second, funding: given the small size of the three Baltic republics' diasporas relative to those of other Eastern European nationalities, the United States had to make policy decisions based on efficient use of limited resources. Finally, symbolism: a basic misunderstanding existed regarding what radio broadcasts meant for the Baltic republics and their exiled compatriots.

An important component of Baltic exile lobbying of the NCFE about the establishment of Baltic consultative panels was the implicit understanding that closer cooperation between Baltic exiles and the NCFE would result in eventual radio broadcasts under RFE. The NCFE and State Department's internal deliberations about formalizing a relationship with the Baltic exile community in January 1951 underscored the centrality of radio broadcasts to the project. Correspondences between the Baltic Desk and the Policy Planning Staff highlight that the core of NCFE cooperation with Baltic exiles should be similar to NCFE cooperation with other Eastern European exiles – that is, centered on radio broadcasts that would occur at regular 15 minute intervals.[39]

When it was announced in May 1951 that Baltic Consultative Panels would be created, Baltic organizations in the United States, along with the exiled diplomats, vigorously continued to push the NCFE to establish Baltic radio desks. Although State Department and NCFE officials sympathized with those that actively promoted RFE broadcasts to the Baltic republics, major policy concerns remained. Of primary importance was what the implications of RFE broadcasts on the non-recognition policy would be. Additional questions included: What would the financial burden of Baltic broadcasts be? How would staff for the possible radio desks be assembled?

Parallel to the push for Baltic RFE broadcasts was an intense lobbying effort to begin Voice of America (VOA) broadcasts in the three Baltic languages. While RFE necessarily involved contacts between legitimate exiles and American interlocutors, the VOA was predominantly an American affair. Lithuanians, who were the most organizationally strong and numerous Baltic nationality in the United States, took the lead in lobbying the State Department and the White House to begin VOA broadcasts. At the annual ALT meeting in New York City on 17–18 November, 1950, three resolutions were passed supporting the initiation of VOA broadcasts to Lithuania.[40] Vedeler responded to Grigaitis's submission of the resolutions by updating him, stating that he had been in New York the previous week discussing Lithuanian matters with United States Information Agency officials and confirming that broadcasts should start in the middle of February 1951.[41]

Lithuanian pressure, however, was not exclusively reserved for the State Department or White House. Republican Representative from Pennsylvania Daniel J. Flood had a number of prominent American Lithuanians among his constituencies. In addition, he also had established a working relationship with Žadeikis. While the debate over whether or not to begin VOA broadcasts continued, Flood kept Žadeikis informed on the current state of affairs. He wrote to Žadeikis on 28 March 1950 informing him that while the present priorities were being given to a series of broadcasts in the Asiatic languages, he should be assured that plans were still underway for the Baltic languages.[42]

Flood served on the House Appropriations Committee and was willing to use his influence over the State Department's annual budget to apply pressure on behalf of Baltic VOA broadcasts. During the appropriations hearings for the 1951 State Department budget, Flood asked the State Department's representative, Kohler, a number of questions pertaining to Baltic broadcasts – particularly stressing the importance of Lithuanian broadcasts. Flood asked: "With reference to your Baltic language programs of the VOA, Estonia, Latvia, and Lithuania, your choice of course, as between the three, the one of superior importance is Lithuania?" Kohler replied, "Yes, due to the increased numbers and for other reasons such as geography, resistance movement, and the ability to organize a larger number of Lithuanians residing in the free world."[43]

VOA Lithuanian broadcasts started on 16 February 1951 with a fifteen-minute daily program featuring Žadeikis along with Under Secretary of State Edward W. Barrett,[44] and on 3 June 1951 they started in Estonian and Latvian, featuring the Estonian and Latvian diplomats and Barrett.[45] While the Lithuanian broadcasts increased their broadcasting time to thirty minutes daily in June 1951 and the Estonian and Latvian broadcasts increased on 26 August 1951, the debate over RFE broadcasts continued to consume the time of American officials concerned with Baltic affairs as well as of Baltic organizations.[46] When the NCFE first began formulating policy for Baltic broadcasts, there were no plans or appropriations within the International Broadcasting Division in New York to broadcast in these languages.[47] The relative ease with which the VOA began broadcasting in Estonian, Latvian, and Lithuanian meant that policymakers and exiles faced a significant policy hurdle going forward if they sought to begin Baltic-language broadcasts over RFE.

Discussions between NCFE and State Department officials reveal the two intrinsically linked policy reservations about continuing plans for Baltic RFE broadcasts. On one hand, there were questions whether Baltic radio broadcasts would be a fortuitous use of the NCFE's perceived limited resources. Coupled with the debate on how to fund Estonian, Latvian, and Lithuanian broadcasts exposed considerable implications for sustaining the non-recognition policy.[48] The total cost of the initial NCFE Baltic plans was estimated at $441,600. RFE documents suggest that the total cost could be reduced dramatically by reducing the broadcasting element of the Baltic proposal.[49]

Despite the existence of VOA broadcasts, NCFE officials continued to seek approval for broadcast funding since it had been part of its negotiations with the Baltic diplomats and other Baltic organizations.[50] The NCFE, however, needed to find some way to justify continuing the plans to broadcast to the Baltic republics. Throughout 1951, regular discussions between State Department and NCFE officials culminated in the NCFE's decision to propose that the Baltic diasporas should make a sizeable contribution of funds towards FEC-sponsored broadcasts to their homelands. As a result, NCFE sent the State Department a memorandum asking whether it would be possible to ask for donations from Baltic Americans to subsidize broadcasts and for the State Department to unblock frozen Baltic funds in the United States to help fund the NCFE's efforts.[51]

Vedeler outlined the State Department's position towards the use of frozen Baltic funds for radio broadcasts. "The Department can see no way clear to unblocking any of the Baltic frozen funds for this purpose." He continued, "We do not wish to see the position or the operations of the Baltic diplomatic missions jeopardized by utilizing these blocked funds in some other way. So long as these funds exist the representatives of the Baltic countries have some measure of independence which supports our doctrine of non-recognition."[52] The implications were clear that the State Department was not willing to allow radio broadcasts over RFE to jeopardize the cornerstone of its policy towards the Baltic republics – the non-recognition policy.

American officials found themselves in a precarious situation in which there were very real policy and economic problems with RFE broadcasts as well as potential political problems with the Baltic exiles to whom they had virtually promised access to the wavelengths of Radio Free Europe. Kohler wrote to Robert Bauer of the PPS in November 1951 asking for documents from the Baltic desk chiefs of the VOA broadcasts giving a rundown of what specifically they were broadcasting. Kohler was hoping to demonstrate that there was an amount of overlap between the VOA and RFE broadcasts sufficient enough to square the circle, so to speak. To create his report, Bauer contacted IBD personnel and several prominent Baltic exiles that were predisposed to VOA, as well as the new Baltic Freedom Committees.

Bauer responded to Kohler on 7 November arguing that the VOA program to the Baltic region had consistently implemented and carried out the clear-cut American policy towards the area. He continued by offering critiques of American broadcasting policy by several notable Estonians and Lithuanians. August Torma, the Estonian Minister in London, stated that he "backs without reservation the American policy toward the area and its implementation by the VOA." The three Baltic Consultative Panels all gave very specific recommendations to the VOA on what their broadcasts should include, and they were all fully implemented. Bauer concluded that Sidzikauskas (who had been promoted to chairman of the Lithuanian Freedom Committee) and Marzins (a member of the Latvian Freedom Committee) had all been actively involved in formulating VOA broadcasts to their respective homelands.[53]

Throughout November 1951, regular correspondences between NCFE and State Department policymakers occurred to finalize what the official policy concerning American broadcasts to the Baltic region would be. In their final analysis, the State Department decided to argue that the non-recognition policy ultimately was a benefit to American broadcasting efforts. One of the original rationales for separating RFE broadcasting from VOA broadcasting in the first place was to allow the United States to broadcast material that might not have been officially acceptable with respect to diplomatic protocols with other states. The non-recognition policy meant that the United States did not have to worry about increasing diplomatic tensions with regimes that they did not recognize. Kohler argued:

> To use a separate and distinct RFE operation to an area controlled by the USSR makes sense only if it can use medium wave facilities not available to VOA and if it can make use of political exiles in a manner denied to the VOA as an official arm of government policy. Neither of these criteria apply in the Baltic States. The contemplated competing shortwave operation of RFE could only serve to confuse target peoples.
>
> If it is deemed advisable to expand broadcasting to these areas – the logical thing to do would be to give VOA a directive to the effect and to provide the necessary funds for carrying on this expansion. In short, we feel that the funds available to RFE could be more profitably and with less confusion be expanded elsewhere.[54]

Going forward, the State Department was going to justify the cancelation of RFE broadcasts to the Baltic republics due to the broadcasts being too expensive and the fact that the VOA would be able to provide the same policy initiatives to both the Americans and the Baltic exiles that RFE might otherwise have been able to provide.

RFE and Operations of Intelligence Branch officials met on 5 December 1951 to discuss what help the State Department could provide to RFE in liquidating their commitments over Baltic broadcasting. Looking back at the meeting, Kohler reported that there was clearly a great deal of suppressed resentment directed at the State Department, creating an environment that was less than cordial. The first point of contention was that that the RFE officials that were in charge of the Baltic programs had not received any specific long-term instructions about how to proceed, but were told only to suspend their activities pending a review and receipt of further instructions. The second and perhaps most important point was that they felt that it was the State Department's responsibility to ensure that the Baltic diplomats were made aware of the official policy line.[55] Concurrently, during regularly scheduled appointments with State Department Baltic Desk officials, the Baltic diplomats were beginning to express their displeasure about broadcasting delays. Throughout December 1951, the State Department utilized these meetings as opportunities to inform the Baltic diplomats of the official broadcasting policy.

Feldmans and Kaarel Pusta Sr. met with Vedeler and Allan on 12 December to ask about the future of American-sponsored radio broadcasts to Latvia and Estonia. Pusta stated in no uncertain terms that the failure to initiate Baltic RFE broadcasts would result in the appearance that the United States was slighting the Baltic States and that the only way to avoid such a falling out was to inaugurate broadcasts. Pusta intimated that this fact alone was significant enough to be a primary reason to begin broadcasts. Pusta and Feldmans asked how the State Department could explain to Baltic refugees in the West or to Balts behind the Iron Curtain why an American organization interested in opposing Soviet tyranny could broadcast to other places in Eastern Europe but ignore the Baltic States? Vedeler asked "what tasks, if any, could be performed by RFE, which are not being done by VOA?"[56] Neither Pusta Sr. nor Feldmans was able to provide a specific answer.

One week later, Kaiv and Žadeikis met with Allan and Vedeler to double down on the Baltic diplomats' position that RFE broadcasts were essential for the Baltic refugees as well as for Balts in the Soviet Union. The diplomats strongly felt that the abandonment of Baltic-language broadcasts by RFE would be misunderstood in the United States and abroad and that the decision would be interpreted widely as a change in the position of the United States towards Estonia, Latvia, and Lithuania. Kaiv continued by stating that Baltic-language broadcasts had been known and widely discussed among exile groups abroad as an excellent medium for providing support and boosting morale for their compatriots fighting for their freedom.

Vedeler stressed that Balts should not take away any political significance from the decision to not support RFE broadcasts and that the decision was "strictly based on the desire to produce the most effective broadcasts in the Baltic languages by concentrating professional efforts in a single organization."[57] Vedeler continued by explaining that the unique relationship between the Baltic States and the United States allowed the Americans to take a much stronger line in its official broadcasts than it could take in broadcasts to countries in which the United States had accredited missions. From the American position, Vedeler felt it was logical to utilize official American foreign broadcasting in as efficient a manner as possible.[58] Kaiv and Žadeikis viewed this reason as illegitimate and left the meeting under the assumption that the State Department vetoed RFE broadcasts due to VOA insistence rather than real policy considerations and that they would file official petitions of protest with both the State Department and the NCFE.

The meeting between the Baltic diplomats and Vedeler did not solve the issue; it only inflamed tensions. Žadeikis submitted his official memorandum on RFE broadcasting to the State Department on 31 December, 1951, followed by Feldmans on 3 January, 1952 and Kaiv on 8 January, 1952.[59] Summarizing the diplomats' argument, Vedeler wrote:

> One of the chief inducements for cooperating with the NCFE had been the promise that RFE would broadcast to the countries of East-

> ern Europe. Žadeikis stated that prior to approving of the affiliation of Lithuanian emigre leaders with the FEC through the establishment of a Lithuanian Panel he had received assurances from Poole that if the Baltic States were associated with FEC, would receive consideration equal to that afforded other East European countries.[60]

Throughout January 1952, RFE officials complained that "the reaction of Baltic exiles to the decision against sending broadcasts is one of deep disappointment. No matter what stand the NCFE and the Baltic Panels may take, it seems that Baltic organizations in the United States will strongly protest the present negative decision."[61]

Kohler, Vedeler, and State Department Press Officer John Devine met on 17 January 1952 to discuss the memoranda that had been submitted by the diplomats as well as all other petitions received from primarily Lithuanian organizations around the country. The three decided that their initial policy was correct and that the Baltic Desk would assume the responsibility for informing the Baltic diplomats that the decision had been settled. They did, however, agree that should the whole question of RFE operations be reviewed by the State Department in the future, the question of whether or not to include Baltic broadcasts could be litigated.[62] In subsequent meetings with the Baltic diplomats at the end of January, Vedeler concisely stated that "the problem had been reconsidered from every standpoint by all officers with a direct interest in it and the various points raised by the Baltic diplomats had been carefully studied ... but the Department could see no other course but to reaffirm its previous position."[63]

Ultimately, Žadeikis's most pressing concern was what sort of provisions would be made for those who had been employed by the FEC to begin work on Baltic radio broadcasts. While Vedeler did not have a specific answer to the direct question, he commented that something probably could be done to take care of these matters through ongoing negotiations between the FEC and VOA representatives in New York. In closing, Vedeler hoped that the diplomats would be willing to cooperate with VOA administrators and the Baltic Freedom Committees, as it was VOA's "sincere desire" to receive and make use of helpful comments.[64]

Ironically, once the Baltic diplomats' concerns were assuaged, the Baltic Consultative Panels that had fully endorsed the idea of streamlining all broadcasting activity through the VOA began protesting the American decision to supplant RFE broadcasts with the VOA. While many of the official memoranda that were submitted to the Secretary of State on the issue deal with the double standard involved – that is, other countries in Eastern Europe were receiving RFE broadcasts – they also offer insight into the symbolic importance that RFE had for the Baltic exiles.

The Estonian Freedom Committee submitted a protest to E. Acker of the FEC on 8 January, 1952 stating:

> The Estonian Panel is of the opinion that broadcasting over the VOA cannot cover the field of broadcasting under the auspices of NCFE because of the different approaches to the problem. The VOA is and will necessarily continue to be the spokesman of American official policy, while broadcasting under the FEC will express the voice of Free Estonia and of the Estonians abroad.[65]

In May 1952, the Latvian Panel wrote to Secretary of State Dean Acheson that "the VOA cannot and does not act as the speaker of Free Latvians. It is for Free Latvians themselves, and not only for the Latvian Panel to take care of their specific problems designed to help their compatriots at home. Our speeches and features would be read not anonymously, but by the authors, known and respected in Latvia, themselves."[66]

The debate over Baltic-language broadcasts over RFE would continue to be an important political issue for Estonians, Latvians, and Lithuanians residing in the United States for the next two decades. Regardless, in January 1952, as in August 1951, the VOA continued to be the sole broadcasting medium for the United States Government as well as for Baltic exiles residing in the United States. Not all factions within the Baltic diasporas felt as if they had achieved anything substantive through the initial debate over radio broadcasts. In reality, however, the VOA was able to broadcast material to the Baltic republics and feature guests that VOA broadcasts in other languages were simply unable to present, mainly due to political protocols. Nevertheless, the ongoing debate between Estonians, Latvians, and Lithuanians who were actively involved in the Voice of America and those who were not would play an important role in all aspects of cooperation among Baltic Americans in the sphere of public diplomacy.

Commemorations and Publications: Impact on Cold War America

Although the Baltic committees continued to play a small consultative role in the development of VOA broadcasts in the Baltic languages throughout the 1950s, the committees' most important audience was the American public. Throughout the duration of the Cold War, various Baltic organizations played an important role in the development of the American anti-communist landscape, and the three FEC-sponsored panels were no exception. Since the Baltic committees consisted of many prominent Estonian, Latvian, and Lithuanian exiles and had more developed contacts with both the White House and the State Department during the 1950s, their privileged access helped their ability to potentially monopolize information about the Baltic republics and present them in a sympathetic light to the American people through the commemoration of holidays and the publication of journals.

The Baltic States Freedom Rally that took place annually in New York City starting in June 1952 was the highest profile rally during the 1950s. It was the product of efforts by the Baltic States Freedom Committee (BSFC). In a March 1952 joint meeting of the Estonian, Latvian, and Lithuanian Freedom Committees, it was decided that the three should pool their efforts to commemorate the annexation of their homelands in 1940 as well as the deportations that took place in 1940 and 1941.[67]

Leading up to the Baltic States Freedom Rally that was to take place in New York City to commemorate the twelfth anniversary of the annexation and eleventh anniversary of the deportations, New York Governor Thomas E. Dewey issued a proclamation that 13 June 1952 would be declared "Baltic States Freedom Day" in New York State and claiming that the United States "has quite properly declined to recognize the incorporation of the Baltic States into the Soviet Union."[68] Throughout the day on 15 June, Baltic exiles handed out leaflets to the public throughout New York City and held an organized protest against the Soviet delegation to the United Nations with signs condemning the "lawless invasion of the Baltic States."[69] The day's events culminated in a rally at Town Hall where Estonian, Latvian, and Lithuanian folksongs were sung and the official messages of John Foster Dulles, W. Averell Harriman, and Harry S. Truman were read.

The White House's willingness to draft a statement for the Baltic States Freedom Rally declaring that the United States continued to not recognize the Soviet annexation and implying that Estonia, Latvia, and Lithuania would regain their independence partly due to the efforts of Balts living in the United States not only added to the expectations of Balts in the United States that the Americans were working towards the liberation of their homelands but also giving the appearance that American policy interests and Baltic exile interests were aligned in the public's eyes.

R.G. Johnson of the Baltic Desk relayed a memorandum to Emmet J. Hughes, Administrative Assistant to President Dwight D. Eisenhower, on a recommended statement that the White House should issue to the BSFC. Johnson stated that the "BSFC was set up, in association with the National Committee for a Free Europe, primarily to coordinate the interests of various organizations of Americans of Estonian, Latvian, and Lithuanian origin in an annual rally to commemorate the two principal tragedies in the recent history of the three Baltic States."[70] The statement recommended to the State Department reinforced the themes that the United States continued to recognize the existing diplomatic missions of the Baltic States and condemned the deportations that were occurring, and that the Baltic States will regain their freedom in the future.[71]

The long-term publishing project, and perhaps the Baltic panels' greatest legacy, was the Baltic Review. In March 1952 the three Baltic panels made the decision to reconstitute the old Revue Baltique that had first been published in 1940.[72] The Baltic Review was a collaborative journal published occasionally by the three Baltic panels through the Free Europe Press. An important component of the Baltic Review's collaborate nature was the rotating editorship, based on nationality. That is, to ensure that one nationality would not dominate all the publication's content, each volume would feature an editor, rotating among the Estonians, Latvians, and Lithuanians. Throughout 1952 and 1953, the three Baltic panels coordinated what their vision for the journal would be with the Free Europe Press, leading to the inaugural volume being published in December 1953.

The inaugural issue explained the origin and purpose of the *Baltic Review*. While acknowledging that the journal hoped to continue the work of Revue Baltique, its editors described its two objectives:

> The main objective of this Review is to inform the Western World of the Communist social, economic, and political system, propaganda and strategy, to acquaint the free world with the sacrifices and struggle of the Estonian, Latvian, and Lithuanian peoples for the restoration of their independence, and to reveal the devious methods and processes of Soviet aggression and occupation. These methods and this strategy have as their aim the suppression of freedom, the extermination of peoples, and Soviet domination of the world.
>
> Finally, and most important for the future, while promoting mutual cooperation among Baltic exile organizations, the Review will foster the idea of federation among Eastern and Central European nations in order that they may be included, after their liberation, in a united Europe.[73]

The Baltic Review's two main audiences were the State Department and the broader American public, which could find the publication in libraries, schools, and research institutions. A careful reading of the publication's articles during its first few years reveals a specific political agenda that its authors hoped to impart to both the American public and policymakers.

The Baltic Freedom Committees hoped to educate the American public about the true nature of the Soviet Union by exposing it as a nation whose values were antithetical to the conservative and religious nature of the United States. Simultaneously, the panels hoped to impress upon American policymakers that there indeed was a high level of cooperation among the three Baltic nationalities that was actually a rooted in shared interwar histories that Baltic exiles thought that the United States should charge the Soviet Union with genocide in the United Nations; and that the Baltic panels supported the American policy of liberating the Soviet bloc.

The *Baltic Review*'s December 1953 volume began by reminding its audience that the Baltic States were among the first victims of "Soviet Russia's aggression and her plans for world conquest" and that the "Baltic peoples form an important part of the anti-communist front" due to their geopolitical situation, Western culture, and Christian traditions.[74] The editorial staff believed that studying the Baltic example and keeping the international community informed on developments within the Baltic republics was important because "what happened to them could happen to the whole world."[75] A prominent theme that the Baltic Review wished to share with international audiences was how the Soviet presence had demonstrably changed Baltic society for the worse, and the discussion included the standard of living trajectory, the educational system, and the risk of Soviet inflicted genocide.

Aleksander Kütt, a prominent exiled Estonian economist, analyzed the deterioration of the Estonian living standard as a result of the Soviet occupation in March 1956. Kütt's article began by arguing that before World War II, Estonia could be seen as a country that did not quite have the standard of living of the Scandinavian countries or the United Kingdom, but it was still higher than most other West European nations.[76] A comparison was also made to the growth of real wages in the United States by stating that from 1932 to 1939 Estonian wages rose 13 per cent per annum, which compared favorably with an American wage growth of 29 per cent from 1939 to 1953.[77] Kütt claimed that before the Soviets arrived in 1940, Estonian farmers had been prosperous and the country's industrial work force had obtained near universal employment.[78]

Using resources made available from the Soviet Estonia media and statistics compiled by the Mid-European Studies Center, Kütt outlined the transformation process required to integrate the Estonian economy into the Soviet economy and the implications for wages and economic freedom in Soviet Estonia. Although, until the German Army arrived in 1941 Soviet authorities gradually increased food prices in an effort to reduce the Estonian living standard,[79] it was the postwar policy of maintaining stable wages while fluctuating the cost of goods that ultimately had a negative impact on wages in Soviet Estonia.[80] Kütt concluded that real wages in 1952 were 27.3 per cent of their 1939 level.[81] Concerning economic freedom, Kütt was concerned that the rapid industrial transformations that were taking place in Estonia were existential threats to the economic freedom of Estonia. The decision to mandate that all factories should work three shifts instead of one, the construction of new production plants, and continuously raising working norms to fulfill the Five Year Plans were all undermining the ability of Estonian citizens to pursue their own economic interests.[82] Additionally, the fact that Estonian economic output was being redistributed through the wider Soviet Union and to nations that the Soviet Union had trade agreements with was eroding the development of Estonia as an economic unit.[83]

It was important to draw comparisons with the economic standards of Western Europe and the United States in order to emphasize the similarities between Baltic economic conditions before 1940 and the changes that were made by the Soviet Union after the annexation. From the perspective of Estonians living in the free world, their home country had been on an economic trajectory similar to the rest of Europe and the United States, but the Soviet annexation imposed a foreign economic system that was ultimately detrimental to the nation's development. Drawing such comparisons bolstered the argument that the Soviet Union was a grave threat not only to small nations but to powerful ones such as the United States as well.

In the same issue, a former lawyer in Latvia, who wished to remain anonymous, wrote about the differences between the Latvian educational system and the changes that the Soviet Union imposed on the way that Latvians were educated.[84] The article attempted to undermine Soviet propaganda that the Soviet educational system was superior to the old Latvian model by making a detailed comparison of Latvia's system during the interwar period with the information available about the educational system in the 1950s.[85] The author argued that the Soviet educational system was actually the inferior of the two as a result of the school system's administrative structures as well as the importance allotted to meeting economic and ideological objectives rather than traditional educational goals.

The author criticized the elementary school system's inability to maintain discipline among Latvia's youth and to have students complete the compulsory seven years of primary education. According to accounts from the Latvian Communist Party's main publication, Cīņa, Minister of Education Vilis Samson revealed that there had been great "deficiencies" in the ability to halt the increase of hooliganism in schools, and many students were leaving school without finishing.[86] The author claimed that the main reason that children had not completed their education was that the Soviet system overloaded students with work outside of regular school assignments without any compensation.[87] Finally, the author described the strong ideological nature of the Soviet educational system. The article cites an editorial from Riga in 1955 that states "schools ... must educate our young generation in the spirit of fierce Soviet patriotism, selfless loyalty to the Communist Party and Soviet Government."[88] This manifested itself in the textbooks that were used in elementary school as well as in entire courses of study at the university level. The author concluded that the Soviet Latvian educational system was incompatible with traditional Latvian values as anti-religious propaganda was taught simultaneously with communist doctrine.[89]

The heavy emphasis placed on the anti-religious nature of Soviet education tied neatly with the conservative and religious anti-communists in the United States during the 1950s, who argued that the best way to combat communism in the United States was to directly associate the

Soviet Union with an assault upon traditional religious values that were mainstream in American culture. The author clearly states that "Communist education is anti-religious education. The children are taught basic sciences in the schools which are not compatible with faith in God."[90] The discussion of communism as being anti-religious fit neatly within the message that religious anti-communist Americans were promoting during the 1950s.[91]

Ultimately, by the very nature of the Baltic Review, its impact proved to be very narrow. Until it stopped being published in 1971, it was largely sent to newspapers, magazines, libraries, public officials, and influential people around the world.[92] Its generally scholarly articles meant that the journal was used as a source for information about the Baltic republics to be distributed by other means, as opposed to a source that the general public would find accessible. Nevertheless, it reflects the ability of Baltic exiles to establish a monopoly on the factual information about the Baltic republics available within the United States. The source material that its authors used was either calculated by scholars associated with the FEC or taken directly from media sources from the Soviet Union and other places in Europe that were initially published in the Baltic languages, Russian, German, or Swedish.

Although other media outlets in the United States had the capability to provide accurate reporting on events in the Soviet Union, access to the Baltic Republics by the foreign media was limited and the marginal nature of the Baltic Republics reduced the American press's interest in them. The contacts that the Baltic panels had with fellow exiles in Europe who had access to Baltic sources, coupled with the resources that the NCFE had to obtain information within the Soviet Union allowed Baltic exiles to become the most reliable source of information on events in their home countries. In the context of anti-communist literature in the United States during the 1950s, the publications of the Baltic exiles contributed by clearly articulating what the Soviet occupation had done to all facets of life in their traditionally Christian and democratic countries. Their literature served as a warning to Americans about the international threat that the Soviet Union posed.

Reassessment of Relations

The events surrounding the 1956 Hungarian Revolution, particularly the possible role that Radio Free Europe played, resulted in a general reappraisal by the United States of its relationship with Eastern European exile groups.[93] While the National Committee for a Free Europe, Inc., renamed in 1954 the Free Europe Committee, Inc. (FEC), acknowledged that the ultimate goal remained to promote freedom from communism, the organization's new objectives, which were deemed more realistic, were "to foster an evolutionary development resulting in the weakening of Soviet controls and the progressive attainment of national independence."[94] It was within this context that in November 1958, the FEC sought to clarify its relationship with its sponsored exiles.

In a 1958 document describing the function of a new European Advisory Committee, the Free Europe Exile Relations wing of the FEC sought to assist exiles in three main ways. First, by promoting the interest of those in the free world in assisting the peaceful restoration of independence in the exiles' home nations; second, by sustaining the morale of all exiles through supporting the efforts of a select few; third, by helping provide information about life behind the Iron Curtain as a means of combatting communist influence in the free world.[95] In addition, the document attempted to offer greater separation between the exile national committees and any notion of political or diplomatic recognition by the United States government. The FEC reiterated that no national committee had the status of a government-in-exile. What was new, however, was the assertion that "it is not the purpose of the Committee to support the ambition of any émigré group to restore, in any sense, the status quo ante bellum in any East European country."[96]

From the perspective of the exiles that cooperated with the FEC, however, there was an implicit acceptance that the national committees would be an important component in reestablishing democratic institutions in Eastern Europe after liberation had taken place. It was significant that the FEC absolved itself from supporting national committees that would be used to restore governments representing the interwar period in the Soviet bloc, should the political conditions for such a transformation become reality. It was representative of a changing belief that political transformation in the former Soviet bloc would consist of a gradual evolution, as opposed to rapid revolutions or Western interventions. It was also representative of the FEC's (and by default the State Department's) interest in reducing the ambition of its relationship with the émigré groups which it sponsored.[97]

The 1960 budget prepared by FEC President Archibald S. Alexander detailed the fundamental changes that were about to take place in the FEC's dealing with Eastern European exile groups. Alexander's number one priority was to reorient the FEC's exile support. He observed that the FEC would spend over one million dollars to support the national committees, the Assembly of Captive European Nations (ACEN), which was established in 1954, and other exile groups.[98] Alexander claimed that such an expenditure was not only beyond the budgetary capabilities of the FEC but also was not essential to accomplish the FEC's program aims. Therefore, he proposed to reduce expenditures by $335,000 and reorganize the structure of FEC exile relations.[99] An important feature of relations between exiles and American officials during the Cold War was the ongoing battle over funding. As early as 1954, coinciding with the establishment of the ACEN, there was a decrease in funding for exiles.[100]

Going forward, the FEC directed the majority of exile activities towards the ACEN in order to allow drastic cuts to be made to the budgets of individual national committees. To achieve this goal, four policy changes were made. First, deserving exile council members who were no longer able to contribute to effective work would be granted small stipends for their prior activities. Second, sixteen of the most effective national committee members from each delegation would become delegates to the ACEN and would only receive a salary for their activities with the ACEN. Third, separate office space and staffs for individual committees would be eliminated and the remaining exiles associated with the FEC would share new office space. Fourth, support for national council programs would be trimmed from $122,200 per year to $51,400 where a portion of the saved funds could be utilized for ad hoc publications in the future.[101]

The FEC hoped that the ACEN would be a cumulatively more effective body than the individual national committees in organizing the political potentials of the exiles. When reducing the scope of the national committees and streamlining exile efforts through the ACEN, officials assumed that this reassessment of the relationships with certain exiles would increase the body's overall quality because it would also trigger an assessment of an exile's abilities and key attributes. Exiles were sought who had the ability to understand the problems that the West faced at the end of the 1950s and the flexibility to meet new international conditions with new programs. Exiles should ideally have a certain degree of stature with other exiles as well as with diplomats, politicians, educators, and journalists. Most importantly, these exiles should have been able to rise above the intermittent strife that had dominated exile politics through the entire decade.[102]

The Estonian, Latvian, and Lithuanian national committees were not immune to the FEC's restructuring of exile relations. The FEC's 1959 operating budget for Baltic operations was $134,200. The proposed 1960 operating budget was $58,200, or a 56% reduction.[103] Ironically, the already minimal activities that the Baltic National Committees had in relation to the FEC's overall agenda meant that the long-term impact of the funding cuts on the national committee's future activities was decidedly mixed. On one hand, the number of exiles that received direct funding from the FEC was slashed. In 1959, five Estonians, four Latvians, and eight Lithuanians were directly sponsored by the FEC. Under the proposed reorganization only two Lithuanians, one Latvian and one Estonian would be affiliated with the ACEN. On the other hand, the Baltic language publications and the Baltic Review continued to be published into the 1960s, which meant that Baltic committees continued to have a level of autonomy despite the prominent role that the ACEN would assume.

In 1960 the newly reorganized ACEN was intended to be a streamlined representational organization that consisted of a general committee and secretary general that would keep the issue of Eastern Europe alive in world opinion, but also keep the international community informed on developments in the Soviet bloc and build relations with anti-communist organizations internationally.[104] In reality, the ACEN continued to function as it had during the post-1956 period. Formal meetings were held regularly where declarations were made, rallies were organized surrounding important anniversaries, and resolutions were passed that were then forwarded to UN delegates.[105] The suppression of the 1956 Hungarian Revolution elicited a strong reaction from within the ACEN. In subsequent years, there was an increase in ACEN activism dealing with the political situation in Hungary. The rehabilitation of relations between the United States and János Kádár's regime, beginning in 1963, and the subsequent era of détente resulted in a general decline in the ACEN's influence, since the majority of ACEN members opposed any rapprochement with the Soviet Union or its satellite states.

Throughout the ACEN's existence, its relationship with Estonian, Latvian, and Lithuanian exiles had always been contentious. Due to the relatively small number of Baltic exiles – compared to larger nationalities such as Poles, Hungarians and Czechoslovaks – and the importance that the FEC placed on satellite countries, issues that were directly related to the Baltic republics were simply crowded out. The fact that ACEN delegates had predominantly been leading diplomats and politicians of Eastern European governments during the interwar period gave a certain amount of legitimacy for the satellite nations but was seen as a potential liability for the Baltic republics, given that it related to the non-recognition policy. The preeminent position that Hungary played after 1956 further diminished the importance of the Baltic issue within the ACEN and resulted in the Baltic national committees continuing their comparatively small activities under the FEC's umbrella.

Conclusion

The construction of the Berlin Wall in 1961 was not only a symbol of a divided Europe, it also symbolized the static nature of the Cold War in Europe and a shift in the Cold War's theater away from Europe and towards the developing world. As a result of the changing Cold War dynamic, it was not surprising that American policymakers reassessed how to best allocate FEC funds. Simultaneously, a generational shift was beginning within the Estonian, Latvian, and Lithuanian exile communities. This shift was accompanied by an assessment of their predecessors' activities for the liberation of their homeland. As a result, the ability of the Baltic Freedom Committees to continue playing a prominent role in either Baltic exile politics or the fight against communism in Eastern Europe was diminished. During the 1960s, the Committees for a Free Estonia, Latvia, and Lithuania became just three of many organizations that represented the interests of second generation émigrés residing in the United States and Western Europe who fought for the continued remembrance of the three Baltic republics.

Perhaps it was ultimately unrealistic for both American policymakers and the Baltic Freedom Committee members to believe that the selective and relatively small organizations based in New York City would have had a strong unifying force over the whole of the Estonian, Latvian, and Lithuanian postwar emigrations. Although Baltic exiles experienced similar circumstances in the post-1940 period – a shared common enemy in the Soviet Union and a shared vision of liberated nations in the future – they did not constitute a monolithic bloc. Indeed, they were politically, economically, and socially a heterogeneous group that had objectives while in exile that did not necessarily converge with the interests of the Free Europe Committee, the American State Department or other agencies, or the Baltic Freedom Committees themselves.

It would be a mistake, however, to describe the Baltic Freedom Committees as merely failures or symbolic organizations that represented fading political memories. Due to FEC funding issues and State Department policy considerations, the Baltic Freedom Committees were unable to directly initiate broadcasts that might have had an impact on their occupied homelands, but the committees had an equally important domestic audience in the United States. Although the FEC's main work was in broadcasting to the Soviet satellite states, it played an important role in buttressing anti-communism sentiments among the American people. The Baltic Freedom Committees initiated publications and commemorative events that made a small but important contribution to the anti-communist tapestry of America during the early 1950s. Most important for the Baltic republics, however, was that the committees' work helped to prevent the legacies of the interwar Baltic republics from going down history's memory hole.

Endnotes

1 Richard H. Cummings, *Radio Free Europe's Crusade for Freedom: Rallying Americans Behind Cold War Broadcasting, 1950–1960* (New York: McFarland, 2010) 6.

2 Ibid.

3 Memorandum from the Assistant Director for Policy Coordination, Central Intelligence Agency, Wisner to Staff Members, 1 January, 1949. *Foreign Relations of the United States, 1945–1950: Emergence of the Intelligence Establishment* (Washington, DC: Government Printing Office, 1996) Document 310.

4 Katalin Kádár Lynn, "At War While at Peace: United States Cold War Policy and the National Committee for a Free Europe" in *The Inauguration of Organized Political Warfare: Cold War Organizations and the National Committee for a Free Europe* (New York: Helena History Press, Distributed by Central European University Press, 2012) 13.

5 Arch Puddington, *Broadcasting Freedom: The Cold War Triumph of Radio Free Europe and Radio Liberty* (Lexington: The University Press of Kentucky, 2003) 12.

6 Ibid., 13. See: "The Free Europe University in Exile" Pamphlet which describes the activities of the University. The purpose of the University was to establish an "invaluable reservoir of informed, trained, democratic leaders among the young people who successfully escaped to the free world." Folder: Free Europe University in Exile - Scholarship Gift, Box 55, C.D. Jackson Papers, Dwight D. Eisenhower Presidential Library, Abilene, Kansas (hereafter DDEPL).

7 Ibid.

8 Romauld Misiunas and Rein Taagepera, *The Baltic States: Years of Dependence, 1940–1990* (Berkeley and Los Angeles: University of California Press, 1993), 354.

9 For more on the non-recognition policy see: Jonathan H. L'Hommedieu, "Roosevelt and the Dictators: The origin of the US non-recognition policy of the Soviet annexation of the Baltic States" in John Hiden, et. Al. eds., *The Baltic Question during the Cold War* (New York: Routledge, 2008) 33–45.

10 On 25 May, 1950, Feldmans met with an FEC official; on 28 July Žadeikis met with an FEC official; and on 1 August 1950, Kaiv met with an FEC official. Folder: B801.4 Consultative Panels, 1950–1954, Records Relating to the Baltic States, 1940–1961. Box 2, RG 59, Stack Area 150, Row 69, Compartment 25, Records of the Department of State, NAII.

11 Fund Memo #51, 25 May, 1950, Ibid.

12 Lithuanian American Information Center Bulletin on 17 March 1950, Ibid.

13 Letter to "William", 26 October, 1950, Ibid.

14 PROJECT #1-1951, 15 March, 1951, Folder: B801.5 Radio Free Europe, Ibid.
15 Ibid.
16 Fund Memo #69, 1 August, 1950 Folder: B801.4 Consultative Panels, 1950–1954, Ibid.
17 Fund Memo #51, 25 May, 1950, Ibid.
18 Ibid.
19 Robert F. Kelley to Robert P. Joyce (Policy and Planning Staff), 9 August 1950, Ibid.
20 FEC Letter to the State Department, 2 October 1950, Ibid.
21 Ibid. Karlis Zarins, the Latvian Ambassador in London representing the interwar government, met with Adolfs Blodnieks, who represented a number of Latvian political parties, in an attempt to create an atmosphere of political unity among various Latvian exile groups.
22 Ibid.
23 Ibid.
24 Fund Memo #117, 19 December 1950, Ibid.
25 Fund Memo #124, "Monthly Report for December 1950, 6 January, 1951, Ibid.
26 Ibid.
27 Fund Memo #139, 25 January, 1951, and Fund Memo #150, 1 February 1951, Ibid.
28 Ibid.
29 Žadeikis and the FEC representative went over the submitted list of names and came to the conclusion that Vaclovas Sidzikauskas was an indispensible member of the future panel. Žadeikis was instructed to meet again on 26 January to discuss the panel, where the number of names was ultimately reduced.
30 Fund Memo #150, 1 February, 1951. "Folder: B801.4 Consultative Panels, 1950–1954" Records Relating to the Baltic States, 1940–1961. Box 2, RG 59, Stack Area 150, Row 69, Compartment 25, Records of the Department of State, NAII.
31 Ibid.
32 Ibid.
33 FEC Memo on Lithuanian Consultative Panel, 8 June 1951, Ibid. On 9 May 1951, Žadeikis had a meeting with an FEC official concerning increasing the size of the Lithuanian Panel due to an oversight on considering an individual from an important Lithuanian political faction. Although there were concerns that Žadeikis was using the Panel as a means of employing Lithuanian refugees, the FEC allowed an 8th member to the Panel in order to avoid any embarrassment to Žadeikis and help foster political cohesion in the panel.
34 Statement by the Members of the Lithuanian Consultative Panel of the National Committee for a Free Europe, Inc., 24 May 1951. Folder: Li801.4 Committee for a Free Lithuania, Records Relating to the Baltic States, 1940–1961. Box 11, Ibid.
35 Fund Memo #287, "Monthly Report for August 1951". Folder B801.4 Consultative Panels 1950–1954, Records Relating to the Baltic States, 1940–1961. Box 2, Ibid.
36 Ibid.
37 Ibid.
38 Fund Memo #391, 27 February, 1952, Ibid.
39 Vedeler to Joyce, 25 April, 1951. Ibid. For more on the establishment of the Baltic Consulative Panels: See Chapter II.
40 Pius Grigaitis, Executive Secretary of ALT to Fred K. Salter, Officer in Charge of Baltic Desk, State Department, 24 November 1950. Folder: B891 VOA, Records Relating to the Baltic States, 1940–1961. Box 3, Ibid. For more on the establishment of the Baltic Consulative Panels: See Chapter II.
41 Harold C. Vedeler, Officer in Charge, Baltic Desk, State Department to Dr. Pius Grigaitis, Executive Secretary, ALT, 28 November, 1950, Ibid.

42 Daniel J. Flood (R-PA) to Povilas Žadeikis on VOA Broadcasts, 28 March, 1950. Folder: Li801.4 Committee for a Free Lithuania, Records Relating to the Baltic States, 1940–1961. Box 11, Ibid.

43 Excerpt from "State Appropriations for 1951." Hearings before the Subcommittee of the Committee on Appropriations, House of Representatives, 2 February, 1951, Ibid.

44 "'Voice' to Add Programs: U.S. to Increase Broadcasts to China, Start One to Lithuania." New York Times (1923–Current file), 13 February, 1951, http://www.proquest.com/ (accessed February 28, 2011).

45 Department of State Bulletin, Vol XXIV, #623, 11 June, 1951. Folder: B891 VOA, Records Relating to the Baltic States, 1940–1961. Box 3, RG 59, Stack Area 150, Row 69, Compartment 25, Records of the Department of State, NAII. The broadcasts were initially supposed to be started on 27 May, but on 11 May the State Department was informed by VOA that they would be delayed due to technical issues.

46 Johnson to Vedeler, 16 August, 1951, Ibid. The Estonian and Latvian programs would emanate from the United States with simultaneous Munich and Tangiers relays. The Estonian program starts at 11:30 (18:30 Estonian time). The Latvian program started at 11:45 (18:45 Latvian time).

47 RFE Broadcasts to the Baltic States, Kohler to Barrett, 12 November, 1951.Folder: B801.5 RFE, Records Relating to the Baltic States, 1940–1961. Box 2, Ibid.

48 While the FEC received most of its funding from the CIA, for appearances' sake the organization did not have a never-ending flow of available resources.

49 Baltic Radio Broadcasts, Kelley to Robert Joyce, 10 April 1951. Folder: B801.5 RFE, Records Relating to the Baltic States, 1940–1961. Box 2, RG 59, Stack Area 150, Row 69, Compartment 25, Records of the Department of State, NAII.

50 From a bureaucratic perspective, it is understandable that the FEC would like to have expanded its presence to cover as many nationalities as possible, if only to increase its own presence in American foreign policy- making. For Baltic broadcasts, the FEC wanted to start Baltic broadcasting from New York City rather than from Munich for two main reasons. First, far better Baltic personnel was available in the United States than in Germany. Second, as a way to streamline costs, they hoped that members of the nascent Baltic panels could double as radio desk personnel.

51 RFE Broadcasts to the Baltic Area, Bauer to Kohler, 7 November 1951. Folder: B801.5 RFE, Records Relating to the Baltic States, 1940–1961. Box 2, RG 59, Stack Area 150, Row 69, Compartment 25, Records of the Department of State, NAII.

52 Vedeler to Joyce, 27 April, 1951. Folder: B801.4 Consultative Panels, Ibid. A related concern was that if blocked funds were to be "raided for this FEC purpose", it would set a disastrous precedent for claims against blocked funds.

53 RFE Broadcasts to the Baltic Area, Bauer to Kohler, 7 November, 1951. Folder: B801.5 RFE, Ibid.

54 RFE Broadcasts to the Baltic States, Kohler to Devine and Barrett, 12 November, 1951, Ibid.

55 Letter on RFE Meeting, Kohler to Barrett, 6 December, 1951, Folder: B801.5 RFE. Records Relating to the Baltic States, 1940–1961. Box 2, RG 59, Stack Area 150, Row 69, Compartment 25, Records of the Department of State, NAII.

56 Memorandum of Conversation on Question of Baltic Language Broadcasts, 13 December, 1951.

57 Memorandum of Conversation on RFE Baltic Language Broadcasts, 18 December, 1951, Ibid.

58 Ibid.

59 See Lithuanian Note #2433, 31 December, 1951; Latvian Note #3, January 1952; and Estonian Note #773, 8 January, 1952, Ibid.

60 Question of RFE Baltic Language Broadcasts, 4 January, 1952, Ibid.

61 Fund Memo on Lithuanians, Monthly Report for January, 1952. Folder: Li801.4 Committee for a Free Lithuania, Records Relating to the Baltic States, 1940–1961. Box 11, Ibid.

62 Memorandum of Conversation on "RFE Baltic Broadcasts" (Foy D. Kohler, Harold Vedeler, and John Devine), 18 January, 1952. Folder: B801.5 RFE, Records Relating to the Baltic States, 1940–1961. Box 2, Ibid.

63 Memorandum of Conversation on Question of RFE Broadcasts to the Baltic Countries, 25 January, 1952, Ibid.

64 Ibid.

65 Leonhard Vahter to E. Acker, 8 January 1952. Folder: E001 Notes, Aide Memoires, Incoming, Outgoing, Ibid.

66 Fund Memo #436, Latvian Consultative Panel to Dean Acheson (Secretary of State), 5 May, 1952. Folder: B801.4 Consultative Panels 1950–1954, Ibid.

67 Unnumbered Fund Report on Baltic Activities in March 1952, Ibid.

68 "Baltic Freedom Day Proclaimed." *New York Times* (1923–Current file), 14 June, 1952, http://www.proquest.com/ (accessed March 17, 2011).

69 Undated Lithuanian Fund Memo, Folder: Li801.4 Committee for a Free Lithuania. Records Relating to the Baltic States, 1940–1961. Box 11, RG 59, Stack Area 150, Row 69, Compartment 25, Records of the Department of State, NAII.

70 Memorandum for the White House, R.G. Johnson to Emmet J. Hughes, 3 June, 1953. Folder: B801.1 Emigre Organizations Abroad. Records Relating to the Baltic States, 1940–1961. Box 2, Ibid.

71 "Message to the Baltic States Freedom Committee" from Eisenhower, Ibid.

72 Fund Memo #407, Monthly Report for March 1952, 1 April 1952. Folder: E801.4 Consultative Panels. Records Relating to the Baltic States, 1940–1961. Box 5, Ibid. See Chapter 1 for more information on *Revue Baltique*.

73 *Baltic Review* 1, 15–16.

74 "To Our Readers", *Baltic Review* 1, 15.

75 Ibid.

76 Aleksander Kütt, "Deterioration of the Estonian Living Standard During Soviet Occupation", *Baltic Review* 1, 15.

77 Ibid, 16.

78 Kütt also emphasized the low unemployment situation in Estonia from 1936–1940 by claiming that only .4 to 1.0 per cent of all industrial workers were registered as unemployed.

79 Ibid, 17.

80 Ibid, 18.

81 Ibid, 19. The article conceded that this had been a phenomenon in other countries, such as the United States, but only 15.6 per cent less.

82 Ibid, 21.

83 Ibid, 22.

84 A.R., "School System in Occupied Latvia", *Baltic Review* 1, 23.

85 Comparisons were made between: the one year of primary school and six years of elementary school in independent Latvia versus the seven years of elementary school in Soviet Latvia; the secondary education systems; and the differences in university life.

86 Ibid, 31. The author pointed out that during Latvia's period of independence, hooliganism had not been a significant problem.

87 Ibid. For example, Cina published on 15 May, 1955 that in the near future thousands of school children would go to help the kolkhozes to sow corn. The paper calculated that 150,000 children would participate in the activity over the course of three days, resulting in 100,000 hectares of fields being planted. In addition, children were allegedly required to perform duties around schools, including but not limited to scrubbing classroom floors and benches.

88 Ibid, 33.

89 Ibid.

90 Ibid.

91 Both Catholic and Protestant anti-Communists dominated the anti-communist discourse during the late 1940s and early 1950s. Richard Gid Powers notes: "All the major religious denominations had anticommunist educational programs." Not Without Honor, 251. See also John E. Hayes, Red Scare or Red Menace? American Communism and Anticommunism in the Cold War Era (Chicago: Ivan R. Dee, 1995) 89–100, for a discussion on the differences between Catholic and Evangelical Christian anti-communism.

92 Fund Memo #811. Folder: B801.4 Consultative Panels. Records Relating to the Baltic States, 1940–1961. Box 2, RG 59, Stack Area 150, Row 69, Compartment 25, Records of the Department of State, NAII.

93 The FEC, CIA, State Department, Council of Europe, as well as the United Nations conducted reviews concerning the role of RFE broadcasting during the Hungarian Revolution. While RFE was generally cleared of any wrongdoing, the internal FEC and State Department reviews were actually quite critical. See Arch Puddington, *Broadcasting Freedom: The Cold War Triumph of Radio Free Europe and Radio Liberty*, (Lexington, KY: University Press of Kentucky, 2000), 127.

94 Ibid, 118.

95 Memo, Proposed European Advisory Committee, 1 November, 1958. Folder: Free Europe Committee, 1958. Box 53: Free Europe Committee Budget, CD Jackson Papers, DDEPL.

96 Ibid.

97 As early as 1955, American officials began to seriously reconsider whether or not the United States wanted to pursue revolutionary changes in Eastern Europe. NSC 5505/1 "Exploitation of Soviet and European Satellite Vulnerabilities," passed on 31 January, 1955, called for "evolutionary rather than revolutionary change" in the satellites. This only deepened the contradictions between stated American policy towards the satellitesin 1955–1956 and the reality of the American position. After Hungary 1956, there were no illusions that the United States could rollback communist influence in Eastern Europe, so policymakers could no longer justify the expenditures associated with emigre national councils.

98 Proposed Budget for Executive Committee and FEC Board of Directors, 27 January, 1960. Folder: Free Europe Committee, 1960 (3). Box 53: Free Europe Committee Budget, CD Jackson Papers, DDEPL. The Assembly of Captive European Nations (ACEN) was founded in 1954 and composed of exiled democratic leaders, diplomats, and intellectuals from Central and East European Nations. The ACEN's purpose was political, action aimed at the restoration of freedom and independence for their homelands.

99 Ibid.

100 Papers of A. A. Berle Jr. Franklin Delano Roosevelt Presidential Library. Box 222: Folder NCFE: Board of Directors 1949–1955. Admiral Harold Blaine Miller to A. A. Berle Jr. July 1954.

101 Ibid. This would result in the discontinuation of FEC support for several national language and other publications.

102 Ibid.

103 Ibid. For a comparison, the Albanian funding was decreased by 59%, the Bulgarian funding by 72%, the Czechoslovak funding by 74%, the Hungarian funding by 62%, the Polish funding by 40%, and the Romanian funding by 65%.

104 The General Committee would establish policy, improve existing programs, and have the ability to employ and dismiss the Secretary General and other officials. The Committee consisted of nine voting members, one from each of the nine captive nations, and there was also one observer representing each of the four international groups represented (International Peasant Union, International Centre of Free Trade Unionists in Exile, Socialist Union of Central and Eastern Europe, and Christian Democratic Union). In an attempt to change the deliberative nature of the ACEN, regular plenary sessions were abolished, and special plenary sessions were to be organized if international developments warranted.

105 Memorandum for the Record: Subject: The Assembly of Captive European Nations (ACEN), 1 July, 1963. Folder: Free Europe Committee Budget, 1963. Box 53: Free Europe Committee Budget, CD Jackson Papers, DDEPL.

Select bibliography

Misiunas, Romauld and Rein Taagepera. *The Baltic States: Years of Dependence 1940–1990, Expanded and Updated Edition.* Berkley: University of California Press, 1993.

Pennar, Jaan. *Estonians in America, 1627–1975: A Chronology and Fact Book.* New York: Oceana Publications, 1975.

Saldukas, Linas. *Lithuanian Diaspora.* Vilnius: VAGA Publishers, 2002.

Zake, Ieva. *American Latvians: Politics of a Refugee Community.* New York: Transaction Publishers, 2010.

V

The Hungarian National Council / Hungarian National Committee Magyar Nemzeti Bizottmány / Magyar Nemzeti Bizottság 1947–1972

Katalin Kádár Lynn

All of the national councils or émigré political groups that emerged in the West after their homelands were folded into the Soviet sphere of influence and became Soviet Satellites at the conclusion of World War II reflected the unique political history and circumstances of their respective nations. In this the Hungarians were no exception. Being on the losing side in World War I resulted in the loss of 71% of their territory, which housed over 66% of their population, including 3.4 million ethnic Magyars. Subsequently, Hungarian inter-war politics and policy were driven by a single goal: revision of the detested Treaty of Trianon that had resulted in the dismemberment of their historic nation. During the inter-war period, the rise of fascism, the rebuilding of the German military on Hungary's western flank and the pressure of the USSR on its northeast, and the fact that it was surrounded by politically unfriendly successor states such as Romania, Yugoslavia and Czechoslovakia all limited Hungary's political and economic options – to the point of placing it in a straightjacket. Hungarian politicians of the post WWI era grew up in a political climate of uncertainty and economic pressure. They were, on the whole, anti-communist and conservative. Differing shades of conservatism are what marked political life in Hungary rather than the full liberal-to-conservative spectrum. Fascists were represented, as were Social Democrats and some liberals, but the general thrust of the nation and its politicians reflected the centrist conservatism of the general populace and was represented by the governments of prime ministers Count István Bethlen (1921–1931) and Count Pál Teleki (1920–21 and 1939–1941). Although it was ruled as a parliamentary democracy, Hungary was unique in that it was a kingdom without a ruler; rather the absent ruler's place was held by a regent, a position filled by Admiral Miklós Horthy from 1920 until 1944.

The political figures who became prominent shortly after World War II, Ferenc Nagy, Zoltán Tildy, Béla Varga, Dezső Sulyok, had all cut their political teeth prior to that war in the Hungary of revisionism and strong Hungarian nationalism and identity. It was a stance with which they identified. Two of the most prominent among them were members of the clergy: Zoltán Tildy, prime minister from 1945–1946 and president from 1946–1948, was a pastor in the Hungarian Reformed Church and Monsignor Béla Varga, a Catholic prelate, served as speaker of the Hungarian parliament in 1946–1947. Both Tildy and Varga were members of the Independent Smallholders Party (Független Kisgazda Párt) since its reorganization in 1930. Ferenc Nagy was of peasant origin and had been secretary of the Smallholders since the 1930s. He served as prime minister from 1946–1947. Dezső Sulyok began his political life as a Smallholder but after WWII formed a splinter faction, the Hungarian Freedom Party, as he was increasingly being pushed out of the Smallholders Party by elements sympathetic to the Soviets. Zoltán Pfeiffer, a lawyer by profession, was also a Smallholder. All but Tildy left Hungary as the Soviets consolidated their control over the nation and emigrated to the United States by 1947. Many other Hungarian political figures and diplomats of note from the 1940s, John Pelényi, George Barcza, Gábor Apor, Paul Auer and the prime minister from 1942–1944, Miklós Kállay, either stayed abroad in their post-war postings or emigrated to various European countries, Latin America and Australia. The co-founder of the Smallholders, Tibor Eckhardt,* traveled to the US in 1941 and remained there in invol-

* Portions of this essay related to Tibor Eckhardt are based on the author's previously published works.

untary exile until his death in 1972. By the time the Hungarian post war political exiles arrived in the United States, Eckhardt was already considered the leader of the Hungarian political emigration, and it was he who helped to organize these new refugees.

Hungary's first free post war elections were held in 1945. The following year, Rusztem Vámbéry, a Hungarian jurist in exile in the United States, wrote *Hungary – To Be or Not To Be*, a book outlining his views on the country's future.[1] When he wrote the book, there seemed to be no fear on his part (or that of many others) of what domination by Soviet Russia would bring, and Vámbéry wrote dismissively, "Journalists not familiar with the Hungarian background are predicting either complete economic ruin or the ultimate communization of Hungary. Political forecasts are always risky, and this one borders on utter nonsense."[2] He does go on to say, however, "Regardless of the orientation of other neighbors, the influence of Russia, the greatest power bordering on Hungary, will be predominant. … Anyone not living in a fool's paradise must admit that Hungary's foreign policy and its army, are de facto going to be controlled by the Soviet Union. Other members of the Allied Control Commission, as was made clear at the conference of the Foreign Secretaries held in Moscow in December 1945, have only an advisory role."[3]

Vámbéry's prediction became fact on 31 May 1947 when the communists took power. After Ferenc Nagy relinquished his position as prime minister and left Hungary, Vámbéry agreed to accept the position of Hungarian ambassador to the United States, continuing to believe in the benign and non-interfering nature of Soviet policy toward Hungary. His tenure was brief and ineffectual. Appointed on 6 September 1947, he was frustrated at every turn in his attempt to do his job, and when he eventually realized that his underlings, Communist Party members, were dictating policy to him, he understood that he was being used as window dressing. He resigned on 19 May 1948, after just nine months in the post, and then wrote an unpublished seven-page memorandum entitled "Failure of a Mission and a Mission of Failure", which outlines his experience in vivid detail.[4] Vámbéry and Michael Károlyi (who remained as Hungarian ambassador to France until the Rajk show trial in September

1949) were among of the last few of the Hungarian émigrés to believe in the benevolence of the Soviet occupiers of Central and Eastern Europe.[5] And in the West during the immediate post WWII period, both men wielded considerable influence as representatives of the liberal element of the Hungarian immigration. Particularly among the liberal media and American intellectuals their following far exceeded that which they garnered in the émigré community. Indeed, if they were known in the latter at all, they were not held in high regard.

Political Leaders Take Refuge in the West

As the Communists consolidated their power in Hungary, the trickle of emigrating Hungarian political figures became a flood and Nagy, Msgr. Varga, Pfeiffer and many others left their homeland. In 1947, after the borders and access to freedom was closed off, James McCargar, a US diplomat and intelligence officer operating in Hungary was personally responsible for assisting the escape of 74 Hungarian political figures to the West.[6] They joined the politicians who had already taken that route during, before and after WWII. By 1947 the West had realized that a Cold War between the world's two superpowers was in full force. Earlier reluctant to publicly endorse or financially support political groups, the US now felt that the time was right to support the efforts of exiles from Soviet satellite countries and sought some means to occupy the émigré politicians' energies and time – as well as to provide them with some form of "employment". The reality of the advent of the Cold War and the descent of the Iron Curtain in Europe provided the conditions that encouraged the organization of national councils, including the Hungarian National Council, which would represent the interests of those forced into exile.

The Establishment of the Hungarian National Council

Encouraged and funded through the US Department of State, the Hungarian National Council (HNC) was organized in 1947.[7] First as the Hungarian National Council and after 1958 as the Hungarian National

Committee, it was to be the longest-lived organization of Hungarian political exiles in America.[8]

The first organizational meeting of what was to become the Magyar Nemzeti Bizottmány or HNC was held in Chicago, Illinois, in November 1947. On November 18 the principals involved – Eckhardt, Nagy, Pfeiffer, Sulyok and Varga – issued a proclamation entitled "Appeal to the Hungarian People". It stated, in part, "... the Hungarian people must survive this darkest period in their history. Resistance at this point in time is futile and purposeless unless the western powers choose to step into the situation. Because of this we are calling upon you; remove yourselves from public life; don't work together with your oppressors; don't listen to those that would deceive you; remain in your homes, but support the passive resistance." The proclamation went on to say, "the problems and direction of the resistance will be accepted as the responsibility of the Hungarian leadership living abroad. We abandon all party politics and divisions and create in the free world a living Hungarian national organization, from whom only the fascists and Communists who intended to deliver Hungary to the foreign powers are excluded." The authors concluded by vowing that the "1000 year old Hungarian nation will rise again."[9]

By 1948 the new organization was established in New York City. It was composed of key Hungarian leaders, almost all of whom had recently fled Hungary, and was regarded by many as a virtual government in exile. Indeed, its executive committee functioned as such, with its president in the role of "prime minister". Msgr. Varga, speaker of the Hungarian parliament until 31 May 1947, headed the council as chairman of the board.

The minutes of the 14 July 1948 preparatory meeting reflect that Varga declared that, in conformity with the resolution passed at the meeting of 10 June 1948, "he sent a notice [to] the former members in exile of the Hungarian Parliaments duly elected in free and unfettered elections informing them about the convocation of the Hungarian National Council as an organ of the Parliament." The notice stated: "On ground of the written approval of the former members of Hungarian Parliaments, Msgr. Béla Varga declares that the members of the Hungarian Parliaments are in agreement with his anouncement [sic] of the convocation of the Hungarian National Council; thereby he declares the Hungarian National Council as legally constituted... The Preparatory Commission of the Hungarian National Council unanimously approves the statement of Msgr. Béla Varga and declares that under the Law Msgr. Béla Varga should preside on [sic] its sessions."[10] This was an important point, stressed throughout, about the formation of the council: Varga was considered the legitimate speaker of the Hungarian parliament, never having resigned his post, and under Hungarian law he could legally head an organization representing the Hungarian people.

The HNC board's Resolution 2/1948 recorded the following elections to its executive committee: "Mr. Dezso Sulyok was elected Chairman of the Committee for Interior [sic]; Mr. Tibor Eckhardt, Chairman of the Committee for Defense; Mr. George Bakach-Bessenyey, Chairman of the Committee for External Affairs; Mr. Francis (Ferenc) Nagy, Chairman of the Financial Committee; Charles [Karoly] Peyer, Chairman of the Labour and Trade Union Committee; Msgr. Jozeph Kozi-Horvath, Chairman of the Committee for Culture and Education; Zoltán Pfeiffer, Chairman of the Committee for Justice and Information; Béla Fábián be elected [sic.] Chairman of the Committee of Social Politics."[11]

The executive committee was composed entirely of Hungarian citizens, most of whom intended to return to Hungary after its liberation from Soviet occupation, which all but the most cynical of them thought would happen in the near future. The work of the committee was encouraged and supported by the Department of State, and after 1949, when the National Committee for Free Europe (NCFE) was established, the HNC was folded into its sphere and was sponsored and funded through that body for its entire existence.[12] (The HNC was joined under the NCFE umbrella by the three other national councils or committees that had been formed at the behest of the State Department at that time.) The HNC's goal was to "represent the nations muted [by Soviet occupation] as well as to care for and to supply spiritual and political guidance to the dispersed Hungarians".[13]

The function or mission of the HNC originally might have been seen somewhat differently by its sponsors than it was by the émigré leaders themselves. While much of the NCFE leadership saw the refugees as tools in the propaganda war against the Soviet Union, the émigré leaders had as a high priority assisting their countrymen who were still living in refugee camps in Europe three years after the end of the war. The desperate plight of almost two million refugees, with thousands still attempting to flee Soviet domination in Central and Eastern Europe, was foremost in the minds of the émigré leadership, and resettling them in nations willing to receive them was a major goal. The United States' Displaced Person Act of 1948, passed by the 80th Congress on 25 June 1948, made provisions for issuing 220,000 visas to be used for two years without regard to national quotas and also made provisions for displaced persons who entered the country prior to 1 April 1948.[14] The trickle of refugees already admitted (some 15,000) became a steady flow. The welfare and resettlement of this influx was an issue foremost in the minds of the Hungarian leadership.

With refugee aid as the HNC's first priority, it was not too long before it set up aid offices in the US and abroad. Eager to recruit the best individuals for these important positions, the HNC did not hesitate to look for talent outside as well as inside the émigré community in the US. As an example, Msgr. Varga sent a letter to Tibor Horányi's home in Rome letting him know it was "imperative that you come over to the US as soon as possible in order to assist Msgr. Jozsef Kozi-Horvath in dealing with refugee problems."[15]Attention was paid to all aspects of servicing the needs of recent immigrants. This included, for example, the refugee aid office assigning George Telegdy (soon after his own arrival in the US in late 1949) to meet each and every ship that docked in New York throughout 1950 and 1951 in order to personally welcome Hungarian émigrés to their new homeland on behalf of the HNC. Some of his observations are recorded in the reports he submitted to the HNC. As an example, he reported on 18 May 1951, after meeting the *SS General C. H. Muir* when it docked, "This was a ship transporting refugees who are stateless. Out of the 1300 DPs transported on the ship, 80 were Hungarian." He went on to list the notable Hungarians on the ship, where the greatest number were being settled and who had been present from the various aid organizations to get the refugees on their way in America.[16] It must have been a great comfort to the DPs to have Telegdy greet them on their arrival and provide some sense that they were not alone in their new homeland.

As the HNC evolved, so, too, did its primary goals, which can be categorized as follows:

- Assist Hungarian refugees both abroad and upon their arrival in the US or other destinations.
- Promote the cause of liberation of their homeland by advocating the cause of freedom from Soviet colonialism by removal of Soviet occupying forces.
- In promoting freedom for their homeland, serve as a thorn in the side of the Soviet Union and utilize the media and all other methods of communication to point out the shortcomings in the Soviet system, including deportations, political repression and control of the economy.
- Promote the maintenance of Hungarian culture and continue the observation of key national holidays.
- Communicate with the Hungarian diaspora worldwide, keep them informed and engaged in the goals of the HNC.

All aspects of these activities developed as the HNC found its footing. However, as is detailed below, the road of the leadership's good intentions, particularly Msgr. Varga's, was paved with many obstacles, not the least of which were placed by the émigré leaders themselves, Varga's colleagues. But despite the obstacles, what also developed was a working relationship and common cause made between the various exile committees that continued throughout the life of the organizations – an amazing development in and of itself. [17]

Funding of the Hungarian National Council

Taking as an example the HNC's financial allocation for November 1949, soon after it was taken under the NCFE's umbrella, we see that the NCFE provided $14,650 per month, which included funding for the New York and Washington, D.C., offices and staff, for "Refugee Services" (including the office and staff and the foreign offices), for the "Communications Office" (which included an office and three foreign-based reporters), and for travel expenses, membership dues in international organizations and the HCN's publication *Bizottmányi Közlöny.*[18] Financial compensation for the members of the executive committee and the ten Hungarians employed by the NCFE-supported Mid-European Studies Center was funded through the NCFE in a separate budget.[19] The first budget discussions with the HNC were held on 27 May 1949 and included Kálmán Sálata, representing the Hungarians as he spoke English well, and Sándor Szász, as well as Frederic Dolbeare, DeWitt Poole and Edgar Dean of the NCFE. In several of Saláta's meeting recaps prepared for the HNC executive committee he also mentions "Mr. Dulles" being consulted.[20]

As outlined in the first chapter of this volume, the growth of the national councils was swift, and by 1954 the HNC had 76 members and included virtually all of the political figures who had left Hungary after 1947, including two former prime ministers, several ministers and the former leaders of all the political parties purged between 1947 and 1949.[21] There were offices in both New York and Washington, D.C., and offices or representatives were established in 18 countries outside the United States.[22] The group was somewhat resistant to including *every* former official, however, and was selective about its choices. This lack of inclusiveness was specifically directed toward the pre-1947 émigrés, who were considered a right wing and pro-fascist group, a situation that troubled the executive committee and was later to become a larger issue. The DP Act of 1948 also specifically excluded from immigration anyone who had been an enemy combatant, which meant that by the terms of that act all members of the Hungarian military who had fought as allies of

Germany were excluded from entering the United States. This provision was broadly interpreted and included national guard members and even members of the Vitézi Rend, a hereditary military order.

> Almost immediately after its establishment, the HNC became a center of political controversy among Hungarian Americans. Whether conservative, right wing or radical left, they accused the HNC of evil intent. The conservatives and the right radicals regarded the participants as pseudo communists and possible agents of the Soviet system in Hungary; the left regarded them as traitors and "agents of United States Imperialism".[23]

The most valid criticism of the HNC was that it did not represent the Hungarian American community. The spokesmen for most of the Hungarian American organizations viewed the HNC's members as recently arrived, appointed agents of certain American political interest groups who were on the US government payroll. In some sectors of the immigrant community it was thought that the HNC had been granted the US government's official recognition and financial support in exchange for representing the interests of US foreign policy with regard to Hungary and the world during the Cold War.

Unlike the recent arrivals among the leadership of the HNC, Tibor Eckhardt had lived in the US since 1941 and established strong ties to the major Hungarian American organizations, whose membership was primarily composed of the immigrants who had arrived in the United States prior to WWI. He had established and cultivated these relationships over a period of several decades, beginning when he was in the United States on several Carnegie Endowment lecture tours in 1929, 1930–31 and on a later trip in 1940. Eckhardt was particularly close to and well regarded by the most prominent of these organizations, the American Hungarian Federation, a hugely influential force in the 1940s that served as the umbrella organization for over 300 American Hungarian groups in the United States. Its president, Tibor Kerekes, was a Georgetown University professor who was well connected and well regarded in Washington, D.C. The AHF's unequivocal support of Eckhardt's Movement for Independent Hungary, the earliest effort to establish a Hungarian council in the United States (1941–1942), had provided him with exposure to many émigré communities and organizations and made him a much sought-after speaker for their groups.[24]

For their part, the recently arrived Hungarian leaders were mostly unknown to Hungarian America. The most prominent among them, Ferenc Nagy, had the prestige of the prime minister's position behind him, and, like Eckhardt, he was invited to give many lectures and make personal appearances – a fact amply illustrated by the 14 file boxes in his archived papers that contain his lecture correspondence. Although there can be no doubt that he was in demand as a speaker, very few of the institutions represented in Nagy's archived correspondence appear to be Hungarian American civic groups, churches or fraternal organizations, which emphasizes his lack of connection with the existing Hungarian American community.[25] When he arrived, Nagy was not only not well known to Hungarian America but he also remained very selective in his contacts with his countrymen who had arrived before or with him. For example, Gabriella Mauthner, who served as a volunteer at Hungarian House (Magyar Ház) in Manhattan from its founding in 1955 until her death in 2011, recalled that Nagy never visited that cultural and political heart of the Hungarian community. The other recently arrived political émigrés were also largely unknown to the Hungarian American community, and as a result that community viewed them with suspicion and mistrust.

After the Movement for Independent Hungary was formed, other Hungarian groups also organized among the earlier arrivals. One being a Committee of Ministers composed of former diplomats (Követi Bizottság, 1944–1945), another was the American Federation of Democratic Hungarians (Demokratikus Magyarok Amerikai Szövetsége, 1941–1945). This latter was a Rusztem Vámbéry-headed group that was pro-Michael Károlyi and wished for him to assume the mantle as leader of the Hungarian diaspora. All these groups, however, had been denied what the US government granted to the HNC after the onset of the

Cold War: official endorsement and financial support. In the immediate post war period, however, even with US government support and the participation of so many key Hungarian émigré politicians and leaders, there were limits to what the HNC could realistically hope to achieve. On behalf of its US sponsors, the HNC served as a propaganda arm of the NCFE, on behalf of its countrymen it served to keep the diaspora united and in communication with each other and to promote the idea of liberation from Hungary's Soviet occupiers.

Not only were the HNC and its leaders initially viewed with great skepticism by the Hungarian American community but its work was also internally fractious. Those who left Hungary during or immediately after WWII were not inclined to compromise with the leaders representing the left wing of Hungarian politics, who had remained in Hungary after the war and only departed when it became clear that they would not be part of the power sharing with the Soviet-backed Hungarian Communists. This was the basis of most of the divisiveness within the HNC and was never to be resolved, only managed by Varga as best he could; in most respects he did a remarkable job.

The first crisis within the leadership came when Dezső Sulyok submitted to the HNC executive committee and the conflict of interest committee a complaint dated 4 February 1950 regarding Varga's leadership.[26] He also submitted the complaint to the Hungarian language newspaper *Az Ember*, which published it on 4 March. The complaint accused Varga of complicity in the fate of Hungarian Jews during WWII and was based on supposedly anti-Semitic comments Varga made in the Hungarian parliament on 1 July 1941.[27] The board took the letter under advisement at their 1 March and 9 March meetings in 1950, as the meeting minutes indicate. Varga was unanimously supported by the board, and Sulyok's complaint was dismissed.[28] Unfortunately, by then Sulyok's public stand against Varga had rendered him virtually persona non grata in Hungarian émigré circles, where Varga's aid to refugees, including Jews from Poland and Hungary, was a matter of public knowledge and he was respected and admired for his activities. In a letter to Otto von Habsburg recounting problems within the HNC during its first few years, Eckhardt commented that Sulyok had "committed hara kiri and had to be eliminated".[29]

A second crisis came in the form of an attack on Eckhardt, an outgrowth of his often-expressed concern regarding the increasingly leftist tilt in the HNC. On 4 October 1950 he provoked HNC President Varga to issue a "Statement of Incompatibility" against him within the executive committee. The convoluted details of Eckhardt's problems within the executive committee are beyond the purview of this chapter, but suffice it to say that ongoing tension between the Nagy camp and the Eckhardt camp escalated rapidly after the HNC was formed, and that was the cause of the friction. The ostensible cause of the incompatibility statement was that in his capacity as the chair of the military committee Eckhardt had joined the Magyar Harcosok Bajtársi Közössége (MHBK), a Germany-based organization of former members of the Hungarian military in exile, which had been labeled pro-fascist. Msgr. Varga was a long-time colleague and friend of Eckhardt and had been a member of the same political party in Hungary, but he was nevertheless determined to be diplomatic as HNC president and to include Nagy in all of his decisions and in the management process. He also deferred to Nagy as a former prime minister, yet attempted, at the same time, also to placate and please the Eckhardt faction. Ultimately, he pleased neither party, as extensive correspondence in both the Eckhardt and Nagy papers reveals.[30] Eckhardt viewed the struggle within the executive committee as a matter of the rightists versus the leftists and felt that in terms of committee composition, the scales were tipping heavily to the left as a result of Varga's leadership. Nagy as his correspondence indicates was suspicious of Eckhardt's ambitions about which he was constantly warned by his coterie of followers, including his translator Steven Swift a US intelligence operative. For his part, Varga was simply attempting to give voice to all groups represented in the Hungarian diaspora, with the exception of the known communists, and trying to keep the HNC on course and functioning, regardless of the factions within.

Although Eckhardt's view of the leftist "threat" may have seemed exaggerated, his and others' fear of communist infiltration of émigré organizations and activities, including sabotage of their work, was very real and not without foundation in fact. The covert and overt threat from the communists was expressed, for example, in activities such as a plan by the Cominform to liquidate the entire Hungarian government in exile. This plan was uncovered in a message from Bucharest to its agents that was intercepted in 1951.[31] Details of other intelligence activities against émigré groups have emerged in recent research into Eckhardt's own intelligence activities regarding the Soviet satellites when he was part of John V. Grombach's US intelligence organization known as "The Pond".[32]

At an ACEN conference in 1955 former Prime Minister Miklós Kállay addressed what he felt was the primary issue with the Soviets, that of communist infiltration of Western institutions, saying that the Soviets utilized the formal problems of disarmament and control of nuclear weapons as red herrings to divert the West's attention from the underground activities of the Cominform and its embedded agents.[33]

While there was intelligence activity against the national councils, it was also true that, like Eckhardt, some of the leadership was actively involved with US intelligence against the Soviet Union and its allies. John Leich served on the NCFE staff as the principal assistant to Vice President Frederic Dolbeare in the National Councils Division, and his successor, Bernard Yarrow, wrote a firsthand accounting of the national councils. In it he mentions that while the councils or council members may have been involved in intelligence operations in their respective homelands, the NCFE was not involved and was not aware of those activities.[34] There is also evidence in intelligence archives that "an underground committee of the HNC" was operational through the CIA.[35]

Almost a year after the accusations against him were aired on 4 September 1951, Eckhardt responded to Varga regarding the Statement of Incompatibility. His words evoke "why" the HNC was formed:

> Since October 4, 1950, when you, Mr. Chairman, had submitted a statement of incompatibility directed against me to the Executive Committee, I have never referred publicly to this accusation, to the smear campaign directed against me or to the injurious decisions

> taken by that sub-committee. By doing so, I wished to respect the public interest ...
> In November 1947, in our Chicago proclamation, we have agreed to set aside 'all party politics' and to create 'the national unity of all Hungarians living in free lands.' It is on this foundation, that in the summer of 1948 the Executive Committee of the Hungarian National council was established from all the leaders of Hungarian political groups who 'form a part of the general political picture of our country.' At that time, in the composition of the Executive Committee, a certain balance was achieved between the pre-war and post-war, Rightist and Leftist political tendencies and it is a real national interest that that balance be maintained continuously.[36]

Eckhardt went on to state his on-going objections to the lack of political balance in the executive committee:

> Contrary to all democratic and reasonable evolution the insistence of the Hungarian extreme Leftist group has put through in recent months an extension to the Left in the composition of the Executive Committee. The original balance does not exist anymore and if the Executive Committee wishes to remain true to its fundamental national program, it has to complete its ranks from the Right in the same proportion as the Left. In its present composition, the Executive Committee is no more the organ of national policy but is rather a representation of the Peasant-Marxist classes and their class-warfare with an extreme Leftist predominance....[37]

The sad truth was that most of the émigré politicians had so little to occupy their time that the committee on incompatibility's report regarding Eckhardt runs to 50 pages.

In analyzing the causes of the schism between Nagy and Eckhardt, it is important to remember that in Hungary both men had been members of the Smallholders Party and shared the same political beliefs and goals. How far Nagy went to the left or Eckhardt was to the right is not the issue. They were simply men whose viewpoints after their emigration diverged from that those they had held at home, and their issues roiled within the HNC for several years, with bitter accusations on all sides.

Eventually, Eckhardt reluctantly concluded that the HNC executive committee's policies were not going to change and his efforts on Hungary's behalf would be better utilized outside that forum. He submitted his resignation on 14 April 1954,[38] thereby relinquished his only regular source of income, the $300 per month stipend the executive committee members received from the NCFE at that time.[39] Since the HNC executive committee could be composed only of foreign nationals, resigning freed Eckhardt to apply for US citizenship, which he did that same year.[40] Although no longer on the executive committee, Eckhardt remained a member of the council and continued to be well regarded by many of its members and by Varga. When the Assembly of Captive European Nations (ACEN) was established in 1954, he was asked to form and chair its first Hungarian Delegation. He was also asked to continue reporting on behalf of the HNC to the Free Europe Committee (FEC) – the by-then re-named NCFE.

HNC members leaked the details of these and other intra-organizational struggles to the Hungarian language press and the Hungarian refugees, and they were dissected and chewed over in Hungarian émigré circles worldwide. Confidentiality was a real issue throughout the life of these major émigré organizations. As an example, only six months after the HNC was asked to join the NCFE fold, the financial plans for the organization were being shopped around to editors of Hungarian publications, causing great controversy.[41] The internal political battles went on for years, while the HNC's credibility, never robust in the eyes of Hungarian Americans, quickly eroded – for as the HNC leaned farther to the left, Hungarian American sentiments, always conservative, were moving farther to the right.

Sadly, these early conflicts between the conservative and liberal camps within the HNC were simply a precursor to later problems that arose when the first of the "freedom fighters" arrived after the Hungarian Revolution.

The NCFE, for its part, was unhappily aware of the internecine squabbles at the HNC; and indeed, it can be difficult to understand why the exile groups and their members often seemed to ignore and go against the wishes of the organization that made their existence possible. In this tendency, the Hungarians were not alone, and many a émigré politician tripped himself up by criticizing the NCFE. A letter from NCFE President C.D. Jackson to Msgr. Varga dated 10 March 1952 is indicative of the situation. Jackson was a former intelligence officer, a prominent publishing executive, a specialist in propaganda and a very politically connected individual. In reviewing his year as the NCFE's president, his letter was making it clear to Varga that the "NCFE does not intend to be hampered or sabotaged by exile political maneuvering".[42]

Jackson's letter provides an objective perspective on the HNC, and its details indicate an intimate knowledge of the operations of the national councils. Large portions of the text are reproduced here for its perspective on the intrigues and personal agendas that seem to have dominated the HNC and hampered its effectiveness.

> Dear Monsignor Varga:
>
> As I wind up my year with the National Committee for a Free Europe, I thought it appropriate to send you a letter – not a letter of farewell, but rather some thoughts on the Hungarian National Council as I have observed it during the year.
>
> In the first place, I would like to congratulate you and your associates on having done an extraordinary job of holding a very volatile situation together. In fact, it was a unique job, and one whose value we may never fully appreciate because so many of the benefits are intangible.
>
> I hope, therefore, that you will continue to work with undiminished will to hold the Council together, as it would present a very serious problem to Admiral Miller if the Hungarian group were to fall apart.[43]
>
> I would also like to congratulate you on the effective work the representatives of the Hungarian National Council have done abroad,

particularly in France and Germany. You know how important I consider this work. It seems to me that the real task and duty of a National Council is to help the exiles, and the front lines of this work are in Europe.

Aside from the obvious necessities of food, clothing, shelter, the most important aspect of the work is what I would call a "consular" service, as these people do not know where and how to turn. In this consular-type work, I think that General Hennyey and Mr. Auer have been doing an excellent job, and personal feelings in this matter are completely confirmed by reactions I have received from the International Refugee Organization and the official foreign and American administrations in these countries.

To my way of thinking, exile political matters in New York and Washington should take a definitely second place to helping human beings in distress, and although there are some who do not agree with this order of priority, I am delighted and grateful that the work of the Hungarian National Council indicates that you share these ideas.

Since this is an honest letter, and not just pro-forma appreciation by a retiring President, I must also, unfortunately, include some observations that are not so pleasant.

I remember very early in my work with NCFE, that you taught me the political meaning of the word "polarization", and since then I have had ample opportunity in the Hungarian National Council to see polarization at work.

NCFE has grown in the past year into a large organization engaged in serious work, and frequently proving its effectiveness behind the Iron Curtain. To put it another way, during the past year NCFE has evolved from just a hope into a professional weapon in the war against the enemy. Therefore, activities which a year ago were deplorable but pardonable, are today inexcusable and intolerable. …

However, I recognize that it is not enough for NCFE to take unilateral action. We must be assisted by you and those of your associates who understand who the real enemy is, and are willing to subordinate fratricidal strife, polarizing attempts, and disloyal activities. …

I have in my possession enough illustrations to fill a volume, but would like to select three in particular to mention in this letter, not because I have any particular desire to single out the individuals for censure, but rather because what they have done not only illustrates the point I am trying to make, but also reveals an attitude of mind which is practically incomprehensible to an American working for a great cause.

The first case that I have in mind is that of Mr. Ferenc Nagy.

Last February, Mr. Nagy wrote a letter to Mr. Frank S. Land of Kansas City, Missouri, complaining bitterly about the National Committee for a Free Europe, accusing it of "supporting outmoded and old-fashioned reactionary political ideologies", and asking Mr. Land to advise him as to how this situation could be brought to the attention of President Truman in order to have him do something about it. As a result of that letter, Mr. Land wrote to the White House, and in the normal course this full correspondence came to me.

I asked Mr. Nagy to come to the office, and tried to explain to him that what he had done was not only bad, but a very silly thing. It was bad in the sense that he had violated our hospitality by secretly attempting to conspire against the organization which was supporting him. It was silly in assuming that he could carry on this kind of intrigue without my knowing about it – in fact, without having the White House check with NCFE, an American organization, as to what action should be taken.

Mr. Nagy seemed to understand what I tried to explain to him, and with what I considered complete honesty and sincerity expressed his regrets and said that it would not happen again. In return for this frank understanding on his part, we shook hands, and I promised that the correspondence would be put away in our files and never referred to again. And as you know, I have never even mentioned it to you.

Mr. Nagy has once again written to President Truman – this time directly. And once again the White House has sent me the memorandum.

I consider that Mr. Nagy has broken his pledge, and therefore I am free to tell you about the incident.
This time, although the words of Mr. Nagy are more temperate, the melody is the same – dissatisfaction with what NCFE has done; dissatisfaction with the Hungarian National Council. Let me quote a passage: "The existing National Committees are not in themselves suitable for this task, partly because of the general intra-Committee controversies between Democrats and reactionaries, and partly because these Committees are not considered by the peoples behind the Iron Curtain international guarantee that promises would be carried out."
I cannot help commenting at this point that in the Hungarian National Council there is probably no one who has contributed more to "intra-Committee controversies" than Mr. Nagy himself. Furthermore, an analysis of Mr. Nagy's definition of "Democrats and reactionaries" would be extremely interesting. It might have been more accurate had he said "people who supported my Government in 1947 and everybody else".
As to the matter of <u>any</u> exile committee, whether the Hungarian National Council or Mr. Nagy's Central Eastern European Committee, being able to "guarantee" to the people behind the Iron Curtain that promises would be carried out, Mr. Nagy's statement is either frivolous or preposterous.
Mr. Nagy winds up with a request that the President give his blessing to Mr. Nagy's proposed super-committee – the Central Eastern European Committee – which represents "a total majority of 70 to 80% of the entire population of Central Eastern Europe."
I am frankly fascinated by the processes of Mr. Nagy's mind. I cannot believe that all he thinks about is the promotion of Leftish Hungarian politicians in exile. I cannot believe that as a human being he does not feel some sense of responsibility toward NCFE and the Hungarian National Council, who have month after month helped him. ... Mr. Nagy has been in this country long enough now to understand that this kind of intriguing is a distressing irritation to everyone, including the White House ...

Jackson goes on to offer a second illustration in which he discusses Nagy's interference in a Radio Free Europe decision by calling upon the NCFE to explain to him, as president of the Hungarian Peasant Federation, their personnel decision to name Andor Gellert to head the New York RFE desk. Nagy's objection, according to Jackson, was that Gellert "does not have the same political colorations as Mr. Nagy"; and Jackson rightly observed that "the Hungarian Peasant Union does not exist as a viable political party: it only exists in the individual persons in exile who happen formerly to have been members of the Hungarian Peasant Union." He goes on to say, "Mr. Nagy is not a member of a government-in-exile, or even of a parliament-in-exile, so that action of his is totally unreal, indicating unwillingness to recognize the world as it exists..."

In his third illustration Jackson mentions that Zoltan Pfeiffer, also a former Smallholder politician, also protested Gellert's appointment, which was made by Gyula Dessewffy, head of RFE's Hungarian desk in Munich.

> Mr. Pfeiffer further stated – and this the really important point – that because of the appointment of Mr. Gellert, Mr. Pfeiffer would have to "attack" Mr. Dessewffy from now on, wherever and whenever possible; in short, a declaration of war.
>
> Again, I would like to understand Mr. Pfeiffer's mental processes. Who does he think he is? Where does he think he is? This is a very serious world, and not a Rufolf [*sic*] Friml operetta. Mr. Pfeiffer is not in Budapest conducting a political campaign against a wayward member of a Left-wing party. Mr. Pfeiffer is in New York, an associate of NCFE, with every opportunity to have his opinion heard and his influence felt. But after a decision has been made, in good faith and after long consideration, to employ a man because of his competence to do a job, it is Mr. Pfeiffer's responsibility as an associate of the same organization to help that man do his work, and not to indulge in declarations of war in order to disrupt the operation.
>
> I am sorry to have had to go into this unpleasant detail, but after a year of patiently observing and listening, I feel that I have earned the right to speak plainly.

> I hope that somehow or other, it will be possible for you to explain to your membership that NCFE does not intend to be hampered or sabotaged by exile political maneuvering.
> I also hope that you will be able to persuade your compatriots that insofar as NCFE can interpret U.S. policy it believes that the Government of the United States, looking forward to the eventual liberation of Hungary, will not permit any political group or individual in exile, to set up a monopoly for himself, his group, or his party.[44]

This lengthy and candid letter clearly illustrates how disruptive and counter-productive the NCFE leadership considered the émigré politicians' actions to be. How was it that Nagy, for example, felt comfortable attacking the US agency that had spirited him and his family out of Hungary, reestablished them in the United States and provided their financial livelihood? While Jackson singled out Nagy and Pfeiffer, it could be said, after reviewing the history of the national councils, that the missteps of the émigré leadership in relation to their patron agency were often a result of the fact that the sheer irrelevance of their own positions simply did not register with many of them. They were used to being important figures in their respective countries and now found themselves marginalized in the US. Their desire to influence the policy and actions of the US State Department was never fulfilled, even at the height of the Cold War, and most of their efforts to effect a difference in policy were dismissed out of hand by US officials. They were told in no uncertain terms to mind their own business and not stray outside their prescribed roles, as seen by the NCFE leadership; some complied, some did not.

Varga as the HNC's Unifying Force

In truth, no matter how rife the HNC was with inter-organizational fighting, it continued to function because Msgr. Varga, while frustrating the left and the right by his unwillingness to take sides, continued his steady, measured leadership. Through all the phases of the Cold War he was able to maintain a functioning organization that was considered the best run of the national councils.[45] Of humble origins, Varga was one of two brothers in his family who became Roman Catholic priests. His brother Andras was a Jesuit who also emigrated to the United States; he taught at Fordham University and later spent several years in Rome. Béla Varga became a member of parliament and a founder of the Smallholders Party in 1930. A the parish priest of Balatonboglár, Hungary, in 1939 he was asked by Prime Minister Teleki, who could not do it officially for fear of raising the ire of the Germans, to organize aid and refuge for almost 50,000 Polish military and civilian refugees who were fleeing the Nazis.[46] During the war he was involved in the anti-German resistance, provided imperiled Jews with forged documents and aided 2,200 French POWs who had escaped from Nazi prison camps after the Battle of France, as well as Polish POWs who had escaped from Nazi camps. His church in Balatonboglar became a center for refugee relief.[47] Varga described his wartime activities in a 1954 television interview: "Because members of parliament enjoy immunity from arrest or police inspection and their homes cannot be searched by policy or any authority, my house at Balatonboglár 100 miles from Budapest became the headquarters for the Polish underground resistance movement." Through his ongoing work helping escaped POW's and persecuted persons he came into contact with the underground movement, "... and eventually became an important link in the communication between the Polish underground movement in exile in London and the Polish government in Warsaw. This is how I became involved in the Hungarian anti-Nazi movement and resistance fight of which I was one of the leaders." At the request of his Bishop, Varga went into hiding, but on 5 November 1944 he was directed to travel to Budapest to try to save the capital's Jews.[48] Arrested and sentenced to death by the Soviets in 1945 he was released when his captors learned that he had also helped Soviet Army POWs. He was elected to parliament in 1945 and was elected its speaker in February 1946. When the communist takeover appeared inevitable, in July 1947 Varga fled Hungary for the US, where he lived at St. Mary's Home in New York City. It was run by an order of Hungarian nuns, the Congregation of Daughters of Divine Charity, and he remained there for the rest of his time in the United States.[49]

Varga's aid to Polish refugees from Nazism in Hungary in the late 1930 was recognized by the Polish government after the overthrow of communism, and his wartime activities also resulted in a personal letter of thanks from General Charles De Gaulle.[50] In January 1960 he was honored as an officer of the Legion of Honor by the French Ambassador to the United States, Herve Alphand.[51]

An unpretentious man, Vargas's unshakeable Christian belief provided the fractious Hungarian émigrés with the steady hand that they needed, and during his tenure at the HCN's helm he showed a remarkable ability to maintain his value system. He was also able to maintain his belief in the goal of the HNC – democracy for the occupied Hungarian nation – while pragmatically adjusting the work of the HNC to reflect changing US foreign policy and creeping détente. A remarkable feat of diplomacy and leadership for which he has never been properly recognized.

What did the HNC provide?

First of all and primarily the HNC focused on activism on behalf of their countrymen. Varga made sure that the aid offices were staffed and providing aid to Hungarian refugees, principally in Austria, Germany and France. They helped refugees find housing and jobs, translated documents for them and generally provided services that the refugees, most of whom spoke only Hungarian, could not obtain elsewhere. Varga's New York office was run capably for many years by his administrative assistant, former diplomat László Acsay, who fielded daily requests for assistance, principally in matters of immigration. A typical Western Union telegram, dated 9 September 1949 and sent from Ellis Island, reads: "Requesting your official visit promptly on Ellis Island to help 50 detained Hungarians"[52]

At the same time, advocacy for those still in Hungary was ongoing. For example, on 18 May 1950 the Voice of America reported a story it headlined "Hungarians Appeal for Prisoner Return":

> The Hungarian National Council has appealed to United Nations Secretary Trygve Lie to intercede on behalf of two hundred thousand Hungarian war prisoners and civilians still said to be held in the Soviet Union. The organization of exiled Hungarian political leaders yesterday cabled Mister Lie, who in Moscow for conferences with Soviet leaders. The appeal, signed by former Hungarian Parliament President Bela Varga, President of the Council, said: "Two hundred Thousand Hungarian war prisoners are still withheld in Russia, part of them civilians captured at random in streets of Hungarian towns and villages by the Russian Occupation Army in 1945. Some of these civilian prisoners had just escaped the gas chambers of Auschwitz (Oswiecim) and other German concentration camps. We ask you to do everything within your power to help all these unfortunate people to return to their families."[53]

A handwritten note on the file copy in the archives indicates that the demand was circulated to 24 UN delegations.

The HNC kept the Hungarian community informed through their publication *Bizottmányi Közlöny* and through their research service, which solicited material from throughout the diaspora. The HNC also collaborated with all of the Hungarian newspapers throughout the world, principally the New York-based *Amerikai Magyar Népszava,* which also received NCFE funding to stay afloat, but also dozens of other news outlets. The publications *Látóhatár* in Germany and *Nyugati Hírnök* and *Courier de l'Occident* in Paris also received funding through the HNC.[54] Modest HNC support went to other publications as far afield as Buenos Aires (*Dél Amerikai Magyarság*) and Australia.[55] In total, by 1950 23 North American, 18 European, 4 South American and 4 Canadian publications were given some form of support by the HNC.[56]

Political activism, largely in the form of lobbying US legislators and keeping the US public informed on the situation in Hungary, was also a major HNC function. Varga arrived in the US speaking no English but within a few years spoke it well enough to be asked to speak annually before the US Senate to give the invocation on the anniversary of the 1848 Hungarian Revolution. A few examples of Varga/HNC activism include: an international lobbying effort to protest the incarceration of Cardinal Mindszenty by the communist government of Hungary in 1949. In 1951 the HNC launched a major protest and media campaign against the deportations and displacement of people thought to pose a threat to the communist leadership in Hungary. Beginning in 1950, some 70,000 Hungarians living in Budapest and rural areas were forcibly deported with 24 hours notice.[57] Messages smuggled out of Hungary revealed an extensive campaign against the non-communist middle and upper classes, with "socially dangerous" people being detained in squalid agricultural work camps, cut off from health care and education for their children.[58] Just a small part of the media campaign included letters of protest to Secretary of State Dean Acheson, UN Secretary General Trygve Lie and the media.[59]

During the first years of the HNC, Varga not only served the Hungarian community in the United States and abroad but also successfully reached out to the other national councils. He became an able diplomat and developed successful ongoing relationships with many other leaders from the Soviet satellites. He was instrumental in the formation of the Central and East European Conference (an NCFE-sponsored coalition of East European exile leaders) and participated in both the Philadelphia and Williamsburg meetings that the conference organized. "The avowed purpose of these meetings was to conduct the fight against communism in concert with all who combat Communism, and particularly in close cooperation with the National Committee for a Free Europe."[60] Eventually the national councils wanted to establish a more formal organization on the UN model, and Varga and the HNC were at the forefront when the Assembly of Captive European Nations (ACEN) was established in 1954.

Varga successfully developed a strong relationship with most of the presidents and officers of the NCFE/FEC, and it was he who was called upon to participate in baptisms, weddings and every other kind of family event. He baptized both of Admiral Harold Blaine Miller's children (NCFE president in 1952 and long time member of its board) and gave them religious instruction as they grew older.[61] It is evident from the warm nature of the communication between Varga and many NCFE/FEC board members that theirs went beyond a patron/grantee relationship. It is apparent from reading the NCFE/FEC documents as a whole that only a few individuals among the refugee groups were socially accepted by the NCFE leadership. The Hungarians among them included, in the US, Varga and Eckhardt, John Pelényi (former Hungarian ambassador to Washington and later president of the FEUE) and Count Anton Szapáry (founder of the Hungarian National Sports Federation), and in Europe, Paul Auer in Paris and Baron Apor in Rome. Members of this group were invited to NCFE/FEC events and were consulted on policy decisions. Varga was even invited to President Eisenhower's inauguration in 1953 and seated prominently on the president's platform.[62] That such preferential treatment was not the case for the majority of HNC members created a two-tier access system to the NCFE/FEC decision makers, a situation that endured throughout the life of the HNC.

The NCFE leadership's confidence in Varga and the HNC was expressed in a note from NCFE President Whitney H. Shepherdson to Mrs. John Chambers Hughes, wife of the chair of the Executive Committee and an activist in her own right for the captive nations of Eastern Europe. Dated 28 April 1953, Shepherdson's letter expresses his belief that "the HNC will be really united, really representative and really working for the liberation of Hungary, and for the restoration of freedom in Hungary after liberation has taken place. That is their aim, and our aim, and your aim. Such a committee now exists."[63] Shepherdson's much more positive view of the workings of the HNC – just a year after the Jackson letter – can in all probability be ascribed to the fact that Jackson was a more hands on manager and understood exile political maneuvering, while Shepherdson likely took the national councils' reports at face value. As Shepherdson's letter makes clear, liberation was a key word and NCFE policy reflected that goal in the early days, when both US foreign policy and the NCFE seemed to provide the HNC with hope that the Hungarians would return to their homeland. Shepardson's letter was written in that period of widespread NCFE sponsorship, financial support and belief – that the refugees could be going home sooner rather than later.

The Refugee Service

In the HNC's Washington D.C. office, Kálmán Saláta headed refugee aid, in New York it was Tibor Horányi, in Salzburg, Austria, István Barankovics and later Colonel Mihály Nagy, in Bregenz, Austria, Lt. General József Vasváry, in Munich, Gusztáv Hennyey, a former Hungarian foreign minister, and in Paris, Imre Gácsér, a Benedictine monk was the refugee director.[64]

While the HNC's political and lobbying function often garnered the most press, the organization's most important and urgent function was refugee aid, as CD Jackson eloquently stated in his 10 March 1952 letter to Varga. This was particularly true given that the International Refugee Organization (IRO) – the principal aid and resettlement agency set up in 1946 by the United Nations to deal with refugees – was disbanded in December 1951. At the time of its deactivation, it had successfully resettled "around ten million people, out of fifteen million who were stranded in Europe". This left some five million persons still to be tended to by the various religious, charitable and government entities that were providing aid on the continent.[65] Gusztáv Hennyey, who in December 1951 headed both the German office of the HNC and the Hungarian Refugee Office in Munich, prepared a comprehensive 14-page report describing in great detail the refugees' circumstances and the shutting down of IRO services. He wrote that remigration in "the tens of thousands" has occurred because the refugees were starving.[66]

The HNC refugee service dispensed absolutely essential services, not only because of the still sizeable crisis but also because limits were placed on immigration by refugees who might formerly have been in the military. There were also limitations on immigration for those with a family member with TB or other communicable diseases.[67] And while the refugee situation became less bleak as the economies of Europe slowly returned to normal, a report written by Tibor Horanyi, head of the refugee service in New York, is worth reflecting on. Dated June 1954, nine years after the end of WWII, the report outlined the scope of work of the HNC's Refugee Service. It stated that to date 62,000 Hungarian refugees remained living in European countries as displaced persons, over 64,000 having emigrated overseas and 120,000 having migrated to Israel. The Refugee Service operated in close cooperation with the HNC's overseas representatives. While the representatives were responsible for political functions, the Refugee Service maintained close contact with and safeguarded the interests of the Hungarian refugees in their region.

The first three of the five major tasks assigned to the Central Refugee Office were: 1) keeping track of Hungarians abroad; 2) the spiritual mobilization of Hungarians abroad; 3) refugee relief and consular activities. The office often was called upon to intervene with the Department of State's Visa Department and was in contact with the judiciary committees of the US Senate and House of Representatives regarding the Refugee Relief Act of 1953 as it related to the Hungarian situation. They also maintained close working relationships with the UN's Office of the High Commissioner for Refugees, the Inter-Governmental Committee of European Emigrants (Geneva), the National Catholic Welfare Conference–War Relief Services (New York), the National Council of the Churches of Christ–Church World Service (New York). The office's other two major tasks were: 4) preparing regular summary reports on the situation of Hungarian refugees for the HNC leaders, and 5) providing assistance in immigration matters to the refugees through their various offices.[68]

For specifics on the services these offices performed on a grass roots level, one can turn to a post-revolution report of activities from 1 January to 30 July 1958 by the Hungarian Refugee Service (HRS) in Austria, the refugee arm of the HNC. At the time, it was directed by Dr. László Taubinger and had evolved into a professional aid organization. In June 1958 there were 17,499 Hungarian refugees living in Austria, with 9,242 still living in camps. During the six month period covered by the report, 394 new refugees who managed to make it out of Hungary arrived in Austria. The HRS office reported that it was in touch with aid agencies and ministries ranging from the federal authorities in Austria, to the Citizens Service of Austria, the United Nations High Commission of Refugees in Austria, and the Austrian relief agencies, employment offices and volunteer agencies.

Taubinger's Austrian HRS office reported that during the six months in question his agency provided services he categorized as intervention, cultural support and special assistance to 7,158 persons who visited the offices. Under the heading of intervention assistance he listed wide ranging activities: welfare and support of refugees in private quarters, emigration opportunities for refugees who were sick or invalided, problems faced by university students, war invalids and refugee farmers. The director and representatives of the HRS also attended conferences related to refugee issues.

> Scholarships for university students were secured for another year. We intervened on their behalf several times with the UNHCR, Rockefeller Foundation and the Ministry of Interior and the rectorates of the universities concerned. Iz [sic] was arranged for a great number of TB patients to go to Sweden for settlement. Only recently, UNHCR informed us that Belgium plans to accept invalids. A positive answer was also received from Switzerland. Intervention on behalf of individuals comprise legal assistance, location of employment, translation of documents and intervention with emigration and other authorities.[69]

In terms of cultural support, the service sponsored language courses in Innsbruck and provided AS 4,680 in funding for that purpose. The Union of Hungarian Students (UFHS Austria) received organizational support and AS 27,000 during the period in question, and AS 15,000 was loaned to students in Graz to cover fees. *Nemzetőr*, the newspaper of Hungarian students in Austria was supported in the amount of AS 1,000 per month, and a lending library in Graz was also supported. Coordinating its efforts through the FEC, Inc., the major funder of scholarships was the Rockefeller Foundation, which provided 712 students located in Vienna, Graz and Innsbruck with funding; the UN High Commissioner of Refugees supported 239 and the Knights of Malta 50.[70]

With the help of Caritas, HRS provided the Hungarian Scouts with a center in Vienna's 16th district and equipment was purchased through a donation of AS 5,143 from the two organizations. A plot of land on the former Esterházy properties in the Burgenland was donated for a camp site. HRS also organized a scout summer camp in Goisern, securing the funding through Austrian Citizens Services and the United States Escapee Program.

Hungarian sports groups were assisted with sports equipment, and funds were provided for groups in Salzburg, Innsbruck and Graz. The water polo team received funds through the World League of Hungarian Refugee Sportsmen. In addition to all of the above, art exhibits, classical concerts and ballet and theater performances were also sponsored through HNC organized and sponsored refugee services, although the FEC also provided direct funds for larger institutions in some cases, such as the Philharmonica Hungarica.

Taubinger mentions providing assistance for 185 refugees with critical needs during the six month period. They received clothing and financial aid. Help was also given for funerals, weddings, and medical expenses; visas and translation fees were also subsidized, as were eyeglasses, dental care and even orthopedic shoes and oversized clothing. In urgent cases, even transportation was provided. HRS also assisted 27 invalids and found two American sponsors in that time frame.[71] Clearly, in Austria at least, attempts were made to address every aspect of refugee need through the refugee service.

The Golden Age of Support of the National Councils

For the various national councils, the peak of ideological and financial support by the NCFE and US decision makers came during a phase falling loosely between 1948 and 1954. This was the period when Cold War warriors who had experience in intelligence and military matters were in control of the propaganda war against communism. This was before Radio Free Europe began to play such a prominent role in the NCFE that the national councils and other organizations took a back seat in terms of visibility and, more importantly, in terms of funding. It was also before there was any appreciable thaw in the Cold War. In this period funding was made available for lengthy trips to Europe, Latin America and even the Far East by members of the HNC, the leadership of the other national councils and even of other sponsored organizations such as the International Peasant Union and later ACEN.

Varga took his first extended trip to Europe in 1951 in his role as chairman of the HNC, arriving in Rome on 24 June and celebrating the silver (25th) anniversary of his ordination at a mass on 27 June. That same day he met with former Hungarian Prime Minister Miklós Kállay at Castel Gandolfo, where he was living in exile. Varga's trip included meetings with Baron Apor (the HNC representative for Italy and a former Hungarian ambassador to the Vatican), the Hungarian Colony in Rome, key members of the Curia, and the Hungarian leadership of the Jesuits, Piarists, Premonsterians, Cistarians and Benedictines. He also met with Chief Rabbi Herskovits of Rome, who was of Hungarian extraction. He gave extensive interviews, including on Rome's Hungarian radio. On 5 July he traveled to Milan, where he met with the Hungarian colony, then went on to Munich, Frankfurt, Baden Baden, Bonn, Stuttgart and Strasberg in Germany. At the latter stop, he met with Otto von Habsburg then traveled to Salzburg, Austria, for two days. His many meetings in Germany were principally related to the Hungarian refugee situation. In all of his travels, he met with US consular officials as well.[72] He also found time to meet with the Bulgarian National Council representative, Mischaikoff, in Munich and sent BNC President George Dimitrov a nice note about his "excellent representative".[73] He departed Germany on 20 July to make his way home via Geneva.

The following year, in his role as president of the HNC, Varga traveled to London to attend a large scale conference on January 21–24 that included representatives of the European Movement, the Central and East European counties and Yugoslavia. The European Movement had been formed in 1947–48 by political figures in Western Europe interested in union after the war. A Central European Commission was formed a few years later when representatives of the countries under Soviet domination were asked to join the Western European members. The European Movement's first major success was to set up the Council of Europe in 1949, and it also set up a special committee on 8 August 1950, chaired by British Prime Minister Harold McMillan, to represent those nations not in the Council of Europe.[74] In 1952 the special committee staged the London conference. The NCFE provided funds for delegates from the various national councils to travel to London for their first international meeting. McMillan was the keynote speaker, and on behalf of the HNC Varga made a major speech to the conference attendees at Royal Albert Hall. The NCFE delegation consisted of Roger Bull, Warren Fugitt (representing the American Committee on United Europe), W.E. Griffith and John F. Leich.[75] The conference passed a resolution that "no arrangement between the Western powers and the Soviet Union can lead to a true and lasting peace which accepts the continued enslavement of the peoples of Central and Eastern Europe."[76] Although the European Movement focused on European unification, the notion seemed to take a back seat with future Western governments, and the organization soon lost its influence.

Like the International Peasant Union and the International Free Trade Unionists in Exile, the Christian Democratic Union of Central and East Europe (CDUCE) was another international political organization supported financially by the NCFE. Founded in 1950 by representatives of the Czechoslovak, Hungarian, Latvian, Lithuanian, Polish and Slovenian Christian Democratic parties in exile, the CDUCE's mission as to "study, propagate and realize Christian Social Doctrine; and to engage in political action looking toward the liberation of Central and Eastern Europe, the federation of Central and Eastern Europe and its integration into a United Europe."[77] The CDUCE was funded not just by the NCFE but by European governments as well, including France, West Germany and Italy – all of which had Christian Democratic governments with a commitment to European unity. Later CDUCE activities included support for the emerging Christian Democratic parties in

Latin America. Although the other NCFE-supported organizations did not have Yugoslav members due to US hesitancy to ire Marshall Tito, the CDUCE made an exception for the Slovenian Christian Democrats. The CDUCE was headed Msgr. József Közi-Horváth until 1961, when it was merged into the World Union of Christian Democrats. It is still a political force today as the Centrist Democrat International (CDI), to which it changed its name in 1999. Current Central European leaders among its leadership include Viktor Orbán, the prime minister of Hungary (FIDESZ Party), the leaders of the Romanian Hungarian Christian Democratic Party and the National Peasant Christian Democratic Party as well as the Christian Democratic Union of the Czech Republic. Leading political figures such as Angela Merkel, president of Germany (Christian Democratic Union) and Antonio Samaras of Greece are also members. Of the many NCFE/FEC-sponsored organizations, it is one of the few still in existence.[78]

The HNC and the Assembly of Captive European Nations

By 1954 the NCFE leadership had begun to realize that the émigré leaders were not going home soon and that the organizations and individuals the NCFE/FEC was supporting seemed to expect permanent financial assistance, which could not be a long term solution. The Hungarians and all the other national councils were told to close their Washington offices, and reorganization and budget reallocation began to be implemented. Initially, it was seen as a matter of shifting priorities, as following the success of their Philadelphia and Williamsburg meetings the national council members of the Central and East European Conference took the initiative to organize the Assembly of Captive European Nations (ACEN), which was founded on 20 September 1954 and funded by the NCFE. Varga asked Eckhardt to form the Hungarian delegation to the ACEN and to choose the subcommittees on which each delegate was to serve.[79] The first delegation consisted of Eckhardt as chairman and Charles (Károly) Peyer as vice chairman. The delegates were László Acsay, István Csicsery-Rónay, Joseph Csákó, Joseph Emődy,

Miksa Fenyő, András Frey, John Gara, Julius Gömbös, General Alexander Homlok, John Mike, Vince Nagy, Leslie Sándor, Béla Teleki and László Varga.[80] In addition, the Hungarian delegation had a secretariat and a press section providing support staff. Not all 16 members of the delegation were members of the HNC,[81] and at the time of the ACEN's inception, all were foreign nationals.

Once established, the ACEN's efforts turned to publicizing the captive nations' aims for liberation and their status under Soviet occupation, resulting in a large volume of reports, resolutions, informational pamphlets, books, and correspondence to key decision makers around the world. One major ACEN function was to lobby for the cause of their captive nations, and the leadership met with key officials, including the US Secretary of State[82] and international heads of state. In addition to its plenary sessions in New York, the ACEN held meetings abroad and its representatives participated in symposia and conferences, established a speakers' bureau and served as voices of protest concerning communism, human rights and the liberation of their homelands. The information generated by the ACEN was used in newspaper articles and television and radio broadcasts. Published literature in many languages was provided to the press and the public at large.

In 1959 the US Congress passed Public Law 86-90 declaring the third week of July as Captive Nations Week, to be celebrated annually. Designed to remind the public and government officials throughout the United States that the citizens of the captive nations should not be forgotten, the event was promoted annually by the ACEN, and it is observed in the United States to this day.

At the request of Bernard Yarrow, vice president of the FEC, Eckhardt had been asked to sit in on the ACEN's organizational meetings, and he participated in drafting the statutes establishing its structure. Eckhardt served as a member of its general- and political committees. During his chairmanship, he authored two extensive memoranda on the resettlement of the Hungarian refugees still in various European camps. He collected data and submitted memoranda to the FEC and the US government on the Hungarian Communist Re-defection Campaign.[83]

Eckhardt resigned from the chairmanship of the Hungarian delegation when he became a US citizen in 1955, but Varga and the ACEN leadership asked him to remain "in charge of the study on Russian colonialism".[84] Baron George B. Bessenyey, who had been serving as the HNC's minister of foreign affairs, was asked to head the Hungarian delegation after Eckhardt's resignation, and that delegation continued to play an important role in the ACEN throughout its existence as an FEC-sponsored organization. In turn, the ACEN member organizations provided a wide range of support for Hungarian issues, particularly after the Revolution of 1956. When the HNC was deactivated in 1972, so, too, was the Hungarian ACEN delegation.

The Situation in Hungary

During their years of exile, Hungarian refugees and refugee leaders attempted to maintain communication with their homeland. Both incoming and outgoing correspondence was censored in Hungary, and letters arrived with portions cut out or crossed through; many letters did not arrive at all. Nevertheless, the Communist government did not halt all private exchanges between East and West. The HNC files contain letters describing the desperate situation in the country, economically and in every other aspect. No matter how much the government attempted to control contact, HNC members, particularly those working in countries adjacent to Hungary, collected fairly good intelligence on its situation; and Varga had good contacts throughout the church and with Apor in Rome, who had good sources in Hungary. The deportations and displacement of the population were taking their toll, as was the heavy handedness of the communist leaders and the Hungarian Secret Police, the AVH. Hungary in every aspect had become a police state.

In 1955, with the organizational and financial support of Varga and the HNC, Dr. László Varga, a Hungarian lawyer, established the Committee for Self Determination, Inc. and the Federation of Free Hungarian Jurists. Their primary functions were to keep pressure on the United Nations regarding Hungarian human rights violations and to work with the press and US authorities to bring them to the attention of the world. The organizations advocated on behalf of individuals whose human rights had been violated in Hungary, cases that simply would not have come to the attention of the world press. Advocating re-establishing human rights in Hungary, the organizations pressed very hard for cases such as those of Dr. Ferenc Matheovitz, a former member of parliament sentenced in 1964 to ten years for advocating setting up a political party after the withdrawal of Soviet troops, and the Jesuit priests arrested in December 1964. In a speech celebrating the tenth anniversary of the Federation of Free Hungarian Jurists, held on 19 November 1965 at the New York Hilton, Béla Varga's statement summed up the "progress" in human rights said to be being made in Hungary: "It might be so that on the everyday level there is a welcome change in Hungary and much progress has been made, yet the sentence and the arrests show that there is no change whatsoever on the political level."[85]

The HNC, Hungarian émigrés and many aid groups attempted to help alleviate the situation by sending packages through the Hungarian government-controlled IBUSZ Külföldi Kereskedelmi Akció or IKKA, the only method by which aid packages could be sent to Hungary. IKKA was part of the government-controlled tourism sector run through IBUSZ, the only Hungarian travel agency that could be used to visit Hungary.[86] Friends and relatives abroad paid in hard currency for aid packages with pre-selected contents, which then were delivered in Hungary to the recipients. The files of Varga and the general HNC files contain many letters of thanks from Hungary for the care packages they sent which contained foodstuffs, clothing and other necessary items.[87] The IKKA system operated for decades, and hundreds of thousands of packages were mailed by exiles living abroad. The service was always the source of enormous controversy, however, as everyone was aware that not only was it a way for Hungary's government to amass both hard currency and data on the émigrés who sent the packages but they also overcharged for all the contents in the packages.[88] Thus, humanitarian relief on any scale, except occasionally the ability to smuggle in desperately needed prescription drugs, was made virtually impossible. A letter from former ambassador and HNC member George Barcza to Msgr. Joseph Közi-Horváth illustrates the efforts made to get drugs into Hungary. Writing from Switzerland on 14 April 1951, Barcza says he had obtained donated drugs from Swiss firms valued at 8,000–10,000 Swiss Francs with a total weight of 39 kilos. The letter discusses how to get the drugs into Hungary and mentions that as the IRO was being disbanded, it could no longer be used as a distributor.[89]

Hungary's borders had miles of no man's land, mines, watch towers and attack dogs and were guarded by ÁVH units, nevertheless, as the refugee statistics reveal, some Hungarians made it to the West. Many others did not. After Rákosi returned to power in 1955, 1,104 Hungarians were convicted of attempting to flee to the West, fewer than 300 of whom were actually arrested on the border, most never having made it that far. Of this group, 65% were under the age of 30, foreshadowing the demographics of the exodus resulting from the 1956 Hungarian Revolution.[90]

After the massive protests in Poznan, Poland, in June 1956, the situation in Hungary, as much a tinder box as Poland, came to a head. On 23 October a demonstration initially organized by university students grew from 20,000 to over 200,000. Violence erupted after a statue of Stalin was toppled, and by 25 October a full scale national uprising pitted largely unarmed and ill equipped protesters against the Hungarian police and military and the occupying Russian troops. Though they retreated for a few heady days, the Soviet military returned and by 10 November had crushed the revolt.

Hungary's borders were essentially open during and immediately after the uprising, until 20 November, although crossing the minefields was dangerous and border police would still fire on fleeing refugees. Nonetheless, during this period some 200,000 refugees fled Hungary. As before the revolution, a great percentage of them were young men under age 25, but a wave of Hungarian leaders who had remained after the Soviet takeover fled as well. Amongst them were General Béla Király, who had organized a Hungarian National Guard on the side of the revolutionaries but had a background as a member of the Communist Party (which the émigré leadership found very suspicious), Anna

Kéthly, a long time leader of the Hungarian Social Democratic Party, and Joseph Kővágó, the former mayor of Budapest. When they arrived in the US, there was no question that they and the other recent arrivals were bearing the standard of the revolution, and they were embraced by the world as representatives of the Hungarian nation.

To the FEC committee that addressed the problems and challenges created by this new wave of refugees and organized aid for them, the ideological clash between the prior wave of exiles and the newly arrived "Freedom Fighters" was apparent from the onset. For example, on 8 November a "Stop the Massacre" protest rally against the Soviet Army's intervention in Hungary was held in New York City. Organized by Christopher Emmet of the International Rescue Committee in collaboration with the American Friends of the ACEN and the Conference of Americans of Central European Descent, it was intended, according to Emmet, not so much to raise funds as "to dramatize a great political protest".[91] Although the crowd of exiles that filled Madison Square Garden was composed of the conservative, anti-communist element of the emigration, the organizers had chosen the recently arrived leader of the Social Democrats, Anna Kéthly, as the main speaker. The attendees had assumed that Béla Varga would also speak as the leader of the emigration, but Kéthly refused to appear on the same program with him. The organizers then made the ill-advised decision to remove Varga from the speakers' lineup, leaving the mostly conservative crowd faced, according to Emmet's papers, with a "left wing Socialist ... whom many in the audience believed to be a Trotskyite" rather than "a Hungarian Catholic Priest who was President of the Hungarian Parliament and is Chairman of the Hungarian National Council". Kéthly further enraged the audience by "giving the communist closed fist salute at the close of her talk".[92] The rally descended into chaos, and although Emmet obtained an extension of time so Varga could speak, it was to a half empty house. The main purpose of the rally had been to pass resolutions condemning the Soviet Union for its actions in Hungary, but as a result of the manipulation of the program, the resolutions were never even presented. The Hungarian left had won the day and the resulting debacle was evidence of their success.[93]

Although their numbers were not large, rather than join with the Hungarian National Council, the Freedom Fighters opted to form their own organization, the Revolutionary Council (Forradalmi Tanács). It was approved by the US government, which, at the onset, had favored establishing an organization composed of prominent leaders of the revolution. After the establishment of the Revolutionary Council, the revolutionary leaders mentioned earlier – Király, Kéthly and Kővágó – then proceeded to form their own organizations, which then competed with each other. All of this was disconcerting to the HNC, and Varga wrote to the FEC board asking what their intentions were regarding the HNC's future:

> ... we have taken due note of the future attitude of Free Europe Committee to be dependent on the development of one question only: That of the integration of the old and new emigration. We wish to establish our stand right away in this respect. In our opinion, integration is absolutely necessary and desirable. However the councils' further expansion and integration depends on some important matters of principle ... I would very much appreciate if your [sic] were good enough to inform me at our earliest convenience as to the stand the Free Europe Committee's Board is inclined to take in at least the four above mentioned basic questions, so the enable me to continue my efforts in the spirit of our past partnership towards the integration of the Hungarian emigree [sic] groups. May I ask you therefore to kindly present this letter to your Board as soon as possible since integration cannot be carried out in practice either on the personal or other lines so long as questions of principle have not been clarified.[94]

The FEC clarified that it wanted the HNC and the revolutionary groups to integrate. Thus, at the behest of its sponsor, the Hungarian National Council was dissolved and a new organization was formed that consolidated the new and old immigrations. This successor organization was established in June 1958, named the Hungarian National Committee (Magyar Nemzeti Bizottság), and including the former Hungarian National Council, the Revolutionary Council of Hungary and the

National Representation of Free Hungary – the latter two being the groups established by the 1956 emigration.[95]

It had 16 members, nine from the 1947 immigration and seven from the 1956. By this time, the more conservative elements of the immigration were no longer represented by the council, and although there had been an upswing of political interest sparked by the Hungarian Revolution, the realization had set in amongst all participants, including the FEC, was that the liberation of the satellites was not an attainable goal to have as a centerpiece of their policy.[96] US decision makers were relinquishing the banner of "liberation", and with that no longer as their goal, the national councils' function as exile governments in waiting was no longer a valid concept. The councils' political capital diminished and "gradually lost is significance among the United States policymakers".[97]

HNC Lobbying and Protests Regarding the Hungarian Revolution

On October 24 1956, immediately after the outbreak of violence in Hungary, Varga sent a letter to Dag Hammerskjöld, secretary general of the United Nations, regarding Soviet violations of the UN Charter, Paragraph 4, Article II. He sent the same letter on the same day to US Secretary of State John Foster Dulles:

> The Hungarian National Council begs you Mr. Secretary, to take urgently appropriate measure in order to induce the government of the Soviet Union to halt the lawless Russian interference in Hungarian internal matters and to allow the Hungarian people free to determine under what government they wish to live.
>
> Intervention by the United States is legally and strongly supported by article 34 of the United Nations Charter and by the continuous violation of the wartime and postwar agreements assuring to the now captive nations the right of self dentermination [sic] through free and unfettered elections.
>
> The Hungarian people urgently need the assistance of the West in their heroic struggle against their oppressors whose recent terroristic

> acts constitute a menace to the peace of our world. In view of these compelling facts, we beg you, Mr. Secretary, to request urgently the Security Council of the United Nations to take energetic action primarily aimed at stopping the massacre of our peace and freedom-loving Hungarian people.[98]

Varga also sent a telegram to President Eisenhower on October 24:

> We, the Hungarian National Council, were always profoundly grateful for all the encouraging statements and messages which you Mr. President have so often addressed to our nation. But today an exceptional and tragic situation calls for exceptional consideration. We beg you, Mr. President, to throw in all the authority of your exalted position to protest against the unlawful and ruthless interference of Russian troops in internal Hungarian affairs to stop the massacre of freedom-loving Hungarian patriots and take all steps in order that the Hungarian nation should be enabled to exercise through completely free and unfettered elections its right to national self-determination, liberty and independence.[99]

Many members of the HNC also sent telegrams to those of their contacts who might be influential. The following telegram was sent to international and national free trade unions:

> We appeal that you protest with Imre Nagy Premier of Hungary against the bloody Soviet Military intervention carried out against the Hungarian workers and people which fight for the freedom, bread and national independence stop please request immediate withdrawl [sic] of Soviet Armed Forces from Hungary and express your solidarity with Hungarian workers.
> Charles Peyer
> Former General Secretary of Free Hungarian Labor Confederation
> Vice President International Center of Free Trade Unionists in Exile
> New York, October 24, 1956.[100]

Varga also sent telegrams to Bernard P. Gentille Cornut, chair of the UN Delegation from France in his capacity as chairman of the Security Council, and to all the other members of the Security Council at the time: Australia, Belgium, China, Cuba, France, Iran, Peru, USSR, UK, Yugoslavia, United States (Henry Cabot Lodge). Telegrams from Varga and the HNC also went out on 24 October to the American, International, Swedish, Danish, Netherlands, and Austrian Red Cross organizations asking for aid for Hungary. On 26 October Varga, who spoke excellent German, wrote to the Viennese newspapers asking for support.

On 27 October, the International News Service, Rotary International, American Legion, Columbia University and Knights of Columbus all received a press release from Varga saying, in part:

> The dilemma of the Kremlin today is whether to return to the Stalinist methods of brutal oppression and face the increasing resentment and inevitable explosions or to agree to a neutralization of the satellites and thereby decrease the potentially hostile forces along its borders...
>
> We supplement our appeals with the present suggestion of neutralizing our country and I personally declare that such as solution would be acceptable to the Hungarian National Council in Exile...[101]

The HNC also found support for its efforts from American groups, including those supporting the ACEN:

> In a statement today, Christopher Emmet, Chairman of the American Friends of the Captive Nations, said, "What the Hungarian people have accomplished virtually with their bare hands, regardless of the final outcome, is a total and dramatic refutation of the defeatism of the so-called realist in the West, who have ridiculed the possibility of the captive nations" liberation and urged us to accept the "finality" of the situation in Eastern Europe. We of the West had too much faith in the omnipotence of the Soviet monolith, and too little faith in the love of liberty of our secret allies, the peoples of the captive nations, The Hungarians are now opening our eyes, but at a fearful cost....

> We must remember that every bullet the Russians fire in Hungary reveals the naked brutality of Soviet colonialism which they have tried so hard to conceal.[102]

On 25 October 1956 Vilis Masens, chairman of the ACEN, telegraphed the Asian and African signers of the 1955 Bandung Declaration declaring their opposition to colonialism in any form and their government representatives in the UN: "ACEN REMINDS BANDUNG DECLARATION SIGNATORIES OF SOVIET INTERVENTION POLAND AND HUNGARY."[103]

On 26 October Ferenc Durugy, secretary general of the Liberal Democratic Union of East Europe in the United States of America (member states: Poland, Czechoslovakia, Bulgaria, Rumania, Albania, Latvia, Estonia, and Hungary), headquartered at 172 Madison Ave., sent Varga a letter expressing support and saying his group had sent telegrams to the UN Security Council. [104]

When it was clear that Soviet troops had returned to Hungary on 4 November 1956 intending to reinforce their occupation of the country, Varga immediately sent another stream of hundreds of telegrams protesting the action to all the major US political leaders and the members of the UN Security council. The telegrams protested that the resolution the UN had made on the Soviet intervention in Hungary was inadequate and without enforcement provisions:

> ... containing no condemnation of this felonious action, no measures to implement the principle points of the resolution and no sanctions in case of non compliance by the Soviet Union. When in 1939 Soviet Russia attacked Finland, she was expelled from the League of Nations. When in 1950 North Korea attacked the Republic of Korea the Security Council determined that the armed attack was a breach of the peace and called not only for immediate cessation of hostilities and withdrawal of troops, but also for the assistance of members in carrying out is resolution... In light these precedents the resolution adopted yesterday by the Security Council appeals [sic] entirely inadequate.[105]

Varga further demanded sanctions, the withdrawal of Soviet troops from Hungary and for Hungary to be secured by a United Nations force. He also demanded that the new government not be recognized.This was the first salvo in an intense six-month program of lobbying on the part of the HNC, principally by Varga.

In his homilies, including one at St. Patrick's Cathedral on 30 November 1956, Varga continued to press the case of Hungary. Additional telegrams were sent in early December to Herbert Hoover Jr., the acting secretary of state, Senators Knowland and Humphrey, and George Meany of the AFL-CIO. In them, Varga stated that "the revolution in Hungary is far from being over" and demanded that sanctions be imposed on the Soviet Union and that the UN Secretary General be allowed into Hungary on a fact finding trip. That December Varga continued to press the case with the international community, contacting Pandit Jawharlal Nehru, then India's ambassador to the US, to ask for his support. This was followed by a letter to all the members of Congress on 2 January 1957. Even as Varga and the Hungarian émigrés were utilizing all of their lobbying resources, Vice President Nixon departed in December 1956 on a fact finding trip to Europe to assess the situation in Hungary and that of the refugees.[106]

Varga and the HNC executive committee continued to exert pressure within diplomatic circles and abroad and on all three branches of the US government, but after the post-revolution refugees arrived in the US and swelled the ranks of the Hungarian refugees remaining in Europe, the HNC's focus was primarily on refugee resettlement, working in collaboration with First Aid for Hungary and other aid organizations. The HNC nevertheless continued to lobby for sanctions against the Soviet Union and for withdrawal of Soviet troops from Hungary. HNC representatives abroad also continued the pressure within the international community with an ongoing public relations campaign against the Soviet Union.

When the realization came that the situation within Hungary would not change, the HNC turned its energy toward preventing the Hungarian Communist delegation from being seated in the United Nations (discussed in further detail below).

First Aid for Hungary/Committee for Hungarian Refugees

At the onset of the Hungarian revolution the HNC leadership realized that they needed to act immediately to assist the new flood of refugees. On 29 October 1956, Tibor Eckhardt called a mass meeting of several prominent Americans of Hungarian descent to initiate the only crisis-oriented aid organization that was founded solely by Hungarian émigrés; it came to be called First Aid for Hungary.

> Eckhardt proposed that the new corporation should be charitable, non-political, non-denominational and established on a temporary basis. It was to serve as a stop gap organization, adapting day by day to the situation in Hungary and on the border and to the needs of refugees who reached the West.[107]

First Aid for Hungary immediately set up a field office in Vienna under the leadership of General Béla Lengyel, a citizen of Austria who had experience in relief work, and was able to begin operations there by 1 November, just three days after its founding. Three committee members had flown to Vienna with funds for Lengyel to establish aid stations on the Austrian border and with a first shipment of medicines destined for hospitals in Hungary, which the Knights of Malta successfully delivered.[108]

The organization was officially incorporated in New York State on 5 November, and at the urging of NCFE Vice President Frederic Dolbeare and President Dwight D. Eisenhower, former president Herbert Hoover agreed to become its honorary chairman, a post in which he was extremely active, well informed and up to date. He made certain that several of his most experienced aides were also involved, among them Tracy Voorhees, his aide at the post-WII Famine Emergency Commission. In December 1956 Eisenhower appointed Voorhees to head the President's Committee for Hungarian Refugee Relief. Indicative of his personal involvement, Hoover sent a personal note to each and every donor who took the initiative to contribute to First Aid for Hungary.[109]

Intended to serve as a non-bureaucratic, stop-gap organization, First Aid was able to respond quickly to the refugee needs in ways the traditional aid organizations could not. According to its documents, it was "the only foreign charity working on the Hungarian border during the hectic first half of November, 1956."[110] Lengyel set up nine refugee centers on the border and later in other provinces of Austria. When the large NGOs started their own operations, Lengyel's field workers assisted in 17 first aid stations and at the Austrian Refugee Collection points, in addition to handling four field kitchens and three mobile pharmacies. First Aid also transferred funds to other charities if it was felt they could more effectively or more quickly respond to refugee needs.[111]

First Aid was also able to deliver medical supplies for hospitals inside Hungary until the border was closed on 20 November 1956 – supplies were flown to Vienna and transported into Hungary by the Knights of Malta and the Red Cross. After the border was sealed, only the International Red Cross was allowed into Hungary and First Aid was able to work with them to supply hospitals until April 1957, although some brave First Aid volunteers managed to deliver medicines to four hospitals in Hungary until February 1957.[112]

The First Aid Sponsors' Committee was composed of prominent citizens and included Mrs. John Chambers Hughes, wife of the former US ambassador to NATO and a long time member of the NCFE board and for several years the chair of its executive committee. She served as Eckhardt's co-chair at First Aid. Hundreds of First Aid volunteers raised funds, received donations, and organized and sent aid packages from their temporary headquarters at 1532 York Avenue in Manhattan. From 23 October after the revolution began until 1 March the following year, food packages were allowed into Hungary duty free, and during that period First Aid sent over 10,000 such packages. The center also packaged and financed the mailing of parcels of donated clothing. Over 12,356 refugee children in Austria received clothing packages from First Aid during its time of operation.[113]

As an integral part of the First Aid effort, the HNC organized aid for the arriving refugees beyond what was supplied by the US government.

István Barankovics was named to head the HNC's Committee for Hungarian Refugees. Operating at Camp Kilmer in New Jersey, the main transit point for the refugees, the committee provided clothing, interpreters and Hungarian-English dictionaries until the new Coordinated Hungarian Relief took over in January 1957. First Aid was also instrumental, along with the Hungarian National Sports Federation and *Time* magazine, in organizing transport to the US for the Hungarian athletes who defected at the Melbourne Olympics in November 1956.[114] Another important partner in the refugee effort was the American Hungarian Federation, headed by its president, Louis Yager. The Federation concentrated its resources on finding placement or sponsorship for the refugees within the United States.[115]

Because many among the influx of post WWII Hungarian refugees still remained in Western Europe in 1956, HNC Refugee Aid Centers had been functioning efficiently there for several years. These centers were now called upon to help handle aid for the new refugees. Having the HNC centers in place and operational made the refugee processing and integration much easier. Once the large international aid organizations arrived on the scene, First Aid, at Voorhees's request, began to deal with the acute problem of higher education for refugee students and through Coordinated Hungarian Relief expanded schools in Austria, Germany and Belgium to accommodate them.[116]

Always intended to be a short-term organization, First Aid wrapped up its mission on 1 May 1957. The funds remaining were disbursed to Coordinated Hungarian Relief and to the Institute of International Education for scholarships in the United States for Hungarian refugee students – there were over 300 student beneficiaries.[117] For the individuals involved with this aid effort, it marked a time when all aspects of the Hungarian emigration came together to aid their former countrymen; and what a First Aid steering committee member praised as the volunteers' "collegiality and unity of purpose" was unique in the refugee aid experience.[118]

Support for the Hungarian Uprising by the ACEN Member Councils and Émigré Groups

Their many years of cooperation within the Central and East European Committee and the ACEN brought the national councils and their leaders much closer together than ever before in the history of their various nationalities, and with the advent of the Hungarian Revolution, the expressions of support and encouragement poured in. A representative example is a telegram sent to Béla Varga by Constatin Visoianu, president of the Rumanian [sic] National Committee (Comitetul National Roman) on 31 October 1956:

> The Rumanian National Committee wishes to convey the most heartfelt admiration for the heroic struggle now being waged by the people of Hungary for freedom and independence. ... we are deeply aware of the sacrifices brought by Magyar patriots to the common cause of our countries, now enslaved by Soviet Russia. We bow our heads in grateful homage to the many who have fallen in this glorious fight.... From the depths of our hearts we wish the people of Hungary victory in their endeavor in behalf of liberty and we pray that Almighty God may be with them.[119]

The Byelorussian-American Association, Inc., sent a letter to Varga dated 5 November 1956 that "hereby expresses its deeply felt solidarity with the heroic struggle of the Hungarian people against the Moscow Bolshevik oppression. ... Let the fire of national revolution, kindled on the streets of Budapest, blaze throughout eastern Europe and liberate from Russia and Communism all enslaved nations, including Byelorussia. Long live Hungarian freedom-fighters!" It was signed by the organization's secretary, George Stankevich, and its president, Micael Tuleyko.[120]

Varga and the HNC also received letters in support of the Hungarian fight for freedom from, among others: the Supreme Ukrainian Liberation Council (1 November to Varga, signed by Mikola Lebed, secretary general for foreign affairs), the Baltic Women's Council, the Council of

Free Czechoslovakia, the Czechoslovak Party of Middle Class Exiles, the Estonian consul general, the Polish minister of foreign affairs (London, A. Zawisza), the Free Slovaks, the Union of Free Romanians, Pavel Avaloff (chairman, Association of Russian Emigrants from Yugoslavia, Inc., former commander in chief, Anti-Bolshevist Army (West) 1919), the All Russian Liberation Committee (Anti Communist Center, 349 West 86th St., NYC, Serge Yourieff, secretary general, 30 October), and the Hungarian Relief Society of Japan. The Polish Government in Exile, London, issued a supportive press release on 27 October (SLO 9323, press officer: S. Leczkowski), and the Asian Peoples Anti-Communist League, Taipei, Taiwan, sent a letter dated 19 February 1957 mentioning a rally at which 3,000 attendees pledged vigorous support to the Hungarian people in their struggle for national independence. An article about the Revolution appeared in the 1 November 1956 issue of *Free China and Asia*.

This partial list of the correspondence indicates the wide range of anti-communist exile organizations that existed during the Cold War and were aware of the HNC and its work. During the Cold War era, the Hungarian National Council and its sister organizations were well known not just within the émigré communities but throughout the nation and abroad. During that era, for example, the *New York Times* published over 150 articles related to Varga alone and a far higher number on the HNC.

Ongoing Protests against the Continued Soviet Occupation of Hungary

The issue of seating the Communist Hungarian delegation at the United Nations provided by far the strongest evidence of collaboration among the exile anti-communist leadership. The HNC-coordinated protests against the continued Soviet occupation of Hungary took several major forms, and the HNC continued its activism while the newly arrived freedom fighters were forming their own organizations. The HNC's first order of business was to try to prevent the Communist Hungarian delegation from being seated at the United Nations.

Hungary had become a member of the UN in December 1955, along with Bulgaria and Romania. The Hungarian delegation to the General Assembly was then seated, but after the revolution broke out, the United States proposed that its membership be suspended unless UN observers were promptly admitted to Hungary.[121] As a provision of Rule 29 of the Assembly Rules of Procedure, the delegation could retain its seat provisionally, with the same rights as the other delegations, until the credentials committee issued its ruling. Imre Horvath, the head of the Hungarian delegation, and its other members were seated under that regulation; France having objected to according the delegation full accreditation.[122] Hungary's provisional UN status, although with no loss of privileges, continued through 1962, with the United States annually taking the lead to protest the delegation's legitimacy.

The UN Security Council had already had been called into session while the Hungarian uprising broke out, and given the power of the Soviet veto, little or nothing was accomplished to address the issue at the 28 October meeting. After the Soviet military returned to Hungary on 4 November, the General Assembly did pass majority resolutions calling on the Soviet government to cease any military action against Hungarians, withdraw its troops and allow Hungary self-determination and free elections. The resolutions also called for the end of deportations and for UN observers to be allowed into the country.[123] None of the items in the resolutions was ever implemented; in fact they were boldly and publicly ignored. On 10 January 1957, the UN adopted resolution 1132/XI establishing the Special Committee on the Question of Hungary for the purpose of investigating the 1956 revolution, the Soviet intervention and the circumstances that had brought the government of János Kádár to power. The special committee produced a report at the end of June 1957 that recounted the history of the events of the Hungarian Revolution, and the Hungarian problem was returned to the assembly's agenda. The special committee continued its work and produced another report before being disbanded at the end of 1958, when its work was pronounced "completed".

By then, the Kádár government had already executed Imre Nagy and two of his associates (June 1958), adding fuel to the protests being waged by the HNC and other émigré groups and proving their point that oppression in Hungary had not subsided as the Hungarian government claimed.[124] Regular protests continued to be staged by the ACEN and the HNC in front of the Soviet UN delegation's headquarters; and the ACEN building situated opposite the United Nations was regularly draped in banners protesting the Soviet Union's actions.

In 1958, the émigrés supported the efforts of Sir Leslie Munro of New Zealand, who had served concurrently as his nation's ambassador to the United States and representative to the UN. He was serving as president of the Security Council at the time of the Hungarian and Suez crises in 1956.When his country's Second Labor Government was elected in 1958, he was dismissed from his posts, but the UN appointed him to the post of Special Representative on the Question of Hungary. He served in that capacity from 1958 until December 1962.According to his biography, he was assigned to:

> ...secure compliance with the United Nations resolutions on Hungary, including the withdrawal of Soviet forces, free elections and respect for human rights. He was refused entry to Hungary and the letters he addressed to the Hungarian and Soviet representatives at the United Nations were returned without reply. For information on what was happening in Hungary, he had to rely on reports from refugees, foreign embassies and European capitals, and from newspapers behind the Iron Curtain.[125]

Munro's assignment kept the Question of Hungary alive in the press; but he was unable to enter Hungary on a fact-finding mission and had to rely heavily on the émigrés and their contacts for information. They had a positive working relationship and considerable mutual respect. Munro had always been one of the strongest anti-Soviet leaders in the UN and the Special Representative assignment was tailor made for him.

The HNC also had a close collaboration until 1960 with the US ambassador to the UN, John Cabot Lodge Jr., who kept the issue of the legitimacy of the Hungarian delegation alive. This was also a public relations boon. However, the number of votes in favor of keeping the Question of Hungary on the UN agenda kept decreasing annually as the Soviet Union worked to normalize relations. It was only a matter of time before the issue was removed from the agenda – which happened on 20 December 1962.

The HNC's annual commemoration of the anniversary of the 1956 Revolution provided an opportunity to keep the Question of Hungary alive in the press, and by 1958, having absorbed the organizations of the freedom fighters, the remembrance became a joint effort of the newly formed Hungarian National Committee. It needs to be mentioned that American labor unions were also major supporters of the national councils and the free trade unionists in exile from the beginning. Not only did they provide financial support for the trade unionists, they also put the lobbying power of the AFL-CIO behind the efforts of all the émigré organizations. In 1959 George Meany, the powerful leader of the AFL-CIO issued a press release on the Hungarian Revolution's third anniversary, addressing efforts to keep the Hungarian Question alive:

> The third anniversary of the Hungarian democratic revolution finds the world in the throes of tension and conflict.
> Berlin, Tibet, Peipings's [sic] seizure of India's territory and Laos and interrelated parts of the whole pattern of Communist aggression against freedom, national independence, and world peace.
> On the third anniversary of the savage Soviet aggression against humanity, Khruschev would have the world forget the historic struggle of the Hungarian people for free nationhood, democracy, and the right to co-exist in genuine peace and friendship with other nations.
> In the interest of their own freedom, liberty-loving people everywhere must thwart this Soviet maneuver to have them ____Moscow's crimes against the Hungarian people.
> The free world dare not forget Hungary.
> The free world must condemn in no uncertain terms the continuous Soviet contempt for the efforts of the United Nations in behalf of the Hungarian people.

> Let us commemorate the third anniversary of the Hungarian democratic revolution by re-dedicating ourselves to the cause of freedom .... It is more urgent than ever that the 14th General Assembly of the United Nations should reject the credentials of the Communist puppet government imposed on the Hungarian people by Soviet tanks and bayonets. This puppet regime has repeatedly trampled on every UN decision in support of human rights for the Hungarian people. It has contemptuously denied the UN Special Representative, Sir Leslie Munro, permission to even enter Hungary. Under these circumstances, self preservation and self-respect demand that the UN should not permit the Kadar delegation to enter and participate in the United Nations.
>
> Before the coming conferences of the "Big Four" enter into new solemn international agreements, they should secure at least some compliance with old pledges for the preservation of peace and human rights.
>
> For the sake of world peace and freedom and mankind's faith in the United Nations, the AFL-CIO urges that the Hungarian question be given full consideration in all forthcoming international diplomatic conferences – including those on the highest level.[126]

In the years before the Question of Hungary was removed from the UN agenda, several events occurred that signaled the beginning of a thaw in US–Soviet relations. Anastas Mikoyan, first deputy premier of the Soviet Union, was invited to visit the United States in January 1959. He was greeted on his arrival at Idlewild Airport on 13 January by 30 members of the Federation of Hungarian Former Political Prisoners, "some dressed in black and white prison garb." They bore signs saying "Mikoyan, war criminal" and chanted the words as well.[127] The HNC organized a committee to stage a major protest. Chaired by Béla Varga, it included Ferenc Nagy, Imre Kovács, Zoltán Pfeiffer and László Varga, with Gyula Szentadorjány as a working member. They worked in collaboration with the Hungarian Freedom Fighters Association and the ACEN, held press conferences on 16 January to protest the visit and filed an official protest with the US government.[128] The ACEN, led by Stefan Korbonski of Poland, also organized protests on behalf of the approximately 100 million persons living under Soviet control and challenged businesses and organizations, such as the First National City Bank and the Economic Club, which had set meetings with Mikoyan.[129]

When Soviet Prime Minister Nikita Khrushchev visited the US in August 1959, the HNC organized a protest committee and mounted its largest ever public relations effort of this type. The records contain a 60-page compilation of the committee's activities, including telegrams, letters, press releases and clippings and long lists of attendees at press conferences, etc. A special delegation consisting of Msgr. Varga, József Kővágó, Imre Kovács and László Varga was even formed to "visit in advance the cities where the Soviet Premier was expected, to inform the American people about the man who crushed the Hungarian Revolution and to caution Hungarian refugees about proper behavior."[130]

The delegation traveled to Los Angeles on 16 September and appeared on Bill Stout's radio program, held a press conference and former Budapest Mayor Kővágó was interviewed for a half hour special on TV Channel 13. The press release from the Hungarian delegation stated: "the man who traveling now in this country and who will arrive in Los Angeles tomorrow is the same Khrushchev who three years ago gave order to the Soviet Army to crush the Hungarian Revolution."[131] The delegation then traveled north to San Francisco on 19 September, where the *San Francisco Call Bulletin*'s headline read: "Hungarians Arrive to Offset Nikita Tour". Kovács, László Varga and Fábián proceeded on to Iowa, where Khrushchev was also traveling. Fábián had been a prison of war of the Russians during WWI and in WWII was held in a concentration camp by the Gestapo. A lawyer and journalist of note, he had organized many protests against the Soviets, and in Des Moines, Iowa, he distributed leaflets saying "Don't have a crush on Khrushchev" and carried placards decrying the Soviet leader's visit.[132] The HNC held press conferences in all the cities it visited, which included Pittsburgh and Washington, D.C., where Kővágó and Béla Király commented on Khrushchev's insulting remarks on the Hungarian Revolution. Protest letters were written to all members of Congress, and the files include many declarations of support for the HNC position.

Such visits to the US by important communist political figures sent a message of looming détente that the émigrés simply did not want to hear. They felt it was their obligation to continue to protest any rapprochement with the Soviet Union and its satellites – no matter what direction US foreign policy was taking. In the 1959 and 1960 protests, over 2,000 people demonstrated in front of the Soviet Union's UN delegation building, and these were among the largest protests organized by the émigrés after the Hungarian revolution.

But the drumbeat of change was sounding. On 1 April 1959, the FEC ceased providing financial support to the Hungarian Refugee Office in Germany. Hennyey wrote to Msgr. Varga that this was done regardless of the fact there were still 30,000 Hungarian refugees in Germany, half of them newly arrived, and that there were 1,363 Hungarian students studying at German universities.[133]

After the United Nations dropped the Question of Hungary from its agenda, the Hungarian community again rallied to the cause of keeping the issue alive and formed the Movement for the Defense of Hungary in the United Nations. Eckhardt headed the organization, and it was the American Hungarian groups (rather than the émigré groups) that took the lead in its founding. The membership included Rev. George Borshy-Kerekes, president of the Hungarian Reformed Federation of America, Aloysius C. Falusy, president of the American Hungarian Federation, John S. Szabó, papal protonotary and president of the Hungarian Catholic League of America and Dr. Alexander Szentiványi, a Unitarian bishop and the last president of the Hungarian Red Cross. These were mainstream leaders who, collectively, represented several hundred thousand members affiliated with their organizations. They had power at the ballot box and did not hesitate to unleash a lobbying effort to reverse the UN decision. The letters in support of their campaign came from notables ranging from former president Hoover (who wrote to Eckhardt, "I have your most interesting letter of August 4 and I obviously agree with your views"[134]) to US Senators Douglas, Keating and Lausche. Even Bernard Yarrow, vice president of the FEC, wrote to Eckhardt, "It is gratifying to know you are spearheading this movement, and I can already see the results of your efforts in the very nice article by Faulkner 'Push for Action'."[135] Although the political support in the US was there, the international community did not continue its initial support, and the Movement for the Defense of Hungary's work was suspended within two years.

The Changing World Created by Détente

In 1966 Msgr. Varga saw one of his personal goals realized: a memorial to the 1956 Revolution was erected at the Andau Bridge in Austria. This was one of the few high points of that period, as by then the HNC had been under his leadership for almost two decades, and despite a temporary increase after 1956, both the financial and ideological support for the national councils was diminishing annually. Varga initiated the idea for the memorial in January 1965 in correspondence with Gyula Klamer, editor of *Bécsi Híradó* (funded through FEC), and Klamer, along with the bishop of Eisenstadt, provided local support for the project. The funds were collected from Hungarians abroad, and the memorial was dedicated in November 1966. Though Varga could not be present for the ceremony, Klamer sent him photos and a full recounting of the event. [136]

In the ten years succeeding the Hungarian Revolution, the FEC made major changes in its mission and its dealings with the exile communities. These changes began with a few major changes just two years after the revolution, first suspending the Free European University in Exile (1958) and cancelling the funding for some exiles living outside the US, which included terminating support for 64 prominent foreign representatives of the various national councils. For the HNC this meant suspending its representation in key countries with a sizeable population of Hungarian exiles. Those whose funding was terminated in 1957 included Thomas Márffy-Mantuano (London), George Barcza (Australia), Gábor Apor (Italy), George Apponyi (Belgium), Christopher Kállay (Brazil),

Tibor Batheldy (Portugal) and Ferenc Marosy (Spain).[137] The principal reason for suspending payments to these exiles was that the FEC wanted the HNC to reorganize after the Hungarian Revolution and incorporate the recent émigrés and the new organizations of the Freedom Fighters – funds were needed for those salaries and stipends. As most of the new émigré organizations were liberal/leftish, the more conservative representatives and former diplomats of Hungary were removed from the newly organized Hungarian National Committee by eliminating their stipends and thus their role as heads of the HNC offices abroad.[138]

In 1961 the FEC de-funded the Paris Refugee Office. In a letter to Father Imre Gácsér, for ten years the head of that office, John Richardson Jr., then president of the FEC, attributed the closure to the good job the office had done in "resist[ing] Communist infiltration … the situation in this area was less dangerous than others with which we must deal."[139] Gácsér wrote back protesting the closing and outlining the value of the Hungarian Refugee Service: "The communists they know it [the value of the service] well themselves. That is why they hasten to establish the organizations in place of those which the Committee must close due to lack of finances." He stressed that the committee should continue to function "as long as the communists rule our country".[140]

Writing to Paul Auer in Paris on 24 August 1966, Varga expressed his concern that the waves of change were very evident at the Free Europe Committee and that the uncertainty of the situation was disconcerting and worrisome.[141]

Among the many official tenth anniversary remembrances was a 17 October letter from the office of British Prime Minister Harold Wilson to Ferenc Nagy. It reflects the very pragmatic policy of forgive and forget that had been adopted by that time by many political figures on both sides of the Atlantic:

> The Prime Minister has asked me to thank you for your letter of September 30. Mr. Wilson is deeply sympathetic for your concern for your country and he is well aware of the ordeals through which the Hungarian people passed after the war and in 1956. He does not,

> however, feel that the attitude which you invite him to adopt would be in the best interest of Hungary and her people or contribute to the better relations throughout Europe to the achievement of which the policy of Her Majesty's Government is dedicated. [142]

By 1971 the gap between the national councils and their sponsor had widened even further. Perhaps an aide memoire written by Varga best expresses the situation that prevailed by the time the CIA's support of the FEC had been made public and further funding of the councils through the American intelligence services had been prohibited by Congress. The councils were looking to continue their efforts, but the prospects seemed slim at best. Varga wrote:

> While those organizations, designated in the Post-WWII years to fight Communism in the West and also in the Soviet orbit are crumbing one after another, a well planned and executed Communist propaganda offensive is on the march. To dramatize this new trend, EAST EUROPE magazine, a professional publication of events in Soviet-dominated and Communist-ruled East Europe, widely read by scholars, journalist, politicians and business men, was terminated on January 1, 1970, the very same day that Communist Hungary launched a new publication, BUDAPRESS, an English, French and German language news bulletin with the aim of penetrating all Western news media.
>
> Exile organizations had been reduced to a skeleton existence by a cruel policy of "self-liquidation". Exile publications and news bulletins, which gave and [sic] objective account of life under communism in East Europe for the large minority groups and feed their press have been forced out of business as the remaining few have been reduced to a starvation level. At the same time, Communist agents are infiltrating émigré organizations and minority associations buying papers and journalists, blackmailing community leaders into collaboration and travel bureaus, forint trade firms with Hungarian ownership into cooperation. Large quantities of propaganda mate-

> rial (books, newspapers, magazins [sic] and leaflets) are sent by mail to Hungarians all over the world. Famous actors and actresses are touring Western countries to deceive Hungarians abroad with repertoirs [sic] ambiguously full of praise for the Communist regime in the "old country".
>
> The change in attitude of the Western governments is motivated by détente, the new dimension in East-West relations, a tragic misunderstanding of the real situation, which is sarcastically (and challengedly [sic]) reflected in the arrogant new communist propaganda offensive, showing that substantially nothing has changed. Thaw or détente is one thing, Communist aim is another, while smiling towards the West with awkward signs of coexistence, Communists are out, without hesitation or qualms, to subvert the free world.
>
> True the institutions of the cold war cannot be used effectively under the new circumstances; the present situation needs more sophisticated approaches and instruments for implentations [sic] of proper counter measures.
>
> The Hungarian Committee, an exile political organization, has created a twin organization in the changed situations for the new tasks. The Hungarian National Committee an already tax-exempt cultural and information center. We are ready to render reference services to scholars, journalist, politicians and businessmen on the changing Soviet orbit as well as its unchanged character. We will publish bulletins, position papers, political and market analyses for interested parties if the funds can be acquired.[143]

And indeed, without the support of the US government the Hungarian National Committee suspended their activities in 1971, as did the other institutions funded by the FEC. Radio Liberty and Radio Free Europe lived on, funded by a public foundation. It seemed the Cold War had come to a standstill.

The Holy Crown

For most Hungarian exiles, however it was not the suspension of the HNC but the return to Hungary of the Holy Crown and Crown Regalia that signaled the real end of their Cold War. The Hungarian Crown Guard had given these treasures into US hands for safe keeping from the communists after WWII, and President Carter returned them to Hungary on 6 January 1978. László Péter notes in his fascinating scholarly history of what most Hungarians refer to collectively as "the crown", "the crown as the source of national sovereignty became a powerful icon in the political rhetoric of modern Hungarian nationalism."[144]

By the early 1950s the crown was in a secure location at Fort Knox in the US. In its contacts with the United States the communist Hungarian government continually demanded the crown's return. It was brought up to every secretary of state and every US diplomat posted in Hungary. When the Rakosi government convicted US citizen Robert Voegler of spying for the US, it offered to exchange the crown for his freedom. Throughout the Cold War years, the US government first denied they had it then admitted possession but refused to return it. While the Cold War was at its height, no US president would consider returning a Christian artifact to a communist controlled government, and regular pressure was brought to bear through the HNC to remind presidents and their aides of that fact.

As time went on, the issue of the crown also created a schism among the liberals and the conservatives within the émigré community and the HNC leadership. Some, Béla Király among them, began to talk about the political benefits that might be gained with its return. Always conservative in its makeup, a great portion of the exile community and the older American Hungarian residents were united in their opposition. Living in exile in Vienna, Cardinal Mindszenty asked Eckhardt to carry his personal letter to President Nixon opposing the return of the crown.[145] As the Cold War thaw continued, the Hungarian exile community's fear that the crown would be returned grew. Hennyey wrote to Varga on 4 June 1970: "In the issue of the Holy Crown we are initiating a large protest against its return. Although the news is not reassuring, I still believe, that the United States will take into consideration what harm it would do if they returned the Holy Crown".[146] Hennyey wrote to Varga again on 18 October 1971 to say that talk of the returnwas continuing and "it is opposed by all in the immigration." He asked Varga to do all he could to make sure it was not returned.[147]

It was clear to the émigré community that the legitimacy of the Hungarian communist regime would be favorably reinforced by the return of the crown, the powerful symbolism of which remained mysterious to Westerners but was nevertheless respected by successive US administrations. For example, President Nixon's advisor Harry S. Dent stated in a 1971 letter, "... there are no plans for giving up the Holy Crown. It is understood that any such eventual action must serve the general goodwill instead of sowing disagreement."[148]

The passing of two giants in the Hungarian American community seems, symbolically at the very least, to have paved the way for the crown's eventual return. The death in September 1972 of Tibor Eckhardt – the "grand old man of Hungarian politics" who had formulated the HNC's anti-communist policy and sustained it with his vigor and intellectual strength – signaled the symbolic end of the émigré community's anti-communist stance. Although Varga was a by far more capable administrator and provided the balanced leadership needed to keep the HNC operational, it was Eckhardt who kept the banner of anti-communism waving throughout the American Hungarian community. In a way, it was fitting that his death coincided with the FEC's defunding and disbanding of the HNC. Eckhardt passed away at the same time that his political belief system became irrelevant in geopolitics.

The death in 1975 of Cardinal József Mindszenty – who had stood in ardent opposition to communism as long as he was alive – may also have made the decision to return the crown possible. Perhaps his passing and the loss of his moral authority finally opened the door to the US rapprochement with the government of Hungary in the late 70s and 80s. For by the time the Carter Administration came into office, relations with Hungary had liberalized, a cultural and scientific agreement was signed, and at the urging of Ambassador Philip Kaiser it was decided to return the crown, despite the fact that correspondence ran 99% against the decision. Carter's chief of staff, Hamilton Jordan, warned him of domestic blowback in the next presidential election.[149] The *New York Times*, however, trumpeted the wisdom of the gesture – "...the decision to return the crown and jewels is regarded by administration officials as a symbol of the changes that have occurred in recent years in Hungary. Under Janos Kadar, Hungary, in terms of internal policy has become, probably the most liberal of the East European countries linked to the Soviet Union..."[150] – never once mentioning the five divisions of Soviet occupying troops stationed in that most "liberal" of countries.[151] In January 1978 the crown was returned, and later that year the normalization of relations expanded to include granting Hungary most favored nation trading status.

The legacy of the Hungarian National Council and the Hungarian National Committee generally mirrors that of the overall mission of the National Committee for a Free Europe/Free Europe Committee. There were, however, significant differences in the organizations' financial status. Over the years, the parent committee expanded and became more bureaucratic, regularly giving itself generous raises in salary and working in an institutional manner, much like any major not for profit organization. The HNC, like the other national councils, lived a hand to mouth existence after the early days of bountiful funding reversed themselves and especially after the radios became the primary focus of the FEC's mission. As examples: Hennyey directed the work of the HNC in Germany from 1952 until 1962 for a salary of $385 a month with $50 for expenses. Varga was finally able to obtain a raise for him in 1962.[152] But by 1969 the Munich Hungarian Institute had such a small budget that its director paid expenses out of his own pocket. When reporting his negative funds for ACEN activities, Hennyey rightfully enquired: "Does the FEC want HNC representation in West Germany or not?"[153] Eckhardt was removed from the FEC payroll in 1958 at the same time that stipends for the "meritorious exiles" were discontinued. Yarrow called him in to tell him in person that he was "fired".[154] Yet the FEC continued to call on Eckhardt when in need of someone to support their efforts or develop a campaign.

Also among the "meritorious exiles" whose FEC stipends were canceled was Ferenc Marosy in Spain. Through the auspices of the Franco government, which did not recognize communist Hungary, Marosy had been able to continue to operate the Royal Hungarian Legation in Madrid on the pittance paid by the FEC. The embassy issued visas and passports, certified documents and generally assisted the refugees of the Hungarian diaspora all over the world, most of whom had left their homeland with no official documents. Two successive US ambassadors to Spain, John D. Lodge and Anthony Biddle Jr., tried to intercede on Marosy's behalf, but the FEC was adamant that this legation, which cost them $350 a month, should be shut down.[155] (At the time, 5,000 well-compensated employees staffed RFE headquarters in Munich.)

After approximately 1958, refugee and cultural aid were clearly no longer permanent FEC priorities. Yet for the national councils and many of the refugee organizations and institutions, this was what was still most needed: funding and support for individuals and families in transition.

In sum, for 22 years, in the final decade on a very tight budget, the Hungarian National Council/Committee performed heroic work on behalf of their countrymen and for the cause of freedom in their homeland. Msgr. Varga, whatever his shortcomings, provided the measured, reasonable, constant leadership that the group needed; and while the HNC never could be said to have been efficient, operationally it was the most successful of the national councils sponsored by the NCFE/FEC. That success can be attributed to Varga. As Otto von Habsburg said of him, "he was a humble man and he didn't have these enormous ambitions".[156] Varga was willing to share the limelight and work in collaboration with others, but he would also diplomatically rein in the more mercurial of his fellow exiles. Although the HNC's intellectual basis and ideology came from Eckhardt, the leadership came from Varga, and without him the organization certainly would not have been held in such high esteem by the NCFE/FEC leadership.

Endnotes

1 Rustem [sic] Vámbéry, *Hungary – To Be or Not To Be* (New York: Frederick Ungar, 1946), 139.

2 Ibid., 183.

3 Ibid., 171.

4 RusztemVámbéry, "Failure of a Mission", Rusztem Vámbéry Papers, Box 3, Folder: Speeches and Writings – 1948, Hoover Institution Archives, Stanford University, Palo Alto, CA. Hereafter HIA.

5 László Rajk, Hungarian Communist leader, organizer of the State Protection Authority (AVH) ran afoul of Mátyás Rákosi the Soviet backed Hungarian leader who saw him as an emerging threat to his authority. He was tried on trumped up charges of Titoism, convicted and executed on 15 October 1949.

6 Christopher Felix [James McCargar], *A Short Course in the Secret War* 4th edition (Lanham, New York and Oxford: Madison Books, 2001), 261.

7 The funding of the HNC prior to the advent of the NCFE was always thought to come from the US government, but confirmations of that support have not been available in archival material. Documents recently made available in the Radio Free Europe Corporate Files at the HIA confirm the funding provided by the Department of State. RFE Corporate Files Box 2319 (temporary), Minutes of the Executive Committee, 17 July 1952.

8 The Hungarian National Council (Magyar Nemzeti Bizottmány) was called that until in 1958. When the Hungarian Freedom Fighters of the 1956 Hungarian Revolution and the emigration they represented were merged into the council, the name was changed to the Hungarian National Committee (Magyar Nemzeti Bizottság). Its name remained the Hungarian National Committee until it was disbanded in 1972.

9 Proclamation, 18 November 1947, Ferenc Nagy Papers, Box 69, File: Émigré Organization/ Hungarian National Council/Appeals, Columbia University Archives.

10 Minutes of the Preparatory Commission of the Hungarian National Council, 14 July 1948. Emigráció. Box 36 (temporary). Országos Széchényi Könyvtár. Kézirattár (Hungarian National Library) Archival Collections. Fond 470: Hereafter OSZK Emigráció.

11 Ibid.

12 Minutes of the First Meeting of the Board of Directors, 17 May 1949. Radio Free Europe Corporate Files, Box 1536 (temporary). HIA.

13 Steven Béla Vardy, *The Hungarian Americans* (Boston: Twayne Publishing, 1985), 127–128.

14 http://immigration-online.org/86-displaced persons-act-united-states-1948.html Accessed 12 February 2013.

15 Béla Varga to Tibor Horányi, 9 November 1949. Emigráció. Fond 470. Box 37 (temporary). Folder: Nemzeti Bizottmány. OSZK.

16 Emigráció. Fond 470. Box 40 (temporary). Folder: Béla Varga to Dr. György Telegdy 1949–1956, OSZK.

17 Program and Speech. Emigráció. Box 40 (temporary). OSZK. In addition to the official meetings and public activities of the coordinating council of Central & East European leaders they also provided support for each other beyond public activities. An example was the memorial mass held on 4 April 1950 in Washington DC at St. Matthew's Church on the 9th anniversary of Pal Teleki's death, organized by Béla Varga. Attending from the émigré community were: Stanislaw Mikolajczik, former Prime Minister of Poland, Vladko Macel, former Prime Minister of Croatia, Joseph Cerni, former Interior Minister of Czechoslovakia, Professor Kojouharoff of Bulgaria as well as HNC members Msgr. JózsefKözi-Horváth, Ferenc Nagy, Károly Peyer and Zoltán Pfeiffer. Program and Speech. Box 40 (temporary). OSZK.

18 Report from Kálmán Saláta to Executive Committee dated New York, November 14, 1949. Emigráció. Fond 470. Box 35 (temporary). OSZK.

19 Frederick R. Dolbeare to Béla Varga, 9 August 1949. Emigráció. Box 35 (temporary). OSZK. "May we appeal to the Hungarian National council to supply us a list of not to exceed ten names of persons in this country whom you recommend to our attention?"

20 Emigráció. Box 36 (temporary). 17 July 1949. OSZK. John Foster Dulles was chairman of the NCFE executive committee and sat in on several such meetings.

21 Tibor Eckhardt Papers, Box 15. File: Magyar Bizottság Membership List. HIA.

22 Ferenc Nagy Papers, Box 71. File: Hungarian National Council – Financial, Columbia University Archives.

23 Vardy, *The American Hungarians,* 128.

24 Eckhardt founded the Movement for Independent Hungary in September 1941 and its work was suspended in mid-1942 as a result of the opposition created by forces led by the Hungarian émigré left and the political pressure and disinformation campaign run by Soviet sympathizers. For details on the history of the Movement for Independent Hungary see: Katalin Kádár Lynn, *Tibor Eckhardt: His American Years 1941–1972* (Boulder: East European Monographs, 2007), 55–97

25 Ferenc Nagy Papers, Index of Collection, Columbia University Archives.

26 Emigráció. Box 53 (temporary). Folder: Varga Béla levelezése. OSZK.

27 Emigráció. Box 63 (temporary). OSZK.

28 Minutes of 1 March 1950 and 9 March 1950 Executive Committee Meetings. Emigráció. Box 22 (temporary). OSZK.

29 Tibor Eckhardt to His Highness the Duke de Bar (Otto von Habsburg), 1 June 1954. Tibor Eckhardt Papers. Box 2. Folder: Correspondence. HIA.

30 Tibor Eckhardt to Msgr. Béla Varga, Chairman of the HNC, 4 September 1951. Tibor Eckhardt Papers, Box 1. File: Bizottmány. HIA.

31 "Red Plot to Kill Msgr. Varga Seen: Warned of Liquidation. Free Europe Group Discloses Order Sent from Bucharest to Blow Up Office Here", *New York Times*, 3 April 1951.

32 Kádár Lynn Katalin, "Tibor Eckhardt and the Grombach Organization: Hungarian Émigré Politics and United States Intelligence 1941–1955". In *ECE in Exile,* ed. Anna Mazurkiewicz. Expected publication Fall 2013. This is the first research article published on Eckhardt's involvement with the Grombach intelligence organization, also known as the POND during WWII and the Cold War.

33 Kállay's speech of 14 December 1955 before the ACEN General Assembly. Emigráció. Box 7 (temporary). Folder: Zoltán Pfeiffer. OSZK.

34 John Foster Leich, "Great Expectations: The National Councils in Exile 1950–1960", *The Polish Review*, Vol. 35, No. 3–4 (1990), 183–196, 186.

35 CIA Historical Staff, The Clandestine Service Historical Series, Hungary Volume II: External Operations 1946–1965, May 1972, 35. www.gwu.edu/~nsarchive Accessed 22 November 2012.

36 Ibid.

37 Ibid.

38 Msgr. Béla Varga to Tibor Eckhardt, 9 June 1954. Tibor Eckhardt Papers, Box 1, File: Bizottmány. HIA.

39 Ferenc Nagy Papers. Box 71. File: Hungarian National Council – Financial, Financial Ledgers of HNC. Columbia University Archives. Initially others who earned the top directors' fee of $300 per month also included some of the directors of the HNC's foreign offices, including Apor in Rome, Auer in Paris.

40 While not an official requirement for participation in the HNC it was agreed that only Hungarian citizens could serve on the council. This rule was later loosened after the council reor-

ganized as the Hungarian National Committee in 1958. Until 1965 it was the practice to ask members who became foreign citizens to resign. Although in some cases after their resignation they simply were hired by a US governmental agency. This happened to Kálmán Saláta who after he became a citizen went to Voice of America. The citizenship requirement was true of the ACEN delegation as well and a practice of the other national councils. Béla Varga to Paul Auer dated 6 January 1965. Re required resignations. Emigráció. Box 4 (temporary). OSZK.

41 Minutes of the Meeting of the HNC Executive Committee 19 January 1950, 3. Emigráció. Box 22 (temporary). OSZK. Eckhardt comments that a Sandor Ungvary was taking the budget/financials of the HNC around town to various newspaper editors and trying to start trouble. The question arose how Ungvary obtained the classified information, and the answer was that it was through Kálmán Saláta.

42 C.D. (Charles Douglas) Jackson was a guiding figure at Time, Inc. for over 33 years, holding positions as general manager of *Life* magazine, vice president of Time, Inc, publisher of *Fortune* and finally senior vice president of Time, Inc. He was a confidant of President Dwight D. Eisenhower, serving as his special White House assistant on the Cold War from 1952–1954. Throughout his career, Jackson took frequent leaves of absence for military, political and diplomatic assignments. One of them was to head the psychological warfare division of General Eisenhower's headquarters in 1944, leading a campaign for support of D-Day in Europe. As a successful publisher, he was knowledgeable about media and was given the assignment to set up Radio Free Europe. He served as president and the American administrator of the FEC/NCFE. After 1954 he served as a delegate to the United Nations. Jackson was a politically savvy and worldly individual, and his assessment of the goings-on at the Hungarian National Council is that of a man who was impatient with the self-destructive nature of some of the Hungarian leadership. It is clear that those Hungarian leaders who crossed Jackson had no idea of his importance and connections, otherwise they would never have disregarded his counsel in such a cavalier manner. See: "CD Jackson Dies, Time Inc. Official: Adviser to Eisenhower had been Publisher of Fortune", *New York Times*, 20 September 1964, 88.

43 Rear Admiral Harold Blaine Miller was an Annapolis graduate who retired from the military in 1946. His last post was as director of public information for the Navy. He was a Navy pilot who served in World War II and was an aide to Admiral Chester Nimitz. He headed the Free Europe Committee in 1951 then went on to a career in aviation at Pan American Airways and in education.

44 C.D. Jackson to Msgr. Béla Varga, 10 March 1952. Ferenc Nagy Papers. Box 69. File: Correspondence 4. Columbia University Archives. Asterisks, underlines and capitalization are all in the original letter.

45 Leich, "Great Expectations", 186. "We always cited the Hungarian National Council...as the model of an efficient and cohesive national exile organization."

46 Solemn Rally in honor of the late General Tadeusz Bór-Komorowski: Supreme Commander of the Polish Armed Forces, Commander in Chief of the Polish Home Army. October 30, 1966. Emigráció. Box 14 (temporary). Folder: Varga Béla Beszedjei: OSZK. Varga's speech ended with "I give thanks to God for granting me the opportunity to work with the Polish underground and General Komorowski, and to help Polish refugees during the last terrible war. In the first week of those hostilities, in September 1939, the tragic Hungarian hero, Premier Paul Teleki, asked me as an opposition leader in Parliament to aid the Polish refugees with the goodwill and love of all Hungarians. He promised every help on the part of the Hungarian government. Though as head of the government he could not officially help the Poles, he was such a protagonist of Polish-Hungarian friendship that when, on German orders, the Polish ambassador had to be expelled from Hungary, he said to him, 'From now on, I will be

the Polish Ambassador'."

47 "Heroes. The Unforgettable Pastor", *Time*, LXXV, No. 6, 8 February 1960.

48 Transcript of interview with Béla Varga on WDTV Pittsburgh, PA, on 21 March 1954. Emigráció. Box 39 (temporary). OSZK.

49 Varga returned to live in Balatonboglár, Hungary, on 2 July 1991. Gyula Borbándi, *Magyar politikai pályaképek1938–1948* (Budapest: Europe Kiadó, 1997), 473–475.

50 Charles De Gaulle to Béla Varga, 22 July 1958. Emigráció. Box 13 (temporary). Folder: Government. OSZK.

51 Telegram invitation to Mr. & Mrs. Allen Dulles dated January 25, 1960. Emigráció. Box 50 (temporary). Folder: Department of State 1959–1971. OSZK. "French Ambassador Herve Alphand will confer insignia of Officer of Legion of Honor on January 27 in Washington at his official residence 2221 Kalorma Road at five thirty pm stop Would deeply appreciate having honor of your presence at ceremony. Msgr. Bela Varga. Chairman Hungarian Committee."

52 Telegram from László Geiger Tatár to Béla Varga dated 9 September 1949. Emigráció. Box 41 (temporary). OSZK.

53 Radio Free Europe Corporate Files. Box 210. Folder 1: Hungarian Refugee Committee. HIA

54 Expenses for Hungarian Newspapers abroad. January 1951. Emigracio. Box 13 (temporary). Folder: Kálmán Saláta. OSZK.

55 Acsay Correspondence 1952–1953 with SzabolcsVajaj. Emigráció. Box 40 (temporary). OSZK.

56 Béla Varga to Frederic Dolbeare,18 July 1950. Emigráció. Box 22 (temporary). OSZK.

57 Partially to ease the housing pressure, as housing damaged or destroyed in WWII still had not been rebuilt, but also to rid the cities and towns of a potential dissident element. Without rhyme or reason regardless of class, economic standing or education, these "socially dangerous" persons and their families were removed from their homes and properties. A virtual Hungarian Gulag was developed on the Great Plain where about 10,000, deportees lived in the most primitive conditions, and for many others their destinations were out of the country into slave labor camps in parts of the Soviet Union then unknown.

58 Hungarian National Council "Memorandum", June 1951. Emigráció. Box 73 (temporary). OSZK.

59 Emigráció. Box 11 (temporary). Folder: Deportations and Polish Relations 1951. OSZK.

60 Report dated 22 March 1951. Emigráció. Box 8 (temporary). Folder: Central and East European Conference. OSZK.

61 The letters of request are in: Emigráció. Box 40 (temporary). Folder: Correspondence Béla Varga with Admiral Harold Blaine Miller. OSZK and Box 53 (temporary). Béla Varga Correspondence. OSZK (the letter from Miller dated 4 November 1957 asking Varga to christen his second born son).

62 Emigráció. Box 10 (temporary). OSZK.

63 Letter from Whitney H. Shepardson to Mrs. John Chambers Hughes dated 28 April 1953. Emigráció. Box 11 (temporary). Folder: Béla Varga Correspondence. OSZK.

64 Gyula Borbándi, *A Magyar emigráció életrajza: 1945–1985* (Bern: European Protestant Hungarian University Press, 1985), 94.

65 Report from Gusztáv Hennyey, "Az 1952 küszöbén", 3–4. Emigráció. Box 73 (temporary). OSZK. In an 18 July 1950 report to NCFE Vice President Frederic Dolbeare Varga states that at that time there were 12,000 Hungarian refugees in Western Austria and over 30,000 in Vienna. Emigráció. Box 22 (temporary). OSZK.

66 Report from Gusztáv Hennyey, "Az 1952 küszöbén",1. Emigráció. Box 73 (temporary). OSZK.

67 Ibid., 2.

68 Tibor Horányi. Report on the Refugee Service of the Hungarian National Council,June 1954.RFE Corporate Files,Hungarian Refugee Committee, Box 210, folder 4. HIA.

69 Activity Report of the Hungarian Refugee Service January – July 1958, report dated7 August 1958. RFE Corporate Files,Hungarian Refugee Committee, Box 210, folder 4. HIA.

70 Ibid.

71 Ibid.

72 Béla Varga's European trip schedule, June/July 1951. Emigráció. Box 39 (temporary). OSZK.

73 Béla Varga to George Dimitrov, 17 July 1951. Emigráció. Box 39 (temporary). OSZK.

74 Leich, "Great Expectations", 194.

75 Emigráció. Box 19 (temporary). Folder: The European Movement. OSZK.

76 Leich, "Great Expectations", 195.

77 Ibid., 192.

78 Home page of the IDC-CDI. www.idc-cdi.com Accessed 23 February 2013.

79 Béla Varga to Tibor Eckhardt, 30 August 1954. Emigráció. Box 11 (temporary). OSZK. "Dear Dr. Eckhardt, I hereby request you, in your quality [sic] as a member of the Hungarian National council to accept the chairmanship of the Hungarian Delegation to the Assembly of Captive European Nations. You are also requested to assign the sixteen members of the Delegation to work on the various subcommittees."

80 Béla Varga to Vilis Masens, 13 September 1954. Emigráció. Box 38 (temporary). OSZK. This letter to the chairman of the newly formed ACEN named the Hungarian delegates.

81 Report on the Political Background of the Hungarian National Council. Emigráció. Box 11 (temporary). Folder: Various. OSZK.

82 Memorandum of a Conversation, Department of State, Washington, January 9, 1956. Subject: US Policy towards Eastern Europe. FRUS, Foreign Relations of the United States, 1955–1957. Volume XXV. Eastern Europe. Document 44. At this meeting, representatives of the delegations to the ACEN, including Vilis Masens, its chairman, and George Dimitrov, its vice chair, met with the secretary of state to discuss US policy regarding the captive nations and the liberation of Eastern Europe. www.history.state.gov/historical documents. Accessed 15 January, 2013.

83 Report by Tibor Eckhardt dated August 8, 1958. Emigráció. Box 11 (temporary). OSZK. This report outlines his contribution to his work on behalf of the Free Europe Committee from 1949–1958.

84 Béla Varga to George Dimitrov, acting president of the ACEN, undated, probably May 1955. Emigráció. Box 11 (temporary). OSZK.

85 Human Rights in Hungary. Emigráció. Box 10 (temporary). OSZK.

86 IBUSZ vouchers had to be prepaid in hard currency abroad prior to departing for Hungary. Not only hotels but also a daily rate were required to be paid for in advance of travel.

87 Emigráció. Box 53 (temporary). Folder: Béla Varga Correspondence. OSZK.

88 In 1965 Charles Szolvai mounted a protest campaign against the Hungarian government's control of IKKA, the commissions it charged and its policies. Letters also went to Dean Rusk, Secretary of State. Szolvai to Béla Varga, 5 March 1965. Emigráció. Box 12 (temporary). Folders: Béla Varga Correspondence. OSZK.

89 Emigráció. Box 11 (temporary). Folder: Közi-Horváth József. OSZK.

90 Karl William Brown, *Regulating Bodies: Everyday Crime and Popular Resistance in Communist Hungary 1948–1956* (Google Books, 2007), 78–80.

91 International Rescue Committee Papers, Christopher T. Emmet Papers, Box 1, File: Help Free Hungary Rally, American Friends of the Assembly of Captive European Nations, 1. HIA.

92 Ibid., 4.
93 See: Katalin Kádár Lynn, *Tibor Eckhardt: His American Years 1941–1971* (Boulder, East European Monographs, 2007), 178–179.
94 Béla Varga to the Free Europe Committee, Memorandum (undated). Emigráció. Box 4 (temporary). OSZK.
95 Hungarian Committee. New International Yearbook. Societies and Organizations, 1961.
96 Leich, "Great Expectations", 187.
97 Vardy, *The Hungarian Americans*, 129.
98 Emigráció. Box 14 (temporary). Béla Varga Correspondence 1956–1957. OSZK.
99 Ibid.
100 Ibid.
101 Ibid.
102 Ibid.
103 Ibid. The Bandung Conference 21–24 April 1955. Organized by Asian and African countries; 29 countries attended. One of the major questions at the conference was that of colonialism, and „colonialism in all its manifestations was condemned", thus censuring the Soviet Union.
104 Ibid.
105 Emigráció. Box 8 (temporary). Folder: 1. Béla Varga Correspondence. OSZK.
106 Ibid.
107 Kádár Lynn, *Tibor Eckhardt,* 182. This quotation is from the First Aid for Hungary papers, HIA.
108 Ibid.
109 Ibid.
110 Ibid., 184.
111 Ibid.
112 Ibid., 185.
113 Ibid., 184.
114 Ibid.
115 Undated memorandum announcing formation of the coordinating committee related to recent Hungarian refugee arrivals. Emigráció. Box 6 (temporary). OSZK.
116 Kádár Lynn, *Tibor Eckhardt,* 186. Quotation from the First Aid for Hungary papers. HIA.
117 Ibid., 186–187.
118 Ibid., 184.
119 Visenau to Varga, 31 October, 1956, telegram [loose in box]. Emigráció. Box 14 (temporary). OSZK.
120 Letters to Béla Varga in support of 1956 revolution. Emigráció. Box 14 (temporary). OSZK.
121 "US Proposes UN Censure Hungary by Barring Aides: Suspension of Delegation is Urged if Budapest Fails to Let Observers Enter: 17 Nations Hold Talks: Assembly May Be Called for Monday to Weigh Bid –Kadar Regime Silent", *New York Times,* 8 December 1956. www.nytimes.com Accessed 15 February 2013.
122 Ibid.
123 Open Society Archives, Budapest. www.osarchivum.org Accessed on 15 February, 2013.
124 Lindesay Parrott, "Nagy Execution Deplored by UN's Hungary Panel: Five- Nation Committee Decides Killings of Premier and other Leaders of Revolt Show Oppression 'Has not Abated'", *New York Times,* 22 June 1958.
125 www.teara.govt.nz/en/biographies. Accessed 3 January 2013.
126 Press Release AFL CIO NA 8-3870, 23 October 1959. Emigráció. Box 24 (temporary). OSZK.

[127] "Mikoyan Arrives in City Under Close Police Guard", *New York Times*, 14 January 1959. www.nytimes.com. Accessed 13 February 2013.

[128] Statement by Msgr. Béla Varga chairman of the Hungarian committee in connection with Mr. Mikoyan's visit to the United States of America, 16 January 1959. Emigráció. Box 29 (temporary). OSZK.

[129] "Mikoyan Arrives in City Under Close Police Guard", *New York Times*, 14 January 1959. www.nytimes.com. Accessed 13 February 2013.
Aide Memoire of the Hungarian Committee on the visit of Mikoyan to the United States of America, 15 January 1959. Special Issue of the "Hungarian Freedom Fighter", January 1959, regarding Mikoyan's visit. Emigráció. Box 29 (temporary). OSZK.

[130] Emigráció. Box 11 (temporary). 1956 material, Béla Varga correspondence. OSZK.

[131] Ibid.

[132] "Bela Fabian, 77, Exile Leader of Anti-Red Protests Here, Dies: Hungarian Refugee Directed Demonstrations and Rallies – Lawyer and Author", *New York Times*, 28 December 1966. www.nytimes.com. Accessed 6 December 2012.

[133] Emigráció. Box 13 (temporary). Folder: Béla Varga Correspondence with Gusztáv Hennyey. OSZK.

[134] Herbert Hoover to Tibor Eckhardt, 7 August 1962. Emigráció. Box 11(temporary). Folder: Movement for the Defense of the Hungarian Nation. OSZK.

[135] Bernard Yarrow to Tibor Eckhardt, 2 August 1962, 2 January 1963. Emigráció. Box 11(temporary). Folder: Movement for the Defense of the Hungarian Nation. OSZK.

[136] OSZK. Emigráció. Box 7 (temporary). Folder: Gyula Klamer.

[137] General Crittenberger (president of FEC) to Bernard Yarrow, memorandum, 6 October, 1958. RFE Corporate Records. Box 235. Folder 12: Ferenc Marosy. HIA.

[138] Ibid.

[139] John Richardson Jr. to Reverend Imre Gácsér, 12 December 1961 and Rev. Gácsér to Richardson, undated. RFE Corporate Files. Box 210. Folder 4: Hungarian Refugee Committee. HIA.

[140] Ibid.

[141] Béla Varga to Paul Auer, 24 August 1966. Emigráció. Box 4 (temporary). Folder: Béla Varga Correspondence with Paul Auer. OSZK.

[142] On behalf of Prime Minister Wilson to Ferenc Nagy, 19 October 1966. Emigráció. Box 11 (temporary). OSZK.

[143] Aide Memoire, Béla Varga, undated but after 1 January 1970. Emigráció. Box 73 (temporary). OSZK.

[144] László Péter, "The Holy Crown of Hungary, Visible and Invisible", *The Slavonic and East European Review*, Vol. 81, No. 3 (July 2003), 507.

[145] Kádár Lynn, *Tibor Eckhardt*, 189.

[146] Emigráció. Box 13 (temporary). Folder: Varga correspondence with Gusztav Hennyey in Germany. OSZK. Letter translated by author.

[147] Ibid.

[148] Kádár Lynn, *Tibor Eckhardt*, 189.

[149] Katalin Kádár Lynn, "The Return of the Crown of St. Stephen and its Subsequent Impact on the Carter Administration", *East European Quarterly*, Vol. 34, No.2 (Summer 2000), 181.

[150] "US to Return Hungary's Crown, Held Since End of World War II", *New York Times*, 4 November 1978. www.nytimes.com. Accessed 25 February 2013.

[151] Adrian Hayde-Price, *The International Politics of East Central Europe* (Manchester: Manchester University Press, 1996), 231.

[152] Gusztáv Hennyey to Béla Varga, 25 October 1969. Emigráció. Box 13 (temporary). Folder: Gusztáv Hennyey. OSZK.

[153] Gusztáv Hennyey to Béla Varga, 30 October 1965. Emigráció. Box 13 (temporary). Folder: Gusztáv Hennyey. OSZK. "Konkrét kérdés: sulyt helyez a FEC arra, hogy Németországban képviselete legyen vagy nem"? Author's translation.

[154] Emigráció. Box 12 (temporary). OSZK.

[155] Ferenc Marosy. RFE Corporate Papers. Box 235. Folder:12. HIA.

[156] Otto von Habsburg, interview with the author, 28 October 2003.

Select Bibliography

Archives:

Hungarian National Library Archives: (Országos Széchényi Könyvtár Kézirattára).
Fond: 470: Emigráció (temporary numbering)
Fond: 488: Tibor Eckhardt

Hoover Institution Archives: Stanford University, Palo Alto, CA
Tibor Eckhardt Papers
Ferenc Marosy Papers
Rusztem Vambery Papers
Radio Free Europe: Corporate Files

Columbia University: Bakhmeteff Archives. New York NY
Ferenc Nagy Papers

Books:

Gyula Borbándi, *A magyar emigráció életrajza: 1945–1985* (Bern: European Protestant Hungarian University Press, 1985)

Christopher Felix (James McCargar) . *A Short Course In the Secret War* (4th Edition – Lanham, New York and Oxford, Madison Books, 2001)

Bela Vardy. *The Hungarian Americans* (Boston, Twayne Publishing 1985)

Articles:

John Foster Leich, "Great Expectations: The National Councils in Exile 1950–1960", *The Polish Review*, Vol. 35, No. 3–4 (1990), 183–196.

Imre Kovács and Cold War Émigré Politics in the United States (1947–1980)

For Imre Kovács (1913–1980) on his centenary

Tibor Frank

Born in 1913, author, journalist, political scientist, and politician Imre Kovács was of peasant stock and early on entered populist politics in interwar Hungary.[1] In 1947 he left Hungary to spend the rest of his life in exile and in exile politics.

Published in 1937, his celebrated *A néma forradalom* [The Silent Revolution] interpreted the social situation in Hungary as a revolution that had failed to erupt.[2] The book is an ingeneous and highly original blend of chapters on Hungarian history, sociology, agrarian socialism, emigration, poverty, and even on religious sects. Published as part of the series *Szolgálat és írás* [Service and Writing], Kovács's book made him nationally well-known as a sociologist of the only child, of poverty and social decline. In his conclusion Kovács asserted, "We are a dying people". Quoting statistician Miklós Móricz, who predicted that the Hungarian population would increase to 10 million by 1960, to be followed by a fall apace, Kovács noted that "there would be no further peasant revolt in Hungary."

During World War II Kovács became thoroughly involved in the national resistance movement as one of the leaders of the *Magyar Front* [Hungarian Front]. He was on the top of the list by the Gestapo when Germany conquered Hungary in mid-March 1944. On the night of December 20–21, 1944, he went over to the Soviet army, where he was mistakenly jailed and kept as a prisoner of war until February 11, 1945, when he returned to Budapest to join the reorganized National Peasant

Party. By the end of April 1945 he had quickly became the party's secretary general and, by March 1946, its vice-president. On April 2, 1945, he became a deputy to the Temporary National Assembly founded in Debrecen, eastern Hungary. He was also the leader of several municipal and national authorities.[3]

In an article on "A demokrácia útja Magyarországon" [The road to democracy in Hungary], written for the November 1946 issue of the journal *Válasz*, he called for strengthening democratic development and for supporting the patient handling of minority views in a democracy.[4] In 1947, when prominent leaders of the Smallholders' Party started to come under lethal attack from the Communists, and the Peasant Party had also lost its prominent role in Hungarian politics, he feared he would lose his own position in Hungarian politics and at the end of that year left via Prague for Zurich, Switzerland. This was indeed a somewhat "premeditated" attempt to leave Hungary – and he meant to return soon afterwards.[5]

He spent the first two years of his exile in Switzerland and France. It was in Switzerland that he wrote *A Szovjetunió árnyékában* [In the Shadow of the Soviet Union], a history of the post-World War II coalition government in Hungary. Published in both German (1948) and French (1949) in Zurich, the book provided the first summary of the Sovietization of Hungary. Kovács soon realized that Switzerland and the West did not consider the Soviet occupation of Eastern Europe to be temporary.[6] He found the Western support given to the members of the Peasant Party inadequate and in marked contrast to that provided to exiled aristocrats, Social Democrats, and victims of Fascism. The Peasant Party was often under attack for anti-Semitism and, more often than not, Kovács felt it necessary to defend his friends and his party against sometimes undeserved accusations.

Kovács initiated cooperation with the International Peasant Union, which was global in scope and instrumental in spreading democracy. Founded on June 4, 1947, the IPU consisted mainly of exiled peasant politicians from East-Central Europe. The Hungarian delegation at the IPU Congress of May 1950 included Imre Kovács as well as former Hungarian Prime Minister Ferenc Nagy (1903–1979). On November 18, 1947, the Hungarian National Council was founded in Chicago;[7] however, Kovács was unhappy with the low level of political activities among émigré Hungarians. In a mid-1948 private letter to his close friend Aladár Szegedy-Maszák (1903–1988), a former Hungarian Minister to the US (1945–47), Kovács expressed his dissatisfaction in no uncertain terms: "[...] when we see that Czechoslovak MPs hold parliamentary meetings in London and the European papers report on them in major articles [...] our exasperation is legitimate – why don't we do something? [...] We should at least create the semblance of being willing to do something."[8] Szegedy-Maszák fully agreed when he stated, "the time is not far away when émigré activities should be speeded up."[9] Kovács also said "my time belongs to émigré politics. As far as I can see, we have to be ready to fight soon. I myself would be happy to take up the battle sword, but I cannot see the chances of a realistic outcome."[10]

After founding the newspaper *Látóhatár* in Zürich in 1950 and *Új Látóhatár* in Munich in 1958, Kovács became thoroughly disillusioned with émigré journalism and authors.[11] In 1949 he sailed for the United States, where he went via New York to Washington, D.C.[12] On November 20, 1949, he became an associate of the Research and Information Center established within the Library of Congress under the auspices of the National Committee for Free Europe (NCFE), an American anticommunist organization, founded the previous May in New York City. Kovács was requested by the NCFE to survey the Hungarian press and prepare political analyses.[13] At the same time, he became editor of the *Parasztszövetségi Értesítő* (Bulletin of the Peasant Alliance), published by the émigré organization of the Hungarian Peasant Alliance.[14] His feverish activities showed that there was a need for the development of political activism amongst the peasant population in Hungary and internationally as well. The peasant movement was also financially sponsored by the NCFE in the Cold War era. Kovács felt it was important not to lose step with political, social and cultural developments in the Western world. He thought highly of the dynamism of US society and the revolutionized means of production introduced in the US. "In a state of constant tension and movement," he wrote, "American society stretches and enlarges the frameworks keeping everything together, which present a complex, fine and sensible task, the most perfect realization of democracy."[15]

In 1950 Kovács moved to New York and started working for the information department of the NCFE. He also worked internationally for most if not all of the Hungarian papers. He was so important in international exile politics that he was asked to serve on the political committee of the Peasant Union in Washington, D.C. Unfortunately, however, one of his letters to a former fellow Hungarian MP, István Pap, was misused, and it revealed Kovács's criticism of the leaders of the Hungarian National Council (HNC) and of the NCFE. Engineered mostly by conservative and Horthyite members of the Hungarian exile community, a press campaign was started to denounce Kovács, who was attacked mainly for his allegedly anti-American views.[16] After a lot of discussions inside the NCFE, Kovács lost his job in 1951. The main reasons for incriminating him were his views on the NCFE and on how the liberation of East Central Europe from Soviet influence should be designed and completed.[17] The NCFE and the Hungarian exiles' to that organization were also criticized by other prominent leaders, such as sociologist and political scientist Oscar Jászi (1875–1957), who labelled the NCFE as Nazi and Stalinist, adding "if the émigrés do not protest against what has happened, all their future activities will come under the pressure of power."[18] Others of Kovács's fellow Hungarian émigré politicians were far less benevolent: former MP Dezső Sulyok (1897–1965) pointed out that Kovács failed to protest against the NCFE before he was dismissed, although "it was the swamp of corruption shown by the abject perfidy of politicians paid with money."[19] Sulyok suggested that the world not be viewed "through the paychecks of the NCFE".[20] Kovács ultimately paid for the intrigues and attacks in exile with his marriage: his first wife, Ilona Földes, divorced him in 1952.[21]

In "A szellem szuverenitásáért" [For the Sovereignty of the Spirit], a 1952 article for *Új Látóhatár*, Kovács staunchly criticized the pro-American orientation of the émigré Hungarians, stressing that the smaller

European nations should preserve their traditions and unique aspects. "In the greater standardizing and synchronizing community we are only worth as much as we include from our own tradition and culture. Our dowry must be the Hungarian soul, it is the sovereignty of the spirit that guarantees our life and liberty. … At least there is one more person now who does not see the world through the cheques arriving from Free Europe."[22]

The early 1950s saw the coexistence of two major Hungarian-American organizations. Kovács was a member of the Magyar Nemzeti Bizottmány [Hungarian National Council], recognized by the US administration and the Western governments and consisting of pre- and post-War members of parliament, members of various Hungarian governments, and party leaders. In 1951 the US government warned the various national committees not to consider themselves governments-in-exile.[23] Older Hungarian-Americans were represented by the Amerikai Magyar Szövetség [American-Hungarian Federation] and were suspicious of the 1945–47 émigrés and the Displaced Persons of the post-War period. Kovács disliked what he saw as an influx of certain Horthyite military officers and government officials who took over some of the clubs and papers from the old Hungarian-Americans.[24] He may have disliked Hungarian émigrés who served in the military, but most of them never had a chance to emigrate to the US until later – and they certainly were not in the first wave of immigrants allowed into the US. This is why military-like groups such as the *Magyar Harcosok Bajtársi Közössége* (MHBK [Comradely Community of Hungarian Fighters]), the *Magyar Szabadság Mozgalom* [Hungarian Freedom Movement] and the *Magyar Királyi Csendőr Bajtársi Közösség* (MKCsBK [Royal Hungarian Comradely Community of Gendarmes]) were all so strong in Germany, particularly the MHBK.[25]

Kovács's correspondence up to 1952 was full of grief about the loss of his native land and his inability to belong to a new society.[26] He was highly critical of the US: "I do not want to besmirch America, but they commit the same mistakes in a small way vis-à-vis those of us who are so very clearly visible throughout the world, from China to Berlin or Belgrade to Washington. The techincal superiority of this nation is undisputable, but they do not understand politics even to the extent of a mediocre cultural educator in Hungary."[27] "America is the cemetery of the great Hungarian desires," he wrote to a friend in 1950, "or, if it is more pertinent, the great cemetery of Hungarian desires."[28] In another letter he wrote, "The great powers that developed over the last half a century, do not allow the will or endeavour of the small nations to develop their own way of life. This is what I experienced during two occupations at home, and this is my sad experience in connection with my émigré politicking in the so-called free West."[29] By mid-1951 he prophesied that he "was already afraid of the time when the Americans would win and want to change the world into their own likeness".[30] His comments on the US sounded hypocritical and unfair, given that the International Peasant Union was funded by the NCFE with US dollars, and he himself was subsidized by the US government in most if not all of the positions he held in America except his manual jobs. *Új Látóhatár* was also funded mostly by the NCFE.[31]

His friend Aladár Szegedy-Maszák was unhappy with Kovács's judgements of émigré politics, which he considered mere "shadow boxing". In Szegedy-Maszák's shrewd opinion, "what goes on here at the level of Hungarian public life is irrelevant from the point of view of the future in the homeland." He wittily compared émigré politics to "the growth of a dead person's beard and nails".[32] This was probably one of the reasons why Kovács turned away from politics in 1952, married American student Rita Deborah Lebanow and decided to continue his university studies, this time at Harvard.[33] He read English Composition, Humanities, the Expansion of Europe since 1815, Problems of Modern Philosophy, and Introduction to Psychology.[34] He enjoyed being a student again and continued at Harvard for a year. "I read these somewhat 'undecipherable' subjects with great determination but hope that the term would lay the foundations of my English, and then I can plan both my career as a political exile and as an American."[35] His English, however, did not prove to develop well enough and was inadequate for university studies. He left Harvard and started writing a novel titled *The Ninety and Nine*, which was published in 1955 and portrayed Communists such as former Minister of the Interior László Rajk (1909–1949) and Jesuits such as József Cardinal Mindszenty (1892–1975). In its conclusion, the majority of credit goes to the Jesuits, who are elevated into martyrdom by their faith alone. It is conceivable that Kovács was impressed by *Darkness at Noon*, a novel published in 1940–41 by his Hungarian compatriot Arthur Koestler (1905–1983).[36] While writing this novel, he was accused in a personal letter of including alleged anti-Semitic details of his second book, *A kivándorlás* [Emigration].[37] He denied the accusation and swept it aside, standing on his reputation and his entire career as an author and politician.[38]

His views of exile politics were characteristically past-oriented. "Here we have to stay in touch with the past, all the more so as everybody profits from his or her own past and takes part with it in [...] émigré public life."[39] He was motivated partly by his own peasant past[40] and partly by his uncertainty about his future in the United States. "I do not know which of my many plans will succeed; whether or not I will succeed in reaching anything at all. America is most merciless to those who follow their own way and do not want to assimilate in the form and sense that is the biggest strength and most perfect melting pot of this gigantic country."[41]

The year 1954 brought changes in international power relations and in the US's appreciation of Imre Kovács as well. Kovács realized that the June 1953 changes in Hungary marked the beginning of a new political course. Bolshevism had received a blow, though it was not a mortal one. There was a sense in the air of the gradual liberalization of Communism. Kovács was suddenly invited back to the NCFE, where he was soon to become involved in Operation Focus, a fictitious national opposition movement. He provided broadsheets for the nationalist movement, each of them 16 pages long and destined to be sent over East Central European countries via balloons to spread political propaganda and market political opposition. His daughter remembered the balloons as having been his idea.[42]

The real change in Kovács's views was brought about by the Hungarian revolution of 1956. From early on he was a member of the Hungarian

National Council, and he became a member of the board of the Hungarian Writers' Association Abroad in 1957.[43] Both the Council and the Association belonged among those Hungarian émigré organizations that constantly developed mistrust, intrigue, and quarrel. The State Department went so far as to voice its political concern, as it did not believe that "the Council was suitable for the representation of Hungarian émigré politics."[44] Kovács found the fragmentation of democratic powers in emigration and the impotence of the Council intolerable, and he was one of those who noticed with sadness the gradual change of the political interests of international public opinion.[45]

After the end of 1956 or early 1957 at the latest, Hungary did not play a major international role in fighting the Soviet Union. Some of Kovács's friends went so far as to allege that the Soviets would not allow Hungary to become free until "NATO survives or functions under the domination of the American voice."[46] One of Hungary's Social Democratic leaders in exile, Imre Szélig, even suggested to Kovács that "the Assembly of Captive European Nations [ACEN, one of the divisions under the NCFE] is an instrument of the Cold War[...] and we have a twofold objection vis-à-vis the body [ACEN], which is an obstacle to our participation. The first is that it serves the Cold War; on the other hand the delegations of the various countries are full of reactionary elements."[47]

Kovács did everything in his power to convince the world of Hungary's just cause by traveling widely in both Europe and Asia. He was part of the Hungarian National Council delegation that was to discuss the Hungarian question, aided by a special department of the Free Europe Committee, Inc. (the NCFE's name after November 1954). He was very well received in Japan and India, and in Europe by the British, French, Italian, and Swedish governments. Both Indian Prime Minister Jawaharlal Nehru (1889–1964) and Swedish Prime Minister Tage Erlander (1901–1985) promised their mediation vis-à-vis Soviet party leader Nikita S. Khrushchev (1894–1971) in an effort to convince the Soviets to introduce a more lenient attitude towards Hungary. These interventions led to no result.[48]

From the mid-1960s Kovács recognized clearly that Hungary had gone through a process of slow consolidation. The 1956 revolution led to a new political order, the combination of planned economy, parliamentary democracy, and individual human rights – a package with the potential to create a new Hungarian social and political order. Kovács then became involved in Latin American issues, arguing that his East European experience would be of great help in interpreting Latin America. In 1961 he became president of the New York-based International Center for Social Research, Inc., funded by the International Development Fund[49] at which he contributed to the understanding of potential structural changes in agricultural production in South America, using his experiences in Hungarian village research in the 1930s. He initiated direct contacts with most of the Latin American centers for agricultural policies, particularly in Colombia.[50] Some of his ideas, however, sounded dangerously socialist to his Latin American and US associates, and he was soon, after a mere two years, dismissed from his job. He then returned to the Hungarian National Council.[51]

Kovács was proud of the direction taken by his journal, *Új Látóhatár*, which, he suggested to Mucio F. Delgado (b. 1910), director for Europe of the FEC's Organizations and Publications division, "never contained any anti-American remarks or insinuations" and represented "the realistic wing of Hungarian exile activities, working in the same spirit which ignited the Hungarian Revolution. We consider ourselves the Free World representatives of Hungarian Populism, a mighty ideological challenge to Communism which already blocked the road for an easy consolidation of Post-Revolutionary Hungary."[52] "Even the Kádár regime," Kovács boasted to Delgado, "has shown many signs of being disturbed by Uj Latohatar [sic]."[53]

In 1963 Kovács was transferred to the press department of the FEC and edited *Magyarországi Hírek* [News from Hungary].[55] He also served as editor of *The Hungarian Quarterly*, an English language journal published by exiled Hungarian journalists and authors. After his brief encounter with Latin American affairs, he returned to the problems of his native Hungary. He considered dialogue with Hungary to be acceptable and necessary but refused to go home, even for a brief visit. He did not accept US citizenship until 1973. After the official citizenship ceremony, he flew to the state of Georgia to view his future gravesite in the family tomb of Edna Harwey Campbell, his third wife – a strange idea for a symbolic farewell to both Hungary and to life.

Throughout his émigré years, Imre Kovács agreed with his London-based friend the author Pál Ignotus (1901–1978), who wrote to him in 1957 that "if we do not want to be nagging, wounded, and old fashioned émigrés, we have to accept that the world belongs to those who suffer at home. And I am happy that you were one of those who accepted all the time that, if voiced at home, a human word in whatever Marxist-Leninist packing [...] can do more than the most enthusiastic anti-Muscovite battle cry voiced outside the national borders."[55] In 1978 Szegedy-Maszák went as far as asking his friend Kovács "whether the emigration consists of émigrés who can only think in terms of regimes, and even that with a negative passion, whether it needs at least a minimum amount of political information and orientation, as well as the recognition of the fact that there is [one] country, one nation which in some basic considerations is independent of the regime?"[56]

"I am quite active in émigré politics and observe the international situation quite soberly, which compels me to an unusually realistic way of viewing and planning," Kovács wrote in 1958 to the Hungarian Writers Association Abroad in London.[57] In an article he signed as "Americanus" and titled "Realistic emigration", Kovács made it clear that

> ... the mandate of us all expired. No one can refer to himself as a representative of the Hungarians, as the people at home have covered a very great distance indeed, together with us. Time has stopped and cruelly torn away the alleged commitments and emotional bonds. Our negation, staunch opposition to the transformation at home, is good for nothing; Hungarian society was restructured and a new nation was formed and forged under Communist rule, which knows and better applies historical methods and everyday tactics, cute and shrewd practices of survival.[58]

Ever the realist, Imre Kovács perceived and assessed the changes in émigré society and politics more clearly than most of his contemporaries. Critical as he was of the United States, as well as of most of his Hungarian fellow-exiles, his straightforward and positive approach to matters Hungarian and the national cause showed him to be a real patriot exhibiting honesty and perseverance. His many contributions to the Hungarian exile press, as both author and editor, as well as his leadership in several of the positions he held singled him out as a major figure of the Hungarian exile in the age of the Cold War.

Imre Kovács died in New York City in 1980.

Endnotes

1 Tibor Huszár, *Találkozások. Beszélgetések a két világháború közötti magyar szellemi-politikai mozgalmakról* [Encounters. Discussions on interwar Hungarian intellectual-political movements] (Budapest: Corvina, 2005), 175 and ff. For his unreliable though detailed biography see, Imre Kovács (1913–1980) (Budapest: Az 1956-os Magyar Forradalom Történetének Dokumentációs és Kutatóintézete Közalapítvány, 2000). For the lectures of a memorial conference remembering Kovács see "Kovács Imre és a népi mozgalom", *Politikatudományi Szemle* 4 (1993), 71–101.

2 Imre Kovács, *A néma forradalom* [The Silent Revolution] (Budapest: Cserépfalvi, [1937]). For other major books by Kovács see *A kivándorlás* (Budapest: Cserépfalvi, 1938); *Kolontó* (Budapest: Cserépfalvi, 1939); *Elsüllyedt ország* (Budapest: Cserépfalvi, 1945); *Im Schatten der Sowjets* (Zürich: Thomas, 1948), franciául: *D'une Occupation à L'autre, la Tragédie Hongroise* (Paris: Calmann-Lévy, 1949); *Magyarország megszállása* (Toronto: Vörösváry, 1979, Budapest: Katalizátor Iroda, 1990).

3 Eszter M. Molnár, *Egy Homo Politicus itthon, Európában és Amerikában. Kovács Imre élete és munkássága* [A *Homo Politicus* at Home, in Europe, and in America. The Life and Work of Imre Kovács] (Budapest: Hét Krajcár Kiadó, 2010), 51–52. For biographical details see also Imre Kovács to unknown, 28 July 1952, Imre Kovács, Letters, mostly copies, Imre Kovács Papers, Bakhmeteff Archive, Box 4.

4 Molnár, *Egy Homo Politicus*, 52; Imre Kovács, A demokrácia útja Magyarországon (*Válasz*, 1946, No. 2), 97–106, republished in Imre Kovács, *Tanulmányok 1935–1947* (Budapest: Magyar Napló, 2003), 347–361.

5 Pál Péter Tóth, "Kovács Imre az emigrációban." In: *Magyarságkutatás. A Magyarságkutató Intézet évkönyve* (Budapest: Magyarságkutató Intézet, 1989), 183.

6 Molnár, *Egy Homo Politicus*, 267–268.

7 Ibid., 268, 270. Cf. Katalin Kádár Lynn, *Tibor Eckhardt: His American Years 1941–1972* (Boulder: East European Monographs, 2007), 218.

8 Imre Kovács to Aladár Szegedy-Maszák, Zürich, 7 June 1948, Imre Kovács Papers, Bakhmeteff Archive, Box 7.

9 Aladár Szegedy-Maszák to Imre Kovács, 1 March 1948, Imre Kovács Papers, Bakhmeteff Archive, Box 7.

10 Imre Kovács to Aladár Szegedy-Maszák, Zürich, 22 March 1948, Imre Kovács Papers, Bakhmeteff Archive, Box 7.

11 Imre Kovács to Gyula Borbándi, New York, 3 June 1975, Cf. Borbándi's answer to Kovács' criticism, München, 19 June 1975, Imre Kovács Papers, Bakhmeteff Archive, Box 1.

12 Tóth, "Kovács Imre az emigrációban", 185.

13 Ibid.

14 Molnár, *Egy Homo Politicus*, 268–269.

15 Imre Kovács, "Elindultam szép hazámból - onnét-e? És hova jutottam?" [I started from my beautiful homeland – from there in fact? And where did I get to?] *Új Látóhatár*, 30 March 1981, 456. Quoted in Molnár, *Egy Homo Politicus*, 269.

16 Imre Kovács to unknown friends, New York, 17 February (Strictly confidential) and 29 March 1951, Imre Kovács Papers, Bakhmeteff Archive, Box 4.

17 Tóth, "Kovács Imre az emigrációban", 185.

18 Ibid.

19 Ibid.

20 Ibid.

21 Imre Kovács to unknown friends, New York, 29 March 1951, Imre Kovács Papers, Bakhmeteff Archive, Box 4.

22 Béla Pomogáts, "A néma forradalom írója" [The author of *A néma forradalom*], *Új Forrás*, XVI (1984), 45. Quoted in Molnár, *Egy Homo Politicus*, 270.

23 Imre Kovács to unknown friends, New York, 4 June 1951, Imre Kovács Papers, Bakhmeteff Archive, Box 4.

24 Imre Kovács, "Elindultam szép hazámból - onnét-e? És hova jutottam?". Quoted in Molnár, *Egy Homo Politicus*, 271.

25 I am most grateful to Dr. Katalin Kádár Lynn for this and several other additions to and comments on the first draft of my paper.

26 Tóth, "Kovács Imre az emigrációban", 186.

27 Imre Kovács to unknown friends, New York, 1 March 1950, Imre Kovács Papers, Bakhmeteff Archive, Box 4.

28 Imre Kovács to Lili Kertay, New York, 30 October 1950, Imre Kovács Papers, Bakhmeteff Archive, Box 5, quoted in Tóth, "Kovács Imre az emigrációban", 187. Repeated in Imre Kovács to unknown friends, New York, 4 June 1951, Imre Kovács Papers, Bakhmeteff Archive, Box 4.

29 Imre Kovács to Béla Justh, New York, 10 May 1954, Imre Kovács Papers, Bakhmeteff Archive, Boksz 3.

30 Imre Kovács to unknown friends, New York, 4 June 1951, Imre Kovács Papers, Bakhmeteff Archive, Box 4.

31 Imre Kovács to Mucio F. Delgado, 11 February 1959 and Imre Kovács to Imre Vámos, 25 December 1952, both in Imre Kovács Papers, Bakhmeteff Archive, Box 2.

32 Aladár Szegedy-Maszák to Imre Kovács, 21 October 1952, Imre Kovács Papers, Bakhmeteff Archive, Box 7.

33 Imre Kovács to Béla Justh, Cambridge [Mass.], 12 November 1951, Imre Kovács Papers, Bakhmeteff Archive, Box 3.

34 Imre Kovács to Aladár Szegedy-Maszák, 3 February 1952, Imre Kovács Papers, Bakhmeteff Archive, Box 7.

35 Ibid. Cf. Imre Kovács to Aladár Szegedy-Maszák, 3 March 1952, Imre Kovács Papers, Bakhmeteff Archive, Box 7.

36 Molnár, *Egy Homo Politicus*, 271–272; Tóth, "Kovács Imre az emigrációban", 186–187.

37 Budapest: Cserépfalvi 1938.

38 Imre Kovács, A kivándorlás [Emigration]. Cf. Imre Kovács to unknown, 15 February 1953, Imre Kovács Papers, Bakhmeteff Archive, Box 4.

39 Imre Kovács to Aladár Szegedy-Maszák, 17 November 1952, Imre Kovács Papers, Bakhmeteff Archive, Box 7.

40 Imre Kovács to Aladár Szegedy-Maszák, 2 November 1952, Imre Kovács Papers, Bakhmeteff Archive, Box 7. Cf. the answer by Aladár Szegedy-Maszák to Imre Kovács, 13 November 1952, Imre Kovács Papers, Bakhmeteff Archive, Box 7.

41 Imre Kovács to Aladár Szegedy-Maszák, 22 September 1952 [?], Imre Kovács Papers, Bakhmeteff Archive, Box 7.

42 Funeral oration by Andrea-Leslie Kovacs, 30–31 October 1980, published in Molnár, *Egy Homo Politicus*, 298.

43 Pál Ignotus to Imre Kovács, London, 21 March 1957, Imre Kovács Papers, Bakhmeteff Archive, Box 3.

44 Dezső Sulyok to Imre Kovács, 27 October 1951, Imre Kovács Papers, Bakhmeteff Archive, Box 7.

45 Imre Kovács to Dezső Sulyok, Cambridge, [Mass.], 12 November 1951, Imre Kovács Papers, Bakhmeteff Archive, Box 7.

46 István Csorba-Mikita to Imre Kovács, 10 February 1957, Imre Kovács Papers, Bakhmeteff Archive, Box 2.

47 Imre Szélig, Social Democratic Party of Hungary in Exile, to Imre Kovács, London, 10 April 1958, Imre Kovács Papers, Bakhmeteff Archive, Box 7.

48 Molnár, *Egy Homo Politicus*, 275.

49 Gyula Borbándi, *A magyar emigráció életrajza 1945–1985* [The Biography of Hungarian Emigration, 1945–1985] (Bern: Európai Protestáns Magyar Szabadegyetem, 1985), 296.

50 Imre Kovács, International Center for Social Research, Inc., to unknown, 30 May 1962; Imre Kovács, International Center for Social Research, Inc., to unknown, 17 July 1962, Imre Kovács Papers, Bakhmeteff Archive, Box 4.

51 Molnár, *Egy Homo Politicus*, 276; Tóth, "Kovács Imre az emigrációban", 187–188.

52 Imre Kovács to Mucio Delgado, 11 February 1959, Imre Kovács Papers, Bakhmeteff Archive, Box 2. English original.

53 Imre Kovács to Mucio Delgado, 4 June 1959, Imre Kovács Papers, Bakhmeteff Archive, Box 2. English original.

54 Molnár, *Egy Homo Politicus*, 276-277.

55 Pál Ignotus to Imre Kovács, 1 April 1957, Imre Kovács Papers, Bakhmeteff Archive, Box 3, quoted by Pál Tóth, "Kovács Imre az emigrációban", 189.

56 Aladár Szegedy-Maszák to Imre Kovács, 25 May 1978, Imre Kovács Papers, Bakhmeteff Archive, Box 7.

57 Imre Kovács to the Hungarian Writers Association Abroad, 3 April 1958, Imre Kovács Papers, Bakhmeteff Archive, Box 4.

58 Americanus [Imre Kovács], "Reális emigráció" [Realistic emigration], MS, Imre Kovács Papers, Bakhmeteff Archive, Box 15.

Select Bibliography

Imre Kovács Papers, Bakhmeteff Archive, Rare Book and Manuscript Library, Butler Library, Columbia University Libraries, New York, NY.

Borbándi, Gyula. *A magyar emigráció életrajza 1945–1985*. [The Biography of Hungarian Emigration, 1945–1985]. Bern: Európai Protestáns Magyar Szabadegyetem, 1985.

Huszár, Tibor. *Találkozások. Beszélgetések a két világháború közötti magyar szellemi-politikai mozgalmakról.* [Encounters: Discussions on interwar Hungarian intellectual-political movements]. (Budapest: Corvina, 2005).

Kádár Lynn, Katalin. *Tibor Eckhardt: His American Years 1941–1972*. Boulder: East European Monographs, 2007.

Kovács, Imre. *A néma forradalom.* [The Silent Revolution]. Budapest: Cserépfalvi, [1937].

Kovács, Imre. *A kivándorlás* [Emigration]. Budapest: Cserépfalvi, 1938.

Kovács, Imre. *Tanulmányok 1935–1947*. [Studies 1935–1947]. Budapest: Magyar Napló, 2003.

Kovács, Imre. *Virtuális Magyarország. Politikai írások 1948–1980*. [Virtual Hungary. Political Writings 1948–1980]. Budapest: Magyar Napló, 2005.

Molnár, M. Eszter. *Egy Homo Politicus itthon, Európában és Amerikában. Kovács Imre élete és munkássága* [A *Homo Politicus* at Home, in Europe, and in America. The Life and Work of Imre Kovács]. Budapest: Hét Krajcár Kiadó, 2010.

Tóth, Pál Péter. "Kovács Imre az emigrációban [Imre Kovács in Emigration]." In: *Magyarságkutatás. A Magyarságkutató Intézet évkönyve* (Budapest: Magyarságkutató Intézet, 1989.

Notes

All the sources have been translated by the present author from the Hungarian original, except where otherwise indicated.

VII

The Schism within the Polish Delegation to the Assembly of Captive European Nations 1954–1972[1]

Anna Mazurkiewicz

Divisions, disagreements, bitter arguments among émigrés are as old as the history of emigration itself. Stefan Korboński, the most influential Polish representative in the Assembly of Captive European Nations (ACEN), pointed out in the third volume of his memoirs: "Essentially, emigration is a quarrel itself; it is a disagreement with the everyday reality of the home country, which is the mother of all emigration."[2] John F. Leich, who worked for over a decade for the Exile Relations Division of the National Committee for a Free Europe (NCFE), wrote in his recollections: "Political exile is a *sui generis* condition, with its attendant frustrations, problems and discouragements. In the absence of an electoral mandate, the political exile can only emphasize his differences with fellow exiles; and he begins to see victory in terms of favors or concessions he has extracted from the protecting power."[3]

The aim of this chapter is to put the uneasy experience of the post World War II political exiles from Poland into the multiethnic context of the Assembly of Captive European Nations. The ACEN was an umbrella organization of Eastern European émigré organizations, officially established on 20 September 1954, under the aegis of the National Committee for a Free Europe in New York.[4] It was comprised of nine national delegations of councils and committees formed in exile. Each national group assigned 16 people to the ACEN to form a single delegation within it – each, that is, except for Poles.

Since the ACEN's inception there were two Polish delegations, each consisting of eight delegates. One, headed by former Polish Prime Minister Stanisław Mikołajczyk, represented the Polish National Democratic Committee, whose delegation was presided over by Karol Popiel; the other spoke on behalf of the London-based Provisional Council of National Unity, which opened its chapter in New York on 11 December 1955. The latter was headed by Otton Pehr, and its delegation to the ACEN was presided over by Stefan Korboński. This duality reflected the divisions among the Polish exiles. However, it did not reflect the American intentions that lay behind the creation of the ACEN.

The second aim of this chapter is to put the interethnic cooperation of Eastern Europeans into the context of American support and control, which was exercised by the National Committee for a Free Europe. The NCFE repeatedly insisted that the Poles unite and form one delegation. Korboński, acting on behalf of the Polish Council of National Unity, unwearyingly attempted to form such a delegation, preferably without Popiel's group representing the Polish National Democratic Committee, which tried to use matching tactics, but in reverse.

What were the reasons for this unbridgeable cleavage? What were the main lines of division among Poles? Did the outside pressure foster any compromise? How did the Polish delegation to the ACEN change from 1954 to 1972? Why did the American sponsors eventually give in to the dual representation of Poles? What consequence did this dichotomy have on Polish effectiveness within the ACEN? How did the other national delegations respond to the Polish divide?

In order to answer these and other pertinent questions one must take a closer look at the system of national councils and committees that was created under the aegis of the NCFE.

The U.S. government was the unofficial creator of the NCFE, for it provided it with opportunities to control and accommodate the various exiled political leaders from Eastern Europe; to employ their potential in a variety of research and propaganda projects; to obtain knowledge regarding Communism, which the exiles were eager to share and which also included sharing intelligence contacts with their respective homelands; and finally, to support them financially.

A typical national council (or committee) consisted of 10 to 15 people – mostly former democratic parties' leaders, members of parliaments, ministers, ex-ambassadors, jurists, journalists, et al. It usually employed a small staff, either in New York or in Washington, D.C. Some had offices or representatives in other counties, occasionally also supported by the NCFE. Any given national council or committee in exile strived to act as a legitimate representation of its respective nation, lobbying the U.S. and international authorities for the restoration of freedom in its homeland. In addition, it served as an information center, usually published a bulletin or a newsletter, and tried to promote its case with both the American and international press. Moreover, the committees and councils that were recognized and supported by the NFCE also served as a particular gateway through which to channel various appeals by the newly emerging exile or ethnic political groups. Once a committee/council was in place, exiles' requests for support (political, financial or both) were directed to their respective organizations, which usually were already a cluster of political or social groups.

Within five years it turned out that cooperation with a number of national committees/councils was difficult, for each had to be dealt with individually, and each pressed its own national agenda. Moreover, internal squabbles within and between the various representations were brought to the NCFE, with each splinter group seeking its support and attention. Most importantly however, in the early 1950s the East Central Europeans began their own interethnic cooperation outside of the framework provided by the NCFE, thus slipping out of its control. Both Korboński and Stanisław Mikołajczyk played important but quite separate roles in this process.

It is therefore important, prior to discussing the topic of cooperation within the ACEN, to briefly characterize Polish post World War II political emigration. First, it must be said that by 1950 it was already deeply divided. The deepest cleavage was caused by former Polish Prime Minister Mikołajczyk's decision to return to Poland in June 1945 in order to accept the posts of vice premier and minister of agriculture in a coalition government created on the basis of the agreement reached by the Big Three at the Yalta Conference in February 1945.[5] When they became public, the Polish government-in-exile immediately repudiated the decisions regarding Poland made at Yalta. Both the prime minister, Tomasz Arciszewski, and many of his political adversaries shared the belief that any form of cooperation with the Communists meant a betrayal of the Polish *raison d'état*.[6]

This cleavage was soon deepened by the conflict that arose on the grounds of presidential succession in exile. Shortly before his death in June 1947, Polish President-in-exile Władysław Raczkiewicz decided to change his earlier decision regarding who should replace him (a provision in the Polish constitution of 1935 gave him the right to do so). However, under the terms of the so-called "Paris agreement" of late September 1939, he should have consulted the political groups prior to changing his designee. He failed to do so. As a result, when August Zaleski took office as the Polish president-in-exile, major groups of the Polish political emigration withdrew their support.[7] The Polish émigrés were now split three ways. By the late 1940s, ideological differences, political disputes and personal disagreements were rife in London, Paris, New York, Washington, D.C. and other places where Polish political exiles were active.

Meanwhile, on 5 February 1947, after fraudulent elections were held, Bolesław Bierut became president of Poland, thus formally completing the Communist conquest. By the end of that year, political persecution had reached such a level that the only way to guarantee security to dissenters was for them to leave the country. Such was the case for Mikołajczyk, who – with American help – secretly left Poland in October, leaving behind many of his friends and colleagues from the Polish Peasant Party (PSL). Soon thereafter, other leaders of the opposition, including Korboński and his wife Zofia, also managed to escape the country.[8]

Once in exile, both Mikołajczyk and Korboński chose to settle in the United States, for they shared not only good contacts with former American Ambassador to Poland Arthur Bliss Lane but also the view that the post-war power center would shift from Europe to overseas, which was where they hoped to lobby for help for their homeland. However, they found themselves on opposite sides in the dynamic struggle for influence over the largest Eastern European ethnic group. The major difference in their political outlook was regarding the constitutionality of the Polish government-in-exile. Already in 1948 Mikołajczyk planned to establish a Polish national committee in the U.S.[9]

Faced with the establishment of the NCFE, the Polish exiles in London and the U.S. resumed talks on unification. In a detailed account of the political developments among the Polish émigrés, Andrzej Friszke mentioned discussions between the representative of the Polish government-in-exile in the U.S., Jan Wszelaki, and Free Europe's representatives.[10] Based on correspondence held in the Polish Institute and Sikorski Museum in London, the Polish historian assumed that the Americans were willing to offer three quarters of their support to a council composed of the major political parties (PPS, SN, NiD and SP), should one be formed, leaving one quarter for Mikołajczyk's PSL.[11] From the very beginning, the Polish exiles had no illusions that the NCFE's offers included both groups.

By the end of 1940s, Korboński and Kazimierz Bagiński of the PSL had decided to join the Polish Political Council,[12] created in London in opposition to President Zaleski. It was headed by Mikołajczyk's antagonist Arciszewski, who believed the Yalta decisions should be renounced. Consequently, acting in his capacity of the head of the PSL, Mikołajczyk ousted Korboński and other dissenters from the Peasant Party in January 1950.

When the Political Council (PPC) opened its U.S. chapter in March 1950, Korboński was selected to chair it. This new organization was sometimes referred to as the "English Committee" by the NCFE.[13]

In response, Mikołajczyk's rival political group created the Polish National Democratic Committee (PNDC) in May 1950. The PSL leader became its president, and Popiel (Christian Labor Party, SP) became chairman of the executive board.[14] The PNDC cooperated closely with international party organizations, chiefly due to Mikołajczyk's leadership of the International Peasant Union and Konrad Sieniewicz's active role in the Christian Democratic Union of Central and Eastern Europe (CDUCEE).[15] It was to Mikołajczyk's advantage, in addition to having its headquarters located in the United States, that this organization had no links to the exiled Polish government – recognition of which by the Americans was out of question. Therefore, this group, already involved in the work of the internationals, must have seemed to the Americans to be more flexible and open to cooperation.

However, the support that the Political Council was winning among the émigrés and the opportunities to influence a wider Polish diaspora worked to the advantage of Mikołajczyk's adversaries. The ensuing disagreements between the leaders of the two groups, of both a political and a personal nature, were extremely hard to bridge and grew even more bitter as the years went by. However, from the American point of view, Mikołajczyk and Korboński were the two men who were crucial to the effort to create a single Polish delegation to deal with.

Already in May 1951, the NCFE prepared a plan for the organization of a Polish Council of National Unity to fit into the framework of national committees and councils that was already in existence. As worded in the plan's outline, this new, united Polish organization was to serve as a "symbol of national unity, a forum for discussion of psy warfare and cold war problems. It would neither be competent nor would it be permitted to discuss post-liberation of polish gov'tal problems ... it would [also] be of great assistance to the NCFE as a symbol and source of names and ideas."[16] Interestingly, according to the plan, the proposed formation of the Council of National Unity in effect would mean "the reunion of the two important factions in the Polish Peasant Party, and as such would make possible for the PSL to participate in resistance activity from which it is now excluded because of the split between Mikołajczyk and Korboński."[17]

In short, the NCFE's idea was to incorporate the representatives of both the PNDC and the Political Council in the proposed Council of National Unity. Furthermore, the American plan encompassed some of the Polish exile leaders from London, such as some of the members of the government-in-exile,[18] military personalities,[19] and prominent individuals,[20] most notably, Count Edward Raczyński. At no point did the plan include recognition of the Polish government-in-exile or include the president-in-exile. While drafting the plan for the Council of National Unity, the Americans were aware of the ongoing unification efforts already underway in London. Regarding as possible the merger between the Political Council and the government-in-exile's National Council,[21] the NCFE was careful not to produce an impression that "the proposal for the formation of a Council for National Unity was only for the purpose of assuring the participation of the Mikołajczyk faction in a unified exile [organization]."[22] The Americans realized that despite the unification efforts in London, a voluntary reconciliation was simply impossible between the Yalta-supportive Mikołajczyk and the government-in-exile (international recognition of which was withdrawn as a result of Mikołajczyk's return to Poland in the summer of 1945). Therefore, they planned to create an attractive alternative for Poles in the U.S., where money and the political benefit of having Free Europe's backing were on hand.

Based on Friszke's research in the London archives, one must conclude that not only was the Polish government-in-exile not willing to give in to American pressure to support the creation of a united Polish committee in the U.S. but, even more importantly, the Americans also were not interested in helping the PPC reach a compromise with the government. For the NCFE, the consolidation of Poles simply meant the Political Council's merger with Mikołajczyk.[23]

Why didn't the NCFE simply choose one of the Polish splinter organizations? It is crucial to note that at this point the Americans from the NCFE seriously considered granting their full support to the London Political Council. However, in their opinion, expressed in the document quoted above, it would bring

> ... political difficulties in the United States due to the prestige of Mikołajczyk and would also alienate the Polish military to the point that they might confuse and obstruct psychological warfare

> and other activities. … If full support were eventually given to Polish Council, especially as in the revised form of a National Council including the government-in-exile personalities, this must be with the full understanding of the difficulties which will be inherent with any dealings with such a National Council. This would be an organization to whose advantage it would be to make insistent demands on the Western nations for nationalistic Polish aims which may be in conflict with the policies of the Western powers. Having certain aspects of a legal Polish government, and having its seat in a foreign country, this National Council would probably be the most difficult of any with which the American authorities have to deal. The [proposed] Council of National Unity on the other hand, would be a purely symbolic organization which, because of its composition from three political centers, would have little likelihood of agreeing on a common policy differing from the general Western policy.[24]

One possible interpretation of this statement is that the NCFE was not interested in assisting in the creation of one, centralized locus of Polish political emigration, if it was not able to exercise control over it. The prerequisites of this hesitance were most likely the result of the then three-month-old experience with exiles' attempts to form an independent, multiethnic lobby.

The idea of acting in concert with the representatives of other national committees/councils was sparked by the NCFE initiative of holding a signing of the "Declaration of the Aims and Principles of Liberation of the Central and Eastern European Peoples" in Philadelphia's Independence Hall.[25] The various émigrés and exile groups from Eastern Europe were invited to sign. However, the unfortunate date chosen for the ceremony (11 February 1951) marked the sixth anniversary of Yalta. Furthermore, the rather hectic way in which the delegates of the committees and councils were invited sowed serious doubts among the Eastern European exiles. Given that Mikołajczyk and Popiel signed the so-called Philadelphia Declaration, the Political Council's representatives eventually decided not to give in to the NCFE's request.

The reasons for declining the invitation to sign the Philadelphia Declaration, as listed by Korboński in a letter to NCFE President C.D. Jackson, were multiple. First, among those invited were both the persecuted victims of Communism and former voluntary supporters of the regime. Second, the organizers ascribed no criminal status to Communist organizations, thus adopting the principle of personal responsibility for specific crimes rather than condemning Communism in the Nuremberg style. Third, the Polish Political Council's representative in the U.S. argued that they were not advised, much less consulted, regarding the text, the names of the speakers, or the program of the Philadelphia ceremony. Furthermore, they believed that the timing of the ceremony was unfortunate, not only due to the Yalta anniversary but also because no liberation policy had yet been proclaimed by the U.S. government. The Political Council's representatives in America disagreed with the Philadelphia Declaration's dominant assertion that the Communist system would collapse from within. Among the issues that were missing from the declaration, the objecting Polish group listed any reference to or mention of: the "gloomy anniversary of Yalta", the return of the lands grabbed by Russia, persecution of the church and religion, Polish fear of German militarism.[26]

This negative response on the part of some of the Eastern European émigrés came at the moment when the NCFE, disenchanted with the uneasy relations it had with the quarrelsome national committees and councils, was tending to shift its cooperation with the exiles to so-called consultative panels. Such issue-oriented, fact-finding and advisory bodies, composed of individual exiles rather than of their national organizations, still provided the NCFE's intellectual sponsors at the State Department with opportunities to use them as a means to legitimize American Cold War policy.[27]

Not surprisingly, such a role was not satisfactory to the majority of exiles, most of whom firmly believed they were the representative voice of the silenced peoples in their respective homelands. As a result, instead of displaying exile solidarity under the aegis of the NCFE in Philadelphia, Korboński's rejection inspired other national councils and committees to take action in order not to be treated like regular employees of the NCFE. Soon thereafter, the Hungarians (Béla Varga), Romanians (Constantin Vişoianu) and members of the Czechoslovak Council (Vaclav Májer, Jozef Lettrich, Juraj Slávik, Adolf Procházka) contacted Korboński, and together they came up with the idea of creating a powerful, multiethnic coalition, thus strengthening its voice and position in the U.S.

The initial meeting of the Central and Eastern European Conference (CEEConf.) was called in March 1951 in Washington, D.C.[28] In regards to the presence of the Polish delegates, Korboński invited both the London government-in-exile's representative and Mikołajczyk to join in. However, Korboński must have been aware that the two men would not stand next to one another in the same room. Therefore, even this multiethnic initiative ended with two separate exile organizations. The creation of the CEEConf. was soon followed by the establishment of the Central–Eastern European Committee. In contrast to the earlier "Washington Conference", this new body was more than occasionally referred to by its adversaries as a "Committee of the Primadonnas". This derogatory term referred to the leaders of this committee – Ferenc Nagy (chairman), Mikołajczyk, and George M. Dimitrov (Gemeto) – powerful individuals, linked not only by their peasant affiliation with IPU but also by their conviction that they must have the dominant role within any new organization.[29]

Both organizations had similar goals: to lobby the U.S. government and Congress, coordinate their own activities for promoting the liberation of their homelands, advise the NCFE and influence Radio Free Europe, which was then just taking its first steps.[30] It is important to observe that in both of the abovementioned multiethnic organizations the Polish leaders assumed important, stimulating roles. Their emergence caused not only confusion among the public but also a problem for the NCFE, which felt that the exiles were slipping out of control.

The Polish émigrés who did not form a single Council could not simply have been left out, mainly due to two factors: the geopolitical importance of Poland within the Soviet bloc in Eastern Europe, and the size of the Polish-American community in the United States.[31] The Polish exiles' military and political record during World War II and the fact that all of the major pre-war political parties were represented in exile were also significant factors in American hesitance to leave the Poles outside of the NCFE programs.[32] The Polish exiles were aware of their special position but also of the fact that due to their inability to unite, they were losing influence over the radio broadcasts and other publicity programs run by Radio Free Europe. Given the changes in NCFE exile programs, absent any sort of agreement they would likely be deprived of American financial means to continue their council's/committee's operations as well. Therefore, provided they kept their political integrity, i.e., were not forced to join together within one organization, they were ready to consider American proposals for cooperation.[33]

The creation of two rival, multiethnic, exile organizations, the members of which were mostly NCFE's stipend recipients but were not officially affiliated with it, was most likely what pushed the Americans to design the plan for the creation of the ACEN – the Assembly of Captive European Nations. Not only did that provide the NCFE with a means of taking over the conference and committee but for Poles it could also have provided a framework comfortable enough to accommodate both groups, the PNDC and the representatives of London's Political Council in America. The latter, however, proved to be a futile hope.

Apart from the trouble in creating the Polish delegation, some other Eastern European committees/councils created in exile were left outside the ACEN, for example: the Croatian National Representation, the Slovenian National Committee, the Serbian Central National Committee, the Slovak National Council Abroad and many others. Some of these organizations were excluded based on the assumption that they represented separatist, nationalistic organizations.[34] Others were left out due to the U.S. policy of not supporting nations of the USSR that were not independent at the time of the outbreak of World War II – most importantly, the Ukrainians. The particulars of American policy towards the German Democratic Republic and Yugoslavia (since Tito's 1948 split with the Kremlin) also prevented their respective representations abroad from joining the structures of the ACEN. On the other hand, representatives of various political internationals were allowed to participate in the work of the Assembly and were granted consultative status.

All in all, due to decisions made by the State Department nine national representations were selected to create the ACEN: the National Democratic Committee for a Free Albania (est. 1949), the Bulgarian National Committee (est. 1945), the Council of Free Czechoslovakia (est. 1948, and since 1967 the Committee for a Free Czechoslovakia), the Committee for a Free Estonia (est. 1951), the Committee for a Free Latvia (est. 1951), the Committee for a Free Lithuania (est. 1951), the Hungarian National Council (est. 1947, and since 1958 the Hungarian Committee), and the Romanian National Committee (est. 1949). As mentioned above, the Polish delegation was comprised of representatives of the Polish Political Council and the Polish National Democratic Committee.

In sum, while all other national groups in the ACEN had one committee or council to represent them in contacts with both the NCFE and the wider world, the Poles had both a committee and a council. Both organizations hoped to gain American recognition as a national representation in exile. Both groups approached Department of State officials, congress members and journalists. Both strived to exercise influence over the FEC's programs in Europe and in the U.S.

However, by the time the ACEN was about to start its operations, the already dynamic political situation regarding Mikołajczyk's and Korboński's groups had changed significantly. In order to understand the reorganization of the Polish émigré groups in the U.S., one must briefly examine the changes that occurred in London in 1954, as they affected both the future of the Political Council's Working Committee in the U.S. and the PNDC.

The creation of a unified political center in London was crucial for the Polish exiles for a number of reasons, most importantly to maintain prestige and legitimacy by showing their compatriots both at home and abroad that the political infighting that marred the history of Poland's Second Republic was not repeated in exile. Therefore a number of initiatives were undertaken during the early 1950s, with Gen. Kazimierz

Sosnkowski's possibly being the one that came closest to success.[35] In response to the general's mediations and faced with a "threat" of the Americans creating a subordinate committee, a substantial majority of Polish political exiles decided to sign the Act of National Unity. Pending President Zaleski's resignation, Gen. Władysław Anders, Arciszewski and Edward Raczyński created the "Council of Three" to take on his presidential prerogatives. On 31 July 1954 a Provisional Council of National Unity was established, which was meant to serve mainly as a consultative body. It was composed of the former Political Council, the Independent Social Group, the League for Poland's Independence, the Christian Democratic Party's fraction, and representatives of social and veterans' associations. It was headed by Tadeusz Bielecki (National Democrat).[36] Soon, it became obvious that not only would one find Mikołajczyk outside of the PCNU but in addition the merger with the supporters of the Polish president-in-exile would not be forthcoming. Due to president Zaleski's decision to remain in office, despite previous promises to step down for the sake of unity, any compromise with the pro-Zaleski "Castle" group was no longer possible. As the quarrels went on in London, the ACEN was already working in New York. However, its Polish delegation was not immune to the European developments.

The ACEN's Rules of Procedure, adopted on 20 September 1954, provided for equal representation of all national councils/committees, each of which was allotted 16 seats, with one chairman usually representing it in the General Committee. The Polish delegation was no different, in that it, too, had 16 seats in the ACEN. Therefore, due to a compromise reached in 1954, both the Political Council and the PNDC had eight seats to fill. However, no single chairman was selected. Both Korboński and Popiel participated in the General Committee's meetings (having only one vote of the Polish delegation on hand), and representatives of both groups were represented in the working committees of the ACEN.[37]

Due to unification efforts in London, by the end of 1954, the Democratic Party left the PNDC and joined the new London-based PCNU. As a result, the Democratic Party representatives in the U.S. (Stanisław

Olszewski and Feliks Gadomski, who thus far had worked in the ACEN as part of the Mikołajczyk-Popiel PNDC delegation) informed the chairman of the Assembly that they'd decided to join Korboński's group, acknowledging his leadership of the Polish delegation.[38] Mikołajczyk's and Popiel's position was thus seriously weakened. Interestingly enough, nobody seemed to care that the Polish Political Council had been dissolved, and thus Korboński's delegation to the ACEN was not yet validated by a new organizational affiliation. As negotiations regarding the PCNU's admission to the ACEN went on, Korboński's group maintained the name Political Council, except that it was no longer addressed as a "Working Committee in the U.S."

On 11 February 1955 Mikołajczyk paid a visit to Lewis Galantiere,[39] Free Europe's influential political adviser, to try to counteract the weakening of the PNDC's position. In a memorandum written by Galantiere after the meeting, one finds a rather unfavorable evaluation of the Peasant Party leader:

> Mr. Mikołajczyk called on me on 11 February and talked almost without interruption for the better part of two hours. I am afraid that I do not always understand what he tells me, owing to his defective English and my hesitancy to ask too often that he repeat his words … . As already remarked, I took little occasion to interrupt; and when I did speak, no dialogue ensued; Mr. Mikołajczyk does not waste his time listening.[40]

During this meeting, the exiled Pole tried to explain the reasons why his adversaries from the Political Council did not sign the Philadelphia Declaration. Galantiere's understanding of Mikołajczyk's words was that "Korboński did not sign it because, on the IPU insistence, it [the declaration] called for free elections supervised by the UN. He [Mikołajczyk] seemed to intimate that PPC would want to rig elections in a liberated Poland." Furthermore, Mikołajczyk tried to convince Galantiere that the various internationals (such as IPU and CDUCEE) deserved full membership in the ACEN, as only they were the true democratic representation of the captive nations, in sharp contrast to the disunited and often reactionary national councils.[41] Naturally, if the internationals' position had been equal to that of the national councils, it would strengthen Mikołajczyk's and Sieniewicz's positions within the Assembly.

Moreover, Mikołajczyk had to face opposition within his own Peasant Party, caused by his "dictatorial style", uneasiness about the lack of financial reporting and decreasing international influence.[42] In March 1955 he'd decided to remove Stanisław Bańczyk, Stanisław Wójcik and Władysław Zaremba from the PSL. As a result, the three expelled leaders orchestrated an opposition group within the party and proclaimed that the PSL had left the PNDC. Furthermore, in April, they informed the General Committee of the ACEN that the PNDC had ceased to exist due to the exodus of its member parties. Formerly representing the PNDC in the ACEN, Wójcik (who was serving as Popiel's alternate), together with Bańczyk and Zaremba announced their decision to continue their work independently within the ACEN.[43]

Popiel and Mikołajczyk decided to ignore the departing individuals and went on to submit the names of eight delegates to the ACEN on behalf of the PNDC. Rejecting claims that the Committee had ceased to exist, in his speech to the ACEN's General Committee, K. Sieniewicz mentioned that actually it was the Political Council's mandates that had expired when that organization was dissolved. During his address, he presented the two Polish ACEN representations in terms of black and white. His – namely the PNDC's – group was the representative of peasant and Christian-democratic parties, whereas the Political Council represented the nationalist and socialist groups in exile. According to Sieniewicz, the ACEN's rules provided accreditation for two organizations and not individuals or parties. Therefore, he suggested that the General Committee of the ACEN maintain the unchanged composition of the Polish delegation: equal distribution of seats between the PNDC and the Political Council.[44] However, due to the significant strengthening of Korobоński's position, this soon proved to be a short-lived solution.

On 16 May 1955, Korboński called a meeting of all Polish delegates to discuss the possibility of creating one common delegation. However,

Popiel and Sieniewicz failed to show up, protesting the ACEN's disregard of the new nominations of PNDC delegates submitted a month earlier. Those who did come, either in person or by proxy, by a 13:1 vote chose Korboński to head the Polish delegation to the ACEN.[45] Popiel and Sieniewicz vigorously protested this ACEN-supported attempt to merge their groups into the Political Council and leave Mikołajczyk and his supporters outside of the Polish delegation.[46]

The General Committee of the ACEN did not want to make changes among the persons in the Polish delegation during its current session (sessions began each year in September) but was forced to take a stand. In order to prevent taking an arbitrary decision, the General Committee agreed to call a meeting of both Polish groups, which was scheduled for 23 May 1955. The PNDC was represented by Mikołajczyk and Tadeusz Paul, the Political Council by Korboński and Andrzej Pomian. The memorandum written after the meeting contains, for the first time, an account of the actual, political differences between the two groups. By then, neither the issues regarding the post-Yalta Polish borders, nor the Western economic help to Poland were as divisive as the attitude towards post-war Germany.[47] According to this document, Korboński staunchly objected to sending any Polish delegates to the ACEN's office in Bonn. It was his firm belief that the Polish emigration should have no official business in Germany. Interestingly, no distinction was made between the GDR and FRG.[48] In response, Mikołajczyk stated that such an attitude would push Germany towards the East and it was in the best Polish interest to keep Germany West-oriented. The meeting concluded with no compromise, Korboński stating that he must refer to London for advice.[49]

The fear of the rebirth of a powerful, militarized Germany posed a greater problem than just differences in opinion between the two groups. The Korboński group's opinions were not in concurrence with the general American policy towards the FRG. It seems that underlining their uncompromising position was a way for Mikołajczyk's faction to weaken the Council's stand with the FEC. One must keep in mind that it was the time when negotiations on the London PCNU's admission to ACEN were underway. Being aware of this process, Popiel supposed that among the conditions stated by the PCNU was elimination of the PNDC, and thus creation of a single Polish delegation and the complete removal of the internationals from the ACEN.[50] In a letter addressed to Vilis Māsēns, Popiel demanded that the General Committee made a decision on the member organizations' rights to replace their delegates during the ongoing session.[51] In his case, it would mean getting rid of Wójcik, Bańczyk, Zaremba, Olszewski and Gadomski. He was not successful in replacing any delegates within the Polish delegation and failed to interfere with the negotiations between the ACEN's General Committee and London's PCNU.

Already in March 1955, the Assembly's chairman, Vilis Māsēns, had discussed the terms of the Council of Unity's access during his visit to London. The PCNU designated the following representatives to carry on the negotiations: Adam Ciołkosz, Zbigniew Stypułkowski (both from London) and Korboński, Pehr and Bolesław Wierzbiański from the United States[52]. The PCNU's conditions, as listed in the minutes of a meeting held on 13 September 1955, included four points: 1. The ACEN should strive to include the Yugoslav delegation in its membership; 2. new organizations should not be admitted to the ACEN without the unanimous consent of all members; 3. matters of crucial importance to a given national delegation should not be posted to the General Committee's agenda without the consent of that delegation; 4. The ACEN should refrain from actions that may incite premature, active resistance among their countrymen behind the Iron Curtain.[53] This unofficial record of talks that took place in New York was not repeated in the PCNU's formal application for membership. That document of 19 September 1955 related strictly to the composition of the Polish delegation. Among the conditions listed there, the London PCNU called for the members of the Polish delegation to the ACEN to get the approval of the Executive Committee of the PCNU. Interestingly enough, by the "Polish delegation" they meant the delegates who had supported Korboński. Second, they pledged to set aside a pre-determined quantity of the Polish seats within the ACEN for the "parties or factions which remain outside of the PCNU". They proposed that the number of these seats should be fixed based on the *de facto* situation at the close of the previous session.[54] In practice, it meant that the PCNU would get 11 out of 16 seats assigned to Poles in the ACEN, leaving the remaining 5 vacant.

Two days later, a crucial resolution was adopted by the ACEN General Committee. Based on the fact that the efforts of both the Poles and the ACEN General Committee "equally failed" and "deserving to have one Polish delegation for each nation", the General Committee decided as follows:

> 1. that the PCNU is succeeding the Polish Political Council as a member of the Assembly;
> 2. that the Polish national representation in the ACEN shall be composed of: PCNU and PNDC;
> 3. that the PCNU shall appoint 11 members and the PNDC shall appoint 5 members of the Polish delegation;
> 4. that the Polish delegation shall be considered as a single unit and have one chairman and one representative in the General Committee.[55]

There was also a "friendly suggestion" added as point 2 to the resolution "that the PNDC be enabled to appoint the alternate Polish delegate to the General Committee". As a result, the PNDC was deprived of any real influence over Polish- and general matters in the ACEN.

Many protests flooded Māsēns desk in an angry reaction by the PNDC, which for the next few years continued to threaten its departure from the ACEN.[56] It is interesting, however, to look at the American reaction to this decision.

On 11 October 1955, Ciołkosz, Stypułkowski and Wierzbiański went to see Galantiere. They informed him of the new developments regarding the Polish delegation to the ACEN, mentioning that Mikołajczyk's continuing role in the Assembly was guaranteed by the fact that he was the president of the IPU. However, they did not waste the opportunity to criticize their political opponent by stating that the dominant trend within the Polish emigration was to turn away from the "isolated" former prime minister and join with the PCNU. Furthermore, they announced that by 8 November the American branch of the Council of National Unity would be created.

In a memorandum written after the meeting, Galantiere offered his interpretation of the new development regarding the Polish exiles:

> I believe the council [PCNU] has a strong case for "recognition" by FEC. It is certainly more broadly representative of its Emigration than any council or committee now recognized by FEC. It possesses an authority over the Emigration incomparably greater than that of any other exile body. The proof is that in our political warfare work we have had to take account of Polish political views to an extent unduplicated in any other emigration – and this as a matter of practice, not of premeditation. I recognize the strength of Mr. Mikołajczyk's personality and the likelihood that he is still more influential at home than any Pole in exile, except probably gen. Anders; but I am also obliged to recognize that Mikołajczyk has, however, admirable reasons of principle, refused to yield a jot in the cause of cooperation and coalition. If there are political (not moral) arguments in his favor on this score, I do not know them. I ask only that there ought to be some way to deal formally with the Council and to support Mr. Mikołajczyk at the same time.[57]

From a more pragmatic point of view, Galantiere went on to observe:

> I must point out that the announcement of "recognition" of the council, coming at this time, would constitute a triumphant retort to a regime in Poland which is funding its re-defection campaign on the argument that the west is not interested in the emigration and therefore émigrés ought to go home we need to bear in mind that the re-defection campaign is a proof that Warsaw regime takes the emigration much more seriously than we could have supposed. Since the chief purpose of that campaign is to destroy the exile organiza-

> tions and their influence on public opinion, both in Poland and in the west, our efforts must be directed to demonstrating unmistakably that the enemy has failed in this task.[58]

The PCNU (most commonly referred to by the Americans as the Polish Council of National Unity) won its place within the ACEN. Its American chapter was opened on 11 December 1955. When it was finally created, it was presided over by Otton Pehr. Given Korboński's role as the new head of the Polish delegation to the ACEN, as well as his aptitude, his well established contacts both with prominent Americans and the Polish-American community and his fluent English, not surprisingly he remained the major partner to discuss the Polish council's future cooperation with the FEC.

However, at about the same time, James McCargar, European Director for Political Programs at Free Europe Exile Relations (1955–1958),[59] warned John F. Leich of the Exile Relations Division that Korboński "has adopted an obstructionist and frustrating attitude with respect to a number of recent events and developments in which our interest has been manifest."[60] As an example, McCargar listed the "shocking arrogance" displayed by Korboński's threat of a walk-out should Mikołajczyk participate in the meeting with the Secretary of State. The Free Europe executive obviously considered Mikołajczyk important because of his position as the head of IPU. In addition he mentioned Korboński's "obdurate refusal" to permit international organizations to appear on telegrams addressed to prominent European politicians and his "singlehanded obstruction" (shown in the ACEN's General Committee) of a request by the Assembly's chairman for the representatives of the internationals to sign public documents and participate in ceremonial visits. Furthermore, McCargar held against Korboński his "singlehanded obstruction" of any General Committee discussion of a European activity that would include representatives in Germany. The list did not end there. McCargar condemned Korboński's "demand for special privileges of Poles in the Secretariat of the ACEN" and mentioned a hint ("information received") that the Polish delegation's chairman would oppose "the Czechoslovak solution" because of PCNU's position towards Mikołajczyk. By that he meant that the Polish leader was to reject a proposed compromise based on naming alternates from opposite groups to the posts of chairman and member in the General Committee, followed by rotation of these functions. The memorandum, aimed at persuading the PCNU to "adopt more reasonable and cooperative policies", ends with a recommendation: "I suggest that any interview which could at this time be interpreted by the Council of National Unity Poles as further evidence that their innate importance is such that the world cannot live without them, and that they are under no obligation to make any concessions whatsoever to our views on our common working problems would be most unfortunate."[61]

As it was preparing for talks with the PCNU's delegates in the ACEN, the FEC was deliberating on how to convince them of the importance of the internationals' presence within it, the IPU in particular. During the first meeting, FEC President Whitney Shepardson and McCargar wanted to make the PCNU delegates aware that they would support their projects on an equal basis with those of the PNDC. A second, lower level meeting with the Exile Relation's Bernard Yarrow and Leich was planned in order to discuss specific projects. At this point, the most important one was to counteract the Communist's repatriation campaign.[62]

McCargar's harsh criticism focusing on Korboński and Free Europe's staff's pressure on the PCNU's representatives in the U.S., overlooked the fact that the PCNU's ability to agree or disagree with the American proposals was limited by its dependence on London's decisions. A day after the abovementioned meetings took place, Korboński sent a telegram to the Council's Executive in London asking for an urgent opinion on the ACEN's European delegations, most importantly, in Bonn.[63] Suffice it to say that a Polish delegate was never sent to the ACEN's German bureau.

The outbreak of riots in Poznań by the end of June 1956 pumped new energy into the Polish infighting. Realizing that the workers' protests had to be publicized and that ACEN delegations should be dispatched to the foreign governments, the U.N. and the Council of Europe, Popiel intensified his efforts regarding the composition of the Polish delegation to the ACEN.[64] The timing was quite right, as the third session of the Assembly was about to open.

According to the memorandum written after the meeting between McCargar and Sieniewicz, the latter quoted Popiel: "Mikołajczyk is in the worst frame of mind since they'd started their cooperation in exile." The Peasant leader was said to be depressed by the fact that he had lost the FEC's support in both the IPU and the ACEN. Furthermore, he complained that all of his financial requests were rejected. In his comments directed to Yarrow, McCargar wrote after the meeting that most likely the Polish budget was withheld pending any agreement on cooperation between the two Polish groups.[65]

The PNDC came up with a compromise similar to the Czechoslovak solution. According to the Popiel–Mikołajczyk plan, the Polish delegation was to be composed of eight members of each group. The chairman of the Polish delegation was to be elected from the PNDC group (presumably Popiel), the Polish representative in the General Committee was to be named by the PCNU (most likely Korboński). Their respective alternates were supposed to be representatives of the opposite groups. This compromise pattern was also meant to be reversed at any time. All the ACEN's working committees and foreign offices were to be manned by representatives of both groups.[66] As this plan required significant concessions on the part of the PCNU, during the next two months no agreement was reached.

In November, Popiel's and Mikołajczyk's plan for compromise was rejected in an unpleasant manner. The ACEN's General Committee decided to uphold its earlier decision in favor of unequal distribution of seats in the Polish delegation. From the list of the eight PNDC delegates to the third session submitted by Popiel, the General Committee simply took the first five names, regardless of party membership, seniority or competence. Not surprisingly, Popiel and Mikołajczyk were furious and regarded this act as a reason to stop cooperating with the ACEN until their proposals for a compromise were given serious attention. By the end of January 1957, the PNDC had backed out of the ACEN, leaving the five allotted seats vacant.[67]

This did not mean that the Polish exile voice in the crucial matters pertaining to the new American policy towards Poland was now single. Even the formerly unanimous voice of the PNDC was now split. According to the documents found in the Polish IPN archive, the interpretation of the October reforms in Poland separated Mikołajczyk and Popiel. The former, together with Paul, now openly spoke against American economic assistance to Gomułka.[68]

On the other hand, one must keep in mind that after the bloody Soviet invasion in Hungary, the majority of the ACEN's General Committee was now wary of aiding any of the East European regimes. This attitude on the part of the ACEN's decisive body was questioned by the PCNU's delegates. Signing their memorandum as "the Polish Delegation to ACEN", they appealed to the General Committee for a more elastic approach to the changes occurring behind the Iron Curtain.[69] In doing so, they expressed views parallel to American foreign policy. At the same time, however, they also questioned the ACEN's hesitance to lobby the U.S. government for final recognition of the Polish–German border, despite the fact that the Oder–Neisse line did not pose a controversial territorial issue among its members. Interestingly enough, the aforementioned PCNU memorandum included a blackmail-like message: if ACEN was not helpful in defending Poland's interests, Polish membership in it might as well be useless.[70] The dominating stance and confidence on the part of the PCNU within ACEN were thus obvious.

The FEC also noticed the *de facto* emergence of a single delegation within ACEN. More importantly, its approach towards Gomulka's Poland, which was similar to the American policy lines, prompted Free Europe's Exile Relations Division to propose that beginning in August the PCNU be granted financial, office and technical assistance.[71]

Realizing their marginalization, and acting on behalf of the PNDC, Mikołajczyk and Popiel addressed the ACEN's General Committee, asking that it stop referring to the PCNU as the Polish delegation. They demanded that in all ACEN publications a proper identification be given.

Simultaneously they announced that they wouldn't be submitting any nominations for the five allotted seats until the ACEN reconsidered the composition of the Polish delegation to it.[72] During the next few years, their continued protests were mostly ignored.[73] The PNDC's situation was further weakened by the fact that in September 1958 Korboński was elected chairman of the ACEN.[74] The process of building a single, PCNU-based, Polish delegation in the ACEN seemed complete.

In the meantime, however, the character of the PCNU's representation in the ACEN changed again. Again it had to do with the delegation's ties to London. It was time to cut away from this dependence, which hindered the activities of the PCNU's representatives in the U.S.

As the PCNU's American chapter (which nominated the Polish delegates to the ACEN) formally operated as an organization representing a foreign body (London's PCNU), they had to be registered with the U.S. Department of Justice.[75] This caused the American PCNU significant inconvenience. As detailed by Gadomski in a letter addressed to Leich, they had to label their publications with information that they were foreign agents and fill out scores of complicated forms regarding their operations. Interestingly, Gadomski stated that the American branch received no money from London and no binding instructions, characterizing their link with the London council as being strictly ideological.[76] Due to its expiring registration period and the inconveniences it had caused the American branch of the PCNU, the leadership decided to change its name to the "Polish Council of Unity in the United States", and – at least ostensibly – to terminate its link with London. Pehr was named chairman; his alternates were Biega and Bohdan Gajewicz. Korboński remained a member of the Council and chairman of the Polish delegation to the ACEN.[77]

After the severance of this link, the PCNU in London planned to send their own representative, Stypułkowski, to the U.S. However, the FEC rejected its plea for financial support, realizing that it was still the same group. In a memorandum prepared by Leich, an American view of these developments was presented:

> Everyone is aware of Korboński's shortcomings as far as a certain lack of subtlety and depth of perception is concerned. Nevertheless, Korboński (with an able assist from Biega) has acquired excellent connections with Polish-American organizations, with Congressmen, and with the U.S. press. He is a liberal, has had intimate experience with post-war Poland, and is untainted by any suspicion of religious or racial prejudice. We are confident that Korboński is responsive to our [FEC's] suggestions. Stypułkowski is a conservative, the party he represents is vulnerable to the charge of anti-Semitism, he is responsive and essential to the general Raczyński-Anders system in London. Stypułkowski needs money, Korboński already has a stipend. Raczyński and Anders support Stypułkowski for the job. [78]

Leich's supervisor, Robert W. Minton, wrote on the document: "Agree: JFL's facts are seemingly correct but I think we should be careful not to interfere with the CNU's selection basing our position purely on the problem of additional support." However, money proved to be the single most convenient excuse. It is evident that despite the formal change in name and termination of links to London, the FEC still treated both groups as one entity.

The new decade, even before the change of administration in Washington, D.C., marked the first serious budgetary cuts in the exile activities run by the Exile Relations Division. While in 1960 the London PCNU received yearly support totaling $21,000,[79] five years later their stipend was reduced to $500 a month ($6000 a year).[80] The first argumentation for cuts that I have been able to find thus far comes from the record of talks held by Yarrow and Albert D. Kappel in December 1962. It was Kappel's recommendation to cut the subsidies "since it is obviously impossible for us to exercise intelligent control."[81] At the beginning of 1963, when the Council still received $1800 a month, London's West European Operations Division of the FEC informed the New York headquarters that the foreign support for the Council (without identifying the FEC as a sponsor) was raising public criticism.[82] These seemed to be the main arguments for phasing out the support for the London

Council and soon for the other exile activities run by the Exile Relations division of FEC. Naturally, as discussed in previous chapters, first and foremost it was the changes in U.S. foreign policy that influenced the FEC's budget allocations.

Regardless of the changes, the pattern of dealing with the Polish exiles in the U.S. remained unchanged: Mikołajczyk vs. the Council's supporters. Just how difficult it must have been to deal with the Polish exile leaders is best exemplified by the testimonies given before the Sub-Committee on Europe of the House Committee on Foreign Affairs in June 1962.[83] On 13 June, Mikołajczyk expressed his negative view of the U.S. Policy towards Poland and actually proposed an economic blockade against the entire Soviet bloc. On 29 June, Stypułkowski (PNCU London) was given, upon his request, a chance to express a dissenting voice and proclaimed that the Council was in favor of the American help to the Polish people. The latter one was naturally in line with the American policy. Not surprisingly, H. Dutton Lee of the East European Division in the State Department chose to pass only one statement, Stypułkowski's, on to the Associated Press.[84]

The John F. Kennedy administration's approach to Polish exile activities was a matter for detailed analysis conducted by Polish intelligence. According to its agents reporting from the U.S., the American government was not willing to support the belligerent rival groups. At the same time, the only reasonable argument that the Americans had in their dealings with the exiles – according to the Polish intelligence informants – was the money to support their activities.[85]

The beginning of the 1960s marked the last major effort on the part of the FEC (namely John Richardson), the ACEN (namely Nagy's negotiations) and Mikolajczyk to resume the talks on creation of a unified Polish delegation. According to accounts found in the Polish IPN archives, the leader of the PSL explained his attempt to resume his work within the ACEN as a reaction to counter Sanacja's influence over this organization.[86] In a letter sent to his friend from the IPU, Nagy, Mikołajczyk stated that the Poles in the ACEN were not truly representative of the nation's political life. Furthermore, he complained that in

1961 the ACEN had ceased to ask the PNDC for their nominations to the next session. As expected, he did not waste an opportunity to criticize Korboński's group.[87]

In reply, Nagy invited Mikołajczyk to a meeting of the ACEN's General Committee.[88] Since the talks on the Polish delegation in the ACEN were thus resumed, on 16 May 1962 Mikołajczyk presented the General Committee with his idea for reaching a compromise based on the return to the 8:8 ratio.[89] Interestingly, neither of the original Polish organizations represented in the ACEN in the 1950s was still in existence. Despite the fact that Mikołajczyk was still addressed as the president of the PNDC, the organization practically was no longer functioning.[90]

This last major attempt to unite and form a complete 16-person Polish delegation to the ACEN proved fruitless again. Based on the information he had on the talks between Korboński and Mikołajczyk, London's Raczyński rejected the IPU leader's proposal. As reported by Mucio F. Delgado (the FEC's program director) to Free Europe's president, the lack of compromise was a result of the "fundamental differences in political views, especially regarding the American economic assistance to Poland and Mikołajczyk's reduced influence in the Polish exile community." Raczyński was reported to have threatened the FEC representatives in the London WEOD office with the Council's withdrawal from the ACEN should the 8:8 ratio be reinstated.[91] This memorandum on the Polish Delegation to the ACEN proves that the American Council's severance of ties with London was only illusory, and that Free Europe's management was well aware of it.

The talks on the possibility of a compromise continued for some time. Two weeks later a meeting presided over by F. Nagy was held. During the talks with Mikołajczyk, Korboński announced that the May proposal of the PSL leader was rejected. The Hungarian chairman of ACEN was sorry to see the Poles still unable to reach a compromise and declared that the decision regarding the Polish delegation was up to the ACEN's General Committee, again.[92] The following year, a subsequent ACEN chairman, and coincidently another companion of Mikołajczyk from the IPU, Dimitrov, organized a meeting to which a representative of FEC was invited. This attempt brought no results as well.[93] Based on the correspondence that followed, no change in the composition of the Polish delegation ensued. Mikołajczyk continued to refuse to submit the nominations for the five vacant seats.[94]

In 1965, in an interview with a representative of the Warsaw press, Nagy called Mikolajczyk "a reactionary and conservative to such an extent that there was not enough patience to deal with him."[95] Deeply offended, Mikołajczyk sent his former colleague an angry reply, copies of which he also directed to all the chairmen of all the national delegations in the ACEN, and to the FEC's Yarrow, Delgado and Kappel.[96]

Even before learning about Nagy's interview with Zygmunt Broniarek, Mikołajczyk published a bitter attack directed at Korboński in the Polish-language bulletin *Orka*, published in Chicago. In it he attacked Korboński for his pro-Gomulka attitude, marginalization of the Polish Poznań riots and neglect of Polish interests in ACEN.[97] The quarrels between the two, which resonated among the Polonia, the FEC, and the political exiles, did not cease until Mikołajczyk's death on 13 December 1966.

The new leader of the re-united PSL in exile, Franciszek Wilk, maintained a much better working contact with the PCU.[98] This however did not affect the shape of the Polish delegation to the ACEN. In 1969 the ACEN was composed of the Free Albania Committee (Rexhep Krasniqi), the Bulgarian National Committee (George M. Dimitrov), the Rumanian National Committee (Constantin Vişoianu), the Committee for a Free Czechoslovakia (Jozef Lettrich), the Committee for a Free Estonia (Leonhard Vahter), the Committee for a Free Latvia (Vilis Hazners), the Committee for a Free Lithuania (Vaclovas Sidzikauskas), the Hungarian Committee (Béla Varga), the Polish Council of Unity (Bolesław Biega) and four internationals.[99] Therefore, the PCU was listed as a single Polish delegation, although the number of its delegates even in 1970 was still 11.[100] This was the last chapter of the ACEN, as the FEC's sponsorship of this organization was about to be completely withdrawn.

Unfortunately, throughout its existence under the auspices of the Free Europe Committee (1954–1972) the Poles were not able to create a single united delegation to the ACEN. When a new organization, the

ACEN, Inc., was incorporated independently of the FEC's control, the question of a Polish delegation was no longer a hot issue. With Mikolajczyk's death and Popiel's move to Europe and his planed return to Poland, the single, dominating voice – and not only of the Polish delegation – became that of Korboński. U.S. intelligence funding for the Free Europe Committee, Inc., including all the organizations that fell under its umbrella, ceased in 1972. Without U.S. funding, Korboński ran the newly established ACEN Inc. from 1972 to 1984, when it was taken over by a Hungarian, László Varga.[101]

One must keep in mind however, that Korboński's position within the ACEN remained firm from its earliest days. Unlike any member of the PNDC group, Korboński was elected the Assembly's chairman in 1958, 1966 and 1971, served as a vice chairman in 1960–61 and 1965–1966 and as acting chairman in 1955 and 1958. Mikołajczyk never served as an ACEN official.

Korbonski's political realism, which proved to be his winning card, is best described in one of his last books, *Behind the Kremlin Walls. A science fiction story.*[102] This book was first published in New York in 1983, when martial law in Poland was just about to be lifted. It contains a quite surprising vision of the end of Communism in Poland. Korboński imagined changes taking place in the Soviet Union as a result of China's growing influence. In his vision, on 3 May 1987, a historic compromise agreement is reached in Poland. Wojciech Jaruzelski apologizes for the imposition of martial law, Lech Wałęsa becomes the new prime minister, with Władysław Bartoszewski and Tadeusz Mazowiecki at his side as vice premiers, and Cardinal Józef Glemp, the head of the Catholic Church in Poland, who oversees the entire transformation.

This vision is striking for a number of reasons. However, in light of this paper, which focuses on the futile attempts to reach a difficult compromise, it seems surprising that the author of such a prophetic, realistic evaluation of current events could not bring about the realization of unity in exile.

First, it must be said that the struggles undertaken for homeland liberation and for uniting the exiles were incomparable. In the post World

War II reality, the future of East and Central Europe was conditioned on the results of the superpowers' confrontation. At the same time no real power was vested in the largely symbolic ACEN, whose members' legitimacy often depended on their maintenance of largely outdated political positions. It should be underscored that this organization was indeed an Assembly – a place to deliberate, discuss, analyze and consequently distribute information on Eastern Europe, evaluate American policy, create, exchange and promote opinions. At every stage, the political future of the countries after their expected liberation from the Soviet yoke was left to be determined by the people of these countries in the outcome of free elections.

Second, the united national representations in the ACEN – committees or councils – were meant to be representative of various political groups. Therefore, each of these was a result of some compromise. In the case of the Czechoslovak delegation, the need for unity reflected the reality of the two-nation state. The representatives from the Baltic nations, turned into Soviet republics, depended on the U.S. government for their legitimacy. In the case of the Bulgarians, unity was a result of a single, dominant leader, Dimitrov. The Romanians clustered around Constantin Vişoianu and for over decade were glad to have Brutus Coste serve as ACEN's Secretary General (1954–1965). In the case of the Hungarians, the organizational framework of their delegation changed a number of times as a result of the 1956 uprising. By 1957 the original Hungarian National Council was faced with the emergence of the Hungarian Revolutionary Council, established in Strasbourg, which by May had taken the name of the National Representation of Free Hungarians in the U.S. In order to elevate their efficiency in building awareness of the revolution and its aftermath, both the pre-revolutionary and post 1956 exiles eventually created the Hungarian Committee. Often referenced as the most efficient and best organized national group, the Hungarians managed to maintain a single delegation. It is important to note that they had excluded most of the pre-1944 exiles from their activities at the very outset.

In the case of the Poles, the cleavage was a direct result of divisions occurring in London, where a government-in-exile continued its operations until 1990. Therefore, the Poles were in a situation different from all other national delegations in the ACEN. Moreover, having fought alongside the Allies throughout World War II, they felt bitterly betrayed at Yalta, which was interpreted not only as a lost chance for free elections but also as an imposed plan that shaped the entire country's geopolitical future. As a result of the Agreements signed on 11 February 1945, the borders of Poland were shifted about 150 miles westward, its area decreasing by roughly 20 percent, which obviously caused great human suffering resulting from resettlement. Despite extensive eviction campaigns, the territories that Poland acquired in the West, according to Yalta and Potsdam, were only under "Polish administration", pending the delineation of the future border at the signing of the Peace Treaty. Ambiguity as to their status was unscrupulously exploited by Soviet propaganda for many years that followed. Moreover, the plan to "reorganize" the usurper Communist government to include the Polish democratic leaders in fact meant acknowledgement of the Soviet-led groups' participation (if not domination) in the political life of Poland. By 1947, the "free and unfettered" elections proved to be a flagrant sham, with the American and British ambassadors having no legal right to intervene. Futile protests brought little comfort to the "betrayed" Poles".[103] As one of the "victors" of World War II, the Poles were convinced of their moral right to demand Western help in liberating their country from the Soviets. The fact that, to begin with, Polish exiles were able to conduct their organizational operations in the United States without American financial assistance[104] and the size of the Polish-American community there, provided for their relative strength in relations with Free Europe. Mikołajczyk's historical links to the Western governments and his later position within the IPU, and Korboński's close ties to London made them the two key actors in the American attempts to form one united delegation to the ACEN. However, their sense of maintaining political integrity, firm belief in the need to preserve the pre-Communist political structure of Poland, and feeling that they had to be loyal to the mandates awarded to them by the Polish people prompted the exiled leaders to see their stubborn maintenance of two Polish groups within ACEN as a sign of independent thinking. As this could easily be said about the other national exile groups' members, Yalta made all the difference in the case of Poland.

The American insistence that the Polish exiles unify was – quite understandably – motivated by the fact that they wanted to utilize the gathering of Eastern European exiled political leaders to offer legitimacy to their Cold War policies. With a split Polish group, there was clear evidence that the exiles differed in their evaluation of the U.S. policy.

Third, it must be underscored that there was always room for representatives of both Polish groups throughout the ACEN's entire history. From 1954 to 1972 the Polish delegation was never composed of 16 members nominated by a single group. Officially, the PNDC was never excluded from the works of the ACEN. The fact that the Council of National Unity grew to dominate the Polish exile milieu was reflected in the uneven distribution of these seats.

Finally, there were a number of personal reasons why overcoming the cleavage between the Mikołajczyk and Korboński groups was not possible. Of course, ambition and idelogical differences spiced up the conflict to the point where it caused exasperation and, in the long run, a decrease in the importance and weakening of the effectiveness of the Polish political exiles.[105] This however, remains true of any political emigration as it faces a new generation's takeover – both at home and abroad.

Endnotes

1 This text is an updated and reviewed version of an article published under the same title by the Polish Academy of Arts and Sciences in Krakow, Poland in: Adam Walaszek and Janusz Pezda, eds., *The Polish Diaspora in America and the Wider World* (Kraków: PAU, 2012) 73–108.

2 Stefan Korboński, *W imieniu Polski walczącej* (Warszawa: Bellona, 1999) 83. (First English edition: *Warsaw in Exile* (New York: Praeger, 1966)).

3 John F. Leich, "Great Expectations: The National Councils in Exile 1950–1960", *Polish Review* 35, no. 3 (1990) 183–196.

4 To date several works on different aspects of the history of the ACEN have been published. Feliks Gadomski, *Zgromadzenie Europejskich Narodów Ujarzmionych. Krótki Zarys* (New York: Bicentennial Publishing Co., "Nowy Dziennik", 1995); Krzysztof Kolęda, *Assembly of Captive*

European Nations – ACEN jako ogniwo systemu wojny psychologicznej Stanów Zjednoczonych (Warszawa: Ośrodek Badania Stosunków Wschód-Zachód, 1972); *Polska emigracja polityczna. Informator*, Reprint, Dorota Piskorska, ed. (Warszawa: Adiutor, 2004) 165–174; Piotr Stanek, *Powstanie i działalność Zgromadzenia Europejskich Narodów Zjednoczonych (ACEN) w świetle Archiwum Feliksa Gadomskiego* in *Prace uczestników studium doktoranckiego* 9: Historia, Anna Filipczak-Kocur, ed, (Opole: Wydawnictwo Uniwersytetu Opolskiego, 2007) 69–99; Anna Mazurkiewicz, "Assembly of the Captive European Nations: 'The Voice of the Silenced Peoples'" in Ieva Zake, ed., *Anti-Communist Minorities: Political Activism of Ethnic Refugees* (New York: Palgrave Macmillan, 2009) 167–185.

5 For a detailed record of the Yalta decisions on Poland and their reception by the Polish leaders in exile see: Zygmunt C. Szkopiak, ed., *The Yalta Agreements: Documents prior to, during and after the Crimea Conference 1945* (London: Polish Govt. in Exile, 1986).

6 It is important to note that three months earlier, in November 1944, when fruitless talks with Stalin and the failed Warsaw Uprising prompted S. Mikołajczyk to resign from the post of prime minister of the Polish government-in-exile, a new cabinet was formed by T. Arciszewski, a Socialist. Already back then, Mikołajczyk perceived the new leader's uncompromising position towards Soviet demands as unrealistic. As a result, the Peasant Party and K. Popiel's faction of the Christian Labor Party (Stronnictwo Pracy) refused to join in. Arciszewski's government was simply ignored at Yalta, where the Big Three provided for the creation of a new Temporary Government of National Unity in Poland with the participation of the Communist-installed Government of National Unity, formerly the Polish Committee of National Liberation.

7 Andrzej Friszke, *Druga Wielka Emigracja*, vol. 1: *Życie polityczne emigracji* (Warszawa: Biblioteka Więzi, 1999) 16–28; Paweł Ziętara, *Misja ostatniej szansy. Próba zjednoczenia polskiej emigracji politycznej przez gen. Kazimierza Sosnkowskiego w latach 1952–1956*, (Warszawa: Trio, 1995) 14–35; Władysław Pobóg-Malinowski, *Najnowsza Historia Polityczna Polski*, vol. 3: 1939–1945 (Kraków: Platan, 2004), 74–82, 153, 162–163.

8 Stanisław Mikołajczyk, *The Rape of Poland: The Pattern of Soviet Aggression* (New York: Whittlesey House, 1948); Stefan Korboński, *Warsaw in Chains* (New York: Macmillan, 1959); Anna Mazurkiewicz, *Dyplomacja Stanów Zjednoczonych wobec wyborów w Polsce w latach 1947 i 1989* (Warszawa: Neriton, 2007). On American assistance in Mikołajczyk's escape see: U.S. Dept. of State, *Foreign relations of the United States. Diplomatic papers, 1947*, vol. IV, *Eastern Europe; The Soviet Union* (Washington, D.C.: Govt. Printing Office, 1972) 400–410, 460–646.

9 By November an Alliance of the Democratic Parties was established there. Soon thereafter, Jan Wszelaki, representative in the U.S. of the Polish government-in-exile (1944–1950), was told by the State Department's official that there was no way the Polish government-in-exile could hope to be recognized by the United States. Friszke, *Życie polityczne emigracji*, 100–104.

10 See correspondence from March to June 1949 at the Polish Institute and Sikorski Museum, London, UK, Jan Wszelaki Papers , fond 39, file 14.

11 Friszke, *Życie polityczne emigracji*, 112.

12 Polish Political Council, Working Committee in the United States, memorandum, 4 February 1955, ACEN, Box 40, file 5, Immigration History Research Center, University of Minnesota (hereafter IHRC); Polish Council of National Unity, U.S. Branch, Polish Political Council, Working Committee in the United States, memorandum, 4 February 1955, Radio Free Europe Corporate Files (hereafter RFE CF), box 254, file 1, Hoover Institution Archives (hereafter HIA); Friszke, *Życie polityczne emigracji*, 130–133.

13 Korboński, przewodniczący Rady Politycznej w Stanach Zjednoczonych do Rady Politycznej, Wydział Wykonawczy (Londyn), 25 March 1950, Korboński Papers, box 19, file 6, HIA. For a detailed description of the arguments see: Friszke, *Życie polityczne emigracji*, 131–134.

[14] It was composed of the Polish Peasant Party (PSL), Mikołajczyk; Christian Labor Party (SP), Popiel and Konrad Sieniewicz; and the Polish Democratic Party (SD), Olszewski and Gadomski. Polish National Democratic Committee, Memorandum to the Assembly of Captive European Nations, February 1955, ACEN, box 40, file 6, IHRC; Ibid., Sieniewicz (vice secretary of the PNDC) to Vilis Māsēns, 4 March 1955.

[15] Ziętara, "Adwokat Konrad Sieniewicz – Rejonowy Delegat Rządu RP na powstańczym Powiślu", *Palestra*, no. 7–8 (2004), http://www.palestra.pl/index.php?go=artykul&id=1328 (accessed: 11 July 2011).

[16] Plan for the organization of a Polish Council of National Unity, 24 May 1951, box 254, file 16, RFE CF, HIA. (hereafter: Plan for the organization of a Polish Council ... .)

[17] On the Political Council's cooperation with American intelligence see: Anna Siwik, "Sprawa Bergu. Współpraca emigracyjnej Rady Politycznej z zachodnimi wywiadami", *Studia Historyczne*, no. 44/2 (2006): 267–288; P. Ziętara, *Misja*, 22.

[18] "Mr. Kuśnierz–or alternate–(Christian) Labor Party faction; Pragier–Socialist Party faction, Luncewicz [Kuncewicz?]–Liberal Party (providing such party really exists), Iwanowski–or alternate–League of Independence". Plan for the organization of a Polish Council ... .

[19] "Gen. Anders – gov't in exile; Kopański – chief of staff – acceptable by Mikołajczyk; Bór-Komorowski, head of the Home Army – member of Political Council; Monter-Chruściel, Commander of Warsaw Uprising, neutral who has agreed to accept Mikołajczyk; Kukiel – former Chief of Staff – gov't in exile". Ibid.

[20] "Count Edward Raczyński – the only recognized Minister in exile, now no longer member of gov't; Count Józef Czapski, prominent representative of Polish cultural life in exile, Mr. Nowak – pseudonym – recognized representative of the WiN in exile". Ibid.

[21] On Gen. Marian Kukiel's attempts to prompt the creation of the Council of National Unity see: Friszke, *Życie polityczne emigracji*, 140–144.

[22] Plan for the organization of a Polish Council... .

[23] Talks between C.D. Jackson, J.F. Leich and R. Walter (the NCFE) and A. Adamczyk, O. Pehr, S. Korboński, A. Niebieszczański, S. Mikołajczyk and K. Sieniewicz (the Polish exiles in the U.S.) that took place in December 1951 are described in: Friszke, *Życie polityczne emigracji*, 162.

[24] Plan for the organization of a Polish Council....

[25] Declaration of the Aims and Principles of Liberation of the Central and Eastern European Peoples, Philadelphia, 11 February 1951, private collection of J.F. Leich.

[26] S. Korboński (Chairman PPC) to C.D. Jackson (President NCFE), 19 February 1951, Korboński Papers, box 19, file 3, HIA.

[27] Examples of such consultative panels regarding the RFE were found at Hoover Institution Archives. According to these documents, the first meeting of the Polish Advisory Committee took place on 16 October 1952. Minutes of the First Meeting of the Polish Advisory Committee, 16 October 1952, Korboński Papers, box 19, file 5, HIA. Korboński reported to London on his fears that the Americans were trying to use the exiles simply as area experts. Chariman of the Polish Political Council in the U.S. to the Political Council's Executive Committee (London), 21 March 1953, Korboński Papers, box 19, file 5, HIA.

[28] Polish Political Council in the U.S. to the Political Council's Executive Committee (London), 10 March 1951, Korboński Papers, box 19, file 6, HIA.

[29] Interestingly, based on the (Mikołaczyk's) PSL paper "Jutro Polski", Friszke wrote that the Political Council participated in the preparations for the Philadelphia ceremony since 1949. Due to last minute changes, including in the list of speakers, the declaration's text and the list of the signatories, the offended PPC members declined to participate. One of the consequences of the PNDC's involvement was the creation of the Central-Eastern European

Committee (16 April 16 1951) without mentioning the almost a month younger Central and Eastern European Conference. Friszke, *Życie polityczne emigracji*, 217–218.

30 In the summer of 1953, Livingston T. Merchant, Assistant Secretary at the Department of State, on behalf of the White House sent a thank you note to both the Central and Eastern European Conference (CEEConf) and the Central-Eastern European Committee (CEEC) for a memorandum signed on 20 May 1953. Livingston T. Merchant to Central and Eastern European Conference and Central-Eastern European Committee, 16 July 1953, Korboński Papers, box 19, file 5, HIA.

31 Based on the 1950 census, the Department of State estimated the size of Polonia (first and second generation Polish-Americans) at 2,786,015, which made it the fourth largest ethnic group (outnumbered by Germans, Italians and Canadians). Memorandum for the Files, Subject: Size of Polish-American Community, 19 January 1961 (revised 30 June 1961), RG 59, EUR, Records Relating to Polish Affairs 1952–1963, box 2, file P. 831 Minorities. 59/250/62/31/01 (MLR: A1 3085), National Archives and Records Administration (College Park, MD) (hereafter NACP).

32 Friszke lists a number of distinguishing features of the exiled Polish government. Regardless of the divisions that occurred after Yalta, it is fair to say that during the war the Polish government was the sole legitimate representation of the Polish state, operating on a constitutional basis with all of the pre-war political parties and groups (with the notable exclusion of the Communist Polish Workers' Party) represented in London. Moreover, Poles put together the most numerous army that fought alongside the Allies and maintained a widespread and efficient underground in Poland. Friszke, *Życie polityczne emigracji,* 15.

33 An interesting interpretation of the American understanding of this problem was given by NCFE President DeWitt C. Poole in his yearly report of 1951: "Prominent figures in pre-exile parties or groups [are] aware of their accountability to that party or group should they return." President's Report (DeWitt C. Poole), NCFE Inc., 5 January 1951 in: Szabad Európa Rádió. Kutatói Peldány, I kötet, 4.1., A-2127/25, k. 11–27, Historical Archives of Hungarian State Security (hereafter ABTL).

34 See: ACEN, box 34, file 2, IHRC.

35 Ziętara, *Misja*, 72–102.

36 Friszke, *Życie poliyczne emigracji*, 193–196.

37 Pro domo: Polish Delegation to ACEN, 1955, (after) 21 June 1955, ACEN, box 40, file 4, IHRC.

38 The decision to leave the PNDC was made by the SD's Executive Committee in London on 29 December 1954. Polish Political Council. Working Committee in the United States, memorandum, 4 February 1955, ACEN, box 40, file 5, IHRC; J. Byliński (Exec. Comm. Polish Democratic Party), S. Olszewski (SD Chairman) to V. Māsēns, 1 October 1955, ACEN, box 40, file 7, IHRC; St. Olszewski, F. Gadomski (SD Sec. Gen. in U.S.) to G.M. Dymitrov (acting ACEN Chariman), 4 April 1955, ACEN, box 40, file 5, IHRC; S. Korboński to V. Māsēns, 14 April 1955, Ibid.

39 Lewis Galantiere directed wartime broadcasts to France for the Office of War Information and was later hired as the Free Europe Committee's political adviser. "He framed sound broadcast policies in a remarkable series of basic guidances". Paul B. Henze, "Recollections of Radio Free Europe. Its Evolution in the 1950s and the Hungarian Revolution", essay based on remarks the author delivered in Budapest on 27 September 1996 at a conference devoted to re-examination of the 1956 Hungarian Revolution. Text received from this author on 9 August 2008.

40 Lewis Galantiere to Mr. Yarrow, memorandum, Remarks by Mr. Mikołajczyk, 21 February 1955, box 238, file 2, RFE CF.

41 Ibid.

42 An interesting account of the September/October 1954 events regarding PSL is to be found in the Polish state security archives, see: Institute of National Remembrance (hereafter IPN), fond 0204/16/2, "Bartek", 15, 21–22, 31–33.

43 S. Wójcik to G.M. Dimitrov, 30 March 1955, ACEN, box 40, file 4, IHRC; Pro domo: Polish Delegation to ACEN, 1955 (after) 21 June 1955, ACEN, box 40, file 4, IHRC; F. Gadomski, S. Olszewski to V. Māsēns, 19 April 1955, ACEN, box 40, file 5, IHRC.

44 Statement of Mr. K. Sieniewicz, Representative of the PNDC, made at 49th meeting of the General Committee of the ACEN, on April 25, 1955, ACEN, box 40, file 6, IHRC.

45 A. Niebieszczański to V. Māsēns, (received on) 20 May 1955, ACEN, box 40, file 4, IHRC.

46 K. Popiel to V. Māsēns, 16 May 1955, ACEN, box 40, file 6, IHRC.

47 Report to the General Committee re: Polish Delegation, 23 May 1955, ACEN, box 40, file 4, IHRC.

48 In the discussions "Germany" refers to the FRG only. The GDR – as not a sovereign, captive nation – was intentionally left out throughout the 1950s.

49 Ibid.

50 K. Popiel to V. Māsēns, 23 May 1955, ACEN, box 40, file 6, IHRC; Memorandum of the PNDC to the ACEN, Concerning the Composition of the Polish Delegation, 23 May 1955, ACEN, box 40, file 4, IHRC.

51 K. Popiel to V. Māsēns, 23 May 1955, ACEN, box 40, file 6, IHRC.

52 J. Starzewski (PCNU's Foreign Dept.), R. Odzierzyński (Chairman of the PCNU's Executive Committee) to V. Māsēns, 9 August 1955, ACEN, box 40, file 5, IHRC.

53 Minutes, New York, 13 September 1955, ACEN, box 40, file 5, IHRC.

54 Application for membership, Korboński, Bolesław Niebieszczański, Adam Ciołkosz, Stypułkowski, 19 September 1955, ACEN, box 34, file 2, IHRC.

55 V. Māsēns to S. Korboński, 21 September 1955, ACEN, box 40, file 4, IHRC; V. Māsēns to K. Popiel, 21 IX 1955, ACEN, box 40, file 6, IHRC.

56 S. Mikołajczyk, K. Popiel, T. Paul to V. Māsēns, 26 IX 1955, IHRC, ACEN, box 40, file 6; On 11 October the PNDC repeated its charges and formulated a two week ultimatum: in case of no reply, the PNDC was about the leave the ACEN. On 24 October they received a reply. This time in a carefully worded letter Māsēns wrote that the 11:5 ratio was a result of secessions from the PNDC that had occurred during the previous session of the ACEN. V. Māsēns to S. Mikołajczyk, K. Popiel and T. Paul, 27 September 1955, ACEN, box 40, file 6, IHRC; K. Popiel to V. Māsēns, 11 October 1955, ACEN, box 40, file 6. IHRC; V. Māsēns to K. Popiel, 24 October 1955, ACEN, box 40, file 6, IHRC.

57 Lewis Galantiere to Mr. Houston, Memorandum: Polish Visitors, 18 October 1955, RFE CF, box 254, file 1, HIA.

58 Ibid.

59 Research Aid: Cryptonyms and Terms in Declassified CIA Files, http://www.archivep.gov/iwg/declassified-records/rg-263-cia-records/second-release-lexicon.pdf, accessed 5 August 2012; M. Nelson, *War of the Black Heavens: the Battles of Western Broadcasting in the Cold War* (Syracuse, NY: Syracuse University Press, 1997) 257.

60 McCargar to B. Yarrow, memorandum, 6 February 1956, RFE CF, box 254, file 1, HIA.

61 Ibid.

62 James C. McCargar, John F. Leich to Whitney H. Shepardson, Bernard Yarrow, 6 February 1956, Memorandum: Polish Council of National Unity (U.S. Branch), RFE CF, box 254, file 1, HIA.

63 S. Korboński to Executive of National Unity, London, Telegram, 8 February 1956, ACEN, box 40, file 5, IHRC.

64 K. Popiel to V. Māsēns, 30 August 1956, ACEN, box 40, file 6, IHRC.

65 James C. McCargar (Free Europe Exile Relations, Paris) to Bernard Yarrow (FEC NY), 17 August 1956, RFE CF, box 238, file 4, HIA.

66 K. Popiel, S. Mikołajczyk (London) to V. Māsēnsa, 6 October 1956, ACEN, box 40, file 6, IHRC.

67 S. Mikołajczyk, K. Popiel to V. Māsēns, 30 January 1957, ACEN, box 40, file 6, IHRC; V. Māsēns to S. Mikołajczyk i K. Popiel, 28 February 1957, ACEN, box 40, file 6, IHRC.

68 Parafraza szyfrówki od "Sędziwego" (Coded message from the "Hoar") (original message: London, 3 February 1957), (paraphrase date: 6 February 1957), MSW (Ministry of Internal Affairs), Teczka sprawy ewidencyjno-obserwacyjnej. "Bartek" record and observation case file, (henceforth "Bartek"), 0204/16/2, vol. 2, 299, IPN,; Notatka informacyjna dot. sytuacji w PSL, 27 May 1957, Ibid., 337–339, IPN.

69 Noticeably, this memorandum was signed: "The Polish Delegation to the ACEN". As not all of its signatories were members of the PCNU, this must have seemed to be the only reasonable title. Bearing 11 signatures, this document pledged for the ACEN General Committee (hereafter GC) reconsideration of the issue of granting economic assistance to Poland. Arbitrarily stating that the entire Polish emigration, the Polish nation, and American Polonia supported the idea of granting economic help to Poland, they listed many arguments for it. Despite the fact that the economic help was likely not going to aid the Polish economy, it had the potential of preventing looming collapse, bringing political and psychological advantages by breaking a hole in the Iron Curtain, renewing Poland's contacts with the Free World. The authors of this memorandum charged the ACEN's GC with having a too orthodox, stiff, unrealistic and politically wrong position. By declining even to discuss the more realistic ways towards liberation (for example promoting a creation of a neutral zone in Central and Eastern Europe in return for the Soviet troops' exit), the ACEN in fact was leaving events to take their own course. Polish Delegation to the ACEN to Chairman of the ACEN General Committee, Memorandum, 2 April 1957, ACEN, box 40, f. 4, IHRC.

70 Ibid.

71 Free Europe Exile Relations (hereafter FEER) recommended that the PCNU – called for „the Polish delegation in the ACEN" to be provided free of charge with a furnished office and $985 a month for its operations. FEER Special Activities Unit, Project Proposal POL-4-58 (Account 5542), Subject: Polish Council of National Unity (American Division), 28 August 1957, RFE CF, box 254, file 1, HIA.

72 S. Mikołajczyk, K. Popiel to V. Māsēns, 16 September 1957, ACEN, box 40, file 6, IHRC.

73 S. Mikołajczyk to V. Māsēns, 7 April 1958, Ibid.; V. Māsēns to S. Mikołajczyk, 9 April 1958, Ibid.

74 On 18 February 1959, Mikołajczyk and Popiel addressed the General Committee rather than the Chairman – Korboński. Due to the latter's absence, the reply was signed by the acting Chairman, Sidzikauskas, who simply refused to discuss this matter before Korboński's return from his trip of the Far East. Upon the Chairman's return, Mikołajczyk was informed that the General Committee decided not to change its earlier decision. Korboński noted however, that the ACEN GC was ready to continue the talks upon composition of the Polish delegation. S. Mikołajczyk, K. Popiel to ACEN General Committee (ACEN GC), 18 February 1959, ACEN, box 40, file 6, IHRC; V. Sidzikauskas to S. Mikołajczyk and K. Popiel, 12 March 1959, Ibid.; S. Korboński to S. Mikołajczyk, 25 June 1959, Ibid.

75 Polish Council of National Unity. Registration entry: 958, registered 29 June 1956, terminated 18 March 1958, address: Hotel Chelsea NY (222 West 23rd Street #705).

76 Foreign Agents Registration Act, United States Department of Justice, Historical List of All Registrants as of 21 June 2010, http://www.justice.gov/criminal/fara/links/qs_primary.html [accessed: 21 June 2010]; F. Gadomski to J. Leich, 19 October 1957, RFE CF, box 254, file 1, HIA.

77 F. Gadomski (Sec. Gen. Polish Council of Unity) to J.F. Leich, 28 August 1958, RFE CF, box 254, file 1, HIA; Polish Council of Unity in the United States, (after June 1958) ACEN, box 40, file 5, IHRC.

78 J.F. Leich to Minton, Memorandum: Comments on PTEX NY 43, 16 February 1960, RFE CF, box 254, file1, HIA.

79 R.W. Minton to A.S. Alexander, Letter from Count Raczyński of February 8, 1960, 16 February 1960, RFE CF, box 254, file 1, HIA.

80 Albert D. Kappel (Director Exile Political Organizations Division) to Count Edward Raczyński, London, 9 June 1965, RFE CF, box 254, file 15, HIA.

81 Excerpt from MFD-66 (Mucio F. Delgado) of 18 June 1963, RFE CF, box 254, file 15, HIA.

82 WEOD Information Item (London), Dissention within the Polish Council of National Unity, 11 January 1963, RFE CF, box 254, file 15, HIA. Despite the attacks, in March 1963, Raczyński asked the FEC's President, John Richardson, not to cut the funding. Count E. Raczyński (London) to J. Richardson, 12 March 1963, RFE CF, box 254, file 15, HIA.

83 H. Dutton Lee, Harolds C. Velder, Memorandum: Testimony in support of aid to Poland before the sub-committee on Europe, House Committee on Foreign Affairs, 30 June 1962, RG 59, EUR, Records Relating to Polish Affairs 1952–1963, box 1. 59/250/62/31/01 (MLR: A1 3085), NACP.

84 Ibid.

85 Mikołajczyk w Londynie. Odpis (Mikolajczyk in London. Duplicate), 30 September 1960, MSW, 0204/16/3, 89, IPN; Notatka "Liny" (A note from "Rope"), February 1961, MSW, 0204/16/3, 94–96, IPN; PSL Mikołajczyka w latach 1960–61 (Mikolajczyk's PSL in 1960–1961), Warszawa, May 1962, MSW, 204/16/3, 117–32, IPN.

86 Mikołajczyk w Londynie. Odpis (Mikolajczyk in London. Duplicate), 30 September 1960, MSW, 0204/16/3, 89, IPN.

87 S. Mikołajczyk to F. Nagy (ACEN GC Chairman), 3 October 1961, ACEN, box 40, file 6, IHRC.

88 F. Nagy to S. Mikołajczyk, 5 October 1961, ACEN, box 40, file 6, IHRC.

89 Zmiana rezolucji z 21 September 1955 (A Change of the 21 October 1955 Resolution), 15 June 1962, ACEN, box 40, file 6, IHRC.

90 With K. Popiel's departure to Europe in 1957, by the late 1950s the PNDC gradually vanished without any formal decision to dissolve it. Ziętara marks the end of the PNDC in 1955, Friszke mentions "years before Mikołajczyk's death". Ziętara, *Misja*, 159; Friszke, *Życie polityczne emigracji*, 360.

91 Mucio F. Delgado to John Richardson, Re: Polish Delegation to the ACEN, 6 July 1962, RFE CF, box 254, file 16, HIA.

92 F. Nagy, memorandum, 24 July 1962, ACEN, box 40, file 4, IHRC.

93 G.M. Dymitrow to S. Mikołajczyk, Telegram, 25 February 1963, ACEN, box 40, file 6, IHRC.

94 V. Germenji to S. Mikołajczyk, 23 August 1965, ACEN, box 40, file 6, IHRC.

95 *Express Wieczorny*, 29 December 1965.

96 S. Mikołajczyk to F. Nagy, 21 April 1966, ACEN, box 40, file 9, IHRC.

97 (S. Mikołajczyk), "Czy to jest obrona interesów Polski za granicą?", *Orka Biuletyn Informacyjny*, Chicago (November 1965) 23–28.

98 F. Wilk to F. Gadomski, 30 September 1968, ACEN, box 40, file 9, IHRC; J. Lettrich, F. Gadomski to F. Wilk, 11 October 1968, Ibid.

99 Christian Democratic Union of Central Europe, International Center of Free Trade Unionists in Exile, International Peasant Union, Liberal Democratic Union of Central and Eastern Europe. Algirdas Budreckis (ACEN Press Officer) to Tibor Weber, 9 January 1969, ACEN, box 38, file 3, IHRC; A. Budreckis to T. Weber, 13 January 1969, Ibid.

[100] During the 17th session of the ACEN, the Polish delegation was composed of: S. Bańczyk, B. Biega, Z. Gross, Adam Galiński, Stanisław Jordanowski, Edward Kleszczyński, Michał Pluciński, Marian Piotrowski, Andrzej Pomian and the chairman, Stefan Korboński. None of the abovementioned became a U.S. citizen. B. Biega to A. Bērziš (ACEN Chairman), 31 August 1970, ACEN , box 40, file 5, IHRC.

[101] J. F. Leich to L. Varga (Chairman of the ACEN Inc.), 18 May 1989, Private collection of J.F. Leich; Roman W. Rybicki lists a different date of Korboński's resignation: 12 September 1985. Cf. *Stefan Korboński 1901–1989*, ed. Małgorzata Ptasińska-Wójcik (Warsaw: IPN, 2010) pp. 319.

[102] S. Korboński, *Za murami Kremla. Opowieść fantastyczna* (Warszawa: Omnipress, 1990) 157–177. (First ed.: New York: Bicentennial Publishing Corporation, 1983.) Stefan Korboński died two weeks after the conclusion of the Round Table Talks in Poland.

[103] Arthur Bliss Lane, *I Saw Poland Betrayed. An American Ambassador Reports to the American People* (New York: Doubleday, 1948). See also: Mazurkiewicz, *Dyplomacja Stanów Zjednoczonych,* 25–28.

[104] They did receive individual stipends and support. For the discussions of means of individual support extended to the exiles (Stanisław Mikołajczyk's case) see: 0204/16/2 „Bartek", IPN.

[105] The internal squabbles delayed the start of the Polish Desk within Radio Free Europe and lowered the authority and position of Polish exile leaders in the U.S. and in Europe. Furthermore, the rivalry weakened ethnic support for the Polish exile groups, and consequently prevented establishment of a powerful political lobby.

Select bibliography

Assembly of Captive European Nations Papers, Immigration History Research Center, University of Minnesota (Minneapolis, Minnesota)

Radio Free Europe/Radio Liberty Inc., Corporate Records, Hoover Institution Archives (Stanford, California).

Archival Records of the state security, The Insitute of National Remembrance (IPN), Warsaw, Gdańsk, Poland

Andrzej Friszke, Rafał Habielski, Paweł Machcewicz, *Druga Wielka Emigracja 1945–1990 [The Second Great Emigration 1945–1990]*, vols. 1–3 (Warszawa: Biblioteka Więzi, 1999)

Feliks Gadomski, *Zgromadzenie Europejskich Narodów Ujarzmionych. Krótki Zarys [Assembly of Captive European Nations. Brief Outline.* (New York: Bicentennial Publishing Co., 1995)

Stefan Korboński, *Warsaw in Chains* (New York: Macmillan, 1959)

Stefan Korboński, *Warsaw in Exile* (New York: Praeger, 1966)

Stanisław Mikołajczyk, *The Rape of Poland: The Pattern of Soviet Aggression* (New York: Whittlesey House, 1948)

The Polish Diaspora in America and the Wider World, ed. Adam Walaszek, Janusz Pezda, (Kraków: Polish Academy of Arts and Sciences, 2012)

Paweł Ziętara, Misja ostatniej szansy. Próba zjednoczenia polskiej emigracji politycznej przez gen. Kazimierza Sosnkowskiego w latach 1952–1956 [*Last Chance Mission. General Kazimierz Sosnkowski's Attempt to Unite Polish Political Emigration*] (Warszawa: Trio, 1995)

VIII

Democracy in Exile: The Bulgarian National Committee and G.M. Dimitrov

Maria Kokoncheva

Often, Eastern Europeans are hesitant to examine their Cold War history. Not only because it is still too personal for many but also because, in large part, we feel we have not yet written that piece of our history, and therefore it doesn't really belong to us. During that time, on the western side of the Iron Curtain, each of the captive nations of Europe had a parallel history, one created by the people who opposed and fled in order to keep working for the cause of their nations and in the hope that change will come. This chapter will introduce readers to the Bulgarian National Committee (BNC), an immigrant organization that took part in this work. Its active efforts and political position not only influenced the lives of the post-war Bulgarian immigration but turned that body into a fundamental building block in the National Committee for Free Europe, Inc. (NCFE), the Assembly of Captive European Nations (ACEN) as well as many other international organizations. This participation brought the BNC to a place of global influence with a role in the international political arena. Many people contributed to the growth of the BNC throughout its active life, but the central role belongs to its founder and leader, Dr. Georgi Mihov Dimitrov.

The way Dr. Dimitrov shaped the image and strategy of the BNC reflected his democratic views and political leadership from the time before he emigrated to the United States from Bulgaria. Growing up in the midst of political chaos and repression, he managed to become one of the most influential and popular political figures in Bulgaria before and during the Second World War. Given his degree of influence, before going into a deeper critique of the role, strategies, and philosophy of the BNC, it is appropriate to introduce the highlights of the life of the man whose vision was embodied in this organization.

The reflections in this essay are based on archival documents, publications of the BNC– the most significant and long-lived among which is the newspaper *Free and Independent Bulgaria*, which spread among the Bulgarian immigration around the world – correspondence and other official materials. Preparation of this chapter also included a personal interview with Hristo Chorelov, a secretary and chairman of the BNC in France until the organization ceased its activities in 1991,[1] and two interviews with Anastasia Moser, a Bulgarian politician and Dr. Dimitrov's daughter, who provided the author with access to her private archives of the BNC's published materials.[2] A small number of published works are dedicated to the life of Dr. Dimitrov, among which I reference here his memoirs and *Dr. G. M. Dimitrov* by Charles Moser.

The Early Years

The story of Dr. Georgi Mihov Dimitrov, generally known as G.M. Dimitrov or Gemeto,[3] began in the small village of Eni Chiflic on the coast of the Marmara sea, less than two decades after Bulgaria won its independence from the Ottoman rule in 1878. Born on 15 April 1903 to a family of Bulgarian farmers whose homeland had been left outside the boundaries of the freed territories of Bulgaria, Dimitrov's childhood was spent among a strong Bulgarian community in the Ottoman valley of Edirne, where he also received his primary education and orthodox Christian religious influence.[4]

The First Balkan War, 1912, which Bulgaria, Serbia, Greece and Montenegro lead against the Ottoman Empire, restored to those countries a large portion of their territories that were still occupied by the Turks. The Bulgarian army advanced to just 90 kilometers from the Ottoman capital Constantinople, thus raising the hopes of many Bulgarians, including Dimitrov's family, that their lands would become part of Bulgaria again. A year later, the Bulgarian monarch, Ferdinand I, turned against his allies and started the Second Balkan War. This time Bulgaria was defeated and suffered great territorial losses. For the final time, Eni Chiflic was left deep within the Ottoman Empire. The Bulgarian military authorities ordered the scattered Bulgarian population to evacuate to Bulgaria. Thus, Dimitrov's family, along with many other Bulgarians residing along the eastern Marmara coast, moved out of their homes and began the difficult journey to Bulgaria. Only 10 years of age at the time, Dimitrov , along with his parents and older sister became immigrants in their own country. The two children were first of the family to arrive, by ship, at the port of Burgas – a southern Bulgarian town on the Black Sea. With the arrival of their parents more than a month later, the family started to search for a home and some land where they could make their living and survive the difficulties of having to adapt to the realities of life in New Bulgaria. After months of wandering, the couple settles in Doirentzi, a village in northern Bulgaria, where Dimitrov helped to support his family and continued his education.[5]

After his high school graduation, G.M. Dimitrov became teacher at the local school, and in 1922 he got involved with the political ideas of the Bulgarian Agrarian National Union (BANU). This political organization represented the peasantry, which constituted a large percentage of the country's population.[6] Very soon, Dimitrov became a figure of considerable influence in his region, and he organized one of the armed peasant revolts that took place in the Lovech region. The revolt was to counter the coup d'état of 1923 and was in support of the government headed by Prime Minister Alexander Stambolijski, who had been elected with BANU's support. The leaders of the coup took Stambolijski into custody and ordered his execution, which took place on 14 June 1923. In the midst of this political chaos, Dimitrov recalled, in his memoires, being taken out of the class room and being detained for first time. He suffered violent interrogations, and the only reason he did not receive a death sentence, as many other political prisoners did, was because he was under the legal age of majority.[7] After he was released, Dimitrov went to Sofia and was enrolled in the School of Diplomacy of the Sofia Free

University. He also became a student of medicine at the University of Sofia. At that time he became involved in intense political activity, putting much effort into restoring BANU's local political structures across northern Bulgaria.[8]

Prior to the parliamentary elections of 1931, BANU participated in forming an oppositionist coalition together with the democrats, the liberal and the radical parties, which they called the People's Bloc. In the elections of June 1931 the coalition surprisingly received the majority of votes and won 152 places in the parliament against only 78 for the ruling party coalition. The distribution of parliamentary seats within the People's Bloc was as followed: 69 for BANU; 43 for the democratic party; 32 for the national liberal party and 8 for the radical party.[9] Dimitrov actively participated in the formation of this coalition and was elected to parliament from the Lovech region. The Bulgarian monarch, Boris III, was so surprised by the People's Bloc's unexpected victory that, according to Dimitrov, he postponed the formation of the new government for over one week – from 21 to 29 June – while trying to work out a political deal with his old partners, who had just suffered a significant electoral loss.[10]

Despite their success at the polls, the parties in the Bloc could not manage to reach consensus on the most important political issues. The BANU also suffered from a number of inner conflicts, which lead to its division and the creation of the Bulgarian Agrarian National Union–Alexander Stamboljski, a political initiative led by Dimitrov.[11] The ensuing government went through a few changes and survived only for three years. In May 1934, Prime Minister Nikola Mushanov and his cabinet resigned. The deep parliamentary crisis that followed was enforced by a military coup d'état and attempts by Boris III to regain his influence over the government. In October 1935 Dimitrov was forcibly taken from his home and severely tortured. This was the beginning of another wave of political persecution against him and other BANU party members.[12]

In May 1936, because of his worsening health caused by the torture experienced during his detentions, Dimitrov went to France for medical treatment. After a short stay in southern France, he visited Paris, where he was introduced to well-known political leaders such as the editor of the socialist journal *Le Populaire* and the French prime minister, Léon Blum. He also met some representatives of the English Labor Party and England's future minister of education, Ellen Wilkinson. These encounters helped Dimitrov build a solid lobby for his party and Bulgaria among European political elites. After he returned to Bulgaria a few months later, the political repression against him resumed.[13]

With the approach of the Second World War, it seemed very clear that Bulgaria would join the German side. Dimitrov's efforts to somehow counter this decision were unsuccessful, and when the Gestapo entered the country, he became one of their first targets. While they searched his home, he managed to escape and flee to Serbia, where he organized armed groups of Bulgarian immigrants and students from the universities of Bratislava, Prague and Zagreb. These groups were to return to Bulgaria and head the anti-fascist resistance there. This initiative was not successful, and after the situation worsened in the Balkans and the Serbians capitulated in April 1941, he left for Egypt with the help of his English friend, Prof. Norman Davis. For the next three years of his exile Dimitrov lived in Cairo, Jerusalem and Istanbul. He engaged in active political work, during which the idea for the Bulgarian National Committee came about for first time. He completed his book, *The Bulgarian Tragedy*, expounding his vision of the direction Bulgarian foreign policy should take after the war. The main political course, according to this work, should focus on finding unity with the neighboring Balkan countries. This thesis attracted the attention of the American Office of Strategic Services, which prepared a resume of Dimitrov's book.[14]

After his escape, Dimitrov's wife Maria was detained, repeatedly interrogated and tortured. Her mother was thrown into a mental institution. For the duration of the investigation, their two children, Alexander, who was 9 years old, and four-year-old Anastasia, were separated and sent to different orphanages. When the children were able to see their mother again, they were seriously ill. In his memoir Dimitrov writes that the doctor who took care of the children later suspected that Alexander was purposely infected with some rare disease, which continued until his death.[15]

In July 1944, speaking on the free radio of Palestine, Dr. Dimitrov addressed three groups of people in Bulgaria – all the Bulgarians, the peasants and the soldiers – condemning the regime of Boris III and urging that the German presence be chased from Bulgaria.[16]

On 25 August, the government announced the disarmament of the German troops on Bulgarian territory and claimed neutrality. This shift was undertaken too late, and on 6 September the Russian army entered Bulgaria. Three days later, the new government of the communist-lead Fatherland Front, with Kimon Georgiev as prime minister, took over. A new series of repressions began. Dr. Dimitrov returned from his first exile on 23 September 1944. At the Bulgarian border with Turkey, he boarded a train, and at every station between there and Sofia he was greeted by multitudes of people welcoming him home.[17]

Dimitrov refused to participate in or support by any means the Soviet occupation and the communist regime. He initiated active work on restoring the local structures of BANU by organizing meetings and massive gatherings, at which he repeatedly set forth his party's political vision in terms of Bulgarian domestic and foreign policies. Because of his position and growing popularity, Dr. Dimitrov was placed under house arrest from January until May 1945, during which time the entire BANU leadership was replaced by communist party activists. On 24 May, and again with the help of his wife Maria, he managed to escape from his apartment – an almost impossible feat given the large number of guards and militia surrounding his home. After hiding from house to house, he was taken by an English diplomat to the residence of the political representative of the United States to Bulgaria, Maynard Barnes.[18]

The early days of fear and uncertainty grew into months of unceasing negotiations between Barnes, Washington, D.C., Sofia and Moscow. The communists tried almost everything possible to detain Dimitrov. Initially, they went about it with open threats. Later on, a unit of Soviet soldiers surrounded the US diplomat's mansion. The regime even tried to sneak under-cover agents dressed as workers inside the house. Finally, Barnes was convinced in personal conversation with Bulgarian Foreign Minister Petko Staynov that Staynov would never sign an official request for Dimitrov's surrender because that would mean Dimitrov's "certain and most cruel death".[19] Despite Dr. Dimitrov's absolute mistrust of such a promise, Barnes was rather inclined to trust Staynov's good intentions – until the day he received a note, signed by the foreign minister, insisting that Dimitrov surrender.[20]

In a secret correspondence of 18 July 1945, in Stalin's archives, it can be seen that after Barnes sent a note to the Bulgarian Ministry of Foreign Affairs asking it to grant permission for his guest to go to the United States, the head of the Soviet Military Mission in Bulgaria, Sergey Biryuzov, after consulting the Bulgarian foreign minister, had contacted the deputy chief of the Soviet Foreign Affairs Ministry, Vladimir Dekanozov. In this correspondence, Biryuzov informed Dekamazov that in reality the Bulgarian government wanted Dimitrov to be handed over to them so Bulgarian officials would be the ones to grant the permission and secure Dimitrov's right to leave the country. Thus, the Bulgarian government would successfully rid itself of the main leader of the political opposition and also gain favor with the United States, which, at that time, had proposed that Bulgaria send its political representative to the US.[21] Maynard Barnes, however, took the note requesting that he turn over Dimitrov as an act of deepest treachery on the part of the Bulgarian foreign minister and refused to act on it. The body of Western diplomats in Sofia was also not indifferent towards Dimitrov's case.[22]

In Exile

In early September 1945, Dimitrov was finally granted political asylum in the United States. His wife was also allowed to leave the country with him; however they were forced to leave their two children behind in the care of his wife's mother. They first saw their daughter Anastasia again seventeen years later, in 1962, when she finally received permission to go to the US. They never saw their son Alexander again. He died in Bulgaria in 1956. On 5 September 1945, G.M. Dimitrov left Bulgaria and never returned.

In January 1946, after a five-month stay in Italy, Dr. Dimitrov reached US soil, where he declared his determination to "continue the fight for the freedom and independence of his people".[23] He was initially disappointed by the US position that it would not be actively involved in the political situation in the Balkan countries, and more specifically would abstain from more radical actions against Russian involvement there. This first disappointing impression did not change over the years and more than once became a point of contention between Dimitrov and the US political oligarchy. In his memoirs, he recalls an interesting incident that took place soon after his arrival. He was called by governmental officials for a meeting in the Social Security office building in Washington, D.C. The people he met with did not identify themselves or their position, and they asked him only one question, "What would you do if you were in President Truman's place today?" The answers Dimitrov gave summarized well his ideas and his expectations of American foreign policy towards the East:

> 1. I would immediately organize the greatest military power in the world.
> 2. I would organize the largest propaganda machine in the world.
> 3. I would organize the most efficient intelligence in the world.
> 4. I would immediately provide all the captive nations in the world with all the help they need to fight against the Soviet-communist aggression, the only purpose of which is to crush the United States, the only fortress of freedom and democracy barring their way to world domination.[24]

After a short moment of silence, Dimitrov was told that even though they well understood and agreed with his program, the US Congress would never agree to support and finance such an agenda.

Political Activity in Exile

Nevertheless, Dr. Dimitrov did not give up his political ideas. He got in contact with other agrarian leaders in exile from Eastern Europe. In September 1946 he, Vladko Machek, leader of the Croatian Peasant Party, and Milan Gavrailovich, leader of the Serbian Peasant Party, united around the idea of recreating the Agrarian Union in exile. Later they were joined by Hungarian Prime Minister Ferenc Nagy, who had recently fled Hungary, and the prime minister of the Polish government in exile during World War Two, Stanisław Mikołajczyk. At the end of May 1948 they held the first congress of the International Peasant Union (IPU).[25]

One of their first initiatives as an organization was to issue a memorandum to the Secretary General of the United Nations insisting that the matters of the captive nations of Eastern Europe be included in the UN agenda. According to the *New York Times*, this document was filled with "the most serious charges" against the Soviet Union made publicly in the United States.[26] The newspaper also expressed its doubts whether the UN would even provide moral support to these nations. [27] One of the strongest and most suspicious critiques the American media expressed at that time regarding the leaders of the IPU was published in the left-leaning *Nation*, a publication very sympathetic to the Soviet Union and its policies, particularly under the editorship of Freda Kirchwey. The article was written by Constantine Poulosq, whose goal was to discredit the IPU leaders, who were not well known abroad. Poulosq had close connections with Alexander Obbov, a political enemy of Dr. Dimitrov who had been at the forefront of the public criticism against him in Bulgaria, after his return from Egypt.[28]

The Founding of the National Committees

Very soon, it became clear to the Eastern European leaders in the US that they could not rely entirely on an agrarian basis for their organization and in order to reach their goals of promoting democracy and bringing awareness to the West of the fate of their nations, they had to base their initiatives on broader political grounds. This is how the idea of the Bulgarian National Committee (BNC), initially laid in Egypt during Dimitrov's first exile, was fully developed into a political organization joining together not only agrarians but also a wide range of political ideas and parties. The main purpose was to fight to establish freedom and democracy in Bulgaria. By 1949, the BNC was an active organization funded through the National Committee for Free Europe, with headquarters in Washington, D.C.[29] The first chairman of the organization was Dimitrov, and he held that position until his death in 1972. In its first years, the BNC brought together democrats, social democrats and independents – all representatives of the opposition in Bulgaria that was formed right after 1945. A main requirement for all active BNC members was that they retain their Bulgarian citizenship as an expression of their conviction that one day they would return to the land of their birth and regain their lawful status as Bulgarian citizens.[30] Along these lines, Dr. Dimitrov wrote in his memoirs:

> ...a capital mistake was that I was still influenced by Mr. Barnes' impression that my stay away from Bulgaria would continue only a few months. ... Therefore, I did not consider even for a moment a longer stay abroad, so the idea of taking my permit for medical practice with me, especially as specializing in radiology did not cross my mind. ... This negligence turned out to be harmful for me personally, as well as for the national liberation work, because I still cannot carry out my plans for work and battle.[31]

The same observation was shared by other immigrants, who had never believed that their exile would continue for so long, for many of them until their death.[32]

The BNC published its official organ, the newspaper *Свободна и независима България* (*Free and Independent Bulgaria*), from 1949 until 1990.[33] Its articles help to provide a better understanding of the nature, the political ideology and ideas of the committee and the way they developed over the course of the years. The newspaper also informed readers of news from Bulgaria and events organized by the committee and served as a place to promote journalist works on the Bulgarian immigration and intellectuals abroad.

Nevertheless, the first text that is of significance is found in another BNC publication, the journal *Освобождение* (*Liberation*). *Liberation* was first published in Paris in 1949. Its editor until 1957 was Vasil Urukov, a journalist and former Bulgarian ambassador to Brussels.[34] The first issue of *Liberation* published the policy statement of the BNC in an article written by Dr. Dimitrov and titled "Program for Battle". This text reveals the vision that Dr. Dimitrov and his organization had for Bulgaria's domestic and foreign policy. In the first paragraph the two main objectives of the BNC are defined as "the liberation of Bulgaria from the communist-bolshevist yoke"[35] and "the gaining of the Bulgarian people's right of to a free and independent existence in tomorrow's free democratic world."[36] Later in the article, Dimitrov stated that the main goal of the committee was not to govern and that its purpose was to involve all Bulgarians in this fight.

In addition, he set forth some more specific ideas for the strategic development of Bulgaria. The first political priority was identified as the restoration of the Tarnovo constitution – the first constitution of Bulgaria. Adopted in 1879 it was very advanced in its legal nature for the time, establishing the separation of powers between the executive, legislative and judiciary branches. The article continued by pointing out the need to elect a new parliament that would serve to guarantee a political atmosphere of respect of human rights and personal freedoms. The political independence of the military as well as spiritual freedom in the area of education and culture were priorities oriented towards the development of young Bulgarians.

In terms of foreign policy, Dimitrov saw as the most desirable path the establishment of effective communication and close cooperation with neighboring countries. The Atlantic Charter and the United Nations Charter were identified as the institutions under whose authority solutions should be sought regarding issues with international relevance. Dr. Dimitrov found this to be the environment where "foes turn into friends", where international competition should be relocated from the military battlefield to the arena of culture and science.

The text continues by placing all of the localized aspirations for freedom, liberation and radical change from the political status quo in Bulgaria and Eastern Europe into a more global perspective in which all the "enslaved and freedom-loving democratic peoples" should stand up against "the red Bolshevist dictatorship".[37] For the sake of this cause, the BNC would be able to make room for a broader political base for the organization and would unite all the strength of the nation to fight, but it would never compromise regarding the democratic principles leading this battle or with respect to the way Bulgaria should be reorganized and governed. It is further pointed out that the BNC would be held accountable only to the Bulgarian people and to history.

At the end of the text, Dimitrov confirmed once again that the main aim of the organization was not to govern or rule but to fight for the independence and the freedom of Bulgaria.

This policy statement does not provide a very clear idea of the practical means by which this fight would be carried out, but it paints a detailed picture of the "ideal" Bulgaria – a country with a modern and independent political system, where individuals not only can exercise the full spectrum of their human right, but are also entitled to power and involvement in the governing of their country. According to the BNC, Bulgaria would also take a position of global cooperation in the arena of international relations and would be respectful towards international institutions, in contrast to the policy of isolationism that the country had fallen into since the beginning of the communist regime. Therefore, it could be concluded that the primary mission of the BNC not only was directed towards bringing to the outside world awareness of the communist reality in Eastern Europe but also was to clearly present the goal toward which BNC members should strive, the pledge of their battle.

Organization and Activities of the BNC

In the next couple of years, the BNC activity and network grew. In its first issue of 1953, *Free and Independent Bulgaria* reported that during 1952 the Committee had issued six memorandums and produced six print publications, four of which were in English. Three new BNC branches and ten sub-branches had been opened in strategic locations; another 38 sub-committees had been opened, and BNC members par-

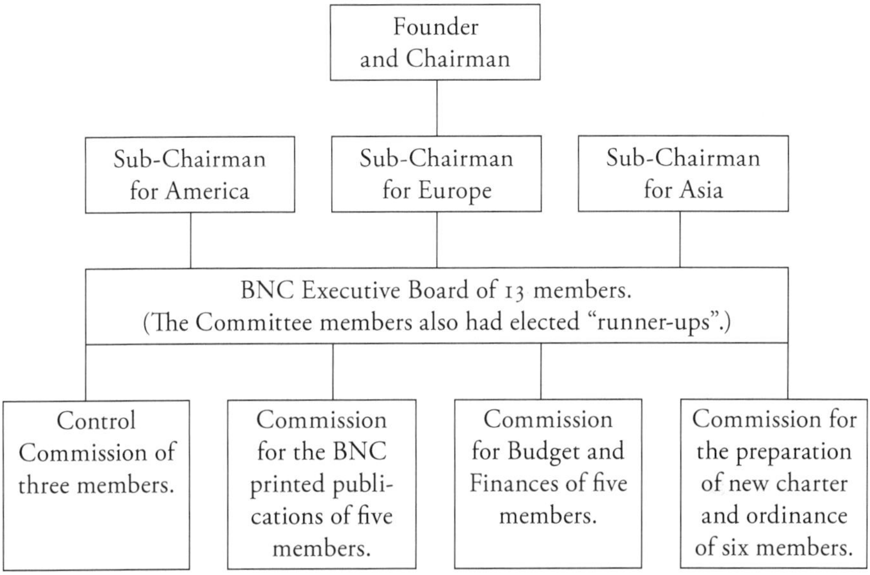

BNC Inner Organization Scheme of December 1953[41]

ticipated in fourteen international congresses, conferences, celebrations and meetings.[38] Representatives of the BNC were located in Italy, Austria, France, England, Germany, Belgium, the Netherlands, Australia, New Zealand, Israel, the United States and Canada. The political structure of the Committee was comprised of the following organizations: the Bulgarian Agrarian National Union, the Bulgarian Labor Social Democrat Party, the Free Labor Syndicates, members of the Democratic Party, a representative of the Bulgarian scientific community and a representative of the Bulgarian army.[39]

The BNC's inner organization was well coordinated. Most of the important decisions were taken during the BNC congresses, which took place once every two years, usually in Paris, France, as that location was most convenient for all the participants. Some of the key founding members of the BNC were: Dr. G. M. Dimitrov, chairman and general secretary; Dimitar Macankiev, former MP and BANU member; Milka Genadieva, journalist and Doctor. of Law; Tzenko Barev, secretary of the BANU Academic Youth Union; Vasil Urukov, former minster plenipotentiary and representative of "Zveno"; Prof. Nikola Dolapchiev, former minister plenipotentiary and vice-president of the Bulgarian Academy of Science; Georgi Petkov, professor at the University of Varna and Social Democratic Party MP in the Grand National Assembly; Tzviatko Penev, representative of the Social Democratic Party abroad; Nikola Balabanov, former minister plenipotentiary; and Konstantin Shopov, former MP in the Grand National Assembly and representative of the Agrarian Union.[40]

In the same December 1953 report the BNC explained that important decisions were taken during the general Assembly and had to be approved by two thirds of the voters. The Committee chairman called and led the meetings of the executive board. He also had the responsibility of representing the organization as its spokesman to the "outside world" and as its representative to international institutions. The executive board chose a secretary, who did not have to be a member of the board, as well as a treasurer and all the rest of the administrative staff. The BNC budget was voted on by the general assembly and was executed by the board.

BNC Sub-Divisions

At the end of the report it was announced that the permanent committee for science and culture had been joined by the following cultural representatives: Professor Ivan Stransky, Professor Vladimir Boukliisky, Dr. G. Shishkov, the writer Loredna and Maria Puidev. Further, the article explains that there was a permanent division of the organization which was dedicated to the development of the scientific work of the Bulgarian immigration. As already mentioned, Dimitrov's aim was to popularize the scientific and cultural activities and work being produced by Bulgarians abroad. In fact, he hoped to find more financial support for the BNC and IPU to support scientific research. He also hoped that more of the Committee members living in Europe would be able to travel to the USA and contribute actively to this specific sphere.

In 1956 a new youth division was added.to the organizational structure of the BNC and its sub-committees. It was placed under the direct leadership of the Paris BNC and had the following goals: to unify the youth in exile; to launch cultural and educational activities; to organize music and dance groups and popularize Bulgarian culture abroad; to launch a youth newspaper; to send monthly reports on youth activity to the leading body of the BNC; to hold political, economic or cultural seminars. Biser Kolev was elected to head the youth division. The goals of this new BNC sub-organization were mostly related to cultural diplomacy initiatives and activities that had the potential to improve and change the image of Bulgaria in the eyes of the outside world. The young people were advised to carefully prepare their programs in such a way that they could "raise admirations in the foreigner and sympathy towards the Bulgarian people."[42]

The committee organized other cultural initiatives, mostly related to the traditional Bulgarian performing arts, and their main goal was again to promote Bulgarian culture. By the end of 1956, we can already see an initiative with a political nature being held by the BNC youth section. It was a lecture by Dr. Dimitrov that took place in Paris in the Société Savant hall. In it the BNC leader called on the international community following the Hungarian Revolution, which broke out in October of that year, to support the Hungarian people and their efforts for freedom and democracy. But at the same time he voiced the opinion that the role of diplomacy had ended and everything was now in the hands of the people behind the Iron Curtain, especially the young people, who had shown courage and made a great sacrifice for freedom.[43] In November 1957, the BNC youth division organized a Bulgarian-German initiative that took place in Germersheim, Germany, where young people from the two countries discussed their concerns, hopes and a common vision for the future of Europe and their place in it. This meeting received a wide and very positive response in the German press, which had been one of the main aims of the organization.[44]

This meeting grew into an annual event and took place again in June 1958 with the cooperation of the local German Christian Democratic Party and the city administration. The main lecture topics covered current issues on the European continent – how it could make itself a whole entity and the role of youth in overcoming the social and political challenges of the separation.[45] The third youth meeting took place in January 1960, and its focus was on the role of Europe in the liberation of the captive nations. At this event, the topics were more specific and diverse and included a discussion of "Collectivism versus the Free Market." At this point, we can already see governmental participation in the event, as represented by the presence of the director of the German government's Institute for Press and Information; and it had grown to become multinational, as well, as there were also official representatives of the Turkish immigration.[46]

Another organization affiliated with the BNC that was established around that time was the Bulgarian Labor Professional Union, which was also a member of the Assembly of the Captive European Nations (ACEN, founded in September 1954[47]) and which unified the working class Bulgarian immigrants in Europe and the United States.

Activities Directed towards the Bulgarian Immigration

One of the basic principles accepted in the BNC's first years was that no member and political immigrant could engage in any political activity related to recruitment by the Bulgarian or any other foreign government unless the activity was coordinated and approved by the Committee.[48] This was a precaution against potential recruitment of the immigrants by the Bulgarian or other secret services. The BNC used *Free and Independent Bulgaria* to inform its readers and the members of the Committee of existing "threats" such as newly formed governmental structures in Bulgaria. An example can be found in the issue of 19 March 1953 in note titled "Important Warning". It warned that recently in Bulgaria a secret section called "partisan" had been formed as a subsection of the Voluntary Organization for Cooperation in Defense (*Доброволна организация по сътрудничество в отбраната*). According to the newspaper, it was under the "control of the Soviet specialists". The text further informed readers that the organization would target anticommunists and movements opposing the Soviets, and therefore they should be attentive and protect themselves from "the perfidies of the communist agent-provocateurs."[49]

In 1963, the February issue of *Free and Independent Bulgaria* published a small note warning the immigrants of dangerous communist activity amongst them that was causing divisions and making destructive attempts on the Bulgarian church. The Bulgarians in exile were asked to do everything possible to prevent any actions undertaken by open or hidden communist agents "dressed in liturgical vestments."[50] Apparently, the Bulgarian orthodox churches abroad, which had naturally become centers of fellowship and activity among immigrants, were easily accessible to the communist regime in Bulgaria, which was in control of the church activity and placements abroad. The BNC often informed its members of such interference and expressed its concern. Similar information was given a couple of months later, when the newspaper mentioned the names of four "betrayers" who had informed on other Bulgarians to the authorities as they attempted to flee the country.[51]

A professional opportunity that was not politically neutral but was encouraged and coordinated by the Committee caused a Bulgarian company, composed of Bulgarian exiles, to be established within NATO in 1951. In light of the growing expense of its units safeguarding US military supply depots and bases in Germany and throughout Europe, the US government decided to hire young immigrants from Eastern Europe to perform the same tasks but at lower salaries. Dr. Dimitrov seized the opportunity and organized a group of over 200 young Bulgarians who became full-time NATO employees until their company was disbanded in 1964. The Bulgarian company was stationed in Germersheim, West Germany, under commander Dimitar Krastev, and was visited yearly by Dr. Dimitrov, usually on May 6, St. George's Day, the patron saint of the Bulgarian military. These meetings were accompanied by a speech given by Dimitrov and celebrations with the local community and the Bulgarians living there. The Bulgarian company did not limit itself to its military duties but took an active part in public life. One initiative, which was very well accepted by the locals, was the Bulgarian soldiers' yearly financial donation to poor orphans. On the tenth anniversary of the company's founding, the mayor of Germersheim asserted that because of their "Christian and humanist values", the Bulgarians had won the sympathy and support of the citizens and the authorities.[52] Another initiative of the Bulgarian company was a dance group that participated in competitions and community celebrations throughout Germany and France. This type of activity continued the cultural diplomacy that was a major element in the Committee's program.[53]

The NATO company of Bulgarian exiles was an undertaking of great significance in times when their homeland was adhering to fostering a policy of political isolationism. The task that the Bulgarian exiles undertook not only spoke of the level of their professional commitment and trustworthiness but also proved Dimitrov to be a person of great political vision, as this took place fifty-three years before Bulgaria became an official member of the NATO Alliance.

Apart from its political agenda, which became its priority throughout its existence, another major Committee commitment was to assist the immigrants coming from Bulgaria.[54] The assistance initiatives were partially sponsored by the NCFE, but even after that sponsorship stopped in 1971, the help continued on a voluntarily basis. These activities had a more humanitarian than political nature and were related to the immediate assistance that the BNC offered to immigrants upon their arrival in the refugee/immigration camps in Austria and Italy. This help included translation of their personal documents, diplomas and so on, assistance with the administrative process, and finding them places to live, a temporary job, and sponsorship for their transfer to other countries, including the United States. The BNC also partnered with different non-governmental and religious organizations, especially Protestant organizations, which provided temporary shelters and food for the newly arrived Bulgarian refugees. Many members of the Committee used their professional positions to help the immigrants administratively. Most of this work was done on a volunteer basis.[55]

The BNC as an International Organization

The value of the BNC's humanitarian efforts notwithstanding, Dr. Dimitrov's main focus was on the political side of his organization. From September to December 1950, he visited Europe in his role as chairman of a number of political organizations, including the BNC and the Bulgarian

National Council for United Europe, and as a member of The International Executive Committee of the European Movement.[56] During these trips, he visited the United Kingdom, France, Italy, Austria, Germany and Switzerland, where he met some of the leading political figures at the time. He also participated over the years in all of the BNC's annual meetings, which were held in Paris, and had the opportunity to communicate personally with other leaders from the Bulgarian opposition who were also in exile. Ferenc Nagy once said of Dimitrov that in all of central Eastern Europe, he was "the most loved political leader among his people."[57] These trips confirmed Nagy's opinion.

Dimitrov and his fellow immigrant leaders also faced criticism and often suspicion concerning the real motives of their work. A small book was published in France in 1948 titled *L'Internationale des traitres* and written by the French communist Renaud De Jouvene, with a forward by André Wurmser. The book's aim was to portray the political immigrants from Eastern Europe and their organizations as leaders of IPU, as fascists trying to undermine the "peoples' republics" with the help of the American and British governments. In the chapter dedicated to Bulgaria, the author painted an extremely negative and false image of the Bulgarian opposition, and especially of Nikola Petkov, who had taken over the Agrarian Union in Bulgaria after Dimitrov and was later hung by the communists. The book repeated the same false charges that the Bulgarian communists had laid against Petrov during his trial in 1947.[58] Dr. Dimitrov, the Romanian Nikola Dianu and the Polish Jan Kovalevsky all found this writing so cynical and undermining of the democratic immigration's image that they decide to sue the author and preface writer for libel. The lawsuit attracted a great deal of attention in the press and the public in France. The Eastern European leaders seized this opportunity to present the case for their nations openly, and thus the court became an arena in which fundamental questions concerning modern European politics were discussed. Sentence was passed on 29 April 1952, and the authors of the book and its preface were convicted and ordered to pay damages, which consisted of a fine of 12,000 Francs and an additional fine of 20,000 Francs if the claimants' names were not removed from all subsequent editions. Dr. Dimitrov and his fellow claimants were granted symbolic compensation of 1 Franc, signifying that they had not filed the lawsuit to benefit themselves but to draw public attention to the fate of their countries. Their stance made the case strongly political, and it marked a significant victory for the political immigration from Eastern Europe.[59]

One of the Committee's initiatives that helped to raise awareness of the realities in Bulgaria and Eastern Europe was to organize an annual day of remembrance for Nikola Petkov, the leader of the Agrarian Union in Bulgaria, who also headed the opposition against the communist regime after 1945. Arrested in the Bulgarian Parliament in June 1947, he was denied a defense at his show trial and sentenced to death. Despite protests and support from the international community for Petkov, he was hanged on 23 September 1947. Commemorating his memory became an annual event since the founding of BNC; and every year until the Committee existed, on September 23 his sacrifice for democracy and freedom was commemorated in the US Senate and marked by meetings, events and Christian services initiated by the Committee. The most significant events took place in Washington and New York, where the guests and speakers included senators, representatives of the State Department, mayors and other high-profile political figures. A good example of the scale and importance these events acquired were the "Days of Bulgaria and Nikola Petkov" held in the US Senate and House of Representatives from 23–25 September 1963. During those three days speeches senators Harrison Williams (New Jersey) and Kenneth Keating (New York) spoke before the Senate, acknowledging Petkov's sacrifice for freedom. In the House, representatives Barratt O'Hara and Edward Derwinski (both of Illinois), Robert Taft Jr. (Ohio) and Clement Zablocki (Wisconsin) all spoke about the hope for liberty and called on the people of Bulgaria not to give up their faith and to fight for free and democracy.[60]

The fate of Nikola Petkov also attracted attention in Europe, where a German Film studio premiered a documentary on Petkov's life on 23 February 1968. Directed by Wolfgang Werner, it was called "The Petkov Case" and was broadcast on the second channel of German television. The documentary also told the story of the opposition in Bulgaria after the end of the Second World War and provoked a number of angry commentaries in the Bulgarian media at the time.[61]

As already mentioned, for many years the BNC and the other national committees received almost no response to any of their actions from the United Nations. Nevertheless, the BNC kept on trying to attract attention to the fate of the Bulgarian people, and in January 1962 Dimitrov sent a letter to the UN Secretary General, explaining in brief how the Soviets had gained complete control over the Bulgarian government and how this had violated all the democratic and human rights and fundamental freedoms of the Bulgarian people. The Bulgarian people never elected the government that was presently in power, and its representation in the UN would undermine the authority of this institution and would discourage and disturb the people of the captive nations.[62] One year later, the national committees decided to change their strategy and use their lobby in the Congress to influence the UN. The approach was similar, but this time it was undertaken by Republican Bob Wilson of California, who put forward a draft resolution in the House calling for free elections to be held in all the captive nations of Eastern Europe – a resolution that should have been passed in the UN.[63] During this period of time, the BNC had started to work actively in the Senate as well, and as a result in 1964 that body proclaimed March 3, Bulgarian Independence Day, the Day of Bulgaria. The proclamation was accompanied by various speeches and events promoting awareness of the Bulgarian past and present.[64]

Dr. Dimitrov saw Radio Free Europe (RFE) as yet another potential tool that could be used to increase awareness of the immigration's activities in the West and behind the Iron Curtain. However, RFE's agenda and that of the US government were often very different from that of the Bulgarian and Eastern European political immigration. Indeed, Dr. Dimitrov disagreed with some general aspects of the radio's policy. His opinion was that information on what people were doing in Bulgaria against the communist regime should have more coverage in the RFE programs. The radio should also inform listeners of the progress and the work of the BNC, so the Bulgarian people could knew that they were not forgotten and that the countries of the free world appreciated their sacrifices. He also advised that RFE pay more attention to the crimes committed by the communists, thus letting the Bulgarians know that what was happening in their country did not remain unnoticed.[65] Nevertheless, further cooperation was not established between the two organizations, as RFE's aim was to directly serve the purposes of American anti-communist propaganda, and the BNC found other means to connect to the Bulgarians behind the Iron Curtain.

One incident for which the Bulgarian section of RFE drew open criticism was related to a program it did on Bulgaria's last monarch, Boris III. The BNC objected to RFE's positive commentary on the kings life in the pages of *Free and Independent Bulgaria*, citing his authoritarian political course during the last years of his rule, with the political repression that members of the Agrarian Union and Dr. Dimitrov had personally endured, and Boris III's decision to join the German side during World War Two. Furthermore, the Committee felt that historical interpretations such as the one by RFE enhanced the communist strategy to present the Bulgarian immigration abroad as fascist.[66]

The BNC in Political Cooperation as a Member of other Organizations

Regardless of the many efforts that the national committees made in their attempt to draw the attention of the big international institutions, and especially the UN, to what was taking place in Eastern Europe, their voice and memorandums did not receive a significant response. The Assembly of Captive European Nations (ACEN) came into existence in this atmosphere and at this time. Just over a month before the ACEN was officially founded in September 1954, *Free and Independent Bulgaria* preceded the event with a lengthy article titled "Unity Makes Strength."[67] The article announced that the idea of federating the national committees was not a new one and had come about as early as 1950 at a BNC meeting in Paris, soon after which, the BNC chairman had tried to reach out with the idea to the rest of the Eastern European leaders. But no further steps were taken until the idea was revived as the ACEN and sponsored by the Free Europe Committee, Inc., the organization that funded and supported the national councils. (The NCFE was renamed the Free Europe Committee, Inc. in 1954.)

The article continued by stating that no matter what kind of arguments and misunderstandings there were within the national committees, those organizations were still the "symbols of the national independence and the integrity of the peoples behind the Iron Curtain".[68] The responsibility that went with this task required that the national committees engage in forming a deeper cooperation among themselves. The BNC saw itself and its fellow organizations as the "most competent" regarding strategies for leading the fight against the communists because the members of those organizations were already involved in that battle in their own countries. They knew best the ethno-psychology of their people and could most adequately plan efficient actions against the communists that would result in the smallest amount of civilian casualties. The article concluded with the statement that their common, methodological and responsible work would become the foundation for future lasting cooperation and liberation of the people of their countries, which would live in one united Europe.[69] In the same issue, the newspaper published the Charter of the United National Committees and Councils in Exile, which announced the decision to launch the organization of the same name. The document was signed on 14 July 1954 by representatives to the National Councils of Albania, Bulgaria, Czechoslovakia, Estonia, Hungary, Latvia, Lithuania, Poland, Romania and Yugoslavia and was officially presented to the State Department and the Committee for Free Europe.

When the ACEN was founded on 20 September 1954, it emerged not only as a response to the efforts to consolidate and make more effective the political activity and influence of the National Committees but also as a parallel structure of the UN. There were two main reasons behind this: the first was because the founders of the organization wanted to underline their attachment to the international cooperation that the UN symbolized. The second was that they also wanted to demonstrate their disappointment in the UN's lack of response to all the memorandums they had released and in the fact that the UN had accepted the Soviet satellite governments as members. Therefore the establishment of the ACEN reflected the national committees' search for an alternative tool for their political agenda. At the first ACEN session, Dr. G. M. Dimitrov was elected vice president of the organization, a post he held until 1962, when he became the organization's president.[70] His role in the Assembly was far from being just an administrative figure, and he became one its key leaders and biggest activists. Nevertheless, the initial enthusiasm of the immigrants who thought they had found the right formula for political cooperation and influence did not last. From the time of its founding, the ACEN leadership and the American sponsoring organization could not reach common ground on the issue of Yugoslavia and whether it should have a place in the ACEN. While the BNC and the rest of the national committees supported its joining, the Americans considered Yugoslavia to be a country of different status and did not want to ratify its membership in the organization. Over the years, these differences grew into larger gaps between the positions that the two sides represented.[71]

The significant contribution the BNC and Dr. Dimitrov made to international organizations was not limited only to the United States, it reached the European Parliament as well. The idea of a Council of Europe was brought forward as early as 1943, but because of the devastated situation Western Europe found itself in after the war, its official beginning can be traced to the Hague Congress in 1948. In addition to Winston Churchill, Leon Blum, Paul Henri Spaak, and many Western European leaders, the European movement included political figures in exile from Eastern Europe. As chairman of the Bulgarian Committee of the European Movement and as a general secretary of the International Peasant Union, Dr. Dimitrov was among these leaders.[72] The first decision, proposed by Dr. Dimitrov and approved by the Council, was that the chairs designated for the nations behind the Iron Curtain would stay empty until the day of their liberation as symbol of their place in a future united Europe. Thus, this European institution, unlike the UN, took an uncompromising position towards the communist regimes in

Eastern Europe. The second contribution of Dimitrov was related to resolution #47 of 28 May 1954, which granted the representatives of the national committees in exile the right to hold hearings in front of the European Parliament on "certain questions related to these committees."[73] Dimitrov often participated and spoke in the parliamentary sessions in Strasbourg as the head of the BNC and ACEN.

Topics of Particular Importance to the BNC

The BNC stood very firm in its position concerning Bulgarian domestic policies, and as already mentioned, it informed its members and supports of all the critical issues emerging in Bulgarian daily life. After its annual meetings, the committee released detailed reports of the decisions made during the meetings and statements of the official BNC positions on current events. One such report, published in June 1959, reflects the organization's deep concerned regarding the fate of the peasants and the working class, as well for the growing centralization of power in the hands of the Bulgarian Communist Party. According to the committee, the worsening living conditions and public health and the low income were caused by poor investments and bad economic strategy on the part of the government. Nevertheless, the Bulgarian people were portrayed as intransigent toward the ideological propaganda they faced at all levels and were acknowledged as being the "one and only constitutional factor."[74] The people themselves were the single democratic factor left in the country.

As already mentioned, Bulgaria's future after the fall of the communism was a subject to which the immigrant leaders attached a great deal of importance. Dr. Dimitrov published a series of articles dedicated to the agrarian reform and restructuring he felt should take place in post-communist Bulgaria. Human rights, religious freedom and church independence, as well as the national administrative structure, were also subjects that were discussed and reflected upon, not just in the pages of the immigrant journals but also in their meetings, official forums and statements issued to the international institutions.[75]

The BNC followed closely the behavior of the Bulgarian governmental representatives in international forums. Dr. Dimitrov often sent letters to the presiding figures of these forums, informing them that the BNC took a completely different position from that defended by the Bulgarian officials and insisting that the latter were not eligible to speak for the people of Bulgaria. In June 1967, Dr. Dimitrov sent a letter to the head of the UN Security Council, Hans Tabor, in which he explicitly differentiated his and his organization's position from that taken by the Bulgarian representative and took Israel's side during the crisis in the Middle East. According to the BNC's leader, that support followed logically from the friendship and bond existing between Israel and Bulgaria. Dimitrov also reminded Tabor that during the Second World War, regardless of the fact that the Bulgarian government had taken the side of Germany, the people of Bulgaria had rescued its citizens with Jewish origins and therefore would never support the communist government's present position on the Middle East.[76]

The BNC was against the attempts at the end of the 1950s by the first secretary of the Bulgarian Communist Party, Todor Zhivkov, to resume diplomatic relations between Bulgaria and the USA. The resumption officially took place on 24 March 1959.[77] The committee continued to stand firm and persisted in its position that complete political and diplomatic isolation was the West's only possible response to the Soviet regime in Eastern Europe. Any other alternative would only encourage this oppressive political course. In the same report, the BNC announced its initiative to call a meeting of all the ACEN members to discuss its reorganization – a necessary process that would pull it out of "its present vegetative stage" which had caused the organization to become "incapable of representing and defending the national freedom and independence of our captive nations."[78] Further, the report also states that the Committee was pleased with its work in common with the Romanian National Committee and with what they had done together to suggest changes in the ACEN. Nevertheless these objections against the ACEN were left just as a voiced opinion and no further actions were taken during that particular time period.

The Bulgarian immigration organizations paid a great deal of attention to one of the most important international events of the late 1950s, the Hungarian Revolution. Dimitrov published a great deal on it. In his opinion, the Hungarian experience proved that no Eastern European nation would surrender completely to communist rule, no matter in what form or shape that rule had been exercised but that the lack of strong oppositionist groups could risk the failure of any attempt to gain back freedom and democracy.[79] A common feature of all the resolutions and declarations that the BNC issued during this time was its discontent with the way the UN held back on making any action or statement vis a vis the events in Hungary. In a resolution of 4 May 1957, the BNC expressed its "deep regret" regarding the UN position and declared that this could only encourage Soviet aggression and delay the liberation of the captive peoples of Europe.[80]

Later, Dr. Dimitrov's dedicated a great number of articles to the events in Czechoslovakia in 1968. The Prague Spring, according to Dimitrov, proved that the people behind the Iron Curtain had not chosen their present fate and had not surrendered to the Soviet domination. At the same time, the indifference of the West that had marked the Hungarian revolution only facilitated the counter action of the Soviet military intervention in Czechoslovakia. To express its disapproval of the intervention and to plead for action, the BNC sent a number of notes of protest to US President Lyndon Johnson, to the UN Secretary General and to major newspapers in Europe.[81] This was one of the few times when the State Department responded to the BNC's formal protest notes. In a letter explaining the US position on the events in Czechoslovakia, Raymond Lisle, the State Department's director for relations with Eastern Europe, noted that the United States condemned the Soviet invasion of the country and the fact that the communists found the Czechoslovakian people's striving for internal freedom to be a threat to the Soviet system.[82]

Among the political acts of support for the Eastern European countries that the BNC found encouraging in the 1960s was a draft resolution put forward in the House of Representatives by Republican Bob

Wilson, asking the US government to insist that the UN hold free elections in all the captive nations of Eastern Europe and in East Germany. A further demand was that Soviet troops leave the territories of these countries and that all people detained in labor camps and prisons be freed.[83] A resolution with identical demands was presented to the US Senate by another Republican, Barry Goldwater, on 30 March 1964.[84]

All of these efforts bore very few practical results, often going no further then to make the West aware that there were people who still had the hope and desire to continue the fight for political and personal freedom in the countries behind the Iron Curtain.

The End of the Dimitrov Era

In the mid 1960s, the BNC put more focus on activities to gather its members and especially the young people, using occasions such as national holidays to bring them together. On the Fourth of July 1965 the BNC held a meeting and a seminar at Niagara Falls hosting over 300 members of the Bulgarian immigration from the US and Canada. The topics ranged within the usual spectrum of political issues in Bulgarian domestic and foreign policy, including discussions on international events taking place in Vietnam, the Dominican Republic, Europe and the Soviet Union.[85] A similar event took place a year later, 2–3 July 1966, in Chicago, organized by the local sub-committee. This time the participants discussed the new administrative structure in Bulgaria and the way the Agrarian Union envisioned the reforms that should take place in Bulgaria after the fall of the communist regime.[86]

When the US funding of the ACEN was suspended in 1971, Dr. Dimitrov refused to accept the demise of that organization and called on the national committees to find a way to continue to support themselves and the organization. At the beginning of the seventies, many Bulgarian immigrants had built a stable life abroad and had a steady source of income; with their contributions, the BNC continued to exist and to publish *Free and Independent Bulgaria* until the fall of the Berlin Wall. The last issue was published in January 1990. [87]

Dr. G.M. Dimitrov led the BNC from Washington, D.C. until the end of 1972. Suffering from a serious heart condition, he died in exile on November 29 of that year. He never returned home. His funeral gathered together numerous immigrants and American political leaders. Of note were Ferenc Nagy, head of the IPU, Stefan Korboński, leader of the ACEN, Teofil Bozarik, representing the Slovak Peasant Party and many others. After Dimitrov's death, Dimitar Petkov, Nikola Petkov's nephew, took over the position of BNC chairman. The Committee ceased its activity completely in 1991, as its founding documents stated that the organization would exist only until the day democracy was restored in Bulgaria.

Seen from an historical perspective, Dr. G.M. Dimitrov is one of those figures whose work has still not been accorded its rightful place as that of other better known immigrant leaders such as Ferenc Nagy, Msgr. Béla Varga and Stefan Korboński. His unselfish dedication to the cause of Bulgarian democracy throughout his life time has yet to be acknowledged by contemporary historians in Bulgaria and abroad. This chapter has modestly attempted to detail some of this political visionary's fundamental contributions to "captive" Bulgaria, which he worked for throughout his life. Dr. Dimitrov, his work and the organizations that he created demonstrated that communism was never organically bound to the people of Bulgaria. In fact, after the end of World War Two anti-communist protests were common in Bulgaria, though they were ineffective in halting the Soviet takeover of the nation or in attracting any international attention. This was why Dr. Dimitrov used every opportunity to remind foreign audiences that Bulgaria was a country where democracy was a value that was pursued and fought for. As a true diplomat he strove to shape for Bulgaria a new national image in the eyes of the West, an image of a people that responded to a different set of codes of political behavior than the one associated with authoritative dictatorship and isolationism.

In addition, the cooperation that the BNC entered into with organizations such as NATO and the Council of Europe began laying the foundations for the international political integration of Bulgaria, which fully took place over half a century later. The political ideology to which the BNC was continuously committed incorporated the principles of democracy, respect of human rights, free market economy and a culture which was a product of a healthy society, free to develop itself, thus creating a parallel history of Bulgaria, marked, but never dominated by communism.

Endnotes

1 Personal interview with Hristo Chorelov, a member of the French branch of BNC and its chairman from 1973 until 1992, taken on 7 August 2012.

2 Phone interview with Anastasia Moser, Dr. Dimitrov's daughter, taken on 18 April 2012; and a personal interview with her on 15 August 2012.

3 Differentiate his name from that of Georgi Dimitrov, a Bulgarian communist politician and the first communist leader of Bulgaria (1946–1949), is important as the two are sometimes confused.

4 G. M. Dimitrov, *Memories* (Sofia: Foundation Open Society, 1993) 14–27.

5 Dimitrov, *Memories,* 50–55.

6 Ivet-Mathilde Chorelov, *The Bulgarian Agrarian National Union 1899–1947: The difficult road to democracy* (Bourgas: Bojich, 2012).

7 Dimitrov, *Memories,* 74–78.

8 Charles Moser, *Dr. G. M. Dimitrov* (Sofia: Voennoizdatelski komplex "Sv. Georgi Pobedonosec", 1991) 47–62 and Dimitrov, *Memories,* 38–42.

9 Moser, *Dr. G. M. Dimitrov,* 53–54.

10 Ibid., *53.*

11 Chorelov, *The Bulgarian Agrarian National Union,* 253–260.

12 Moser, *Dr. G. M. Dimitrov,* 47–62.

13 Dimitrov, *Memories,* 121–125.

14 National Archives, Washington, D. C., Bureau Research and Analysis, #2301 3 [Bulgarian politics as seen from the Agrarian perspective]: Resume of Manuscript by Dr. G.M. Dimitrov, 25 January 1945.

15 Dimitrov, *Memories,* 148.

16 Stratia Skerlev, *Dr. Dimitrov: Person, Ideas and Activity* (Paris: Bulgarian National Committee, 1970) 29–39.

17 Dimitrov, *Memories,* 184–186.

18 Moser, *Dr. G.M. Dimitrov,* 183–184.

19 Dimitrov, *Memories,* 236. "явна и най-жестока смърт..." Translated by the author.

20 Ibid.

21 Dimitar Genchev, *Bulgaria in* Stalin*'s Secret Archives: From Kimon Georgiev's Government until Stalin's Death* (Sofia: Geny Agency, 2005) 60–61.

22 Dimitrov, *Memories,* 245.

23 Ibid., 270. "...да продължа борбата си в защита на свободата и независимостта на народа си..." Translated by the author.

24 Ibid., 271.

1. Аз бих веднага организирал най-мощната военна сила в света.

2. Аз бих организирал най-широката пропагандна машина в сшета.

3. Аз бих организирал най-ефикасното разузнаване в света.

4. Аз бих веднага дал възможност на всеки народ в света всякаква помощ, за да организира една мощтна съпротива срещу съветско-комунистическата агресия от световен мащаб, чиято главна цел е сломяването на Съединените американски щати като единствена крепост на свободата и демокрацията, която им пресича пътя към световното господство!" Translated by the author.

25 Chorelov, *The Bulgarian Agrarian National Union,* 515.

26 George Barrett, "UN Asked To Free Soviet Satellites", *New York Times*, 29 September 1947. Section 1, Page 1

27 Ibid.

28 Constantine Poulosq, "Front Men for Reaction", *The Nation*, 21 February 1948, 203–207.

29 The mission statement of the NCFE issued on 17 May 1949 is quoted in Katalin Kádár Lynn's essay in this volume. It states ... "we will encourage these leaders to maintain in this country National Committees which will stand as symbols of democratic hope to their peoples – the peoples of Bulgaria, Czechoslovakia, Hungary, Poland, Rumania and Yugoslavia to whom at Yalta we promised *free elections and fundamental freedoms.*"

30 Toncho Karabulkov, *G.M. Dimitrov 1949/72: Sentence on Communism* (Sofia: Canko Cerkovski Publishing, 1991) 8.

31 Moser, *Dr. G.M. Dimitrov*, 270. "... капитална грешка беше, че все пак се повлиях от от внушението на Г-н Барнс, че моят престой вън от България ще е само няколко месеца. (...) Така че аз нито дори за миг не помислих за дълго оставане в чужбина и не ми мина през ум да си взема позволително за практикуване на медицината, особено като специалист по ренгенология. (...) И този пропуск се оказа пакостен и за мене лично, и за народното ни освободително дело, защото аз и досега не можах да осъществя своите начертани планове за работа и борба." Translated by the author.

32 Karabulkov, *G.M. Dimitrov 1949/72*. 6–7.

33 The author was given access to copies of *Free and Independent Bulgaria* from 1949 to 1972, courtesy of Anastasia Moser. The full collection is also available in the St. Cyril and Methodius National Library, Sofia.

34 Karabulkov, *G.M. Dimitrov*, 6–7.

35 G.M. Dimitrov, "Program for Battle", *Liberation* 1, November 1949. "...освобождението на България от ...комунистическо-болшевишко иго." Translated by the author.

36 Ibid. "...осигуряване правото на българския народ на свободно и независимо съществуване в утрешния свободен демократичен свят." Translated by the author.

37 Ibid. "...червената болшевишка диктатура". Translated by the author.

38 "What Did You Do for Bulgaria?" *Free and Independent Bulgaria* 1, 1 January 1953, 4–5.

39 "Decisions of the BNC", *Free and Independent Bulgaria* 5, 4 December 1953, 1.

40 Zemedelsko Zname, Bulgarian Democratic Political Organizations in Exile, http://www.zemedelskozname.com/bnk/. Accessed on 12 October 2012.

41 "Decisions of the BNC", *Free and Independent Bulgaria* 5, 4 December 1953, 2.

42 Toncho Karabulkov, "Advance in the Organizational Life of the Youth in Exile", *Free and Independent Bulgaria* 12, 20 September 1956, 3. "...те да събуждат възторг у чужденеца и симпатии към българския народ." Translated by the author

[43] Chernorizetc Hrabar, "The Struggle for Freedom in Critical Stage", *Free and Independent Bulgaria* 16, 23 November 1956, 8–9.
[44] "A Bulgarian-German Youth Meeting Took Place", *Free and Independent Bulgaria* 19, 10 December 1957, 4–5.
[45] "The Warrior's Voice of Bulgaria Heard again in a Successful German-Bulgarian Youth Meeting", *Free and Independent Bulgaria* 8, 31 August 1958, 9–10.
[46] "The Third Youth Meeting in Firnheim: Contribution to the Cause of Freedom", *Free and Independent Bulgaria* 3, March 1960, 4–6.
[47] Immigration History Research Center, Assembly of Captive European Nations: http://www.ihrc.umn.edu/research/vitrage/all/am/ihrc246.html. Accessed on 26 September 2012.
[48] Personal interview with Hristo Chorelov, taken on 30 July 2012.
[49] "Important Warning", *Free and Independent Bulgaria* 4, 19 March 1953, 2. "...коварствата на комунистическите агент-провокатори." Translated by the author.
[50] "A Call to the Bulgarians Abroad", *Free and Independent Bulgaria* 2, February 1963, 6.
[51] "Remember! Write it Down!", *Free and Independent Bulgaria* 2, March–April 1964, 7.
[52] "Ten Years Bulgarian Company in Germany", *Free and Independent Bulgaria* 9, December 1964, 7–8.
[53] "One More Dance Group Gains Victories for the People's Cause", *Free and Independent Bulgaria* 7, October–November 1962.
[54] Personal interview with Hristo Chorelov, taken on 7 August 2012.
[55] Ibid.
[56] Moser, *Memories*, 227.
[57] Ibid.
[58] Ibid., 233–234.
[59] Nicolas Dianuet, *Les communistes démasqués: D'après les comptes rendus sténographiques du procès contre "L'internationale des traîtres"* (Paris: Société Roumaine D'éditions, 1953).
[60] "The Days of Bulgaria and Nikola Petkov in the Senate and in the House of Representatives in the USA", *Free and Independent Bulgaria* 5, August–September, 1963, 1–2.
[61] "The Film 'The Petkov Case'", *Free and Independent Bulgaria* 2, July 1968, 9–10.
[62] "BNC Documents", *Free and Independent Bulgaria* 3, March–April 1962, 4.
[63] *Free and Independent Bulgaria* 1, January–February 1964, 5.
[64] "Day of Bulgaria in the US Congress", *Free and Independent Bulgaria* 2, March–April 1964, 4.
[65] Moser, *Memories*, 228.
[66] "The Image of Free Europe", *Free and Independent Bulgaria* 9, 8 September 1956, 3.
[67] "Unity Makes Strength", *Free and Independent Bulgaria* 6, 30 July 1954, 1.
[68] Ibid. "символи на националната независимост и на честността на народите зад желязната завеса". Translated by the author.
[69] Ibid.
[70] Moser, *Memories*, 229.
[71] Ibid.
[72] Ibid., 232.
[73] "Europe and the Captive Nations", *Free and Independent Bulgaria* 12, 26 November 1954.
[74] "The Decisions of the Plenum of the Bulgarian National Committee", *Free and Independent Bulgaria* 6, July 1959, 4–5.
[75] These were the main topics occupying the major part of the BNC annual meeting reports, especially during the 1960s when a new administrative regional division within Bulgaria took place.
[76] "The BNC and the Middle East Crisis", *Free and Independent Bulgaria* 3, August 1967, 2.

[77] US Department of State, A Guide to the United States' History of Recognition, Diplomatic, and Consular Relations, by Country, since 1776: Bulgaria. http://history.state.gov/countries/bulgaria. Accessed on 27 September 2012.

[78] "The Decisions of the Plenum of the Bulgarian National Committee", *Free and Independent Bulgaria* 6, July 1959, 4–5.

[79] Moser, *Memories*, 236.

[80] "Resolution of the Bulgarian National Committee", *Free and Independent Bulgaria* 9, 31 May 1957.

[81] "Protest against the Invasion in Czechoslovakia", *Free and Independent Bulgaria* 3, October 1968, 8–9.

[82] "BNC Documents", *Free and Independent Bulgaria* 3, October 1968, 8.

[83] "Resolution", *Free and Independent Bulgaria* 1, January–February 1964) 4.

[84] "A Resolution was Presented to the US Senate Requesting the UN to Hold Free Elections in the Captive Nations", *Free and Independent Bulgaria* 3, May–June 1964, 4.

[85] "Heavily Attended BNC Seminar in Niagara Falls", *Free and Independent Bulgaria* 4, July–August 1965, 3–6.

[86] "BNC Seminar in Chicago", *Free and Independent Bulgaria* 3, September 1966, 7–8.

[87] Personal interview with Anastasia Moser, taken on 18 April 2012.

Select bibliography

Г.М. Димитров. *Спомени.* Фондация «Отворено Общество», София 1992. (G. M. Dimitrov, Memories. Sofia: Foundation Open Society, 1992)

Ивет-Матилд Чорелов. *Български земеделски народен съюз 1899–1947. Трудният път към демокрацията. Божич.* Бургас 2012. (Ivet-Mathilde Chorelov, The Bulgarian Agrarian National Union 1899–1947: The difficult road to democracy. Bourgas: Bojich, 2012)

Чарлз Мозер. *Д-р Г.М. Димитров.* Военно-издателски комплекс „Св. Георги Победоносец, София 1991. (Charles Moser, *Dr. G. M. Dimitrov.* Sofia: Voennoizdatelski komplex "Sv. Georgi Pobedonosec", 1991)

Стратия Скерлев. *Др. Димиров-личност, идеи и дейност.* Париж: Български национален комитет, 1970. (Stratia Skerlev, *Dr. Dimitrov: Person, Ideas and Activity.* Paris: Bulgarian National Committee, 1970)

Димитър Генчев. *България в секретния архив на Сталин: От правителството на Кимон Георгиев до смъртта наСталин.* София, 2005. (Dimitar Genchev, Bulgaria in Stalin's Secret Archives: From Kimon Georgiev's Government until Stalin's Death. Sofia: Geny Agency, 2005)

Тончо Карабулков (предг.). *Д-р Г. М. Димитров 1949/72. Присъда срещу комунизма.* София: Цанко ЦерКовски, 1991. (Toncho Karabulkov, *G.M. Dimitrov 1949/72: Sentence on Communism.* Sofia: Canko Cerkovski Publishing, 1991)

IX

The Relationship Between the Assembly of Captive European Nations and the Free Europe Committee in the Context of U.S. Foreign Policy, 1950–1960

Anna Mazurkiewicz

Established in 1954, the Assembly of Captive European Nations (ACEN) was a U.S.-based organization of exiled East European leaders from Albania, Bulgaria, Czechoslovakia, Estonia, Latvia, Lithuania, Hungary, Poland and Romania.[1] According to its members, the ACEN functioned as a quasi-East European parliament, or a lobby of exiled politicians who strived to maintain the case of liberation of Eastern Europe from the Soviet yoke on the agenda of international relations. The formal structure of this organization included a Plenary Assembly, chairman, General Committee, secretary general and working committees.[2] Its activities included coordination of exile voices on Cold War developments and their dissemination via its own publications (the most notable being the *ACEN News*), rapports, organization of public meetings, rallies, demonstrations, as well as issuing policy evaluations and recommendations addressed to U.S. and foreign leaders and the press. Although the exiles played active roles outside of the ACEN framework as well (individually or via other organizations – ethnic, party internationals etc.), it was within ACEN that they were able to establish and maintain contacts with the American government and Congress and cooperate with other East European leaders and anti-communist organizations of the "free world". Founded at the initiative of the Free Europe Committee (FEC), the ACEN operations enjoyed that committee's support and were obviously influenced and monitored by official American policy. (A brief history of the FEC is included in the introductory chapter on the NCFE/FEC.)

In order to examine the extent of American control and to exemplify the political and public activities of the ACEN, I have selected a period during which the exiles began to openly disapprove of American foreign policy. This chapter focuses on the years 1959–1960, during which the ACEN vehemently opposed both the decision to invite Soviet Prime Minister Khrushchev to the U.S. and the subsequent courteous treatment extended to him during his appearance before the United Nations General Assembly.

Cold War relations during the selected period were characterized by attempts to resolve the post-World War II stalemate in Europe in an early effort to establish a peaceful coexistence. The Eisenhower–Khrushchev exchanges during these years marked a brief interlude between the heightened East–West tensions related to the crises in Hungary (1956) and Cuba (1961, 1962). The selection of such a chronological framework for analysis of the ACEN–FEC relations is further validated by a number of occurrences.

By 1958 C.D. Jackson – President Dwight D. Eisenhower's trusted adviser, an expert on psychological warfare, and president of the FEC in 1951–1952 – noted that the FEC had already embarked on a new policy in regard to its propaganda policies. In "probably the most painful" letter he ever wrote to Allen Dulles, Jackson not only tendered his resignation from the FEC Board but also included his evaluation of how recent changes had affected the organization.

> As you doubtless know, I have been increasingly disturbed over the past year to eighteen months over the fact that the management of FEC's affairs seemed to reflect a concerted plan, first to isolate and then to get rid of what I would call the "editorial" brains of the organization, and to replace them with more administratively "tidy" people. The result has been that by the first of the year there will literally not be left in the organization a single American in a high-level

> policy position whom I would consider a top-flight expert in political warfare. ... If, for whatever tactical reasons, the United States Government cannot support an unequivocal U.S. position on denying the credentials of the Kadar[3] representatives, I cannot see why the United States Government considers it worthwhile to continue to support the Free Europe Committee.[4]

Jackson pointed to attempts by the U.S. government to curb the FEC's relative independence regarding propaganda actions, but there were changes within the ACEN as well. After Latvian Vilis Māsēns's four terms as chair, the Assembly members decided to change its rules. Since 1958 the chairman's post was held in rotation by each national delegation on a yearly basis. Following Māsēns, in 1958–1959 the post went to a Pole (Stefan Korboński), in 1959–1960 it was held by a Czech (Petr Zenkl), and in 1960–1961 by a Lithuanian (Vaclovas Sidzikauskas).[5] Therefore, one may look into the changes in ACEN policies and actions that were stimulated by the changing leadership.

The above mentioned changes occurred against the background of changing American–Soviet relations. In May 1959 U.S. Secretary of State John Foster Dulles, considered a close ally of the exiles, passed away. It happened only few days after the opening of a foreign ministers' conference in Geneva that brought no solution to the problem of Berlin. Despite the Soviet ultimatum on Berlin of November 1958, the next year, which opened with the victorious Cuban revolution and the Dalai Lama's escape from Tibet, brought a summer invitation from the Department of State to Nikita Khrushchev to visit the United States. No preconditions were mentioned.[6]

This was the first visit to the U.S. by a Soviet leader.[7] Khruschev's was not the only top-level Soviet visit of 1959–1960, however; it was preceded by the arrival of two Soviet vice premiers, Anastas I. Mikoyan and Frol R. Kozlov. In July 1959 Vice President Richard M. Nixon visited Moscow. In the fall of 1960 Khrushchev attended a United Nations General Assembly session in New York City. Both the FEC and the ACEN might have interpreted these visits as an indication of a change in the character of U.S.–Soviet relations, a change that might consequently result in the weakening of anti-communist sentiment among the American public.

What was the ACEN reaction to the mutually expressed desire to ease tensions between the two empires? What actions did the exile organization plan to confront Khrushchev with during his American trip? How did the ACEN react to the notion of United States foreign policy moving toward peaceful coexistence and disarmament? How did the East European exiles respond to the fact that the U.S. president who proclaimed liberation was now reaching out to the Soviets with a message of mutual trust and need for dialogue? The widening gulf between the American policymakers' and the exiles' opinions on these visits seems all too obvious. It is therefore intriguing to examine the relations between the ACEN and the FEC during the final years of the Eisenhower administration.

This is an analysis of the ACEN's activities and its relationship with the American authorities at a time when the exiles' positions/opinions and those of the U.S. Department of State were clearly at odds. On the basis of a thorough analysis of the documentary records, periodicals and press, memoirs and interviews, I will offer a partial answer to a larger question regarding the constraints placed on the exile activities that were carried out under the aegis of the Free Europe Committee.[8]

***

In November 1958 Khrushchev issued an ultimatum to the United States, the United Kingdom and France regarding West Berlin, which signaled the likely coming of another European crisis rather than the coming of a summit meeting. Two years after the crushing of the Hungarian Revolution, the Soviet prime minister was trying to force the Western powers into signing a common European peace settlement. He wanted the West to recognize the German Democratic Republic, and his ultimatum demanded that within six months the West sign a German peace treaty that included a provision turning West Berlin into a demilitarized "free city". Otherwise, he would sign a separate treaty with the GDR and turn "control of access", meaning control of the routes to Berlin, over to the

East German government.[9] In this awkward manner he was soliciting a summit meeting to foster U.S.–Soviet détente. The American response was one of wait-and-see. The deadline Khrushchev set was May 1959.

Hearing news of the ultimatum, the exiled Central and East European political leaders were concerned by the likelihood that the signatories of the Yalta and Potsdam agreements might meet again to sign a German peace treaty. The ACEN demanded that any international pact signed by the wartime allies include "the restoration of the independence and freedom of the presently captive nations of Albania, Bulgaria, Czechoslovakia, Estonia, Hungary, Latvia, Lithuania, Poland and Romania, and the withdrawal of Soviet armed forces and agents from the territories of these countries." For the exiles, the problems of Central and Eastern Europe and of Germany were indivisible.[10]

Mikoyan's Visit

On January 4, 1959, Soviet Vice Premier Anastas I. Mikoyan's arrived in the United States with the aim of easing the tensions aroused by Khrushchev's erratic position on the German question. ACEN members believed that the true aim of Mikoyan's visit was to confuse public opinion in the West in order to pave the way for acknowledgement of a *status quo* in Central and Eastern Europe. As a sympathetic reception of Mikoyan by the Americans would further imperil the cause of the captive nations, the Assembly was desperate to counteract any outcome of his visit that might further the Soviets' agenda.

The ACEN organized a campaign using its own periodical, the *ACEN News*, and its contacts with the U.S. press. A special press conference was scheduled for January 13. In a press release issued that day the Soviet first deputy premier was described as follows:

> One of the architects of the Soviet colonial empire, founded on the violation of nearly one thousand international treaties; on the subjugation of nine formerly independent and sovereign states …; on the mass murder and mass deportation of millions of men, women,

> and children ... on the infamous system of forced labor camps; on total disregard for human rights and fundamental freedoms, and on the organized economic exploitation of the subjugated countries. As a close collaborator of Stalin, Mr. Mikoyan directly shares responsibility for Stalin's national and international crimes. Last but not least must be mentioned in this context the perfidious role played by Mr. Mikoyan in the recent Soviet military intervention in Hungary, resulting in the bloody suppression of the national revolution.[11]

Additionally, the ACEN organized a mail campaign targeting prominent individuals who were to meet with the Soviet official. A list of six questions that should be addressed to Mikoyan was sent to U.S. congress members, business leaders, state-level officials and the U.S. media.[12] A telegram to John J. McCloy from ACEN Assembly Chairman Korboński asked that the following questions be asked during the January 15 Council on Foreign Relations (CFR) meeting with the second most important Soviet official:

> 1) As one of Stalin's closest associates for almost 40 years, did you or did you not participate in and agree with the decisions which, as partially admitted by Mr. Khrushchev at the 20th Party Congress, brought about the imprisonment, torture and death of countless millions of men, women and children in your governments forced labor camps?
> 2) As a member of the highest Party and government organs, did you or did you not approve of Molotov-Ribbentrop Pact of August 23, 1939, the ensuing joint attack on Poland by Hitler and Stalin and the forcible incorporation of Estonia, Latvia and Lithuania into the Soviet Union?
> 3) As one of Stalin's closest associates at the end of World War II, did you or did you not agree with the decision to occupy and to impose puppet Communist governments on the formerly independent nations of Central and Eastern Europe, while under the solemn obligation (set forth in several wartime and post-war agreements) to respect the right of the respective peoples to set up governments of their own choice?

4) In its Note of December 27, 1958,[13] on the question of Berlin, the Soviet Union called for an end to foreign occupation in the former capital of Germany, to be followed by free elections under some kind of United Nations supervision. Soviet leaders have repeatedly declared that the regimes established in Albania, Bulgaria, Czechoslovakia, Hungary, Poland and Romania were established by the free choice of the respective peoples and that the incorporation of Estonia, Latvia, and Lithuania into the Soviet Union was based on the freely taken decision of the peoples of those nations. If so, in order to end any controversy on this subject, is the Soviet Union prepared to permit the peoples of those nations freely to express their will under the conditions which the Soviet Government itself proposed for the city of Berlin?

5) As the highest official of the Soviet Union on economic matters, are you aware of allegations to the effect that from 1944 to date the Soviet Union has exacted from Albania, Bulgaria, Czechoslovakia, Estonia, Hungary, Latvia, Lithuania, Poland and Romania, through various devices (such as war reparations, joint companies, unequal trade relations) goods and services estimated at between 10 and 15 billion dollars? To further confidence among nations, are you prepared to render public the entire record of the economic and financial relations between the Soviet Union and each one of the abovementioned countries?

6) Is it true or false that, as the official representative of the Soviet government, you formally assured the Hungarian government of Imre Nagy, in Budapest, on October 30, 1956, that all Soviet troops would be withdrawn from Hungary? Did you know that the representatives of the Hungarian government invited by your subordinated to discuss the withdrawal would be arrested and shot?[14]

In the last sentence of the telegram to McCloy, and acting on behalf of the ACEN, Korboński expressed the hope that at least some of these questions would be asked during the CFR meeting. Identical missives were sent to other CFR members and were widely distributed in the press release.[15]

Understandably not willing to cause further deterioration of American–Soviet relations, few hosts of the meetings with Mikoyan were willing to raise the issue of Central and Eastern Europe; even fewer asked questions similar to those prepared by the exiles. However, in the exiles' struggle to weaken early Soviet propaganda regarding détente, to prevent the popular acknowledgement of a status quo in Europe, at the time the ACEN enjoyed the full support of the FEC. On January 13, FEC President John Richardson Jr. sent a letter to the editor of the *New York Times* which opened with a critical evaluation of a "remarkably friendly" reception extended to Mikoyan by "American business, professional, labor and political leaders". Richardson's letter repeated the entire list of ACEN-prepared questions, "respectfully suggesting that those who, in all sincerity, welcome an opportunity to entertain, debate with and learn from Mr. Mikoyan, consider the implications of these questions." Richardson was certain that none of the ACEN questions would be asked of Mikoyan due to "the dictates of courtesy and hospitality", but he hoped that "before Mr. Mikoyan leaves our shores, perhaps he will learn what I sincerely hope to be the fact that most American leaders in private and public life cannot be bamboozled so easily."[16] At this point in their relationship, the ACEN and the FEC were working in concert with each other. The aims of both organizations were identical: to weaken the propaganda effect of Mikoyan's visit. However, the ACEN aspired to influence U.S. Cold War policies as well.

In a letter to John F. Dulles sent on January 14, the ACEN chairman expressed his hope that "the issue of Central and Eastern Europe would be an integral part of any negotiated European peace settlement."[17] The Assembly-prepared "Statement on Mikoyan's visit" was sent as a press release to the White House and to the Office of European Affairs at the Department of State, as well as to U.S. senators. It listed the exiles' reasons for concern: the "sinister nature of the Soviet First Vice-Premier", his "intention to confuse the public opinion of the free world" and to "disarm it morally", and the fact that the visit occurred during a period of heightened tensions (Berlin, Soviet technological advances).[18] A number of U.S. senators, the director of the Office of European Affairs, and members of the CFR replied to this ACEN communication with polite "thank you" letters.[19]

Neither were the non-governmental leaders who extended invitations to Mikoyan willing to irritate the Kremlin's second in command by asking him questions that could have been considered offensive. Nonetheless, Mikoyan's hosts could readily recognize the hostile crowds that cursed (and at times threw eggs at) Mikoyan in the streets of the cities he visited (Cleveland, Detroit, Chicago, San Francisco, Washington, New York) as a clear indication of popular sentiment in the U.S. The ACEN archival collection contains sixty-three clippings from U.S. newspapers (most of them based on Associated Press releases) related to the tense atmosphere surrounding the preparations for Mikoyan's visit.[20] The *New York Times* quoted the U.S. President asking for moderation. It was one thing to abhor Soviet crimes but quite another to threaten Mikoyan's safety and make it impossible for him to travel. "Be Courteous", asked Eisenhower.[21] In fact, the Soviet leader received courteous treatment from the majority of American business and political leaders whom he encountered during his visit. There were, however, notable exceptions.

The ACEN exploited all opportunities to promote any unfavorable reaction to Mikoyan by members of the American establishment. On January 5, the Assembly's chairman sent a letter to Congressman Walter H. Judd expressing gratitude for Judd's refusal to participate in an official dinner organized for the Soviet dignitary by Eric Johnston of the Motion Picture Association of America. In reply, Judd sent Korboński a copy of his January 2 telegram to Johnston explaining the motives behind his decision:

> Appreciate your courtesy in inviting Mrs. Judd and Me to a dinner for Mikoyan Monday evening but regret you are giving it and we will not be present for the same reasons we would not attend a social function honoring Hitler, Himmler, Nero, or Genghis Khan. Ghosts of too many enslaved, tortured and murdered human beings will be looking down on the dinner. Private negotiations with tyrants actually in power in a country are one thing. Conferring of respectability

> on them and increasing their prestige and power by acceptance into civilized society is quite another ....[22]

The ACEN also thanked George Meany, president of the American Federation of Labor-Congress of Industrial Organizations, who had acted in a similar fashion. The AFL-CIO was the single most powerful labor organization in the U.S., and Meany met with ACEN representatives on a number of occasions and publicly expressed views similar to those of the exiles.[23] Unlike Meany, former U.S. President Harry S. Truman believed that the possible gains outnumbered the dangers involved in the negotiations with the Soviets. However, he also criticized the sympathetic treatment extended to Mikoyan by American politicians and businessmen. The ACEN expressed gratitude for Truman's stand in the January/February issue of the *ACEN News*.[24]

Kozlov's Visit

Soon after Mikoyan's departure, the ACEN leadership set out for a world tour. Its aim was similar to an earlier Latin American trip in 1956 – to drum up support for a UN resolution demanding the withdrawal of Soviet troops from East and Central Europe and to issue a call for free elections under international supervision.[25] Throughout, the ACEN strived to present the USSR as the largest colonial empire in the contemporary world. Such initiatives were in concurrence with FEC programs[26] and generally in line with American foreign policy.

Although the ACEN and the FEC had seemingly parallel objectives, there were differences in the ways the FEC and the ACEN saw their priorities while addressing European organizations. Utilizing its European delegates, and during the relatively frequent visits to Europe by its U.S.-based members, the ACEN unvaryingly lobbied in Western Europe for the restitution of freedom in their homelands. The exiles operated within the Committee on Non-Represented Nations of the Council of Europe, were received by the Consultative Assembly of the Council of Europe, and organized special ACEN sessions in Strasbourg.[27] Concurrently, the

Free Europe Committee was working on the creation of the West European Advisory Committee. The advisory committee was composed of fifteen to twenty prominent and well known European leaders and was designed to promote West European interest in captive nations.[28] Working with the FEC, these leaders would help to educate West Europeans about the importance of East and Central Europe and its future role in a united Europe. According to the 1959 plans, the task for the exiles, their organizations and leaders, would be to connect the émigré organizations in the U.S. with those in Western Europe and to convince exiled leaders (in both culture and politics) to help promote European integration, including the future incorporation of Central and East European countries into a single "Europe Whole and Free".[29]

Although the ACEN charter listed cooperation with the Council of Europe and European Movement "with the aim of assuring an adequate representation of the captive European nations in those bodies, and of preparing the way for the integration of these nations to a United Europe", the intent was for the Assembly was to be dissolved the moment the captive nations were liberated. Promotion of European integration was not the ACEN's chief aim. Rather, it was the "peaceful liberation" of the Soviet Satellites by free elections and immediate withdrawal of Soviet troops.[30] In their statements of policy the ACEN leadership repeatedly stated that their focus was on the present. The ACEN charter listed the goals of the Assembly: to sustain the morale of the peoples behind the Iron Curtain, strengthen their will to resist, preserve democratic ideals, promote research on Eastern Europe and provide assistance to refugees but also to supply information to the free world on the Soviet's colonial policy in relationship to her satellites and seek international support for liberation of Central and Eastern Europe.[31] Interestingly enough, the ACEN attempts to reach compatriots behind the Iron Curtain were not carried via Free Europe's primary engine: Radio Free Europe. The FEC did not want to establish a direct connection between the ACEN and the Radios for fear of spreading exile internal squabbles. News about the ACEN activities was broadcast occasionally, but its central publication, the *ACEN News*, was not distributed in the captive nations.[32]

U.S. policy regarding the ACEN was clearly outlined in a document found in the C.D. Jackson papers in the Eisenhower Presidential Library. The FEC's president, Willis D. Crittenberger, described the exile activities in the following words:

> FEER [Free Europe Exile Relations] covertly directs the so-called National Committees and the ACEN and its organizations. These National Committees are propaganda agencies of FEC, which is why all personalities involved, though separated politically, follow the same line. Though there are some dissenting people in ACEN to lend it an aura of respectability, it is an American propaganda agency and the people in it are not free... .[33]

It would be wrong however, to consider the ACEN activities as merely a part of the U.S. Cold War propaganda machine. The exile activities, while based on the U.S. founding, were chiefly focused on political activities and strived to influence the course of affairs, most importantly not letting the free world acknowledge the *status quo* in Europe despite U.S. policy fluctuations.

In order to advance its goals, from 1956 to 1963 the Assembly rented a small warehouse opposite United Nations headquarters in Manhattan. Although plans to create a captive nations center there never materialized, many demonstrations and pickets were organized in front of it. Most importantly however, the façade of the building was used as a huge billboard (24x20 feet).[34] Images of Khrushchev and quotations such as "We will bury you"[35] were among the ACEN's favorite themes for its posters. Interestingly enough, it was an image of the Soviet leader in military uniform saying "I freed Hungary. I will 'liberate' all nations"[36] that caused the ACEN its first round of trouble connected with its operations at the warehouse, already referred to as ACEN House, even in official correspondence. On 9 September, 1958, the building's owner, Irma M. Tomich, asked that the poster be taken down, as the city authorities had informed her there was no permit for its display. This is interesting, given that – judging by the correspondence gathered in the IHRC – the

ACEN had obtained the appropriate permits and had been mounting displays since 1956.[37] As the 13th UN session, opened on 16 September, 1958, the ACEN was ready to begin its next campaign against "Kádár's usurpers" seated in the UN. Instead, they had to focus on consultations with various city officials and lawyers regarding how to keep the poster up in the "special zone" at the UN Plaza.[38]

The FEC's reaction to these complications can be described as ambiguous on the surface; although the Boys' Clubs episode that followed was clearly a behind the scenes attempt to remove the highly visible displays from the building facing the UN. According to the ACEN secretary general's note, on 16 September Edward McHalle recommended that the ACEN give in and take the poster down, not mentioning that it would be replaced with any other.[39] It "turned out" that behind the trouble were the Boys' Clubs of America, which were interested in purchasing the Tomich building. Negotiations regarding the possible purchase were carried out via FEC officials. During a meeting on 14 October, Brutus Coste and Korboński were informed about an offer that Herbert Hoover (the Boys' Clubs' honorary president) had made to FEC President Crittenberger. The offer was presented to the ACEN leadership by John F. Leich, the assistant director of the FEC's Exile Relations Division. The ACEN was supposed to terminate its lease on the warehouse. In return, the Assembly would be able to rent rooms in a new building owned by the Boys' Clubs called the "Hoover Building". However, there was no provision for the display of posters on the façade or for flying the nine captive nations' flags, thus far proudly flown from masts installed on the warehouse roof.[40] This offer was promptly rejected by the exiles, and the FEC acknowledged their decision. For the time being, the poster displays were secured.

On 10 December, 1958, the ACEN unveiled a new, and soon to become the most popular, poster depicting Boris Pasternak.[41] After Mikoyan's departure, in April 1959 the next poster on ACEN House was a direct reference to foreign ministers' talks in Geneva, which were about to be resumed (11 May). Marianne, Uncle Sam, and John Bull were depicted as a group about to follow Khrushchev up a steep path leading to the summit. As they passed by caves turned into prison cells holding captive nations, they wondered, "Shall we pass them by and help Khrushchev – 'bury us'?"[42]

As before, the foreign ministers' talks in Geneva stalled, bringing no solution to the German question. East and Central Europe were not even mentioned. However, the ACEN appeals were noticed by the U.S. press.[43] On 28 June, 1959, another Soviet dignitary visited the U.S., which signaled ongoing American–Soviet dialogue. First Deputy Vice-Premier Frol R. Kozlov visited the U.S. for fifteen days, the official reason being to open a Soviet exhibition in New York. Unofficially, his visit was a Soviet-designed step to secure an invitation for Khrushchev to visit the U.S. With the Berlin ultimatum deadline having quietly passed by, the Americans were open to such an idea in order to force Soviet concessions in Geneva.[44] Undersecretary of State Robert Murphy delivered the invitation to Khrushchev (via Kozlov), which the Soviet leader gladly accepted on 21 July,[45] since it carried no preconditions.

Before the exile leaders learned about the invitation to Khrushchev, they were confronted with Kozlov's visit. When the Soviet exhibition opened in New York, protesters showed up. One man held a sign saying "rope products", depicting a man dangling from a gibbet.[46] However, this time, rather than focusing on public opinion, the ACEN exiles seized the opportunity to influence the course of affairs. Three days before the Soviet dignitary's visit, ACEN Secretary General Coste wrote to Senator William Langer asking for assistance in organizing a meeting with J. William Fulbright, chairman of the Senate Foreign Relations Committee. The aim of the meeting was to discuss the issues pertaining to the announced exchanges: Kozlov's U.S. visit and Vice President Nixon's trip to the USSR.[47] The ACEN wanted to receive a confirmation of the American position, expressed in January 1958 by the U.S. president, that during all summit meetings the fate of Central and Eastern Europe would be debated. At that time, Khrushchev replied that should the European *status quo* not be accepted, no meeting was possible.[48] Neither during Geneva talks, nor during Mikoyan's visit was the tough American position on captive nations reinstated. On 26 June, 1959 Korboński addressed an appeal directly to Vice President Nixon.[49] Three days later, the ACEN sent a letter to the U.S. president in which they asked that the issue of freedom and independence of the Central and East European nations be raised during the imminent American–Soviet conversations in Washington and Moscow.[50] On 30 June, the ACEN delegation met with the chairman of the House Foreign Affairs Committee, and as in their prior communications asked for the U.S. to push the Soviets for a comprehensive, all-European settlement "based on the honest application of the principle of self-determination".[51]

On 2 July the *New York Times* carried an article titled "U.S. denies Dulles Softened Views" describing the Freedom Day celebrations in which representatives of both the FEC and the ACEN were present.[52] A week before Nixon's departure for his Moscow trip (23 July–2 August, 1959),[53] the exiles were to receive a tremendous boost for their activities from the U.S. president and Congress – the designation of the third week in July as "Captive Nations Week."[54]

Before the official presidential announcement and with Kozlov's visit underway, the ACEN was actively monitoring American attitudes towards the Soviet dignitary. On July 8 Kozlov met with Michigan Governor G. Mennen Williams. The governor interrogated the vice premier on the situation in Central and Eastern Europe.[55] Some of the questions he asked might have been influenced by the materials supplied by the ACEN. After the meeting, Williams telephoned Korboński and apprised him of the course of the meeting. A detailed transcript of this talk was published in the *ACEN News*, and the governor's stance and support were promptly rewarded by the Assembly.[56] On 10 July the ACEN chairman sent a letter to the *New York Times* asking for a correction of a text published the day before. The New York daily had quoted Kozlov saying that the Central and East European governments were established on the basis of free and unfettered elections. Korboński stated that since the Soviets had recently demanded free UN-supervised elections in Cameroon (4 March), they should be asked to approve a similar solution in Central and Eastern Europe.[57]

It looked as if – despite J.F. Dulles's death and U.S. policy shifts toward détente – the exiles would be able to keep the momentum going toward influencing international affairs.[58] However, Kozlov's visit was just a prelude to Khrushchev's triumphant visit to the U.S. – of which the ACEN still had no information. Khrushchev accepted the invitation on the day that the ACEN delegation received a copy of the Captive Nations Proclamation of 17 July from Undersecretary of State Douglas Dillon (21 July). During the ceremony, Dillon said the United States would never acknowledge the Soviet domination of Central and Eastern Europe.[59]

The exiles considered the Captive Nations Week Proclamation a "milestone", "an act of historical significance":

> Never before have the rights of these nations to live in freedom under governments and institutions of their choosing been given a more authoritative support. And never before have the tyrants of the Kremlin been forced to a more open confession of the precariousness of their hold on the once free nations they are keeping in bondage at the very time when they are masquerading the world over as champions of the emancipation of colonial peoples.[60]

Their convictions were further strengthened by President Eisenhower. When asked about Khrushchev's furious response to the news about Captive Nations Week during a press conference on 29 July, the president said that there could be no true peace until all nations were able to decide their fate themselves.[61] Some of the press comments admitted that the timing of the Captive Nations Week Proclamation, coinciding with Nixon's visit, was unfortunate, but the media nevertheless supported Eisenhower by openly voicing support for the captives' aspirations for freedom.[62] The Harrisburg, Pennsylvania *Patriot* commented that "resolution accomplished what the State Department has never succeeded in doing – it got Eastern Europe on the agenda for the high-level US–Russian talks. Moreover, it was Soviet Premier Khrushchev who brought it up during the Nixon visit."[63] It appeared then that the Central and East European exile agenda would continue to receive unwavering American support.

Waiting for Mr. K

The ACEN's initial reaction to the news of the American visit by the Soviet leader, by that time popularly referred to by the media as Mr. K, was one of a "great shock".[64] In August, the ACEN opinion that Khrushchev's visit would "sow some confusion that may result in a kind of moral disarmament of the American people" was often quoted in the U.S. press.[65] Their voice was not the only one expressing concern. On August 3, 1959, the ACEN ally, Congressman Walter H. Judd of Minnesota, commented:

> The Khrushchev visit to our country is a major victory for him in his relentless political offensive to soften up the West preparatory to the kill. ... To us such an exchange of visits represents a chance to lessen world tensions. To Communists it represents a chance to use the tensions to win still further victories. After all, they created the tensions for that purpose.[66]

However, by the end of that month the press focused its attention on the likelihood of violent public protests during Khrushchev's visit, the prospect of which the ACEN representatives vigorously condemned.[67]

Being well aware of the Soviet tactics, the exiles soon understood that Khrushchev's arrival could possibly provide them with an excellent opportunity to promote their goals and advance anti-communist propaganda. Series of telegrams were sent by the ACEN to American leaders in various fields (diplomats, labor leaders, foreign affairs advisory bodies and organizations), all contained an identical message: "We respectfully urge you to raise the question of the restoration of freedom and independence to captive nations in your meeting with Soviet Premier Khrushchev."[68]

Moreover, the exiles planned a widespread propaganda campaign to convince the American public that there was nothing likeable about the Soviet leader. There was however a significant limitation on their domestic activities. According to the FEC's guidelines, the ACEN had to refrain from interfering with the domestic policies of the U.S. The leadership of the ACEN was composed of non-U.S. citizens who were working on behalf of their enslaved compatriots. Only a few of the Assembly members ever adopted American citizenship; in fact the early criterion was not to allow anyone to serve in the ACEN delegations if they were naturalized citizens. Thus the first head of the Hungarian delegation, Tibor Eckhardt, resigned as chair of the delegation when he became an American citizen in 1955. There were however organizations that supported the ACEN agenda and initiatives, such as the American Friends of Captive Nations (AFCN), headed by Christopher Emmet, and the Conference of Americans of Central and East European Descent (CACEED), chaired by John Balkunas, which were not subject to such limitations, although they were supported financially by the U.S. government as well as ACEN. Their cooperation allowed the exiles to converge their aims with those of an American public that was anti-communist, regardless of whether or not they were of Central or East European descent. A month before Khrushchev's visit, the ACEN prepared a document addressed to the AFCN titled "Brief Arguments Against Khrushchev's Visit".[69] Among the many arguments listed there, one can hear the bitterness of the exiles: "No one ever dared to suggest that Hitler or Stalin be invited to this country. Why then Khrushchev, whose personal record is just as amoral and ruthless?" Now the "Hangman of the Ukraine" and the "Butcher of Budapest" was to be received with the honors of a head of state, which *de jure* he was not.

Khrushchev's visit to the U.S. was in fact a summit meeting with no preconditions. As such it was to be interpreted as indicative of the weakness of the West and its acceptance of the *status quo* in Europe. In short, the impending visit was to be complete diplomatic victory for the Soviets. This was the ACEN official line to be promoted during Khrushchev's September visit:

> The smiling hospitality with which he will be greeted by everyone, from the President on down, will prevent Khrushchev from learning the two things which it is vital that he must learn if his visit it to serve the cause of peace. These are: a) the depth of the American peo-

> ple's conviction that the captive peoples must be free before the Soviets can be trusted or peace be secure; b) Our determination to stand firm on Berlin, even if it means war. ... It is essential that American anti-Communists, while abjuring violence would defeat its own end, do everything possible to see that Khrushchev learns these things. This is our greatest challenge.[70]

On August 6 the ACEN organized a meeting of anti-communist organizations in preparation for Khrushchev's visit in New York. Among the participants were various unionists, political, religious and ethnic groups (Hungarian, Jewish, Ukrainian), as well as representatives of the press.[71] Tentative agreement reached at this meeting provided for a joint petition to the U.S. president asking that he condition the continuation of a dialogue on Soviet withdrawal of the Berlin ultimatum and agreement to free elections in Central and Eastern Europe. The petition was designed to set off a public information campaign. It was not meant, however, to serve as a criticism of the Eisenhower administration. Rather than criticize the decision to invite Khrushchev, the anti-communist groups wanted to issue a warning that "unless the Administration pursues the firm policy we recommend in its discussions with Khrushchev, there is a serious danger (1) that it will deal a crushing blow to the morals of the peoples of the captive nations; (2) that it may make a miscalculation by Khrushchev on Berlin more likely by giving him the impression that we are soft and will continue to back down before threats and ultimata."[72] Such theses were included in the ACEN letters to Eisenhower and Nixon and were repeated by Korboński during interviews with the U.S. press.[73]

The other common initiative taken by the assembled representatives of the various American organizations was to encourage the "thousands or tens of thousands of people in every city he [Khrushchev] visits" to wear black armbands. While remembering the victims of communist tyranny, it would be the "most dignified and effective" form of protest. Other ideas tentatively agreed upon included a call for people to turn their backs to the Soviet leader's motorcade as it passed by. Such a campaign was an effort "to help Khrushchev understand how the American people feel on the specific issue of the captive nations."[74] No pickets or mass demonstrations were planned for two reasons: no permission was likely to be granted and due to "the danger that a mass of people might get out of control".[75] Throughout its preparations, the ACEN members promoted "dignified" forms of protest and called on the exiles "not to join disorderly demonstrations".[76] Instead, it was suggested that people ask church leaders for special services and a tolling of church bells in commemoration of the victims of communist tyranny. In addition, a mass rally with U.S. senators' participation (Thomas J. Dodd, former senator William F. Knowland, Paul H. Douglas, Kenneth Keating) was planned to take place in New York on the day before Khrushchev's arrival.[77] Although approached by them on many occasions, the ACEN was cautious not to associate itself with extremist, far-right groups and individuals.

Khrushchev's 1959 Visit

The welcome extended to Khrushchev by the ACEN consisted of a new poster displayed on ACEN House. For the first time it was black, with white letters saying: "UN: We Demand Freedom and Independence, the peoples of Albania, Bulgaria, Czechoslovakia, Estonia, Hungary, Latvia, Lithuania, Poland, Romania".[78] Twelve days of mourning were advocated by its leaders.[79] ACEN representatives were present during the White House press conference on the Khrushchev visit, and right afterwards the ACEN organized its own as a form of reply. The slogan behind the speaker proclaimed: Khrushchev not welcome in the home of the free.[80] United appeals from the ACEN, AFCN and CACEED were printed in the press.[81]

Seemingly, the effect of the ACEN actions was not great. Peter Carlson, author of a book devoted to Khrushchev's visits, did not mention the ACEN at all, and he word "captive" appears only in regards to the July 17 resolution.[82] However, an examination of the U.S. press reveals many mentions of repeated exile calls for action.[83] Protests on UN Plaza being strictly prohibited, the ACEN's black poster was the sole remainder of the true nature of the Soviet rule. It was frequently quoted by journalists covering Khrushchev's visit.[84]

Interestingly, Carlson's book did describe the cold welcome extended to the Soviet leader by the American public. Those who stood by as the motorcade carrying Khrushchev passed from Andrews Air Force Base to the White House on 15 September did not cheer. President Eisenhower, squeezed in between Khrushchev and his wife, saw crowds of about two hundred thousand quiet, almost emotionless people.[85] This could have been the result of major American media participation in an action propagated by many exile and anti-communist organizations.[86]

Similarly to the tactics employed during Mikoyan's earlier visit, the ACEN prepared a questionnaire for Khrushchev. It consisted of twenty-six questions which were distributed among U.S. journalists, members of Congress, business and culture leaders. Obviously, the exiles found the method effective. Some of these questions pertained to the same issues – inquiring about the role played during the Hungarian revolution, support for the Ribbentrop-Molotov pact, the development of forced labor camps, lack of free elections in Central and Eastern Europe. While repeatedly calling Khrushchev "one of Stalin's close associates", the novel questions included the Berlin ultimatum, Soviet prisoners jailed without trial, deportations from the Baltic countries, the annexation of Kaliningrad, Boris Pasternak's case, liberalization of international travel, etc.

Many of the questions were meant to expose the true nature of the Soviet system. Question fourteen said:

> Mr. Khrushchev, at the 8th Party Congress, Lenin has stated: 'The existence of the Soviet Republic side by side with imperialist states for a long time is unthinkable. One or the other must triumph in the end.' Do you subscribe to this view? And if you do, where does that leave co-existence?

Question fifteen went even further: "Mr. Khrushchev, Lenin has stated once that:

> 'The strictest loyalty to the ideas of Communism must be combined with the ability to make all the necessary compromises, to talk, to make agreements, zigzags, retreats, and so on, in order to accelerate the coming into power of the Communist.' As a faithful Leninist will you implement this advice during your visit into USA?"

The ACEN couldn't refrain from quoting Khrushchev's own "We will bury you" statement in the next question, asking if this was his interpretation of a peaceful co-existence.[87] It is extremely difficult to establish how influential this questionnaire and other ACEN-disseminated materials were for the journalists and attendees at various meetings with Mr. K. However, scholars of the period have established that the questions asked of the Soviet leader regarding East Central Europe's fate were among the most irksome and caused the most tension.[88]

From the first days of the Soviet leader's visit, the ACEN disseminated its own answers to and interpretations of Khrushchev's statements. For example, after a meeting at the Press Club, the Assembly sent a statement to the U.S. press commenting on two issues: Khrushchev's call for the removal of vestiges of World War II in Europe and his reference to the case of Hungary as a problem which "has stuck like a dead rat in [the] throat of some people – they are disgusted with it and yet cannot spit it out."[89] In a brilliant remark, József Kővágó, the mayor of Budapest at the time of the 1956 Revolution and an ACEN delegate, observed that Khrushchev tended to choke each time he mentioned coexistence.[90]

Naturally, the ACEN reaction was one of indignation, but they focused instead on future steps to be taken to free Central and East Europe from the Soviet yoke. The Assembly recommended focusing on UN-supervised free elections in East Central Europe in order to solve European problems and calling for the removal of Soviet troops from Hungary in concurrence with the UN General Assembly's call.[91] On September 25 a letter by ACEN Chairman Korboński and Secretary General Coste, titled "Lest We Forget", was published by the *Christian Science Monitor*.[92] More importantly, the ACEN was ready with its third volume on developments in Hungary following the suppression of the revolution there.[93]

The report, the ACEN House poster and the materials supplied to the U.S. press were more influential by far than the street protests, as the ACEN-organized demonstrations during Khrushchev's visit were overshadowed by hundreds of other protests, pickets and demonstrations.

However, one event was a success, and was referenced both in Carlson's book and in other accounts of the 1959 visit.[94] It was a rally and meeting at the Carnegie International Center that proved to be the most effective protest against Khrushchev's visit.[95] The rally, with approximately 2,500 participants,[96] was the realization of an earlier plan agreed upon in August. The plan was to hold the rally on the eve of Khrushchev's arrival in New York, but for obscure reasons the event took place one day after the Soviet leader's departure for Los Angeles. Despite that, the 20 September rally "We Answer Khrushchev" – officially sponsored by CACEED and AFCN – received widespread media coverage.[97]

During the rally the Soviet leader's visit was described as "detrimental to the national interest of the United States and to the cause of universal freedom". In addition to repeating the pleas for Soviet troops to be removed from Central and Eastern Europe and calls for free UN-supervised elections there, the rally ended with a call addressed to Eisenhower to confirm during the talks with Khrushchev the American determination to stand fast by its promises extended to the "brave people of Berlin" and to raise the issue of Central and Eastern Europe in the spirit of the Captive Nations Week Proclamation "unanimously passed by the U.S. Congress". The participants gathered in the Carnegie International Center called on the American people to boycott any and all occasions honoring the Soviet prime minister and party leader and to decline to welcome him "except with dignified restraint when necessary".[98]

Among the speakers addressing the rally participants were Balkunas, Emmet and Korboński, but also General Béla Király representing the Hungarian Freedom Fighters, Harry Gideonse, the president of Freedom House, Dmytro Halychyn, the president of the Ukrainian Congress Committee, and Congressman Ray Madden (on the House of Representatives' Select Committee to Investigate the Katyn Forest Massacre). Republican Congressman Alvin O'Konski was also among those present, and Democratic Senator Paul H. Douglas sent a letter in which he supported the exile aims.[99] Just before the meeting opened, a real threat of discomposure occurred. As the Ukrainians had special reasons to hate Khrushchev,[100] their representation at the meeting was strong. However, when they entered the room they saw the ACEN-prepared map (identical to its logo), which represented only nine captive nations, the Ukraine borders not being shown, the country (republic) being a part of the USSR.[101] This was nothing new, as since the 1953 decision by the U.S. Psychological Strategy Board, Ukraine, Belorussia and other "separatists movements" were not treated as Soviet satellites.[102] The ACEN's wish to cooperate with the nations forcibly incorporated into the USSR, as well as political exiles from Yugoslavia, was limited by the decisions of its sponsors.[103] The crisis was resolved in the name of the greater good, but the bitterness remained.[104]

During the meeting a resolution was passed, which was generally supported by the U.S. press.[105] In the documents prepared for the meeting, the ACEN members stated that the so-called liberalization or thaw seemingly allowed by the Kremlin was just a tactical propaganda move and did not affect the actual workings of a police state. Furthermore, the aim of Khrushchev's visit was not to eliminate the sources of tensions in Europe but by threatening West Berlin to obtain recognition of the status quo. At the same time, the visit would serve the Soviet aims behind the Iron Curtain, as the captive nations would realize that their fate was no longer of interest to the West. The ACEN called on the American president and the American people to abide by the words of the Captive Nations Week resolution.[106] Three days later ACEN sent a telegram based on the abovementioned arguments to President Eisenhower, who was already at Camp David. Almost identical letters were sent to Vice President Nixon and Secretary of State Herter.[107]

In his memoirs, ACEN Secretary General Gadomski assumed that the "manifestations and pickets against Khrushchev did not influence the official course of the visit."[108] However, in a manner contrary to the protesters' intentions, the lukewarm reception extended to Mr. K on the East Coast did in fact influence the visit. After Khrushchev's patience with the chilly welcome and irksome questions ran out in Los Angeles, the U.S. administration decided to undertake initiatives to cheer him up before the meeting with Eisenhower at Camp David.[109] The crowds that welcomed Khrushchev in California and the "media craze" surrounding his visit to Roswell Garst's farm in Iowa[110] overshadowed earlier public responses. Many photos were taken showing the Soviet leader in the midst of an enthusiastic crowd.[111] Of course, the U.S. media reported promptly on scandals connected with Khrushchev's uncontrolled fits of anger as well.

Khrushchev's first visit to the U.S. did not cause any dramatic differences or tensions between the American administration, the FEC and the ACEN. The dignified and self-restrained forms of protest, to a large extent influenced by the Captive Nations Proclamation, were obviously in line with the expectations of the sponsoring organizations. The exiles hoped that at some point in the Soviet leader's visit the issue of Central and Eastern Europeans would be brought up – preferably at Camp David. Their hopes were dashed. Khrushchev left the United States on September 27 in triumph.

Khrushchev's Return, 1960

Almost exactly a year later, Khrushchev returned to the U.S. – this time, however, uninvited. The Soviet leader arrived in New York on 19 September 1960 as a USSR delegate to the United Nations session. Yet again, his arrival was overshadowed by the unresolved German issue. In the aftermath of the 1 May U-2 incident, when the Soviets shot down a U.S. spy plane with pilot Gary Powers on board, hopes for Eisenhower's reciprocal visit were doomed by the frenzy at the Paris summit in mid May 1960. Khrushchev's arrival was volatile even before it begun. From the Central and East European exiles' point of view, the situation was even more tense due to the fact that during the Soviet leader's visit to France in March, East European exiles living in France were interned in Corsica in order to avoid trouble.[112] While in the U.S. for the UN session, it was Khrushchev's own ability to move that was restricted. For his own security, he was not allowed to leave Manhattan.[113]

Both the American and the foreign media reported widely on Khrushchev's second U.S. visit. The ACEN plans of actions related to the Soviet leader's arrival were covered extensively during the last two weeks of September.[114] As the American authorities were anxious about the possibility of the émigrés' vehement reaction to Khrushchev's presence in the U.S., tensions between the authorities and the exiles surfaced.

Upon his second arrival, Khrushchev was not welcomed with the honors usually extended to a head of state but by angry crowds, signs and posters. The ACEN was not planning on showing restraint either. But further escalation of tensions by the émigrés' actions was not in line with the aims of the U.S. government-connected organizations. Consequently, when the exile Assembly started preparations for the unveiling of yet another anti-Khrushchev poster on ACEN House opposite the UN, it was halted by the authorities.

On the occasion of the issuing of the second Captive Nations Proclamation, the ACEN presented a poster depicting Khrushchev riding in a sedan chair carried by the nine captive European nations. The description below was a quote from Khrushchev's February speech in Indonesia: "We feel bound by close ties to the colonial peoples."[115] Perceiving the USSR as the world's largest colonial empire, the ACEN wanted to ridicule Soviet efforts in the UN General Assembly to promote the total eradication of colonialism. In his memoirs, Korboński depicted the ACEN efforts to counteract the Soviet propaganda and inform the UN delegates about Soviet tactics. Calling on all free world delegations, the ACEN representatives sent out over a hundred communications and personally addressed sixty delegations, including the new members of the UN. Moreover, they disseminated their own publication, specially prepared for the occasion, titled "The New Colonialism".[116] This brochure, sent to the American and foreign media, stimulated great interest and thus added to the generally unfavorable popular reception of Khrushchev.

In the meantime however, the chairman of the ACEN, Petr Zenkl, was informed that there had been a change to the ACEN poster on ACEN House. The problem was, no ACEN official had requested such a change.[117] On the day of Khrushchev's arrival, the ACEN poster had been covered with a plain, white sheet.[118] On 4 October the new ACEN chairman, Vaclovas Sidzikauskas, and Secretary Coste sent a telegram to William Boswell, addressed as a director of security at the State Department. They asked for permission to immediate uncover the poster, as an anti-communist demonstration was scheduled to take place in front of ACEN House on 5 October.[119] The permission was not granted, and photos of the covered poster were widely reproduced in the media.[120] One reader commented: "We have become so polite that we have lost all our sense of moral indignation. And that is what really harms American prestige among other nations."[121]

This obvious censorship of ACEN activity had to be explained somehow. In the *ACEN News* the organization explained it as an "embargo imposed by the authorities".[122] This ambivalent statement did not satisfy many of its readers. The ACEN received letters and postcards from many radically anti-communist citizens who learned about the incident. McCarthyite statements were common: "We, true Americans, want to know who are the pro red enemies in American Midst", or "We must get the home rats first to be successful to the outsider red enemies". Despite the fact that ACEN distanced itself from such radical statements, it had to answer at least a few of the letters it received. A reply was sent to retired US Air Force Reserve Colonel Tom R. Hutton, director of SPX Associates, an organization collecting and evaluating information on communist subversion.[123] Hutton had inquired of the ACEN secretary what authorities had asked the exiles to cover the poster, for how long, and whether this was an order or a "request".[124] Coste did not answer any of these questions directly. Instead, he sent Hutton the following reply:

> For the reasons you will, I hope, understand, our exile organization has felt unable to go beyond the statement that 'in compliance with measures taken by the proper authorities on UN Plaza, the poster prepared for the opening of the UN session had to be covered.'[125]

The scheduled protest had to be moved away from ACEN House as well. With Senator Thomas J. Dodd in attendance, acting on behalf of Democratic presidential candidate John F. Kennedy, the exile rally took place on the corner of UN Plaza and 46th Street. A photo printed in the *ACEN News* shows the exiles holding their national flags in their hands, with the UN building clearly visible in the background. During his speech, delivered on the street, Dodd officially criticized the "arbitrary decision of local and federal authorities", which he called "a violation of civil rights" similar to methods employed by the Soviets.[126] Interestingly, a few days earlier, Archibald S. Alexander, the president of the FEC, had addressed the ACEN delegates during the ceremonial opening of the Assembly's seventh session, emphasizing "the harmonious cooperation" between the two organizations.[127]

The debates of the 15th session of the UN were characterized by Khrushchev's and Fidel Castro's tirades, as well as by uncontrolled fits of anger from the former. Thus, the UN session that went down in history as the one during which the "Declaration on the Granting of Independence to Colonial Counties and Peoples" was adopted, is most commonly associated with Khrushchev's bizarre behavior, including the banging of his shoe.[128] In his memoirs Korboński observed: "By taking off his shoe, Khrushchev showed his Achilles Heel, but no one tried to get him there."[129] Few people remembered that it was the issue of Soviet colonialism in Central and Eastern Europe that drove Khrushchev mad.[130]

After twenty-five long days, on 13 October the Soviet Premier eventually departed from the U.S. – to great American relief. The ACEN billboard was unveiled eleven days later, on the fourth anniversary of the Hungarian Uprising. On 24 October an ACEN special session was inaugurated during which prominent guests voiced support for the captives. Among them were: the Chinese (nationalist) delegate to the UN, Tingfu F. Tsiang; a member of the Philippines' delegation, Ramon Bagatsing, whose fellow delegate Lorenzo Sumulong had driven Khrushchev into shoe-banging fury; William C. Wentworth of the Australian delegation; and Estonian defector Viktor Jaanimets, who had arrived with the Khrushchev delegation on the *Baltika*.[131] During this special session, the ACEN adopted a resolution addressed to the 15th UN session calling for withdrawal of the accreditation given to the Hungarian regime's representatives and – as usual – demanding that the issues of free elections in Central and Eastern Europe and Soviet troop withdrawal be included in the text of the Declaration.[132] Despite the media attention, little was achieved toward these ends.[133] U.S. foreign policy was already on a course towards "Peaceful Engagement" and "Bridge Building", accommodating East European leaders while promoting "evolutionary" change.

By November a new poster was unveiled on ACEN House. This time Khrushchev was a jailer who commanded the captives "Shout: down with imperialism!", while the other prison cell doors (British, French, and Belgian) stood wide open. The subheading read: "U.N. open all the doors."[134] This proved to be the last influential poster displayed by the ACEN. In the years that followed, only few of its posters garnered media attention. By 1963, financial cuts forced the ACEN to give up its lease on the warehouse. More importantly, the exile assembly was drifting farther away from American Cold War policies.

The ACEN and its Relationship to its Sponsor, the Free Europe Committee

The first cuts in the ACEN budget were debated by representatives of the Department of State, the CIA and the FEC already in mid-1960.[135] Although they coincided with but were not directly caused by the ACEN activities during Khrushchev's visit, it is crucial to connect the budget cuts for émigré activities with the emerging policy of détente. By 1960, the FEC limited its support for the ACEN to individual exiles. In the amendments to the memorandum of April 1960 submitted by FEC President Alexander for discussion with the sponsors, a list was included of prominent exiles on whom the Americans wanted to base their future operations.[136] Written two years later, the FEC's 1963 internal evaluation of the ACEN actions reveals a divergence in aims.

> ACEN has always to some extent functioned as a lobby for Eastern European interests on the U.S. political scene and in respect to the United Nations. Most of its formal and most energetic activity

> of this sort has been directly or indirectly sanctioned by U.S. policy – especially its activities following the Hungarian Revolution. There have always been other peripheral activities by ACEN and its members which are less clearly in the basic U.S. interest. Such activities have up until now usually been quite well contained. During the past year or two, however, there has been increasing evidence of divergence between the exile views and interests, as expressed by ACEN and some of the exile national committees and councils, and the basic interests of the U.S. Government. This is also applicable to some extent to problems with which the U.S. becomes involved in the United Nations. ACEN found it difficult to reconcile itself to a more moderate U.S. policy on Hungary. ... On this and many other facets of relations with Eastern Europe, ACEN appears to be basically out of sympathy with the current U.S. policy of encouraging gradual loosening of ties between Moscow and the East European Satellites and capitalizing on freer U.S. – East European contacts.[137]

By 1963 the FEC was already debating how to phase out the ACEN activities:

> Far from considering an expansion of ACEN in Latin America or anywhere else at his point in time, we should be considering how to disengage from ACEN during the next few years, how gradually to phase it back and reduce it (at most) to nothing more than a brass nameplate, a letterhead and a list of names who can sign proclamations when there is some real need for them.[138]

The changing nature of West–East Cold War relations caused increasing apprehension among the exiles, who closely followed the announcements of consecutive secretaries of state. The straw that broke the camel's back came with Secretary of State Dean Rusk's speech of February 25, 1964, "Why We Treat Different Communist Countries Differently".[139] The ACEN criticized the administration for softening its policies. Coste prepared a highly critical letter, signed by ACEN Chairman Alexander Kutt, which was sent to Rusk on April 9, 1964.[140] The exiles soon found out that the ACEN budget for 1965 had been reduced by 56 percent![141] Naturally, the financial cuts and the FEC's attempts to phase out the ACEN influenced the latter's operations (travel, publishing, public meetings etc.) and consequently its effectiveness. Whereas individual ACEN members continued to enjoy the respectful attention of members of the U.S. Congress,[142] politicians and/or journalists – their texts were published in the Congressional Record, prestigious American dailies and magazines – the ACEN was steadily losing its role as the "voice of the captive people". By 1972 the FEC's financial support for the exile activities had come to an end.

***

The years 1959–1960 undoubtedly mark a watershed in relations between the exiles and their FEC-affiliated sponsors. Since the heyday of the Captive Nations Proclamation of July 1959 to obvious case of censorship of its activities in 1960, the Department of State and the Free Europe Committee begun to slowly but steadily phase out – politically and financially – the ACEN. Based on fragmentary analysis of just a few selected themes in the ACEN history, it is easy to see how complicated and how delicate a balance they had to maintain with their sponsor. The Assembly's unwavering struggle to promote Central and East European liberation in the forum of international organizations and among the American public was becoming less and less in harmony with Department of State policies of reestablishing diplomatic and trade relations with the Soviet Bloc.

Despite the émigré leadership's self-restraint and adherence to the FEC-imposed rules, the moment the ACEN activities diverged from official U.S. policy, it lost American support. The FEC's reaction to the ACEN activities shows that the ACEN mission had to remain compatible with U.S. foreign policy objectives. The early days of the Cold War when support was bountiful were over, the foreign policy thaw had begun and accelerated, leaving the leaders of the Captive Nations behind as they evolved. The ACEN retained its stance, while American policy changed.

Compromise was the price that some of the émigré leaders were willing to pay for many years following their disillusionment in 1959. However, it was not a matter of personal or financial gain, indeed, many of them would have been far better off adopting U.S. citizenship and pursuing private careers. Their essential objective was to keep the ACEN alive and continue the concerted Central and East European émigré effort not to let the world forget about their approximately one hundred million captive compatriots. For them it was a matter of being able to act on behalf of their captive nations, and it was this goal that forged their dedication and commitment for the life of the organization.

Endnotes

1 For a general overview of the ACEN activities see: Anna Mazurkiewicz, "Assembly of the Captive European Nations: 'The Voice of the Silenced Peoples'" in: *Anti-Communist Minorities: Political Activism of Ethnic Refugees*, ed. Ieva Zake (New York: Palgrave Macmillan, 2009) 167–185.

2 The ACEN chairmen were: Vilis Māsēns (Latvia) 1954–1958, Stefan Korboński (Poland) 1958–1959, Petr Zenkl (Czechoslovakia) 1959–1960, Vaclovas Sidzikauskas (Lithuania) 1960–1961, Ferenc Nagy (Hungary) 1961–62, George M. Dimitrov (Bulgaria) 1962–63, Alexander Kutt (Estonia) 1963–64, Vasil Germenji (Albania) 1964–65, V. Sidzikauskas 1965–66, S. Korboński 1966–67, G. M. Dimitrov 1967–68, Jozef Lettrich (Czechoslovakia) 1968–69, Alfreds Bērziņš (Latvia) 1969–1970, V. Germenji 1970–1971, S. Korboński 1971–72. Brutus Coste (Romania) served as the ACEN secretary general from 1954 to 1965, followed by Edmund Gáspár (1965–66, Hungary), and Feliks Gadomski (1966–1972, Poland). After the withdrawal of FEC funding, the exiles continued their operations as an independent organization, the ACEN Inc. (1972–1989).

3 Following the Hungarian Revolution in November 1956, János Kádár became the head of the Soviet-controlled government. Although the relations between the two countries remained tense (ambassadors were recalled) until 1966, the U.S. administration was widely criticized for "not having the courage to propose and to insist on the expulsion of the Hungarian Red representatives from the UN". See editorials quoted in: *ACEN News* 42–44, (September–November 1958) 2–3.

4 C.D. Jackson to A. Dulles, 9 December 1958, C.D. Jackson Papers, 1931–1967 (hereafter CDJ Papers), box 53, file FEC 1958 (2), Dwight D. Eisenhower Library (Abilene, KS), (hereafter DDEL).

5 For biographical information see: *Biographical Dictionary of Central and Eastern Europe in the Twentieth Century*, eds. Wojciech Roszkowski, Jan Kofman (Armonk, NY, London, England: M.E. Sharpe, 2008) 490, 637, 908, 1153.

6 Kenneth A. Osgood, *Total Cold War. Eisenhower's Secret Propaganda Battle at Home and Abroad* (Lawrence: University of Kansas, 2006) 357; See also, Richard P. Stebbins, *The United States in World Affairs 1959* (New York: Harper, Council on Foreign Relations, 1960).

7 Formally, Nikita Khrushchev was not the chief of the Soviet state. Such title belonged to Kliment Voroshilov, chairman of the Presidium of the Supreme Soviet of the Soviet Union (1953–1960). Despite that, in 1959 Khrushchev, the first secretary of the CPSU since 1953 and the chairman of the Council of Ministers of the Soviet Union since 1958, received a state welcome upon his arrival in the U.S. with the honors reserved for heads of state, which of course he was in practice. William Taubman, *Khrushchev: the Man and His Era* (New York, London: W.W. Norton & Company, 2004) 420–421; Peter Carlson, *K Blows Top: A Cold War Comic Interlude Starring Nikita Khrushchev, America's Most Unlikely Tourist* (New York: Public Affairs, 2009) 61–62.

8 This article is based on my research in the archives of the Immigration History Research Center (Minneapolis, MN), the National Archives and Records Administration (College Park, MD), the Dwight D. Eisenhower Presidential Library (Abilene, KS), and the Hoover Institution Archives (Stanford, CA). My research was made possible by support from the Kosciuszko Foundation and the Foundation for Polish Science.

9 Taubman, *Khrushchev*, 396–397, 399–402.

10 *ACEN News* 46/47 (January/February 1959) 6.

11 Ibid., 5–6; ACEN Press Release no. 274, 13 January 1959, ACEN, box 152, file 7, Immigration History Research Center, University of Minnesota (Minneapolis, MN), (hereafter IHRC); Stefan Korboński, *W imieniu Polski walczącej* (Warszawa: Rytm, Bellona, 1999) 591, (U.S. edition: Stefan Korboński, *Warsaw in Exile* (New York: Praeger, 1966)). Charles Gati described Mikoyan's role during the Hungarian Revolution differently: Charles Gati, *Stracone złudzenia. Moskwa, Waszyngton i Budapeszt wobec powstania węgierskiego 1956 roku* (Warszawa: Polski Instytut Spraw Międzynarodowych, 2006) 331, 337, 343 (U.S. edition: Charles Gati, *Failed Illusions: Moscow, Washington, Budapest, and the 1956 Hungarian Revolt* (Washington, D.C.: Woodrow Wilson Center Press; Stanford CA: Stanford University Press, 2006)).

12 "Mikoyan Here Today, Will Get Top Security", *New York Herald Tribune*, 13 January 1959; Mary Hornaday, "Mikoyan Roves into Wall Street", *Christian Science Monitor*, 14 January 1959, both in: Scrapbooks, ACEN, box 163, IHRC.

13 This date is incorrect in the telegram. It should be 27 November.

14 S. Korboński to John J. McCloy (CFR Chairman), telegram, 13 January 1959, ACEN, box 152, file 7, IHRC.

15 S. Korboński to Henry M. Wriston, Howard C. Sheperd, R. T. Hurley, 13 January 1959, ACEN, box 152, file 7, IHRC; Press Release no. 275, "ACEN Asks Mikoyan's Hosts In New York Put Pertinent Questions to Moscow's Second In Command", 13 January 1959, ACEN, box 152, file 7, IHRC.

16 J. Richardson to the Editor of the *New York Times*, 13 January 1959, ACEN, box 152, file 7, IHRC.

17 S. Korboński to John F. Dulles, 14 January 1959, ACEN, box 152, file 7, IHRC. The letter contained both the questions and the statement (as in press releases nos. 274 and 275). Copies of this correspondence were sent to Foy D. Kohler (Deputy Assistant Sec. for European Affairs), Edward L. Freers (Director, Office of Eastern European Affairs, OEEA), Henry P. Leverich (Deputy Director OEEA).

18 Press Release no. 274, "Statement on Mikoyan's Visit", 13 January 1959, ACEN, box 152, file 7, IHRC.

19 See: ACEN, box 152, file 7, IHRC.

20 Scrapbooks, ACEN, box 163, January 1959–June 1959, IHRC.

21 Felix Belair Jr., "Eisenhower Bids U.S. Be Courteous; President 'Hopes' Mikoyan Will Be Given Accurate Picture of America", *New York Times*, 9 January 1959, 4; "Mr. Mikoyan on Tour", *New York Times*, 10 January 1959, 16.

22 Copy of a telegram sent to Eric Johnston by Walter H. Judd, 2 January 1959, attached to a letter from Walter H. Judd to S. Korboński, 7 January 1959, ACEN, box 152, file 7, IHRC; S. Korboński to W.H. Judd, 5 January 1959, ACEN, box 152, file 7, IHRC.

23 S. Korboński to G. Meany, telegram, 13 January 1959, ACEN, box 152, file 7, IHRC; "Meany Belittles U.S.-Soviet Talks; Speech at labor Parley Held a Rebuke to Aides Who Met With Mikoyan", *New York Times*, 9 January 1959, 5.

24 *ACEN News* 46/47 (January–February 1959) 8.

25 Stefan Korboński, József Kővágó and Vilis Māsēns left the U.S. on January 29, 1959. "Dziennik podróży dookoła świata" in: Korboński, *W imieniu Polski walczącej*, 377–498.

26 "Agreed Policy Governing Free Europe Committee Operations, 7 August 1956", CIA FOIA Document, access: www.foia.cia.gov, accessed 23 April 2010; E. Acker, "Suggested shift of emphasis for National Councils and Committees (fiscal year 1958)", 12 June 1957, Radio Free Europe/Radio Liberty Inc., Corporate Records (Hereafter RFE CR), box 198, file 5, Hoover Institution Archives (Stanford, CA), (hereafter HIA); R.E. Walter to R. Minton, Memorandum, 18 March 1960, RFE CR, box 198, file 1, HIA.

27 Five ACEN special sessions took place in Strasbourg in July 1955, April 1956, April 1957, April 1958, and in October 1961. Korboński, *W imieniu Polski walczącej*, 498–506; Feliks Gadomski, *Maszynopis: Zgromadzenie Europejskich Narodów Ujarzmionych. Krótki zarys*, New York, 1991 (book manuscript), Feliks Gadomski Archive, 108/02–1, Zakład Narodowy im. Ossolińskich (Wrocław, Poland), (hereafter ZNiO). See also: *ACEN News* 4/5 (July–August 1955), 13/14 (April–May1956), 25/26 (April–May 1957), 38/39 (May–June 1958), 79 (October 1961).

28 C.D. Jackson to J. Nowak, 15 April 1959, CDJ Papers, box 53, file FEC 1959 (2), DDEL.

29 Proposed West European Advisory Committee, memorandum, 1 February 1959, CDJ Papers, box 53, file FEC 1959 (2), DDEL.

30 Assembly of Captive European Nations, Charter and Rules of Procedure, ACEN, 136, b.1, file 2, IHRC.

31 Ibid.

32 Interview with Alfred Reisch, Warsaw, 16 October 2008. Reisch is the author of the forthcoming book: *The West's Secret Plan for the Minf: Book Distribution to East Europe during the Cold War*. See Alfred Reisch, "Ideological Warfare during the Cold War: The West's Secret Book Distribution Program behind the Iron Curtain," *Military Power Revue der Schweizer Armee 3* (2008) 44–56.

33 W.D. Crittenberger, Opposition to European Advisory Group, memorandum, 21 April 1958, CDJ Papers, box 54, file FEC 1958 (2), DDEL.

34 The Captive European Nations and the U.N., memorandum, 31 May 1956, ACEN, box 1, file 10, IHRC; B. Coste to E. Packer, 25 July 1956, ACEN, box 1, file 10, IHRC; ACEN House Progress Report and an Outline of Alternative Solutions, September 1956, ACEN, box 1, file 10, IHRC.

35 Quote of November 1956, in: Taubman, *Khrushchev*, 427.

36 *ACEN News* 42/44 (September/November 1958) 1.

37 B. Coste to R. Wagner, 8 November 1956, ACEN, box 1, file 10, IHRC; B. Coste to H. Jack, 8 November 1956, ACEN, box 1, file 10, IHRC.

38 In his pleas, B. Coste received support from the Civil Liberties Union and Workers' Defense League. B. Coste, Memorandum for the Record, 12 September 1958, ACEN, box 1, file 11,

IHRC; B. Coste, Memorandum of the Meeting, 15 September 1958, ACEN, box 1, file 11, IHRC. It was not the last time that the ACEN experienced this sort of trouble. An almost identical situation occurred in 1961.

39 B. Coste, Memorandum for the Record, 12 September 1958, ACEN, box 1, file 11, IHRC.

40 B. Coste, Memorandum for the Record, 17 October 1958, ACEN, box 1, file 11, IHRC.

41 Scrapbook 1959, ACEN, box 162, IHRC; B. Coste to Turner Construction Company, 4 November 1959, ACEN, box 1, file 11, IHRC; R.M. Hettem to B. Coste, 5 November 1959, ACEN, box 1, file 11, IHRC; *ACEN News* 57 (December 1959) 15.

42 *ACEN News* 49 (April 1959) 24; "Anti-Reds Paint Khrush as Jailer", *New York Daily News*, 16 April 1959, in: Scrapbooks, ACEN, box 163, IHRC.

43 E[lon] F. Tompkins, "Re-Mapping Europe. Packages for Geneva", *New York Journal American*, 5 May 1959; "Herter Pledges East Europe Aid", *New York Herald Tribune*, 11 May 1959, in: Scrapbooks, ACEN, box 163, IHRC.

44 Taubman, *Khrushchev*, 415; Vladislav M. Zubok, "Khrushchev and the Berlin Crisis (1958–1962)", Cold War International History Project Working Paper no. 6, Woodrow Wilson International Center for Scholars, Washington 1993, 13–16; Carlson, *K Blows Top*, 39–41.

45 Letter from Chairman Khrushchev to President Eisenhower, 21 July 1959 in *Foreign Relations of the United States 1958–1960*, Vol. X, Part 1: "Eastern Europe Region; Soviet Union; Cyprus" (Washington: U.S. Government Printing Office, 1993) 324.

46 A. Cooke, "Russia on Show. Some Myths in New York", *Manchester Guardian*, 1 July 1959 in: Scrapbooks, ACEN, box 162 (July–November 1959), IHRC.

47 B. Coste to W. Langer, 25 June 1959, ACEN, box 11, file 1, IHRC.

48 Bennet Kovrig, *Of Walls and Bridges. The United States and Eastern Europe* (New York, London: New York University Press, 1991) 105.

49 S. Korboński to R. Nixon, 26 June 1959, ACEN, box 11, file 1, IHRC.

50 Press Release no. 310, President Eisenhower urged raise captive nations problem, 30 June 1959, ACEN, box 152, file 7, IHRC.

51 A month before Nixon's departure to the USSR, in a letter addressed to the vice president, ACEN referred to Nixon's speech of 27 January 1959, in which he said that "Mikoyan's meeting with American officials would be exploited by the Soviets as an indication that the U.S. has resigned itself to the captive status of the countries of Central and Eastern Europe". ACEN Chairman (Korboński) to Vice President Richard M. Nixon, 26 June 1959, IHRC, ACEN, box 152, file 7; S. Korboński to Christian A. Herter (Secretary of State), 29 June 1959, ACEN, box 152, file 7, IHRC; J.W. Fulbright to S. Korboński, 13 July 1959, ACEN, box 152, file 7, IHRC.

52 "U.S. Denies Dulles Softened Views", *New York Times*, 2 July 1959, in: Scrapbooks, ACEN, box 162 (July–November 1959), IHRC. The ACEN representatives were also active in Europe. Commenting on the ACEN-related exile activities in London, the *New York Journal American* wrote that if the Soviets really wanted world peace, they should relinquish its East European base for war. E[lon] F. Tompkins, "European Peace: Atlantic Congress Plan", *New York Journal American*, 16 July 1959, in: Scrapbooks, ACEN, box 162 (July–November 1959), IHRC.

53 Taubman, *Khrushchev*, 416–419.

54 *ACEN News* 52/54 (July–September 1959) 13. Since 1959, Captive Nations Week has been proclaimed every year. See: Presidential Proclamation, *Captive Nations Week 2011*, 15 July 2011, http://www.whitehouse.gov/the-press-office/2011/07/15/presidential-proclamation-captive-nations-week , accessed: 4 May 2012.

55 Korboński, *W imieniu Polski walczącej*, 592–3.

56 *ACEN News* 52/54 (July–September 1959): 29–30; "Captive Nations Honor Williams", *Lansing State Journal*, 27 July 1959, in: Scrapbooks, ACEN, box 162, IHRC.

57 S. Korboński to the Editor of the *New York Times*, 10 July 1959, ACEN, box 11, file 2, IHRC.

58 S. Korboński, "Mr. Dulles' Policies. He Is Memorialized as a Spokesman for Europe's Enslaved Nations", *New York Times*, 9 June 1959, 36.

59 *ACEN News* 52/54 (July-September 1959) 9.

60 Ibid., 1.

61 Ibid.

62 "Crossfire in Moscow", *Christian Science Monitor*, 25 July 1959; "Gesture to Captive Nations", *Toledo Blade*, 27 July 1959; "Spark of Freedom Still Burns", *Erie (Pennsylvania) News*, 1 August 1959, in: Scrapbooks, ACEN, box 162, IHRC.

63 "The Captive Nations", *Harrisburg (Pennsylvania) Patriot*, 29 August 1959, in: Scrapbooks, ACEN, box 162, IHRC.

64 Gadomski, *Maszynopis: ACEN (book manuscript)*, 56, ZNiO; *ACEN News* 55 (October 1959) 9.

65 Mary Hornaday, "Anti-Red Groups Strive for Khrushchev Visit", *Christian Science Monitor*, 22 August 1959, in: Scrapbooks, ACEN, box 162, IHRC; Milton B. Freudenheim "Exiles Warn on Nik Visit. Its Effect Might Soften Our Moral Fiber Says Anti-Red", *Chicago Daily News*, 5 August 1959.

66 Representative Walter H. Judd on the announcement of exchange of visits of President Eisenhower and Khrushchev, 3 August 1959, ACEN, box 152, file 7, IHRC.

67 "Hungarians Pledge No Insults to Mr. K", *New York World Telegram*, 10 September 1959, in: Scrapbooks, ACEN, box 162, IHRC. In early September many small newspapers around the country printed parts of the Associated Press wires. Many of them repeated: "The ACEN says that in promoting the cause of freedom for the captive peoples it has 'never resorted to or encouraged, and never will, violent means or means incompatible with the laws and customs of this country', but it expressed hope that the 'Soviet visitor will be forcefully reminded of the unresolved issue of freedom and independence for the nine captive European nations'". "Chairman of ACEN told a reporter his organization opposed Khrushchev visit but did not plan any public demonstrations"; "Korboński said refugee groups did not want to be accused of 'poisoning the atmosphere' in the event that the Khrushchev talks with President Eisenhower fail to ease international tensions". Headlines of the articles in which the exile voice was mentioned said: "Courteous, Lukewarm. Attitude toward Khrushchev Visit", "Reactions to Khrushchev's Visit Vary Across Country", "American Attitude toward Nikiti's Visit 'Lukewarm'", "Is Khrushchev's Visit a Genuine Peace Mission, or Just Propaganda", "Just In Case, Niki to Get Top Shield". See: Scrapbooks, ACEN, box 162, IHRC.

68 Copies of S. Korboński telegrams to: Walter Reuther, Vice-President AFL-CIO, Averell Harriman, George Meany (AFL-CIO President), 14 September 1959, ACEN, box 152, file 7, IHRC. United Automobile Workers President Walter Reuther's exchanges with Khrushchev are described in: Taubman, *Khrushchev*, 434.

69 ACEN to American Friends of Captive Nations [AFCN], Brief Arguments against Khrushchev's Visit, 12 August 1959, ACEN, box 152, file 7, IHRC.

70 Ibid.

71 The Jewish Labor Committee, National Catholic Welfare Conference, AFCN, *The New Leader*, *National Review*, American Committee on Liberation, Ukrainian Congress Committee, Lithuanian Information Center, Committee of One Million, CACEED, Aid Refugee Chinese Intellectuals, Hungarian Committee, *Jewish Forward*. ACEN Secretariat to the General Committee, Khrushchev's Visit to the U.S., 12 August 1959, ACEN, box 152, file 7, IHRC.

72 Ibid.

73 *Chicago Daily News*, 5 August 1959, quoted in: *ACEN News* 52/54 (July–September 1959) 40–41.

74 *ACEN News* 55 (October 1959) 2–3.

75 ACEN Secretariat to the General Committee, Khrushchev's Visit to the U.S., 12 August 1959, ACEN, box 152, file 7, IHRC.

76 "Four Hungarians Arrive Here to Rap Khrushchev, but Countrymen Are Urged Not to Join in Any Demonstrations Against Premier", *Los Angeles Times*, 18 September 1959; "Top Hungarian Exiles Praise Discipline of Refugees in US", *Washington Post*, 25 September 1959, in: Scrapbooks, ACEN, box 162, IHRC.

77 ACEN Secretariat to the General Committee, Khrushchev's Visit to the U.S., 12 August 1959, ACEN, box 152, file 7, IHRC.

78 H.E. Salisbury, "Khrushchev and the intellectuals", *San Francisco Chronicle*, 14 September 1959; "Captive Nation Unit Raises Black Flag", *New York Times*, 16 September 1959, in: Scrapbooks, ACEN, box 162, IHRC.

79 "Honor Poland's Heroes", *The Chicago American*, 12 September 1959; "Nikita's Visit Seen as Policy Shift", *Chicago Daily Tribune*, 12 September 1959, "12 days of mourning urged during Khrushchev's visit", *Chicago Sun Times*, 13 September 1959, in: Scrapbooks, ACEN, box 162, IHRC.

80 "Khrushchev Welcome Plans Are Announced", *Wilkes Barre (Pennsylvania) Times Leader News*, 11 September 1959, in: Scrapbooks, ACEN, box 162, IHRC. Photos of the ACEN conference were published in renowned papers such as the *New York Times*, as well as in such local papers as the *Wilmington (Deleware) News*, *Cumberland (Maryland) News*, and *Norfolk Virginian Pilot*.

81 S. Korboński, "Surest Road to Peace", letter to the Editor, *Indianapolis News*, 15 September 1959, in: Scrapbooks, ACEN, box 162, IHRC.

82 Carlson, *K Blows Top*.

83 T. Kelly, "Black Armbands and Tolling Bells", *Washington News*, 11 September 1959, in: Scrapbooks, ACEN, box 162, IHRC.

84 "Tough Police Bans Made for UN Talks", *Abilene (Texas) Reporter News*, 18 September 1959; "Public is Barred from UN Today", *Baton Rouge (Louisiana) State Times*, 18 September 1959; M. Besser, "U.N. Bars the Public; Area Heavily Guarded", *Utica (New York) Observer Dispatch*, 18 September 1959, in: Scrapbooks, ACEN, box 162, IHRC.

85 Carlson, *K Blows Top*, 74.

86 Ibid., 53–54.

87 Questions to Khrushchev, 11 September 1959, ACEN, box 152, file 7, IHRC; S. Korboński to E. Weintal, 11 September 1959, ACEN, box 152, file 7, IHRC.

88 Taubman mentions Gardner Cowles' September 18 question on co-existence compatibility with the triumph of Communism. Taubman, *Khrushchev*, 429.

89 Quoted in: Carlson, *K Blows Top*, 95; Taubman, *Khrushchev*, 428.

90 P. McConomy, "Kovago Questions Khrushchev's Statements; Is in California to Help Cool Off Demonstrators", *Wilmington (Delaware) News*, 18 September 1959, in: Scrapbooks, ACEN, box 162, IHRC.

91 ACEN, The Visit of Khrushchev and Captive Nations. A Statement, 11 September 1959, ACEN, box 152, file 7, IHRC; ACEN Press Release no. 322: ACEN Answers Khrushchev, 16 September 1959, ACEN, box 152, file 7, IHRC.

92 S. Korboński, B. Coste, "Lest We Forget", *Christian Science Monitor*, 25 September 1959, in: Scrapbooks, ACEN, box 162, IHRC.

93 "Hungary Under Soviet Rule, Vol. 3: Rapport on Hungary" by the AFCN, ACEN and the Hungarian Committee, ACEN, box 156, file 3, IHRC. "Report Charges Budapest Terror. Private Document Compiled Here Says Intellectuals Are Still Prosecuted", *New York Times*,

18 September 1959; "Picketing Shifts to U.N. Report New Hungary Terror", *New York Post*, 18 September 1959, in: Scrapbooks, ACEN, box 162, IHRC. Between September 21 and 25 six more articles were published from Connecticut to Arizona on the third report on Hungary submitted to the United Nations by the ACEN and AFCN.

94 *ACEN News* 55 (October 1959) 8; Korboński, *W imieniu Polski walczącej*, 595–607; Carlson, *K Blows Top*, 137–138.

95 "Visit Denounced At Carnegie Rally" *New York World Telegram*, 21 September 1959, in: Scrapbooks, ACEN, box 162, IHRC; ACEN Secretariat to the General Committee, Khrushchev's Visit to the U.S., 12 August 1959, ACEN, box 152, file 7, IHRC; ACEN, Khrushchev's Visit - A Challenge which Must Be Answered, 20 September 1959, ACEN, box 152, file 7, IHRC; ACEN Secretariat to Gen. Comm., Memorandum, 26 August 1959, ACEN, box 152, file 7, IHRC; P.H. Douglas to S. Korboński, 18 September 1959, ACEN, box 152, file 7, IHRC.

96 "Visit Denounced at Carnegie Rally", *New York World Telegram and Sun*, 21 September 1959; "Rally Bids President Put Issue of Captive Nations to Premier", *New York Times*, 21 September 1959; "Appeal Made for Enslaved People. Msgr. Balkunas Urges President Put Issue to Khrushchev", *Brooklyn Tablet*, 26 September 1959, in: Scrapbooks, ACEN, box 162, IHRC.

97 "Rally Bids President Put Issue Of Captive Nations to Premier", *New York Times*, 21 September 1959, 19; Korboński, *W imieniu Polski walczącej*, 268–9: M. Hornaday, "Hungarians in U.S. Hone Barbs for Visit", *Christian Science Monitor*, 14 September 1959; "Rally Here Assails Reds Khrushchev's Visit", *The Chicago American*, 13 September 1959, in: Scrapbooks, ACEN, box 162, IHRC. The latter reference contained the following call: "As displaced persons living as guests in this country it would not be fitting for us to organize demonstrations against a guest of the American President. However, we will wholeheartedly support any such demonstrations led by American citizens".

98 *ACEN News* 55 (October 1959) 3–4.

99 P.H. Douglas to S. Korboński, 18 September 1959, ACEN, box 152, file7, IHRC.

100 Dr. Lev E. Dobriansky summarized Khrushchev's terrible legacy in Ukraine in eight points, citing famine, purges, resettlements, persecution and repressions. "Crimes of Khrushchev against the Ukrainian People", *The Ukrainian Weekly*, http://www.ukrweekly.com/old/archive/1960/1796003.shtml, (accessed: 4 May 2012).

101 "'We Answer Khrushchev' Rally Draws 3000 Persons, Mostly Ukrainians to Carnegie Hall", *Svoboda. Ukrainian Weekly* 186, 26 September 1959, 1. http://ukrweekly.com/archive/pdf1/1959/The_Ukrainian_Weekly_1959-35.pdf, accessed: 4 May 2012. Interestingly, in an article a month earlier the ACEN is not mentioned as one of the organizers: "CACEED to Stage Peaceful Demonstration Against Khrushchev's Visit", *Svoboda. Ukrainian Weekly* 163, 25 August 1959, 1. http://ukrweekly.com/archive/pdf1/1959/The_Ukrainian_Weekly_1959-32.pdf, accessed: 4 May 2012.

102 Psychological Warfare and the Soviet Union, 10 February 1953, General Records of the Department of State, 59, Psychological Strategy Board, Working File 1951–1952, Executive Secretariat, box 7, E Series, National Archives and Records Administration (College Park, MD), (hereafter NARA); Draft Memorandum Concerning the Report on Soviet Economic Integration of the Captive Countries, 16 March 1960, ACEN, box 41, file7, IHRC; Alexander D. Bunescu, letter [no date], ACEN, box 42, file4, IHRC.

103 V. Māsēns to Z. Stypułkowski, 23 January 1956, ACEN, box 6, file 6, IHRC.

104 Lev Dobriansky played a pivotal role in lobbying for the Captive Nations Week Proclamation. In order to advance their goal he created the National Captive Nations Committee, which from the moment of its inception was continuously confused with the ACEN.

105 The text of the Resolution: ACEN, box 152, file 7, IHRC; "Captive Issue Pressed. Exile Leaders Here Ask Word by Eisenhower in U.N.", *New York Times*, 22 September 1960, 13; Korboński, *W imieniu Polski walczącej*, 594–595; ACEN Secretariat to the General Committee, Khrushchev's Visit to the U.S., 12 August 1959, ACEN, box 152, file 7, IHRC

106 A. Popa, Draft Statement concerning premier Khrushchev's visit to the USA, ACEN Political Committee, 9 September 1959, ACEN, box 152, file 7, IHRC.

107 *ACEN News* 55 (October 1959) 6.

108 Gadomski, *Maszynopis: ACEN (Book manuscript)*, 56, ZNiO.

109 Taubman, *Khrushchev*, 429–433; Carlson, *K Blows Top*, 177.

110 S.J. Frese, "Comrade Khrushchev and Farmer Garst: East-West Encounters Foster Agricultural Exchange", *The History Teacher* 38, no. 1 (2004) 37–65.

111 Aleksej I. Adżubej, *Twarzą w twarz z Ameryką. Reportaż z wizyty N.S. Chruszczowa w USA* (Warsaw: Książka i Wiedza, 1960).

112 *ACEN News* 61 (April 1960) 12; S. Fliegers, "Paris Goes All Out to Honor K.", *New York Mirror*, 13 March 1960; V.D. Hurd, "Motive: Khrushchev's safety. France's Vacation for Exiles Hit", *Christian Science Monitor*, 10 March 1960, in: Scrapbooks, ACEN, box 163 (Nov. 1959–Jul. 1960), IHRC. The *New York Herald Tribune* commented on the same day as well.

113 "8000 Cops to Guard K and Castro", *Long Island Press*, 16 September 1960, in: Scrapbooks, ACEN, box 164, IHRC.

114 ACEN pickets were reported mostly by the New York papers. Well over twenty articles appeared from September 18 to 22, including the opinion-making *New York Times, New York World Telegram, New York Daily News, National Review*, and *New York Telegram and Sun*. Scrapbooks, ACEN, box 164, IHRC.

115 *ACEN News* 64/66 (July–September 1960) 6.

116 "The New Colonialism", ACEN, box 152, file 5, IHRC; Korboński, *W imieniu Polski Walczącej*, 609–613: F. Hailey, "Exiles Assembly to Meet Near UN", *New York Times*, 16 September 1960; R. Dole, E. Salveson, "'Greeters' set for K.", *New York Mirror*, 17 September 1960, in: Scrapbooks, ACEN, box 164, IHRC. The *New York Herald Tribune* and *New York Mirror* cited the data contained in the ACEN rapport on Soviet colonialism. Until the end of October, 115 articles that contained reference to the "New Colonialism"were clipped by Burrelle's Press Clipping Bureau for the ACEN records.

117 E.K. Kexdi to P. Zenkl, 19 September 1960, ACEN, box 1, file 11, IHRC.

118 "What Khrushchev Won't See", *New York Herald Tribune*, 23 September 1960, in: Scrapbooks, ACEN, box 164, IHRC.

119 B. Coste, V. Sidzikauskas to W. Boswell, 4 October 1960, ACEN, box 1, file 11, IHRC.

120 P. Vajda to W. Loeb (*Manchester Union Leader & New Hampshire Sunday News*), 14 October 1960, ACEN, box 1, file 11, IHRC. All together there were over 30 articles announcing the new anti-Khrushchev poster, including: J. Grant, "How NY Greeted the 'Uninvited Ones'", *New York National Guardian*, 3 October 1960; S. de Garmont, "What Khrushchev Won't See: State Dept. Covers Cartoon Near U.N. Attacking Red", *New York Herald Tribune*, 23 September 1960; B.W. Munn, "Assembly Invaded by Red Bloc Chiefs", *Indianapolis Star*, 20 September 1960; S. Pelletiere, "UN Has Its Diplomatic Chuckles", *New York Journal American*, 23 September 1960; "A Course in Manners Might Aid Us at UN", *Washington Post and Times Herald*, 25 September 1960. See: Scrapbooks, ACEN, box 164, IHRC.

121 B. Smits, "Turmoil in Manhattan", *New York Journal American*, 29 September 1960, in:Scrapbooks, ACEN, box 164, IHRC.

122 *ACEN News* 67 (October 1960): 8.

[123] E.V. Toy, Jr., "The Right Side of the 1960s. The Origins of the John Birch Society in the Pacific Northwest", *Oregon Historical Quarterly* 105, no. 2 (2004). Article Stable URL: http://www.jstor.org/stable/20615422 .

[124] T. Hutton to P. Zenkl, 27 September 1960, ACEN, box 1, file 11, IHRC.

[125] B. Coste to T. R. Hutton, 6 October 1960, ACEN, box 1, file 11, IHRC.

[126] *ACEN News* 67 (October 1960) 9; Scrapbooks, ACEN, box 164, IHRC.

[127] Ibid.

[128] *ACEN News* 68 (November 1960) 2–5; Carlson, *K Blows Top*, 286–290.

[129] Korboński, *W imieniu Polski Walczącej*, 614.

[130] On October 12 the U.N. delegate of the Philippines, Lorenzo Sumulong, suggested that the USSR was to be blamed for colonization itself. He conditioned support for the "Declaration" on including East Central Europe among the regions subjugated to foreign domination and exploitation. The chaos that followed was nicely described by Carlson. See: Carlson, *K Blows Top*, 292–295; Taubman, *Khrushchev*, 475.

[131] *ACEN News* 68 (November 1960) 2–5. Victor Jaanimets, the Estonian sailor who defected from the *Baltika*, made his first public statement in the ACEN. J. G. Rogers, "Baltika Defector Asks Stronger Action by West", *New York Herald Tribune*, 25 October 1960. The ACEN Scrapbook collection contains 75 press articles on the case published from October 25 to 29.

[132] *ACEN News* 68 (November 1960) 2–5.

[133] Korboński, *W imieniu Polski Walczącej*, 616–617.

[134] *ACEN News* 68 (November 1960) 6.

[135] Archibald S. Alexander to Board of Directors, Executive Committee, Free Europe Organizations and Publications, Reorientation of Exile Support (1 April 1960), 4 April 1960, CDJ Papers, box 53, file Free Europe Committee 1960 (2), DDEL.

[136] Archibald S. Alexander to Board of Directors, Executive Committee, Free Europe Organizations and Publications, Reorientation of Exile Support, 27 January 1960, CDJ Papers, box 53, file Free Europe Committee 1960 (3), DDEL.

[137] Memorandum for the Record, The Assembly of Captive European Nations (ACEN), 1 July 1963, CDJ Papers, box 53, file FEC Budget etc., 1963 (1), DDEL.

[138] Ibid.

[139] D. Rusk, "Why We Treat Different Communist Countries Differently", Department of State Bulletin, 16 March 1964, no. L/1920, 390–396.

[140] *ACEN News* 108/109 (April–May 1964) 20–22.

[141] See: Coste Brutus, RFE CR, box 164, file 9, HIA; Gadomski, *Maszynopis: ACEN (book manuscript)*, 48, ZNiO.

[142] Among ACEN most faithful allies one should list: Representatives R. Madden, Edward J. Derwinski, William O. Lipinski, and Daniel J. Flood, and Senators Karl E. Mundt, T. Dodd, and William F. Knowland.

Select bibliography

Assembly of Captive European Nations Papers, Immigration History Research Center, University of Minnesota (Minneapolis, Minnesota)

Radio Free Europe/Radio Liberty Inc., Corporate Records, Hoover Institution Archives (Stanford, California).

Anti-Communist Minorities: Political Activism of Ethnic Refugees, ed. Ieva Zake (New York: Palgrave Macmillan 2009) 167–185.

Biographical Dictionary of Central and Eastern Europe in the Twentieth Century, eds. Wojciech Roszkowski, Jan Kofman (Armonk, NY, London, England: M.E. Sharpe, 2008)

Peter Carlson, *K Blows Top: A Cold War Comic Interlude Starring Nikita Khrushchev, America's Most Unlikely Tourist* (New York: Public Affairs, 2009)

Feliks Gadomski, *Zgromadzenie Europejskich Narodów Ujarzmionych. Krótki Zarys* (New York: Bicentennial Publishing Co., „Nowy Dziennik", 1995)

Stefan Korboński, *W imieniu Polski walczącej* (Warszawa: Rytm, Bellona, 1999) 591, (U.S. edition: Stefan Korboński, *Warsaw in Exile* (New York: Praeger, 1966))

John F. Leich, "Great Expectations: The National Councils in Exile 1950–1960", *Polish Review* 35, no. 3 (1990) 183–196.

Tajny oręż czy ofiary zimnej wojny? Emigracje polityczne z Europy Środkowej i Wschodniej [Secret weapon or the victims of the Cold War? Central and Eastern European political émigrés], ed. Sławomir Łukasiewicz (Lublin, Warszawa: Instytut Pamięci Narodowej, 2010)

William Taubman, *Khrushchev: the Man and His Era* (New York, London: W.W. Norton & Company, 2004)

X

The Free Europe University in Exile Inc. and the Collège de l'Europe libre (1951–1958)

Veronika Durin-Hornyik

This essay briefly presents the history of the NCFE's educational corporation called The Free Europe University in Exile Inc. (FEUE Inc.), based in New York, and its joint entity, the Collège de l'Europe libre (CEL), which operated in Strasbourg-Robertsau, France. Its aim is to provide an introduction to the NCFE's institution of higher learning, which during the height of the Cold War between the two world superpowers, the Soviet Union and the United States, gave grants to Central and Eastern European youths residing in Western countries. These grants allowed them to complete at Western European universities studies which had been interrupted because of Communist takeover in their respective countries. The NCFE attempted to train future leaders in anticipation of collapse of Soviet control in Central and Eastern Europe by complementing the students' studies with seminars—intended to keep national sentiment alive in exile—and with series of lectures taught by Western lecturers, both held in the CEL. The article attempts to demonstrate the undertaking's successes and failures from 1951 to 1958, emphasizing the NCFE's point of view in this "three-cornered-undertaking" between the U.S., France and Eastern Europe.

The Origin of the Idea of the University and its Place in the Context of the Cultural Cold War (1948–1950)

In the aftermath of World War II, American foreign policy strategists very soon recognized that the United States needed a plan of action to counteract the Communist takeover in Central and Eastern Europe. While 1946 was a time of reflection, 1947 was for action, leading to the conceptualization of the "Truman Doctrine" – which became the premise for organizing American foreign policy and attempting to contain Soviet influence -, and the launching of the Marshall Plan. The Soviet response was the creation of the Communist Information Bureau, called Cominform – a Soviet-dominated organization of European Communist parties -, and the announcement of the "Zhdanov Doctrine" at its first conference on 22 September 1947. The Soviet party secretary stated that the world had been divided into two parts: on one hand, the "imperialist" and "anti-democratic" world, and on the other hand, the "pacific" and "democratic" one. Zhdanov called for resistance against the establishment of American "imperialist world domination".

To this end, the USSR pushed the processes of "Sovietization" in the Central and Eastern European countries, with the aim of creating identical and servile Soviet people's republics. In the cultural domain, this meant introducing a new education policy which aimed to put an end to illiteracy, to help create a modern, industrial generation, and to support youth from the peasant class to pursue studies in higher education. It also means giving greater access to cultural events, which were overwhelmed with political content; the control and censure of press and radio to serve the political agenda; and the manipulation of human sciences to promote political ideology. These measures were implemented in order to demolish national identity, introduce cults of personality, eliminate religion, and ultimately declare the primacy of the Soviet Communist Party ideology.

This ideological conflict between the superpowers, accompanied by political-economic and military competition, led to the construction of two spheres of influence. As the Iron Curtain began to descend, before escape became virtually impossible, thousands crossed the borders into Western Europe out of fear of the consolidation of power by Communist regimes in their nations. The majority of these refugees were accommodated in hundreds of Displaced Persons camps in Germany, Austria, Italy and other European countries, most of them still harboring hundreds of thousands of refugees who left during WWII.[1]

The fear of Sovietization and of its destructive consequences gave birth to the idea of a university for Eastern European youth, first put forth in the Polish exile politic and literary journal *Kultura*. *Kultura* originated from a publishing house established in 1946 in Rome by Polish publisher-editor and former soldier of the Polish II Corps Jerzy Giedroyc as a sign of protest against Communist takeover in Eastern Europe. After a short stay in Rome, the publishing house moved to the Parisian suburbs, where a review was launched, also called *Kultura*. Giedroyc believed that the exiles had to take a position and act against Communist oppression and that only the intelligentsia could form a potent force for change in Eastern Europe. An inner circle of exiled Polish intellectuals worked closely with Giedroyc, among others, the writer and painter Joseph Czapski, also a former soldier in the Polish II Corps and one of a few survivors of the Katyn massacre in 1939.[2]

The university project originated from a spontaneous friendship between Czapski and the conservative American philosopher and political theorist James Burnham. Formerly a Communist but by that time an ardent anticommunist, Burnham covertly headed one of the branches of the newly formed Office of Policy Coordination (OPC), an intelligence organization independent from the CIA.[3]

Czapski and Burnham met in early 1948 in Saint-Etienne in France at a conference held by General de Gaulle. They were both intellectual and deeply engaged in the struggle against Communism. Czapski held a talk about the university project at this first meeting in France and Burnham became so interested in the idea that upon returning to the U.S., he started putting Czapski in touch with key contact officers at the State Department, beginning in June 1948.

The first detailed draft outlined by Czapski explains that the idea for a university emerged from the Communist takeover in Central and Eastern Europe and its results, which not only made the intellectual development of these countries impossible but also caused the destruction of their intelligentsia due to Sovietization. The Communist takeover led to massive emigration from these countries to Western Europe where, through lack of opportunities and money, refugees in exile were living in unclear and uncertain conditions.

Under these circumstances, the University would act with a double purpose. First, to educate Eastern youth about democratic values, and second, to involve the U.S. in the struggle against Communism on behalf of the Soviet satellite countries, which had, until then, been neglected by the U.S. Czapski wrote in the draft:

> With the idea of creating an European Union and the reconstruction of its culture in our mind, the fact of finding a solution – at least a provisional one, even it be only for the refugees – cannot be left out. It is of great importance therefore to educate the Central-European elite that will represent the intellectual values of their countries and who shall be penetrated with the American democratic ideas – forming in the future a group that could be relied upon for the building up of the Pax Americana. …This would be easily attainable by creating a University for the Youth coming now from behind the iron curtain. This sort of action would have a deep mental effect on the people under Soviet occupation as they would certainly regain faith in the reality of America's plan in finding a solution for their difficulties and would as well be an encouragement to further struggle, a much more effective one than any purely propaganda action.[4]

To Czapski's mind, the University would be a type of higher education institution, established possibly in France and affiliated with an existing institution. France offered numerous advantages. The country, enjoying great popularity among Eastern European countries, was always a destination for intellectual émigrés due to its democratic values and respect of human rights. European integration was flourishing there with the Council of Europe in Strasbourg. Furthermore, France had a good geopolitical position and well respected universities.

The University would have three faculties: political, social and economic sciences; humanistic studies on Central and Eastern European literature, history and languages; and lastly a series of lectures on the history and literature of the U.S. and England. Students desiring to study applied sciences would study at the local French university. It would be obligatory for all students to study American and English history and literature, under the conditions of the university project. At the end of their studies, a degree would be awarded to students, on agreement with the local university. Due to the destructive nature of Sovietization, it would be important to create a library, specializing in literary and historical books, and a periodical review on intellectual problems and concepts of federation for these countries.

The students would be mainly recruited from behind the Iron Curtain in Poland, Rumania, Hungary, Bohemia, Slovakia, Balkan and Baltic countries, and Ukraine. Czapski also suggested inviting American students learning about these countries, who would later become political consultants in the U.S. The number of pupils would be five thousand, and a quota would be set up for each nationality to be represented in the University in accordance with the total of refugees from the respective countries. The teachers would be refugee and American professors, depending on the faculty. The University would have a standard academic structure, with the addition of a vice chancellor chosen by the American authority funding the University, who would be responsible for financial and organizational issues. All students would be housed together, with the dual purpose of creating a healthy community and providing accommodation for refugee students. They would also be provided with necessary assistance, such as a living allowance, clothing and pocket money.

In his plan for the organization of the University, Czapski intended to avoid the problems which characterize international organizations ("rigidly shaped routine, leading to a wasteful financial economy") and problems arising from Central and Eastern European national divisions. Supporting the vice chancellor would be a commission of three people whose task would be to work out the University's legal, educational and financial aspects in order to permit it to open at the beginning of the 1949/50 academic year. Exile professors would be recruited through American universities where they were already teaching or in Western European DP camps, on the basis of their qualifications. Student recruitment would be left to scientific and national organizations; the University would only require proof of their qualifications by documents and certificates. If the University wanted to select candidates itself, it would have to set up an examination board in Europe, after advertising in the various national presses. Czapski's budget plan notes that "it would seem logical to include in it the Marshall Plan as part of the cultural reconstruction of Europe."[5]

Burnham kept Czapski informed of his opinions on the University project every month. Answering a letter in which Czapski had summarized his impressions about the first meeting with one of Burnham's contacts – William G. Casey, general counselor for Averell Harriman on the European Cooperation Administration, the U.S. governmental agency to administer the Marshall Plan – Burnham argued for the creation of a more political institution:

> Let me make a few brief comments, first, from my own point of view: 1. In general, the idea is an admirable one. 2. I have certain doubts about it in relation to the present time. I proceed, in my own mind, from the point of view that the war is not something in the future, but is already on. Its specific objective is the destruction of the Bolshevik regime, – that is, from what must become the perspective of the West. I therefore judge particular proposals in term of this outlook. If what you have in mind is a long-term rather academic and "objective" institution, it has little interest for me (though I have nothing against it). It would accomplish nothing from the standpoint of the central issue, and would probably end up in the hands of American fellow-travellers. But a center which would be in effect an institutional weapon in the war, and a training ground for the liberation of Eastern Europe would be another matter. Whatever formula

might be used (and an academic formula might be a good one), the latter is what is relevant today.[6]

The Kultura group agreed with Burnham's suggestions. On one hand, they supported collaboration between the U.S. and Eastern European countries through the University, believing it would act as a weapon and have an enormous impact on Soviet propaganda behind the Iron Curtain. On the other hand, all of them agreed that the ultimate aim should be to create an anticommunist and antinationalist current among the youths, to defend liberty and overcome strong nationalism in Central and Eastern Europe respectively. Furthermore, this would encourage the creation of a core of European ways of thinking. As the project required huge funds, Kultura argued that it would only be feasible if funded by the State Department, American foundations, or if it could be part of the Marshall Plan and considered as part of the cultural reconstruction of Europe. Czapski trusted Burnham and shared his plan with him confidentially and exclusively. As Czapski did not have many contacts in the U.S., he asked Burnham to become the "advocate", the "propagator" of this project, and even its first rector "to insure that it won't be an abortive, academic institution for the American fellow-travellers."[7]

Burnham subsequently promoted the project in the U.S., and also invited Czapski to get in touch with several influential people. In February 1949, after having received the detailed draft of the University plan, Burnham let Czapski know he intended to distribute three copies: one to his friend Sidney Hook (also a former Marxist and already leading anti-communist and anti-totalitarian intellectual), another to the Institute for Advanced Studies, and a third to "a friend of [him] in a certain branch of the government". Burnham added that these three, already acquainted with the general idea, would be "test cases": "If they are enthusiastic, they can do much. If their response is negative – either because they do not approve the project or because they think its practical realization impossible – it will be a bad omen indeed."[8]

The *Kultura* circle conceived the draft with their close and confidential friend Anatol Mulhstein, a writer on international affairs and an

American citizen since 1946, formerly minister-counselor of the Polish Embassy in Paris between wars. It was Mulhstein who met Hook in the U.S. shortly after Czapski received Burnham's letter. However, the talk "was not really encouraging."[9] In Hook's opinion, the Marshall Plan would never give money for that kind of project because it did not want to redirect funds from the economic field. He also thought it would be impossible to get serious funds from foundations such as Ford or Carnegie. Hook suggested getting in touch with the State Department but added information about a similar institution in Germany, the Baltic University, which had been running for some years but was now close to bankruptcy. Thus, the 'test' did not succeed.

In spring 1949, Burnham came to Europe and sent a short letter to Czapski from London, on March 19, to tell him that he would also come to Paris at the beginning of April in order to meet him. In summer 1949, Czapski sought to engage Burnham who, already back in the U.S. after his European visit, was absent due to writing his new book, *The Coming Defeat of Communism* (published in 1950). In his correspondence, Czapski informed Burnham of his coming trip to Canada and the U.S. to give lectures. He also made allusions to a "new foundation", supposedly mentioned by Burnham in their talk in Paris. In a letter dated 8 June 1949, Czapski wanted to know if Burnham had met the "representative of this foundation" concerning the university project.[10] On 12 July 1949, he sent another letter to inform Burnham that general but non-serious conversations had taken place with American officers in France and to ask again about the talk on the university project in June "to the people from this foundation under creation."[11] It is not hard not to guess that the "foundation" in question was the National Committee for Free Europe (NCFE). However, its time hadn't yet come. First, another American propaganda initiative would intervene to support the project.

It was during Czapski's American lecturer tour in April 1950 that Burnham got in touch with his Polish friend to inform him of a new event, the Conference for Cultural Freedom. Burnham enthused about the Conference and encouraged Czapski's participation in it:

> A fairly impressive list of participants has already accepted. In my own opinion, this Conference is potentially of the very greatest importance. With luck, it can be the most important anti-Communist affair of this kind that has been held during the past fifteen or twenty years. I consider it really essential that you should attend. (If you have not already been invited formally, I know that you are on the list of those who will be.) I will write about this further – or talk about it if we are able to see each other – but I mention it now in order to try to make sure that you will plan to be in Berlin for the Conference.[12]

Held for the first time in June 1950 in West Berlin, the Congress for Cultural Freedom (the CCF – its original name in Berlin was *Kongress für kulturelle Freiheit*) was one of the most successful CIA operations and ran until 1967, when it was uncovered.[13] It acted to attract and divert the Western European intelligentsia from Communism and Marxist influence and promote liberty of expression, thus helping to create a non-Communist left.[14] The CCF fulfilled its missions through thirty-five offices, published about twenty magazines, organized exhibitions and important conferences, had an information and news bureau, and granted awards to artists from all over the world.

The idea for a cultural initiative was born out of the recognition that American economic aid had to be accompanied by cultural undertaking in Europe to educate people about the effects of communism. Communist infiltration was ubiquitous in Europe: in syndicates, feminist movements, youth organizations, cultural institutions, press and publishing houses.

To counteract the prestigious Soviet-sponsored and Cominform-shaped cultural conferences, such as the First German Writers Congress in Berlin in 1947 or the World Congress of Intellectuals in Wroclaw in 1948, several conventions were organized, utilizing American support in Europe. However, it was the Scientific and Cultural Conference for World Peace, held in New York's Waldorf-Astoria Hotel in March 1949 – the first conference to convene in a Western country – which mobilized an organized American counterattack.

In the U.S., right after the conference, thirty anticommunist left-wing intellectuals created the American Committee for Cultural Freedom under the presidency of Sidney Hook. In Paris on 30 April 1949, the OPC organized an anticommunist counteraction called the International Day of Resistance to Dictatorship and War. This was orchestrated by French socialist David Rousset and the leftist newspaper *Franc-Tireur*, with the participation of Sidney Hook and other prominent anti-Communists. It was Averell Harriman (Czapski had met his advisor in the summer of 1948 through Burnham) who transferred funds for the counteraction, at the direct request of OPC Director Franck Wisner.[15] Despite some success at the conference, the tone was too neutral for the Americans.

It was American journalist Melvin Lasky, who resided in Berlin with Arthur Koestler, a Hungarian-born British writer, who drafted the proposal for organizing a counter-conference.[16] Promoting the idea, Michael Josselson transferred the proposal to the OPC in late 1949. He was an Estonian-born American military intelligence agent in WWII, who stayed in Berlin after the war. Josselson worked in the Office of Military Government, U.S., as cultural affairs officer and then in the High Commission for Occupied Germany as public affairs officer. In these positions, he was responsible for the de-Nazification of top German intellectuals and leaders and for the editing and dissemination of anticommunist propaganda. Later, in November 1950, he would resign his job to become the future CCF's life-long administrative secretary until 1967.

In the U.S., Burnham and Hook worked on the organization of the American delegation to the CCF. The sixth key person in the organization of the CCF was Irving Brown, the American Federation of Labor (AFL) delegate in Europe, and in this position he acted to counter Communist influence in trade unions. Also, having close contact with OPC officers, he intervened in the distribution of the Marshall Plan's funds for secret operations.

The *Kongress für kulturelle Freiheit* was held in West Berlin from 26–29 June 1950, coincidentally starting one day before the outbreak of the Korean War. It brought together 108 intellectuals, world-renowned philosophers John Dewey, Bertrand Russell, Benedetto Croce, Karl Jaspers, and Jacques Maritain, and thousands of participants. The lecturers were mainly from the U.S. and Germany,[17] and they included former Communists, people from the antifascist and anti-Nazi non-Communist resistance, European federalists, and intellectual exiles from countries under Soviet control such as Joseph Czapski and Jerzy Giedroyc. The fully public and open debates dealt with four topics and were titled: Science and Liberty; Arts, the Artist and Liberty; Citizens in the Free Society; and Peace and Liberty. All of them, of course, urging participants to define a moral and political answer to counteract the "Communist threat".

The congress's final meeting on 29 June brought together approximately ten to fifteen thousand people. As the crowning moment, Koestler presented the *Manifesto for Free Men*, co-written by him and French writer Manès Sperber. As a result of this manifesto, the congress produced six papers: three general manifestos and three proposals, all advanced during the debates, including Czapski's paper on the creation of a University for Eastern European youths.

In the summer of 1950, the embryo of the future international intellectual organization started running under the guidance of Lasky, with an International Committee of twenty-three members (among others, Burnham, Hook and Czapski) and with an Executive Committee of five (including Irving Brown and Koestler). Lasky divided the future organization's tasks into two categories: Actions and Long-term Projects. The university project was classified as a long-term project, along with other plans such as the production of films, a series of conferences, and a research institute.

The first meeting of the International Committee took place in Brussels on 28–30 November 1950, with the participation of all its members. The Secretariat organized six commissions to deal with concrete projects and to define the position of the international movement before these questions were discussed more widely at the plenary assembly. The three concrete projects were: a publication programme, a proposal for the Fund for Intellectual Freedom, and the creation of a university for exiled youths. Czapski presented his project at the assembly of the International Committee as he had outlined it before, and he asked for the congress's support to get funds for the creation of the University. However, the ensuing discussion was divided over the project, with some participants arguing that this kind of institution would "quickly encourage the 'fermentation' of extreme national sentiments".[18] Despite deep reservations, the proposal was finally adopted, and a Commission designated to advance the project in Paris and in New York. The Commission included Czapski, Hook, an exiled Latvian law professor working at the University of Stockholm, Mintauts Cakste, Chairman of the Department of Slavic Languages and Literatures at Harvard University, Michael Karpovich, Professor Adam Rose, and American historian and former OSS member, Arthur Schlesinger Jr.

Burnham had always remained in close contact with Kultura. Before and after the meeting in Brussels, he continued to give Czapski contacts from the State Department and also personally promoted the university project, with the aim of finding sponsors. On 19 October 1950, Burnham wrote to Czapski: "I do not want to raise false hopes that may hereafter be blasted. However, I think that it is advisable for you to know that there have been some very favorable developments in relation to the University. There seems to be a reasonable chance that before the Brussels meeting something rather more definite will be at hand."[19] On 15 December 1950, Burnham addressed another letter to Czapski with some notes on how to advance the Commission's exploratory work: "2. Serious interest in the University increases, I am becoming quite optimistic that something is really going to be done in the near future. 3. You certainly, as representative of the Congress Committee, should come to this country. Right now it looks to me that the time for your trip should probably be the latter part of January. However, I want to be sure that things here will be in a condition that will make your journey as fruitful as possible."[20]

After the resolution of the Brussels Congress, Czapski started inquiring about the creation of the University in France independently from

Burnham and as the only really active member of the University Commission. From December 1950, thanks to his previous acquaintances, he started meeting officers in the Ministry of Foreign Affairs and the Ministry of National Education and members of the Council of the Republic. In February 1951, he went to visit French universities in the cities of Nancy, Grenoble and Strasbourg. Even if the idea was generally appreciated on the ministerial level, Czapski also met serious reluctance concerning the instruction of Eastern European youth in France: "The meetings that followed with the French gave me the impression that we have to act here with lot of caution. I highlight first the completely human and academic side [of the project]. There is a general fear of worrying and of frightening anything, and the Communist infiltration within the scientists is so large, that tactically, first of all, we must create a concrete ground in a university, and after act as we find necessary."[21]

Despite this negative reaction, Czapski still believed that France was the best place to create the University. In a letter dated 11 January 1951, he clearly told Burnham that even if the negotiations with the French had moved forward, the American proposals seemed serious to him: "I am not a pessimist and I think we can overcome the French difficulties. What matters most to me, are the American negotiations. The existence of University project has meant that we have already received quality proposals with of great potential."[22] Thus, the university project had been developed enough at this point that the NCFE came onto the stage.

The Appropriation of the University Project by the NCFE (1950–51)

Kultura had already worked with the NCFE on some typesetting work in October 1950. Having become interested in this process, the editor, Giedroyc, even suggested an eventual printing business.[23] However, it was not the printing press idea which excited the NCFE so much as Czapski's university plan for exiled youths.

In a short letter of 13 February 1951, written on his way to India, Burnham informed Czapski that the NCFE had a "suddenly revitalized interest in *some* university project; they have done some work on the subject."[24] Burnham encouraged Kultura to "break out of the present self-imposed limitations", and to contact all parties which had declared an interest in the university project, and, of course, to get in touch with NCFE.[25]

On 27 February, Burnham wrote again to tell Czapski that he would come to Europe soon and visit Kultura in connection with the university project. In this letter, Burnham also mentioned Czapski's trip to the U.S. with regards to the meetings he was preparing with potential sponsors for the University. The main question was one of timing, but in talking about these details, the American "propagator" of the project also expressed his early fears:

> I am inclined to think that the latter part of March will in any case be just about right for your arrival here. The developments in connection with the University are exceedingly complex, and in many respects delicate. A large variety of interests is intervening, and the whole issue is also indirectly caught in the play of state policies – and not only those of the government here. I repeat my conviction that something substantial is going to be done in the comparatively near future, but my doubts about the exact content.[26]

Two weeks after this correspondence, the NCFE's "suddenly revitalized interest" turned to action with its first president, Dewitt Clinton Poole, personally visiting France. Beyond his pre-war diplomatic career and intelligence background, Poole was also an educator at Princeton University, where he helped establish the School of Public and International Affairs in 1930. He came to France in order to discuss the outline of the university project with the Kultura staff, and specifically Czapski as the head of the CCF's University Commission, and to start negotiations with the French authorities. Poole made a very good impression on Czapski and Giedroyc during their first informal meeting, held in mid-March, having "a lot of good will" even though there was still only a vague notion of the university project[27]. Czapski scheduled a plan for meetings with Poole and Burnham, who was soon to arrive in France.

In spite of Poole's good will and of the NCFE's interest in the university project, this interest seemed so far theoretical. As a matter of fact, the NCFE had been following the development of the project for a long time, and had already made an attempt to create the University without Kultura's knowledge[28]. However, these early attempts failed, leading the NCFE to get in touch with Kultura, and become involved in Czapski's plan.

The NCFE's interest in the university project began in summer 1950, for many reasons. First, Burnham had been promoting the university project in the State Department since its conception, and had helped Czapski to get in touch with some of his contacts. Czapski met these people but reported in his letters to Burnham that the conversations always remained general. These tentative conversations aside, Burnham must have talked about the project to the NCFE, which is proved by Czapski's letters sent to Burnham in the summer of 1949 asking about the "foundation under creation". The NCFE became definitively interested in the project after it was considered by the *Kongress for für kulturelle Freiheit.*

The NCFE's proposed original structure included three operating committees to mount the propaganda program but also to help exiles and refugees behind the Iron Curtain: Intellectual Cooperation (Committee I) established programs at the Research Center at New York University and the Library of Congress (later at the Mid-European Studies Center) to provide suitable occupations for Central and Eastern European intellectuals; Radio and the Press (Committee II) was to broadcast news and programs to their native countries in their own languages; and last, the Committee on American Contacts program (Committee III), of which the Subcommittee on Exile Relations was intended to bring exiled leaders into direct contact with American people. From the beginning, the NCFE also welcomed new ideas, as its chairman, Joseph C. Grew, expressed in an introductory statement to the press on 1 June 1949: "I have no doubt that as we go along other activities will be added to our program. ... We wish and need suggestions from all those who share our feelings about the final goal."[29] Thus, the university project, which would help Central and Eastern European refugee youths, fit perfectly within the NCFE's objectives.

Even the more appealing was Czapski's aspiration to form a future generation of democratically spirited intellectuals who would return to their native countries to introduce democracy and build up the Pax Americana. This objective correlated with American foreign policy objectives in the very early years of the Cold War, targeting the liberation of Central and Eastern European countries from Soviet orbit.

The NCFE's active interest in the university project dates from the aftermath of the June 1950 *Kongress für kulturelle Freiheit*. In August, the NCFE sent Edgar Ansel Mowrer, journalist, foreign affairs expert and former deputy director of the Office of War Information, to Europe in order to explore the possibility of creating a university in France. His note of 14 August summarized his impressions of three cities; Strasbourg, Grenoble and Paris. Of the three, he preferred the first:

> ... Strasbourg seems to me preferable for the following reasons: two major languages (French and German) with most of the many refugees already speaking one or the other; town accustomed to strangers; quarters available and cooperation pretty sure; nearest to Frankfurt and ultimately to Munich; young people out of refugee bickering and hatreds which already poisoning Paris; European atmosphere owing to location of Council and Assembly of Europe. Grenoble lies eccentrically. Paris is already overcrowded.[30]

The NCFE started using its French connections to get support from the government and from local contacts to get the University of Strasbourg's backing for the project. On 11 August 1950, Mowrer sought to get in touch with the president of the University of Strasbourg through a French professor, Jules-Albert Jaeger, director of the Institute of European Studies of Strasbourg. Jaeger gave a note to the president, René Hubert, inquiring into the possibility of the NCFE establishing a University Center for young Eastern European refugees at the French university. The outline was very similar to Czapski's plan. It proposed the creation of a University Center which would help approximately four hundred Central and Eastern European youths exiled in Western countries to pursue their studies at the local university and to have seminars in the center, conceived and sponsored by the Carnegie Foundation. Jaeger asked the university president if Strasbourg would be a candidate to host the university, expressing that this city and its university would be the best place for the University Center. He also suggested that the American sponsor would lease the Pourtalès Chateau from the University of Strasbourg, and would build further accommodation for students in the chateau's park.

The note expressly points out that the university project was conceived during an informal conversation between Mowrer, Jaeger and Hubert Ripka. The latter[31] was, at the time, the leader of the National Committee for Free Czechoslovakia. He was involved in the project first to give official and moral weight to the undertaking; second to ease its high political sensitivity, due to his status as an exile political leader working as a middleman between the French authorities and the NCFE; and third, to encourage local support, as he was married to a French woman from Alsace. The Mowrer-Ripka-Jaeger delegation claimed that the NCFE had the support of Georges Bidault, the former president of the Council of Ministers (the Prime Minister), and Robert Schuman, the foreign minister. They highlighted that this note was sent only with the intention of examining the possibilities and "at the initiative of a Czechoslovak leading figure and a particular friend of Alsace, whose good will for Strasbourg, in this case, is undeniable."[32]

While waiting for the deliberation of the Committee of Deans of the University of Strasbourg, (expected to be held in October after the summer vacation and at the beginning of the academic year), the NCFE started outlining its first project proposal called "Education of Young Eastern European Exiles" and dated 30 August 1950. The proposal stated that this project was only in its initial stages. Most of the work done over the summer was by Edgar A. Mowrer, although it was still discussed with prominent NCFE members Poole, Allen Dulles, Frederic R. Dolbeare, Royall Tyler and Spencer Phenix.

According to the proposal, the aim of the project was to train selected Central and Eastern European refugee youths in order to form a future post-liberation leadership, and through education to save the national cultural heritage of the countries now caught in the Soviet orbit. The proposal highlighted that when these countries were liberated, many prominent exiles would be "too old to play any active role in reconstruction; it therefore becomes imperative to begin immediately with training younger elements; only thus can a continued reservoir of leadership be obtained."[33]

The NCFE project proposal was very similar to Czapski's proposal, but with three major divergences. First, it was a brief but very well constructed plan giving concrete details (for instance, to situate the University in Strasbourg). Second, it proposed that the students be selected from among the exiled youths already residing in Western countries, so they would not arrive directly from behind the Iron Curtain, as Czapski had planned.[34] Third, the main divergence lay in the objective of the proposed institute. While the NCFE was primarily concerned with the formation of a future leadership, Czapski had a much more noble goal in mind: to save the Eastern European intelligentsia and to form an enthusiastic and responsible generation of youths who were democratically minded and European in spirit.

The NCFE discussed the project proposal during an informal conversation on 22 September 1950 between, among others, Mowrer, Adolph A. Berle, Phenix and Alan Valentine. Because of its educational nature, the proposal was of interest to the NCFE's Committee on Intellectual Cooperation, headed by Berle, which already included the newly formed Mid-European Studies Center (MESC). This conversation outlined further measures to be taken in order to find personnel for the future University and sponsors in the U.S., to approach French personalities at the ministerial and local levels[35], and to "arrange for an official liaison man to be chosen, perhaps from U.S. Embassy Staff or E.C.A. Staff, who would help negotiate with the French government on the financial side of the undertaking."[36] This "liaison man" would later be Royall Tyler. The American historian was a U.S. member of the U.S. delegation to the Paris Conference, then financial advisor to the League of Nations in Hungary in 1924. During WWII, he stayed in Geneva, and using his European connections, cooperated with Allen Dulles and the latter's intelligence network. After the war, he was the director of the International Bank for Reconstruction and Development in Paris, then representative of the NCFE in Europe.

Aside from details on setting up the University, the conversation centered on the proposed objectives of the institute, which provoked disagreement among the NCFE members. Valetine urged that the objectives needed to be clarified and that the NCFE had to decide to produce first-rank specialists or political leaders because the political atmosphere in European universities was so bad. Berle stated that the NCFE was interested in "providing the raw material for democratic leadership", and "it was necessary to train raw material in Europe because there was a chance of only one in three of those who had been brought to the United States ever going back to their native lands."[37]

Valentine argued that if the project must be carried out in Europe, the NCFE had to create an American educational, social and political environment, but "to this there was general objection on the grounds that there should be no attempt to impose the United States stereotype."[38] In Valentine's opinion, the primary concern was to distribute students in small groups throughout Western Europe and not to concentrate this educational activity in one point. Expressing his disagreement, he "left the meeting at this point."[39] Despite this opposition, Berle continued to draw up the project as it has been defined in the first proposal. Furthermore, he would later become the life-long chairman of the Board of Trustees of the NCFE's educational corporation.

The NCFE's proposition, submitted by Jaeger, was finally refused by the University of Strasbourg on 2 October 1950. During the deliberation, the Committee of Deans of the French university argued that there was no need to create a separate institution; the young people in question were free to attend the University of Strasbourg itself. In spite of this decision, the NCFE did not stop developing the project and made helping exile youths part of its official policy.

The NCFE policy statement, dated 20 October 1950, declared four operating divisions: the Division of Intellectual Cooperation, Radio Free

Europe, the American Contacts Division, and the National Councils Division. The Committee on Intellectual Cooperation, its first division, had established its main activity on 3 April 1950, i.e., the MESC, which provided grants for exiles doing research into the political, economic and social conditions in the Iron Curtain countries and also sponsored two major projects, the Legal-Index Digest and the Danubian Inquiry.[40] Furthermore, the MESC initiated a scholarship program to aid young exiles in the U.S. to attend American universities, sending four youths to the Massachusetts Institute of Technology (MIT). The NCFE policy statement concluded that NCFE had broadened its activities to Europe because of the large number of exiles present in Europe. It was with the purpose of training young exiles to replace elderly exiled leaders that a project for the creation of an Eastern European Institute was put "under consideration by the NCFE"[41] in October 1950.

Thus, by October 1950 the NCFE had started two programs within the framework of its "Training-Education Program." These programs were described by Poole in November 1950 as the assistance of 12–15 young political exiles studying at MIT and other American universities, and the development of a Western European program, establishing a "beach head university."[42] This label gave an element of propaganda to the university project, whose four guiding principles were Dedication (the will to return home to introduce democracy being criteria of selection), Contacts and Future Reference (keeping files on students for further purposes), Concentration (consolidating the activity at one or in a small number of universities), and Normalcy (special favors, especially financial, would not be given). Scheduling the opening of the University for autumn 1951, the project also developed the idea of a "doubling program", resulting in one or two "beach head universities", with the second possibly in Salzburg, Austria, but "this [depended] on how far the sponsors of NCFE [wished] to carry the program."[43]

At this point the NCFE's undertaking to assist exile youths was not as intense and dynamic in practice as its development of theoretical policies and projects. Tyler, the NCFE's European representative, wrote a letter to Poole on 26 December 1950 which illustrates the committee's absence: "Since I left New York last September, I have had nothing from the NCFE about the plan for helping refugee boys of university age to pursue their studies in Europe, which we were discussing when I was with you. I should be very much interested to know if anything has happened since then, and in what form you now propose to cast the idea."[44]

However, as Burnham had expressed to Czapski, the NCFE "revitalized" its interest in February 1951, and Poole came to France in March in order to manage the negotiations with French authorities. It has to be clarified that Burnham definitely knew about the NCFE's plans for the creation of the University before it officially got in touch with Kultura in March 1951. However, he did not agree with what the university project was to become in the NCFE's framework – this is why he informed Czapski of his fears in February 1951.[45] During the negotiations, he would act as consultant for the NCFE and later would become a member of the NCFE's educational corporation with Hook. Because of his devotion to the original university project and his life-long intellectual friendship with Czapski and Giedroyc, he would always try to defend the fundamental idea among FEUE officials.

Negotiations continued for exactly two months, from the opening talk at the Ministry of Foreign Affairs on 21 March until the deliberations at the University of Strasbourg on 21 May 1951. Poole and Tyler worked as European representatives for the NCFE and took over the negotiations with the same people that Czapski had previously been in touch with: Louis Joxe, director of cultural relations at the Ministry of Foreign Affairs, and Pierre Donzelot, director of higher education at the Ministry of National Education. Joxe was responsible for conducting discussions with Americans on the juridical side of the University Center's implementation in France, and Donzelot dealt with academic questions. Their personal support and assistance with the project contributed enormously to the establishment of the study center, along with the backing of Minister of Foreign Affairs Robert Schuman.

In general, the French officials agreed to the project. However, changes to the final agreement had to be made due to the juridical feasibility of creating the institute in France and to the political connotations of the project. The final structure of the so-called Free Europe University in Exile fulfilled the NCFE's objectives concerning the form and content of the University but was conceptually a shadow of the original proposal envisaged by Czapski on behalf of Kultura and voted on at the CCF's Brussels meeting. This absence also took physical form. After the first opening talk, the NCFE appropriated the whole project, and Czapski and Kultura were completely removed not only from the negotiations but also from the entire future existence of the institution.

The opening talk took place at the Ministry of Foreign Affairs on 21 March 1951 where a tentative plan took shape based on extended talks between, among others, Tyler, Poole, Charles Torem (an attorney from the Coudert Brothers law firm, based in Manhattan), U.S. Ambassador to France David Bruce, Czapski, on the behalf of CCF, and Joxe. This plan concerned two subjects: the juridical and the educational aspects of the proposed University. With regards to the juridical aspects, the Coudert Brothers recommended that a new membership corporation be formed in New York under the title The Free Europe University in Exile, Inc. which would then, at its trustees' insistence, establish a branch in Paris to be run by a branch manager.[46] On the educational side, the NCFE planned to set up a Free Europe Institute at a cooperating French University, with the approval of the Ministry of National Education. The institute would have an American dean, and would include "national seminars" taught by "competent and politically suitable professors" exiled from Central and Eastern European countries in order to preserve the national heritage of these countries. Joxe's impression of the plan was generally positive. He agreed to the American corporation but rejected Czapski's proposal to create a university in France, as Poole reported to C.D. Jackson.[47]

At a later conversation between Poole, Tyler and Joxe on 31 March, Joxe made two points about the plan. First, even if the proposed University would be entirely American, it would be necessary to include some prominent French faculty members. Second, as the French government was already assisting some one hundred 'Satellite' students (albeit with very limited grants), the NCFE should introduce in its plan a competitive examination to win scholarships.

On 4 April, Poole and Tyler met director of higher education Donzelot to discuss the academic side of the University. The director, introduced by Joxe, listened to the plan "with evident understanding and sympathy."[48] He asked if an academic degree or certificate would be provided when students finished their studies, but Poole and Tyler confirmed that they would not set anything up outside of the existing French system. Donzelot understood the choice of location, but he added that "Strasbourg (speaking confidentially) could not be regarded as altogether a French town ... he would prefer Poitiers or Bordeaux, for instance."[49] Ultimately, the advantages of Strasbourg as the location for the University (its international character, bilingual and bi-confessional – Catholic and Protestant – environment, resident exile professors) outweighed the disadvantages. Donzelot concluded that all further questions must be discussed with the University of Strasbourg itself, as in France the universities were autonomous entities whose independence and sovereignty were well respected. Confirming his "complete understanding" of the plan and giving "his full-hearted support", he invited the president of the University of Strasbourg, rector René Hubert, to Paris to informally discuss the proposal. At the meeting with Rector Hubert, held on 10 April, the iconic NCFE President C.D. Jackson was also present, having come to France specifically to move negotiations forward.

After the meeting in Paris, the two NCFE representatives went to Strasbourg on 12 April to discuss the proposal with the Council of Deans. Here, they outlined three main points. First, they aimed to convince the council that creating the University Center in France would strengthen French cultural influence in Central and Eastern Europe, which had been undermined in the inter-war period due to increasing German influence from 1930. Second, the content of the national seminars would lean towards saving cultural heritage rather than political indoctrination. Third, the concentration of approximately 100 students of different nationalities in one place could help to overcome and manage nationalist tendencies and to teach these youths to live together. As a result of this conversation, the NCFE representatives outlined an aide-memoire summarizing the proposal's main points and gave it to various official French bodies for consideration (including the Ministry of Foreign Affairs, Ministry of National Education, Prefecture of the Bas-Rhin Region, and University of Strasbourg as well as the U.S. Embassy in France).

The meeting with the deans of the University of Strasbourg held an extraordinary importance due to the amount of autonomy the French universities had. It was entirely the university's prerogative to decide whether or not it would proceed with the creation of the institution. If refused, the project could not continue, even if it had ministerial approval. Following the meeting, Rector Hubert sent a letter to the deans and to the director of the Institute of Political Studies to ask for their decision on the university proposal[50].

Meanwhile, C.D. Jackson, Poole and Tyler met Joxe and Donzelot at a luncheon in Paris on 19 April to discuss the juridical side of the University Center again. Joxe still believed that the best solution was to create an American educational institute which would establish a branch in Paris. This branch, however, would be an administrative and financial office and nothing more. Donzelot believed the future institution would ideally be a center, having close working contact with the University of Strasbourg, although that university would not establish the center and the center would not be a part of the French university. French law did not allow foreigners to become professors at university. Thus, the American staff officer would be a head of the center or "President", as Joxe suggested. He also added that the center should have some French members on a council, remaining, of course, under American control, "for the sake of public relations here, but the Paris unit could be simply American; he saw no need for conspicuous participation here."[51] Aside from these concerns, Joxe and Donzelot had no objection to the library or publication plans, or to the seminar idea, on the condition that students spend most of their time on university studies.

On 21 May 1951, in the light of preliminary agreement by the faculties,[52] the University of Strasbourg expressed its agreement to the creation of the "Center for Refugee Students". The deliberation highlighted two main questions: the refugee students' relationship with the University of Strasbourg and the relationship between the two institutions. The students' rights and obligations would be devised on a basis of absolute equality with French students. They would be able to study at every faculty, use all facilities and take advantage of benefits (on the condition of being admitted and fulfilling all university requirements). They would be answerable to the rules and jurisdiction of the University of Strasbourg, and "they must undertake in particular to abstain, within the University, from all activity, propaganda or discussion of a political or confessional nature."[53]

Regarding the Center for Refugees, the University of Strasbourg would transfer the lease of the Pourtalès Chateau to the American Committee so that the students could establish accommodation there. The Center would "function in a manner completely independent of the University [of Strasbourg], as function at the present moment, alongside but disassociated"[54] from the university and its other entities. This would mean that the Center was banned from using the name of the University of Strasbourg as its partner, and wouldn't be represented at its Council, stating that "the independence of the two establishments is the best guarantee for a good functioning of the system."[55] The University of Strasbourg could offer special courses (French literary and linguistic preparation or perfection) in collaboration with the Ministry of National Education if needed, but if the Center wished to compliment the university studies "with courses and lectures directed towards particular ends" at its lodging center, it would be "without official collaboration and disassociated from all responsibility of the University [of Strasbourg]."[56]

Thus, the University of Strasbourg gave the NCFE the go-ahead to create the University Center, whilst also expressing its regret "that the question of refugee students … has not been made the object, by the receiving countries, of a coordinated examination, of inter-governmental agreements and coordinated legislatives measures", expressly by UNESCO.[57] The NCFE president, Jackson, was delighted with the resolution, which "could hardly be better" and seemed "to be animated by a genuinely friendly spirit and an effort to go the limit in meeting what [the NCFE] put up to them."[58] Poole was more cynical, believing that "the UNESCO paragraph [was] no more than a flourish which [the NCFE] can ignore."[59]

The NCFE could now start organizing and setting up the Free Europe University in Exile (FEUE) in order to open in autumn 1951.

The NCFE clearly appropriated the university project from Czapski and the CCF, as can be demonstrated by three principal facts. First, neither Czapski nor the CCF as an organization would ever again be involved in the FEUE. There were suggestions that some CCF members would be invited to participate in the future institution (Burnham and Hook would be later incorporated into the FEUE Inc., but at the NCFE officials' invitation and not as CCF delegates), particularly Czapski as a consultant to the NCFE, representing the CCF's University Committee. Yet Czapski was informed by Hook and Burnham that the CCF decided to disassociate from the university project, now being run by the NCFE, as they didn't want "too-close collaboration with Free Europe because in Europe that organization [was] regarded as a branch of the State Department and such a collaboration would be inconvenient, from a tactical point of view, for the Congress; the Congress [wished], consequently, to leave all the responsibility for the University to Free Europe, merely delegating certain members to take an interest in the project as individuals."[60] Burnham argued to Czapski that the University idea was "so correct and so powerful that once any kind of real start [was] made, it [would] develop, in part at least, from its own inner dynamism."[61] He added that it was better for the CCF not to have co-sponsorship so that it didn't have control or direct influence over the University Center. Czapski was not at all satisfied by what the university project was to become, believing that, under the NCFE, it would be characterized by propaganda and simple philanthropy.[62] From the moment that the negotiations started, Kultura was kept only vaguely informed of their progress, Giedroyc and Czapski were not even invited to the FEUE's opening inauguration. Despite some personal visits to Strasbourg, they were kept away and were excluded from the University operation right from the early stages by the NCFE.[63]

Second, the NCFE removed all institutions running parallel to the university project in order to establish its own dominant Center. For example, one prominent rival project was a Central and Eastern European Institute, outlined by the International Federation of Free Journalists under the presidency of Boleslaw Wierzbianski and with financial support promised from the International Rescue Committee, some foundations and divisions of the U.S. State Department. As a result of swift NCFE intervention, this project was not realized. There were also several meetings and correspondences between NCFE officials and the Ford Foundation about sponsorship, ending without any concrete or provable plans.

Third, the most compelling evidence was the NCFE's plan to set up its own institutions, and refusal to work with other entities, in order to demonstrate the variety of actions, interest and ambitions which it was undertaking in the fight against Communism.[64] Although many organizations dealing with exiles existed, the NCFE was the top-ranked corporation.[65]

The Organization and Launching of the "Collège de l'Europe libre" in France (1951)

Following the University of Strasbourg's deliberations, the FEUE's Study Center was scheduled to open in November 1951, leaving the NCFE with two urgent tasks – writing a press announcement and starting to organize the University in earnest. On 24 May 1951, Tyler met Donzelot and Rector Hubert again to discuss, among others things, the press release. When shown the written proposal, the French agreed to it with two exceptions. First that the center would not be "intimately associated with" the University of Strasbourg but rather the "students [would] attend courses of" the French university, avoiding any association between the two institutions.[66] Second, Donzelot emphasized that "the press release [may be] held back until the elections [are] over (say June 19)."[67] French requests concerning the press release show the political complexity of creating this Center in France in 1951.

Aspiring to political change after WWII, France finally voted acceptance of the referendum on the Constitution of the Fourth Republic on 13 October 1946, establishing parliamentary democracy with a bicameral form of government. This allowed the president of the Republic a symbolic role while executive power rested in the hands of the president of the Council. The main aim of the constitutional law was to guarantee ministerial stability in parliament, owing to the return of a party system.

Following the first election of the Fourth Republic, held on 10 November 1946, the balance of power in the National Assembly was as follows: the French Communist Party (PCF) and its allies received 29% of the seats, the Christian democratic political party (MRP) 27.6%, and the Socialists (SFIO) 16.3%, leading to the coalition of the so-called Three-Party Alliance. However, this union split in early May 1947 following disagreements over international and internal politics under the increasing threat of the Cold War.[68]

Directly after, another coalition, the Third Force, was created, bringing together the SFIO, the center right party UDSR, and the MRP, who opposed the PCF and the Gaullist movement (RPF). At the end of the five year parliamentary mandate, this coalition could have been eligible to win the elections held on 17 June 1951, due to a change in the voting system.[69] The Third Force parties and their allies won a combined 51% of the votes, while the PCF had 25.9%, and the Gaullist RPF 21.7%. However, like its predecessor, the Third Force was not strong enough to manage internal politics, and the coalition split four months after the second election of the Fourth Republic. Subsequently, the predominant groups in government were radical socialists and conservatives until the 1956 socialist majority. This majority failed to cope with the mounting internal crises and problems with decolonization during the Algerian war, leading finally to the collapse of the Fourth Republic in 1958.

Despite the aims of the constitutional law there was permanent instability under the Fourth Republic, which hosted twenty-five governments in twelve years. Nevertheless, internal political instability did not influence France's post-war economic recovery and the establishment of important institutions, such as the Atlantic Alliance, due to the "disassociation between political and administrative and economic power."[70]

Referring to the previous facts, two major observations must be made. First, the PCF constituted a strong, leading political power not only in the early 1950s but throughout the entire Fourth Republic (in 1956, the PCF got 26% of electoral votes, and in 1958 it got 19.2%). As the PCF was also a Cominform member, along with the Italian CP in Western Europe, serious attempts were made by the U.S. to counteract their influence. Thus, early CIA operations concentrated on counteracting communist infiltration in Italy and France. They manipulated the Italian election in 1948 – two months after the Czechoslovak coup d'état – by funding Italian center parties to oppose strong communist and leftist parties. They also established the CCF headquarters in Paris to fight against European neutralist and communist intellectual tendencies.

Second, it is necessary to highlight the importance of Robert Schuman's support for the NCFE in this context. Being one of the leading politicians of the MRP, along with Georges Bidault and François de Menton, and having previously held several ministerial posts, Schuman was minister of foreign affairs for almost five successive years, through nine governments, from July 1948 to January 1953. While prime minister (November 1947–July 1948), his government put forward plans for the creation of a European Assembly, which was realized in the Council of Europe on 5 May 1949, the first European intergovernmental organization. During his tenure in foreign affairs Schuman also promoted the principles of supranational democracy (announced in the Schuman Declaration on 9 May 1950, now annual European Day), which resulted in the creation of the European Coal and Steel Community on 18 April 1951. He played a key role in the creation of NATO and signed the Washington Treaty for France on 4 April 1949. It was also during his tenure in foreign affairs that the Economic Cooperation Administration and its joint entity (OECD) were established in order to administer the Marshall Plan.

Schuman was a proponent of European integration and the Atlantic Alliance and was known to the American officials at the State Department as a "friend of the United States."[71] The NCFE referred to him as a key contact for the university project from the very beginning, as demonstrated during the meeting to discuss the educational program for exile students held on 22 September 1950 between Berle, Mowrer, Phenix and Valentine: "Except for Mr. Valentine, there was substantial agreement on the conclusions to the conversation listed by Mr. Berle as follows: … (8) Approach Robert Schuman to get authoritative high level approval before he leaves New York and before any publicity leaks should lead to communist or other unfavorable reaction in France."[72]

At the end of May 1951, as in September 1950, Joxe wished to consult Schuman about a FEUE press release, both to get his approval and out of fear of future communist attack on the future university project. On the day of French elections, 17 June 1951, Poole informed Berle:

> Donzelot thought we must defer any public announcement until after the elections, lest the Communists make an issue of the project. Joxe tells us now that M. Schuman has taken such a personnel interest in the project that he feels he must clear the release date with him, more particularly since Schuman comes from Strasbourg region. That defers it until June 25 at least. Now Torem at Coudert Brothers suggests, sagaciously I think, that we ought to defer public announcement until the French association – to be called Collège de l'Europe Libre – has not only been formed but declared by the Ministry of Interior to be "d'utilité publique". Otherwise the Communists, being apprised, might set up a road-block. ... Today the French are voting.[73]

Faced with a strong Communist and Gaullist opposition, the Third Force finally won the elections in 1951 with a slight majority. On 2 July, Schuman required a "press release altered so as to stress still more the purely cultural"[74] intention of the University Center, and according to a memorandum dated 24 July, "from Paris [came] the definite proposal that between July 23 and early August all announcements about FEUE [should] be kept in pretty general terms."[75]

However, nothing and nobody could get away from communist criticism in France. Schuman was the target of communist attacks, reproaching him for leading France to war with the Atlantic Alliance while the U.S. were treated as the new Nazi Germany, seeking to enslave France and get her into debt, as shown in the lyrics of a period French Communist song, sung to the tune of Jingle Bells: "It was president Truman / Who said to old Schuman: / 'You should sign my treaty / As it's got Hitler's Label.'/ He is calling for a war / Against the Soviet Union / And the People's Republics, to benefit the U.S."[76]

The Communists also violently opposed the FEUE long before its official opening in November 1951. On 7 May, the French Communist newspaper *L'Humanité* wrote that "recently the American authorities (with threats of reprisals in case of refusal) have requested the University of Strasbourg to organize a special section for émigrés ... 'to prepare to take over the administration of their countries after their liberation'."[77] "This university," continued the article, "would in actual fact group the spies who are now circulating in Strasbourg and gravitate around the European Council."[78] Criticism also arrived from behind the Iron Curtain. In its 20 May issue, Bucharest's *Romania Liberia* referred to an unnamed French magazine as a source of information, stating that the NCFE was establishing a special section at the University of Strasbourg, a "Spy University," in order to "prepare the traitors who have fled from the people's democracies, because of fear of the legitimate wrath of the respective populations, 'in order to grab power again' over those countries which have freed themselves forever of exploitation and oppression."[79]

With the opening scheduled for November 1951, the NCFE had to start concentrating on the organization of the University, in spite of any Communist criticism. According to the agreement with the French authorities, an educational corporation was established in the U.S. under New York State law on 20 July 1951 called the Free Europe University in Exile, Inc. in order to organize, direct and finance the whole enterprise.[80] The chairman of the Board of Trustees was Berle, the president of the Corporation, Poole, and the treasurer, Spencer Phenix. Levering Tyson was designated secretary of the FEUE, Inc, and director of the NCFE's Division of Intellectual Cooperation. He had been president of Muhlenberg College since 1937, former director of the national advisory council on radio and education at the Carnegie Corporation of New York, and also a member of the Wartime Commission of the U.S. Office of Education from 1941 to 1945. The corporation included NCFE officials, such as Frederic R. Dolbeare, Joseph C. Grew, C.D. Jackson, and Arnold J. Zurcher; CCF members Burnham and Hook; and other prominent American citizens, such as diplomat and philanthropist Robert Woods Bliss (also an NCFE member), the president of Princeton University, Harold W. Dodds, and the chairman of the International Rescue and Relief Committee, Reinhold Neibuhr. As Poole explained to Allen Dulles, the FEUE Inc. incorporated new names "as a means of widening interest and support", but the active and executive staff were recruited from the existing NCFE group.[81]

This corporation, through its Board of Directors, created a Western European Branch, headed by its Resident Branch Manager – initially Tyler – for management of funds, administration and general supervision. Its office was at 7 rue de la Paix in Paris, with an administration staff composed of Ian Forbes Fraser, head of the American Library in Paris and a former teacher at Columbia University, Charles A. Foster, who had done his PhD at the Sorbonne, was married to a French lady and had been an NCFE member since 1950, and Richard Sears, former secretary of the U.S. Delegation to the Paris Peace Conference and Assistant to the NCFE European Representative from 1950. AGJ Sabalot, a retired member of the U.S. Navy who was at that time an IRO (International Refugee Organization) officer, was designated special advisor to the branch in Paris, to maintain informal contact with French Security and to carry out security checks on applicants.

For academic purposes, the Board of Directors set up a committee of five in Paris dedicated to awards and placement, in order to select applicants, award scholarships and place students at universities. This committee included the American dean of the center at Strasbourg-Robertsau; Foster, Fraser and Sears from the Paris office; and a French member to be the assistant to the American dean. This latter, the "Trojan horse," was Maurice Galy, a young officer at the Ministry of National Education, personally recommended and transferred by Donzelot.[82]

Additionally a French legal entity called the *Association de Collège de l'Europe libre* had to be set up in order to operate and maintain the Pourtalès Chateau as a study center and living quarters. Thus, the organizational chart was as follows: the FEUE, Inc. in New York was an

American educational corporation; the CEL Association in Paris was a non-profit organization; and the study center in Strasbourg was called *Collège de l'Europe libre* (CEL). Similar to the FEUE, Inc., the CEL Association included French and American citizens from varied backgrounds, at Joxe's request, to maintain public relations in France. However, the CEL Association remained under American control, with the key positions being held by American officers to ensure a connection between the different FEUE entities. Its honorary president was Swiss historian Carl Burckhardt, formerly chairman of the International Red Cross and Swiss ambassador in Paris; the president was the American resident branch manager. The association had two vice presidents (the Americans Dean and Fraser), a secretary (Foster) and two treasurers. French members were the financial expert, René Charron; historian and visiting professor at Princeton, Gilbert Chinard; Charles Eyselé from the Catholic Institute of Paris and the French Philosopher Jacques Maritain. Additional members were Sabalot, Mulhstein, the Russian-born composer and CCF Secretary Nicolas Nabokov, the Belgian John Goormaghtigh, in charge of the Paris office of the Carnegie Endowment for International Peace, and Dorothy Flagg Leet, principal of Reed Hall in Paris.

The NCFE's favorite candidate for the post of American dean was Princeton's Professor John B. Whitton. Besides his teaching experience, he had been director of the Geneva Research Center and was interested in the increasing use of radio as a weapon of propaganda – especially by the Nazis. He conceptualized the Princeton Listening Center in 1939 in order to monitor and analyze shortwave propaganda. However, he had a health problem which made him unable to travel and work in France. The NCFE staff was looking for another candidate when they found Malcolm Davis.

Davis had all the qualities required to be American dean. He had a familiarity with Eastern Europe and also with France. In 1917, he served on the Committee on Public Information in Russia, then he was chairman of the Danubian Economic Inquiry at the League of Nations for some years. Later, he was also director of the Geneva Research Center, from 1931–1935, then was in charge of the European Center of the Carnegie Endowment from 1935–40 in Paris. During WWII, he became principal officer of the OSS's Foreign Nationalities Branch. He spoke French, German and Russian, and had "been one of the Americans most intimately associated with the East European exiles in the U.S.", enjoying "their esteem and confidence."[83]

Concerning his personality, NCFE officers agreed that Davis was "no ball of fire",[84] but that this could be advantageous during the first year, when it would be necessary to consolidate relations with the University of Strasbourg and to manage conflicts of any sort. He was also generally accepted by French authorities, namely by Joxe who knew Davis from his Carnegie years in Paris and "liked and estimated him and thought him a very good choice as Dean."[85] Poole, who both organized the FEUE and conceptualized the CEL's structure, acknowledged Davis's qualifications and ability not only to conceive and direct the program of national seminars and lectures series, due to his previous experience in the League of Nation's Danubian Inquiry, but also to take it "under his own direct, management and personal inspiration."[86]

However, the preparation for the University Center in the summer of 1951 was not as visionary as the NCFE hoped it would be. Poole wished to launch several ideas and projects in connection with the FEUE which were being developed in conversations and correspondence. These ideas included a larger scope of students including Russians, Ukrainians, and Caucasians; placing students in other cities besides Strasbourg; cooperation with other NCFE entities; publications and correspondence courses. However NCFE President C.D. Jackson was more anxious about the scheduled opening in November, and he redefined the targets to Poole and Tyler in July:

> Quite frankly, I am somewhat worried. Owing to a lot of circumstances, practically all of them beyond our control – for instance, the delay by the New York Board of Regents and the consequent delays along the line – I have feeling that we are going to have one hell of a time opening on November 1st. And open we must! The only way that this can be accomplished is if you and Royall will get together and set up a firm schedule of priorities, wherein everything but the

> absolute basic essentials are put at the bottom of the list or even postponed for a year. ... Aside from the legal formalities and the announcement, the basic essentials, to my mind, are: 1. Robertsau in shape, 2. A well-selected student body, 3. An adequate faculty.[87]

According to these priorities, negotiations started with the owners of the Pourtalès Chateau over the transfer of lease, which was agreed between the French owner, Madame Bérard, and the CEL Association. The Pourtalès Chateau was constructed in the eighteenth century and stood in a 40 hectare wooded park six kilometers from the center of Strasbourg in the suburban area called Robertsau. Although it was in good shape structurally, renovation works were proposed, with the owner's approval, including creating a heating system, a modern cafeteria kitchen, cafeteria eating arrangements, showers and additional toilets. The chateau provided apartments for the FEUE resident staff, and the dormitory rooms provided accommodation for one hundred students. The renovations were finished on 26 October 1951, one week before the CEL opened.

Selecting a good student body required an efficient campaign to find the best young exiles and successful selection by the Committee on Awards and Placement. Due to internal political conditions in France, it was decided to spread the word from New York: "At a meeting on this aspect in New York August 6, under Mr. Jackson's chairmanship, New York was agreed to be the base from which to spread the word – for practical reasons, and because we must not abuse French hospitality. To have France as the principal base of our educational work, to tap its incomparable resources in this regard, is enough. To attempt to use France also as a base of agitation (or what could be adversely construed as agitation) would be to jeopardize the enterprise."[88] The means of campaigning included RFE, the Voice of America, exile organizations, the foreign language press in the U.S. and in Europe, American official agencies, the IRO and similar international agencies.

When the status of the Committee on Awards and Placement was established, the aim was to create an autonomous and responsible unit, able to select applicants. As such, in each case the decision of the committee was final, no appeal could be entertained, and no other organization was allowed to intervene in the relationship between the committee and the candidate as an intermediary or broker. The first committee was composed of Dean Davis, French Assistant Dean Galy, Foster, Fraser and Sears. As a result of the press announcement and the campaign, 3630 application forms were sent out, and 626 applications received. Scholarships could only be awarded if an application was made by the candidate. First, the committee examined the application to determine if the candidate was eligible. Criteria for selection were: 1) to be in exile or refuge from Albania, Bulgaria, Czechoslovakia, Estonia, Hungary, Latvia, Lithuania, Poland, Rumania or Yugoslavia, regardless of race, creed or sex, 2) to be between the ages of 18 and 32 (except in cases of special dispensation by the committee), 3) to have passed the baccalaureate in Europe or a qualification that European universities recognized as equivalent, 4) to be capable of following university courses in French, and 5) "by reason of previous academic performance, character and estimated capacity for leadership in a free society [to] commend themselves to the University's Committee on Awards and Placement as likely to return to their countries of origin as soon as becomes possible and [to] fulfill there useful and constructive roles."[89]

Ineligibility was largely due to "being over 32 years of age (with a few exceptions), or already having university degrees and needing to [be finished] elsewhere, or wishing to study a subject not taught at Strasbourg, or not possessing qualifications required by the university, or not knowing enough French to profit by the Strasbourg university courses, or not having refugee status."[90] Eligible applications were shared among committee members for personal interviews, which mainly took place in Paris but also in England, Belgium, Germany, Greece, Spain, Italy, Turkey and Switzerland. After the interviews, the committee held several meetings where candidatures were examined and discussed.

Summarizing the results for the first year, 87 candidates (76 men – of whom 5 were theological students – and 11 women) were accepted, and 349 notifications of non-acceptance were sent out. Although a quota of

100 students was originally contemplated, the committee thought it preferable to maintain high quality over fulfilling the quota for two reasons. First, promising applications were still coming in. Second, and mainly, a high percentage of the candidates (including some promising ones) did not wish to study in Strasbourg but hoped to obtain scholarships to remain in Paris or at other universities. For this reason, following consultation with Poole and Tyler, 19 partial scholarships were granted to external students to study in Paris (3), Barcelona (3), Caen (2), London (2), and one each in Malmaison, Lille, Aix-en-Provence, Brussels, Louvain, Rome, Geneva, Tübingen, and Bonn. Statistics show that students accepted at the University of Strasbourg were mainly between the ages of 22 and 28, originated from Czechoslovakia (22), Poland (19), Rumania (14), and Yugoslavia (13), and wished to study at the Faculty of Law (23), Medicine (16), Letters (15), Political Sciences (11) and Applied Science (10). The scholarship granted by the CEL was 800 dollars for a twelve-month year, half of which had to pay for food and accommodation at the Pourtalès Chateau. Thus, a net sum of 400 dollars was provided to the students for paying tuition fees, buying books, clothing and so on.

The official opening of the CEL was held on 14 November 1951, "without public fanfare"[91] at French request. Davis and Dean Redslob of the Law School at the University of Strasbourg, representing the absent Rector Hubert, addressed speeches to the exile youths, and NCFE President Jackson spoke briefly. Deans from the University of Strasbourg participated in the ceremony, while the NCFE and the RFE were represented by a group of Americans, Czechs and Hungarians. Poole also visited the CEL on 4 November, and talked to the students already living there: "My impression of the human quality of the students there present was favorable. Upon hearing their individual stories one recognizes by way of qualification how turbulent, or twisted, some of the inner lives must be."[92]

In order to complete the unforeseen and growing number of tasks, the original body of CEL staff in Strasbourg-Robertsau was increased gradually beginning in November 1951. The FEUE's trustees approved the appointment of Georges Straka to the post of French Academic Consultant to plan and administrate French language courses for FEUE students. The American dean, Davis, had authority over and supervised all of the FEUE's European educational and academic operations. In January 1952 he started collaborating with new arrival Assistant Dean and Administrative Officer Eugene L. Metz, whose task was to deal with "technically non-academic affairs", including looking after the students' well-being, with his ultimate responsibility being to the trustees in New York through the Paris office. Although these technically non-academic affairs were not educational in character, they inevitably turned out to be extremely important to the educational process as a whole. For this reason, the relationship between the academic operation and its technically non-academic features, as well as between Davis and Metz was crucial. Franklin G. Balch was appointed as an administrative assistant to help Metz, while C. Mildred Thompson, formerly dean of Vassar College (1923 to 1948) and a prominent figure in American education, became dean of women in August 1952.

With the aim of increasing student numbers for the year 1952–53, 123 new candidates were accepted for Strasbourg and 47 for external universities, out of 1105 applicants. Thus, 204 students started their studies in November 1952. The predominant student nationality was Polish (51), followed by Yugoslav (37), Czechoslovak (30), Rumanian (29), then Bulgarian (17), Hungarian (15), Latvian (9), Lithuanian (7), Albanian (6), and Estonian (3). In January 1952, Fraser was appointed head of the Committee on Awards and Placement, replacing Davis because of the dean's growing workload (although Davis still kept his membership on the committee). From August 1952 the enlarged student body was housed in newly constructed buildings on the grounds of the chateau, including dormitories for male students (women lodged in the chateau) and a bedroom and office for the administrative assistant, Balch. In line with the increase in students, the chateau's service staff went up to 32 people, including one French supervisor, catering and laundry staff, chambermaids, handymen and chauffeurs to transport the students between the chateau and the university.

In order to fulfill the purpose of the FEUE - which was "by no means limited simply to helping the recipients continue their general education; a more intensive purpose [was] to equip them for future leadership in their native lands"[93], the students' curriculum was comprised of three components. First, they had to follow university studies at Strasbourg or the external universities where they had been admitted. They could renew their applications for FEUE scholarship for the next academic year on condition of achieving good marks and passing university exams. Dean Davis and Assistant Dean Galy helped the students academically. Second, a Central and Eastern European Seminar was organized and entrusted to an exile professor in the Pourtalès Chateau. This played an integral part in the students' studies for each national section (except for external students), instructing them in national cultural heritage, specifically the historical, political, economic and cultural structures of these countries. Third, throughout the year, a series of lectures in French and English was organized, also in the chateau, offered by French, American and other visiting scholars, intellectuals or public figures. These dealt with Western democratic values, international relations, the USSR and Marxism, and current political, economic and social issues. Programs for the national seminars and lectures were conceived by Davis with the help of Galy and approved by both the Paris office and the Board of Trustees in New York. Supplementing the CEL's educational training, a library was established – specializing in Central and Eastern European countries – whose collection reached twelve thousands books in 1955.

During the academic year, the CEL received frequent visitors: NCFE members, exile leaders and representatives of various anticommunist organizations. The institution organized sports and cultural events for its students, and the national holidays of the countries represented in the CEL were also celebrated each year.

Parallel to its Western European program, the NCFE also granted scholarships, through the MESC, for exiled youths residing in the U.S. In the first year, 15 students could follow university studies on the other side of the Atlantic, while in 1952 their number increased to 90. During the Christmas holiday season, a regular conference was held in New York to gather these students together. The Third Annual Student Conference of the FEUE's U.S. Scholarship Program, held on 29–30 December 1953 in the Barbizon-Plaza Hotel in New York, dealt with the question of European integration and ended with a recording for the RFE.

The condition for being granted a CEL scholarship in Europe was that the recipient follow university studies, with the obligation to attend special courses at the Pourtalès Chateau. The NCFE's aim was not simply to grant fellowships but to create a distinguished institution. A little before his resignation as president of the FEUE Inc., Poole summarized the results of the year 1951 in a memorandum in March 1952 and defined the CEL's overall mission. He promoted not simply a scholarship institution offering grants but also national seminars as the whole undertaking's distinctive effort and self-justifying purpose:

> Strasbourg was selected as seat because it is one of the best of the French universities. To give well chosen youngsters a chance to sit at the feet of the Strasbourg faculties must always remain a major purpose and justification for the FEUE; but it is no less the case that FEUE will miss achieve full successs until Robertsau, as distinct from Strasbourg University but still in cooperation with the University, has been built into a leading center – soon it ought to be the leading center – for study of the East European cultures and the over-all problems of that region. FEUE scholarships should come to be prized above all because those who hold a certificate of satisfactory performance at Robertsau are marked for future leadership on their native heaths.[94]

The workability of this policy remained to be tested in the first years.

Facing Reality: the Challenges of the First Years and the Transformation of Ideas (1951–1954)

The NCFE and FEUE officers either underestimated or failed to predict the number and nature of challenges they would face in the University Center, abandoning any idea of creating other "beach-head universities". First, the establishment of the official FEUE entities was rushed, with some being established after the CEL was already running, illustrating the strength of American ambitions to open the institution as soon as possible. The American corporation was created on 20 July 1951 in New York. The Committee on Awards and Placement started its work on 24 August with no office in Paris, so applications had to be sent to New York or to Foster's Paris address. At the beginning of November, the Paris office at 7 rue de la Paix still did not have legal footing. The opening ceremony was held on 14 November, the French association received its ministerial authorization on 21 November, and the lease on the chateau's rental was only signed on 11 February 1952.

Second, the FEUE in New York and the operation at Strasbourg-Robertsau required more staff than anticipated, which impacted on the budget. The original plan from November 1950 estimated a budget of $110.000 for the first year, including salaries for only three administrators, one professor at the University of Strasbourg and one visiting professor, 60 scholarships, and expenditures for travel and staff maintenance. The final structure, including administration in New York, Paris and Strasbourg-Robertsau demanded a budget four times as big. The total predicted budget was $481,000 for the year 1951, which increased to $624,086 for the year 1952, in accordance with the increased student body.

However, the main problem was related to the FEUE's essential purpose, or "raison d'être" for the exile body (including students and national tutors) and the national seminars and lecture series. The CEL officers faced an unprecedented situation with the exiled students. They were young refugees who came from a wide range of backgrounds, and for whom residence and a future in Western Europe were uncertain. Not to mention the administrative difficulties of organizing visas and correlating their international qualifications with the various French universities' acceptance criteria. Students were suspicious of the administration, their national tutors and each other.[95] This negative atmosphere gradually dispersed, to be replaced by a friendlier climate at the beginning of the second year thanks to "old" students conveying the nature of the institution to new arrivals. Visa and diploma issues were resolved thanks to good relations between French local authorities and the University of Strasbourg.

The recruitment of exile teachers only started in October 1951, with a preference for young tutors in line with French expectations,[96] with recommendations for posts coming through NCFE channels: "... the main facts regarding two possible candidates which have come to our attention for the Czechoslovak section may make clearer the type of individual tentatively thought to be suitable for a tutorial post. They are a Czech and a Slovak, both younger scholars in the early thirties. Each has academic degrees approximately equivalent to the doctorate and each has had experience in research and seminar teaching."[97] Tutors were chosen by personal interviews with Poole, Tyler or Davis. In February 1952, three tutors were in residence at Strasbourg, by the end of June there were five, and in January 1953 there were eight tutors representing the following nationalities: Bulgarian, Czechoslovak, Hungarian, Lithuanian, Polish, Rumanian, and Yugoslav. With two exceptions (the Czech and Slovak tutors), they had no teaching experience. The Czech and Slovak tutors were specialists in the field of literature and comparative culture; the Romanian and Bulgarian tutors in law and philosophy; the Hungarian tutor had done a great deal of advanced work in political science and law, and the Yugoslav tutor in history and political science. They were mainly between the ages of 30 and 40. They, too, had to face the students' mistrust, but by summer 1952 a sense of team spirit started to develop in each national group.

Davis and Galy conceptualized the program of national seminars at weekly meetings with the growing group of tutors, after which the proposed program was sent to New York for approval. The topic of the national seminars during the winter of 1951 and spring of 1952 was the recent history of the Central and Eastern European countries which were represented in the CEL, their relations with their neighbors and with the great powers, and their present situation, emphasizing the contrast between "free" and "police or Soviet states". In the summer term, seminars briefly reviewed the recent history and political development in these countries, and participants studied Communist methods of grasping control that led to loss of independence.

In October 1952, Michel Potulicki joined the CEL for the large Polish seminar in order to help guide the resident tutors and plan the overall program. He was a Polish citizen, experienced in law and diplomacy, and a former IRO employee. For the 1952–1953 academic year, the program for the national seminars was divided into two parts: the first dealing with the "European Idea and Lifestyle" from a cultural and religious point of view (contrasting Western liberal and Soviet dictatorial attitudes and activities), and the second with "Political Problems" through comparative analysis of the application and effects of Western political democracy and Soviet political constructs on the national systems.

The lecture series program was planned in accordance with the students' need to learn more about political concepts of confederation, federation, integration, and regional relations resulting from "the fact that the majority [did] not possess such an understanding ... explained by the evidence that they [have] never lived in their own lands under conditions affording any chance to observe processes of this type or to exercise freedom individually and that they have never taken part in such experience anywhere else in exile."[98] For this reason, the first lecture series program held in April and May 1952 was on "Determining elements in European Unity", with the participating exile professors teaching in Western universities and professors from Strasbourg and around France. The Summer Lecture Program in September and October 1952 was on the United States (presented by the chairman of the FEUE trustees, Berle, and CEL Association member, Professor Chinard) and European integration (held by a group of lecturers from the Institute of Political Sciences in Paris.)

However, this entire curriculum, including university studies and special instruction in the CEL, required a knowledge of French, which the majority of the students did not have. This handicap was the major cause of students' lack of comprehension of lectures and failure in university exams. French language courses were organized by French professor Straka, resulting in an intensive study schedule for the students: "National seminars and French courses during the university year had to be held in the evenings, since the students [were] at the university during the day, and this [was] the arrangement from November to June. During the summer term the program divided for two hours of French in the morning, a general lecture in the afternoon followed by national seminars, and finally an hour of group instruction based on translating from the national language into French."[99]

The question of giving priority to university studies over instruction in the CEL was already raised among FEUE officers in August 1951. Poole sent Davis the notes from an "evening-long discussion" amongst Berle, Dolbeare, Tyson and himself to use as guiding principles for the curriculum at Robertsau. During this conversation, Poole put forward the idea of having the students "attempt to carry no more than, say, a two-thirds load of courses in Strasbourg University and so to leave them with ample time and energy for the Central and Eastern Seminar."[100] However, Berle argued that these students "would be the recipients of a very special favor and [the NCFE] could and should expect from them an extraordinary effort", insisting that they "should carry a full load at Strasbourg and do the Seminars as well ...".[101] To conclude, Poole summarized: "I did not want the Seminar, I said, to fall to a second level, to become an incident or boondoggle. That was agreed; but in the end I think the main issue was left open."[102]

This indicates what would later become the CEL's main problems: first, the vast and confusing guiding principles conceived by the Board of Directors in New York; second, the effect of the physical distance between the entities, which meant that projects conceived were often not workable in reality. Meanwhile, the situation in the CEL at Strasbourg-Robertsau was determined by the limited ability to act on French territory, and by the complexity of the problems occurring with the exile body. Thus, the goal of fulfilling FEUE's aim under the circumstances at hand shaped the CEL's spirit and program. Nevertheless, the way the CEL was being run did not appeal to several key figures in the Study Center. The CEL seemed to fail to fulfill the mission it was conceived for, but for a different reason for each figure. Unclear ideas led to controversial interpretations, provoking a series of clashes and fateful changes in the CEL.

The main issue for American officials was that students spent most of their time learning French and working on their university studies. They felt that learning French and integrating into the French university system prioritized French requirements over preparing a devoted generation of young people for the Pax Americana. This obviously differing interpretation of the CEL's mission – helping young Eastern refugees to follow university studies versus producing educated youths for future leadership – led to a conflict in the CEL administration in early 1953. Assistant Dean Metz, with Balch and Thompson, reproached the Davis-Galy-headed institution for involving French elements too heavily in the CEL (through permanent collaboration with the University of Strasbourg and conception of the CEL program with Galy, despite emphasizing the American guidelines) and for emphasizing French culture much more heavily in the CEL courses than the anti-communist teaching, which was the institution's original purpose. Contrary to Metz, Davis argued that the CEL was founded on French soil with French support, so it was necessary to involve and inform the French of the institution's activities. The security branch of the police headquarters of the Bas-Rhin Region, which followed the institution's activities, also observed the rift within the CEL leadership in its "information notes". These notes spoke of an opposition within the leadership between two "clans": on the one hand the "Francophiles", who emphasized the human mission of the CEL, and on the other hand the "Francophobes", who, based on information in the notes, alerted the Board of Trustees in New York that anticommunist teaching had been minimized in the CEL's program of courses.

However, discontent also occurred on the French side. French professor Straka reproached the institution for failing to carry out its original mission, that is to say, helping exile youths to follow studies. He criticized the American CEL officials' views, which seemed "always obscure or in any case contrary to [his] own; the point of view of those who inexperienced or unaware of the mission they are charged with accomplishing, lack a sense of justice with respect to the students, preferring high society and the planning of endless parties and mixers to university work, intriguing and undermining the authority of the Dean and his closest academic associates, criticizing everything that is French, and above all as profoundly unaware of the needs and the mindset of the refugees as they are of European problems, French and Central European alike."[103]

Last but not least, Burnham and the Kultura staff also discussed the crisis occurring in the CEL in their correspondence. In a letter to Giedroyc and Czapski, Burnham, being a member of the FEUE's educational corporation, emphasized the seriousness of the affair: "The College, too, is discouraging. I gather that it is at present in an administrative crisis. A meeting of the Board of Trustees is supposed to be held this month, and I understand that the question of a complete change of direction will be up for decision."[104] In his answer, Giedroyc suggested a number of changes to the functioning of the CEL and argued for a more active institution, which would also offer employment in other FEC entities, thus predicting the CEL's future.[105] Furthermore, *Kultura* published a Polish student's article on the CEL in its December 1953 issue which portrayed an incompetent administration, the scandalous nature of the CEL courses and a program more concerned with westernizing the students than with preparing them for their return to Central and Eastern Europe.

As a result of Tyson's personal investigation in Strasbourg-Robertsau (he transferred there from New York from February to May 1953 to study the situation at the institution, questioning officials and students) and of the decisions of the FEUE trustees, the crisis was resolved through a series of personnel changes between May and October 1953. Dean Davis tendered his resignation, effective 30 June 1953, much to the regret of Galy and the Strasbourg body of scholars who appreciated his work and character. The chairman of the FEUE's Board of Trustees, Berle, sent a letter to Rector Hubert on 8 May 1953 in order to explain the reason for the dean's resignation, citing Davis's personal objection to the FEUE president and his belief that the CEL was changing its original mission. Berle stated again that the CEL's principle aims, as they were confirmed to French authorities at the creation of the University, had not changed: it meant to help students follow university studies, and to instruct them in national cultural heritage with lectures on the possible future of their respective countries.

Not only did Davis leave the CEL but Metz, Balch and Thompson were also dismissed and replaced by new staff members. However,

Thompson became a FEUE trustee, and Metz was also kept in the FEUE framework, being assigned to the position of Director of Admissions and Placement, which he would hold throughout the CEL's existence. After the Board of Trustees found a pretext, French professor Straka was dismissed at the end of August 1953. Reacting against this discriminative decision, he sent the previously quoted open letter to FEUE officials criticizing the institution. Galy remained as assistant dean in order to maintain relations with the French.

After a short period with Potulicki as interim dean, the FEUE officials found a new person to head the CEL, to be called its president from then on. Tyson introduced the new president at the CEL's inaugural assembly on 22 October 1953. He argued that the new president fulfilled the NCFE's requirements, which were to "be resident in Europe, and ... possessed with basic qualifications to perform such a task."[106] John Pelényi, a distinguished former Hungarian diplomat, agreed to assume the presidency of the CEL. Born in 1885 in Budapest, he completed his studies in the Consular Academy of Vienna under the Austro-Hungarian Monarchy, then served as Hungarian consul general in Cleveland, Ohio. In 1930, he became a permanent Hungarian delegate to the League of Nations and to the International Labor Organization. Later he served as a diplomat in Cuba and Mexico from 1933. He served as the Hungarian minister to the U.S. until he resigned in November 1940, when Hungary joined the Axis. He remained in the U.S. as a professor of international relations at Dartmouth College, where he taught for thirteen years and retired as professor emeritus. He was active in Hungarian-American affairs, including serving on the Hungarian Council of Ministers formed at the end of WWII. Of all the former Hungarian diplomats who emigrated or remained in the U.S., he had the strongest ties to the U.S. Department of State as well as access to the executive office.[107] Pelényi's role was mainly representative, while academic issues were forwarded to Potulicki as acting dean and Galy. The new president also reaffirmed in his introductory speech that the institution was "not simply humanitarian":

> The College was intended to give young exiles from countries on the other side of the Iron Curtain the chance to undertake their studies in an atmosphere of total academic freedom, something which is only possible in a democratic environment anticipating that, after the liberation of the respective countries, those exiles who have benefited from the program would have the patriotic zeal to return to their native countries in order to take part in the reconstruction of their countries and in the creation of a happier future within the framework of a Europe, no longer divided and poor, but unified and prosperous.[108]

During 1953–1954, lecture series and national seminars continued and adapted to actual needs. The Summer Lecture Program, held from 10 August to 15 October 1953, dealt with three topics: the USSR and its foreign policy from 1917; Germany from the Third Reich up to the present day, and its possible integration into a European Union; and the question of Europe's unification, emphasizing the integration of Central and Eastern European countries. Although Tyson outlined the program in May 1953, its organization was rushed because of the changes in the CEL staff: "... the setting up of [the program] by Dr. Potulicki in about three weeks' time was a remarkable "tour de force" on his part for which the term brilliant is not too much."[109] Students were grouped in two seminars: "Seminar A" for advanced students, and "Seminar B" for students whose knowledge was not sufficiently developed, followed by an informal discussion to help these students to draw full benefits from the lecture program.

Although the plan for holding national seminars was long established in the CEL, there was a permanent insufficiency of national tutors. RFE Vice President Bernard Yarrow wrote to Pelényi in April 1954:

> Dr. Tyson spoke to me again today about recommending names of candidates as tutors for the Estonian, Latvian, Lithuanian, Czechoslovak, Romanian, Bulgarian, Yugoslav and Albanian groups. ... As I understand from Ty, the Board [of FEUE trustees] on April

> 8 approved the whole project of getting in new tutors for all these groups and now it is up to us to find them. We shall do our very best. I know how important it is to be surrounded by the right caliber of men who will put into effect a farsighted program.[110]

This problem called into question whether national seminars would be still part of the Summer Lecture Program.[111] The 1954 summer program, covering the period of 16 August to 7 October, dealt with a wide range of subjects: development of the Federalist idea in various parts of the world; comparative analysis of the practice of Communist and Western doctrines; communist activities within the Western trade unions; study of the foreign policy of the Great Powers; and a special conference on European integration held by SFIO party leader André Philip. In this enlarged context and to avoid "nationalistic tendencies", resident tutors "have been guided increasingly this year to stress their national heritage and contribution to the common treasury of Western civilization, rather than the aspects of differences in national history that would stimulate a divisive reaction."[112] To supplement national seminars, separate lectures were given by exile representatives to familiarize the student body with the culture and development of their respective countries and with the effects of Soviet domination.[113] Three groups were established according to the students' levels of knowledge and development. As an entirely new experiment, an international students' conference was also held on European integration, with the participation of Western European students and auditors.

In May 1954, FEUE officials were reassured of French support for the CEL by Gaston Berger, director of higher education in the French Ministry of Education. In 1952 Berger had succeeded Donzelot in the post of director of higher education at the French Ministry of National Education, the latter having become the permanent representative of French universities in the U.S. Following a lunch held in Paris with NCFE President Whitney H. Shepardson, Pelényi, Potulicki, CEL Association President René Charron, and other French state officials, "Mr. Charron indicated definitely after the meeting that Mr. Berger assured him of his agreement with the Aide Memoire".[114] This aide-memoire stated the aim of the CEL as declared in 1951 and reconfirmed in October 1953 (to form a future leadership in which "the countries of asylum refrain from applying a policy of systematic assimilation vis-à-vis the students from FEUE/CEL"[115]) and the collaboration between the American institution and French authorities, including academic (coordination of grants with French scholarship institutions, French presence in the CEL administration approved by the Ministry of National Education) and legal aspects (visa demands, regulations relating to the residence and the employment of the exiles in France).

From Big Expectations to Unexpected Closure (1955–1958)

By 1954, FEUE officials had to face another issue: the increasing number of graduating students and the question of their resettlement. Times had changed since 1951. In light of the evolution of international relations, the U.S. recognized that the Cold War was going to be a long war to win. Talk of peaceful coexistence between the superpowers became a topic of diplomatic discussion and a campaign directed at liberation of Central and Eastern European countries seemed to have been postponed. For this reason, FEUE officials sought to find suitable employment for former CEL students.

In the academic year 1953–54, 237 scholarships were granted, in 1954–1955, 211. The majority of CEL scholarships were granted to students who renewed their fellowship from year to year. To give an indication of how many students needed to find employment: in December 1953, there were 120 ex-CEL students out of 393 grants in total, allocated for 1951–52 and 1952–53. In his new position as admissions director of the CEL, Metz reported that of these 120 ex-students "83 may be considered alumni; 5 expellees; 32 were of such short stay at the College that they cannot be counted at all."[116]

The obvious "what's next?" question was raised by among everyone – the Americans, the French and the students alike. In late 1953, this question was under early consideration according to Metz's report:

> The Placement possibilities have been more widely studied, but still the same answer: there is practically no opening for intellectually trained people in the present French economy. …. It is my intention to explain this to the students at Strasbourg, making it clear to them that the College was founded to train intellectuals for their return to their own countries, not merely to give them a profession for their immediate practice, that it is their responsibility to train themselves in practical lines while we are training them professionally, so that they will be able to fit into the economy of their countries of exile until that time when they can be intellectual forces in the nations of their origin.[117]

However, in his report Metz also outlined the intention to organize regular series of receptions, with the purpose of bringing together members of organizations from governmental, philanthropic and private spheres with which NCFE and FEUE were in contact.

Thus, the resettlement of graduating students became a preoccupation from early 1954. Other Free Europe entities sought to seize on the human resources trained by the CEL, whose aim ran parallel to that of the FEC[118] Policy of August 1954, as highlighted by Tyson: "3. FEUE can be a political warfare instrumentality particularly as a supplier of personnel for FEC operations. 4. In respect to program, while liberation objectives can always be maintained to a limited extent service to free world should be highlighted. Goal should be for equipping students to further free world objectives which can be done particularly at the trade school level."[119]

According to this policy, several types of action were taken. In January 1954, Yarrow's proposal suggested the possibility of utilizing CEL students within the International Labor Organizations, FEC-sponsored national councils and committees, and as counselors and teachers in refugee camps and kindergartens with the Free Europe Citizens' Service. In December 1955, Tyson listed for Yarrow the names of 84 students who were considered likely candidates for participation in the activities of the Crusade for Freedom. In the summer of 1955, CEL students helped with secretarial work at the first session of the Assembly of Captive European Nations (ACEN) held in Strasbourg. Furthermore, the ACEN's special sessions were held in the Pourtalès Chateau from 1956 to 1958. In November 1953 under the guidance and direction of Potulicki, the CEL created the Advanced Study Group from among its best students to monitor and analyze the communist press (also collecting articles about communist attacks on the FEUE/CEL and publishing them in its "Black Book") and do research on Central and European Communist countries. This research group started working more intensively from November 1954, also preparing materials for RFE scripts, monographs, and conferences. Its best members found their work acknowledged in the form of an invitation from the FEUE to the U.S. in order to participate in its Student Conference.

Despite these promising developments, serious doubts over the CEL were coming to light. The FEUE's Board of Trustees held an important meeting in New York in September 1954 to discuss the institution's future. Burnham informed Giedroyc about this situation and his actions in support of the CEL: "On September 23rd there is to be a most important meeting of the University Board of Trustees. I have submitted a memorandum in which I decided to omit all secondary questions and concentrate on what I feel to be the three critical points: (1) The College should be kept going; (2) Its intellectual, political and spiritual level must be raised; (3) It should orient toward transformation into an East European Center or Institute."[120]

As a result of the trustees meeting, "the dominant outlook had been to reduce the importance of the Robertsau center (perhaps moving towards its gradual liquidation) and to expand the program of subsidies to students at other universities, and also – a new departure – subsidies for 'vocational training' in crafts and various mechanical arts."[121] The Trustees agreed to keep the CEL alive and to turn it into a "center". In this guise, all students would be required to attend the Summer Session, also attended by American students and scholars. The intellectual level of the program and the staff in the CEL were supposed to be raised in order to fulfill this new goal. Pelényi also suggested developing plans for the publication of books or periodicals, and exploring the possibility of having some sort of conference or meeting held in at Strasbourg-Robertsau.

This new policy was implemented through the establishment of the Advanced Study Group and by hosting the ACEN's special sessions in the Pourtalès Chateau. Meanwhile, the changing FEUE policy was also adapted to the changing international situation by the mid 1950s, in the era of "peaceful coexistence". Recognizing the Cold War as a long war to win, the American foreign policy objective towards Central and Eastern European countries was no longer to liberate them but to contribute to their liberalization. In other words, it entailed a shift from a "revolutionary approach" to an "evolutional approach" towards the liberation of East European countries.[122] Waiting for expected democratic changes from behind the Iron Curtain, the CEL's principal aim changed in late 1954 to one of helping young refugees integrate into their country of exile, as Burnham pointed out it to Giedroyc: "There was also discussion of the political dilemma in which the College finds itself. In original theory, it was started for the sake of young exiles oriented toward returning to their liberated countries. But in fact the perspective of liberation becomes slow and dim. Most young exiles consider it unrealistic, and wish actually to integrate themselves into a non-Communist nation."[123]

On 30 December 1954, President Pelényi announced to the president of the University of Strasbourg that the CEL had changed its function from a boarding school to a non-residential scholarship organization. This meant that each fellow could freely choose a European university at which to pursue his or her studies, with the only obligation being attendance at the summer conferences (the same obligation as existing external students were under up until this point). The FEUE trustees decided that the CEL office should move to Paris in order to centralize the administrative work. The CEL library was also transferred to Paris and housed in the Polish Library.

In this new framework, FEUE and CEL officials in key positions remained in the same posts they had been appointed to before. The chairman of the trustees was still Berle, Tyson its chancellor, while Shepardson became vice president of the FEUE Corporation in 1953.

The resident manager of the Western European branch was U.S. Naval Attaché Henri Smith-Hutton, succeeding Sabalot, who substituted for Tyler after his death in March 1953. Metz remained director of Admissions and Placement, Galy was still director of External Affairs to ensure relation with French, and Potulicki retained his post as academic counselor.

In light of these operational changes, the purpose of the CEL Summer Lecture Program was also transforming. The notion of the "return to homeland" had been dismissed and replaced by the new CEL mission: emphasizing Western indoctrination to create young promoters of democracy who were conscious of "communist danger" and willing to fight against Communist expansion in the "free world".

The CEL's new orientation gave hope to some and filled others with despair. FEUE Chancellor Tyson described it as a "significant change" and "reversion to the most important element in the whole idea from which the University was conceived."[124] Tyson pointed out that this new orientation was a kind of deviation from the institution's original purpose because the CEL itself did not fulfill the mission it had been dedicated to, being only an academic institution and neglecting to play a role in political warfare.[125] With the arrival of Pelényi and this new policy, NCFE officials were called upon to indicate ways in which the FEUE training program could be exploited to support FEC activities.

However, for Burnham, who had always promoted both a more active institution and firmer political action against the Soviet Union, it meant the end of the CEL. His reflections, sent to Giedroyc in January 1955, indicate that parallel to the international situation the French political climate had also changed:

> I suppose that by now you have had news of the projected drastic changes at Robertsau. A sudden meeting of the Board was called … . Nearly every decision that had been taken two months previously, was reversed. The actions were motivated by the development of the Coexistence policy, the state of European opinion, and especially the condition of France. Very little is salvaged. At best, a skeleton is left that

> could conceivably take on flesh again if the political climate changes. ... In strict realism, it is likely that this present result is inevitable. It is hard to see how you can have a subordinate institution functioning on the implied basis of a Policy of Liberation when the western world is proceeding basically on the premises of a Policy of Coexistence.[126]

The year 1954 embodied the image of a France independent of the U.S., inaugurated by the election of Pierre Mendès France in June and the rejection of the European Defense Community (EDC) in August, which was a major issue in French internal politics. The origin of the idea to create a supranational European army and a European defense community went back to the outbreak of the Korean War in 1950, when the world was afraid of an eventual Third World War and Europe of an invasion of Russian tanks. European states appealed to the U.S. for military assistance, and in return the Americans required the rearmament of West Germany. Rearming the former enemy only five years after WWII was, however, considered unacceptable. Thus, Prime Minister René Pleven, inspired by the political economist Jean Monnet, proposed the creation a supranational European Defense Community among France, Italy, West Germany and the Benelux countries. The treaty was signed on 27 May 1952 but was still to be ratified by the French National Assembly.

Meanwhile, France had been involved in the Indochina War since 1946, which from 1950 demanded increased military and, consequently, financial support (funded increasingly by the U.S.). In this context, there was uncertainty among French politicians concerning the EDC because if France went more deeply into colonial war, she could probably not take a leading role in a new European security frame. The final vote on the EDC treaty at the French National Assembly took place only in August 1954, due to hesitancy which poisoned French internal politics, dividing politicians into "ECDists" and "anti-ECDists." When Prime Minister Mendès France submitted to European cooperation on defense in the National Assembly, he did so without really supporting the idea. After being ratified by other countries, the treaty was finally refused by the French for various internal political reasons. It was also refused because the international political climate was beginning to calm, particularly following the death of Stalin in March 1953, and the signing of the Geneva Accords to end the Indochina War by, among others, the Vietnamese Communist leader Ho Chi Minh and Mendès France, on 21 July 1954. The U.S. acknowledged that the Geneva Accords existed but refused to sign in order to avoid being legally bound to them. Both the Geneva Accords and Mendès France's negotiations and agreements with the Maghreb colonies (Tunisia, Morocco and Algeria) for independence frightened U.S. officials and increased American mistrust of the French prime minister. They feared that France was allowing global communist expansion. This was the end of American influence in France.

In line with the new international and French political climate, the perspective of CEL activities also changed. For the academic year 1955–1956, 160 students were granted CEL fellowships (including full-time grants for the whole academic year and so-called "one-time grants" for specific purposes, varying from $100 to $400 per student) with the opportunity to choose freely the university at which they wished to study as long as they attended the Summer Lectures Program. In accordance with the CEL's new mission and operational reorganization, the 1955 summer lecture series aimed to shape young people with a democratic spirit and willing to fight against Communism. With this aim in mind, the 1955 summer program, held in French and English from 1 August to 17 October for CEL fellows and representative students from other universities, had two principal objectives: "1) a long-term objective – to attempt to frame a statement of the ideal of the Free World, so cast as to be meaningful and vital to thinking men anywhere in the world; to explore the mechanism which will be necessary to the attainment of those ideals; 2) a more immediate objective which aims at making young people conscious of the danger of communism through an intensive examination of its principles and methods of operation."[127]

The first part of the Summer Lectures Program followed a theoretical line, attempting to define "free world" ideals (which was hard work because these ideals "[could] not be found anywhere expressed in a universally applicable doctrinal form"[128]) compared to Marxian communist ideals. Lectures were given by, among others, the chairman of the FEUE's Board of Trustees, Berle; French MRP party leader, George Bidault; the Italian ambassador to France, Pietro Quaroni; the rector of the University of Saar, J.F. Angelloz; professor of theology of the University of Fribourg, J. Bochenski; Governor of Puerto Rico, Luiz Muñoz-Marin; and former Communist French writer Michel Collinet. The second part of the summer program dealt with both theoretical and practical questions through round-table discussions by lecturers and students on "techniques and purposes of Communist infiltration in various areas and groupings in the Free World" (such as youth organizations, trade unions, sciences, legislation, woman rights, education and art) and the means of counteracting this infiltration.[129] This latter phase on communist counteraction was devised entirely by the CEL's Advanced Studies Group, and discussions were run by its members in order to define tactics, arguments, and slogans against communist action. The second part of the summer program was supplemented with a series of national seminars and lectures on the respective languages of CEL students held by Bulgarian, Czech, Estonian, Hungarian, Latvian, Lithuanian, Polish, Slovak and Yugoslav tutors.

What the CEL fellows learned in the Summer Lectures Program they could put to use during the academic year when they were spread all over Europe. In the university cities where the biggest CEL-fellow communities existed (such as London, Louvain and Stockholm), CEL groups had been created under the "Foyer Program". These groups were led by the most impressive CEL students and were run with the purpose of keeping CEL students together and continuing to increase their awareness of anticommunism. Metz, along with another colleague from the Paris office, was responsible for visiting and reporting on the Foyer groups.

The evolutionary spirit and the concept of spreading democracy were best expressed in the plan for the 1956 Summer Lectures Program, created by Peter Beers, a CEL staff member in Paris since 1955:

> ... I found that clear thinking required me to outline the FEUE objectives. The evolutionary process has basically reflected the changing

> international situation. You will notice that I have not mentioned the 'return to the homeland' feature which was prominent in the original conception. I consider that our present objective will do more to further the success of a 'return', when and if such becomes possible, for the reason that our students will have gained special training and, I hope, free-world action experience, which they will sorely need if they are to become effective in the radically changed situation which they will find on return to their eventually liberated homelands. ... To answer this fundamental question I propose that we consider an idealized end-product of a FEUE program assuming for the moment the money, personnel, time and talent necessary. The desired end-product is the Berle-styled 'dedicated missionary'. [130]

Understanding the nature, appeals, aims and tactics of communism, and the ideals and goals of the West, this missionary would believe that "the conflict of ideologies between the Free World and communism overshadows all other factors of importance in the world".[131]

After announcing the FEUE's new inclination towards political warfare, the 1956 Summer Lectures Program, held from 7 August to 16 September, dealt with three topics: Western ideals and resolutions versus the attraction of Communism; infiltration of totalitarian ideals in democratic countries; the superpowers' foreign policy, focusing on the Soviet Union and the problem of underdeveloped countries. The inaugural address was made by Berle and Pelényi. Lectures were given by American, French and other respected international scholars, politicians and intellectuals, and complemented by national seminars.

The 1957 summer program, held from 6 August to 7 September, interrupted the CEL's increasingly militant agenda, due to events occurring in the summer and autumn of 1956 in Poland and Hungary. Lectures attempted to analyze current international situations, emphasizing the conditions in Eastern European countries from cultural, social and economic perspectives. The inauguration was held by Berle, while, as in previous years, prominent international speakers came to Strasbourg-Robertsau, such as, Bochienski, Professor Jacques Freymond (director of the Institute of International Studies in Geneva), Sidney Hook and the exiled Polish writer Czeslaw Milosz. The closing conference, on the integration of Central and Eastern European countries into Europe, was presented by André Philip. Lectures were presented in English, French and German and supplemented by national seminars.

Concerning the number of CEL students, 216 grants were given the year of 1956–1957, of which 137 were full-time grants and 79 part-time grants. With respect to the events occurring in Central Europe, the FEC launched the Hungarian Emergency Program, which consisted of two activities. First, in winter 1956 the Pourtalès Chateau was reopened to house for six months approximately 80 Hungarian youth exiles coming from Austrian and French refugee camps. They were provided with medicine and clothing and beginning in January 1957 French language courses (funded by the French Ministry of National Education) were organized for them at the University of Strasbourg. Second, the FEUE granted more than 200 fellowships to young Hungarian refugees who had escaped into Western Europe (44 students in Austria, 40 in Belgium, 10 in France, 111 in Italy, and so forth).

Despite all these remarkable undertakings and the farsighted educational program to form democratic militants, the CEL was by now nothing more than a sinking ship, enjoying less prominence in the FEC's framework from 1956[132] – with more and more of its leaders taking their leave. In 1956, Galy left the CEL to join the embassy of France in the U.S. as cultural counselor. In June 1956, the distinguished FEUE official Tyson, who was president of FEUE's corporation from September 1952 (substituting for Poole after his death) until the arrival of Pelényi, also retired because of his dissatisfaction. As Tyson explained to Sidney Hook: "It has been good to know you because I feel we have thought alike – certainly, on all major points. I regret that the adventure, so far as I am concerned, should not have met with the success I think it deserves. I have been butting my head against a pretty firm stone wall ever since 1953 and there is no sense in continuing that – certainly not under present auspices."[133]

One year later, following his lecture at the 1957 summer program, it was Hook who wrote a brief report to FEUE officials on his dissatisfaction with the CEL. He based his report on his two weeks long participation in the Summer Lectures Program and talks with its officials – Pelényi and Potulicki – and students. He wrote: "No one has requested me to write this report, but I feel that it may be helpful to the members of the Board of Trustees, responsible for shaping policy, to get my fresh and unauthorized impressions."[134] Hook argued that the CEL could not fulfill its educational political activity while its double purpose consisted of assisting Central and Eastern European refugee students with scholarships to undertake academic training and in keeping alive their cultural heritage to make them capable of holding leadership in their respective countries once they were liberated from Soviet orbit. He saw the biggest problem in the summer program's curriculum of studies as being what he qualified as "miracles of improvisation", lacking not only integration and organization, but also "systematic exploration of basic themes."[135] The lecturers were not distinguished enough on an educational level (with some exceptions), while the students were neither affected by them nor followed them seriously. Finally, all these problems were also due to the fact that there was no one at the topmost administrative level in the FEUE's corporation in New York who would coordinate the educational plans on both sides of the Atlantic. Hook highlighted that the CEL was considered as just "another operational political instrument of the Free Europe Committee, comparable to Radio Free Europe."[136] Meanwhile the undertaking could not build up intellectual prestige without publicity ("There is not sufficient of an echo in the European and world press about what is said and done in the College."[137]) and farsighted educational planning.

Although Hook presented some recommendations in his report, they would not be taken into consideration by the FEUE officials. At a special meeting of the executive committee of the FEUE's Board of Trustees, held on 22 May 1958, a resolution was unanimously passed on the closure of the FEUE program and on the liquidation of the undertaking according to which no more fellowships would be provided after 30 September 1958, except for the Hungarian student scholarship holders for 1958–1959. It was also agreed to hold the 1958 Summer Lectures Program along the lines worked out by Potulicki, to conclude arrangements "with appropriate European grant-making agencies to the end that Free Europe University in Exile scholarship- and grant-holders may be placed under the supervision of such agencies",[138] and to maintain contact with alumni students trained under the FEUE program.

The last Summer Lecture Program was held for approximately two hundred students from 29 July to 30 August 1958, dealing with three main topics (the problem of underdeveloped countries; reunification of Europe; the recent situation in Central and Eastern Europe) and organized by the same guiding principles as in the previous years (lectures held by American and other prominent interveners in French, English and German, followed by discussions and supplemented by national seminars). As it was the last CEL summer program, following Berle's opening address representatives of the French authorities gave speeches paying tribute to the American organizers for this successful undertaking.

On 1 October 1958, the Pourtalès Chateau ceased to serve as the CEL study center, and the French CEL Association was also soon to be dissolved. On 4 February 1959, the MESC director dealing with the liquidation, Stetson S. Holmes, handed to Rector Joseph Angelloz of the University of Strasbourg his set of keys to the chateau and the surrounding buildings as his "last" act, a "symbolic act"[139] in Strasbourg. Despite the creation of a CEL student association in Switzerland, formed to protest against the FEUE trustees' decision and to keep the institution alive, in accordance with FEC policy the FEUE scholarship program was being phased out.

The FEUE and its joint entity, the CEL, were dissolved and closed as quickly and as controversially as they were created and administered. This controversy can be best demonstrated in the FEUE's press release on the closure, issued on the same day as the meeting of the FEUE's executive committee, and announced by the chairman of the Board of Trustees in New York, Berle. The press release did not mention the initial aim of the institution at all, denying its whole "raison d'être". Moreover, the same argument on the CEL's closure was expressly repeated in the foreign press and in Berle's opening address at the 1958 Summer Lecture Program:

> The Free Europe University in Exile and its companion organization, the Association du Collège de l'Europe libre, were organized in 1951 to assist in providing university education for young men and women, originating in the countries behind the Iron Curtain, who had been displaced from their native lands by World War II and by the subsequent Communist seizure of these countries. It was recognized at that time that this project by its nature would continue only for a relatively few years. Few other organizations were then concerning themselves with giving assistance to this particular group of students. Now, after nearly seven years, most of the young men and women so displaced have achieved their education or have reached adult life. The project on which the Free Europe University in Exile embarked in 1951 has thus reached its end. During the seven years of its existence, Free Europe University in Exile through the Collège de l'Europe libre at Robertsau (Strasbourg) has made possible, education in European universities for approximately 1000 young men and women originating in the Iron Curtain countries. Some of them have taken highest academic honors; many have attained distinction. Most of them have found permanent places of occupation and usefulness in the life of Europe. It is proper now to announce termination of this project, and of the operations of the Free Europe University in Exile and the Collège de l'Europe libre. This means that no further applications will be taken for bourses by the Collège de l'Europe libre.[140]

The history of the FEUE Inc. and the Collège de l'Europe libre demonstrates the NCFE's grandiose ambitions for Central and Eastern European countries in the 1950s, its supplementing of U.S. foreign policy, and the limits of these objectives and policies. It also highlights a major point for understanding the origins of the Cold War, in that this American venture to fight against communism in support of Central and Eastern European countries was initiated and promoted mainly by political and intellectual exiles of those countries.

The NCFE's early activities attempted to maintain the faith of populations living under the Soviet orbit in regaining their political, social and cultural liberty, and to prepare them for liberation into the "free world". It was with the aim of training exile youths for future leadership that the FEUE Inc. in New York and the CEL at Strasbourg-Robertsau were organized.

However, the arrival of the idea of "peaceful coexistence" in the mid 1950s challenged this policy, leading to the new goal of liberalizing Central and Eastern European Soviet countries by means of persuasion. Obviously, the FEUE/CEL could hardly fit in with this new strategy. The FEC's educational division sought to be as strong as other Free Europe activities, but because of its own internal problems and controversies and the Cold War's changing climate, it could not accomplish the goals its organizers had set.

The FEUE/CEL faced a continuous identity search, during which its existence and its purpose were directed and defined according to changing international relations and depending on American foreign policy. This explains the extreme make-overs that the FEUE/CEL underwent during its seven year existence, each time denying all previous statements of purpose and mission.

It became what its originators, Czapski and Burnham, always disapproved of – an academic institution for American fellow-travelers – and the opposite of what the NCFE's representatives, Poole and Tyler, had promised to French authorities in 1951 – to concentrate exile youths at one center, giving priority to university studies while strengthening French culture among Central and Eastern European countries. Thus , serious scissions were provoked inside and in connection with the institution. When the CEL was launched in 1951, national seminars were conceived in order to keep alive national sentiment and cultural heritage in the country of asylum. The intention was not to interrupt the exiled youths' national life, and thus, prepare them for future leadership when they returned to their liberated homelands. The Aide-Mémoire regarding the FEUE/CEL's aim, agreed to by the French authorities in May 1954, expressly stated that the country of asylum must refrain from applying any policy or act of assimilation to CEL fellows. Nevertheless, four years after this declaration, the official press release on the CEL's closure cited as a reason for the undertaking's success the fact that it had helped to integrate Central and Eastern European refugee youths into Western European life.

In his 1952 report, the American dean, Malcolm Davis, described the FEUE/CEL as a "three cornered-undertaking", referring to its American, French and Eastern European elements. In a figurative sense, the FEUE/CEL was the result of great American ambitions that were limited by their workability on French soil and by the American's inexperience in the face of unexpected challenges, their failure to comprehend what the exile world really meant. Although the FEUE/CEL failed to accomplish its purpose according to NCFE's officials, it gave hope and backing to some one thousand refugee youths already living in the "free world".

The story of the NCFE's scholarship activity did not finish in 1958. Everybody, including NCFE officials, thought that the CEL had definitely closed. However, with a change in its objectives, it would continue to run for years in the Pourtalès Chateau.

Endnotes

1 WWII forced 20 million people to leave their original homes because of combat operations, ethnic cleansing, genocide and general fear. The so-called displaced persons were first assisted by the Allied nations' military missions. From 1 October 1945 the United Nation Relief and Rehabilitation Administration (UNRRA) took the majority of responsibility for the administration and the care of DPs in the so-called DP camps, helped by a number of charitable organizations providing humanitarian relief and services. These camps – including former military barracks, airports, hotels, castles, hospitals and private homes – became more or less permanent homes for thousands of "non-repatriable" DPs waiting for the outcome of their fate.

2 Joseph Czapski (1896–1993) was a war prisoner in WWII following the Polish Defensive War and miraculously survived the mass execution of nearly 22,000 Polish nationals (including mainly police officers, officers taken prisoner during the Russian invasion of Poland in 1939, and falsely accused civilians) in the Katyn Forest in Russia in April and May 1940, carried out by the Soviet secret police (NKVD). Joining the Polish II Corps, Czapski led investigations in 1941–1942 into the disappearance of Poles who had been in NKVD captivity and were massacred. Never receiving any satisfactory answers, he wrote of his experiences in two books, *Reminiscences of Starobyelsk* (1944) and *The Inhuman Land* (1949, published in English in 1951), which proved Russian guilt that was not, however,

officially acknowledged until 1990, the Russians having denied the massacre and laid the blame on Nazi Germany.

3 James Burnham (1905–1987) started out as a political activist of the American Trotskyite movement in the 1930s along with another philosopher, Sidney Hook. Burnham left Marxism, and joined the first intellectual organ of anti-Stalinist left, *Partisan Review*, in 1938. Soon, he turned to the political right and became a life-long contributor to the U.S.'s leading conservative journal, *National Review*, in 1955. He became a well-known intellectual in 1941 after writing *The Managerial Revolution* (1941). In *The Struggle for the World* (1947), based on his 1944 paper written for the Office of Strategic Services (American wartime intelligence service) on Soviet post-war ambitions, Burnham articulated the "opposition between the West as a precious heritage to be defended and Communism as a murderous tyranny to be defeated" (citation: Roger Kimball, "The power of James Burnham", *The New Criterion*, 21 (September 2002) 4). This book and the context of the Truman doctrine made Burnham, at Kennan's invitation, the head of the political and psychological warfare division of the OPC during a time when, "officially", he had left New York University to do research.

4 Untitled draft on the university project, James Burnham Papers, Subject File, Free Europe University (FEU) (1949–1952), box 9 folder 2, Hoover Institution Archives (Stanford, CA) (hereafter HIA), copyright Stanford University.

5 Ibid.

6 James Burnham to Joseph Czapski, 20 October 1948, Giedroyc – Burnham Correspondence (1948–1952), Institut Littéraire Kultura (hereafter ILK).

7 Czapski to Burnham, 9 November 1948, Ibid.

8 Burnham to Czapski, 10 February 1949, Ibid.

9 Anatol Mulhstein to Czapski, 7 March 1949, Miscellaneous documents, ILK.

10 Czapski to Burnham, 8 June 1949, Giedroyc – Burnham Correspondence (1948–1952), ILK.

11 Czapski to Burnham, 12 July 1949, Ibid.

12 Burnham to Czapski, 10 April 1950, Ibid.

13 To read more on the CCF, there is a study about the origins of the CCF on the webpage of the CIA's Center for the Study of Intelligence: https://www.cia.gov/library/center-for-the-study-of-intelligence/csi-publications/csi-studies/studies/95unclass/Warner.html For its entire story, see: Frances Stonor Saunders, *Who Paid the Piper?: CIA and the Cultural Cold War* (London: Granta, 1999).

14 To read more on the history, the politico-cultural content and the impacts of the CCF, see: Pierre Grémion, *Intelligence de l'anticommunisme: Le Congrès pour la liberté de la culture à Paris 1950–1975* [Intelligence of Anti-Communism: Congress for Cultural Freedom in Paris1950–1975] (Paris: Fayard, 1995).

15 "Wisner cabled Averell Harriman of the Economic Cooperation Administration (managers of the Marshall Plan), seeking five million francs (approximately $16,000) to fund a counter-demonstration. Harriman, a great supporter of propaganda and psychological warfare, was one of the first amongst America's political mandarins to understand that Russia had declared ideological war on the West, and to think up ways of countering 'the blast of abuse which was propelled from Moscow'. He was more than happy to provide Marshall Plan funds – referred to as 'candy' by Wisner – for covert operations." Stonor Saunders, *Who Paid the Piper?*, 68.

16 Melvin Lasky (1920–2004) participated in the First German Writers Congress in Berlin in 1947, which was organized in the same month as the Cominform. At this congress, Lasky violently attacked the Soviet Union, denouncing the similarities between Nazi Germany

and the new Soviet police state. His proposals and actions for a cultural undertaking against Communism resulted in him being called the Father of Cultural Cold War. He founded the intellectual review *Der Monat* in October 1948, supported by the Office of Military Government, U.S. with the approval of General Lucius D. Clay. Lasky later became the editor of the England-based CCF magazine *Encounter*. Arthur Koestler (1905–1983) was a former member of the "Munzenberg trust", a network of covert Soviet organizations existing before WWII under the guidance of Willi Munzenberg, in order to broaden the Comintern's (Communist international) influence. After WWII, he joined the Information Research Department in the British Foreign Office, dealing with anticommunist activities. Koestler also gave lectures in the U.S. and it was through Burnham that he was presented to American officers, counsellors, journalists and syndic representatives. Thanks also to his other contacts, he started working closely with the CIA.

17 The interveners mainly came from Europe – Austria, Belgium, Denmark, France, Greece, Holland, Italy, Norway, Spain, Sweden, Switzerland, Turkey and the United Kingdom – and from Colombia and India. Exiled intellectuals were Russian, Czechoslovakian, one Latvian and two Poles (Czapski and Giedroyc).

18 Grémion, *Intelligence de l'anticommunisme*, 64.

19 Burnham to Czapski, 19 October 1950, Giedroyc – Burnham Correspondence (1948–1952), ILK.

20 Burnham to Czapski, 15 December 1950, Ibid.

21 Czapski to Burnham, 27 December 1950, Ibid.

22 Czapski to Burnham, 11 January 1951, Ibid.

23 "Maybe the idea of a small 'domestic' printing press would appeal to them. In case you consider this project an interesting one – please help us in the Free Europe." Giedroyc to Burnham, 4 October 1950, Ibid.

24 "I believe that you should also write a formal letter to Mr. C.D. Jackson, the new director of the NCFE. Tell him of the long background that you and your associates have in the development of the University project. State that you have heard of a renewed interest in the matter by NCFE, and that you would like to make available to him your experiences in the matter and the material which you have assembled. Add, then, that James Burnham is well versed on the whole matter, and that he might do well to consult said Burnham." Burnham to Czapski, 13 February 1951, Ibid.

25 Ibid.

26 Burnham to Czapski, 27 February 1951, Ibid.

27 Czapski to Burnham, March 1951, Ibid.

28 Czapski's university project was first presented in June 1950 in the *Kongress für kulturelle Freiheit* in Berlin. The proposal was officially adopted by the CCF's International Committee in November 1950 in Brussels, creating a University Commission with the aim of acting toward the creation of the proposed institution. The NCFE president, Poole, came to France in March 1951 in order to meet Czapski and talk about the project. Meanwhile, the NCFE had already made an attempt to create the University Center in Strasbourg in August 1950, but it was refused by the Council of Deans of the University in Strasbourg in October 1950. That Czapski and Giedroyc did not know about the NCFE's early attempt to create the University Center in Strasbourg is confirmed by three facts. First, there is no mention of the NCFE's attempt in the correspondence between Kultura and Burnham, which consists of very detailed and confidential letters, especially about the university project. Second, the NCFE's first documents on the FEUE (from August to October 1950 in the RFE/RL Corporate Records' collection at the HIA) do not mention at all the name of Kultura or its members.

Third, the Kultura's enthusiastic reaction, which produced the NCFE's interest in the university project in February and March 1951, makes it evident that Czapski and Giedroyc had not previously been contacted by the NCFE or met its officials regarding the university project. Burnham supposedly knew that the NCFE was developing an educational training program in autumn 1950. This may be the reason why he wrote enthusiastic letters to Czapski in October and December 1950. However, Burnham certainly was also not aware of the NCFE's first attempt toward the creation of the University Center in August 1950.

29 Portion of Introductory Statement to the Press by Joseph C. Grew, 1 June 1949, RFE/RL Corporate Records, Free Europe Committee, Inc. (FEC), box 188, folder 1, HIA.

30 Excerpt from letter from Edgar A. Mowrer to Frederic R. Dolbeare, 14 August 1950, RFE/RL Corporate Records, Free Europe University in Exile (FEUE), box 201 folder 1, HIA.

31 Hubert Ripka (1895–1958), politician, secretary of state in the Czechoslovakian government-in-exile in England. After WWII, he returned to Czechoslovakia and became minister of foreign trade but thanks to the diplomatic relations of his French wife, Noémi Ripka, he was exiled to France after the Communist seizure of power in Prague in February 1948.

32 Jules-Albert Jaeger to President René Hubert, Note, 11 August 1950, Rectorat de Strasbourg [Board of Education of Strasbourg], Vie universitaire [University Life], quotation 1161 W, box 43, Departmental Archives of Bas-Rhin Region (Strasbourg, France) (hereafter DABR).

33 Project Draft on Education of Young Eastern European Exiles, 30 August 1950, RFE/RL Corporate Records, FEUE, box 201, folder 1, HIA.

34 Czapski had argued for the inclusion of students behind the Iron Curtain so that the institution would have a counter-propaganda effect on Soviet propaganda and openly demonstrate the U.S.'s interest in Central and Eastern Europe.

35 The NCFE's project proposal, dated 30 August 1950, already stated that "preliminary investigation indicated that the University and the French Government are, in general, favorable to the idea".

36 Memorandum on conversation between Messrs. A. A. Berle, Jr., Edgar A. Mowrer, Spencer Phenix, Alan Valentine, and Richard Sears regarding an educational program for exile students, 22 September 1950, RFE/RL Corporate Records, FEUE, box 201 folder 1, HIA.

37 Ibid.

38 Ibid.

39 Ibid.

40 The Legal-Index Digest was to analyze and digest the laws promulgated in Central and Eastern European countries since 1945, sponsored jointly with the Library of Congress. The Danubian Inquiry, sponsored jointly by the Carnegie Foundation and New York University, was to keep the exile world and American public informed of conditions in those countries.

41 "The possibility that the exile of these leaders, many of whom are already well advanced in age, may be of long duration makes advisable some provision for the education and training of selected young exiles. The younger exiles are, for the most part, living in Western Europe. A project for the creation of an Eastern European Institute which could handle some 100 students, and which could be under the aegis of an established European university is presently under consideration by the NCFE. All indications point to the University of Strasbourg as being the most suitable choice." NCFE Policy Statement, 20 October 1950, RFE/RL Corporate Records, FEC, box 191, folder 5, HIA.

42 A NCFE Training - Education Program in Europe, 10 November 1950, RFE/RL Corporate Records, FEUE, box 201, folder 1, HIA.

43 Ibid.
44 Royall Tyler to Dewitt C. Poole, 26 December 1950, Ibid.
45 See the previously quoted letter from Burnham to Czapski of 27 February 1951, Giedroyc – Burnham Correspondence (1948–1952), ILK.
46 This possibility seemed the best solution for many reasons: "A 'fondation' would require the transfer to France and immobilization here of a considerable capital sum, and the French authorities would insist upon French citizens largely participating in, if not controlling, its administration ... [a legal entity under New York State law and a branch in Paris] would keep the legal situation in France to the simplest and easiest. It would be desirable to obtain as soon as possible from the Ministry of Interior a declaration of 'utilité publique'; but even before that the Chase Bank would no doubt be ready to effect all needed financial operations. No question of taxation would arise beyond the ordinary social security taxes having to do with the staff. The conduct of business would remain in American hands to full extent or any extent desired." Poole to C.D. Jackson, 22 March 1951, RFE/RL Corporate Records, FEUE, box 201, folder 2, HIA.
47 "The usefulness of the Coudert proposal was confirmed when we talked with M. Joxe at the Quai d'Orsay. Czapski had disturbed Joxe by proposing the establishment of a university-in-exile in France. Joxe was emphatic in rejecting this idea as inadmissible 'juridiquement', if not politically and psychologically. He was relieved and apparently satisfied when we outlined the Coudert plan as that now tentatively in mind." Ibid.
48 Note of Conference between Dewitt C. Poole, Royall Tyler and Pierre Donzelot, 4 April 1951, RFE/RL Corporate Records, FEUE, box 201, folder 3, HIA.
49 Ibid.
50 Each faculty had to choose from among the following possibilities: 1) if it supported the creation of one center at the University of Strasbourg, 2) if the University of Strasbourg should participate at the work of this center, 3) if undergraduate students would follow studies in Strasbourg while graduate students would be gathered in different European universities and the University of Strasbourg would take responsibility for national seminars, or 4) the faculty rejects the proposal.
51 Poole to Berle, 20 April 1951, RFE/RL Corporate Records, FEUE, box 201, folder 3, HIA.
52 Donzelot informed Tyler on 28 April 1951 that he received a letter from Rector Hubert on 25 April concerning the preliminary opinion of the faculties of the University of Strasbourg. They agreed with the creation of the future institution, which would run autonomously and would be completely independent from the French university; while regular university studies would be radically separated from the institution's student program.
53 FEUE Interim Report as of 6 August 1951, Appendix A: Resolution of the Conseil de l'Université de Strasbourg adopted 21 May 1951, RFE/RL Corporate Records, FEUE, box 203 folder 7, HIA.
54 Ibid.
55 Ibid.
56 Ibid.
57 Ibid.
58 C.D. Jackson to Tyler, 30 May 1951, RFE/RL Corporate Records, FEUE, box 201, folder 4, HIA.
59 Poole to Levering Tyson, June 16 1951, RFE/RL Corporate Records, FEUE, box 201, folder 5, HIA.
60 Untitled and undated document [CCF University Committee's document written by Czapski], James Burnham Papers, Subject file, FEU, box 9, folder 2, HIA, copyright Stanford University.

61 Burnham to Czapski, 22 May 1951, Giedroyc - Burnham Correspondence (1948–1952), ILK.

62 "The essential goal of the University is not simply to furnish Radio Free Europe with a propaganda theme for countries behind the Iron Curtain, but the creation of a study and youth center where conditions for creative work in a cultural sense would exist and where the purpose would be not simply a detached study of the history of our countries, but also an attempt to draw from such studies a conception for the future capable of uniting, in a spirit neither nationalist nor Stalinist, but democratic, a student youth which would feel itself part of a European organism and which would have a vision of the world worth fighting for culturally and, if necessary, military." Untitled and undated document [CCF University Committee's document written by Czapski], James Burnham Papers, Subject file, FEU, box 9, folder 2, HIA, copyright Stanford University.

63 "The Congress of Cultural Freedom I find to the rather a pain the neck, but they're abroad and that's that. Joseph Czapski, who as a human being is precious, upset first the Quai d'Orsay and then the boys at Robertsau by his belligerent interpretations of our enterprise, so that Tyler and I had in both instances to do a good deal by way of mollification before we could put the proposition forward in our own more gentle and humanitarian terms. Now Czapski has announced to me – this befell a couple of days ago – that "the movement" (meaning the Congress of Cultural Freedom) wants him to go to NY to join Burnham as collaborator with us in creating the university in exile. ...There is nothing I can do by way of remedy at this end. I believe Burnham returns to Washington about April 26. A talk with him would see to be in order. If Czapski, God bless him, deserves a trip to the US, let it not at least be fanfared as part of the university in exile lying-in, for that will renew the apprehensions, which I am sure we've done no more than damper, lest France is to be made the base of a new loud-trumpeted anti-Muscovite campaign." Poole to Tyson, 21 April 1951, RFE/RL Corporate Records, FEUE, box 201, folder 3, HIA.

64 "I will bear in mind the interest felt by you over there, including Allen [Dulles], in finding suitable European organizations to sponsor us. For the moment, my mind is rather a blank on the subject, but something may occur to me later. Personally, I am rather inclined to feel that our position would be stronger if we were alone, without any sponsors." Tyler to Poole, 12 May 1951, RFE/RL Corporate Records, FEUE, box 201, folder 4, HIA.

65 "I have not run across a single one that has anything even approaching the prestige that NCFE has, so I would not be worried on this score. ... I always hate to see waste motion and duplication of expense. Besides, I believe that if something like this could be effected, our own position in the field at the moment is such that we would be out in front". Tyson to C.D. Jackson, 9 May 1951, Ibid.

66 Tyler to Poole, 24 May 1951, Ibid.

67 Ibid.

68 Communist ministers were dismissed by Prime Minister Paul Ramadier on 5 May 1947 because PCF deputies disagreed with the funding of the Indochina War and the government's social politics in France.

69 The electoral law on grouping of electoral lists was introduced on 7 May 1951 by the Third Force parties in order to reduce Communist and Gaullist representation at the National Assembly.

70 Summarizing the major ambiguity of the Fourth Republic: "A system of government based, like that of the Third Republic, on rapidly shifting alliances within a class of political nobles and election by proportional representation was inherently unstable. Governments with impermanent majorities were not best suited to dealing with the problems of reconstruction, the rapid expansion of the state's responsibilities, with colonial war, repeated financial

crises, or the social tension caused by unequal access to the rewards of economic growth. However in contrast with the Third Republic, when the state has appeared as the helpless spectator of economic and social change, the result was no longer stalemate. Economic and social forces, and in particular the internationalization of economic activity resulting from American predominance and the moves towards European integration, were too strong. Moreover guidance and continuity had been provided by an increasingly self-confident and assertive bureaucracy. In this respect, one of the regime's weakness, the disassociation between political and administrative and economic power, had facilitated reconstruction, the establishment of a welfare state, and inaugurated an unprecedented period of sustained economic growth and improvement in the standard of living. … Thus alongside the ill-advised efforts to hang on to empire, major moves had also been taken towards Franco-German reconciliation and greater European unity within the OEEC (1948), the Council of Europe and NATO (1949), the European Coal and Steel Community (1951) and finally with the signing of the Treaty of Rome in 1957." Roger Price, *A Conscience History of France* (Cambridge: Cambridge University Press, 1993) 318.

71 Irwin M. Wall wrote an excellent book on the American role in French diplomacy, economic reconstruction, military policy, politics and the reshaping of French society after WWII up to the Radical Socialist Pierre Mendès France's government in 1954, *The United States and the Making of Postwar France, 1945–1954* (Cambridge: Cambridge University Press, 1991). He argues in this book that it was not American pressure which intervened in French internal political life but, on the contrary, French and European fears led to the creation of the Atlantic military alliance. However, American influence in France, also tamed by the financial support of the Marshall Plan, became ubiquitous and intervened in unprecedented ways. In this book, Wall alludes to French President Vincent Auriol's visit to the U.S. and meeting with Truman in March 1951, making the following remark: "Auriol was an activist president with strong personal views, the Pleven government had just fallen, which served to accentuate Auriol's role as the guarantor of the continuity of French state, and he was accompanied by Foreign Minister Robert Schuman, who the Americans knew would remain in that post in any successor government." After describing Auriol and his wife, Wall also quotes the description of Schuman from Truman's Briefing Book: "Robert Schuman was austere, shy, devout, ascetic, 'saintly' and a mystic, but endowed with common sense; he remained a friend of the United States." Wall, *The United States and the Making of Postwar France*, 207.

72 See the previously quoted document: Memorandum on conversation between Messrs. A. A. Berle, Jr., Edgar A. Mowrer, Spencer Phenix, Alan Valentine, and Richard Sears regarding an educational program for exile students, 22 September 1950, RFE/RL Corporate Records, FEUE, box 201, folder 1, HIA.

73 Poole to Berle, 17 June 1951, RFE/RL Corporate Records, FEUE, box 201, folder 5, HIA.

74 Poole to C.D. Jackson, 2 July 1951, RFE/RL Corporate Records, FEUE, box 201, folder 6, HIA.

75 Levering Tyson to NCFE members, memorandum, 24 July 1951, Ibid.

76 Philippe Roger, *L'ennemi américain: Généalogie de l'antiaméricanisme français* [American Enemy: Genealogy of French Anti-Americanism] (Paris: Seuil, 2002) 427.

77 Poole to Berle, 23 May 1951, RFE/RL Corporate Records, FEUE, box 201, folder 4, HIA.

78 Ibid.

79 Article attached to a memorandum from C.A. Davila to C.D. Jackson on Communist Press in Romania, in reference to the projected Universities in Exile, 22 June 1951, RFE/RL Corporate Records, FEUE, box 201, folder 5, HIA.

80 "To organize an educational institution to be known as THE FREE EUROPE UNIVERSITY IN EXILE; to maintain this institution financially, to carry on its operations in the United States and in foreign countries; and to operate branch offices in foreign countries as needed – all to the end of providing suitable educational facilities for persons presently in exile from the countries of Central and Eastern Europe, and possibly other regions who, because of their non-citizen status in the countries of their sojourn, are unable to obtain adequate educational assistance and facilities; to solicit gifts and receive, hold and distribute monies; to employ suitable academic and administrative personnel; to award according to discretion scholarships, fellowships and academic grants-in-aid of all sorts; to purchase and publish books and papers for educational uses; to hire, purchase, construct or otherwise acquire necessary living and academic quarters; and generally to do here and abroad everything necessary and appropriate to the end in view." FEUE, INC.- Statement of purpose for incorporation in the State of New York, RFE/RL Corporate Records, FEUE, box 201, folder 2, HIA.

81 Poole to Allen Dulles, 14 May 1951, RFE/RL Corporate Records, FEUE, box 201, folder 4, HIA.

82 "Donzelot has offered us as Registrar and Executive Secretary of the Committee on Awards and Placement, a youngster (about 35), named Maurice Galy), with excellent personality, good experience, entrée through the needed doors, and undoubtedly one of the most promising young men of the National Education Ministry. One sniffs, of course, a Trojan horse, but why not? We have no secrets for Donzelot." Poole to Berle, 17 June 1951, RFE/RL Corporate Records, FEUE, box 201, folder 5, HIA.

83 C.D. Jackson to Tyler, 30 May 1951, RFE/RL Corporate Records, FEUE, box 201, folder 4, HIA.

84 Ibid.

85 Poole to Berle, 17 June 1951, RFE/RL Corporate Records, FEUE, box 201, folder 5, HIA.

86 Dewitt C. Poole, memorandum to the Executive Committee of FEUE, 3 October 1951, RFE/RL Corporate Records, FEUE, box 201, folder 9, HIA.

87 C.D. Jackson to Poole, 11 July 1951, RFE/RL Corporate Records, FEUE, box 201, folder 6, HIA.

88 The Free Europe University in Exile – Interim Report as of August 6, 1951: First Section, RFE/RL Corporate Records, FEUE, box 203, folder 7, HIA.

89 Free Europe University in Exile – Announcement for 1951–1952 (Preliminary edition), RFE/RL Corporate Records, FEUE, box 202, folder 3, HIA.

90 Interim Report of the Committee on Awards and Placements, 20 October 1951, RFE/RL Corporate Records, FEUE, box 201, folder 9, HIA.

91 Document from the Crusade for Freedom on the opening of the FEUE, RFE/RL Corporate Records, FEUE, box 203, folder 6, HIA.

92 Poole to Berle, 19 November 1951, RFE/RL Corporate Records, FEUE, box 201, folder 10, HIA.

93 Free Europe University in Exile – Announcement for 1951–1952 (Preliminary edition), RFE/RL Corporate Records, FEUE, box 202, folder 3, HIA.

94 Dewitt C. Poole, memorandum on the Free Europe University in Exile , 15 March 1952, Ibid.

95 "When the students arrived last fall, most of them had never seen any one of the others before, and they were mistrustful among themselves and uncertain of us. ... Emphasis should be given to the fact that the students are a very varied group, of ages ranging from 19 or 20 to over 30, from all sorts of social and family environments, and with backgrounds of conflict and dictatorship, of discontinued or disordered education, of escape and exile, and all the personal strain and stress that such a situation means. Hardly any

of the students, certainly few indeed, could have a natural youth. Most have lost homes and families, as well as countries. They are less formed in some ways, and more mature in other ways, than any ordinary set of students. Comparisons are sure to be wrong. Relations between them and with them are unprecedented, and the operation is unique." Dean Malcolm W. Davis, report to the President and the Chairman of the Board, FEUE on Progress and Prospects, 1951–1952, 27 October 1952, RFE/RL Corporate Records, FEUE, box 203, folder 8, HIA.

96 "Malcolm Davis and I have come to a clearer idea about the Central and Eastern European seminar. ... In short, there would be two classes of teachers under Malcolm's direction in the Central and Eastern European seminar: (1) a cohesive, full-time working group of tutorial rank, resident in Strasbourg and immediately at Malcolm's hand; (2) a list of more mature and distinguished lecturers; the latter no more than occasional visitors but chosen nevertheless in a discriminating and coherent fashion. The academic and political advantages seem to us obvious and hardly to need argument. An additional result would be to facilitate relations with the French. As you know, the French take education very seriously, and themselves also in that connection. Despite a general friendliness, some uncertainty of feeling inevitably persists toward an educational activity such as the Central and Eastern European seminar, which is to be carried on in France but not by the French; a sort of extra-territorial operation. While Malcolm and I are impelled to our present recommendations by what seems to us their inherent north, we take note of some incidental advantages. The proposed limitation of the full-time staff to younger men of no more than tutorial rank would, we believe, tend to assuage French uneasiness and jealousy; and the inclusion of a certain number of French intellectuals or public figures among the occasional lecturers (including professors from Strasbourg University) should have the same effect." Poole to Tyson, 26 October 1951, RFE/RL Corporate Records, FEUE, box 201, folder 9, HIA.

97 Ibid.

98 "This is the student material with which we are dealing – interested, intelligent in the main, of good character on the average, but frequently ill-informed and needing to be prepared for progressive study and realistic thinking. Conferences and general lectures on the ideals of liberty and the great objectives of federation or union would, it seems, be wasted largely. Most of the students do not know the differences between confederation, federation, and a centralized system. ... The study of their own region and their own countries can be the basis and background for such teaching to a group in which all except a few have known little but authority and its acceptance. They are anti-Communist and need no arguments about that because they have felt in their own lives the operation of the Soviet system, but they do need to learn the implications of freedom and its duties." Malcolm Davis to Executive Vice President and Chairman of the Board, FEUE, memorandum on Central Eastern European Seminar and Other Projects, 10 April 1952, RFE/RL Corporate Records, FEUE, box 202, folder 4, HIA.

99 Dean Malcolm W. Davis, report to the President and the Chairman of the Board, FEUE on Progress and Prospects, 1951–1952, 27 October 1952, RFE/RL Corporate Records, FEUE, box 203, folder 8, HIA.

100 Poole to Davis, 6 August 1951, RFE/RL Corporate Records, FEUE, box 201, folder 7, HIA.

101 Ibid.

102 Ibid.

103 Georges Straka to Tyson, 1 October 1953, Rectorat de Strasbourg [Board of Education of Strasbourg], Vie universitaire [University Life], quotation 1161 W, box 43, DABR.

104 Burnham to Czapski and Giedroyc, 23 April 1953, Giedroyc - Burnham Correspondence (1953–1959), ILK.

105 "The graduates are leaving the College and disperce all over the world – or some posts are searched for them: the College should not be a charity institution. I think that the graduates should be employed by such institutions as Free Europe or Voice of America in their technical or editorial staff, as well as in the other institutions dealing with the problems of Eastern Europe, giving them the possibility of making a success of their posts and events. ... The American staff (administration) of the College should be composed of dynamical personalities, politically educated and adherents to liberation. The personnel now is composed of old, weary men like Davis, neutralists like Fraser or French agents. The same is to be noticed in the line of the administration where emigrants are: there are people chosen by the French government (the tutor of the Czech group of students) or employed there by a pure chance (Poles) ex-diplomats in the worst meaning of this word, who do not understand the youth, studying in Robertsau, having nothing in common with them, without any possibility to understand the students, or kind-hearted nationalists, for whom 'federation' or 'United States' are nothing more than words." Giedroyc to Burnham, 2 May 1953, Giedroyc - Burnham Correspondence (1953–1959), ILK.

106 "When DeWitt Poole relinquished the Presidency of the University, he was convinced early, just as I was – for the University is part of the overall responsibility of our Division of the National Committee for a Free Europe, of which I am Director – that the administrative affairs of the Robertsau College and of FEUE should be placed in the hands of a President who would be resident in Europe, and who, possessed with basic qualifications to perform such a task, would be vested with full authority for the accomplishment of this mission. When I succeeded Poole as President, it was with this in view. My sojourn at the College last winter and spring was to survey general conditions as the second year was about to close, submit information to the Board as to what was needed in all areas of the College's activities for the future; and generally report, as intelligently and objectively as I could, what I found." Dr. Levering Tyson, address to the Inaugural Assembly at Robertsau, 22 October 1953, RFE/RL Corporate Records, FEUE, box 202, folder 7, HIA.

107 Katalin Kadar Lynn, *Tibor Eckhardt: His American Years 1941–1972* (New York: East European Monographs, 2007) 116.

108 John Pelényi, introductory speech, undated document, Rectorat de Strasbourg [Board of Education of Strasbourg], Vie universitaire [University Life], quotation 1161 W, box 43, DABR.

109 Pelényi to Tyson, memorandum on Summer Program, General courses given in French, 27 February 1954, RFE/RL Corporate Records, FEUE, box 202, folder 8, HIA.

110 Bernard Yarrow to Pelényi, 20 April 1954, Ibid.

111 "Attached for your consideration prior to the April 8 meeting of the Board of Trustees is a recent report received from Dr. Pelényi embodying his ideas and suggestions for the conduct of the 1954 Summer Program and an outline of the general courses planned. As you will note, the proposed program envisages the continuation of national courses." Tyson to the Board of Trustees of the FEUE, 9 March 1954, Ibid.

112 CEL item for 1954 Annual Report on FEC, 18 October 1954, Ibid.

113 Beyond two national tutors from the CEL, exile representatives were from various backgrounds, among others: the Estonian Karel Pusta, former minister in Paris; Edward Raczynski, former Polish ambassador to London and member of the Polish government in exile during WWII; and Ladislaus Szabó, former professor of literature in Hungary, at that time an employee of the BBC's Hungarian Section.

114 Levering Tyson, memorandum to the Board of Trustees of FEUE, 19 May 1954, RFE/RL Corporate Records, FEUE, box 202, folder 8, HIA.

[115] "3. The College – supported exclusively by American funds, was founded in France in 1951. It seems now appropriate, in the light of three years' experience, to examine in what ways its purpose can be further promoted. CEL supports only young men and women, who at the moment of their admission to the College have clearly expressed their intention to return to their homelands if and when the totalitarian regimes disappear. They are living in an atmosphere largely inspired by the fact of the presence of the Council of Europe in Strasbourg. They all pursue their studies at the University of Strasbourg. 4. The policy of the College was clearly stated by the President of FEUE when he assumed office in October 1953... . The above statement expresses that the spiritual and intellectual education — free of any element of political indoctrination — given to the students of FEUE/CEL aims at making them able to play some day a constructive role ('un rôle de cadres' in French text) in their respective countries. This goal is being aimed at in order to oppose the systematic destruction of the national cultures of Mid-Eastern Europe as practiced at present by the communist regimes. It is consequently advisable that the countries of asylum refrain from applying a policy of systematic assimilation vis-à-vis the students from FEUE/CEL, since their presence in their countries of origin will be highly desirable after liberation." Aide-Mémoire concerning the Free Europe University in Exile and the Collège de l'Europe libre; 18 May 1954, RFE/RL Corporate Records, FEUE, box 202, folder 8, HIA.

[116] Eugène L. Metz, Report on Admissions and Placement for the month of November, 1953, 8 December 1953, RFE/RL Corporate Records, FEUE, box 202 folder 7, HIA.

[117] Ibid.

[118] The name of the National Committee of a Free Europe, Inc. (NCFE) was changed to Free Europe Committee, Inc. (FEC) on 5 March 1954.

[119] Free Europe College – Statement by Dr. Tyson, 29 August 1954, RFE/RL Corporate Records, FEC, box 191, folder 5, HIA.

[120] Burnham to Giedroyc, 8 September 1954, Giedroyc - Burnham Correspondence (1953–1959), ILK.

[121] Burnham to Giedroyc, 19 October 1954, Ibid.

[122] For further reading on American foreign policy toward the Soviet bloc from the aftermath of WWII until 1956 and the Eisenhower administration's transition from a revolutionary strategy to an evolutionary strategy see: Gregory Mitrovich, *Undermining the Kremlin: America's strategy to subvert the Soviet bloc (1947–1956)*, (Ithaca: Cornell University Press, 2000).

[123] Burnham to Giedroyc, 19 October 1954, Giedroyc - Burnham Correspondence (1953–1959), ILK.

[124] Levering Tyson, memorandum on FEUE as FEC Personnel Training Agency, 19 July 1955, RFE/RL Corporate Records, FEUE, box 202, folder 9, HIA.

[125] "There is no point here in indicating how deviation from this original idea came about, but it is pretty clear that the major difficulties which have arisen in connection with the University's past operations are all traceable to determination on the part of the European operating staff at the outset to make of FEUE a strictly academic enterprise, paying no attention to the political warfare possibilities. ... In operations, all efforts were expended to facilitate the students' careers at the University of Strasbourg. The so-called seminars, originally designed as political warfare devices, were a farce. Until Dr. Pelényi's arrival, the College was nothing more than a boarding and rooming house for a group of exile students attending the University of Strasbourg. ...The point of all this is to indicate the training program possibilities now inherent in FEUE for all FEC activities. Cooperation with RFE in this direction has already been effected and can be expanded." Ibid.

[126] Burnham to Giedroyc, 31 January 1955, Giedroyc - Burnham Correspondence (1953–1959), ILK.

[127] Collège de l'Europe libre – Summer Program 1955, Documentation of Antoni Nowak-Przygodzki, box 6792, Polish Library of Paris (Paris, France) (hereafter: PLP).

[128] Ibid.

[129] The second part of the 1955 Summer Program was composed of two phases: "Techniques and Principles of the Communist movement compared with those of the Free World" and "Individual relation to the problem raised by Communist Problems in the Free World". In the first phase, former Communists presented the Communist movement (Collinet) and its infiltration among intellectuals—for instance, on other continents (André Ferrat, former Communist French professor); in Spain (Julian Gorkin, former Spanish Communist Party member, editor, and CCF member); and in England (Douglas Hyde, until 1949 assistant director of the *London Daily Worker*, associate editor of the *Catholic Herald*) – and in education (August Gallois, French specialist on youth problems and communist infiltration in educational circles) as well as organized labor (André Vassart, former Communist, writer and lecturer). These lectures were complemented by round-table discussions, with the participation of the lecturers themselves, on the topic "Why I became a Communist and later left the Party". The second part's second phase, conceived entirely by the CEL's Advanced Studies Group, consisted of discussions in small groups of students on two topics: the legal status of refugees in the West, lead by lecturers, and anticommunist actions through individual participation in existing organizations, followed by members of the Advanced Studies Group.

[130] Peter Beers to Pelényi on Relations of the Summer Program to the Overall Objectives of FEUE, 5 January 1956, Documentation of Antoni Nowak-Przygodzki, box 7083, PLP.

[131] Ibid.

[132] The FEC Policy, dated 12 November 1956, presented three operating divisions (Free Europe Exile Relations, Radio Free Europe, Free Europe Press), while the FEUE, Inc. was only mentioned briefly as the "Free Europe Committee cooperates with" for the selection "of exile students attending European universities and in their placement". Free Europe Committee Policy 1956, RFE/RL Corporate Records, FEC, box 191, folder 5, HIA.

[133] Tyson to Sidney Hook, 8 June 1956, Sidney Hook Papers, Correspondence, box 29, folder 4, HIA, copyright Stanford University.

[134] Report on the Free Europe University in Exile (Collège de l'Europe libre) at Strasbourg, France by Sidney Hook; Sidney Hook Papers, Subject file, FEUE (1955–1958), box 133 folder 4, HIA, copyright Stanford University.

[135] Ibid.

[136] Ibid.

[137] Ibid.

[138] Minutes of special meeting of the Executive Committee of the Board of Trustees of the FEUE, 22 May 1958, RFE/RL Corporate Records, FEUE, box 202, folder 9, HIA.

[139] Stetson S. Holmes to J.R. Reid, 4 February 1959, Ibid.

[140] Press Release, 22 May 1958, RFE/RL Corporate Records, FEUE, box 203, folder 6, HIA.

Select Bibliography

Unpublished source material

Hoover Institution Archives, Stanford (U.S.)
RFE/RL Corporate Records
James Burnham Papers
Sidney Hook Papers
Institut Littéraire Kultura, Maisons-Laffitte (France)
Jerzy Giedroyc – James Burnham Correspondence (1948–1952, 1953–1959)
Miscellaneous documents
Departmental Archives of Bas-Rhin Region, Strasbourg (France)
Rectorat de Strasbourg [Board of Education of Strasbourg], Vie universitaire [University Life]
Polish Library of Paris, Paris (France)
Documentation of Antoni Nowak-Przygodzki

Published material

Article

Roger Kimball, "The power of James Burnham", *The New Criterion*, 21 (September 2002) 4

Web site

Origins of the CCF on the webpage of the CIA's Center for the Study of Intelligence:
https://www.cia.gov/library/center-for-the-study-of-intelligence/csi-publications/csi-studies/studies/95unclass/Warner.html

Books

Pierre Grémion, *Intelligence de l'anticommunisme: Le Congrès pour la liberté de la culture à Paris 1950–1975* [Intelligence of Anti-Communism: Congress for Cultural Freedom in Paris 1950–1975] (Paris: Fayard, 1995)

Katalin Kadar Lynn, *Tibor Eckhardt: His American Years 1941–1972* (New York: East European Monographs, 2007)

Roger Price, *A Conscience History of France* (Cambridge: Cambridge University Press, 1993)

Philippe Roger, *L'ennemi américain: Généalogie de l'antiaméricanisme français* [American Enemy: Genealogy of French Anti-Americanism] (Paris: Seuil, 2002)

Frances Stonor Saunders, *Who Paid the Piper?: CIA and the Cultural Cold War* (London: Granta, 1999)

Irwin M. Wall, *The United States and the Making of Postwar France, 1945–1954* (Cambridge: Cambridge University Press, 1991)

To read more

Gregory Mitrovich, *Undermining the Kremlin: America's strategy to subvert the Soviet bloc (1947–1956)*, (Ithaca: Cornell University Press, 2000)

XI

The Cold War Activities of the Hungarian National Sports Federation [1]

Toby C. Rider

We may never know the full extent of the Free Europe Committee's (FEC) activities during its nearly two decades in operation.[2] The history of Radio Free Europe is considerable enough on its own, not counting the range of other groups that were touched in some way by one of the CIA's most famous conduits. The men who established the FEC, and those that later administered it, were possessed by a profound purpose to defeat the Soviet Union by mobilizing whatever resources that could be put at their disposal. As part of a broad mandate of psychological warfare, supplying émigré organizations with financial and logistical assistance was not intended to be a mere sideshow in the Cold War. Exile organizations were provided with FEC funds so that they could give hope to people behind the Iron Curtain. Perhaps, over time, hope could be converted into change. When Abbott Washburn, deputy director of the U.S. Information Agency from 1953 to 1961, discussed his own role with the Committee in 1951, he made this objective clear: "[The Soviet Union's] purpose is to convince the prisoner peoples that it is hopeless to resist. They want to create a vacuum of despair. Into this vacuum we must shine a new light of hope – a new vista of a very different future." Washburn continued, "Today the concept of self-determination … still holds tremendous power. The people behind the Iron Curtain long for a chance to control their own destiny, their own culture, their own security." "The American ideal has within it the dynamism to undermine the Soviet empire," he concluded, "provided we can get it across and show that we mean it. Our success in this job may well determine whether we can, indeed, win World War III without fighting it."[3]

The FEC indeed tried to "shine a light" into Eastern Europe, through various means and missions, some of which involved using sport. This approach took several forms. For one, Radio Free Europe filled hours of its programming with sports coverage which trumpeted the achievements of East European athletes in exile and drew attention to the "poor sportsmanship" of Soviet competitors.[4] The same theme inspired articles in the FEC publication *News From Behind the Iron Curtain*. One column in the magazine observed, "To the Communists, sports are a grim and serious business. They form an integral part of the regimented Communist State System and are assigned a specific function in the Communist propaganda machine."[5] At one stage or another, the FEC also provided meager funds to a small number of exiled sport groups in Europe. However, the focal point of sport-related propaganda which received FEC backing was on initiatives orchestrated, in most instances, with the Hungarian National Sports Federation (HNSF), a refugee group based in New York. For over a dozen years the HNSF functioned as an opposition in exile to communism in Hungary and, furthermore, to communism in general. By helping Hungarian athletes to escape from communism, and even participate in competitions against the regime they had fled, the HNSF made its own small contribution to the Cold War objectives of Washburn and his colleagues. This chapter will provide an outline of the HNSF's main aims and explore some of the ways in which the group sought to fulfill them.

Sport in Hungary

It is a notoriously hard business to accurately pinpoint when sport took a "modern" form. Although we can roughly trace the process back to the Renaissance, certainly by the eighteenth century it is possible to discern the emergence of sports which were characterized by codified rules, professionalism, commercialization and rational bureaucratic organization. Moreover, increasing levels of urbanization and industrialization produced large markets for spectator sports, as opposed to the local and unruly contests so evident in Feudal society. It is, at least, rather less disputable that a key ideological and organizational thrust was applied to the evolution of sport by the children who attended the elite Public Schools of England throughout the middle portion of the nineteenth century, especially with regard to soccer and rugby. At any rate, if England is the cradle of modern sport, it did not keep them to itself. Wherever the British set foot, their sports tended to follow them.

The physical culture of Britain became the source of much admiration from abroad, and several aristocrats in Hungary were among the admirers. While Hungary's sporting culture took its cues from several European nations – for instance, fencing was encouraged in schools run by French and Italian masters – it was for English sport that the deepest respect was held. In particular, a small group of Hungarian aristocrats attempted to take the sports of England and plant the seeds for their growth in Hungary as a way of improving the general fitness and character of the national population.[6] Count Miksa Esterházy, for example, desired to "raise muscularity to a national religion", for, he argued, the "'Hungarian belly' is a truly national 'specialty.'"[7] Wealthy social elites put time and personal resources into the establishment of sporting facilities, clubs, events and organizations to stimulate wider interest in the benefits of physical activity to the mind as well as the body. Under the guidance of Esterházy, the Magyar Athletikai Club was founded in 1874 so as to form a nucleus for the spread of athletics across the country, and before long the urge to participate in a range of sports was evident up and down the class spectrum. "Fashionable" sports included cycling, weightlifting, fencing, swimming, wrestling and gymnastics. Toward the end of the nineteenth century, both water polo and soccer reached Hungary from English shores, and both sports would become a national obsession, particularly the latter. The formation of the Hungarian Football Association in 1901 ensured that soccer was given direction on a national scale. As such, foreign influence and the patronage of the upper classes were decisive contributors to the rise of Hungary's sporting culture, which, by the close of the nineteenth century, was firmly established.[8]

This was representative of a broader phenomenon. At the dawn of the twentieth century, modern sport had moved far beyond the confines of any one country or continent. Governing bodies for individual sports were followed by national and then international organizations.[9] By the 1930s, argues Barbara Keys, international sport was "governed by distinctive laws and practices, linked by its own repertoire of invented symbols and traditions, referring to a common past and heroes." Sporting festivals such as the soccer World Cup and the Olympic Games were transformed into global and commercial mega events, where competition between athletes wearing the uniforms of their country was interpreted as a measure of national strength. As a site where victory or defeat could be universally understood and athletic performance celebrated, modern sport, in this sense, became a perfect venue for governments to promote their way of life to the world.[10]

Hungarian sports administrators were not oblivious to these developments. Some were at the center of them. For instance, Count Csáky, Alexander Hegedüs, Count László Hoyos and Ferenc Kemény attended a congress at the Sorbonne in 1894 which determined the establishment of the International Olympic Committee (IOC). The congress was organized by Baron Pierre de Coubertin, a French aristocrat who nurtured a vision of gathering the very best athletes in the world to compete in a spirit of peaceful "internationalism." As a result of the baron's work, the ancient Olympic Games were revived in their modern form. Coubertin and Kemény were firm friends; both undertook their studies in Paris and it was there that they met and discussed the need for pedagogical reform in the French educational system. They also agreed on the importance of physical education. Kemény not only attended the Sorbonne congress but was also a founding member of the International Olympic Committee. A year later he formed the Hungarian Olympic Committee (1895) and, in 1896, played a major role in ensuring that Hungarian athletes were among the competitors at the first modern Olympic Games in Athens.[11] Coubertin was fond of his links to Hungary and wrote in 1911:

"…I should like to pay tribute to Hungary for having, right from the start, shown herself to be particularly understanding of the spirit of Olympism and for having remained one of its most loyal adherents right up to the present day."[12] Hungary's association with the Olympics became far more than administrative. Although facilities, funding and training techniques were often lacking, Hungary managed to make its mark on the Olympic stage. Prior to World War II, Hungarian athletes won numerous titles in swimming, boxing, wrestling and gymnastics. In fencing they were often supreme, dominating the sabre contest for individual and team events.[13]

Although the sporting infrastructure of Hungary was greatly hampered by the destruction from World War II, sport was still, nonetheless, an important part of the national culture and a passion of the people. Soon, however, the organization of sport in Hungary was to change. By the end of the 1940s, the Soviet Union had tightened its hold on Eastern Europe. The U.S. government's effort to win favor in Europe through the Truman doctrine and the Marshall Plan was combated by Stalin with the creation of the Cominform. The actions of Tito in Yugoslavia served to quicken the process of Stalinization throughout Eastern Europe in an increasingly brutal manner. There would be no national road to communism or independent ideological doctrine in the Soviet satellites; they were forced to toe the Communist Party line, a line which inevitably emanated from the Kremlin.[14]

In the field of sport, too, the Soviet system provided a blueprint for replication. At home, sport contributed to the ideological education of the population, especially the youth, while keeping the people fit and healthy for production or war. Abroad, the very best athletes the system could produce served to sell communism as a better way of life.[15] Sport was a tool at Stalin's disposal and strictly under state control. A Communist Party resolution from 1948 declared that government sports committees were "to spread sport to every corner of the land, to raise the level of skill and, on that basis, to help Soviet athletes win world supremacy in major sports in the immediate future."[16] Bulgarian sports officials journeyed to Moscow as early as 1945 for education in what would become their country's centrally organized and state-directed sport structure. In 1949, the Polish government formed the General Committee for Physical Culture, and soon after, all non-communist sports clubs and federations were brought under the autonomy of this apparatus. Similar developments occurred throughout Eastern Europe in the late 1940s and early 1950s.[17]

For decades following the Russian Revolution, the Soviet Union ignored "bourgeois" sports festivals and organizations. This policy was rescinded after 1945, and the USSR began to join international sports federations and to compete on a regular basis against teams from outside the communist bloc. International sport, when it saw sportsmen from the East competing against sportsmen from the West, had an added political flavor in the post-war years. Commenting on the Moscow Dynamo tour of Britain in 1945, George Orwell famously wrote, "Serious sport has nothing to do with fair play… in other words it is war minus the shooting."[18] The Olympic Games, like so many other events, provided yet another space for the reproduction of ideological differences; and athletes from either side of the Iron Curtain competed for more than just the personal honor of a gold medal. A sporting triumph became, in essence, the demonstration of political superiority. The Free Europe Committee recognized this state of affairs. An FEC planning report argued that athletic victories were part of the Soviet Union's "ceaseless assault on the morale of the free world as they push toward their goal of total world domination."[19] Psychological warfare experts in the U.S. government became preoccupied by the possible ramifications of a U.S. defeat by the Soviet Union on the Olympic stage, fearing the impact it could have on American global prestige. Congress even considered state funding for the U.S. Olympic team in order to strengthen its chances of finishing first in the unofficial medal count.[20] Orwell's words were far from just hyperbole.

The transformation of sport in Hungary was quickly apparent to the outside world. When the Hungarian national soccer team demolished England in 1953 and 1954, the British Foreign Office was in little doubt that the Hungarian government was using both victories for political propaganda.[21] Labouchere, the British Minister in Budapest, argued that, "Until we can win or at least hold our own in such contests it would be better to avoid arranging them with countries such as the Satellites whose propaganda made largely at the expense of our own prestige it cannot be our policy to further."[22] The media in Holland was quick to denounce a potential meeting between swimmers from the Royal Dutch Swimming League and participants from Hungary. One editorial charged that Hungarian teams "are not composed on purely sportsmanlike considerations."[23] In a similar fashion, the American legation in Budapest reported that "the [Hungarian] state is using sports teams and their participation in international contests as a medium of propaganda for the Communist regime."[24]

The communist sport model may well have made bold promises of "sport for all" but it did not always conform to "Western" sporting ideals. In truth, long before the Cold War era even began, most nations in the East and West considered sporting victories to be a symbol of national vitality, and state funding was hardly a rarity. Still, the doyens of international athletics were ardently against this. The IOC, for one, was committed to the complete separation of politics from sport and abhorred the payment of athletes, whether it came from commercial sponsors or a government. The Soviet Union and other East European countries were in clear violation of these rules. The IOC was aware of this. The organization's vice-president, Avery Brundage, wrote in 1950: "It is impossible, therefore, to find a [National Olympic Committee] in any Communist country that is free and not under complete state control."[25]

Of course, it would be too much to claim that the Soviet sport model was accepted without qualms in Eastern Europe. Indeed, American Embassies behind the Iron Curtain were always keen to inform the U.S. State Department of instances when satellite athletes, teams, or spectators showed dissent toward the USSR. During sporting events, the Hungarian public sometimes heckled Soviet competitors and celebrated their errors.[26] As such, sport was used as a further avenue to resist the dominant Soviet influence over Hungary. And while athletes in Eastern Europe could benefit from a higher standard of living than the average citizen, they were also privy to opportunities to strike back at the communist regime. Crucially, the best athletes in Hungary could travel abroad for international competition, which, George Eisen points out, gave them a perfect opportunity to "choose freedom."[27]

The Hungarian National Sports Federation

Sport has long been a part of the American immigrant experience, performing a complicated role of "uniting, integrating and socializing" newcomers into mainstream American society.[28] For those who fled to America after a communist takeover in their respective countries, it was not enough simply to adjust to the different surroundings. A great many of those who arrived at America's gates had terrible tales of life under communism and a profound desire to overthrow it. To convey this sentiment, a vast array of organizations, federations and congresses were formed to express the wishes of certain ethnic minorities and, amongst other goals, to retain ethnic and cultural identity.[29] For some of these ethnic groups, sport became an instrument for political resistance, a way of attacking and undermining a communist regime. In 1956, a Ukrainian sports organization based in Washington D.C. called for the removal of the USSR from the Olympic Movement for its "subversive system of genocide, murder, bloodshed, force and violation of human rights."[30] Needless to say, sport functions as far more than simple diversion, it can be used "to make a political statement about events not directly related to sport."[31]

The Hungarian National Sports Federation was formed in December 1949, under the auspices of the Hungarian National Council (HNC). The aim of the Federation was very straightforward: "deal the greatest possible blows whenever and wherever possible to the communists in the field of sports."[32] This project thus contributed to a broader general mission: "Our Federation is in the service of anti-communist propaganda and our main purpose is to gain the free, democratic world for the fight against communism."[33] The HNSF tried to fulfill these aims in two main ways. First, it facilitated the defection of athletes from Hungary, or aided those that had defected to start a new life on "free soil." Second, the HNSF helped exiled athletes to continue their sporting careers and compete in local, national and international competitions. This last objective required constant lobbying, as some international sports bodies such as the International Olympic Committee refused to allow stateless athletes to enter their events.

The HNSF's prime objectives were simultaneously pursued in a number of ways and not for financial gain. The individuals involved in the Federation were dedicated anti-communists and they hoped that their own small contribution would one day lead to the collapse of communism in Hungary. And while the HNSF had hundreds of members and numerous vocal supporters, two men in particular were synonymous with the group's activities. The first, Count Anthony Szápáry, was the president of the Sports Federation. His arrival in the United States, and his desire for a free Hungary, were based upon some almost catastrophic experiences at the time of, and after, Hitler's attempt to master Europe. During the war he served as an officer in the Hungarian Red Cross and helped to aid the Polish refugees who swarmed into Hungary. He was arrested by the Germans in 1944, imprisoned in the Mauthausen concentration camp, and "condemned to die." To his considerable good fortune, an intervention by the king of Sweden saved his life. He arrived in the U.S. in 1948, found employment at the Chesapeake & Ohio Railroad, and later married the granddaughter of Cornelius Vanderbilt, a descendant of the great Commodore.[34] Szápáry possessed a sound knowledge of international sport and was familiar with the training methods in the Soviet Union and its "imprisoned countries." He was always keen to compare the difference in ideology between sport in the East and West, with the former always taking the brunt of his criticism: "In these countries competitors and their performances are used for political propaganda, athletes are forced to make political statements, to sign political petitions and to solicit political funds."[35] Szápáry provided the HNSF with a sober and measured leadership; his correspondence with international sports officials was always thoughtful and considered. His letters were filled with passion but also with reason. Indeed, at times his arguments for the inclusion of exiled athletes into international competition were so convincing that they could not be refuted other than through tried and tested diplomatic ramblings on the part of the recipients.

Dr. George Telegdy approached his work in an entirely different way. Telegdy was associated with the HNSF from its early days but gradually became the driving force in the organization. Born in Hungary in 1921, Telegdy graduated from the University of Budapest with a doctorate in political science. His professional career was spent in the Budapest city administration where, for a time, he was the personal secretary to the city's mayor. In 1948, he escaped from Hungary and eventually made his way to America. Telegdy enjoyed a prominent reputation in Hungarian sporting circles. He was an outstanding fencer during his time at university, and later became a member of the Hungarian Fencing Association and president of the Budapest University Athletic Club.[36] He was characterized by an often misguided passion. This endeared him to some; not so to others. One Free Europe Committee employee described him as a "megalomaniac," prone to "exaggeration of his own importance."[37] Szápáry was told about the "incompetence" of his colleague, but the count looked past this. He appreciated Telegdy's "energy" and "dynamic personality," not to mention his "extraordinary ideas." When Telegdy set foot in America, Szápáry once recalled, "he continued his vocation, rather than his job ... and that was fighting against communism."[38]

Archival sources suggest that the leaders of the HNSF were highly proactive. On at least one occasion, Telegdy and Szápáry even requested the support of Fulgencio Batista, the president of Cuba.[39] After all, the HNSF may have been fortified with drive and ambition but it could not achieve its goals alone. Additional assistance came from the Hungarian National Council and other organizations with ties to the Free Europe Committee. Nonetheless, the FEC was the main source of HNSF funds, and the Committee also worked in tandem with Szápáry and Telegdy on a range of operations. The FEC functioned as a big brother, sometimes encouraging the HNSF, sometimes reeling it in. This relationship also yielded another vital connection for the Federation when a very significant individual in the U.S. government's psychological warfare establishment took an interest in the group's activities.

Charles Douglas Jackson was the president of the FEC from 1951–1952 and later took a role as Special Assistant on Cold War Planning in the Eisenhower Administration. After graduating from Princeton, Jackson's early career was spent ascending through the ranks of Time Incorporated. He became a vice-president of the company and acted as a publisher for *Fortune* and, later, *Life* magazines. A highly creative and imaginative expert in the craft of psychological warfare, Jackson advocated a diverse range of methods to shatter Soviet control of Eastern Europe.[40] This included the use of sport. Jackson knew that athletes were prized possessions for communist regimes: "These are important people in the eyes of the world," he asserted, "particularly in the world behind the Iron Curtain."[41] Without question, the HNSF benefitted a great deal from Jackson's connections in the government and also from his belief that exiled athletes living and competing in America were potent weapons in psychological warfare.

In order to make an impact in international sport, the HNSF also required the relevant patronage of influential sports organizations. Over time they managed this. For instance, the HNSF had membership in, and support from, the Amateur Fencers League of America and the People-to-People Sports Committee. Telegdy also established correspondence with several key administrators. Daniel Ferries, the secretary-treasurer of the Amateur Athletic Union of United States, had immense authority in American sporting circles. Telegdy developed a cordial relationship with Ferris, attended AAU national meetings, and became acquainted with the machinery of the organization.[42] Further links were formed with members of the United States Olympic Committee (USOC), especially Lyman Bingham, the USOC's executive director. Telegdy once referred to Ferris and Bingham as "my good honorable friends."[43] This friendship perhaps reached its height when the HNSF and FEC arranged a fund raising evening for the U.S. Olympic team on the eve of the 1960 Rome Summer Games. As Szápáry put it, even though exiled athletes could not represent the United States in Rome, they could at least help to make sure that an American team was present in Italy.[44]

Before the group had even invested in its own official stationary, Szápáry initiated correspondence with the most powerful sports administrator in America, and possibly the world. Avery Brundage had, at one stage, been president of the AAU and the USOC, and in 1952 he was elected president of the International Olympic Committee. The count began writing to Brundage in 1950 and continued to do so for the next dozen years. Due to his position in the IOC, Brundage was accustomed to socializing with European aristocrats, and he treated Szápáry with the utmost respect, responding to every letter sent to him, even though his news was normally not what the count wished to hear. Nevertheless, if the HNSF wanted exiled athletes in the Olympics, then Brundage had to be courted. Thus, by the end of the 1950s the HNSF had become acquainted with an array of sports organizations.

In addition to its base in New York, the HNSF had thirty-one affiliated sports clubs worldwide, in locations such as Brussels, Buenos Aires, London, Paris, Rome and Salzburg. It claimed to have representatives in 23 countries, and it published sport newspapers in Canada and Argentina. In 1958 the Federation was incorporated.[45] By the end of the 1950s, the FEC was providing an office and regular funding for the group. However, it is unclear in the records whether Szápáry knew about the origin of the FEC's financial support. That said, he was a well-respected member of the Hungarian exile community and familiar with other Hungarian groups that received money from the FEC. As such, it is perhaps worth considering the opinion of former FEC employee John Foster Leich: "The exiles without exception assumed that government funds were involved, and were glad of this evidence of United States interest in their cause."[46]

It is hard to be precise about the total amounts the FEC provided the Federation over the years. On multiple occasions it is indicated that the FEC gave the HNSF funding from the outset. A confidential budget review for fiscal year 1959–1960 indicates that the HNSF received $18,486 (the equivalent of approximately $140,000 in 2012) for its program, and there is every reason to believe that it was given an allowance before that.[47] It does appear, however, that the funding subsided in 1960 and was cancelled in 1962. In return for its investment, the FEC gained access to the rich propaganda potential of sport.

Defection and Resettlement

The HNSF took risks to achieve rewards. Aiding an athlete to defect following a sporting competition was one thing, making sure that they did not return to Hungary was quite another. Szápáry and his colleagues were convinced that defecting athletes inflicted a blow to the communist regime and offered hope to the people of Hungary that a more favorable existence could be found beyond the Iron Curtain:

> Assistance given to the defecting Hungarian athletes and the activities of the HNSF will seriously damage the communist regime's prestige, and on the other hand it would be a gesture greatly appreciated by the Hungarian nation, to see that the greatest democracy in the world has not failed to help those who have chosen freedom. The Hungarian regime would again lose an effective propaganda weapon, the cream of the nation in sport, who in turn would be a gain for the West.[48]

In 1956, the HNSF instigated its most ambitious project. The scheme would never have succeeded without a rather notable collaborator, C.D. Jackson's employer, Time Inc. During the early Cold War years, an extremely close relationship was developed between the CIA and Time Inc., a company run by anti-communist crusader Henry Luce. Spurred on by religious zeal and a deep confidence in America's capacity to lead the world, Luce pitted *Time* magazine against communism in a "private war."[49] Luce, a founding member of the Free Europe Committee, was well connected in covert circles, and the presence of Jackson at *Time* meant that Luce had a direct contact to the government's psychological warfare machinery.[50] The magazine provided "cover" for CIA staff and assisted in various Agency projects. Taking all this into account, Hugh Wilford has commented that "it was difficult to tell precisely where the Luce empire's overseas intelligence network ended and the CIA's began."[51]

In 1954, Time Inc. created *Sports Illustrated* (*SI*), a magazine which quickly assumed a cooperating role in some of Jackson's plans to use sport as a propaganda weapon in the Cold War.[52] The main contribution of *SI* in this regard came in 1956, when the magazine organized the defection of 38 Eastern European Athletes, coaches, and sports administrators after the Melbourne Summer Olympics. At least, this is how *SI* told the story to its readers. In fact, the idea for the Melbourne defection came from the HNSF and was driven by the events of the Hungarian Revolution.[53]

Indeed, both the Hungarian Revolution and the Suez Crisis cast a shadow over the 1956 Olympics. While some countries debated whether or not to send a team to the Summer Games due to the "world situation," a decision also had to be made by the Hungarian Olympic Committee. Some athletes on the Hungarian Olympic team fought in the revolution, marched in protest against the Soviet Union, and wielded machine guns against Soviet troops.[54] There were doubts that they could get to Australia at all. Only when the IOC intervened did the Hungarian Olympic team manage to secure safe passage to Melbourne.[55] The Hungarian Olympic Committee sent a cable to the Olympic Organizing Committee to confirm that its athletes were traveling to Australia, albeit one week later than originally planned. The understated message blamed "unforeseen circumstances."[56]

These developments were carefully monitored by the Hungarian National Sports Federation. Just under two weeks before the Melbourne Games were due to begin, Szápáry entertained Whitney Tower (a relative of Szápáry's wife, Sylvia) at his home in Pound Ridge, New York. Szápáry had just returned from Vienna, where he had been trying to organize relief for Hungarians in the wake of the revolution. The count had contacted Tower for a meeting, primarily because Tower was the associate editor of *Sports Illustrated*. Szápáry inquired whether *SI* and *Time Inc.* could assist in the defection of Hungarian Olympic athletes, many of whom had decided not to return home upon the conclusion of the Games in Melbourne.[57] Tower agreed to run the proposal by the *SI* hierarchy, and his memorandum on the subject soon landed on Jackson's desk. Within days, Tower wrote to Szápáry that "things definitely look promising" and that "Jackson is at the moment probing deeper into the matter in Washington."[58] A mere plan soon became a reality. Telegdy, who enjoyed naming HNSF projects, called this one Operation Griffin.

Shortly after Tower's conference with Szápáry, *SI* reporters in Melbourne were made aware of Operation Griffin, and they were soon joined in Australia by Telegdy. Through contacts in the Argentine and Italian Olympic teams, word of Telegdy's presence in Melbourne was conveyed to Hungarian athletes. Friends in the city found him private accommodation in North Brighton, and, wrote Telegdy, "... this became a second home for Hungarian Olympians, whom we welcomed at all hours of the day or night."[59] Operation Griffin was the most elaborate and publicized project in which the HNSF was involved, and it was only able to succeed due to the financial and logistical contribution of *SI*, which oversaw the entire endeavor. Telegdy provided guidance for the defectors and offered them reassurances about settling in America. When the athletes managed to elude the state security officers that watched over the Hungarian team, *Sports Illustrated* took responsibility for their welfare. Jackson was able to use his "influence" within the U.S. government so that immigration laws were bent to accommodate the defectors. He even convinced Pan American Airways to fly the athletes to the United States at no cost. Considering the time frame within which the defection was conceived and then executed, the mission was a resounding success, with the athletes landing in San Francisco on Christmas Eve. All told, thirty-four Hungarians and four Romanians stepped off the Pan American flight arranged by Jackson. They included five fencers, three of whom were part of the gold medal winning sabre team, five swimmers, two divers, two from track and field, a canoeist and a rowing coxswain. There were four gymnasts, two of whom, Andrea Bodó and Margit Korondi, had taken gold in the team exercise on apparatus. Five members of the gold medal winning water polo team were part of the group, along with a total of six coaches, one of whom was the famed Mihály Iglói, the mentor of another defector, László Tábori.[60] "Fleeing from Red oppression," commented the *Los Angeles Times*, the athletes "arrived here ... to start a new life in a land of freedom."[61]

In the midst of the defection, Telegdy had named the group of athletes the Hungarian National Olympic Team. This group became the focus of HNSF activities in the ensuing years, and due to the worldwide attention which the defection received, the FEC rewarded the Federation with higher levels of funding. Still, the HNSF did not take sole responsibility for the athletes. Once again, decisive contributions came from *Sports Illustrated* and Jackson. Telegdy named this next phase Operation Eagle.

Within weeks of landing in America, *SI* paraded the team around the country in a nationwide "Freedom Tour." The athletes were presented as symbols of "freedom," both in terms of their choice to flee from communism and as living proof that the people of Hungary wished to be released from Soviet domination. The Hungarian and Romanian athletes left New York on 10 January to start the six week tour. They were carried from "coast-to-coast," staging ninety-five performances at fifty-nine different locations. Every time the athletes competed, it "dramatized" their story. In a random assessment of news outlets, the *Sports Illustrated* team found nearly 800 references to the tour in forty-eight states, while movie and television newsreels across the country showed the athletes arriving in San Francisco and departing for the tour. Some of the athletes gave interviews on radio and television, including an appearance on the Ed Sullivan Show.[62]

For the Melbourne defection to strike the right note, the athletes had to appear to have made the transition to life in America in the smoothest manner possible. This fell in line with an overall propaganda strategy devised by the U.S. government, which was itself trying to ease a further 38,000 Hungarian refugees into American society in the wake of the revolution. By April 1957, *Sports Illustrated*, Jackson, and the HNSF had placed all of the athletes in employment or higher education. For example, the fencer, Jenő Hámori, secured a job and an apartment in Philadelphia; the swimming coach, János Gergely, chose to settle in California; Mártha Nagy, a gymnast, was studying at the University of Colorado; the diving coach, Bálint Papp, accepted a job offer in Florida; and Gábor Nagy, the Romanian water polo player, was given a scholarship at the University of Southern California.[63]

Soon after the conclusion of the Freedom Tour, *Sports Illustrated* ceased to provide financial assistance to the athletes because all were either working or in educational institutions. The HNSF maintained its interest in the Hungarian National Olympic Team and worked on the implementation of a "re-defection program." One strategy involved looking after the dependents of the exiles still living in Hungary by sending them goods and medicines only available in the United States. Over fifty packages were sent on four occasions to family members in Hungary, and the HNSF received word that they "meant a great deal" to the dependents.[64] However, not all of the refugees adapted to their new life in America. Zoltán Török, the rowing coach, learned that his mother was deeply ill and flew home. The swimmer, László Magyar, and two of the water polo players, László Jeney and György Kárpáti, all "re-defected." Others talked of doing the same thing.[65] Coupled with personal and unforeseen dilemmas, Szápáry underscored that the communist regime was "desperately" trying to entice athletes back to Hungary.[66] Telegdy even claimed that due to his prompting, a separate branch of the Federal Bureau of Investigation was "engaged in supervising the affairs of the Olympic athletes and of other sportsmen" in order to prevent the communist regime from "luring" the athletes home.[67]

Over 200,000 people fled Hungary as a result of the 1956 revolution. The majority made their way by foot across Hungary's poorly guarded border with Austria.[68] The Eisenhower administration relaxed its hitherto strict immigration procedure in order to allow for a large influx of refugees. Before escapees could move from Vienna to the United States, they had first to complete an array of tasks. Amid the list of requirements, each person had to be interviewed and pass through health and security checks. Agencies staffed by volunteers matched refugees with sponsors who, in turn, helped them find a job and somewhere to live. When the refugees landed in America, they where further government checks and bureaucratic measures followed.[69]

Many athletes were among the refugees who came to America after the revolution. The HNSF sought to reach as many of these individuals as it could and, in January 1957, established an office at camp Kilmer.

By April, around 240 refugee athletes reported at the HNSF facility. Telegdy and his colleagues found employment for over sixty individuals, and university scholarships for seven more. Other relief organizations placed a portion of the athletes elsewhere in the United States. The HNSF sent athletes Hungarian newspapers published in the "free world," textbooks, FEC bulletins and reading material that could inform them about American culture. In all these efforts, Telegdy claimed to have the "close" cooperation of Ferris at the AAU, the Amateur Fencers League of America, *Sports Illustrated*, the Free Europe Committee, the National Catholic Welfare Conference and the International Rescue Committee. Through this network of contacts, the HNSF tried to introduce athletes to the broader Hungarian community in America and integrate them into American society.[70]

Returning to Competition

Throughout the 1950s, the HNSF and the FEC constantly lobbied the International Olympic Committee to change its rules on the admission of stateless athletes. The *Olympic Charter* dictated that in order to compete at an Olympic Games, an athlete must be a member of a recognized National Olympic Committee. Even more importantly, if an athlete competed for one country, they were excluded from competing for another unless, in the case of a woman, she accepted a new nationality in marriage.[71] The rules posed a serious problem to the activities of Szápáry's group. An exiled athlete could compete at some non-Olympic events, but the sheer propaganda value of an exile competing on the world stage at an Olympic festival had clear potential.

In 1952, the HNSF and FEC formed an Olympic committee of exiles called the Union of Free Eastern European Sportsmen. The timing of this plan was perfect. The 1952 Summer Games in Helsinki were the first Olympics ever attended by the Soviet Union. While Stalin expected Soviet athletes to dominate in Finland, a group of exiles competing in defiance of communist control in Eastern Europe was sure to raise a few eyebrows in the Kremlin. The project gathered considerable momentum, with both Jackson and Szápáry contacting Avery Brundage on the matter with some degree of success. Although Brundage never promised that athletes representing the Union would be able to compete at the Games, he did put the issue on the agenda of an IOC meeting. The media attention which surrounded the application of the Union, and the fact that it reached the inner sanctum of the International Olympic Committee, was regarded as a success by staff at the Free Europe Committee. Eventually, however, the IOC members voted the proposal down, refusing to change the *Charter* to accommodate a small minority which had no country to represent.[72]

The Union of Free Eastern European Sportsmen effectively ceased as an organization following the IOC's decision, but this failed to stem Szápáry's determination to restate the question. Prior to the 1960 Rome Olympics, the count once again wrote to Brundage. Szápáry thought it "absurd" that proven competitors like Tábori were excluded from the Games. He asked that the IOC consider altering its rules "which were fashioned in another era" and by leaders who "could never have foreseen the circumstances existing in our world today." Szápáry suggested that a team could be formed that could compete "under the flag of the United Nations." "I cannot imagine anything which could be more in the true spirit of the Olympics," he added. [73] In his response, Brundage repeated that the problem of exiles had been debated at length but no solution had been forwarded which did not require reorganizing the basic structure of the IOC.[74] This made little sense. The IOC did change its rules in 1964, and could have done so some years earlier.

Despite the determined letters written by the leaders of the HNSF to members of the IOC's hierarchy, Brundage and his colleagues do not appear to have grown frustrated with the Federation's promptings. If anything, Brundage harbored sympathy for their cause. Likewise, the Melbourne defection did not register to any considerable degree in the IOC. This is understandable. Due to the sheer controversy of the Hungarian Revolution, coupled with the Suez Crisis, the IOC had to focus on promoting a united front, while trying, as ever, to insist that political incidents should not impinge on the Olympics. After the Games, Brundage casually mentioned to the Hungarian IOC member, Ferenc Mező, that some of the defectors were touring around the U.S. but did not seem to have been vocal about it.[75]

On a further occasion, Brundage displayed no animosity to the HNSF or the defected Hungarians when it came to a request for Olympic diplomas. George Telegdy wrote to Otto Mayer, the IOC chancellor, on behalf of the members of the Hungarian National Olympic Team. Telegdy sent a list of the athletes who had finished either first, second or third in their respective event and asked that the appropriate diplomas be sent to the HNSF, which would distribute them accordingly. He added: "Should the diplomas be sent to the Communist Hungarian Olympic Committee, the just owners of the diplomas would never receive them."[76] Brundage had no objections, and the IOC informed the Melbourne Organizing Committee that it should forward the relevant articles. Telegdy was thrilled with this minor success, although a few months later, Brundage once again stated that the IOC could do nothing about the participation of exiles at the Olympics.[77]

The entry of stateless athletes into the Olympic Games may have been of paramount importance to the HNSF, but it was not the only sporting event which attracted the group's attention. Szápáry wanted to make sure that the athletes who desired to keep competing had the financial backing to do so, whatever the competition. In one sense, he thought that keeping the athletes active might help in the process of resettling. On the other hand, Szápáry added, "Now we have the chance to use the appearance of the Hungarian athletes as well as their results in the service of the Hungarian national cause and the athletes themselves are anxious to serve this cause."[78]

Some of the athletes were already taking part in local, regional and national competitions around the United States, and the HNSF set up a "campaign fund" so that the practice could continue. Szápáry made the first donation and the FEC put $4,000 into the pool. Despite their recent defection, the exiles managed to secure some solid results after six months in America. László Tábori, the world class middle distance runner, proved his caliber by never finishing outside the top three in his seven races, and winning twice. The male and female fencers made a dramatic impact in various competitions, including the U.S. national championships, where, among the notable achievements, Lídia Dömölky finished second in the women's foil and Daniel Magay won the men's sabre. József Gerlach secured two top-five finishes at the U.S. National Indoor Diving Championships, and Zsuzsa Ördögh took a respectable seventh at the U.S. National Swimming Championships.[79]

By this stage, the Free Europe Committee began to intensify its support for the HNSF and the Hungarian National Olympic Team. Perhaps spurred on by the level of public awareness directed at the exiled athletes, the FEC supplied more money to the Federation than it ever had before. The period 1957 to 1960 were the golden years of the relationship. For instance, the FEC paid for an HNSF soccer team to fly to Stockholm for the World Cup, for Zsuzsa Ördögh to compete at the U.S. National Swimming Championships, and for a Hungarian chess player, Paul Benkő, to fly to a tournament in Yugoslavia.[80]

One of the competitions isolated for special attention was the 1958 World Fencing Championships, scheduled to take place in Philadelphia. Not only would the exiled fencers stand a good chance of winning but representatives of the Hungarian regime were also sure to be there. It also served as a reminder that grave problems still had to be overcome with regard to immigration. While the Hungarian athletes could compete in America at various national or state competitions, international events were a different matter altogether. The athletes that fled Melbourne entered the United States on "parole," and were thus not American citizens. Jackson and the HNSF had intended to fast-track the exiled athletes onto the U.S. Olympic team, only to face obstructive immigration laws. Along with the AAU, the parties had been investigating ways to force special legislation to expedite citizenship for refugee athletes.[81] They were not alone. In 1959, Texas Senator Lyndon Johnson submitted a bill to the Senate for the purpose of speeding up the immigration process for a Polish-born athlete who relocated to America. Johnson argued that it was an exceptional case. The individual could compete for the U.S. at the 1960 Olympics if he were granted citizenship in advance of the standard five year waiting period. The Senate passed the bill in May. When it reached the House Judiciary Committee, it was given to a subcommittee on immigration. Here it faltered. The chairman of the subcommittee, Francis Walter of Pennsylvania, said he would "use every effort to block its approval." Walter charged that if the United States were to pass such legislation, then it could be accused of "bootlegging" communist athletes.[82]

Initially, the participation of the exiled Hungarians in the World Fencing Championships was doubtful. The athletes had no country to compete for and the International Fencing Federation was reluctant to permit the entry of the refugees. The exiles had to provide evidence of their "statelessness." Through *SI*, Jackson, and contacts at the State Department, preparations were made to attain the necessary documentation.[83] It was enough for the time being. The long term challenge remained. Jackson could not hide his frustration with the laws of the land. He berated the State Department:

> Does the Government of the United States, under constant attack for inadequate handling of the cold war problem, consider it important enough to go through the necessary bureaucratic motions to arrange for these people to do for the United States and for the West the thing at which they are supremely competent – something which will make headlines throughout the world?[84]

The FEC underwrote all the costs for a five person team to participate at the World Fencing Championships, amounting to just under $4,000.[85] It transpired that prior to the event, the Hungarian delegation attempted to exclude the exiles from the competition, only for the motion to be defeated by the other nations represented at the tournament. During the competition, three fencers from the Hungarian squad were set to face three from the exile team. The official Hungarian fencers were subsequently withdrawn from the tournament by their coaches.[86] The American legation in Budapest reported that the Hungarian press was groping to find excuses.[87] Telegdy was ecstatic: "The participation of the Free Hungarian team at these Championships echoed very loudly in Hungary, and the Hungarian public opinion acknowledged with satisfaction that finally there has been an international event at which the communist government had to back out in front of the free Hungarians."[88]

Over the Dam

There can be little doubt that the HNSF was largely dependent on the financial backing of the Free Europe Committee. When, for instance, Telegdy ignored policy guidance, the FEC leadership was quick to check his plans. Indeed, one FEC official wrote of Teledgy: "The only way he can be brought to heel ... is to convince him that he does not, in fact, have the unqualified support of FEC or the Hungarian sports world that he would like to have, and that unless he cooperates with the many other person's involved he and his Sports Federation are finished."[89] Yet, the relationship between the government and the private sphere cannot be simply reduced to private groups working in straightforward compliance with the state. It was often the case, as in many other "state–private" initiatives, that the impetus for action came from the private side.[90] After all, the Hungarian National Sports Federation approached the FEC for help, not the other way around.

Needless to say, the secret nature of the HNSF's ties to the U.S. government was also crucial to its success. Had Brundage and other IOC members been "witting" regarding the HNSF or the FEC, doubtless they would have kept the organization at more than arm's length.[91] When, in fact, Brundage was approached by U.S. government officials for cooperation in efforts to stymie Soviet propaganda, he was generally unhelpful. If Brundage had known that America's intelligence community was behind the HNSF, it is unlikely that his correspondence with them would have been quite so civil.

Unfortunately for the HNSF, the halcyon days of the late 1950s were not to last. While the Federation's stock had been rising, the Free Europe Committee faced a period of declining morale and organization. When John Richardson, a New York investment banker, took over the presidency of the FEC in 1961, he streamlined the operation, giving it direction and purpose.[92] A larger percentage of the committee's budget was funneled to Radio Free Europe, and other programs were cut. Richardson regretfully made the decision to sever FEC funds for the Hungarian National Sports Federation. As of January 1962, regular payments to the HNSF ceased. The FEC provided an allotment for three more months to "phase-out" the Federation's activities and to buy time for George Telegdy to find alternative employment.[93] Count Szápáry attempted to recover the situation, and wrote to C.D. Jackson for assistance. Szápáry argued that the discontinuance of FEC funds might cause "panic" in the HNSF's affiliated clubs and "greatly affect the Hungarian morale and spiritual resistance of Hungarians in Hungary." The end result, he added, "would only satisfy the Hungarian Communist regime."[94] Jackson did what he could, sending a message to Bernard Yarrow, vice president of the Free Europe Committee. "Is this over the dam, or can something be done?" he asked Yarrow.[95] There was some optimism in Yarrow's response. He explained that "there is no assurance as yet that we will get the necessary funds to keep it going at its old level, but we shall try to do our very best."[96] For a time, the HNSF received a few more installments, but these were temporary, and soon ground to a halt. Telegdy was employed by the FEC until 1963 and then released when his services were no longer required.[97]

It is difficult to judge the overall success of the Hungarian National Sports Federation. Of course, the individual athletes that were given invaluable support after defecting no doubt felt a debt of gratitude to the group. No doubt, too, there were some repercussions in Hungary. Telegdy insisted that the Hungarian regime was fully aware of the Federation and that "a special section of the Hungarian Sports Ministry" worked exclusively to "counterbalance the activities of the HNSF."[98] The Melbourne defections troubled Hungary's government, sporting establishment, journalists and academics, to a sufficient degree that few wrote about it in that country for years to come. Hungarian sport historians lingered over the 1956 Summer Games in only the briefest manner.[99] As the end of FEC funding neared, Szápáry told Jackson that athletes competing for Hungary in Western competitions "commented with sad irony that the Hungarian regime spends more on the counter-activities regarding the HNSF than the Hungarian National Sports Federation receives."[100]

It is also possible to argue that the HNSF raised a considerable amount of interest for the general cause of stateless athletes around the world. In some small way this contributed to the International Olympic Committee finally altering its *Charter*. In 1964, the IOC decided that an athlete could compete for their new country of residence once they had become a naturalized citizen.[101] With the change to the *Olympic Charter* ratified, three former Hungarian citizens took part in the Tokyo Games wearing the colors of the United States. Jenő Hámori and Attila Keresztes were part of the fencing team, while Róbert Zimonyi was the coxswain in the eight-oared shell.[102] All three men were part of the Melbourne defection.

The media coverage given to exiled athletes further suggests that the choice of a world class athlete to defect from Hungary served to "dramatize" the difference in life on either side of the Iron Curtain. Creating dissension in Eastern Europe was preferable, but rallying support in the "free world" could not be neglected. As one article in the *New York Times* read:

> There is no surcease of sorrow in the whole story of the refugees from terror. But these athletes are not pitiful creatures. They are proud men and women who have attained recognition at home and honor abroad. Their flight is therefore the more impressive, because it is completely rational. They cannot stomach the regime in Budapest. Neither can we.[103]

A plethora of American newspapers reported defections and quoted the experiences of athletes in exile. Of course, these personal stories included scolding comments about sport in the satellites, with athletes accusing the communist regimes of using international competitions as nothing but a vehicle for propaganda. These claims were mostly true. Still, the same accusations can be directed at the HNSF. Never once did Szápáry deny that the Federation was an instrument of propaganda, or that sporting events were a stage on which to parade exiled athletes in front of a global audience. The moral high ground could not be claimed without some qualification. It was claimed nonetheless.

Endnotes

1 The author would like to thank the International Olympic Committee and the International Society for Olympic Historians for research grants which supported this work, and also Gladys and Paul Szápáry for access to the their father's personal papers.

2 It is acknowledged that the Free Europe Committee was called the National Committee for a Free Europe until 1954. For the sake of clarity and consistency, it shall be referred to as the former throughout this chapter.

3 Abbott Washburn to C. D. Jackson, 22 October 1951, RFE/RL INC. Corporate Records (hereafter RFE/RL), Box 355, (13) "Alphabetical File, Washburn, Abbott, 1949–1963," Hoover Institution Archives (hereafter HA), Stanford University, California.

4 "Radio Free Europe Policy Handbook," 30 November 1951, United States Declassified Documents Reference System (Woodbridge, CT, 1986), document number 1974.

5 "Olympics Preview," *News from behind the Iron Curtain* 1, no. 7 (July 1952) 42.

6 Miklós Zeidler, "English Influences on Modern Sport in Hungary," *The Hungarian Quarterly* XLVII, no. 181 (Spring 2006) 36–54; Zeidler, "English Influences on Modern Sport in Hungary, Part 2," *The Hungarian Quarterly* XLVII, no. 182 (Summer 2006) 27–47; József Vető, ed., *Sports in Hungary* (Budapest: Corvina Press, 1965), 9–20.

7 Cited in Zeidler, "English Influences, Part 2," 28.

8 Zeidler, "English Influences," 36–54; Zeidler, "English Influences, Part 2," 27–47; Vető, *Sports in Hungary*, 9–20; Deobold B. Van Dalen and Bruce L. Bennett, *A World History of Physical Education: Cultural, Philosophical, Comparative* (Engelwood Cliffs, NJ: Prentice Hall, Inc., 1971) 339–40.

9 Barbara Keys, *Globalizing Sport: National Rivalry and International Community in the 1930s* (Cambridge, Massachusetts: Harvard University Press, 2006); Pierre Arnaud, "Sport and International Relations Before 1918," in *Sport and International Politics*, eds., Pierre Arnaud & James Riordan (London: Routledge, 1998) 14–30; Peter C. McIntosh, *Sport in Society* (London: C. A. Watts & Co, 1968) 188–203.

10 Keys, *Globalizing Sport*, 2–4. See also Barbara Keys, "The Internationalization of Sport, 1890–1939," in *The Cultural Turn: Essays in the History of U.S. Foreign Relations*, eds., Frank A. Ninkovich and Liping Bu (Chicago: Imprint Publications, 2001) 201–19.

11 "Hungary and Olympism," *Olympic Review* 105–6 (July–August 1976) 383–407; József Keresztélyi, "Ferenc Kemény," *Olympic Review* 174 (April 1982) 212–13. In 1912, Hungarian sports officials were also involved in the formation of the International Amateur Athletic Federation (IAAF).

12 Cited in Norbert Müller, ed., *Pierre de Coubertin 1863–1937: Olympism: Selected Writings* (Lausanne: International Olympic Committee, 2000) 431.

13 Denis Echard, "A Well-Anchored Olympic Tradition," *Olympic Review* XXV, no. 3 (June–July 1995) 4–9; "Hungary and Olympism," 383–407.

14 Vladislav M. Zubok, *A Failed Empire: The Soviet Union in the Cold War from Stalin to Gorbachev* (Chapel Hill: The University of North Carolina Press, 2007) 73; Norman Naimark, "The Sovietization of Eastern Europe, 1944–1953," in *The Cambridge History of the Cold War: Volume 1: Origins*, eds., Melvin P. Leffler and Odd Arne Westad (Cambridge: Cambridge University Press, 2010) 189–92.

15 For the standard treatment on this subject see James Riordan, *Sport in Soviet Society* (London: Cambridge University Press, 1977).

16 Cited in Jenifer Parks, "Red Sport, Red Tape: The Olympic Games, the Soviet Sports Bureaucracy, and the Cold War, 1952–1980" (Unpublished PhD Dissertation: University of North Carolina at Chapel Hill, 2009) 42.

17 Vassil Girginov, "Capitalist Philosophy and Communist Practice: The Transformation of Eastern European Sport and the International Olympic Committee," *Culture, Sport, Society* 1, no. 1 (May 1998) 125; Adam Fryc and Mirosław Ponczek, "The Communist Rule in Polish Sport History," *The International Journal of the History of Sport* 26, no. 4 (March 2009) 505; Gyöngyi Szabo Földesi, "From Mass Sport to the 'Sport for All' Movement in the 'Socialist' Countries in Eastern Europe," *International Review for the Sociology of Sport* 26, no. 4 (1991) 243–47; Riordan, *Sport in Soviet Society*, 380; G. A. Carr, "The Birth of the German Democratic Republic and the Organization of East German Sport," *Canadian Journal of History of Sport and Physical Education* 7, no. 1 (May 1976) 1–21.

18 Cited in Peter Beck, "The British Government and the Olympic Movement: The 1948 London Olympics," *The International Journal of the History of Sport* 25, no. 5 (April 2008) 621.

19 "Round-up of FEOP Projects for the Rome Olympic Games," 22 July 1960, RFE/RL, Box 245, (5) "Olympic Games General, 1960," HA.

20 Toby C. Rider, "The Olympic Games and the Secret Cold War: The U.S. Government and the Propaganda Campaign Against Communist Sport, 1950–1960" (Unpublished PhD Dissertation: The University of Western Ontario, 2011).

21 Peter Beck, "Losing Prestige On and Off the Field: England Versus Hungary, 1953–54," *Sport in History* 23, no. 2 (Winter 2003–4) 15. See also Ronnie Kowalski and Dilwyn Porter, "Cold War Football: British European Encounters in the 1940s and 1950s," in *East Plays West: Sport and the Cold War*, eds. Stephen Wagg and David L. Andrews (New York: Routledge, 2007) 64–81.

22 Cited in Peter Beck, "Britain and the Cold War's 'Cultural Olympics:' Responding to the Political Drive of Soviet Sport, 1945–58," *Contemporary British History* 19, no. 2 (June 2005) 177.

23 George Copeland to Department of State, 10 March 1952, Record Group 59 (hereafter RG), Central Decimal File, 1950–54, Box 5296, 864.45/3–1052, National Archives (hereafter NA), College Park, Maryland.

24 George M. Abbott to Department of State, 2 July 1952, RG59, Central Decimal File, 1950–54, Box 5296, 864.453/7-252, NA. Brackets mine.

25 Avery Brundage to J. Sigfrid Edström, 7 December 1950, Avery Brundage Collection, 1908–75 (hereafter ABC), Box 149, Reel 84, International Centre for Olympic Studies Archives (hereafter ICOSA), University of Western Ontario, London, Canada. Brackets mine.

26 See for instance Ravndal to Department of State, 11 August 1954, RG59, Central Decimal File, 1950–54, Box 5296, 864.453/8-1154, NA.

27 George Eisen, "The Hungarian Sport Culture," *Quest* 22 (1974) 103.

28 George Eisen, "Introduction" in *Ethnicity and Sport in North American History and Culture*, eds., George Eisen and David K. Wiggins (Westport, Connecticut: Greenwood Press, 1994) xi. See also Grant Jarvie, "Sport, Parish Life, and the Émigré," *Journal of Sport History* 25, no.3 (Fall 1998) 381–97.

29 John Radzilowski, "Ethnic Anti-Communism in the United States," in *Anti-Communist Minorities in the U.S.: Political Activism of Ethnic Refugees*, ed., Ieva Zake (New York: Palgrave Macmillan, 2009) 8; Vic Satzewich, *The Ukrainian Diaspora* (London: Routledge, 2002) 139.

30 Drawn from a memorandum appended to Osyp Zinkewytch to Brundage, 24 September 1956, ABC, Box 116, Reel 63, ICOSA.

31 Peter Donnelly, "Resistance Through Sports: Sport and Cultural Hegemony," in *Sports et Sociétés Contemporaines, VIII Symposium de L'ICSS* (Paris: Société Française de Sociologie du Sport, 1983) 398.

32 Count Anthony Szápáry to C.D. Jackson, 2 February 1962, C.D. Jackson Papers, 1931–67, Series II Time INC. File, 1933–64, Subseries A. Alphabetical File, 1933–64 (hereafter Jackson Papers), Box 53, "Free Europe Committee, 1962," Dwight D. Eisenhower Presidential Library (hereafter DDEL), Abilene, Kansas.

33 Szápáry to Brundage, 17 January 1950, ABC, Box 132, Reel 73, ICOSA.

34 "Anthony Szapary, Led Sports Group," *New York Times*, 26 December 1972, 27; "Sylvia Szechenyi Fiancee Of Count," *New York Times*, 12 February 1949, 20; "Sylvia Szechenyi Married to Count," *New York Times*, 24 April 1949, 75.

35 Szápáry to Members of the IOC Executive Committee, 20 May 1952, ABC, Box 116, Reel 63, ICOSA.

36 "Curriculum" of Telegdy, no date, RFE/RL, Box 343, (20) "Telegdy, George," HA; "Biography of George Telegdy," no date, the Private Papers of Count Anthony Szápáry (hereafter Szápáry Papers), Box 2, "misc," Pound Ridge, New York; Tibor Szy, *Hungarians in America* (New York: The Kossuth Foundation, Inc., 1966) 428.

37 John Matthews to R.W. Minton, 21 July 1960, RFE/RL, Box 245, (5) "Olympic Games General, 1960," HA.

38 Szápáry to John Richardson, 30 April 1962, RFE/RL, Box 343, (20) "Telegdy, George", HA. For Telegdy's "incompetence" see Whitney Tower to Szápáry, 10 January 1957, Szápáry Papers, Box 2, "HNSF, *Sports Illustrated*, 1956–57."

39 Telegdy and Szápáry to Fulgencio Batista, no date [circa 1957], Szápáry Papers, Box 2, "AAU of U.S."

40 Blanche Wiesen Cook, "First Comes the Lie: C. D. Jackson and Political Warfare," *Radical History Review* 31 (1984) 42–70; David Haight, "The Papers of C.D. Jackson: A Glimpse At President Eisenhower's Psychological Warfare Expert," *Manuscripts* XXVIII (Winter 1976) 27–37; H. W. Brands, Jr., *Cold Warriors: Eisenhower's Generation and American Foreign Policy* (New York: Columbia University Press, 1988) 117–137; Valur Ingimundarson, "Containing the Offensive: The 'Chief of the Cold War' and the Eisenhower Administration's German Policy," *Presidential Studies Quarterly* 27, no. 3 (Summer 1997) 480–95.

41 Jackson to Rod O'Connor, 10 July 1958, Jackson Papers, Box 104, "Sports Illustrated – Hungarian Olympic Team Defectors," DDEL.

42 See for instance Telegdy to Ferris, no date [circa 1959], Szápáry Papers, Box 2, "AAU of U.S."

43 "Operation Griffin," by George Telegdy, no date, Szápáry Papers, Box 2, "Confidential Reports – Operation Eagle."

44 "Olympic Evening Festival Program," no date [circa 1960], Szápáry Papers, Box 2, "Misc"; FEC press release, 8 July 1960, RFE/RL, Box 245, (5) "Olympic Games General, 1960," HA; "Olympic Drive Opened," *New York Times*, 12 July 1960, 43.

45 Szápáry to Robert McKisson, 25 May 1950, RG59, Central Decimal File, 1950–54, Box 5296, 864.453/5-2550, NA. This information on the HNSF was drawn from a "Pro-Memoria" appended to the letter. For the HNSF's incorporation see Stein to George Telegdy, 27 March 1959, Szápáry Papers, Box 2, "B." For more on the aims of the HNSF see "The Role of the Hungarian National Sports Federation in the Free World," no date, Szápáry Papers, Box 2, "Misc." Among the athletes associated with the HNSF in its early days were world-class trap and skeet shooters, István Strassburger and Sándor Dóra, the wrestler István Kiss, the fencing champion Béla Mikla, the fencer József Vida, and swimmer, József Szegedi.

46 John Foster Leich, "Great Expectations: The National Councils in Exile, 1950–60," *The Polish Review* XXXV, no. 3 (1990) 185. Leich was familiar with the work of the HNSF although he does not mention this fact in his article.

47 "Reorientation of Exile Organizations," 1 April 1960, Jackson Papers, Box 53, (2) "Free Europe Committee, 1960," DDEL. This report is appended to a letter from Archibald Alexander to Members of the Free Europe Committee Executive Committee, 4 April 1960, Jackson Papers, Box 53, (2) "Free Europe Committee, 1960," DDEL.

48 George Telegdy to John Matthews, no date, Jackson Papers, Box 53, (3) "Free Europe Committee, 1960," DDEL.

49 Frances Stoner Saunders, *Who Paid the Piper? The CIA and the Cultural Cold War* (London: Granta Books, 1999) 281.

50 Kenneth Osgood, *Total Cold War: Eisenhower's Secret Propaganda Battle at Home and Abroad* (Lawrence, Kansas: University Press of Kansas, 2006) 82.

51 Hugh Wilford, *The Mighty Wurlitzer: How the CIA Played America* (Cambridge, Massachusetts: Harvard University Press, 2008) 227–32, quote on 232; Carl Bernstein, "The CIA and the Media," *Rolling Stone*, 20 October 1977, 55–63.

52 For more on this see Rider, "The Olympic Games and the Secret Cold War."

53 "Down A Road Called Liberty," *Sports Illustrated*, 17 December 1956, 14–19. One of the few scholars to explore *Sports Illustrated*'s role in the Melbourne defection is Thomas Domer. However, Domer did not link the HNSF to the FEC. See Thomas M. Domer, "Sport in Cold War America, 1953–1963: The Diplomatic and Political Use of Sport in the Eisenhower and Kennedy Administrations," (Unpublished PhD Dissertation: Marquette University, 1976) 90–95. The defection is also mentioned very briefly in Michael MacCambridge, *The Franchise: A History of Sports Illustrated Magazine* (New York: Hyperion, 1997) 92–93.

54 "Hungary's Heroes In Their Hour Of Staggering Strain," *Sports Illustrated*, 3 December 1956, 22–23.

55 Otto Mayor to Brundage, 30 October 1956, Correspondence of Avery Brundage, 1956–60, Box 5, International Olympic Committee Archives (hereafter IOC Archives), Lausanne, Switzerland; Mayor to Brundage, 28 October 1956, Correspondence of Avery Brundage, 1956–60, Box 5, IOC Archives; Richard Espy, *The Politics of the Olympic Games* (London, England: University of California Press, 1979) 54–55.

56 "Olympic Newsletter No. 19," Olympic Games Organizing Committee of Melbourne, 1956: Circulars, Communications, Organizing Program and Press Releases, 1954–56, IOC Archives.

57 Tower to Sid James in "Documentary Chronology," 15 November 1956, Jackson Papers, Box 104, "Sports Illustrated – Hungarian Olympic Team Defectors," DDEL.

58 Tower to Szápáry, 19 November 1956, Szápáry Papers, Box 2, "HNSF, Sports Illustrated, 1956–57."

59 "Operation Griffin," by Telegdy, no date, Szápáry Papers, Box 2, "Confidential Reports – Operation Eagle." This report is Telegdy's personal account of Operation Griffin.

60 This information was drawn from a special supplement of *Sports Illustrated* called the *Hungarian Athletes Freedom Tour*.

61 "Hungarian Athletes in San Francisco," *Los Angeles Times*, 25 December 1956, C1.

62 Neale memorandum, no date, Szápáry Papers, Box 2, "HNSF, Sports Illustrated 1956–1957."

63 Neale to Team Members, 14 May 1957, Szápáry Papers, Box 2, "HNSF, Sports Illustrated 1956–1957;" Neale to Szápáry, 15 May 1957, Szápáry Papers, Box 2, "HNSF, Sports Illustrated 1956–1957." For more on the U.S. government's resettlement strategy see Carl J. Bon Tempo, *Americans at the Gate: The United States and Refugees During the Cold War* (Princeton, NJ: Princeton University Press, 2008) 75–82.

64 Szápáry to Jackson, 8 July 1957, Szápáry Papers, Box 2, "Misc."

65 Neale to Team Members, 14 May 1957, Szápáry Papers, Box 2, "HNSF, Sports Illustrated 1956–1957" ; "Across a Free Land," *Sports Illustrated*, 8 April 1957; "Operation Eagle – Sum-

mary Report on six months' activities," 10 July 1957, Szápáry Papers, Box 2, "Confidential Reports – Operation Eagle"; "2 Hungarian Athletes Change Minds, Go Home," *The Hartford Courant*, 5 February 1957, 3.

66 Szápáry to James, 18 June 1957, Szápáry Papers, Box 2, "HNSF 1956."

67 "Operation Eagle – Summary Report on three months' activities," 15 April 1957, Szápáry Papers, Box 2, "Confidential Reports – Operation Eagle."

68 Michael R. Marrus, *The Unwanted: European Refugees in the Twentieth Century* (New York: Oxford University Press, 1985) 359–61.

69 Bon Tempo, *Americans at the Gate*, 66–70; Michael Gill Davis, "The Cold War, Refugees, and U.S. Immigration Policy, 1952–1965" (Unpublished PhD Dissertation: Vanderbilt University, 1996) 128–33.

70 "Operation Eagle – Summary Report on three months' activities," 15 April 1957, Szápáry Papers, Box 2, "Confidential Reports – Operation Eagle"; "Operation Eagle – Summary Report on six months' activities," 10 July 1957, Szápáry Papers, Box 2, "Confidential Reports – Operation Eagle."

71 International Olympic Committee, *Fundamental Principles Rules and Regulations* (Lausanne, Switzerland: 1958) 19.

72 "International Olympic Committee 47th Session," Helsinki, 16 July 1952, IOC Archives. For more on the Union of Free Eastern European Sportsmen see Rider, "The Olympic Games and the Secret Cold War," 171–212.

73 Szápáry to Brundage, 1 August 1960, ABC, Box 132, Reel 73, ICOSA.

74 Brundage to Szápáry, 6 August 1960, Ibid.

75 Brundage to Ferenc Mező, 18 February 1957, Ibid.

76 Telegdy to Mayer, 29 April 1957, Correspondence of the NOC of Hungary, 1907–1969, Box 166, IOC Archives.

77 Brundage to Mayer, 12 August 1957, Correspondence of Avery Brundage, 1956–60, Box 5, IOC Archives.

78 Szápáry to Jackson, 8 July 1957, Szápáry Papers, Box 2, "Misc;" Jackson to Tibor Eckhardt, 9 July 1957, Jackson Papers, Box 52, "First Aid for Hungary," DDEL; "Operation Eagle – Summary Report on six months' activities," 10 July 1957, Szápáry Papers, Box 2, "Confidential Reports – Operation Eagle."

79 "Meeting of the Hungarian National Olympic Team," 8 December 1957, Szápáry Papers, Box 2, "HNSF;" "Operation Eagle – Summary Report on six months' activities," 10 July 1957, Szápáry Papers, Box 2, "Confidential Reports – Operation Eagle."

80 Yarrow to Szápáry, 2 June 1958, Szápáry Papers, Box 2, "Free Europe Committee"; Delgado to Szápáry, 1 August 1958, Szápáry Papers, Box 2, "Free Europe Committee"; Delgado to Szápáry, 24 July 1958, Szápáry Papers, Box 2, "Free Europe Committee"; Bernard Yarrow to Szápáry, 10 December 1958, Szápáry Papers, Box 2, "Free Europe Committee"; "FEC Special Project," no date, Szápáry Papers, Box 2, "Free Europe Committee."

81 Matthews to Jackson, 21 January 1960, Jackson Papers, Box 53, (3) "Free Europe Committee, 1960," DDEL; Matthews to Jackson, 2 February 1960, Jackson Papers, Box 53, (3) "Free Europe Committee, 1960," DDEL; Telegdy to Edward Rosenblum, 16 December 1959, Szápáry Papers, Box 2, "Roma."

82 "How to Try Too Hard," *Sports Illustrated*, 15 February 1960, 55.

83 Neale to Hamori, 16 June 1958, Jackson Papers, Box 104, "Sports Illustrated – Hungarian Olympic Team Defectors," DDEL; Neale to Rod O'Connor, 16 June 1958, Jackson Papers, Box 104, "Sports Illustrated – Hungarian Olympic Team Defectors," DDEL; Neale to Jose de Capriles, 20 June 1958, Jackson Papers, Box 104, "Sports Illustrated – Hungarian Olympic

Team Defectors," DDEL; Neale to Jackson, 20 June 1958, Jackson Papers, Box 104, "Sports Illustrated – Hungarian Olympic Team Defectors," DDEL; Jackson to O'Connor, 10 July 1958, Jackson Papers, Box 104, "Sports Illustrated – Hungarian Olympic Team Defectors," DDEL.

84 Jackson to O'Connor, 10 July 1958, Jackson Papers, Box 104, "Sports Illustrated – Hungarian Olympic Team Defectors," DDEL.

85 Yarrow to Szápáry, 7 August 1958, Szápáry Papers, Box 2, "Free Europe Committee."

86 "Hungarian Move Blocked," *New York Times*, 19 August 1958, 34; "3 Americans Gain in World Fencing," *New York Times*, 24 August 1958, S5.

87 James W. Pratt to Department of State, 8 October 1958, RG59, Central Decimal File, 1955–59, Box 4062, 800.453/10-858, NA.

88 Telegdy to Laurence Dawson, 23 January 1959, Szápáry Papers, Box 2, "HNSF."

89 Matthews to Minton, 21 July 1960, RFE/RL, Box 245, (5) "Olympic Games General, 1960," HA.

90 For more on this see Scott Lucas, "Beyond Freedom, Beyond Control: Approaches to Culture and the State-Private Network in the Cold War," *Intelligence and National Security* 18, no. 2 (2003) 58–61.

91 "Witting" is a term used within American intelligence. The term denotes whether a person is aware that a certain fact or piece of information is connected to the intelligence establishment.

92 A. Ross Johnson, *Radio Free Europe and Radio Liberty: The CIA Years and Beyond* (Stanford, CA: Stanford University Press, 2010) 131–32; Arch Puddington, *Broadcasting Freedom: The Cold War Triumph of Radio Free Europe and Radio Liberty* (Lexington, KY: The University of Kentucky Press, 2000) 130.

93 John Richardson to Szápáry, 3 January 1962, Szápáry Papers, Box 2, "Antal Szapary;" Szápáry to Richardson, 5 December 1961, Szápáry Papers, Box 2, "R."

94 Szápáry to Jackson, 2 February 1962, Jackson Papers, Box 53, "Free Europe Committee, 1962," DDEL.

95 Jackson to Bernard Yarrow, 16 March 1962, Ibid. Jackson told Szápáry that he read the count's letter with "the utmost sympathy and will be glad to do what I can." See Jackson to Szápáry, 16 March 1962, Ibid.

96 Yarrow to Jackson, 27 March 1962, Ibid.

97 J.W. Brinkley to Christopher Emmet, 3 September 1963, RFE/RL, Box 343, (20) "Telegdy, George," HA. The HNSF appears to have continued its operations on a more limited scale for years to come.

98 George Telegdy to John Matthews, no date [circa January–February 1960], Jackson Papers, Box 53, (3) "Free Europe Committee, 1960," DDEL.

99 Emese Ivan and Dezső Iván, "The 1956 Revolution and the Melbourne Olympics: The Changing Perceptions of a Dramatic Story," *Hungarian Studies Review* XXXV, no. 1–2 (2008) 16–17.

100 Szápáry to Jackson, 2 February 1962, Jackson Papers, Box 53, "Free Europe Committee, 1962," DDEL.

101 "IOC Executive Board Meeting," Lausanne, 26–27 June 1964, IOC Archives; "Minutes of the International Olympic Committee 62nd Session," Annex 10, Tokyo, 6–8 October 1964, IOC Archives.

102 Asa Bushnell, ed., *The United States Olympic Book* (Providence, RI: Riverhouse Publishing Company, 1964) 38, 39, 50.

103 "Hungarian Sidelight," *New York Times*, 9 December 1956, E6.

Select Bibliography

Beck, Peter. "Britain and the Cold War's 'Cultural Olympics:' Responding to the Political Drive of Soviet Sport, 1945–58." *Contemporary British History* 19, no.2 (2005): 169–185.
Bon Tempo, Carl J. *Americans at the Gate: The United States and Refugees During the Cold War.* Princeton, New Jersey: Princeton University Press, 2008.
Domer, Thomas M. "Sport in Cold War America, 1953–1963: The Diplomatic and Political Use of Sport in the Eisenhower and Kennedy Administrations." Unpublished PhD Dissertation: Marquette University, 1976.
Espy, Richard. *The Politics of the Olympic Games.* London: University of California Press, 1979.
Keys, Barbara. *Globalizing Sport: National Rivalry and International Community in the 1930s.* Cambridge, Massachusetts: Harvard University Press, 2006.
Lucas, Scott. "Beyond Freedom, Beyond Control: Approaches to Culture and the State-Private Network in the Cold War." *Intelligence and National Security* 18, no.2 (2003): 53–72.
Rider, Toby C. "The Olympic Games and the Secret Cold War: The U.S. Government and the Propaganda Campaign Against Communist Sport, 1950–1960." Unpublished PhD Dissertation: The University of Western Ontario, 2011.
Riordan, James. *Sport in Soviet Society.* London: Cambridge University Press, 1977.
Wiesen Cook, Blanche. "First Comes the Lie: C. D. Jackson and Political Warfare." *Radical History Review* 31 (1984): 42–70.
Wilford, Hugh. *The Mighty Wurlitzer: How the CIA Played America.* Cambridge, Massachusetts: Harvard University Press, 2008.

Biographies

Veronika Durin-Hornyik

Veronika Durin-Hornyik is a Hungarian PhD student at the Université Paris-Est (France) doing research on the National Committee for Free Europe's cultural activities during the Cold War. She earned degrees in French literature, Communication and Law in Hungary. In 2006 she continued her studies in France for her Master's Degree on the Marxist interpretation of the French Enlightenment in the work of Hungarian literature historians. Her deep interest in the relation of Culture with Politics and its use for political purposes led to her research on the Cultural Cold War under the supervision of Professor Fabienne Bock. Having completed a Research Masters in History on the Free Europe University in Exile at the Université Paris-Est Marne-la-Vallée (France) in 2009 as a fellow of the Regional Council of Île-de-France, she began her PhD studies in 2010 as a contract researcher on the extended topic of the NCFE's overall cultural activities to fight against Communism in Europe from the 1950s-mid 1960s.

Tibor Frank

Holds positions as Professor of History and Director of the School of English and American Studies at Eötvös Loránd University in Budapest (1994–2001, 2006–), where he is head of the Ph.D. program in American Studies. He has been doing research on transatlantic relations, international migrations, imagology, and historiography. He was a Fulbright visiting professor at the University of California, Santa Barbara and UCLA (1987–90), the University of Nevada-Reno (1990–91), and vis-

iting professor at Columbia University (2001, 2007, 2010). Recipient of the Humboldt Award (Germany, 2002) and corresponding fellow of the Royal Historical Society (London, 2006-), he has been board member of *Historical Abstracts* (Santa Barbara-Oxford, 1989-93, 2000-), *Nationalities Papers* (New York, 1989-2009), *Polanyiana* (Budapest, 1994-), the *European Journal of American Culture* (Nottingham, England, 1998-), *Apprasial* (2010-), *Külügyi Szemle* (2011-), *Öt Kontinens* (2011-). Elected c. member of the Hungarian Academy of Sciences in 2013.
His recent books in English include *From Habsburg Agent to Victorian Scholar: G. G. Zerffi 1820-1892* (New York: Columbia UP, 2000), *Picturing Austria-Hungary: The British Perception of the Habsburg Monarchy 1865-1870* (New York: Columbia UP, 2005), and *Double Exile: Migrations of Jewish-Hungarian Professionals through Germany to the United States 1919-1945* (Oxford: Peter Lang, 2009). He has edited *Discussing Hitler: Advisers of U.S. Diplomacy in Central Europe, 1934-1941* (Budapest–New York: CEU P, 2003), *Ever Ready to Go: The Multiple Exiles of Leo Szilard* (Berlin: Max-Planck-Institut für Wissenschaftsgeschichte, 2004), and (with Frank Hadler, eds), *Disputed Territories and Shared Pasts: Overlapping National Histories in Modern Europe* (Palgrave Macmillan, 2011).

Jonathan H. L'Hommedieu

Jonathan H. L'Hommedieu, currently a faculty member in the History Department at Armstrong Atlantic State University, received his B.A. in History from Armstrong Atlantic State University, his M.Soc.Sc. in Contemporary History from the University of Turku in Finland where he was awarded a Ph.D. in Contemporary History 2011. His doctoral dissertation was titled „Exiles and Constituents: Baltic Refugees and American Cold War Politics, 1948–1960." His current research has continued to be focused on Baltic history, immigration history, and public diplomacy.

Katalin Kádár Lynn

Katalin Kádár Lynn is an independent scholar based in Budapest and California and a senior researcher at Eötvös Loránd University in Budapest. Her principal area of scholarship is WWII and the Cold War with an emphasis on Central and East European exile leaders, their organizations and activities. She earned a PhD from Eötvös Loránd University Faculty of Humanities in 20th Century Hungarian history and a Masters in Liberal Arts from Washington University in St. Louis, MO. Her undergraduate degree with dual majors in History and English Literature was earned at the University of Colorado.

Kádár Lynn is the biographer of the Hungarian political figure Tibor Eckhardt. Her book on Eckhardt, *Tibor Eckhardt: His American Years 1941–1972* was published in the US (East European Monographs) and in Hungary (L'Harmattan Press). She edited and published Eckhardt's memoir *Tibor Eckhardt: In His Own Words* in English and in Hungarian. Her most recent book in collaboration with Hungarian historians Károly Szerencsés and Péter Strausz is titled *Through an American Lens, Hungary 1938: Photographs by Margaret Bourke-White* (English edition: East European Monographs 2010 – Hungarian edition, L'Harmattan Press 2009). She is the editor this compendium of essays on the history of the National Committee for a Free Europe, *The Inauguration of Organized Political Warfare: Cold War Organizations Sponsored by the National Committee for a Free Europe/Free Europe Committee* which includes her essays on the history of the Hungarian National Council and the NCFE as well as contributions from scholars worldwide. She is currently researching and writing an expanded biography of Tibor Eckhardt, which will encompass his Hungarian years and his wartime and Cold War intelligence activities. Her current research also includes a biography of Béla Varga and a history of the Hungarian National Council.

In 2012 she founded Helena History Press, a publisher specializing in scholarship related to Central and East European history of which she serves as editor.

Maria Kokoncheva

Based in Sofia, Bulgaria,Maria Kokoncheva has a degree in journalism and a Masters in International Relations from Aalborg University, Denmark. She has done an extensive study on the content and corporate aspects of the strategies of Radio Free Europe and other Western Media broadcastings in Bulgaria during the Cold War. She has been published in academic reviews of University of Plovdiv and Burgas Free University (Bulgaria).

Anna Mazurkiewicz

Anna Mazurkiewicz Assistant Professor at the Institute of History, University of Gdansk, Poland. In 2012/2013 Kosciuszko Foundation Visiting Scholar, State University of New York Buffalo. She earned her Ph.D. in History 2006, and the award of the Polish National Centre for Culture. Books and articles on U.S. policy towards Poland; *Dyplomacja Stanów Zjednoczonych wobec wyborów w Polsce w latach 1947 i 1989* (Warsaw: Neriton, 2007) and *Prasa amerykańska wobec wyborów w Polsce w latach 1947 i 1989* (Gdańsk: University Press, 2009). Recipient of the Kosciuszko Foundation Fellowships and grants from the Foundation for Polish Science and the Visegrad Fund. Second Vice-President of the Polish American Historical Association. Mazurkiewicz is writing a book about the Assembly of Captive European Nations-U.S. based émigré organization of east European exiled political leaders.

Marius Petraru

Was awarded a Bachelor of Arts degree with a double major in History and Geography from the College of Letters and Science, at the Ştefan cel Mare University of Suceava, in Suceava, Romania in 1995. In 1997 he received an International Scholarship from the Polish Government to attend Łodz University in Poland. In 1998, he was admitted to doctoral studies at the History Institute of Jagiellonian University of Kraków, Poland. In 2002, after the presentation of his doctoral dissertation "Poles in the Bukowina in the Years 1775–1918: From the History of

The Polish Settlement", he was awarded a Doctor of Humanities in History. His doctoral dissertation was published by Jagiellonian University Press in 2004. Until his emigration to the United States he participated at different international symposium in Romania and Poland published a series of articles related to the Austro-Hungarian Empire and political and civilian Polish emigration to Romania during XIX-XX century. From 2003 he continued his academic career as a professor of Geography at American River College and the Department of Geography at California State University of Sacramento.
His recent research concentration is on the history of the Romanian government in exile in the United States and its relationship with the National Committee for Free Europe/Free Europe Committee as well as the activity of the Romanian political elites in the Assembly of Captive European Nations during the Cold War.

Francis D. Raška

Francis D. Raška is an associate professor of modern history at the Institute of International Studies, Department of American Studies, Faculty of Social Sciences, Charles University in Prague. He also teaches at Anglo-American University in Prague. He was awarded his PhD. In Modern History from Charles University, Faculty of Social Sciences, Prague, 2000. His research interests include Cold War-era Czechoslovak exiles, U.S. immigration policy, and dissent in the 1960s and 1970s. He is the author of three books, *The Czechoslovak Exile Government in London and the Sudeten German Issue* (Prague, 2002), *Fighting Communism from Afar: The Council of Free Czechoslovakia* (Boulder, 2008), and *The Long Road to Victory: A History of Czechoslovak Exile Organizations* (Boulder, 2012). Articles 2012: 1. The Council of Free Czechoslovakia and the Issue of Human Rights in Communist Czechoslovakia, In: Young Czech and Slovak Professionals in America, New York, 2012, pp. 152–163. 2. The Journal Svědectví and the Struggle for Democracy in Coomunist Czechoslovakia, In: Kosmas: Czechoslovak and Central European Journal, Volume 26, Number 1, Fall 2012, pp. 23–59.

Toby Rider

Toby Rider is Assistant Professor of Kinesiology at Pennsylvania State University, Berks. He specializes in the history of sport in the Cold War era and the history of the modern Olympic Games.. He earned a Bachelor of Arts at the University of Birmingham and a Master of Arts at the University of Brighton. He earned his PhD in Sport History at the University of Western Ontario in 2011. In his doctoral dissertation he explored the U.S. government's use of sport in propaganda operations from 1950–1960.

His publications include: Article Review in *Olympika*, 2007: Stephen Wassong, "Pierre De Coubertin's Studies In and About the USA," 115–116. Article Review in *Olympika*, 2008: Anthony Moretti, "*New York Times* Coverage of the Soviet Union's Entrance into the Olympic Games," 190–191. Encyclopedia entry, "1932 Lake Placid Winter Olympics," in *Sports Around the World: History, Culture, and Practice*, ed. John Nauright (ABC-Clio, 2011). In print. Encyclopedia entry, "Ping-Pong Diplomacy," in *Sports Around the World: History, Culture, and Practice*, ed. John Nauright (ABC-Clio, 2011). In print."From Resistance to Revolution: The Struggle for Control of the Cuban Olympic Committee, 1953–1964," *Olympika* XVIII (2009). In print. "The Olympics and Cold War Propaganda: the Use of Exiled Athletes by the United States Government," *Journal of Olympic History* 17, no.2 (August, 2009), 49–51.

Photo Gallery

The Case

FOR AMERICANS, the highest political value is freedom. Knowing that our freedom can survive only in a free world, we have fought two world wars to preserve freedom in the world.

In 1945, as World War II drew to a close, we (along with the United Kingdom and the U.S.S.R.) gave a particular pledge to the peoples of Eastern Europe who were about to be liberated from the Nazi yoke. We promised that they should—

> **"solve by democratic means their pressing political and economic problems."**

These were the peoples of Bulgaria, Czechoslovakia, Hungary, Poland, Rumania and Yugoslavia. But the promise to them has not been kept. Instead, the Nazi oppression has been replaced by a Communist oppression that daily grows more vicious.

Eighty million sturdy people living between Germany and Russia are now in bondage. Their democratic

leaders have been liquidated by the score. But some have escaped to the freedom of the West.

Several hundred have reached America. More may come. They are the leaders who refused to knuckle under: those who have risked everything for their democratic faith.

Our American tradition calls for hospitality to political exiles of democratic faith. And, lest we forget, we on our side need the help of these proven democratic leaders in the struggle to preserve freedom in the face of the Communist assault.

The NCFE—What and How

THE NCFE begins with the tangible fact of the presence in the United States of several hundred of these democratic leaders. The Committee was formed in June, 1949—

- To help keep these leaders (while they are with us) alive and in vigor, bodily and spiritually;
- To couple their efforts with ours in the fight to halt Communism and save freedom, and with it our American way of life.

The NCFE is now energetically at work. To implement its objectives, three operating committees have been organized:

1. Committee on Intellectual Activity

THE FIRST JOB of the Committee on Intellectual Activity has been (and still is) to find suitable employment for escaped political and intellectual leaders, who usually come here despairing and unequipped, to maintain themselves financially.

Within four months after the NCFE's incorporation, the operating Committee on Intellectual Activity had these concrete achievements to its credit:

a It had catalogued the political and intellectual leaders who came here from behind the Iron Curtain in order to place them where they can be most useful in the fight against Communism.

b It had assisted the Library of Congress by assigning two exiled jurists from each of the six Iron Curtain countries for the purpose of analyzing and indexing the new laws and decrees of their respective countries. As a result, the Library is now in a position to answer authoritatively the many inquiries it receives from Congress, Government departments and private sources regarding these new laws and decrees.

c It was well advanced in organizing, with the Carnegie Endowment for International Peace, a systematic study relating to the future of the Danube Valley. This work is now being carried out jointly by American scholars and technicians and their counterparts exiled from the Danube countries. The object of this study is someday to help the peoples of this key area in working out their regional problems cooperatively and to their mutual advantage.

In addition, the Committee on Intellectual Activity has been finding for the exiles opportunities for intellectual studies in their particular professions.

2. Committee on Radio and Press

RADIO PRESENTS many technical difficulties but this operating Committee is getting on with the acquisition of facilities which will enable the exiled democratic leaders to speak to their countrymen at home. Had the Yalta promise been kept, these democratic voices would have been heard directly in free elections in the homelands. It is felt that that promise will be in some part kept when they are heard by radio: to that extent, free political life will have been restored, as was promised.

The sturdy millions living between Germany and Russia will know that their friends in the West have not forgotten them. They will hear news and views now denied them by their quisling governments. They will still share in the life of the West and may look forward to the time when freedom will return. A serious counter-attack will be under way against the Communist assault.

The Committee's broadcasting will not duplicate or compete with the Voice of America. It will be a helpful unofficial supplement.

3. Committee on American Contacts

THIS COMMITTEE had already gone some distance in building up contacts between the exiled leaders and the American public. Through lectures, informal discussions and forums with trade unions, farm organizations, civic groups, colleges and universities, the exiles are letting the American public know about Communism as they have seen it work. By the same operation, they themselves are now seeing freedom and democracy as they work in the United States. On both sides, ideas are enlarged and understanding grows.

The radio facilities, which the Committee on Radio will in due course offer the exiles, will enable them to tell their countrymen in Europe what they hear and see of life in the United States.

NATIONAL COUNCILS

IN ADDITION to the foregoing activities, the National Committee for Free Europe is assisting the exiled leaders to form effective working groups representative of democracy in each of the six Iron Curtain countries. These National Councils stand as symbols of democratic hope to the millions now under Communist oppression. They actively assist the NCFE to accomplish the purposes already outlined for Committees 1, 2 and 3.

The Struggle for Men's Minds

IN SUM, the National Committee for Free Europe has taken up a well defined and practical role in the defense and counter-attack against Communist expansion.

In this defense and counter-attack, three main sectors are apparent:

- **MILITARY**
- **ECONOMIC**
- **PSYCHOLOGICAL**

Currently, the United States is spending billions on military defense. Certainly this expenditure is indispensable as safeguard. But even military victory would bring no ultimate solution, because a third World War would destroy freedom everywhere, whoever the victor.

The economic efforts of the Marshall Plan promise enduring contributions to world peace with freedom. But it is plain that only on the psychological front can we as individuals effectively combat world Communism.

> **Only in the contest of ideas can there be final victory which will yield us one world dedicated to peace with freedom**

It is in this sector of the battleground that the NCFE has come into action. To achieve the ultimate victory in the struggle for men's minds, the Committee is keeping Eastern European leaders alive and vigorous. It is preparing radio facilities to enable these leaders to speak to their own people and convince them that the forces of freedom are more alive and powerful than ever before. It is working toward the day when the Iron Curtain will fade out and the exiled leaders we now befriend will return to their homelands as champions of democratic thought and faith.

What You Can Do to Halt Communism and Save Freedom

THE NCFE is a practical organization formed for a practical purpose. Conceived and carried on by men with long experience in international affairs, it offers you a chance to do something direct and concrete to preserve our highest value—freedom. You can—

1. **Join the NCFE as Contributing Member by mailing the coupon below, today, with your contribution.**
2. **Discuss these problems with your spiritual advisor. Tell your best friend about the NCFE and get him to join it, too.**
3. **Dedicate yourself, your family to the cause of freedom and to the defeat of Communism.**

National Committee for Free Europe, Inc.
350 Fifth Avenue, New York 1, N. Y.

Please enroll me as a Contributing Member of the NCFE, and send me a membership card immediately. I enclose my contribution of $........... to be used in the fight against world communism—*the fight for freedom!*

Name..

Street..

City.. State..............

Haskins and Sells, Certified Public Accountants, are the Committee's auditors.

TO HALT COMMUNISM

And Save Our Freedom

The

NATIONAL COMMITTEE FOR FREE EUROPE

350 Fifth Avenue, New York, N. Y.

Telephone: BRyant 9-3563

Members

EDWARD W. BARRETT	CHARLES R. HOOK
LAIRD BELL	ARTHUR BLISS LANE
A. A. BERLE, JR.	HERBERT H. LEHMAN
FRANCIS BIDDLE	HENRY R. LUCE
ROBERT WOODS BLISS	JOSEPH V. McKEE
JAMES B. CAREY	ARTHUR W. PAGE
WILLIAM L. CLAYTON	ROBERT P. PATTERSON
CECIL B. DeMILLE	SPYROS SKOURAS
WILLIAM J. DONOVAN	CHARLES M. SPOFFORD
HUGH A. DRUM	CHARLES P. TAFT
DWIGHT D. EISENHOWER	DeWITT WALLACE
MARK F. ETHRIDGE	W. W. WAYMACK
JAMES A. FARLEY	MATTHEW WOLL
VIRGINIA C. GILDERSLEEVE	MRS. QUINCY WRIGHT
WILLIAM GREEN	DARRYL ZANUCK

Officers and Directors

JOSEPH C. GREW	Chairman of the Board
DeWITT C. POOLE	President
FREDERIC R. DOLBEARE	Vice-President and Secretary
FRANK ALTSCHUL	Treasurer
ALLEN W. DULLES	Chairman, Executive Committee

> **"The State Department is very happy to see the formation of this group. It thinks that the purpose of the organization is excellent, and is glad to welcome its entrance into this field and give it its hearty endorsement."**
>
> Dean Acheson
> Secretary of State
> to the Press, June 23, 1949

Gifts to the NCFE are Deductible for Income Tax Purposes

◄ National Committee for Free Europe
Brochure 1949
"To Halt Communism and Save Our Freedom"

DeWitt Clinton Poole
First President
National Committee for a Free Europe, Inc.
(NCFE)
1949–1951

A. A. Berle, Ambassador Joseph Grew, Jerry Voorhis, President of the Carnegie Endowment for Peace and historian James T. Shotwell at the Mid European Studies Center opening of the Danubian Inquiry

Alexander Szasz, Ferenc Nagy, Stanisław Mikołajczyk and George M. Dimitrov at an organizational meeting of the International Peasant Union, 1 December 1947

Dwight D. Eisenhower announcing the launch of the Crusade for Freedom
4 September 1950

Major General Maxwell D. Taylor, US Commander, Berlin; General Lucius D. Clay, former military governor of Germany and Professor Ernst Reuter, Lord Mayor of Berlin meet at Tempelhoff air base as General Clay, President of the Crusade for Freedom arrived 24 October 1950 to take part in a historic ceremony dedicating the World Freedom Bell at the Berlin City Hall.

General Lucius D. Clay helps launch the United States Tour of the Freedom Bell.
"Help Lift the Iron Curtain Everywhere Join the Crusade for Freedom"

World Freedom Bell

A Berlin crowd estimated at over 400,000 attended the dedication of the World Freedom Bell 25 October 1950

Thousands of Freedom Balloons filled with Western propaganda were launched over the Iron Curtain to Czechoslovakia, East Germany and Hungary by the Crusade for Freedom

Demonstrations of Freedom Balloons were used by the Crusade for Freedom to raise funds for the Crusade in the United States. Denver, Colorado 22 February 1956

Crusade for Freedom Billboard, Denver Colorado in support of Radio Free Europe

Thomas Dewey, Governor of the State of New York broadcasting over Crusade for Freedom Radio, 1 January 1950

Whitney H. Shepardson (left) with General Willis D. Crittenberger. Crittenberger assumes the presidency of the Free Europe Committee, Inc from Shephardson, 1 October 1956

George Meany president of the AFL-CIO being honored by the International Rescue Committee. Left to right front row: George Meany; Leo Cherne, Honorary Chairman, International Rescue Committee, U. S. Vice President Hubert Humphrey. In the rear Brutus Coste, Vasil Germenj, Peter Pirogov, 1965

A. A. Berle Jr. speaking at a Press Conference at the Overseas Press Club discussing the importance of the Hungarian Question in the United Nations and for American Foreign Policy. Left to right: Alexander Kutt, vice chairman of the ACEN; Leo Cherne, executive director of the Research Institute of America; Christopher Emmet chairman of ACEN; Mr. Berle and Msgr. Béla Varga president Hungarian National Council, 29 November 1955

At a ceremony launching the Foreign Language Drive of the Crusade for Freedom the nationality groups honor C.D.Jackson president of the National Committee for a Free Europe, Inc., 23 October 1951

Bernard Yarrow, Vice President of the Nationalities Division of the Free Europe Committee, Inc. visiting Radio Free Europe in Munich. 1962

Mojmír Povolný
Chairman of the Council of Free Czechoslovakia
1974–1989

Jiří Horák and Mojmír Povolný

Mojmír Povolný speaks at the signing of the Czech-Polish Declaration on 19 January 1986 in London

Leaders of the Council of Free Czechoslovakia meet with President Václav Havel

Ivan Medek and Mojmír Povolný

The final meeting of the Council of Free Czechoslovakia in 1993

Michael I, the former King
of Romania and his family
21 April 1955

Former King Michael of Romania and his mother Queen Elena, 10 January 1948

Ex Romanian Foreign Minister Grigore Nicolescu Buzesti, 1 December 1947

Romanian Peasant Leader Iliu Maniu April 1949

Former King Carol II of Romania and his wife Magda Lupescu, 1950

Vice President
Richard M. Nixon
visits with US bound
refugees of the
Hungarian Revolution
in Austria
1 January 1957

Msgr. Bela Varga, Sir Leslie Munro, Christopher Emmett and Alexander Kutt
discuss the Question of Hungary

Msgr. Béla Varga and Tibor Eckhardt of the Hungarian National Council meeting with Senator Brian Mcmahon in Washington DC., 1 December 1947

Tibor Eckhardt, Zoltán Pfeiffer and László Acsáy meeting in the Hungarian National Council Washington DC office, 1 December 1947

Hungarian Natioanal Council leadership, Msgr. Béla Varga, Tibor Eckhardt, László Acsáy and Zoltán Pfeiffer emerging from a meeting in the US capitol
1 December 1947

Imre Kovács around 1943 in Hungary

Imre Kovács at the Dózsa Celebrations in Cegléd, 13 May 1945
(with Imre Nagy, Péter Veres, Ferenc Erdei, József Darvas and Gyula Illyés)

1514

Imre Kovács at the Assembly of the National Peasant Party, Budapest, 24 August 1947 (with Péter Veres and Lajos Jócsik).
The sign says „Good bye, Imre Kovács, don't count on your supporters"

Upon arrival on a Panagra flight
in Latin America

Imre Kovács and his first wife
in Zermatt, Switzerland

Imre Kovács in Latin America. On the left is András Hamza, Calvinist priest, important member of the Hungarian exiles in post-World War II New York

Left to right: Imre Kovács, Mrs. Uhlir, Mr. Uhlir, Professor Oyarzún of the Universidad de Chile and Secretary in the Parliament. Picture taken upon Imre Kovács's arrival

Imre Kovács with Msgr. Béla Varga, Hungary's first post-War speaker of Parliament, in 1967

Imre Kovács, New York, 1978

Stefan Korboński and ACEN Delegation including Vilis Masens and József Kővágó in Panmunjon Korea viewing communist fortifications

Meeting of the General Committee of the Assembly of Captive European Nations

Banner flying at ACEN headquarters across from the main United Nations buildings. ACEN effectively used the building for propaganda opportunities because of its highly visible location.

ACEN Leadership meeting with Prime Minister Lester Pearson of Canada.
Left to right: Ilmar Raamot, Stefan Korboński, PM Lester Pearson,
Ferenc Nagy (not in view) and Wing Commander Stefan Szmik

Dr. George M. Dimitrov shaking hands with Polish peasant leader Stanisław Mikołajczyk, 1 December 1947

George M. Dimitrov speaking at the European Movement Conference, 1 march 1949

ACEN leaders meet with US Secretary of State John Foster Dulles, 9 January 1956
Left to right: N. Bessenyey, (rear; Brutus Coste) Stefan Korboński, Vilis Masens, Secretary Dulles, George Dimitrov, Vaclovas Sidszikauskas, Leonhard Vahter, Constantin Viscianu, N. Doesti, Juraj Slavik

ACEN celebrating Captive Nations week 1963.
George Dimitrov with Senator Kenneth B. Keating at the Washington Press Club

Joseph Czapski, Polish writer and painter contributor to the Polish exile newspaper Kultura. Originator of the idea of creating a university in Western Europe with the aim of saving East European intelligentsia from the destructive consequences of Sovietization

Joseph Czapski and the writer Jerzy Giedroyc at the first meeting of the future internaitonal cultural organziation Congress for Cultural Freedom held in West Berlin 26–30 June 1950. Giedroyc the publiher editor of the Polish exile newspaper Kultlura participation at the Congress at the inviation of the American Philopher James Burnham in order to represent intellecutal exiles from the Soviet satelltes

The Chateau at Pourtales and the FUEU residentail buildings in the park in Strasbourg-Robertsaud. Photo shows the Hungarian national tutor Dezso Albrecht sitting on the right side of the bench with students

The leadership of the Hungarian National Sports Federation. Left to right Dr. George Telegdy, Secretary General, Count Anthony Szapary, President, Frank Chase, Vice President

Count Anthony Szapary
Founder and President of the
Hungarian National Sports
Federation

Hungarian Olympic Athletes who defected during the 1956 Sydney Olympic Games Arrive in New York

Photo Credits:

Page 554: NCFE Brochure courtesy of the Franklin D. Roosevelt Presidential Library Archives, Hyde Park, New York.
Page 555: Images courtesy of the Hoover Institution Archives (further HIA), Stanford, CA. Radio Free Europe Corporate Files.
Page 556/1: Image courtesy of Getty Images.
Page 556/2: Image courtesy of the HIA, Stanford, CA. Radio Free Europe Corporate Files.
Page 557: Images courtesy of the HIA, Stanford, CA. Radio Free Europe Corporate Files.
Page 558: Images courtesy of Getty Images.
Page 559/1: Image courtesy of the HIA, Stanford, CA. Radio Free Europe Corporate Files.
Page 559/2: Image courtesy of Getty Images
Page 560: Images courtesy of Getty Images
Page 561: All images courtesy of the HIA, Stanford, CA. Radio Free Europe Corporate Files.
Page 562: Images courtesy of the HIA, Stanford, CA. Radio Free Europe Corporate Files.
Pages 563–565: All images courtesy of the estate of Mojmír Povolný.
Page 566: Images courtesy of Getty Images.
Page 567: All images courtesy of Getty Images.
Page 568/1: Image courtesy of Getty Images
Page 568/2: Image courtesy of the HIA, Stanford, CA. Radio Free Europe Corporate Files.
Page 569: Images courtesy of Getty Images
Page 570: Image courtesy of Getty Images
Page 571: All images courtesy of the Hungarian National Museum, Budapest
Page 572: All images courtesy of the Hungarian National Museum, Budapest
Page 573: All images courtesy of the Hungarian National Museum, Budapest
Page 574: All images courtesy of the Rare Book and Manuscript Library, Columbia University Libraries, New York.
Page 575/1: Image courtesy of the Rare Book and Manuscript Library, Columbia University Libraries, New York.
Page 575/2: Image courtesy of the Hungarian National Museum, Budapest. Photo Miklós Molnár.
Page 575/3: Image courtesy of the Rare Book and Manuscript Library, Columbia University Libraries, New York.
Page 576: Images courtesy of the Stefan Korboński Foundation, Warsaw.
Page 577/1/3: Images courtesy of the Stefan Korboński Foundation. Warsaw.
Page 577/2: Image courtesy of the HIA, Stanford, CA. Radio Free Europe Corporate Files.
Page 578: All images courtesy of Getty Images
Page 579: All images courtesy of the HIA, Stanford, CA. Radio Free Europe Corporate Files.
Page 580: All images courtesy of the Institut Litteraire Kultúra Archives, Paris.
Page 581: All images courtesy of a private donor, Paris.
Pages 582/583: All images courtesy of Gladys and Paul Szapary, New York.

Index

C

E

F

Q

R

T